Basketball
Offenses
& Plays

Ken Atkins

Human Kinetics

Library of Congress Cataloging-in-Publication Data

Atkins, Ken, 1952-
    Basketball offenses & plays / Ken Atkins.
        p. cm.
    ISBN 0-7360-4847-2 (softcover)
        1. Basketball—Offense. 2. Basketball—Coaching. I. Title:
Basketball offenses and plays. II. Title.
    GV889.A84 2004
    796.332'2–dc22   2003026703

ISBN: 0-7360-4847-2

Developmental Editor: Cynthia McEntire; **Assistant Editors:** Scott Hawkins, Cory Weber; **Copyeditor:** Bob Replinger; **Proofreader:** Jim Burns; **Graphic Designer:** Fred Starbird; **Graphic Artist:** Kim McFarland; **Cover Designer:** Keith Blomberg; **Photographer (cover):** Dan Wendt, Les Woodrum; **Art Manager:** Kareema McLendon; **Illustrator:** Mic Greenberg; **Printer:** Versa Press

Human Kinetics books are available at special discounts for bulk purchase. Special editions or book excerpts can also be created to specification. For details, contact the Special Sales Manager at Human Kinetics.

Printed in the United States of America   10 9 8 7 6 5 4 3 2 1

Human Kinetics
Web site: www.HumanKinetics.com

United States: Human Kinetics
P.O. Box 5076
Champaign, IL 61825-5076
800-747-4457
e-mail: humank@hkusa.com

Canada: Human Kinetics
475 Devonshire Road Unit 100
Windsor, ON N8Y 2L5
800-465-7301 (in Canada only)
e-mail: orders@hkcanada.com

Europe: Human Kinetics
107 Bradford Road
Stanningley
Leeds LS28 6AT, United Kingdom
+44 (0) 113 255 5665
e-mail: hk@hkeurope.com

Australia: Human Kinetics
57A Price Avenue
Lower Mitcham, South Australia 5062
08 8277 1555
e-mail: liaw@hkaustralia.com

New Zealand: Human Kinetics
Division of Sports Distributors NZ Ltd.
P.O. Box 300 226 Albany
North Shore City
Auckland
0064 9 448 1207
e-mail: blairc@hknewz.com

I would like to extend my deepest gratitude to the two most important women in my life, my mother, Elizabeth Atkins, and my wife, Betsy Atkins. They helped me in countless ways as I wrote this book. They have been my foremost supporters and have consistently encouraged my writing. Although I now have some serious physical limitations, they have enabled me to maintain a positive outlook. Their assistance and suggestions have been invaluable. Their belief in my abilities inspired me to write and endeavor to assist my fellow coaches.

Contents

Acknowledgments

For the fans:
Basketball fans throughout the world are responsible for the upsurge of the sport. Professional and college basketball have become huge businesses with significant financial power. Television revenues are astronomical because of the millions of people who watch basketball through the media. The rising popularity of the game has enabled coaches to pursue a full-time occupation connected to the game they love. I was among the fortunate, able to earn a living through my involvement with a game. The National Basketball Association, its developmental league, and the professional leagues located in multiple countries outside the United States employ thousands. College basketball in America is played at over 310 NCAA Division I institutions, more than 260 Division II schools, and in excess of 390 Division III colleges and universities, where I was employed for 13 years. Another 150-plus colleges compete as part of the NAIA, an alternative administrative body. Well over 200 two-year institutions field basketball teams. These numbers roughly double when counting men's and women's teams separately. Women's basketball is growing at a much higher rate than men's basketball.

Fans are an integral part of the game. They inspire players and coaches to perform at a higher level. They are the reason that many teams have a home-court advantage. The excitement and intensity generated in a gymnasium full of fans produce an exceptional experience for the participants. When their numbers are few, games take on a completely different feel. The best fans are those loyal to the team, win or lose. Such fans seek to bolster the players' spirits and not destroy their confidence. These fans understand that the players do not know everything. True fans do not pester or harass. They are enlightened enough to know that mistakes are a natural part of the game, and that no team or individual plays the perfect game. Even the world's best players do not make every shot, grab every rebound, block every shot by an opponent, or complete every pass. They know that the pace of the game mandates that players and coaches make decisions swiftly. Decision-making skills are essential for anyone connected with a basketball team. Fans enjoy the competition and strategy. They know that winning a basketball game is better than losing it, but they understand that the outcome is not crucial in the grander scheme of life. Basketball is a game. They enjoy it for what it is.

Introduction

Almost 20 years have passed since publication of my first book, *Winning Basketball Drills*. At the time I was just beginning my career as a collegiate head coach at King's College in Wilkes-Barre, Pennsylvania. After 13 years as a head coach, I had to abandon my coaching career. While my team was on a six-game tour of Ireland, I was thrown backward into the dashboard of a bus. The extensive damage to my lower back (disc damage, nerve injury, a fracture, and internal bleeding) has made it physically impossible for me to coach basketball now or at any time in the near future. My disability stems from the constant pain associated with the damage done to my lower back. Although my body has failed me, my mind is still active. In my estimation, what is stored inside it could be worthwhile for my fellow coaches. I believe I can help.

I used the tactics and plays described in this book during my coaching tenure, the vast majority of it at King's College. The analysis encompasses all aspects of offensive basketball. My first book focused solely on drills, but *Basketball Offenses & Plays* concentrates on the process involved in scoring as a team. I learned the material in many ways while serving as a head coach—by watching games on television, attending games through the years, operating and working summer basketball camps, coaching against and with some creative people, and talking with numerous coaches. Many of the plays I created from scratch. One of my strengths as a coach was my ability to work with the Xs and Os. I enjoy formulating productive motion and have never been shy when it comes to experimentation.

Even before publication of *Winning Basketball Drills*, I saved everything I did in connection with the game of basketball. I added to my collection of pertinent information and organized it into various categories. My knowledge of offensive basketball has culminated in the writing of *Basketball Offenses & Plays*. As need arose while I was coaching, I either sought specific

plays that covered the targeted topic or formulated them on my own to achieve specific objectives. Although I sat down and physically tinkered with the Xs and Os to fabricate many of these player movements, I cannot claim that the information is original. I could not begin to estimate what percentage of material created by coaches is without duplication. It seems to me that truly original creation in basketball is uncommon. I am certain that some coach, somewhere, at some time, combined actions in the same manner I did.

During my years at King's College I established one of the best win-loss records in the country on the NCAA Division III level. My teams were able to set plenty of institutional records. I also learned a great deal more about basketball and the best way to teach it. Competing in the Middle Atlantic Conference against some superb coaches pushed me to be my best and brought out my creative side.

Basketball Offenses & Plays includes five parts. Each part deals with a particular piece of offensive basketball: man-to-man offense, zone offense, quick-scoring and delay offenses, plays for special situations, and inbound plays. The text is designed to be an easy reference for coaches at all levels of competition. Consistent headings within each part of the writing further break down each item. These divisions enhance the search for information by making it easy to identify specifically relevant information.

Several topics are described for every play or offense: personnel, scoring, execution, and keys. Illustrations throughout the book clarify player motions on the court. I have tried to make the book reader friendly. My goal is to provide coaches with one source that reviews all aspects of offensive basketball pertaining to player motion. This Xs and Os book covers well over 300 plays, offenses, movement variations, and special calls.

The introductory portion of each play identifies the conditions under which the tactic or play will be most successful. Any tips concerning deployment appear here. The first two headings will help you narrow your search for beneficial material. The personnel section tells you what traits or characteristics your players should possess and the skills they need for completing the play. Under the scoring heading is a listing of the scoring occasions likely to arise as a result of the play. The section describes who secures the shot and where on the court the shot originates.

The discussion then turns to player motion and timing. The execution portion of each description supplies the precise means by which the team can find scoring opportunities. Detailed descriptions with accompanying diagrams show the coach how to run every play. Player movements are laid out in sequential fashion. The keys section identifies the instructional methods necessary to build a successful offensive basketball program and includes information that could assist instruction.

When you improve how players function in given circumstances and provide them with tools to enhance performance, you take a giant stride toward extracting a favorable outcome. I included drills and other helpful means of teaching, noted anything that players may find difficult to grasp, and outlined suggestions that can aid the educational process.

I assigned a title to each play or offense. Feel free to change the names as you deem fit. I am partial to calling systems, an effective way to disguise the name of a given play. If you use only one call for a motion, your opponent likely will figure out what is coming as soon as the word is out of your mouth. Create a system that assigns each play a category. Use NBA teams, colors, foreign countries, and so on. Some categories can include further divisions. For example, continents—South America, Asia, Europe, and so on—provide a way to group countries. NBA teams fall into divisions or conferences. My favorite categories are letters and two- or three-digit numbers. I use the names of states, cities, colleges, or universities with letters. For example, South Carolina, Seattle, Susquehanna, or Stanford all denote the S play. That way, the opponent has to break the code to know the precise call. Surprise is a positive element during competition. Any time you hit your opponent with the unexpected, your team gains an advantage.

I am confident that you will find this book a valuable reference for offensive basketball. You can be confident that the material fulfills its objective—to provide coaches with player motions that achieve a desired outcome. The offenses and plays create scoring moments or beneficial actions.

A coach's primary job on offense is to devise a plan for player movement that will create specific shots for individual players. You want the right person releasing the right shot. Players have to put the basketball through the net, but you have to provide them with openings to do so. Players also need ways to generate certain results in response to opponents' defensive actions. They must be able to bring the ball up the floor when confronted with a full-court press, inbound the ball without creating a turnover, and keep the ball away from the opponent when putting it in the deep freeze at the close of a game.

This Xs and Os book does not consider individual player personalities. Instead, I explain how to move players on the playing surface to create openings for shots or minimize turnovers. Many factors determine whether a player is going to do what is asked at the proper time and in the preferred manner.

One factor you can control is your players' perception of the depth of your knowledge about the game. When you supply players with productive motions, you build their confidence in your ability. If they believe in what you are teaching, they believe in you. Your credibility increases. The information provided in this book will increase your basketball wisdom and provide the means to conquer any defensive situation.

Key to Diagrams

B1, B2 = Big players

S1, S2 = Shooters

G = Point guard, lead guard

‐ ‐ ‐ ➤ = Pass

〜〜➤ = Dribble

⟶ = Run/move

⟶⊣ = Move and screen

⊦➤ = Move, screen, and move again

N = Highlighted player

● (S2) = Player with the ball

X = Defender

O = Offensive player

PART I

Man-to-Man Offenses

CHAPTER 1

Passing-Game Offenses

Unlike continuity offenses, which use specific sequences of movements, passing-game offenses are rule oriented. Passing-game offenses require continuous action, but players do not perform a set movement pattern. They have a great deal more freedom of mobility. This independence permits team members to be creative and do certain tasks spontaneously. Instead of repeating predetermined moves in a sequence, players choose actions by reading the defense and executing countermoves. A mental breakdown or defensive disruption during execution of a continuity offense can create a serious obstacle for a team. With a passing game, players learn to respond to various defensive techniques.

A freelance offense should be incorporated into a team's offensive scheme. After players reach junior high school age, they are able to comprehend and execute a rule-oriented offense. They learn how to play the game and the concepts behind specific player movements. A team can function better when players have some latitude in terms of their actions on the court. A passing game is harder for opposing teams to scout, and opponents are less able to produce plans that will disrupt the offense. Defending a passing offense requires constant reaction to multiple offensive maneuvers. In addition, a freelance offense allows players to play through mistakes more easily. The freedom

of motion permits the coach to add quick-hitting plays to the system to generate a variety of scoring opportunities for designated players in a short period. A passing-game offense is the logical deployment at the conclusion of a quick hitter. Players can execute it regardless of where they are positioned on the floor when the quick-hitting play ends.

Patterns have advantages too. Chapters 2, 3, and 4 present a number of patterns to consider. Patterns provide more control over player motion. The coach can determine what types of offensive movements take place, who can make shot attempts, and from where players can take shots. This control factor is certainly not as great in a passing-game offense. In a pattern offense, the order of actions is known, and coaches teach the counters to defensive overplays as part of the offense.

A wide variety of coaches employ passing games. I believe that Bob Knight was one of the coaches who propelled its use nationally. His Indiana University teams were national powerhouses, and their success was largely due to their exceptional execution of a passing-game offense. Dean Smith at the University of North Carolina was also a proponent of the passing-game offense. His squads won regularly and operated the freelance-style offense to perfection. Development and extensive use of a passing game offense by two Hall of

Fame coaches catapulted its popularity. Now, the majority of college teams in America use some form of passing game against man-to-man defense.

When discussing multiple man-to-man offenses, review of several points that occur frequently in the descriptions of various plays is necessary. For example, setting a screen is an important component in most offenses. To avoid having to repeat the methodology of common actions, the sidebar "Man-to-Man Offensive Fine-Tuning" provides the details. The sections about the various offenses refer the reader back to the relevant point when appropriate.

Man-to-Man Offensive Fine-Tuning

Screening Between Post and Perimeter Players

The interaction between the exterior and interior players is my preferred method of screening because the defense finds it more difficult to switch assignments. When a post player picks for a perimeter player, or vice versa, the opposition is reluctant to allow any mismatch in size or quickness. Mismatches invariably favor the offense.

Setting a Screen

A player sets a screen by flexing his or her knees, fists on chest, elbows up just short of shoulder level. The player needs to maintain a wide base with his or her feet. The screener goes right at the targeted defender (headhunts) and becomes stationary just before making contact. He or she keeps the arms near the body and does not extend the fists out after making contact.

Players should indicate that they are screening by raising a fist in the air or calling the name of the intended recipient of the pick. This communication allows the recipient to do whatever is necessary to make the screen effective.

The screener plants the screen at an angle so that his or her back is turned to the area where he or she anticipates that the recipient will get open. The screener steps toward the ball after the teammate uses the pick. The screener seals the opponent by keeping him or her on rear or hip and gives a target to the passer.

Slipping a Screen

The screener slips a screen (darts to the basket or an open area early before the pick is actually set and used) when he or she recognizes that the defense is switching too soon or cheating prematurely to bump the offensive player using the screen. The screener cuts to an open space or alley.

Using a Pick

To use a pick, the recipient must wait for the screen to be set on the defender. The player makes the defense think that he or she is heading in one direction but then moves in the opposite way. The use of V-cuts is encouraged. The receiver is patient and understands that it is better to go off a screen late rather than early. The player using the pick runs the defender into the pick and adjusts his or her movements based on the reaction of the defense. The recipient reads the defense and comes off the pick, in a manner most difficult to defend. In general, the recipient of the pick has three choices: rub closely off the screen to an open area, fade to a region away from the defender if the defender tries to cheat over the pick to maintain coverage, or curl around the pick when the defender is trailing underneath the screen.

Rescreening

Rescreens are back-to-back picks for the same player. When one pick is ineffective, the same player quickly establishes another, either unintentionally or intentionally. A big player normally rescreens. Usually, rescreening requires a down pick followed by a back screen, or vice versa. But the rescreen also could be a down screen and then a flare screen, or vice versa. Occasionally, a pick on the ball can be rescreened.

Down Screen

The down screen at a block on the foul lane usually requires a big player to move from the perimeter to pick for an exterior player low along the lane. The screener pivots on the foot farther from the baseline to open up to the ball after the recipient uses the pick. The screener steps to the ball and attempts to pin the defender on his or her hip or rear to gain a position advantage. He or she is prepared to receive the toss from a teammate and supplies a target. The player using the down screen has three basic choices. First, the recipient of the down screen can come off the pick tight and head to the open area near the same-side wing. Second, he or she can fade to the near corner if the defender motors over the top of the pick some distance away from the offensive player. (In either case, the screener seals and steps to the ball.) Third, when the defender is trailing under the screen, the recipient of the down screen can curl around the pick and head back across the lane while looking for the ball. In this case, the screener steps out to a spot about 15 feet from the basket along the baseline after the recipient of the screen wraps around.

Back Pick

For the back pick, one player is near the hoop or baseline and the other player, the recipient, is on the periphery. The back screen for a passer is best because the player with the ball is the only one who can score. Therefore, the defender is likely close by. The player setting the pick is ready to move as soon as his or her teammate passes the ball. The screener must give the defender one step before contact if the defender is unable to view the pick. Players react to defensive maneuvers.

The player using the pick races to the basket. He or she rubs off either of the screener's shoulders. The screener pops out for a possible pass reception and outside shot attempt. The recipient of the pick fades to the near corner or open area as the defender is caught going over the top pick. The receiver heads to the area farthest from the defender. Their actions capitalize on a defender who gets caught in or near the foul lane. This time the screener could bolt to the hoop but most likely will pop out after his or her teammate rubs off the screen. If the defense switches, the player using the pick fades as the screener seals the new defender and bolts to the basket. The screener should be open with the

defense trailing. The player securing the pick fakes a cut to the basket and pops back off the pick to the perimeter. The screener can bolt to the basket. The defender on the recipient of the pick tries to cheat over the screen and beat the player to the basket. It is a swift rescreening situation.

Two-Player Game

In the two-player game (pick-and-roll or screen on the ball), a big player usually screens for a perimeter player. The screener often sets the pick so that the dribbler moves toward the center of the floor. The ball handler dribbles off the screen to drive to the basket, looks for a jump shot, or passes to a teammate. The screener normally rolls to the basket by pivoting on the foot farther from his or her teammate, swings the other foot in the direction of the dribbler, puts the inside arm up to provide a target, and cuts on a line to the hoop. If one or both big players are effective shooters from the periphery, the coach may decide to allow them to move to an open area or step out for an outside shot rather than roll straight to the hoop. Players adjust based on defensive movements.

By rubbing off the pick tight, the ball handler may generate a shot. If the defender on the ball goes underneath the pick to maintain coverage, the screener rolls early to the goal. The screener slips the screen when his or her defender steps out too soon to hedge. The screener sees a lane to the hoop and immediately exploits it. The dribbler has not yet used the pick when the screener begins the dash to the basket.

If the defender on the ball handler tries to cheat over the top of the pick too early, the dribbler may head to an open area away from the pick (usually toward the baseline) for a shot. The screener maintains the screen slightly longer than usual.

If the defense switches the screen, the player with the ball takes advantage of any mismatches. He or she may have to dribble back toward the original location to send the ball into a post player with a height advantage inside. The big player with the mismatch yells, "Hot!" The screener immediately heads to the basket to secure the ball. The other three players vacate the region to enable the two teammates to exploit the mismatch.

(continued)

(continued)

Flare Screen

The flare screen begins with the player receiving the pick acting as though he or she is cutting into the foul lane from above the foul line. He or she usually runs a straight line parallel to a lane line. The screen comes from the perimeter on a 90-degree angle. The recipient flares over the top of the pick and replaces the screener on the perimeter. The player with the ball uses a skip pass to deliver the ball to a teammate on the exterior. Normally a big player sets the flare screen for an outside player. A post player can receive a flare pick only if he or she is a capable outside shooter.

Double Screen

For the double screen, two players establish a pick by standing side by side. The players performing the double screens can be stationary or can move together to pick. Screeners never allow a defender to split them to maintain coverage on their teammate using the twin pick. The recipient of the double screen has several options:

- Cut over or under the double screen to location directly opposite starting spot.
- Curl around the twin screen by moving under and then twisting over the top of the pick into the foul lane. The defender trails under the double screen. One screener bolts out to a spot at least 15 feet away from the lane.
- Fake using the double screen and instead fade back toward the original location. The player uses this option when the defender cheats over the twin pick too soon.

Low Exchanges and Cross Screens

Low exchanges and cross screens are similar movements. For the low exchange, one player is on the ballside block and another is on the opposite box. The ball is at the wing or corner. The player nearer the ball plants a screen for the player on the other block. The recipient steps toward the baseline and races to the high post or steps to the foul line and bolts low to the other box. The screener seals back heading to spot opposite recipient. If the defense switches, the person using the pick always goes high. The screener seals back low and

should be open to secure a pass after sealing defender on rear.

Teams use the cross screen when the ball is above the foul line within the lane width. One player is on one side of the foul lane, and another player is on the other side at approximately box level. Either player can initiate the pick, although usually the one away from the strongside initiates it. If the defense switches, the screener actively seals new defender and is the primary target. The screener always steps to the ball after picking. The player using the cross screen slides over the top or underneath the pick. He or she uses whichever method is toughest on the defense, steps one way, and goes the other.

Throwing the Ball Inside

When throwing the ball inside, the player with the ball on the exterior reads the positions of the defenders and passes away from the defense toward the appropriate target. Most post feeds are completed with a bounce pass. When a size difference favors the offensive interior player, it is possible to throw the ball over the head of a defender who is trying to full front or side front in the post. The offensive player positions his or her body to place the defender on a hip. The forearm on the same side as the hip is up at the defender's throat or neck, making contact. The player uses his or her thigh to push the defender farther away from the basket, if possible, to provide more room in which to work. The offensive player extends the other arm up to supply a target for the passer. The passer tosses the ball over the top as the inside player moves to gain control. The post player maintains position advantage and is careful not to push off with the forearm when releasing to retrieve the ball.

Passing Into the Low Post

Passing into the low post with the back to the foul lane triggers one of several movements. Remaining consistent and using one method regularly against man-to-man defense is beneficial.

For the first option, the passer cuts to the hoop, ending at the opposite block on the foul lane. He or she cuts to either the baseline side or the foul-line side of the receiver. The nearest perimeter player replaces the passer at the wing or corner in front of the low post. The post player who is not the recipient rushes to the weakside elbow when the pass goes inside. He or she tries to screen for an exterior player, moving from the weakside to above the strongside elbow. The motion occupies the defense to isolate the low post.

In the second option, players spot up. The only person to cut is a big player, who instantaneously sprints to the other box on the lane. The other three players move within each of three exterior regions: to the ballside wing or corner, above the strongside elbow, and to the weakside elbow.

In the third option, players spot up to specific areas. The passer moves but remains in the wing or corner on the periphery. A post player hustles to the offside elbow to act as a screener. A perimeter player from the offside uses the pick to relocate above the ballside elbow. The other player motors to the block opposite the pass receiver.

For the fourth option, players execute a split maneuver. The passer races to screen for the closest player on the periphery. The two players switch positions. The other two players head to the offside elbow and weakside block.

L-Cut

Players use the L-cut to get open to catch a pass on the wing (extended foul line). The team clears a side of the floor for the play. The player begins at a block on the foul lane and moves straight up the lane line to the elbow. He or she pushes off the inside foot to bolt on a 90-degree angle to the wing. The player extends the outside arm to provide a target for the passer. If the defense overplays, the player initiates a backdoor cut immediately after reaching the wing. The passer executes a ball fake, which starts the back cut. The player pushes off the foot closer to the sideline and darts to the hoop, extending the outside arm as a target. If no pass comes by the time the player hits the near block, a second L-cut begins. The player repeats the process as necessary.

Duck-In

Usually, a post player performs the duck-in maneuver. The post player begins just outside the foul lane near the weakside box. He or she steps at the defender and walks into or toward the lane while facing the defender. The player initiates contact with the defender and quickly pivots on the foot nearer the ball. The foot is thrust at the center of the defender's feet just before the pivot. The timing of the action is vital. The pivot coincides with the placement of the ball in the middle of the foul line and above it. The other foot swings away from the defender, placing the defender on the hip or backside. The offensive player stays low with knees flexed, establishing a wide base, and moves his or her feet to maintain a position advantage on the defender. The body shields the defender from interfering with a passing lane. The player provides a target by extending the arm opposite the defender's position. The player with the ball at the top may have to dribble to the post player's side to achieve a proper passing angle to feed the ball inside. The inside pass can come from the top or the ball may need to be reversed to a wing on the post player's side. The pass is completed to the wing when the player out top sees the defense on the topside of the post player. Tosses inside are likely to be bounce passes.

Pinning the Defender

Unlike the duck-in maneuver, pinning the defender does not require a weakside block location or ball positioned above the center of the charity stripe. The locations of the ball and the defender determine which foot is the pivot foot. The player uses the foot that permits him or her to seal the defender on the hip or rear for a potential post feed.

Twist Move

The twist move regularly occurs between two big players who are positioned next to each other within 10 to 12 feet of the hoop. The players read their locations in relation to the ball to ensure that the screener steps down or in toward the foul lane. The teammate swoops over the top of the pick, heading to the player with the ball, not away from him or her. The player stepping down and in usually is the one closest to the ball. Players' roles are defined so that the recipient of the screen can move to the ball handler. The player who darts over his or her partner's backside presents a target for the player with the ball. Generally a bounce pass is used to dump the ball inside.

This chapter discusses two types of passing games. The difference between them is how many players work in the low-post region. The first type is the most common and uses two post players. The second type uses only one post player. With each offense, I provide specific rules and particular types of movement that coaches should teach their players.

RULES OF MOVEMENT

Regardless of which type of passing game a coach chooses to use, players must learn the rules associated with both styles. First, let's look at the rules for the player in possession of the ball.

After receiving a pass from a teammate, the player turns, faces the basket, and establishes triple-threat position. This position gives the player the option to shoot, pass, or drive. This rule has two exceptions:

1. If a defender is denying the perimeter and tries for the steal or deflection but misses, the offensive player may have an opportunity to execute a reverse turn. Following the catch, the player with the ball quickly dribbles toward the basket by spinning away from the defender and stepping with the foot farther from the defender. The poor defensive gamble opens a clear path.

2. If a player receives the ball near the basket, a turn-and-face move may not be necessary. The player can catch the pass on a cut to the hoop or in a post-up situation near the foul lane.

The player with the ball dribbles for these reasons only: to penetrate to the basket, to maintain floor balance or proper spacing with teammates, to improve a passing angle, or to get out of trouble. Players must be aware of opportunities to penetrate to the basket to create scoring chances. Putting the ball on the floor also is required if the player wants to use a screen on the ball. The player with the ball needs to let the screens develop and come to a completion. He or she must realize that the screener is often the one who is open.

All players should maintain floor balance and spacing, keeping 12 to 15 feet between one another. Team members should use the entire half-court and keep the offense spread.

Players do not stand in one place for more than two or three seconds. They move with purpose. They know what they want to accomplish with their movement before beginning it. Players must move the basketball and themselves. They are never stagnant.

Players should demonstrate some patience. They should not be afraid to make a set number of passes before taking a shot. Coaches can control the patience level of their teams by establishing a minimum number of passes before players may launch a shot. Setting other conditions is acceptable, too. Perhaps the coach wants the low post to touch the ball at least once or a particular person to secure ball twice before the team attempts a shot. The coach may or may not fix certain restraints on players.

Coaches should communicate with their players to ensure that each player knows exactly what types of shots he or she is allowed to release. Individual restrictions are beneficial.

Players need to be quick, but they should not hurry. Players without the ball, including the person who just passed the ball, can cut to the basket or open areas, set a screen for a teammate, use a screen from a teammate, or run away and come back to the same general area, an action called replacing.

Players do not fight defensive overplays when coming to the ball. They react by cutting to the hoop or screening for a teammate. The move is known as a backdoor cut or back cut. Two cutters cannot go to the same area at the same time.

Refer to "Man-to-Man Offensive Fine-Tuning" on page 4 for guidelines about setting a screen, slipping a screen, using a pick, back pick, rescreening, throwing the ball inside, and pinning the defender. These elements are important parts in operating an effective passing-game offense.

To improve the team's performance of the passing game, coaches can use each of the maneuvers involved as a separate entity for practice. These are referred to as breakdown drills. For example, coaches can drill their teams on rescreening techniques, perhaps a down screen followed by a back or flare screen, or a back or flare screen preceding a down screen. Establishing a drill that focuses on a specific technique is an excellent way to refine various offensive movements. Coaches can work with perimeter players only, big players only, or they can drill the interaction between the two groups.

Coaches must be patient when teaching a passing-game offense. Players will need some time to execute at a high level. At first, the action may look like mayhem. The best way for players to learn is by doing. Throughout the season, coaches can periodically review specific items that players have forgotten, are not performing well, or are not coordinating properly on the floor. Teams should practice the movements and rules using a five-on-none framework before adding defense. No form of practice, however, can substitute for playing live.

Coaches should consistently reinforce, positively and negatively, the rules they require players to adhere to during performance of the offense. Coaches should pay strict attention to the team's implementation of those regulations.

A useful drill is simply to practice delivering the ball inside to reinforce the precise motion that squad members are to carry out. The drill begins with no defense. Defenders are then gradually added for each offensive player.

Coaches should emphasize the necessity for players to think during the execution of the offense. Players need to have an idea of what they would like to accomplish before they act. The squad should play through mistakes, not stopping just because they make an error.

Players should not get into the habit of putting the basketball on the floor as soon as they catch it. Players dribble only if there is an opening to the basket right off the pass reception.

Players should not resist defensive denials. When players read that an overplay has developed, they either back cut to the basket, screen for a teammate, or flash to the foul line. Players do not fight the denial; they counter it.

For each passing game, coaches can mandate specific moves to gain some control over the players. Although players still have a great deal of discretion regarding their actions, the introduction of the movement options reviewed in each subsequent section enables the coach to set parameters on the players' motion.

Now let's discuss each passing-game offense. I include specific types of movements that are taught as part of each passing game. The actions described are not sequential. The items are specific movements available within a passing game. This lets the coach have a little more control of the players' actions than he or she would have in a true freelance offense.

TWO-POST PASSING GAME

The two-post passing game is a half-court offense used when a breakdown occurs during the execution of another offense, or after a quick-hitting play finishes without a shot attempt. Coaches should have faith in their players' ability to make decisions and rely on them to execute the movements that are most likely to be productive. Players have to accept responsibility for their actions on offense. Coaches must be comfortable relinquishing some control over their motion. For teams composed of players who are of roughly equal offensive ability, the passing game provides balance for scoring opportunities.

Personnel

The two-post passing game is designed for three perimeter players and two big players. Big individuals should possess not only the skills to score around the bucket but also the ability to handle the basketball on the perimeter. Players need to be capable of feeding the ball to a post. If all three perimeter players are strong outside scoring threats, the floor will open for the offense.

Scoring

With a passing-game offense, pinpointing the particular types of shots that will occur is difficult. Available shots will vary with each trip down the court. What is important is that the coach let players know precisely what shots each player can attempt. The coach should make clear to the squad the tempo he or she wants to establish. All forms of shots develop. The coach sets the limitations for each player.

Execution

The general rules of movement give an idea of the type of motion that is allowed and what players should be doing while performing the offense. The two-post passing game includes specific rules.

One big player is high and the other is low on a consistent basis. They are positioned roughly within the foul-lane lines. The big players are aware of spacing with the perimeter players.

The high-post player may operate a two-player game out front with an exterior teammate. The high post usually steps out following his or her pick instead of rolling to the basket. He or she rolls to the hoop only if the ballside low post is vacant for the cut. The high post also serves as a screener for a perimeter player without the ball and may perform a rescreen action. The high post acts as a passer. He or she regularly glances inside to the low post.

The low-post player is ballside or weakside. If on the ballside, the low post tries to post up strong along the foul lane to receive an entry pass. If the low post sees the basketball above the foul line, he or she may attempt to seal the defender in the lane to secure a feed from the top. The low post also can step out to execute a back screen for a perimeter player directly in front of the low post when the ball is near the top of the key. The low post also can rescreen. The low-post player in either passing game does not always set up shop on the ballside. He or she periodically (roughly 30 to 50 percent of the time) assumes a position on the weakside.

Post players periodically change positions. When the high post sees the low post on the ballside vacant, the high post dives to fill the opening while the low post moves high. They screen for each other and react to the defense. The low post on the ballside may move away, creating an opening for the high post to dive into. The low post continues movement to the high-post position as the high post cuts to fill the void left by the low post. If the low post recognizes that a perimeter player on his or her side of the floor is vigorously denied, the low post flashes upward directly to the ball to receive a pass. On the pass, the overplayed teammate cuts to the basket for a possible layup. The low post sets a stationary baseline screen for a perimeter player directly in front when the ball crosses the foul lane from one side to the other. The player who sets the pick always steps to the ball after screening. The perimeter player cuts off the screen on the foul-line or baseline side or fades back toward his or her original position when the defender cheats over the pick too early.

In figure 1.1, one big player is low (B1) and the other is high (B2). Their positions can be reversed. The three perimeter players (S1, G, and S2) space themselves on the exterior approximately 15 feet apart. The lead guard (G) receives the ball from a perimeter player (S2). The high post (B2) sets a screen for the point guard (G), who is in possession of the ball. The other player on the periphery (S1) drops toward the corner to give the pick on the ball a chance to work. The low post (B1) may or may not flash to a spot on the ballside. The high post (B2) does not roll to the basket if the strongside block is occupied or is about to be occupied. More often than not, B2 will slide out to the exterior after screening for the ball. The high post (B2) also could establish a rescreen for the guard. The playmaker reverses direction and uses another pick from the high post. Once a teammate on the perimeter (S2) sees the rescreen, he or she drops toward the near baseline to create more space for the lead guard. If the ball handler passes to the exterior (to S1), players adhere to the rules for motion within a passing game.

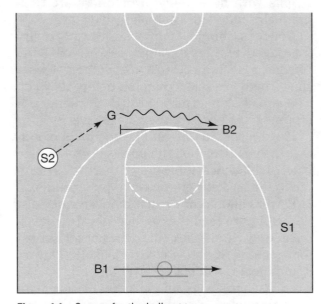

Figure 1.1   Screen for the ball out top.

In figure 1.2, the ball is on the exterior, and the high-post player (B1) sets a down screen for the nearest perimeter player who does not have the ball (S2). The low post (B2) establishes a back screen for the guard (G). The low- and high-post players can elect to rescreen for S2 and G,

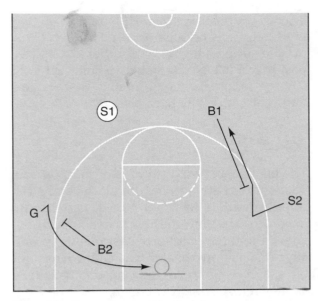

Figure 1.2 Down screen and back pick.

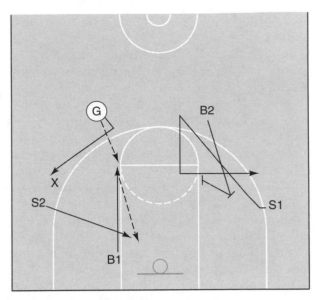

Figure 1.3 Wing denied.

respectively. Refer to the discussions of the back pick and rescreening on pages 4 and 5.

Whenever the ball goes inside to the player low along the foul lane, players execute specific movements. The passer (S1) cuts to the basket, ending near the weakside block. He or she cuts the foul-line or baseline sides of the post. The closest perimeter player replaces the passer. The post player who does not receive the entry pass hustles to the weakside. He or she looks to screen for any weakside perimeter player who moves to the area above the strongside elbow. Players keep defenders occupied. The low post is isolated and executes a solid inside-scoring maneuver. See techniques for throwing the ball inside and passing into the low post on page 6 for various movement options.

In figure 1.3, the low post (B1) flashes high in recognition that the defender is overplaying the nearest perimeter player (S2). The point guard passes to the low post (B1), and the perimeter player (S2) instantaneously performs a backdoor cut to the hoop. The passer (G) replaces the cutter (S2), and B2 screens for S1. These two players keep the defenders busy. In figure 1.3, S1 uses a flare screen by B2 as part of a rescreening maneuver. Initially, B2 would have down picked for S1. Refer to the section about rescreening on page 4.

The big players could also set at a high-post location near the foul line and a low-post position away from the pass receiver. The ballside

block is vacant. A passer from out top cuts to the bucket while using a high-post screen. The pass receiver observes the interior and delivers the ball if the passer is open on the dash to the hoop. If no return pass goes to the cutter, the passer screens across for the low post. The movement alternative is viable as part of a two-post passing game.

Figure 1.4 shows the basic movement described previously, except that the high post (B2) is not at the foul line but above the key. The passer (G) cuts to the hoop. There is no high-post screen to use. The cutter (G) picks

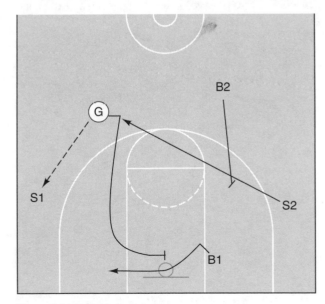

Figure 1.4 Ballside low vacant.

across for the low post (B1) when no return pass comes. The low post (B1) comes to the ball. The high post (B2) screens for the remaining perimeter player (S2). See the discussion of low exchanges and cross screens on page 6.

One method by which big players exchange spots is by screening for each other. The low post picks for the high post. The player accepting the screen cuts high or low (over or under). The screener steps to the ball and assumes position on the opposite side. The high post could also pick for the low post. The recipient goes over or under the screen, stepping in one direction and heading in the other. The screener reacts to his or her teammate's cut by moving opposite (cut low, go high, or vice versa). Post players also switch positions (high to low and vice versa) by cutting to spots. They constantly react to each other to ensure that they continually occupy high- and low-post sites.

The two-post passing game has one more option—a through call. Figure 1.5 details this play. Players can execute the same action in the one-post passing game. The player with the ball (G) yells, "Through," causing the weakside wing (S2) to motor to the ballside corner. The low post (B2) is on either box and screens for S2 on his or her cut. After G makes the through call, the player on the periphery closest to the ball (S1) must get open to catch the pass from G. G throws to S1. A back screen develops as B1 picks for the passer (G). G exploits the back pick and moves to an open area on the weakside to receive a skip pass.

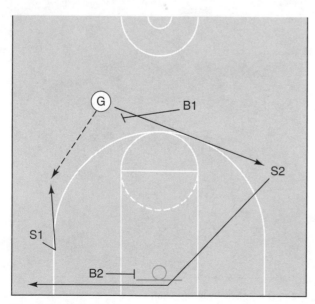

Figure 1.5   Through call.

In a one-post passing game, this action happens more frequently because of the post players' rule to keep one post high and the other low. When a post player is next to the ball handler out front (G), the action may be promoted. Go to page 5 for discussion of the back pick.

Keys

The high post should vary his or her position. Sometimes the high post should be along the free-throw line; at other times, usually the majority of the time, the high post should be out above the three-point arc. Post players generally remain approximately within the lane lines but may venture outside occasionally as long as they return shortly thereafter.

A small forward may also happen to be a power forward. He or she plays both a post spot and a perimeter position in the two-post passing game. This arrangement places a great deal of pressure on the player. His or her capacity to comprehend and perform effectively from both positions will definitely be strained. Coaches must decide whether the individual is capable of taking on the added responsibility.

Post players must understand that they change roles by different methods. They mix up the various means they use to accomplish the task.

When performing the stationary baseline screen in the two-post passing game, the post player setting the pick signals the move. He or she sees the ball thrown out front to the weakside and immediately recognizes the situation, places a fist in the air, and calls to his or her teammate stationed on the same-side wing. The screener steps to the ball after the pick is used.

The two-player game is a viable option in the two-post passing game. The high post sets the pick for the exterior player in possession of the ball above the foul line. The movement options listed in the discussion of the two-player game (page 5) are limited by the positioning of the low post. If the ballside block is open, then options that involve heading to the basket are available. When the strongside low post is occupied, the screener must step out after the pick is used.

Coaches can best teach the two-post passing game using the part-whole method. They drill individual components before developing the entire offense. Coaches provide separate instruction before bringing the post and perimeter players together. Post players must know how to change positions. Perimeter people will have to learn to incorporate the high- and low-post players into their movements. Breakdown drills are useful for review sessions. For example, if a team has trouble grasping the motion required when the ball goes into a low post, the coach can drill the specific action.

ONE-POST PASSING GAME

Teams that have an outstanding interior player are excellent candidates to run the one-post passing game. The one-post passing game allows a team to take advantage of an inside mismatch. The offense is arranged to send the ball to a specific person in the post area. If the team has two strong inside players on the floor at the same time, the two-post passing game is the better option. Coaches must be confident in their players' ability to make decisions. The non-sequential nature of a passing game's motion should appeal to coaches.

Personnel

To run the one-post offense effectively, a team needs an excellent inside-scoring post player. The post player needs to be willing to work on obtaining position along the lane for possible post feeds to materialize. He or she should crave the ball inside and finish the play after receiving the ball. The offense benefits if the second big player is competent from the outside, especially if he or she is a serious scoring threat in the 15- to 20-foot range. This offense provides some flexibility in terms of personnel because it is possible to install a fourth perimeter player to replace the big player on the exterior. The more productive the perimeter people are at scoring from the periphery, the more success a squad will have.

Scoring

This offense provides an adequate mix of scoring situations. The highlighted player must be able to produce shots in and around the paint. The other four players are encouraged to throw the basketball in. They score from the outside to open up the inside. Players on the exterior must be capable of putting the ball on the floor to penetrate to the basket.

Execution

In the illustrations, N is the highlighted player. The highlighted player assumes position in the post area, either high or low, strongside or weakside. The other players take up positions on the perimeter.

In figure 1.6, the highlighted player (N) occupies the low post (strongside or weakside). Players execute the pass and cut. The point guard (G) passes to S2 and sprints. If the ballside low post is not occupied, G moves to the basket. If N is strongside, then the cutter (G) moves as shown. At the ballside elbow, the cutter breaks to the offside of the lane. B1 and S1 rotate for spacing and floor balance. If the low post (N) is on the weakside block, the passer (G) makes a hard cut to the hoop, performing a give-and-go. If the guard does not catch the ball, a cross pick is set for N. The other two players (S1 and B1) still rotate for spacing purposes. The pass and cut action can also be used if N occupies the high post just above the foul line. This time the cutter (G) uses a pick from N after passing to S2. B1 and S1 again rotate.

When the wing catches the ball, the low post (N) could also vacate and head to the high post. This move gives S2 a chance to go one-on-one along the baseline. N dictates the option by moving high. Once the wing (S2) sees

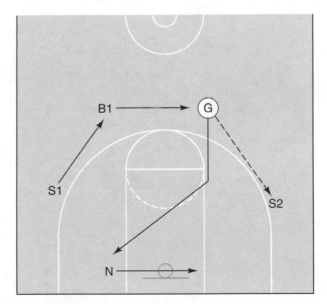

Figure 1.6   Cutting short.

the move to the high post, he or she considers putting the ball on the floor as part of a one-on-one maneuver. The other players perform cutting short (at the elbow) and replacing movements. They do not allow defenders to get into positions that would allow them to help their teammates easily.

In figure 1.7, the players execute a down screen when the ball is passed across the top. B1 passes to S2 and down picks for S1. If another post player (B1) is in the lineup, I prefer using him or her as a screener the majority of the time. If B1 had been on the wing and S1 was the passer when the ball was tossed across the key, a back screen is set. The closest player on the exterior screens for the passer. The player using the back pick (S1) either cuts to the basket for a lob if the weakside low post is vacant or fades toward the near corner. Establishing a rescreen action is also possible. In either case, the original screener (B1) turns to set another pick for the same player. Players do not hesitate to exercise the rescreen if the initial one does not produce results. When the ball is passed across the top of the key, the flare screen is another option that players can implement. The passer cuts down the foul-lane line. The nearest player on the perimeter reads the move and heads toward the lane to set a flare screen. The recipient fades over the top of the pick. The screener steps out after the pick is used. See further information on setting a screen, using

a pick, back pick, rescreening, and flare screen on pages 4-6.

In figure 1.8, the highlighted player (N) is on the strongside block. N recognizes that a teammate is being aggressively denied on the ballside wing. He or she flashes high toward the ball and catches the pass. On the pass from S2 to N, the point guard (G) back cuts to the bucket, seeking a bounce pass from N. The guard cuts as soon as the ball leaves the passer's hands. The passer (S2) replaces the guard (G), while the other two players (B1 and S1) keep the weakside defense occupied by screening for one another on the offside. If the defense is aggressively overplaying the wing when the low post (N) is on the weakside box, there is no flash high. The denied player (G) makes a backdoor move, looking to receive a direct pass from S2 for a layup. If he or she does not gain control of the ball, an L-cut is performed to secure the ball on the wing. See details about the L-cut on page 7.

When the ball goes to the highlighted player on the ballside low post, players create movement to make it hard for the opposition to double-team or rake the post. The same acts transpire as with the two-post passing game when the ball is dumped inside. Refer to the sections on throwing the ball inside and passing into the low post on page 6.

In figure 1.9, players counter defensive denial of the pass across the top. B1 is overplayed. The player on the weakside perimeter (S1) realizes

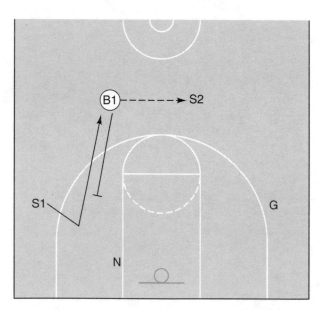

Figure 1.7   Pass across the top.

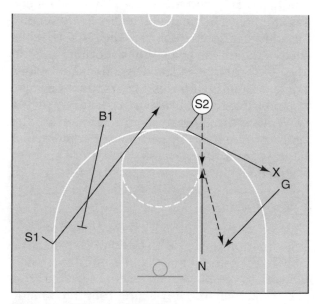

Figure 1.8   Wing overplayed.

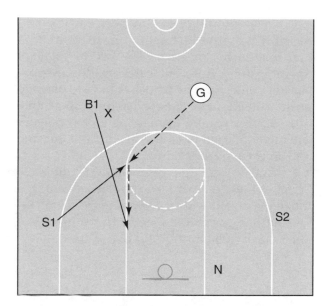

Figure 1.9 Pass across the top denied.

the predicament and flashes toward the player with the ball (G). B1 or G may initiate the option by calling S1's name. Quick recognition of denial is essential. The overplayed player creates space and provides an area where S1 can flash to catch the pass from G. Once the ball leaves the passer's hands, B1 back cuts to the basket in anticipation of a bounce pass from S1.

The one-post passing game includes several rules. Unlike in the two-post passing game, the four perimeter players do not establish two-player games. Screens on the ball do not occur. Players move without the ball to create scoring opportunities.

The designated low-post player stays active. He or she cannot stand still for more than three seconds. The post player moves weakside to strongside and high to low and vice versa. High-post positioning is restricted to just above the foul line, not out past the arc.

The highlighted player is a worker. He or she willingly expends energy to post up. The four players on the perimeter constantly make an effort to send the ball inside to the post player before putting up shots from a distance. The players on the perimeter maintain spacing with each other and with the post player. Players keep play off the baseline as much as possible. Players must also be careful not to get too close to the foul lane.

Keys

Coaches may wish to break down the offenses to specific actions for practice. The through call and overplay options of passes to the wing or across the top require recognition as the key to implementation. Coaches should drill players on the circumstances necessary to perform each option. Repetition in practice should carry over to better execution during a contest.

When the through call is used with the one-post passing game, the perimeter player with the ball out front runs the option only if he or she recognizes a post individual alongside. If the offense is using four perimeter players, it is likely that the defense will just switch on the back pick, decreasing the effectiveness of the call. Refer to the discussion of screening between post and perimeter players on page 4.

The one-post passing game is probably best taught through the whole-part methodology. Five players are on the floor initially because the four stationed on the exterior are working together while the highlighted person operates solo. They learn to maintain proper spacing and how to interact with each other.

Coaches should encourage players to dribble penetrate from the perimeter, especially when the highlighted player is away from the ball. Drives to the basket are more likely in the one-post passing game because two big players are not constantly moving within the lane area. Players also learn to get into position for shot opportunities after penetration occurs.

In the one-post passing game, the low post is the highlighted player. Therefore, he or she should spend more time on the ballside than on the weakside. The player should be away from the basketball only about 30 percent of the time.

To execute the through option, players must quickly recognize appropriate player placement. Call recognition is important in the one-post passing game because the second big player could be anywhere on the periphery.

Coaches who normally use two big players may want to set aside some practice time to work with four perimeter players in the one-post passing game. A circumstance may arise during a game when having four outside players on the floor at one time would be beneficial.

In the one-post passing game, the highlighted player occasionally vacates the low post and goes high to allow a one-on-one chance for a wing with the ball. The highlighted player does not choose this option if the player with the ball is not an effective one-on-one player. The passer reads whether a cut to the basket is desired off a high-post screen. The highlighted player raises a fist and calls the passer's name if he or she wants the high-post screen consummated. Otherwise, the passer just darts to the weakside while staying above the foul line, allowing the player with the ball on the wing to go one-on-one.

Coaches should place any player who could possibly play the highlighted post position in that role during practice. The two big players operate under different rules in the one-post passing game. Anyone who may have to play the position needs to be exposed to the responsibilities before an actual game. Some post players will have to learn both the inside spot and the one on the periphery.

Passing games are rule-oriented offenses. Coaches must determine the rules and enforce them. If a coach wants players to perform certain actions or exhibit specific traits, he or she must make them aware of those wishes.

CHAPTER 2

Offenses From 1-4 High Sets

The 1-4 set enables a team to combat an aggressive man-to-man defense. Teams initiate the seven patterns covered in this chapter from a 1-4 high set. Before going into details on each pattern, let's review the beginning of the offenses and the counters required to combat defensive overplays. All seven patterns start in the same fashion. Analysis of the individual plays shows that all begin when the initial movements conclude.

STARTING SET FOR 1-4 HIGH OFFENSES

My primary consideration when creating these actions was to use the placement of personnel as a starting point for scoring possibilities. The consistency of activity creates a smooth transition into multiple offenses. The movements described here are introductory. Although not continuous on their own, they allow players to execute the seven offensive patterns.

Post players need to be able to handle the ball away from the basket and have the decision-making skills to make appropriate passes. Ideally, the two players in the wing positions can score 15 to 20 feet from the basket.

Layups for wings result from back cuts to the hoop to counter defensive overplays. The two wings achieve good looks for shots in the 15- to 20-foot range between the foul line extended and the baseline. Either a big player or a point guard could receive an inside scoring chance by stepping to the ball after establishing a screen.

In the beginning set, four players take up positions across half-court above the foul line. The point guard (G) brings the ball up the middle, giving him or her the ability to complete the first pass to any of the other players. Each post player (B1 and B2) is positioned just above one of the elbows. The two perimeter shooters (S1 and S2) are on the wings, slightly above the foul line extended.

If G passes to S1 or S2, then each subsequent offense begins at that point. A situation may develop, however, in which the defense denies a wing (S1 or S2), preventing the start of the offense. The point guard (G) may toss the ball directly to the wing, back cutting to the hoop for a layup. This action also is possible if the defense overplays the big players. The lead guard sends direct passes if his or her teammates are open and heading to the basket.

Players need to know what to do if the defense denies the wings. As shown in figure 2.1, the point guard (G) automatically passes to one post player (B1 or B2) to counter denials of the wings. The ball goes to B1 because the wing on his or her side (S1) is denied. As the ball leaves the passer's hands, S1 executes a backdoor cut, anticipating a bounce pass from

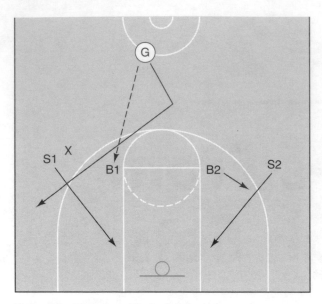

Figure 2.1   Wing denied in the 1-4 set.

B1 for a layup. The other three players (G, S2, and B2) hesitate before making their moves. G replaces S1 (the cutter) on the wing. The other wing (S2) moves to the near box on the lane. The big player (B2) slides out short toward the closest wing. They do not interfere with the back-cut opportunity.

As the action continues, the three all set down screens (figure 2.2). G sets a single screen on one side of the floor, and S2 and B2 set staggered screens on the other side for S1. S1 has the choice of which screening action to exploit. The player nearest the other block (S2) always heads opposite S1 and uses a lone down pick.

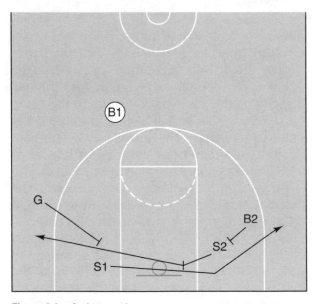

Figure 2.2   Action continues.

The rule is that the original wings (S1 and S2) finish opposite one another. The big player with the ball (B1) passes to either S1 or S2 or inside to G or B2, stepping to the ball after picking. Refer to the discussion of the down screen in "Man-to-Man Offensive Fine-Tuning" on page 4.

The seven offenses that follow pick up at one of two points, either after a wing (S1 or S2) receives the first pass in the 1-4 alignment or when the initial toss goes to a big player in the 1-4 alignment, who in turn throws the ball to either wing (S1 or S2). Coaches should teach these movements before beginning instruction on any of the seven offenses that follow.

Refer to "Man-to-Man Offensive Fine-Tuning" in chapter 1 (page 4), especially the discussions of setting a screen, slipping a screen, and using a pick.

Players need to know how to recognize defensive denials. Any of the four players may be able to receive a direct pass from the point guard following a backdoor move.

The ball handler reacts spontaneously and executes the pass to the same-side post player when the defense overplays the wing. The ball handler reads the defense and acts quickly.

If the initial pass goes to a post player, he or she then selects the next pass. The big player who catches the first pass pivots and faces the basket immediately after looking for the back-door cutter over his or her outside shoulder. The coach chooses how to teach the pivot (front or reverse).

The ballside wing needs to know to start his or her back cut to the hoop as soon as the ball leaves the point guard's hands and is on its way to the big player on the same side. The big player who catches the first pass uses a bounce pass if the wing is open while going backdoor.

Wings are slightly above the post players in the initial 1-4 high set. The team must understand that wings and post players are interchangeable. Coaches should give special attention to any player who may be required to know both positions. He or she must learn twice the amount of information.

The playmaker needs to take charge of the offense. He or she should know each teammate's responsibilities. The playmaker has to be able to point out mistakes and get people into their proper locations. If the point guard does not possess convincing skills around the basket, passes should not go inside when the point guard steps to the ball after picking.

FLARE

I first saw a flare screen when the University of Kentucky under Coach Rick Pitino used it. The effectiveness of a flare screen increases because the defense is screened while in help position, when the space between the defender and player being guarded is at its maximum. I wanted to incorporate the flare screen into a continuous action that included a pick-and-roll, which draws the attention of the uninvolved defensive players. When a flare pick is used in conjunction with the pick-and-roll against man-to-man defense, defenders away from the basketball are in optimal positions to be exploited by a flare screen.

Personnel

The flare is more effective if all three outside players are strong exterior shooters. They need to be able to put the ball on the floor with either hand. The two post players need to be effective screeners and capable of scoring around the basket.

Scoring

Players can use any shots associated with a two-player game: a shot off the dribble by a perimeter player heading toward the top of the key or baseline, a score secured by a big player going to the basket on the roll or through a slip-the-screen maneuver, or a shot made when a big player posts up when the defense switches and a mismatch occurs. Perimeter players receive jumpers in the vicinity of the foul line extended by way of flare picks.

Execution

In figure 2.3, the initial pass to the wing (S1) occurs from the 1-4 set. After passing, G heads to a spot just off center at the foul line toward the weakside. The opposite wing (S2) moves to a position above the three-point arc along the extended lane line on the offside. The weakside big player (B2) steps off the lane at the foul line extended.

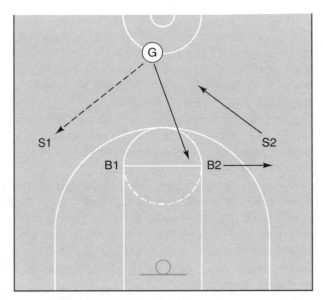

Figure 2.3   Weakside spots filled.

The ballside big player (B1) picks for the ball handler (S1) (figure 2.4). After S1 dribbles toward the middle, the player out front on the weakside (S2) begins to cut straight down the near lane line and uses the flare screen set by B2. See the discussions of the two-player game and flare screen in "Man-to-Man Offensive Fine-Tuning" on pages 5-6.

S1 throws a skip pass to the perimeter player (S2), who used the flare screen if open. Three players immediately fill the spots on the weakside. The perimeter player at the foul line (G)

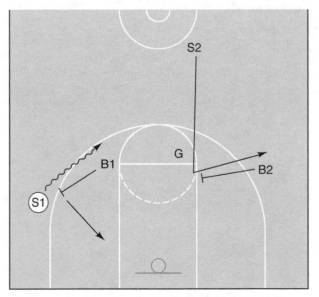

Figure 2.4   Continuation to the two-player game and flare pick.

goes above the offside elbow. The lone big player (B1) races to the offside foul line extended, while the passer (S1) occupies a place on the foul line close to the center. Players are then in the same formation shown in figure 2.3 except on the other side of the court. Action continues as players execute the two-player game (B2 picks for S2) on the ballside. The weakside action begins once S2 dribbles toward the top of the key. B1 sets the flare screen for G.

What happens when the player using the flare screen is denied the basketball? He or she recognizes the overplay and immediately cuts to the weakside box. The player at the foul line reads the denial and cuts off a second screen by the post player (the original flare screener) to the same-side wing.

Whenever the wing secures the ball, the nearest big player sets a pick for the pass receiver, while the other three players go above the elbow, to the center of the foul line, and to the foul line extended (lone post player). The team runs the offense continuously. Two players are involved in the two-player game on the ballside, and the other three players fill sites on the offside to perform flare screens.

In figure 2.5, player positioning coincides with personnel placement when the first pass goes to a post player (B1) from the 1-4 formation. B1 subsequently passes to the wing (S2) and heads to set a screen for the recipient. G, S1, and B2 fill the weakside slots. The team runs the play continuously.

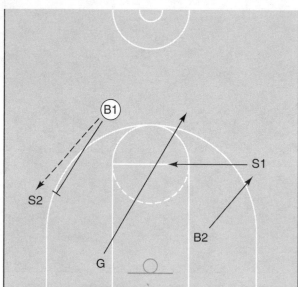

Figure 2.5 First pass went to the post in the 1-4 set.

Keys

In "Man-to-Man Offensive Fine-Tuning" on page 4, refer to the following topics: screening between post and perimeter players, setting a screen, slipping a screen, using a pick, throwing the ball inside, L-cut, and passing into the low post.

This offense is not difficult to teach. Players consistently fill spots on the ballside and weakside, which leads to implementation of the two-player game and flare screen. Execution levels possibly will be satisfactory after one hour of teaching the offense. Coaches may find it valuable to break down the offense to practice the two-player game and flare screen separately.

The weakside player's timing when beginning the cut down the lane line for the flare screen is crucial. He or she starts as soon as the ball handler takes one or two dribbles and heads toward the key.

The big player moving to establish the two-player game does not have to hurry. He or she takes time to permit teammates to fill proper positions on the weakside.

Perimeter players should glance inside. They must send the ball to post players who are open and rolling to the basket.

If a breakdown in the pattern occurs, players should pass the ball to a perimeter player on a wing. To get back into the basic pattern, the nearest big player moves to set a pick on the ball and three other players fill spots on the weakside.

STACK

I created the stack offense early in my college head-coaching career and used it consistently thereafter. It played an integral role in my team's success. Players couple a two-player game with a variety of actions on the weakside. The maneuvers complement one another. Coaches need to be confident in their players' ability to operate a two-player game. The offense does not ignore the exterior players. Scoring activities occur simultaneously on both sides of the court.

Personnel

Big players need to be potent screeners with the capability to score around the hoop. The offense benefits if all three perimeter players can stick the outside jumper. They need to be proficient at handling the basketball with either hand. Players are required to read the defense so that they can respond to a variety of defensive techniques.

Scoring

Perimeter players shoot jump shots off the dribble after using screens on the ball. They can attempt shots toward the baseline or at the top of the key. The big players roll to the bucket for layups or slide to open areas for jump shots. If the defense switches, the post player may benefit from a mismatch and score by posting up along the lane. Perimeter players attempt exterior jump shots near the key by using staggered screens, double down screens, or single down picks. They may or may not be beyond the three-point line. Post and perimeter players might enjoy inside scoring attempts or outside jumpers, respectively, because of the screening maneuvers associated with a stack along the foul lane.

Execution

In figure 2.6, the first pass goes to the wing (S1) in a 1-4 set. The players are immediately in the basic formation of the offense. Three players (B2, G, and S2) assume weakside positions, forming a line along the foul lane, with the big

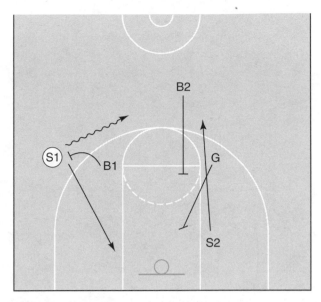

Figure 2.7   Primary action continues.

player (B2) out past the three-point line, the passer (G) at the weakside elbow, and the other perimeter player (S2) at the block.

The ballside post player (B1) establishes a screen for the player with the ball (S1) (figure 2.7). B1 and S1 play a two-player game. S1 takes one or two dribbles toward the top of the key. G and B2 on the weakside set staggered down picks for the shooter (S2) stationed on the block below. S2 gets open above the closest elbow. See the discussion of the two-player game on page 5.

If the next pass goes to the player coming to the top using the offside screen (S2 in figure 2.7), the weakside big player (B2) continues down and plants a second screen for the perimeter person below (G). The screen recipient pops out to the closer wing, and the post player steps to the ball after the screen is used. See the discussion of the down screen on page 4.

Whenever the ball is thrown to a wing, the nearer big player sets a pick for the receiver. The remaining three players form a line on the offside lane line, with the post player farther from the hoop.

Occasionally, the defense denies the person coming up off the weakside picking action (figure 2.8). The overplayed player (S1) back cuts to the basket and curls around the post player (B2), who just rolled to the hoop. B1 and S2 perform the same maneuver out of the stack formation—B1 picks for S2. If G completes the

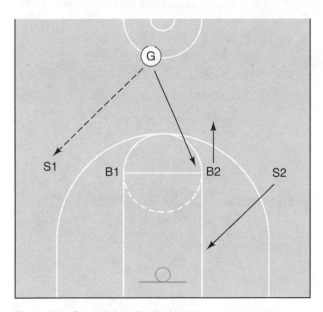

Figure 2.6   Pass to the wing in the 1-4.

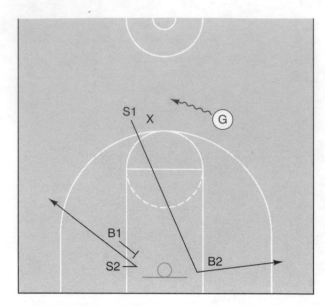

Figure 2.8 Defense denies the toss across the top.

pass to either wing (S2 or S1), the squad returns to normal motion.

The first pass went to a post player out of the 1-4 set (figure 2.9). The big player (B1) tosses to the wing (S2) and then establishes a screen on the ball. The other three players (G, B2, and S1) scurry to weakside spots. Instead of staggered down screens, G and B2 come together to form a double screen. S1 still races to the weakside box. If B1 had thrown to the far wing (S1), the other post player (B2) would have screened for the pass receiver. The closer big player plants the pick consistently. Refer to the section on

the double screen in "Man-to-Man Offensive Fine-Tuning" on page 6.

G and B2 double pick for the player directly below (S1) (figure 2.10). S2 dribbles once or twice toward the top of the key as part of the pick-and-roll with B1. Two offside players head down. S1 uses the twin screen to get open up top.

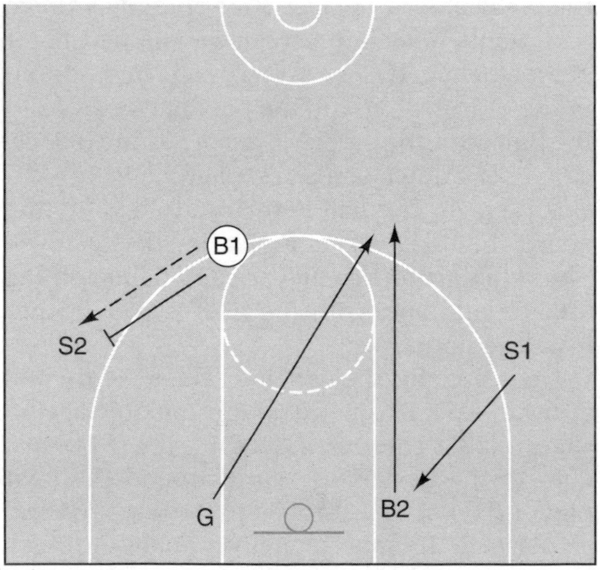

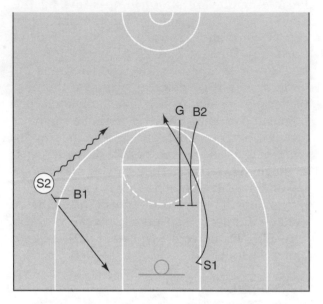

Figure 2.10 Two-player game and the double down screen.

Figure 2.11 illustrates the third option in place of the staggered or double screen. The players on the weakside occupy three spots.

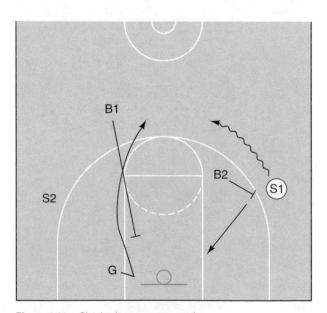

Figure 2.9 Pass was thrown to the post in the 1-4 set.

Figure 2.11 Single down screen option.

The post player (B1) is out behind the three-point line, directly above the weakside elbow. One perimeter player (G) is on the box, and the other (S2) bolts to position behind the arc on the wing. After S1 takes one or two dribbles at B1, he or she sets a single down screen for G. If the ball is tossed to G out front, S2 stays wide and B1 posts up strong along the foul lane. If G does not have a shot, he or she flings the ball to S2 on the wing or B1 inside.

Keys

Refer to "Man-to-Man Offensive Fine-Tuning" in chapter 1 on page 4, especially the following topics: screening between post and perimeter players, setting a screen, slipping a screen, using a pick, throwing the ball inside, and passing into the low post.

Coaches should decide which of the weakside options they will teach to their teams. The coach might wish to instruct his or her team in the execution of two, or possibly all three, weakside options (staggered screen, double pick, or single screen). The advantage of using the staggered or single down screen is that a big player is last to set a pick for a perimeter player. With the double screen, the pick takes up more space but defenders on the two perimeter players may switch defensive assignments.

The coach can exert more control if he or she decides which of the three weakside options the team should execute during a given possession. As long as the coach feels comfortable in the team's ability to handle the variety, he or she can teach more than one. The coach can even allow the three weakside players to choose their activity. The passer decides which option to use. If he or she moves to the weakside elbow, staggered screens occur. If he or she heads to a spot out front with the post player, the double pick happens. If he or she cuts wide to the weakside wing, the single screen is the proper selection. Regardless, the big player moves above the weakside elbow past the key, and the other perimeter player heads to the offside block.

The overplay countermove is the same for the player coming toward the top regardless of which weakside option the team is using. He or she employs a back cut down the lane and curls around the big player rolling to the hoop out to a position behind the three-point line.

The backdoor move cannot occur too early. The coach wants the ball delivered to the big player heading to the basket if possible.

The perimeter players are obliged to glance consistently to the interior at the post players. This offense is not just for jump shots.

With staggered and double-screen options, the big player involved in the offside pick should execute a second screen for the outside player below when ball is tossed out front.

The post player heading out to set a screen on the ball can attempt to post up along the foul lane before moving to pick. Hesitation enables the three weakside players to reach their proper locations. If the post player is open, the ball goes inside for a possible score. The screener does not hurry to set the screen but is aware of the potential five-second violation on the ball handler.

Players will not have difficulty understanding this offense. Instruction is not extensive. Players consistently fill spots on the ballside and weakside, which leads to the implementation of the two-player game and some action by the other three players. Execution levels possibly will be satisfactory within one hour of teaching the offense.

Coaches may wish to break down the pattern for practice, especially when educating a team on the proper execution of the two-player game. Performing the offense initially on a dummy (no-defense) basis is probably a good idea. Coaches can add defense after they are comfortable with the team's operation of the pattern and elements contained within it.

When the perimeter player out top has the ball and uses the staggered, double, or single down screen but does not have a shot, he or she pursues a pass to the near wing to complete the ball-reversal action. If desperate, the team could assume the 1-4 alignment at this point to counter overplays if defensive denials persist.

CUTTERS

Teams have used the cutter offense since before I was in high school, well over 30 years ago. This pattern rushes two cutters to the ballside whenever the ball is reversed. Players handle the basketball on the periphery and may be able to obtain shots from three-point range.

The cutter offense is an equal-opportunity offense. No one or two players take the majority of shots. The offense sends multiple cutters to the hoop.

Personnel

All players, including big players, must be able to handle the ball on the perimeter and be capable of making sound pass decisions. Each player should have the ability to score around the basket. The effectiveness of the offense increases if players are proficient from the outside.

Scoring

Any player can take a shot in the foul lane off a cut to the hoop. Outside shot attempts from the foul line to the top of the key are options for all players. Players may be open for layups by making back cuts to the basket.

Execution

Figure 2.12 shows the start of the pattern. The initial pass goes to a wing (S1) in the 1-4 formation. The point guard (G) cuts to the ballside corner, moving through the ballside elbow. The weakside wing (S2) heads to a position near the offside box, while the ballside post player (B1) screens so that the other big player (B2) can cut to the basket. Once the job is complete, B1 sprints to the top to receive the next pass.

The next pass goes out top to B1. S2 executes an L-cut up the foul-lane line and then out to the wing, timing the movement with B1's reception of the ball. S2 makes a backdoor cut if the defense aggressively denies him or her at the wing. B1 reverses the basketball as soon as possible by throwing to the opposite wing (S2). Refer to the discussion of the L-cut on page 7.

Figure 2.13 illustrates the continuing motion, which happens as soon as B1 releases the ball to S2. S1 is the first player to cut off a screen by B2. He or she always sprints to the ballside corner unless the pass is secured for a scoring chance. The player in the corner (G) is the second cutter. The first and second cutters may rub off either side of B2's screen. The passer out front (B1) delays before heading down to screen the screener (B2). B1 pops out to the near sideline.

With the completion of the motion shown in figure 2.13, S2 flings the ball back to the top (to B2) and the ball is reversed again. Players execute the same actions with one possible exception. The second cutter does *not* cut off the screen along the lane but stops short of it. The passer (B2) still sets a screen for the screener. The second cutter may or may not choose to use the down pick. If the second cutter does use the pick, the screener moves across the foul lane and switches roles with the second cutter. The second cutter yells, "Me" when he or she wishes to use the pick from the top to

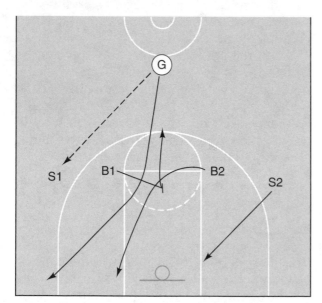

Figure 2.12 Pass to the wing in the 1-4 set.

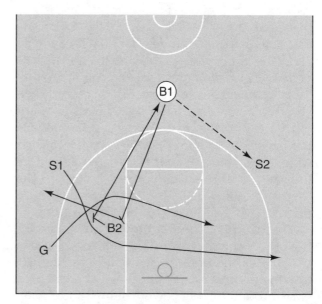

Figure 2.13 Ball reversed from the top.

let both screeners know his or her intentions. When S2 chooses not to use the pick, he or she becomes the next screener along the lane. The player moves to the appropriate location across the lane as soon as the ball heads to a player at the top. Play is continuous. The team reverses the ball and sends the cutters to the basket off the pick along the lane.

In figure 2.14, the initial pass went to a post player (B1) in the 1-4 set. B1 screens away for the opposite wing (S1 or S2). The player low on the ballside (G) pops out to the closer corner. As soon as S2 casts the ball to the top, the person away low (B2) zips to become the screener along the lane (figure 2.15). B1 pops out to receive the reverse pass from S1.

Players must be ready to adjust to defensive overplays. If the defense denies the player coming to the top, he or she automatically screens away for the nearest teammate. If the defense overplays the wing and the team cannot fully reverse the ball, the player coming to the top executes a back cut to the basket. If no layup opportunity develops, he or she performs an L-cut. Other players demonstrate patience and wait to make moves until the ball is completely reversed.

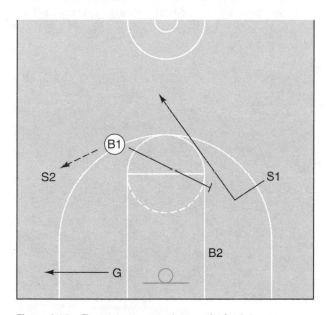

Figure 2.14 First pass went to the post in the 1-4 set.

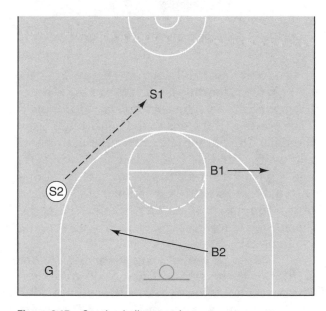

Figure 2.15 Starting ball reversal.

Keys

See the following topics in "Man-to-Man Offensive Fine-Tuning" on page 4: setting a screen, slipping a screen, using a pick, throwing the ball inside, and passing into the low post.

The offense may be hard for some players to comprehend. A fair amount of time will be required to teach it. Coaches will likely spend approximately two hours of instruction time getting the execution of the play to an acceptable quality level.

Coaches should review the overplay options to counter denials out front and on the wings. Players need to react swiftly to combat an aggressive defense.

Coaches cannot put this pattern on hold for long. They must thoroughly reexamine the team's implementation on a weekly basis.

Players need to stay in the pattern. They cannot afford mental breakdowns. The second cutter must understand that he or she is the next screener along the lane and choose whether to use the pick along the lane or stop short of it. If the second cutter elects to stop, he or she screams, "Me" and decides to exploit the pick from the top or remain put.

The player out front *always* screens the screener after the ball is reversed. The move does not begin until the second cutter approaches the screen. He or she reacts to the second cutter's me call, if necessary. The screener reads the second cutter so that he or she knows the precise target of the pick. The second cutter nods toward the screener along the lane if he or she is staying put.

Cutters need to take responsibility for running defenders into the screens along the lane. They do not hesitate to step as though going over and slice under or vice versa.

Rapid ball reversal is important. The quicker the team achieves it, the better.

Coaches should tell players what type of shots each can attempt. Players should not be shooting the ball from the top of the key if they are not capable of making it.

The me option is a good way to counter the defenders' switching in reaction to the cutters off the screen along the foul lane. The coach may also give the first cutter the alternative. When the first cutter makes the call, the second cutter goes first and heads to the ballside corner. The first cutter then chooses whether to stay or use the pick from the top. Giving a second player the option increases the complexity of the offense.

Coaches should instruct players that the pattern rotates all five people on the floor. All players have the same responsibilities in terms of what they must learn.

ARIZONA

Coach Lute Olsen at the University of Arizona has used the basics of the Arizona offense, but I added some subtle changes to fit my personnel better. The offense proved to be highly productive, especially in getting the ball to the interior for a scoring chance. The Arizona offense is a good choice for a team that has two strong post players capable of scoring in the paint. By choosing this offense, the team makes a commitment to sending the ball inside.

Personnel

Post people need to possess strong inside-scoring skills and be capable of making 15- to 18-foot jump shots near the foul line. Perimeter players must be able to shoot the outside shot, especially from three-point range. This outside scoring threat opens the interior for the main action. The offense is even more effective if one of the perimeter players can score in the paint.

Scoring

Interior shots occur close to the hoop in or near the foul lane. Players attempt jump shots from 15 to 20 feet near the key. Exterior players get chances for long-range jumpers on the two wings.

Execution

From the 1-4 set, the point guard (G) passes to a wing (S1) (figure 2.16). As the ball leaves the playmaker's hands, the opposite wing (S2) cuts to the ballside low position off a high-post screen by the weakside big player (B2). S2 ends approximately five to eight feet off the lane along the baseline. The lead guard (G) immediately replaces S2 on the wing. B1 picks for B2 (screener), establishing the screen closely following B2's pick for S2.

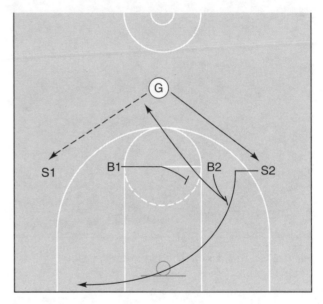

Figure 2.16 Pass to the wing in the 1-4 set.

The pass goes to B2 out front (figure 2.17). B1 cross screens for the player at the ballside baseline spot (S2). S2 slides over or under the pick. The screener (B2) steps to the ball after S2 uses the pick. The passer (B2) views the action low and waits until it is completed. Both wings (G and S1) maintain positions at or slightly above the foul line extended whenever a teammate at the top has possession of the ball. See the discussion of low exchanges and cross screens in chapter 1 on page 6.

B2 passes to either wing (G or S1) (figure 2.18). He or she sets a diagonal down screen for the teammate low opposite (B1). At the same time, the wing away from the pass (S1) bolts to the closest corner. The ballside low player

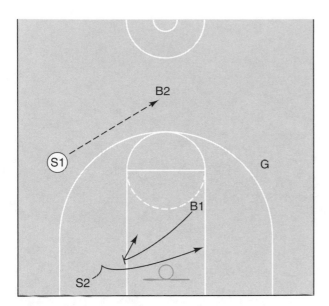

Figure 2.17   Pass to the top—cross screen.

(S2) moves to the baseline approximately five to eight feet off the foul lane. The screener (B2) *always* seals toward the ball. G endeavors to deliver the ball to the screener (B2) if he or she is open, especially when defense switches.

When the post player receives the initial pass in a 1-4 set, the ballside low player darts to the baseline. The passer sets a diagonal down screen for the teammate at the weakside block and seals toward the ball. The weakside wing drops to the corner. The point guard is part of the three-player movement around the lane. The other two perimeter players are on the wings.

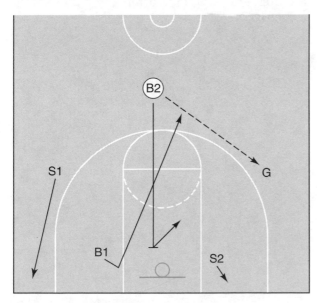

Figure 2.18   Pass to the wing and finishing the pattern.

The first pass to the post brings the lead guard into the screening action. When the starting toss goes to a wing, the other wing is in the three-player motion.

Players are prepared to handle two defensive overplay situations. First, when the player out front with the ball sees both wings aggressively denied, he or she has a one-on-one chance as the two low players step off the lane. Second, when the defense overplays the player heading toward the top, he or she recognizes the denial and simply cuts to the block opposite the ball while yelling, "Up." This call informs the teammate who originally screened for him or her to pop out top to receive the next pass. Regular offensive motion resumes.

Keys

See the sections about setting a screen, slipping a screen, using a pick, passing into the low post, and throwing the ball inside in "Man-to-Man Offensive Fine-Tuning" in chapter 1 (page 4).

This offense is not difficult to teach. Players should be able to comprehend the motion within one hour of instructional time. Coaches may first want to teach just the three-player rotations before adding the wings. They may also wish to have the squad practice on a dummy (no-defense) basis initially.

All perimeter players need to practice playing at both wing positions as well as being part of the three-player rotation around the foul lane.

The ballside low player slides to the baseline when the basketball is in the hands of a wing. This act creates space for the diagonal down screener in case of a defensive switch. The screener should be open if the opponent switches.

The low player away from the wing who sent the ball to the top *always* initiates the cross-screening action.

If the ball is in a wing's hands and the player heading out front off the diagonal screen is overplayed, he or she yells, "Up" and motors to the offside block. The denied player must not make the cut and call too early. He or she must first take the defender out past the top of the key. This action enables the screener to gain some space to seal the defender while looking for a pass directly from the wing. See the discussion of pinning the defender on page 7.

The perimeter players on the wings need to be ready for shot attempts. Their defenders may be caught trying to help teammates inside.

Post players are always part of the three-player rotation around the foul lane. They need to know the wing spots only if they can play on the perimeter as a small forward.

POWER

The power offense focuses on sending the basketball to the paint for scoring purposes. This basic pattern revolves around the post-up. The motion is uncomplicated. The power offense is effective when a team has two big players who are proficient with their backs to the basket. Post players should have good physical size and strength. In this offense, players make an effort to send the ball inside.

Personnel

The big players must be able to score around the basket and play physically to gain position low against defenders. Perimeter players need to have the ability to stick the outside shot so that the defense cannot concentrate on stopping the interior players.

Scoring

Post players receive the ball around the basket and attempt shots in and around the foul lane. Shots above the elbows are also feasible if defense sags off coverage. Perimeter players procure shots by using the down screen set by a big player at a box on the lane, by attempting corner jumpers by using a fade move when exploiting a baseline screen, by cutting off the baseline screen to get near the hoop, or by attempting jump shots from the periphery if defenders are more concerned with helping inside.

Execution

As shown in figure 2.19, the first pass goes to the wing (S1) in the 1-4 formation. The ballside big player (B1) screens away for B2. B2 dives to the ballside block. The screener (B1) pops out beyond the three-point line above the weakside elbow. The post players also have the option for B1 to fake the pick for B2. B1 then dives to the strongside box, and B2 steps out above

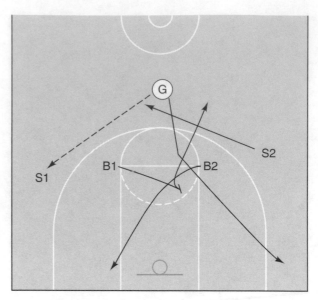

Figure 2.19   First pass to the wing in the 1-4 set.

the offside elbow. The passer (G) cuts to a spot behind the three-point arc below the weakside wing, while the offside wing (S2) sprints to a place above the ballside elbow.

If a post player (B1) secures the first pass in the 1-4 set, he or she has the option shown in figure 2.20. The ball then goes to a wing (S2). The player below (G) sets a high-post screen, allowing the passer (B1) to cut to the hoop. The opposite big player (B2) sprints up the lane line to a spot beyond the three-point arc. The screener (G) moves out eight feet or so past the elbow, replacing the cutter (B1). If B1 passes to the opposite wing (S1) originally, B2 posts up

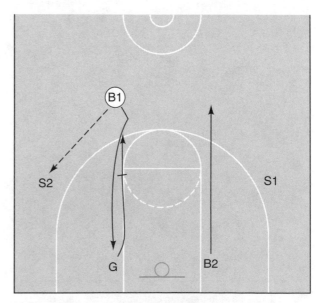

Figure 2.20   First pass went to the post in the 1-4 set.

strong while the other wing (S2) hustles to a spot above the ballside elbow. G breaks to the closest wing past the three-point line, while the passer (B1) stays put.

A wing (S1) passes the ball to a fellow perimeter player at the top (S2) (figure 2.21). One way to change sides is for the pass receiver (S2) to dribble at the post player (B1) next to him or her. Once S2 begins to dribble, the perimeter player on the ballside (G) heads into the foul lane and receives a down pick from the same-side big player (B1). See the discussion of the down screen on page 4. The other post player (B2) races out high past the arc and above the offside elbow. The weakside shooter (S1) drops down toward the near corner. G may shoot or feed the ball inside to B1.

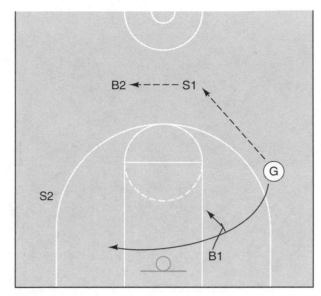

Figure 2.22   Reversing the basketball.

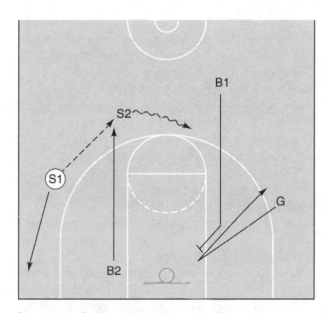

Figure 2.21   Basic motion of the power offense.

Instead of reversing the ball by using the dribble, the team can get the ball to the big player out front by passing (figure 2.22). S1 throws to B2. The wing on the same side as the passer (G) uses a baseline screen set by the near post player (B1) to dart to the ballside block. The screener (B1) steps to the ball. The wing (G) also has the option to fake cut to the ballside box and fade back to the same-side corner. B1 flashes to the ball. B2 looks to throw a skip pass to G or toss the ball directly into B1. If instead B2 tosses the ball to the same-side wing (S2), he or she dives to the ballside low post. If the wing (G) cuts to the ballside block, he or she heads

up the lane line to set a pick for B2's move to the basket. If G fades to the corner on the baseline screen, B2 dives to a vacant low post. Regardless, the other big player (B1) races about eight feet beyond the offside elbow when the ball is passed to the opposite wing (S2).

Players must commit one rule to memory. Whenever a perimeter player out front throws the ball to a wing, the passer cuts through to the offside corner at the elbow. The weakside wing immediately scampers to replace the cutter. The two exterior players exchange positions.

Figure 2.23 shows a big player (B1) throwing the ball to same-side wing (S2). After using the baseline screen, G heads up to set the high pick for the passer (B2). Meanwhile, B1 bolts up on the weakside. S1 fans out below the wing on the offside. Instead of passing the ball to the ballside wing (S2), B2 may decide to throw the ball back to S1 out front. On the pass, G comes back to the ballside wing, employing another screen by B1. The screener (B1) steps to the ball after the pick.

A skip pass completed from the wing to the post player on the weakside periphery is treated identically to a ball thrown to a big player from the perimeter player out front. The action is the same as changing sides with the pass. The passer chooses to cut off the baseline screen to the basket or fade back to the corner if the defender cheats over the screen. The passer and low-post player understand that if the skip pass is thrown, the big player may want to seal the

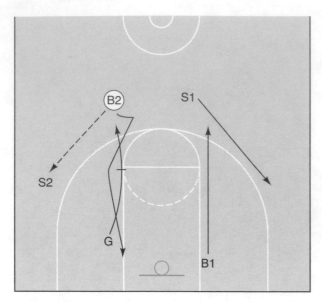

Figure 2.23   Big player tosses to the closest wing.

defender immediately and step toward the pass receiver. If the passer gives a genuine effort to feed the ball low and cannot accomplish it, the interior defender is probably either full fronting or side fronting from the baseline side. The low-post player has a position advantage if he or she seals *immediately* and prepares to catch the ball in the lane from the pass recipient out top opposite.

Coaches must teach the counter to denial of the pass out from the wing. The wing cannot throw to the exterior player at the top, toss a skip pass to the big player, or dump the ball inside to the low post. The wing reads the inability to pass and begins a one-on-one maneuver. The low player steps to the baseline while the two players out top slide farther out to maximize space for the dribbler.

Keys

Refer to "Man-to-Man Offensive Fine-Tuning" in chapter 1 on page 4, especially the following topics: screening between post and perimeter players, setting a screen, slipping a screen, using a pick, and pinning the defender.

Coaches should stress to big players that the offense focuses on them. If they are not willing to work to get position down low, this play will not be successful. Coaches want the ball thrown inside. Therefore, it is important to decide what action players are to execute whenever the ball goes to the low post. See the discussions of

throwing the ball inside and passing into the low post in chapter 1 on page 6.

When a post player has the ball out front, he or she must view the baseline screening action that is taking place. He or she looks to the baseline *before* tossing to a wing.

Drilling this offense into players' minds requires approximately one hour of instructional time. The offense is not a complex series of moves. It involves a big player posting up low and spreading the other four players around the periphery.

Coaches should review the two methods of ball reversal (dribble and pass) and tell team members to mix up their use. The dribble triggers a down screen, and the pass across to the big player puts the baseline screen into action.

The wing in possession of the ball must read the defense. He or she makes every effort to get the ball inside. The wing uses the dribble to improve passing angles as needed. In addition, the wing considers a skip pass to the other post player at the weakside top, especially if the low post is full fronted or side fronted from the baseline side. Players on the wings should dribble penetrate if no pass is available.

Coaches may wish to practice the baseline screening maneuver as a separate breakdown drill. The down pick at the box is another possibility. I strongly suggest teaching the offense as a whole using a dummy system at first and adding the defense later.

The three perimeter players are interchangeable. The two post players also perform identical tasks. Any player who plays both positions has a much tougher job. The best way for this player to learn is to memorize the pattern as a whole.

SCRANTON

The Scranton offense gets its name from one of the favorite actions used by Coach Bob Bessoir at the University of Scranton, my chief rival while I was at King's College. The success of his teams enabled the school to gain an excellent reputation nationally. Big players need to be proficient in the two-player game. The coach needs to have confidence in his or her players' abilities to take advantage of the screen-and-roll and staggered picks.

Personnel

Perimeter players need to be good exterior shooters and possess the ability to shoot successfully off a dribble while using either hand. Post players need to be effective screeners and have the ability to score as a result of a pick-and-roll.

Scoring

Shots develop through execution of the two-player game. Perimeter players get distant shots in the wing to baseline regions on both sides of the half-court. The screeners step to the ball and may receive interior passes and shot attempts in the paint. Layup opportunities arise for perimeter players by way of a cut to the basket using a high-post screen.

Execution

The opening pass goes to a wing (S1) (figure 2.24). The passer (G) cuts hard to the hoop, taking advantage of the pick by the high post (B1). The weakside perimeter player (S2) races to the near box. The offside big player (B2) is stationed above S2 near the weakside wing.

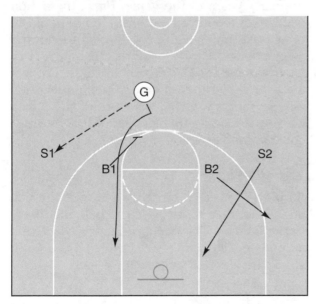

Figure 2.24   First pass to wing in the 1-4 set.

The high-post screener (B1) drifts and establishes a pick on the ball for S1 (figure 2.25). The player on the ballside box (G) capitalizes on the staggered screens by S2 and then B2 on the offside as soon as S1 takes one or two dribbles toward the key. After G uses the staggered

screens, the first screener (S2) heads to the opposite wing. S2 hesitates briefly to keep the side clear for B1 to roll to the basket. Refer to the discussion of the two-player game in chapter 1 on page 5.

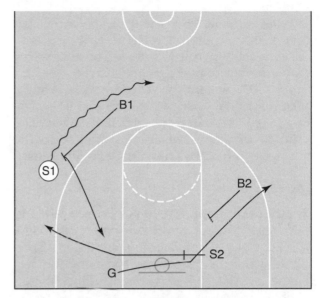

Figure 2.25   Primary motion of the Scranton offense.

If S1 sees a scoring opportunity arise from the two-player game, he or she takes advantage of it. But if S1 recognizes that no scoring opportunities are developing, he or she must dribble outward to create distance to make the next cut off the high-post screener (B2). See figure 2.26. The weakside players (S2 and B1) circulate to spots to set the stage for the staggered screens (B1 outside S2). The dribbler (S1) throws the

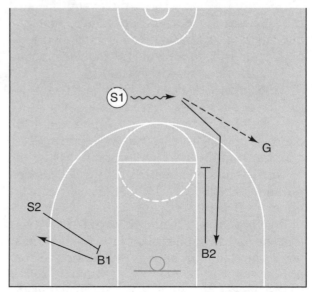

Figure 2.26   Dribble across the top and pass to the wing.

ball to the wing (G) and then runs off the screen set by the big player (B2), who is coming high. Players enact the standard motion of play (the two-player game and staggered screens) whenever the ball goes to the wing. They run the play continuously.

What happens when a post player catches the first pass from the 1-4 set? The next pass is to either wing. The rule is simple: The nearest big player moves to pick for the pass receiver. The other three players (two exterior players and a post player) fill three sites. The closest perimeter player is located on the ballside block. The other two are on the weakside, getting set for the staggered picks. The basic pattern proceeds.

Keys

See the sections on screening between post and perimeter players, setting a screen, slipping a screen, using a pick, passing into the low post, pinning the defender, and throwing the ball inside in "Man-to-Man Offensive Fine-Tuning" in chapter 1 (page 4).

The perimeter player on the same-side box as the pick-and-roll needs to time his or her movement off the staggered screens. He or she takes advantage of the picks after the ball handler takes one or two dribbles.

The post player involved in the staggered screens must realize that the defense could switch the first screen. His or her job is to headhunt and pick the appropriate defender.

I cannot emphasize enough that the exterior player with the ball in the two-player game must recognize a nonscoring opportunity instantaneously and dribble out toward half-court. He or she builds distance from the high post before making the next pass to a wing.

If the defense overplays the wings at any time, the player out front with the ball simply motions the post players up and the team executes the overplay option discussed in the beginning of the chapter from the 1-4 high formation (page 18).

With the limited number of movements incorporated in this play, teaching time will probably not exceed 45 minutes.

Coaches should drill into perimeter players that the one dribbling toward the top is actually filling the role of point guard. If he or she does not have a shot or pass to a teammate rolling to the bucket, he or she not only stretches the space but also directs traffic and calls big players up if the wings are denied. When a teammate capitalizing on the staggered screens is open for a shot, the passer tosses the ball to him or her regardless of the spacing with the high post.

Initially, teams should practice the offense as a whole on a dummy basis. Of course, there is no substitute for live action. Under game conditions, the coach can accurately evaluate the reaction of the perimeter player dribbling to the top of the key. The player wants to secure a layup if possible from the high pick. When necessary, the coach can use breakdown drills to work on the two-player game, setting staggered picks, and the pass and cut off the high-post pick.

Anyone playing both small and power forward positions has to learn the actions involved in total execution of the offense. Big players and perimeter players have different assignments in this offense.

AWAY

The away offense has taken on many forms over the years. It employs the screen away as the primary weapon. The passing and picking in the direction opposite the toss goes back to the early years of the game. Here, the action becomes a sequential pattern. Teams should be of at least junior high school level to run the away offense. This offense teaches players to move without the basketball. Scoring prospects are evenly distributed among personnel. This offense meets the requirements of the coach who desires a man-to-man offense that includes constant movement and screening.

Personnel

All players need to be able to handle the ball on the perimeter and pass the ball effectively to the interior. The offense is more effective if all players (including big players) are able to shoot the ball well from 15 to 18 feet.

Scoring

Jump shots develop near the top of the key or the wings. These shots may or may not be three-point shots. Low-post opportunities occur for anyone. A layup opening develops as a result of a cut to the basket. Shot chances originate from the high post, including jump shots or the creation of shots by exercising one-on-one plans.

Execution

The point guard (G) passes the ball to the wing (S1) in the original 1-4 high formation (figure 2.27). G screens away for the weakside wing (S2). The ballside big player (B1) picks for the other post player (B2). B2 steps high and goes low or vice versa. The screener (B1) steps back opposite. The player using the pick runs over the top whenever the defense switches.

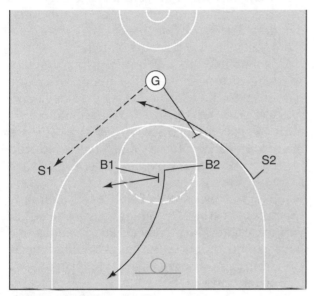

Figure 2.27 First pass to the wing in the 1-4 set.

A wing (S1) throws the ball to the player moving to the top of the key (S2) (figure 2.28). As soon as the ball leaves the passer's hands, the high post (B2) back screens for the passer (S1).

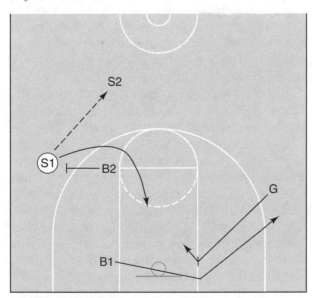

Figure 2.28 Pass to the top.

S1 cuts over the top or below the obstacle. The cutter (S1) is the first look for S2. B2 steps out to the wing after S1 uses the pick. As the back pick occurs, the offside wing (G) races to set a down pick by the near box. The low post (B1) uses the down pick while cutting to the opposite wing. The down screener (G) steps to the ball after B1 uses the pick. See the discussions of the back pick and down screen on pages 4 and 5. The fade options in each are conceivable. To maintain the pattern, however, the players involved may have to adjust or switch their positions swiftly. For example, with the back pick the wing fakes a cut into the lane and fades toward the closer corner while the screener cuts to the basket. Players just exchange roles. This wrinkle is effective if the opponent switches the back screen.

Action continues (figure 2.29) as the pass is completed from the top (S2) to the wing (B1). S2 screens away for the other wing (B2). The ballside low player (G) operates a low exchange with S1. S1 darts to ballside high, while the screener (G) seals back opposite low. The player exploiting the screen dashes high whenever the defense switches. Refer to the discussion of low exchanges and cross screens on page 6.

Play continues as the ball is passed back out front. But what happens if the defense denies the player coming to the top off the screen away (B2) (figure 2.30)? When the overplay occurs, the wing with the ball (B1) counters by dribbling at B2 (the denied player). B2 executes a shallow cut and replaces B1. To facilitate the counter,

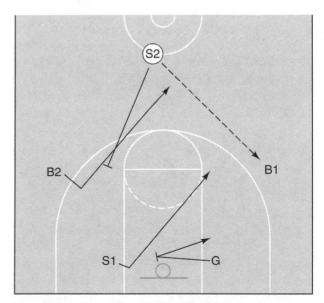

Figure 2.29 Continuing motion—low exchange and screen away.

the ball handler calls, "Shallow" after putting the ball on the floor. The ball arrives near the top of the key. The team then executes the same action as if the pass was thrown to the top. B2 cuts off the back screen by G. S1 moves opposite off the down screen by S2.

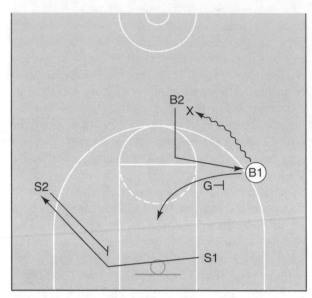

Figure 2.30 Defense denies the pass to the top.

The wings (S1 and G) are denied (figure 2.31). The player with the ball (B2) yells, "Down" to instruct the two wings (G and S1) to set down picks for their teammates below (B1 and S2, respectively).

When the initial pass was delivered to a post player in the 1-4 set, players finished aligned in a 1-2-2 formation. This alignment fits the offense

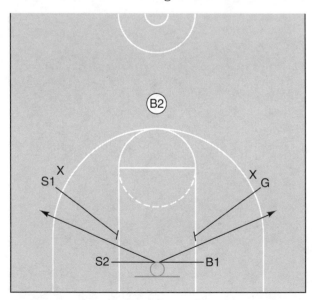

Figure 2.31 Defense overplays both wings.

perfectly. The ball is tossed to a wing, triggering the low exchange and screen-away player movements (standard motion when the ball is at a wing).

Keys

Refer to the following topics in "Man-to-Man Offensive Fine-Tuning" on page 4: screening between post and perimeter players, setting a screen, slipping a screen, using a pick, and passing into the low post. The coach must decide whether or not to permit rescreening. For details, see rescreening on page 4.

Coaches need to teach two primary action sequences: movements that occur when the pass goes to the wing and player actions when the pass goes out top. Instruction should last no more than one hour. Once players grasp the two main motions, coaches should focus on educating them about the two overplay options (shallow and down). I suggest that coaches begin teaching the offense as a whole using a dummy (no-defense) style. By yelling, "Overplayed" at various points during execution, coaches can have players practice the denial circumstances. Drilling in this way trains players to react quickly to the defensive tactic.

Coaches can use breakdown drills to review movements that have become troublesome or that players do not execute consistently. Each part is a candidate (back pick, down screen at the block, low exchange, and so forth.).

If a post player has a limited shooting range and possesses the ball on a wing or out top, the defense likely will slough into the paint. He or she can dribble at the defender to make him or her guard the ball. Otherwise, the passing lanes inside could disappear.

If the high post catches the ball, he or she turns and faces the hoop, looks low, and then goes one-on-one if given the chance. The low player actively seals his or her defender, especially if the defender is fronting him or her, so that the pass from the high teammate is possible. See the discussion of pinning the defender in "Man-to-Man Offensive Fine-Tuning" on page 7.

Coaches should instruct the team to take advantage of any mismatch that arises in the low post. Refer to the discussion of throwing the ball inside in chapter 1 on page 6.

All positions are interchangeable. Squad members need to learn the entire pattern.

CHAPTER 3

Tried-and-True Man-to-Man Offenses

Most coaches will recognize the man-to-man offenses included in this chapter. They are widely used across the country by both men's and women's coaches. Some have been in the forefront for decades, whereas others have enjoyed publicity in more recent seasons. One, the flex offense, has its own series of books detailing its operation. Elizabethtown College, the 2002 NCAA Division III runner-up for the men's national championship, uses the flex offense as its main attack against man-to-man pressure.

The flex offense includes dozens of movement variations. The alternatives presented in this chapter have been productive for me in my coaching career. When different versions exist for a particular pattern, I describe the one with which I have the greatest familiarity.

FLEX

The flex offense enjoys widespread use at all levels of play from grade school to college. I used it when I broke into coaching as a ninth-grade varsity coach as well as during my tenure as head coach at Division III King's College. One year the flex offense produced the game-winning shot for King's against NCAA Division I Drexel University. Drexel was coming off an NCAA tournament year during which they lost by 10 to the eventual national champion Louisville. The flex offense generated the deciding shot, allowing a Division III school to knock off a quality Division I opponent.

Many variations of the flex offense are currently in use. Over the years I have seen teams run it in countless ways. My description is based on what I found to be useful with my teams during my coaching career.

The flex offense forces man-to-man defenders to change constantly from weakside to strongside and vice versa. The coach needs to be confident in the big players' capability from the exterior. All players are actively involved. Players are obliged to shoot the basketball effectively inside 16 to 22 feet from the hoop. A squad that has two or more players with limited shooting ranges may see a decrease in the productivity of the pattern.

Personnel

Each player must possess sound ballhandling and passing skills. Having post players who shoot well from the periphery is an advantage because the defense must extend out to counter the team's shooting ability. The flex offense requires everyone to be capable of setting strong, solid screens. Each player should be prepared to take advantage of chances around the basket.

Scoring

Players will find 15- to 20-foot jump shots available near the two elbows. Shot attempts occur close to the three-point arc at midlane to baseline sites on each side of the half-court. Scoring chances appear around both blocks or within the foul lane. Layups result from backdoor moves. The player with the basketball can create shot attempts by penetrating to the hoop.

Execution

Players begin in a 1-4 low formation. The point guard (G) is out front, and the other players stretch along the baseline (figure 3.1). Two perimeter shooters (S1 and S2) are in the corners, and each of the two post players (B1 and B2) is stationed on or just above one of the boxes on the foul lane. Play starts with the point guard (G) choosing a side. He or she heads toward either elbow. The big player opposite the ball (B2) steps in toward the lane and then hustles along the lane line to receive the initial pass across from G. On the pass, the weakside corner (S1) cuts off a baseline screen set by B1. S1 goes over the top (foul-line side) or underneath (baseline side) the pick by B1. B1's baseline foot is on the block or above it. After making the pass, the passer (G) establishes a down pick for the screener (B1). G pops out behind the three-point line at the near wing following B1's use of the pick. When B2 receives the pass, he or she turns and faces the hoop imme-

diately. B2 assumes the triple-threat position and considers a possible dribble penetration. The same action occurs on each pass across the top (figure 3.2).

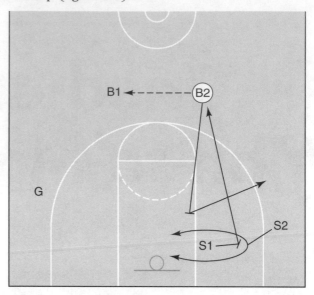

Figure 3.2　Same motion on a pass across the top.

Figure 3.3 illustrates the me option. When the ball is sent across the top (B1 to S1), the player using the baseline screen (G) can yell, "Me" as he or she nears the screener (S2). This tells S2 to move from box to box. The passer (B1) adjusts and picks G's defender before moving out wide. G heads up off the down screen, anticipating the pass from S1. Players use the me option when the defender on the cutter jumps into the foul lane well before the cutter does so.

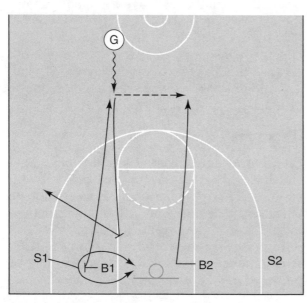

Figure 3.1　Basic flex motion.

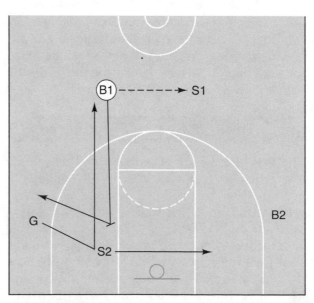

Figure 3.3　Me option.

Players are prepared to counter denials of the pass across the top. The defense aggressively denies the player coming up to catch the pass across the top (G in figure 3.3). Once above the foul line, G executes a backdoor cut to the basket. The player on the same-side wing (B1) reads the back cut and sprints to replace the player at the top. G heads out to a spot beyond the three-point arc if he or she does not receive the pass for a layup with a backdoor move.

There is a second counter to strong defensive denial of the player opposite the ball out front. The player with the ball dribbles at the denied player (in figure 3.3, S1 dribbles at G). The overplayed player (G) sets a down screen opposite for S2 and pops out wide. G and the dribbler (S1) have switched roles. The player on the far wing (B2 in figure 3.3) motors off a baseline screen as soon as there is recognition that the ball (S1) is heading away. Therefore, instead of passing to change sides, players use the dribble. The pattern continues normally at this point.

Obviously, the team will not just keep transporting the ball out front from one side to the other. The coach will instruct his or her team to use the player in the ballside corner. Figure 3.4 shows the corner option. When the ball is hurled to the corner, the player on the strongside box (S2) remains there and actively posts up, looking for an entry pass. The passer (B1) immediately cuts through to the weakside by way of the ballside elbow. The other two players (S1 and B2) rotate to fill places out front. If the next player

coming toward the ball (S1) is denied, he or she instantly cuts in the same manner as B1 did. Three people (B1, S1, and B2) cut and replace, keeping three spots (two on top and one on the offside wing) filled on the periphery.

Two other movements are connected to the corner option. First, if no toss from the corner is feasible, the player in the corner attempts to dribble penetrate. When this happens, the low post steps out to the baseline three to eight feet off the lane and the other three players stay put to give the player with the ball room to operate. In most cases, the dribbler uses the hand on the foul-line side. Second, the coach decides what motion players should enact when the pass goes inside to the low post. Refer to the discussions of passing into the low post and throwing the ball inside in "Man-to-Man Offensive Fine-Tuning" in chapter 1 (page 6).

Keys

Review relevant topics by referring to the discussions of setting a screen and using a pick in "Man-to-Man Offensive Fine-Tuning" on page 4.

Approximately one hour of instructional time is required for a team to attain an acceptable level of performance. All spots are interchangeable. Players concentrate on learning the entire continuity. The basic pattern is not difficult to teach, but players will need time to learn the various options needed for specific circumstances. The coach should review the offense periodically throughout the season. Otherwise, some slippage is likely to occur. Players may have difficulty recalling some of the special options.

This is a good offense to teach on a dummy basis at first. After players demonstrate that they understand the regular continuity, the coach can call out various options. He or she asks for the me option or corner option, or designates certain players as overplayed.

Teaching the flex offense in segments may be desirable. For example, the coach teaches only the normal pattern first, adds the corner option the next day, adds the overplay counters the day after that, and perhaps puts in the me option later in the week.

Players must set the baseline screen with their baseline feet on or above the box. If the defender on the cutter heads above the screen, the cutter moves below and vice versa. The player establishing the baseline pick concen-

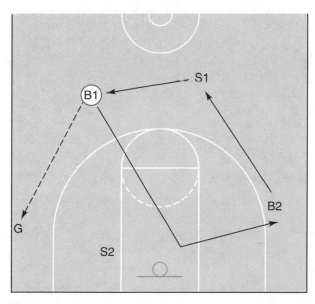

Figure 3.4 Corner option.

trates on completing that job before moving to the top.

The player who uses the baseline screen is responsible for running the defender into it. He or she deploys the me option periodically to keep the defense honest.

The player out front with the ball is obliged to face the basket and become an offensive threat. He or she may have an opportunity to put the ball on the floor. The player regularly observes the baseline screening action before sending the ball to a teammate and docs not force the pass inside.

The team must demonstrate patience and wait for good scoring opportunities to develop. They keep running defenders into screens. With patience, defensive breakdowns will occur. Players react quickly and decisively to defensive overplays. They do not hesitate.

The coach will likely need to insist that players use the player in the ballside corner. Players have a tendency to ignore the corners. The ballside low player aggressively works to gain position. The entry pass comes from the corner to reward the player's effort.

If the player out front deploys the dribble option to counter a defensive overplay, he or she has to be aware of the five-second closely guarded rule.

TWO-SCREEN OFFENSE

When I began my coaching career, I regularly used the two-screen offense against man-to-man defense. If I recall correctly, the offense came to my attention through an article in a monthly coaching periodical. The two-screen offense was successful for my junior high, high school, and college teams. This offense is most effective when all players are capable of handling the basketball from the outer regions. If more than one player must stay within 15 feet to shoot, the offense loses its productiveness. The more the opponent has to respect the players' shooting skills from distance, the more the lane opens to traffic. This offense engages all five players in continuous scoring actions.

Personnel

All players must have strong ballhandling and passing skills. Players must be capable of scor-

ing in the paint. This offense is highly productive if all players can shoot the ball from 15 to 20 feet.

Scoring

Jump shots develop around the extended foul line. Shot attempts arise at the basket through a cut or a post-up play. Players receive jumpers from the foul line to the top of the key. Corner jump shots occur because of the execution of a fade.

Execution

The team begins in a double-stack formation with the post players (B1 and B2) setting screens on either side of the foul lane just above the boxes. Two shooters (S1 and S2) start below the big players and either cross or fake the action before rubbing off screens. They begin their movements just as the lead guard (G) gets into position to make the initial pass.

Figure 3.5 illustrates the basic actions that occur when the pass goes to a wing. G passes to S1 and screens away for the opposite wing (S2) near the weakside elbow. G sets the pick with his or her back to the ball. The weakside wing (S2) employs the screen and cuts to the basket. As soon as the ball is tossed to a wing, the ballside player directly below (B1) pops out behind the three-point arc in the near corner. After screening for S2, G sets a second pick for the player below (B2). B2 heads toward the top

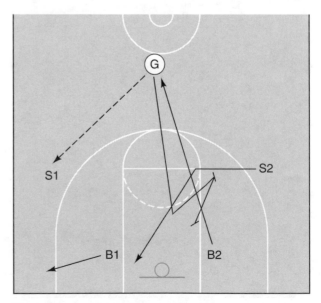

Figure 3.5 Pass to a wing.

of the key. S2 or B2 might attain a good scoring chance.

Figure 3.6 shows the required movements each time the ball is passed from a wing to a player out front. On the release of the pass, G performs an L-cut to get open on the offside wing while the person in the corner (B1) uses a baseline pick by S2. B1 goes over or below S2's screen and ends at the opposite block. The baseline screener (S2) steps to the ball. B2 first tries to pass to B1 and S2 on the inside. If not open, B2 flings the ball to either wing (G or S1). If the defense denies both players, B2 yells, "Down." Wings immediately establish down picks for teammates below. The players using the screens may cross or fake before employing the down screens. This sequence is called the wings overplayed option.

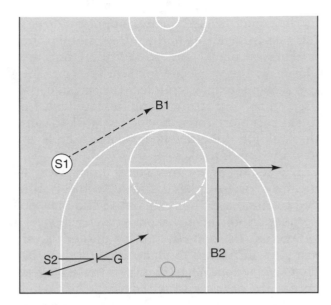

Figure 3.7 Fade maneuver.

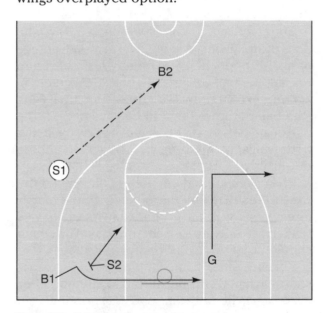

Figure 3.6 Pass to a player out front.

Instead of cutting off the baseline pick, the player in the corner (S2) can run a fade maneuver (figure 3.7). The cutter (S2) physically pushes the screener (G) across the lane. The corner player decides to use this move when he or she notices that the defender is cheating over the baseline pick. The player in the ballside corner has two options. He or she can either cut off the baseline screen to the opposite block or push the screener across the lane and fade back to the same-side corner.

Figure 3.8 shows another choice available to players when a pass goes to a wing. B1 passes and screens for G (weakside wing) at the oppo-

site elbow, allowing G to cut to the basket. But B1 recognizes that the defense is switching assignments, so he or she counters by yelling, "Me." B1 cuts to the ballside box and changes roles with G. If the defense is switching, the screener should have a position advantage on the new defender. He or she yells, "Me" just before the cutter (G) reaches the screener's location. After G hears the call, he or she turns and sets a down screen for the player below (S1). B2 still pops to the ballside corner immediately after B1 releases the pass from the top to the wing (S2).

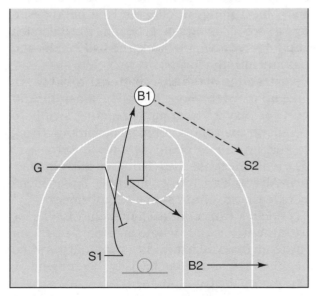

Figure 3.8 Me option on the pass to a wing.

The counters used when an opponent denies the pass from a wing to the top are simple. The overplayed player cuts to the hoop, and the player on the weakside bolts to the top. The two players just switch roles. The ballside low player posts up strong along the foul lane. He or she has more room in which to work toward the foul line if the defender denies the player near the top of the key.

The team cannot rely solely on passes to the wing or top. Players need to direct the ball to the player popping out to the ballside corner periodically to keep the defense honest. Otherwise, the defender on the corner player just sags in toward the lane and clogs up the offensive action. When the ball is tossed to the corner, the passer cuts to the offside block and changes positions with the low player opposite. The passer watches for two things. First, he or she cannot move too close to the player posting up on the strongside block. The coach wants the ball tossed inside if possible. Second, he or she does not want the action to be too near the player on the offside box. Players do not let defenders switch. When the ball is thrown out from the corner, the player at the top sets a diagonal screen for the player at the weakside box. The top-overplayed option is available if needed. The team continues to execute the pattern.

Keys

See the following topics in "Man-to-Man Offensive Fine-Tuning" in chapter 1 on page 4: setting a screen, using a pick, pinning the defender, slipping a screen, throwing the ball inside, and passing into the low post.

Instruction of the basic pattern probably will take no more than one hour. The most difficult part for players to grasp is reacting swiftly to defensive overplays. A long lapse in practicing or reviewing this offense should never occur. The team must use the offense regularly in practice. All spots are interchangeable. Squad members learn the entire series of movements.

Coaches can more easily teach this offense with the whole-part-whole method. They want the team to absorb the basic continuity first, so beginning on a dummy basis is recommended. During this instruction, the coach can call out, "Overplayed" periodically to see if the team reacts rapidly and correctly to the defensive

denial. Once the players learn the pattern, the coach can break down specific parts of the offense (baseline screen, for example) to make execution of a particular phase even more precise. Then the team can go back to operating the offense as a whole.

The player using the baseline pick has three options. He or she can cut over the baseline screen to the opposite box, go under the pick, or fade back to the corner when the defender races over the screen too early.

The passer at the top of the key has options when the ball is sent to a wing. He or she can screen away so that the weakside wing can cut to the basket. If he or she recognizes an impending switch, he or she executes the me option and bolts to the hoop. The passer and wing swap roles. The passer usually sets two screens on the weakside unless he or she yells, "Me."

The player out top receives the ball. He or she does the following in sequence: takes advantage of a shot opportunity if one arises, considers tossing the ball toward the baseline screening action, or contemplates a pass to either wing (the ball does *not* have to be reversed). If the player notices that the defense is overplaying both wings, he or she calls, "Down" to initiate down screens from the wings.

The coach should encourage players on the wing to toss the ball periodically to the player directly below in the corner. Players will have a tendency to shy away from the pass. The coach should insist upon and reinforce its use.

Coaches should inform players of the exact shots each player is permitted to attempt. After all, coaches do not want players shooting from deep if they are incapable of hitting the shot consistently.

Coaches must preach patience. Players should make the defense work. Drills should reinforce the rule that the person above the key reacts instantly by planting a diagonal screen whenever a pass is completed out of the corner to a wing. When teaching the L-cut maneuver, coaches should be aware that the backdoor opportunity is not available because of interference from the baseline-screening activity. Refer to the discussion of the L-cut in "Man-to-Man Offensive Fine-Tuning" on page 7.

If a wing possesses the ball, he or she focuses on the cutter down the lane while reading the defender on the player in the near corner. If the defender is sagging, a throw to the corner may be the best way to enable the feed inside.

SHUFFLE CUT

The shuffle cut became part of the game in the mid-1900s. Some teams still use it as part of their offensive arsenal against man-to-man defense. Placing three people in motion simultaneously can cause some confusion for the defense when the paths of the offensive players begin to intersect. Because the techniques do not currently enjoy widespread use, the offense can prove fruitful. Personally, I have always had a soft spot for the methodology involved. What follows is my version. This offense uses multiple cutters to the hoop. Each player's ability to shoot from the outside dictates the amount of spacing available for cutters. Players likely will create shots off the dribble. This pattern is more appropriate when there is no shot clock because patience is required for quality shots to develop.

Personnel

Players must be able to score around the basket. All five may receive opportunities. Players must possess sufficient perimeter skills because everyone handles the basketball on the periphery. The offense works best if all five players can shoot 15- to 20-foot jumpers.

Scoring

Shots around the basket crop up for anyone. Layups occur as a result of backdoor moves or cuts. Jumpers develop at the foul line or the top of the key. One-on-one chances may arise from the high-post area or the baseline.

Execution

Play starts from a 1-3-1 set (figure 3.9). The point guard (G) is out top with the ball, and the other two perimeter players (S1 and S2) wait at each foul line extended. The post players (B2 and B1) are at the high post just above the foul line and low post, respectively. They are interchangeable. Motion begins with the lead guard (G) passing to the wing (S1) *away* from the low post (B1). The release of the ball triggers the high post (B2) to screen down diagonally for the low post (B1). B1 heads toward the high post. The weakside wing (S2) cuts to the basket off

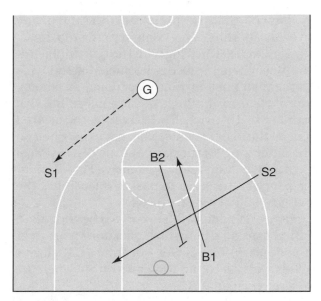

Figure 3.9 1-3-1 starting set.

the original high post, who is the screener (B2). They make some physical contact.

Movement continues (figure 3.10). After the point guard (G) tosses the ball to S1, he or she moves to screen diagonally. This pick is actually for the original high post (B2) following B2's diagonal down screen for the original low post (B1). The lead guard's and high post's picks take place along the same plane. B1 curls over G's tail to the ballside high post. B2 comes out top to the key off G's pick. Notice that S2 moves along the baseline about 5 to 10 feet off the foul lane on the ballside if he or she does not catch the pass from S1 on the first cut to the hoop.

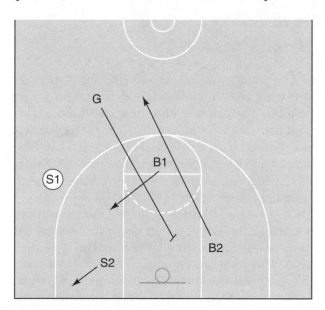

Figure 3.10 Action continues with the second down pick.

Players must be prepared to counter any overplay of the player coming to the top. Reaction is simple. The wing with the ball dribbles at the player being denied, who immediately heads to the high post currently occupied by a teammate. In turn, the high post replaces the ball handler on the wing. The player on the cleared side of the floor executes an L-cut to get open on the other wing for the pass. See the discussion of the L-cut in "Man-to-Man Offensive Fine-Tuning" on page 7. A back cut to basket is feasible if the defense still denies the pass.

Figure 3.11 shows the pass to the top (S2 to B2). G uses an L-cut with a backdoor maneuver if necessary. The player out front (B2) always sends the ball to the wing away from where he or she received it (G).

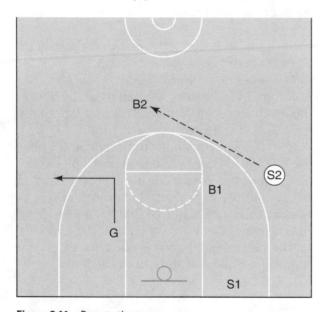

Figure 3.11   Pass to the top.

The action continues (figure 3.12). The opposite wing (S2) has already cut to the hoop off B1's tail, the original high post, who moved to pick for the original low post (S1). The passer (B2) heads to set a diagonal pick for B1, the first screener. S1 slices across to the opposite side of the high post using the rear of the second screener (B2). B1 (low post) hustles out front following the pick from B2. The wing's first option is to send the ball to S2 on his or her cut to the hoop. If S2 receives the ball along the baseline, he or she goes one-on-one. When the low post (S2) catches the pass, the high post (S1) cuts to the basket opposite to clear the defense. G may also be able to deliver the ball to the high

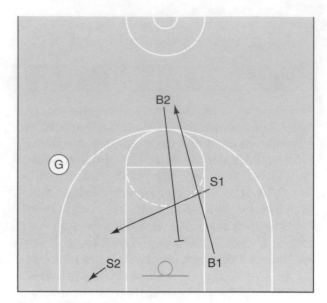

Figure 3.12   Shuffle cuts continue.

post (S1) on his or her movement toward the ballside. Again, the pass to the high post signals a one-on-one opportunity.

The following movements occur when the ball heads to a wing. The weakside wing cuts to the ballside low position off the rear of the high post, who is setting a diagonal pick for the weakside low player. The passer at the top of the key races to pick for the previous screener. The player who used the first pick curls off the rear of the second screener and heads to the strongside high post. Finally, the first screener receives the second pick and bolts to the top of the key.

Keys

See the following topics in "Man-to-Man Offensive Fine-Tuning" in chapter 1: setting a screen, slipping a screen, using a pick, pinning the defender, throwing the ball inside, and passing into the low post.

Players should grasp the operation of the offense well within a one-hour period. The series of actions is not complicated, but timing must be precise. Players must understand the offense as a whole. All team members rotate spots. Coaches should teach the offense on a dummy (no-defense) basis initially. Coordination of moves is essential. The coach may elect to yell, "Overplayed" during practice to ensure that players react quickly and properly to the defensive tactic. Breakdown drills are not particularly useful in promoting better comprehension and execution of the offense.

Timing is important. The high post cannot hesitate when moving to pick low on the pass to a wing. The first cutter anticipates the ball reversal and races off the high post's tail. The second cutter moves upward and curls over the second screener's rear. Movement by the cutters either too soon or too late jeopardizes the effectiveness of the action. Going five-on-five is necessary to achieve the right timing and spacing when pressured by a defense. Players must watch for the five-second closely guarded call, using the dribble to negate an infraction if necessary.

The wings, contemplating a catch from the player at the top, realize that their side of the court has been cleared so that they can operate. L-cuts with back cuts are great weapons. Cutters should coordinate the motion with reception of the ball out front because ball reversal from the top-of-key vicinity occurs swiftly. If ball movement is too slow, cutters have more difficulty getting open.

Players must know exactly who is permitted to shoot the ball from the top of the key or wings.

Any time the high-post or low-post player catches the ball, he or she can go one-on-one. The post turns and faces the basket right after reception unless the defender gambles on a steal, misses it, or loses leverage on the receiver. Then the receiver goes to the hoop immediately.

Coaches should drill players on the counters to defensive overplays. There are only two. First, on a pass to the wing, the player executes a back cut followed by an L-cut. Second, when the toss out front is denied, the player at the top, the high post, and the wing with the ball all rotate and replace each other. The player with the ball dribbles at the teammate above, and the other two players rotate.

The positioning of the high post is important. If he or she is too low, there will not be enough time for the wing to cut off his or her tail as the down screen begins. Players should maintain approximately 12 to 18 feet between the high post and low post.

The movement of the low post to the baseline 5 to 10 feet from the lane creates space for the high post to use as the second cutter. If the first cutter catches the ball off the foul lane near the baseline, the player in the high post cuts quickly to the weakside box.

FDU–MADISON OFFENSE

Fairleigh Dickinson University's branch campus in Madison, New Jersey, was recently renamed to Fairleigh Dickinson University's College at Florham. I have referred to it as FDU–Madison since it was a member of the Middle Atlantic Conference along with King's College. Coach Roger Kindel uses this pattern every year. He has had some excellent teams during his tenure, and this offense has been a staple of his program. The team using this offense should have four people who are potent from the exterior. This man-to-man offense sends cutters to the basket and achieves a slower pace with the repetitive actions of the play.

Personnel

One post player serves duty as a screener and does not play on the periphery. The other big player must be an effective outside scoring threat and be able to handle the ball on the exterior. The three perimeter players are required to hit shots from the outlying areas. All players should be proficient scorers around the basket.

Scoring

Any team member can have a scoring chance in the midpost region on either side of the foul lane. The big player who serves primarily as a screener is least likely to see an attempt unless it occurs through an offensive rebound. A layup using a back cut to the hoop is possible for the other four players. They also may see jumpers near the foul line or top of the key. A layup appears because of a direct or scissors cut off the high post. A shot by way of a one-on-one maneuver erupts for one of four players working on the periphery.

Execution

The offense begins in the 2-1-2 set (figure 3.13). Two guards (G and S1) are stationed out front opposite one another. The post player who is not going to be involved in the four-player rotation is at the high post (B2). The two forwards (B1 and S2) begin at the boxes. The ballside forward (B1) executes an L-cut to receive the pass from the point guard (G). Refer to the discussion of the L-cut in "Man-to-Man Offensive Fine-Tuning" on page 7. Players also can throw the ball from guard to guard to begin the offense to the other side. On the pass to B1, the guards (G and S1) scissor off a high-post screen (B2). The passer (G) cuts first and ends up as a screener for the other forward (S2) stationed near the weakside block. Alternatively, instead of a scissor off the high player, the guards can run straight cuts after faking the scissors. S2 heads to the top of the key after using the pick. S1 is the second cutter and heads to the ballside. Once B2 knows that S1 is not going to receive the ball from B1 for a shot, he or she dashes along the lane on the strongside. B2 and S1 become a twin screen. If the ball is not tossed inside, it must be thrown to the player near the top of the key.

In figure 3.14, the ball has been tossed to B1

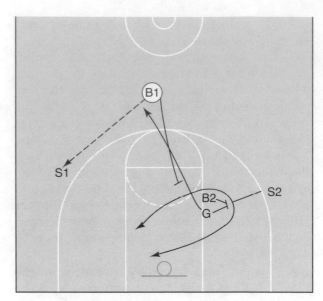

Figure 3.14 Ball reversed from the top to the wing.

movements. S2 darts over the top or below the double pick to the ballside lane. S1 glares into S2 and relinquishes the ball if possible. The passer (B1) deposits a diagonal down screen for G as soon as he or she releases the ball.

If no pass is available to the cutter, the big player (B2) slides over to the ballside when the wing (S1) releases the ball to G at the top. B2 forms a twin screen with S2. B1 heads out to the wing on his or her side (figure 3.15). G reverses the ball to B1. B1 may be able to back cut if his or her defender overplays. After catching the ball, B1 has a brief chance to go one-on-one. S1

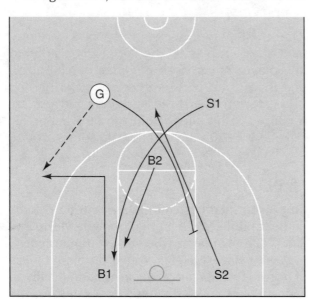

Figure 3.13 Starting in the 2-1-2 set.

out front. The other four players align themselves as part of the normal rotation of the play. B1 could be open for a shot attempt. On the pass to the top, S1 (the player away from the double screen) hustles out to a wing. An L-cut is not necessary at this point. If denied, S1 still has a backdoor opportunity followed by the L-cut. B2 and G plant a double screen along the foul lane. The two come together at approximately midlane. B1 reverses the ball to S1. The reversal pass to the wing keys the next

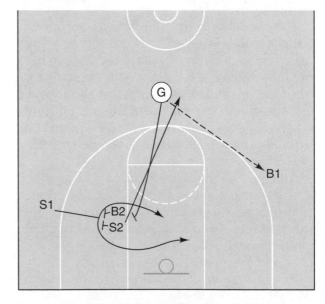

Figure 3.15 Action continues back to the other side.

adjusts the cut off the double screen to prevent defensive help on B1's dribble penetration. If no one-on-one commences, the normal pattern continues. S1 busts high or low off the double pick. The passer (G) diagonal screens for S2 to sprint to a position around the key.

The team reacts quickly to any defensive denial of the pass toward the top of the key. The player does not fight it, does not dance with the defender. He or she immediately cuts to the basket and eventually ends up replacing the weakside wing. The offside wing sprints to replace the cutter out front.

Keys

See the following topics in "Man-to-Man Offensive Fine-Tuning" in chapter 1 (page 4): setting a screen, using a pick, double screen, throwing the ball inside, pass into the low post, and pinning the defender.

Instructional time required to teach the offense thoroughly should not exceed one hour. The series of movements is not complex.

The offense is best taught as a whole on a dummy basis. Five-on-none practice allows the team to grow accustomed to the basic rotation. The coach may call out, "Overplayed" to get the team to react quickly and appropriately to defensive denials. All five players should practice together so that they can work on timing and reactions. Breakdown drills are not likely to be worthwhile. After players master the basic rotation, the coach should add defenders. Five-on-five enables players to become accustomed to the congestion in the lane area.

Coaches should urge players to vary the beginning of the offense. They should use straight cuts off the high post only after performing the scissors several times. Reversing the ball from guard to guard is another alternative.

Players always strive to reverse the ball. The player near the top of the key may have a shot opportunity when he or she first receives the ball. If one does not develop, the player throws the pass opposite.

The player rubbing off the double pick knows it is better to go off a screen late than early. The cutter varies movement over or under the double. Once at ballside, he or she actively posts up. The cutter needs to sell the move in one direction and go the opposite way.

The big player who is not involved in the four-player rotation has an important role. He or she may net a post feed from up top when sliding across the foul lane. His or her defender may be more concerned about helping teammates. The big player may occasionally flee early to the ballside as a surprise. Offensive rebounding is the player's primary job.

Shooting the ball from distance is under the coach's control. The coach chooses who is permitted to take the shots and at what point in the possession shots are acceptable.

The team should keep turning the offense to wear down the defense. If the team maintains its discipline, a defensive breakdown is probable. Opponents will not enjoy constantly running into screens.

DIAGONAL OFFENSE

This pattern has been around for decades and still helps numerous teams score points against man-to-man defense. Most coaches have used at least some portion of the action. Motion is perpetual, and all positions are interchangeable. This offense requires a squad that is adept from the outer regions. Scoring chances are evenly distributed in this equal-opportunity offense. The offense provides moments to toss the ball inside.

Personnel

All players need to be effective outside shooters from at least 15 feet (the greater the range, the better), must be able to handle the ball well on the exterior, and must have sound passing skills. Players need to be able to feed a post, obtain position in a low post, and score when they receive the ball near the basket.

Scoring

Low-post moves produce shots. Jump shots occur from the wings and perhaps corner and baseline sites. Players attempt outside jumpers from the area above the foul line. The cutters to the hoop can gain layups off back screens.

Execution

The offense begins with a double-stack set. The shooters (S1 and S2) are stationed above the post players (B1 and B2) along the foul lane. The point guard (G) brings the ball up court and tries to maintain position within the lane lines. The lead guard is able to toss the ball to either side of the half-court at the start. B1 and B2 establish screens at the boxes. S1 and S2 may cross before using screens, or they can fake and slice off the same-side pick. If the defender goes too high over the pick, the shooters complete a fade maneuver to the corner. The big players seal the defenders and step to the ball after teammates use their screens.

The playmaker (G) passes to either wing (S1 or S2). (Figure 3.16 shows the ball going to S1.) The passer (G) immediately scampers to affix a diagonal screen for the player on the weakside block (B2). B2 sprints above the foul line. The screener (G) steps to the ball after B2's cut. The strongside low post (B1) aggressively posts up. The wing away from the ball (S2) remains stationary.

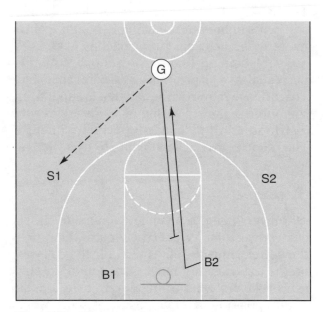

Figure 3.16 G passes to the wing.

The ball is thrown to the top (figure 3.17). S1 tosses to B2. As soon as S1 releases the ball, the low post on the passer's side (B1) hustles to set a back screen for S1. See the discussion of the back pick in "Man-to-Man Offensive Fine-Tuning" on page 5. On the other side of half-court, the wing (S2) heads to the lane to establish a down pick for G. G has just completed a diagonal screen. S2 steps to the ball after G uses the pick. Refer to the discussion of the down screen in chapter 1 on page 4. The player with the ball at the top of the key (B2) can toss to either wing,

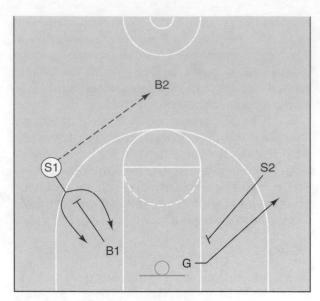

Figure 3.17 Ball is thrown to the top.

inside to S2, or to S1 on a cut off the back pick. Whenever the ball goes to a wing, the diagonal screen is executed.

If the opponent denies the player coming to the top (S1), S1 does not fight the overplay (figure 3.18). He or she simply back cuts to the basket to counter the denial. This action begins replacement moves as the wing away from the ball (B1) races to replace S1 and the weakside low player (B2) darts to replace B1. S1, B2, and B1 continue triangular motion until one opens at the top of the key. S2 (ballside low) is posting during the entire exercise. The player with

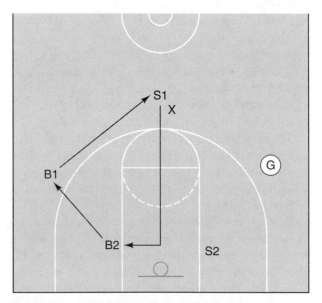

Figure 3.18 Defender overplays the player at the top.

the ball (G) is aware of the five-second closely guarded rule.

If the opponent denies a pass to a wing when the ball is out front, the player recognizes the inability to complete a pass and immediately yells, "Down." On this command, the wings rush to plant down screens for players at the blocks. The players using the picks may cross or fake before using the picks.

Keys

Refer to "Man-to-Man Offensive Fine-Tuning" on page 4 to review these topics: setting a screen, slipping a screen, using a pick, throwing the ball inside, pass into the low post, and pinning the defender.

Instruction should require no more than an hour. Players will not find this a difficult play to learn. Repetitive movements enable players to familiarize themselves with the offense swiftly. Five-on-none practice should come before any live action. Coaches will not likely need to break down the various components of the offense for specific instruction.

Players must recognize and react quickly to defensive denials. When the defense overplays a player coming to the top, the three offside players cut and replace consistently. If the defense denies the wings, the player on top with the ball yells, "Down" so that the wings will set down screens.

When screens occur at each box, players at the boxes sell movement in one direction and go the other way. The fade to the corner or baseline is effective against a defender who moves too high over the pick. The corner baseline area opens, not the wing vicinity.

The passer out front must headhunt during his or her diagonal pick. The defender will most likely sag toward the middle of the lane.

Players should not throw the ball inside to the low post unless that player is vigorously trying to establish and maintain a position advantage. The low post must offer a target to the passer.

The player coming to the top of the key contemplates a shot attempt if open and cleared to shoot. The coach sets each player's shooting limitations.

With the back pick, the fade-to-the-corner option is usually not part of this offense. A player may make a rare exception if he or she is sure that a good scoring chance will arise.

The wing with the ball should look in to the player setting the diagonal pick. The screener may be open when stepping to the ball, especially if defenders switch the screen. Coaches should stress the need to demonstrate patience. Players do not have to attempt distance shots early in a possession. They wage a significant effort to procure the ball inside first.

A one-on-one opportunity could develop for the player out top with the ball. If the defense denies both wings, space is available for the ball handler. The one-on-one is an alternative to yelling, "Down" to combat the denials. Coaches may wish to designate which people have permission to perform the one-on-one option.

WING SHOOTER

Many coaches throughout the country make extensive use of the wing-shooter offense. I have transformed it to use repeated movements instead of the quick-hitter format. Used with the quick hitter, this productive movement happens only once. Putting it into continuous action enables the coach to keep pounding at the defense with something difficult to stop. The wing shooter is an excellent choice for teams who want to keep the big players near the hoop. Players regularly attempt to send the ball to the interior. Outside opportunities follow quickly. The offense consistently highlights the interaction between post and perimeter players.

Personnel

Perimeter players must be able to hit 15- to 20-foot jump shots. They are required to handle the ball equally well with either hand and must be adept at directing the ball to open teammates around the basket. Post players need to be able to score in the paint and set convincing screens.

Scoring

Post players catch the ball by a box and execute a back-to-the-basket move for a score. They may also attain shots in the heart of the foul lane. Perimeter players acquire shot attempts near the foul line and top of the key. They may acquire layups through cuts off high-post picks. Outside players might secure shots from the foul line extended.

Execution

Players begin in a 1-3-1 set (figure 3.19). The point guard (G) is out top with the ball. Two shooters (S1 and S2) are stationed at the wings. One big player is high (B2), and the other (B1) is at either box. Whichever side B1 selects determines which shooter (S1 or S2) becomes part of the upcoming three-player motion. The shooter opposite the low post (S2) takes part in the movements first. Therefore, the playmaker (G) dribbles at S2. The lead guard always dribbles at the wing away from the low post. S2 moves to screen across for the low post (B1). B1 may cut over or under the pick and ends up posting near the ballside block. The high post (B2) then screens the screener (S2), who moves out front for a shot attempt. Moreover, the weakside wing (S1) slides down toward the baseline once he or she sees S2 approaching B1 with a pick. S1 tries to take defensive help away from S2's cut to the top.

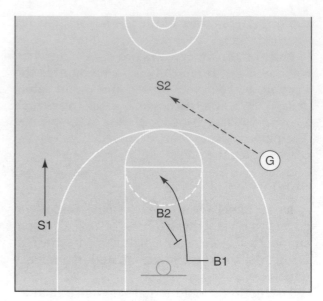

Figure 3.20 Pass to the top.

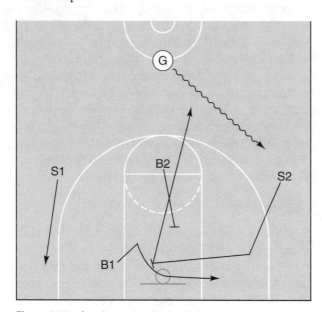

Figure 3.19 Starting action from 1-3-1 set.

When the ball goes to S2 out front and he or she does not have a shot opportunity, S1 slides back up to the same-side wing (figure 3.20). The big player in the center of the lane (B2) steps down to run a twist with his or her partner (B1). The low post (B1) twists over the top of B2. See the discussion of the twist move in "Man-to-Man Offensive Fine-Tuning" in chapter 1 on page 7. S2 tosses the ball inside for a quality scoring chance if possible. If B1 does not procure the

ball from S2, then he or she heads to the high post above the foul line. B1 must read quickly that no pass is coming.

After the player out front (S2) catches the ball and notices that he or she has no shot and cannot pass inside to B1, he or she dribbles at the opposite wing (S1). See figure 3.21. S1 glides to screen across for the low post (B2). B2 cuts over or under the pick to the ballside block. The high post (B1) screens the screener (S1). As soon as S1 makes his or her move to cross pick, the weakside wing (G) drops toward the nearer baseline to clear the region out top. The action

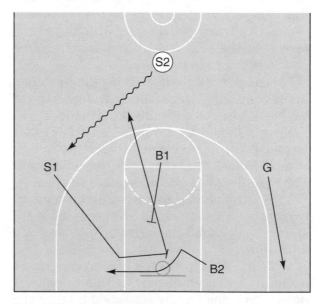

Figure 3.21 Play continues.

is the same as that shown in figure 3.19 except that it occurs to the other side of the court.

The motion continues with the ball conveyed by S2 to S1 near the top of the key. The opposite wing moves up to the foul line extended, while the post player in the lane steps down to run a twist with B2. B2 cuts over B1 and anticipates an entry pass from S1. If he or she does not catch the ball, then B2 slides to a position above the foul line. This action is the same as that described earlier for figure 3.20.

The team has to be able to adjust quickly to a defensive overplay of the player coming to the top of the key. The ballside low post races up to the high post near the elbow, while the other big player hustles to the weakside box. The posts move spontaneously as they realize that the player out front is denied. The player being overplayed may have to yell, "Up" to spur post players to slide upward, although it is best if the post players can accomplish the action without the call. To counteract the overplay, the player out front cuts off a high-post screen to the basket, expecting a pass from the wing. If the player does not receive the ball, he or she completes an immediate move across the foul lane to pick for the low post. The high post screens for the screener, and the player runs back out front. The wing must avoid being in jeopardy of committing a five-second violation.

Keys

Refer to "Man-to-Man Offensive Fine-Tuning" in chapter 1 (page 4) for details on screening between post and perimeter players, setting a screen, slipping a screen, using a pick, cross screens, throwing the ball inside, passing into the low post, and pinning the defender.

This offense is not overcomplex because the number of movements is limited. Coaches have to teach only three steps:

1. Dribble the ball to a wing.
2. Pass the ball to a teammate near the top of the key.
3. Counter a denial of the pass to the top.

Coaches should initially teach the offense as a whole on a five-on-none basis. After gaining confidence in the team's ability to execute the sequential movements and react to a denial of the pass to the top, the coach can add defense. This offense does not benefit from a breakdown into smaller components. The coach should conduct periodic reviews to keep players' memories fresh and accurate. The offense plays to the strengths of both post and exterior players.

The high post dashes to affix a down pick for the screener as soon as the player setting the screen reaches the foul lane. The high post goes right at the targeted defender. He or she becomes still just before a physical bump occurs.

The player out front with the ball does the following in order:

1. Considers a shot attempt if one is available. The coach should instruct players when they can take a shot during a possession and who is cleared to do so.
2. Peeks inside to the post player twisting over the top of his or her partner. The player sends the ball there if feasible.
3. Dribbles at the wing away from where he or she received the ball.

The team needs to exhibit some patience. They conduct a serious effort to toss the ball inside.

The player dribbling at the wing keeps the dribble active. He or she watches that no five-second closely guarded violation occurs. Perimeter players regularly view the interior while maintaining their dribbles.

CHAPTER 4

Creative Motions

The offenses in this chapter are part of my history. Some evolved as I matured as a coach. Some are the result of my creative side. Some I learned along the way through my association with outstanding mentors. These productive man-to-man offenses manufacture a variety of scoring opportunities. The plays constitute an assortment of offensive maneuvers, each of which is unique. I have used all of them and found each to be worthwhile.

BASELINE SHOOTER

The idea of running the premier shooter from the periphery off baseline screens has been around for a long time. Coach Bob Knight at Indiana did it for Steve Alford, his main outside shooter. Allen Iverson uses baseline picks to gain freedom for ball possession. I began using the motion when I had one of the most proficient three-point shooters in all of NCAA Division III basketball. The movements form a continuous action that presents many scoring opportunities.

The baseline-shooter offense is ideally suited for teams that have an exceptional shooter from three-point land. The two big players are integral to the success of the play. The baseline-shooter offense generates good scoring distribution because it manufactures shots from both the inside and the outside. The offense also offers a good way to wear down a defender on the predominant shooter from the outlying regions.

Personnel

Big players should be good inside scorers and substantive screeners. They must be able to perform back-to-the-basket moves. The three perimeter players can use screens on the ball. At least one of the outside players needs to be an efficient three-point shooter. The other exterior players also receive shots from the periphery.

Scoring

The primary distance shooter obtains shots in each corner. Big players attain chances in the paint. Perimeter players achieve shots off the dribble near the foul line. Layup opportunities may develop as a result of back cuts to the hoop against defensive overplays. A three-point attempt by a shooter could develop above an elbow. If no shot is available, a scoring chance may come through a one-on-one move. The big player in the high post sees shots develop by facing the basket or driving to the goal.

Execution

Play begins in the set shown in figure 4.1. The perimeter player in the corner (S1) is always on the ballside and is the best outside-shooting threat. Post players (B1 and B2) are positioned

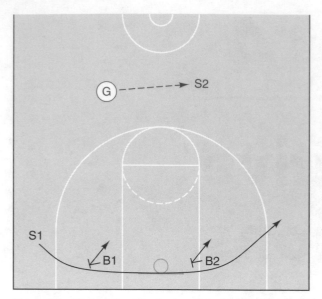

Figure 4.1 Beginning set for the baseline-shooter offense.

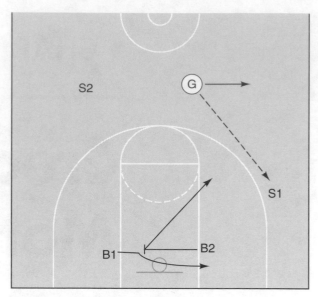

Figure 4.2 Ball tossed to the corner.

on each block, and the other two perimeter players (G and S2) establish a two-out front. The point guard (G) fires the pass to S2. On the pass release, the player in the corner (S1) runs baseline using screens set by the big players (B1 and B2). Post players always step to the ball after S1 rubs off them. The shooter in the corner has a second option—to fade back to his or her original location. He or she implements the fade if the defender races over the first screen too soon. If no skip pass comes, the shooter runs the baseline again.

The point guard may counter a defensive denial of the teammate out front by dribbling at him or her. The targeted teammate slides below the ball handler and replaces him or her. This action begins a change in sides. The playmaker has to be aware of the five-second closely guarded rule, if it applies. On the dribble, the shooter in the corner has the same options described earlier. The dribble exchange is one way of countering a denial of the pass across the top. I discuss another way of doing so later in the chapter in the description of the action in figure 4.5.

Figure 4.2 depicts the action that transpires when the player out top (G) passes the ball to the shooter working the baseline (S1). The passer (G) (or player directly above) always steps toward the sideline after sending the ball to the corner. The pass triggers a low exchange; the ballside big player (B2) picks across for the weakside post player (B1). See the discussion

of low exchanges and cross screens in "Man-to-Man Offensive Fine-Tuning" on page 6 for further details about operation of the motion. In figure 4.2, the opponent does not switch, so the player using the screen (B1) steps high and goes low toward the ball. The screener (B2) heads to a location opposite the cutter (in this case, to the ballside high post).

The receiver in the corner may have an immediate shot opportunity. If not, he or she tries to get the ball inside to the low post. If the toss goes inside, the high post always cuts to the basket while the perimeter players spot up on the periphery. When the defender full fronts the low post, an opportunity for a lob pass over the defender may be available. Refer to the discussion of throwing the ball inside in chapter 1 (page 6).

The second option for the person with the ball in a corner is to pass to the high post. The corner player wants to toss the ball to the high post whenever he or she sees that the low post is full fronted or side fronted on the baseline side. The pass receiver immediately looks to the other post low. The pass from high to low may be a quick touch pass. If no pass low is available, the high post puts the ball on the floor and goes to the basket.

Another alternative for the player with the ball in the corner is to throw a skip pass to the player at the weakside top site. Players use this option when the defender on the player out front on the diagonal cheats down into the lane to help defensively. The recipient of the diagonal pass takes advantage of a three-point shot opening or goes one-on-one to create a scoring opportunity. He or she has an entire side of the court in which to work.

Finally, S1 (the player in the corner) can pass directly above to G (figure 4.3). The pass signals players that ball-reversal movements are to take place. The high post (B1) sets a screen on the ball for G, resulting in a two-player game. See page 5 for further information on the two-player game. B1 rolls to the basket, while G attempts to get open for a shot near the foul line. G may also penetrate and kick the ball out to S2, who is drifting toward the far corner. After G tosses to S2, he or she steps out wide to a spot above the receiver near the ballside sideline. The player who originally passed the ball out of the corner (S1) moves to replace G as soon as the pick-and-roll maneuver takes shape. The low post (B2) remains stationary. Play continues as described when the ball goes to the new player in the corner, in this case S2.

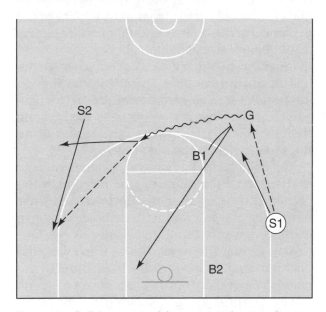

Figure 4.3 Ball thrown out of the corner and reversed.

A defensive overplay of the pass directly out of the corner is possible. If denied, the player immediately above the ball handler cuts toward the foul line and replaces the teammate at the top on the opposite side, who rushes to ballside position. The player countering the overplay must not react too quickly. He or she has to give the player in the corner with the ball a chance to throw it elsewhere. After all, three other pass options, described previously, are available.

Figure 4.4 depicts the regular ball-reversal motion. S2 throws the ball out to S1. The high post (B1) screens for the pass receiver (S1), and they execute a pick-and-roll. S2 replaces S1 out front when the dribble begins. The other perimeter player (G) slides toward the corner as S1 penetrates and is ready to catch a kick-out pass from G. The low post (B2) stays put.

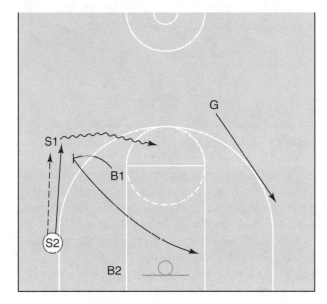

Figure 4.4 Ball reversal.

During the ball-reversal process, the ball handler has another choice. Rather than passing to the player in the far corner, the dribbler can send the ball back to the player heading to a site opposite out front. *Any pass across the top dictates that the player in the corner run baseline off screens by both big players.* The fade option is possible.

In the situation illustrated in figure 4.5, the player with the ball (S2) recognizes that the defense is denying passes to the corner (to G) and across the top (to S1). Instead of dribbling at the teammate out front to change sides (as reviewed previously), he or she calls the opposite big player's name (B1), who responds by flashing to the foul line and catching the next pass. The player across the top (S1) cuts backdoor as soon as the ball leaves the passer's hands. B1 looks over his or her outside shoulder for a bounce pass to the cutter. If the pass is not available, the cutter (S1) slides out to the same-side corner. The passer screens down for the perimeter player in the corner (G) to head

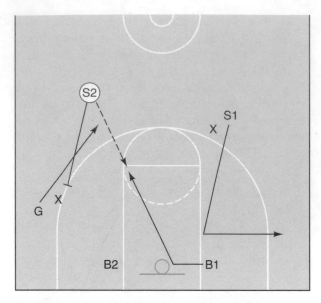

Figure 4.5   Passes denied.

out front. If the post player (B1) gives the ball to the player moving out top, he or she quickly sets a screen for the pass recipient (G). The team is now in its normal ball-reversal pattern.

B1 also could choose to toss to S1, who has back cut and then popped out to the corner (figure 4.6). When the bounce pass is completed, S1 creates space by dribbling out to the near corner if a scoring chance is not present. After S1 has the ball in the corner, the other perimeter players (G and S2) occupy two positions out top. B1 (the passer) cuts to the basket on release of the ball to the corner. If no return pass comes, he or she screens across for the other

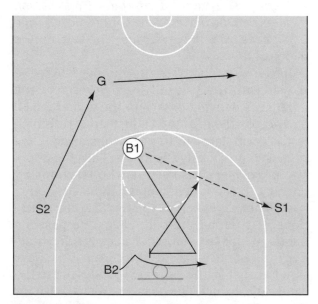

Figure 4.6   High post passes to the opposite corner.

big player (B2). In this case, B2 runs below as part of the low exchange. The team operates the offense continuously until they can take a quality shot.

Keys

Refer to the following topics in "Man-to-Man Offensive Fine-Tuning" in chapter 1 (page 4): setting a screen, slipping a screen, using a pick, and pinning the defender.

A team will be able to perform the baseline-shooter offense at an acceptable level after approximately 60 to 90 minutes of instructional time. Initial education should be on a dummy (no-defense) basis. This approach enables the team to learn the continuity as well as how to execute specific movements (for example, when an overplay is present on a pass across the top). Coaches should start instruction by giving the team the basic continuity first and saving the overplay options until a day or two later. After players know the required movements, coaches can add defense. They must avoid overloading players mentally at the beginning. Review of the dynamics of the offense should occur regularly throughout the season.

Coaches should instruct players to throw the ball across the front periodically rather than to the perimeter player in the corner off the two-player game. This action initiates a run along the baseline by the player in the corner using the screens set by the big players.

The point guard has several options available at the start of the offense: pass directly to the corner, throw the ball across the top to the other perimeter player, conduct a dribble exchange with the player out front to counter a defensive denial, or call the name of the opposite post player to flash to the foul line in reaction to the defensive overplay of the pass across the top.

The shooter sprinting along the baseline needs to run his or her defender into screens set by the big players. The player in possession of the ball out top regularly observes the baseline screeners. They might be open.

The player in the corner with the ball has these choices: attempt a shot, read the defensive positioning on the high- and low-post players after a low exchange and send the ball to the appropriate spot, execute a skip pass to the weakside top player, or throw the ball directly above and begin a change in sides.

The perimeter player with the ball in the two-player game has these options: shoot, penetrate for a score or kick the ball out to the far corner, pass back across the top to the perimeter player who moved up from the other corner, or call the name of the other post player (nonscreener) if the defense denies tosses to the corner and across the top. The dribble exchange is not available because the dribble is currently in use.

When the defense overplays the toss directly out from the corner, the perimeter players out front let the low exchange conclude before adjusting to the denial and exchanging positions.

The team must show some patience. Perimeter players focus inside. Players should feed the ball to big players before launching jumpers from a distance. Coaches who have an exceptional outside shooter may want to make an exception for him or her, especially after the player has exploited the baseline screens.

The duties of the perimeter players and post players differ. Any player who ends up playing both positions must know the entire pattern.

TRIANGLE AND TRIANGLE OVERLOAD

The triangle and triangle overload offenses are discussed together because of their similarities. The basic motion is the same for both offenses. One difference is that in the triangle the two players out of the main action are stationed on the wings. In the triangle overload, these two players are in a stack on one side of the half-court. In addition, in the triangle offense both post players are included in the primary action around the foul lane with one perimeter player. In the triangle overload, two perimeter players and one big player conduct the main motion near the foul lane.

When I first went to Widener University as an assistant coach, these were the first two man-to-man offenses I learned from Head Coach C. Alan Rowe, one of the all-time leaders in several coaching categories in NCAA Division III history. A few years before my arrival, the offenses were important instruments in Widener's drive to the NCAA Division III National Championship. I used them regularly when I became a head coach. These offenses work well for teams that have at least two and preferably three excellent offensive players. An accomplished trio is the featured group, the players on whom the action centers. If a coach has one or more outstanding one-on-one players, the triangle overload is the perfect fit because one side of the half-court is free of traffic. Because the bulk of the activity involves only three players, the other two players may not be content with their supporting roles.

Personnel

In the triangle, the three perimeter players should be solid outside-scoring threats. Both big players need good ballhandling skills and must be proficient shooters from 15 to 20 feet. Running the triangle offense successfully is difficult if one perimeter player is a weak exterior shooter or if both post players can score only inside 15 feet. In the triangle overload, including a perimeter player with relatively weak shooting skills or a post player with a shooting range of only 15 feet is more feasible.

Scoring

The players involved in the three-player movement will find shots in the paint and jump shots above either elbow in the 15- to 20-foot range. As a result of a two-player game, the dribbler obtains jump shots within 20 feet and a post player secures shots from the hoop out to 20 feet based on his or her movement. Defensive overplays may produce back cuts to the basket for layups. Back picks manufacture shots close to the goal through lob tosses at the hoop. Shots develop from a one-on-one on the cleared side of the court in the triangle overload offense.

Triangle Offense Execution

Players set up with four across the baseline (figure 4.7). Each of the post players (B1 and B2) is located on a block, and the shooters (S1 and S2) are in the corners. The point guard (G) picks a side and dribbles toward that elbow. The opposite big player (B2) steps inward, performs a V-cut, and then races straight up the lane line to a location opposite the ball to receive the first pass. He or she times the movement with the positioning of the lead guard.

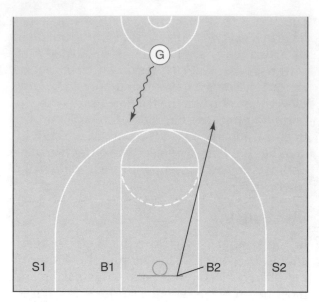

Figure 4.7   Start with four players across the baseline.

Figure 4.8 shows the initial pass completed from the lead guard (G) to the post player positioned opposite (B2). On the release of the ball, the perimeter player in the same-side corner as the pass receiver (S2) moves to the ballside wing at approximately the level of the foul line extended. Figure 4.8 shows the first movement option available for the three players around the foul lane (G, B2, and B1). G passes to B2 and then down screens for the player on the block directly below (B1). After picking, G pivots on the inside foot, opens up to the ball, and slides to the opposite box.

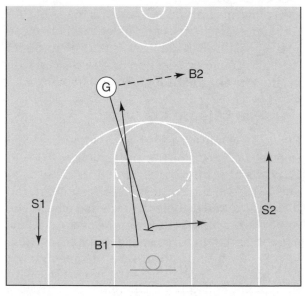

Figure 4.8   First movement option—down screen.

The second movement option for the passer is for the player below (B1) to move up, establishing a back pick instead of the down screen. Refer to the discussion of the back pick in chapter 1 (page 5). The player below calls out the name of the pick recipient (G) immediately after his or her teammate releases the pass. This call tells the passer a back screen is going to be set. A lob pass to the cutter may or may not be feasible. The cutter off the pick ends up on the opposite block below the player with the ball (B2) if there is no reception. The back screener (B1) steps out opposite the ball after the passer uses the screen.

The third option is for the passer (G) to act as though he or she is going to set a down screen below but instead cuts it short, plants the outside foot, and performs a V-cut to the other box, anticipating the pass from the top (B2). The player on the block below the passer (B1) darts upward opposite the pass receiver (B2). This maneuver is called a speed move.

The final option in the three-player triangle action around the lane is for the player on the block below the passer (B1) to fake a move up off the down pick and yell, "Me!" The passer (G) races to fix a down screen for the player below. The pick recipient (B1) calls, "Me" and then cuts to the other box. Once the screener (G) hears "Me," the player moving to pick runs back to his or her original site. Players use the me call if the defender on the player on the block tries to cheat over the down screen too early. The pass receiver (B2) looks inside to the teammate who made the call (B1).

Figure 4.9 shows the pattern continuing. B2 passes across to G. The two players out of the three-player action (S2 and S1) follow one simple rule. When the ball is on their side, they move up to the area of the foul line extended. If the ball goes away, they slide down to the corner. S1 moves up to the wing. S2 drops toward the corner. The passer (B2) establishes a down screen for the player below (B1) and then cuts to the other block. The down screen option is the primary move. Players mix in the back screen, speed move, and me call. The three-person action continues constantly, employing one of the four methods reviewed previously.

The team may use one of two methods to counter aggressive defensive denials of the pass across the front. First, if the pass receiver

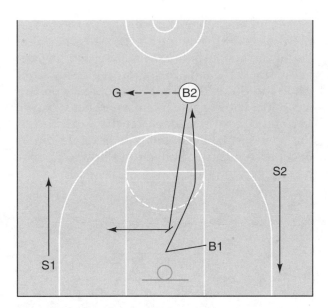

Figure 4.9 Motion continues.

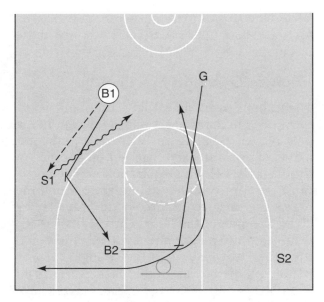

Figure 4.10 Ball passed to the player out of the triangle motion.

is overplayed, he or she simply back cuts to the hoop and expects a pass. If the player does not receive the ball, he or she returns to his or her original position. The second option is for the player with the ball to dribble at the player being denied. When the ball handler uses the dribble to change sides, the player in the corner on the side of the dribbler's destination bolts up to the wing. When the denied player sees the ball handler coming at him or her, he or she immediately races to down screen for the player on the opposite-side block. The screener achieves a good angle by swinging to the other side of the lane. The player below exploits the down pick. The screener opens to the ball following the pick and slides across the foul lane. The denied player (the pass receiver) and the ball handler (the passer) have just exchanged roles.

The activity should not include only the three players around the lane. The team must get the shooters (S1 and S2) involved periodically by having B1 fire the ball to S1 (see figure 4.10) instead of across to G. Once either S1 or S2 catches a pass, players perform the subsequent actions. Because a big player (B1) passed the ball to S1, he or she establishes a screen on the ball. See the discussion of the two-player game in chapter 1 (page 5). Meanwhile, the other three players fill specific spots. S2 stays in the corner, the other post player (B2) darts to the weakside box, and the other perimeter player (G) hurries above the weakside elbow. After S1 dribbles off B1's pick, the screener (B1) rolls to the basket.

G down screens for B2 to cut up top opposite S1. After screening, G heads to the far corner where S1 was originally stationed. The squad is now back into the normal offensive motion except that S1 is in the three-person triangle movement and G is out of it.

Figure 4.11 illustrates what happens if B1 skip passes the ball to S2, the shooter in the opposite corner. The nearer big player (B2) always dashes to set a screen for the pass receiver (S2). The other three players fill slots on the weakside of half-court (G above the elbow, B1 on the box, and S1 in the corner). B2 and S2 execute a pick-and-roll. As S2 approaches, G down screens for

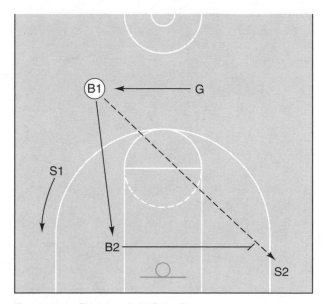

Figure 4.11 Skip pass from B1 to S2.

B1 and then heads to the corner away. B1 flashes up to the spot opposite S2. G is now out of the triangular action, and S2 is in.

Triangle Overload Execution

The triangle overload employs the same movement used in the triangle offense except that a post player (B2 in figure 4.12) and a perimeter player (S2) are stacked together on one side of the court out of the triangular action. Their positions are approximately at midlane about three to five feet inside the three-point line. Players clear one side of the floor. The playmaker (G) dribbles up to a spot above either elbow, and the other two players in the triangle (S1 and B1) are on the blocks. In this case, B1 darts up to catch the first pass from G. The players have the same four movement options discussed in the triangle offense: down screen by the passer, back screen for the passer, speed move by the passer to the other block, and the me option for the player receiving the down pick.

When the pass goes to B1 up top (figure 4.12), the perimeter player in the stack (S2) uses a screen by a nearby teammate (B2) and pops out past the three-point arc. The defense may deny the player coming out top opposite the ball (S1). The back cut is an effective weapon against an overplay on the cleared side of the court. The cutter may catch a direct pass for a layup or a lob pass tossed at the weakside of the rim. The dribble option described previously may also be used against denials.

Instead of flinging the ball across the top to G, B1 tosses to the shooter (S2), who is popping out of the stack (figure 4.13). The two players in the stack (B2 and S2) operate a pick-and-roll, while the other three players fill slots on the weakside. The big player and a perimeter player (B1 and S1) form a stack on the weakside of the half-court. The remaining exterior player (G) occupies a position above the elbow.

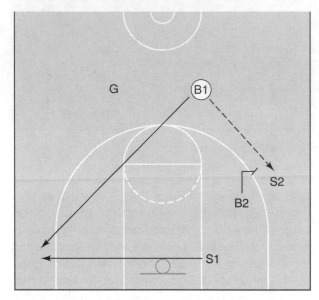

Figure 4.13 B1 passes to the shooter out of the triangle motion.

Figure 4.14 illustrates what occurs after B2 and S2 have executed the two-player game. The other three players are in positions outlined

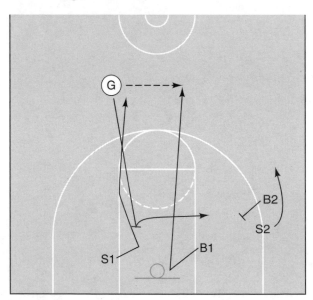

Figure 4.12 Beginning set for triangle overload.

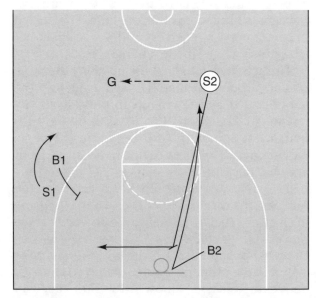

Figure 4.14 Completion of the two-player game in triangle overload.

previously (B1 and S1 are in a stack, and G is above the offside elbow). After S2 slings the ball to G, S2 and B2 do one of the four movement options in the triangle. Two important changes have occurred. First, the players in the stack have changed (from B2 and S2 to B1 and S1). Second, they have cleared the other side of the floor (from right looking in to left). The team executes the triangle overload offense until a quality shot develops.

Keys

Refer to the discussions of screening between post and perimeter players, setting a screen, slipping a screen, using a pick, and pinning the defender in "Man-to-Man Offensive Fine-Tuning" found on page 4.

These offenses are easy to teach. Players should fully understand either the triangle or triangle overload within one hour. Coaches may choose to teach only one of the offenses. Teams need not use both. After players learn one, however, they do not need long (no more than 30 minutes) to memorize the other.

Coaches may want to teach the squad one part at a time before going through the whole motion. The team must initially be drilled in the triangular action and the down screen, back screen, speed move, and me options. Next comes a review of the moves required when the other two players are on the floor. Finally, the coach puts the whole offense together, using a no-defense (dummy) basis first. Teams should practice the four movement options in the triangle versus a defense (going three-on-three) before going five-on-five. Coaches can use breakdown drills periodically to reinforce proper execution.

Coaches should insist that team members vary their motions in the triangle. They must use all four alternatives. The down screen is the primary move.

The player catching the ball out front turns and faces the hoop immediately after receiving the ball. In the triangle overload, the player securing the ball at the vacant-side elbow has a quick opportunity to go one-on-one. Teammates need to adjust if they see a one-on-one in progress. The passer should not end up on a block in front of the one-on-one.

The cleared side in the triangle overload provides chances for dribble penetrations and

encourages the use of the backdoor to counter overplays. Additionally, the vacant side permits the player at the top to feed the ball directly to the box below if the player low establishes a position advantage. The me option can produce layups when the player is heading toward the open side.

Players must react quickly and accurately to defensive denials. The team needs to know the two overplay options—to back cut or to dribble at denial. Another way to counter an overplay is to burn it before it can take place. The me option comes in handy here. The defender tries to slide over the down screen early to achieve a denial. The player using the down pick sees his or her defender cheating, fakes up, yells, "Me," and heads to the opposite box.

The two players out of the triangular movements cannot be lazy. They must move based on the location of the ball. They need to stay focused and be ready to make the defense pay if the defense ignores them.

To keep the defense honest, players in the triangle should use their teammates who are out of the action. They do not want the opponent to think that those two players are worthless.

Coaches should drill players on what spots they should fill on the weakside when a perimeter player out of the triangle motion touches the ball. Sites differ in the triangle and triangle overload. Both have a perimeter player above the elbow, but the post player is on a block in the triangle and outside in a stack in the triangle overload. The last shooter is in a corner in the triangle and in a stack for the triangle overload.

Players do not begin the execution of the two-player game too quickly. Players let teammates nearly arrive at their designated weakside locations.

The playmaker declares a side when beginning the offense. He or she must not confuse teammates.

In the triangle, if the ball is tossed to one of the shooters out of the triangle action, the nearest big player dashes to set the screen for the pass receiver, even if the perimeter player makes the pass.

Players must know that a poor pass across the top will most likely be very damaging. A clean, defensive interception means a layup at the other end of the floor.

Players must be patient. These two offenses are continuities. Therefore, the team must wear down the defense and wait for a quality shot to develop.

In the triangle overload, the coach may want to designate which players start in the triangle movement. The point guard is always involved. The coach may call names of the two players that are in or out of the triangle. Uninvolved players must understand how important they are to the success of the play. If ignored, they may feel inferior and useless.

Post and perimeter players have some jobs that differ. Players who play both post and perimeter positions must know the offense as a whole and must learn the added responsibilities.

TENNESSEE OFFENSE

The Tennessee offense is an easy-to-teach pattern that provides an opportunity to get the ball to the prime post player near the hoop. The offense creates strong scoring payoffs for perimeter players in alternating sequence. I used it periodically throughout my career. Tennessee is an unceasing motion that players enact until a satisfactory scoring opportunity surfaces. Because players constantly repeat the movements, the defense adjusts quickly to the pattern. Therefore, the offense is not a man-to-man system that can serve as the principal means to procure shots. When deployed infrequently, however, Tennessee is valuable. The team needs an exceptional post player who will gain ball possession around the hoop.

Personnel

Perimeter players need to be adept at handling the basketball with either hand. The three should possess the ability to shoot 15- to 20-foot jumpers. One big player needs to be a prolific inside scorer. The team wants to secure back-to-the-basket chances for this player. The other post player is the better perimeter shooter of the two and has the capacity to take a defender one-on-one in either direction. The exterior players' capacity to shoot outside is important.

Scoring

The offense achieves an interior-scoring chance for a designated big player. Perimeter players attain exterior shot attempts at the top of the key. An outside player gains scoring chances by using cuts off the high post with a payoff in the foul lane. The high post obtains a prospective shot by way of a drive to the bucket or a jumper near the three-point line out front following a step-back action after picking for the ball. Exterior players can gain shots off the dribble through picks on the ball.

Execution

The beginning set is a 1-3-1 with the featured post player occupying the low-post position (B2 in figure 4.15). B2 takes a position on either block. The other big player (B1) is at the high post. The point guard (G) brings the ball up the floor and always dribbles at the wing (S1) away from the low post (B2). At the same time, the opposite shooter (S2) drops toward the corner. The wing at which the lead guard dribbles (S1) screens across the lane for the low post (B2). The screener (S1) receives a pick from the high post (B1) and races near the top of the key. The lead guard (G) focuses inside on B2 first and then considers a toss to S1, who is moving to a region out front. Players strive to throw the ball low. The coach must be sure that players know the goals of the offense. See the discussion of passing into the low post in "Man-to-Man Offensive Fine-Tuning" on page 6.

Figure 4.16 depicts the continuation of the play. When the shooter (S1) catches the ball

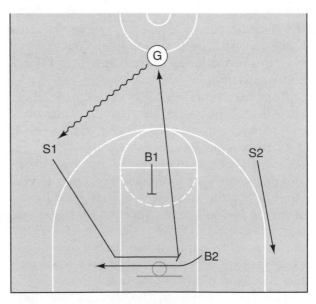

Figure 4.15 1-3-1 beginning set and movements.

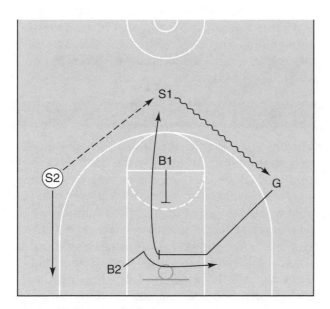

Figure 4.16 Same motion to the other side.

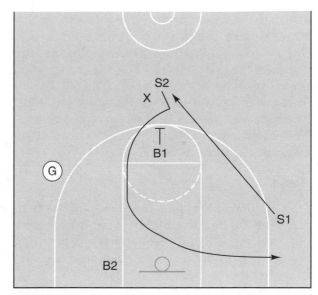

Figure 4.17 Pass to the top is denied.

out front, he or she must dribble to the side away from the passer (S2). The ballside wing (G) then sets a screen for the low post (B2). The high post (B1) down picks for the screener. The other wing (S2) drops to the corner to keep the defense away from the screen-the-screener action. This is a repeat of the basic motion of the offense.

The high post (B1) can periodically deploy a twist to the motion. The coach should allow the high post to use this option only if the player is an effective outside shooter with range to about 20 feet. The pattern is the same except that the high post steps out to establish a pick for the pass receiver out front (S1 in figure 4.16). S1 uses the screen and dribbles toward the wing away from the passer. The high post (B1) steps out after S1 uses the pick. No roll to the hoop occurs. The ball goes to the high post only if he or she is open for a shot. If the pass does not go to the high post, the regular pattern continues.

In figure 4.17, the player coming to the top (S2) is denied the pass from a wing (G). Therefore, he or she cuts again off the high post (B1), only this time the cut is straight down the lane and out to the offside. The opposite wing (S1) sprints to replace S2 out front. S2 and S1 have simply exchanged positions.

Figure 4.18 shows another deviation from the pattern. Before the player out front (S2) puts the ball on the floor and heads opposite, he or she may elect to toss the ball into B1 at the high post. B1 has screened the screener and

moved back to a spot at the foul line, awaiting the ball. No attempt was made to pick for the pass receiver out top (S2). After B1 grabs the pass, he or she views the low post (B2), executing a duck-in maneuver. Refer to the discussion of the duck-in on page 7. The playmaker (G) moves up to the near wing as soon as he or she sees the ball thrown to the high post. Another option available to the high post after receiving the pass is to go one-on-one, preferably away from the low post (B2). The high post either throws the ball into the low post, dribble penetrates, or flings the ball back out top to S2.

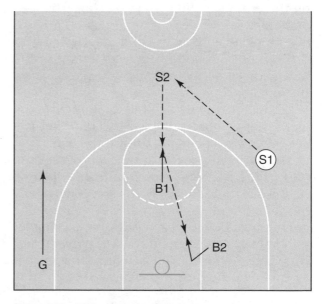

Figure 4.18 Ball sent to the high post.

The defense, however, may deny the target (S2). If that occurs, the player out front cuts hard to the hoop off the high post heading to the side opposite the low post. The bounce pass goes to the cutter if he or she is open. The wing away from the low post replaces the cutter out front. The high post passes to the teammate out top. The receiver dribbles at the wing away from the low post (normal motion).

Keys

See the following topics in "Man-to-Man Offensive Fine-Tuning" in chapter 1 (page 4): screening between post and perimeter players, setting a screen, slipping a screen, using a pick, and throwing the ball inside.

Tennessee is an easy offense to teach. Movements are not complicated or intricate. Total instruction time should be about an hour. The best method of instruction is whole-part-whole. Coaches should instruct players in the repeated actions of the play on a dummy (no-defense) basis initially and add the defense after players grasp the movements. The coach should periodically concentrate on one action, for example, the pick across the lane, the screen on the screener, or the duck-in. Frequent review of the pattern will help ensure that players react automatically and correctly to defensive overplays.

The primary post player using the low screen steps one way and goes the opposite way (over and then under or vice versa).

The high post heads directly at the defender on the cross screener when picking. The high post must be careful not to slide too far down into the lane and must maintain spacing with the low post. A good rule is to establish the down screen no more than a few paces below the foul line.

Perimeter players need to keep their heads up as they dribble to the wing so that they can see the low post coming toward the ball.

The perimeter player at the top always dribbles in the opposite direction from which he or she caught the pass. He or she consistently heads to the wing away from the low post. The counter to a defensive overplay of this shooter is ingrained in players. The denied player reacts by slicing off the high post to the hoop and out to the weakside corner. The weakside wing sprints to replace out front.

Perimeter and post players have different movements and responsibilities. Anyone who plays both positions must clearly comprehend the actions of both.

POST OFFENSE

For one season at King's College, my personnel mix steered me to playing three post players at one time. Because they were three of my best players, I wanted to come up with an offense that would take advantage of their interior skills. The normal three-out, two-in arrangement is the preferred configuration of personnel for a reason. Having three players on the perimeter pulls the defense away from the hoop and creates an inside-outside balance. When three big players are on the floor at the same time, it is difficult to space the offense sufficiently to spread the defense. The post offense let me put the three big players together while minimizing congestion.

If a squad has three strong post players or the trio contains its better players, then the offensive action in the post allows the coach to group the players together on the court. The offense can forge mismatches with the opponent—will the opposing team's small forward be able to handle the third big player man-to-man? Coaches must remember that mismatches can work against them if the foe is quicker. With three big players on the floor at the same time, the squad will have less overall ballhandling ability and may have problems defending on the periphery. Coaches must determine whether the advantages of placing a majority of post players in the game at once outweigh any of the potential negatives.

Personnel

This offense accommodates a team in which all three frontline players have good size but are not particularly effective shooters from the periphery. Coaches most often use it when they want to play three post players together and only two perimeter players. The personnel dictates that the frontline players have opportunities to post up to take advantage of their size. The two guards need to be quality outside-shooting threats, especially because the other three players are not.

Scoring

Players cut to the basket for layups. Backdoor maneuvers produce layups against an aggressive denial defense. Jump shots are available for frontline players near the foul line. The three big players receive passes in or near the paint for close-range shots. Guards attain jump shots from the wings. Shots arise from two-player games. Guards receive jumpers off the dribble, and screeners roll to the bucket, anticipating passes from teammates.

Execution

The offense begins in a two-guard set with G and S1 out front. They are the only two perimeter players (figure 4.19). The small forward (S2) is actually a third big player and occupies a spot at the foul line extended away from the ball. Two post players (B1 and B2) start on the boxes along the lane. S2, B1, and B2 are interchangeable. Motion starts with B1 doing an L-cut to get open to catch the first pass. Refer to the discussion of the L-cut on page 7. After G sends the pass to B1, the guards (G and S1) scissor as G establishes a diagonal down screen for B2. S1 ends at the ballside box. B2 heads to an area above the foul line. He or she may be open for a midrange jumper. S2 moves to the weakside block.

The next pass goes to B2 out front (figure 4.20). The passer (B1) hustles to establish a down screen for the shooter below (S1). See

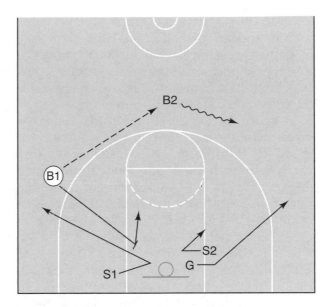

Figure 4.20   Pass completed to B2 at the top.

the discussion of the down screen in chapter 1 (page 4). The other guard (G) darts out past the three-point arc at the foul line extended as S2 ducks into the foul lane, awaiting an entry pass. See page 7 for the discussion concerning the duck-in. The pass inside to S2 could come directly from B2, or he or she may have to throw to G first. Regardless, the next pass likely heads to G if it cannot go in to S2.

If the pass goes to G and he or she cannot throw the ball into S2, the passer (B2) sets a screen for the receiver. The pick-and-roll between G and B2 takes place (figure 4.21).

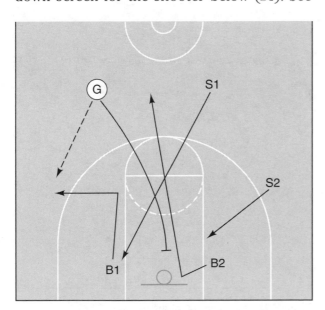

Figure 4.19   2-1-2 set to begin the motion.

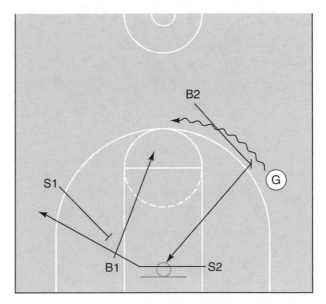

Figure 4.21   Pick-and-roll between G and B2.

Refer to the discussion of the two-player game in "Man-to-Man Offensive Fine-Tuning" on page 5. As the screen on the ball forms, B1 moves to a high-post position at the foul line. As G begins to dribble, S1 scampers to set a down screen for S2, who ends near the opposite wing.

In figure 4.20, the ball could just as easily go to the other wing (S1) rather than the point guard (G). Regardless, when the guard at a wing catches the ball, he or she looks to deliver to a teammate low. If he or she cannot do so, the player nearest the top of the key (B2) races to establish a pick for the ball handler and the team executes the action shown in figure 4.21.

When the guard at the top (S1 in figure 4.22), who has been involved in the pick-and-roll, recognizes that a shot attempt or toss to a rolling teammate (B2) is not feasible, he or she dribbles out above the top of the key. This movement increases the distance between the ball and the high post (S2). As soon as the guard on the box (G) realizes that a pass will not be thrown to B2, he or she slides to the opposite block to form a stack with B2. S1 passes to B1 and cuts to the hoop off a high-post screen by S2. If the defense aggressively overplays the intended pass recipient (B1), B1 contemplates a backdoor move followed by an L-cut to get open to receive the next pass. The player dribbling off the two-player game (S1) *must* pass to a teammate on the wing away (B1) if no shot is forthcoming or if he or she did not throw the

ball to the screener who is rolling. There are no exceptions to this rule.

The ball goes to the high post (S2 in figure 4.23), who steps out following S1's use of his or her pick. B1 flips the ball to S2. The team returns to the down screen by the passer (B1) for the player on the same-side box (S1). The other guard (G) pops out to the closest foul line extended behind the three-point line. B2 ducks into the lane. S2 dribbles toward B2's side to improve the passing angle, if necessary.

The offense continues replicating the movements discussed. Figure 4.24 shows the pick-

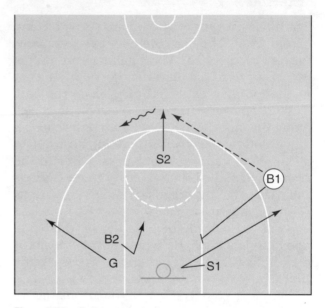

Figure 4.23 Ball goes to the top.

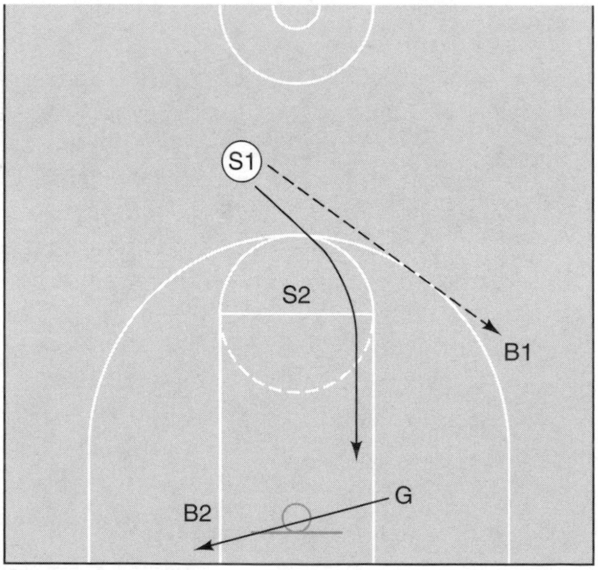

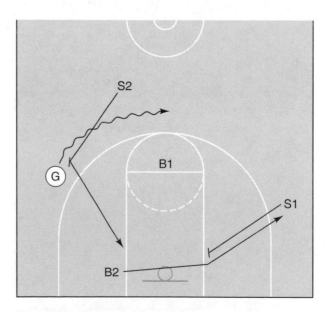

Figure 4.22 Guard involved in the pick-and-roll tosses the ball to the wing away.

Figure 4.24 Pick-and-roll sequence.

and-roll sequence. The final overplay option players may confront is denial of the pass to the high post (B1 in figure 4.24), who steps out after picking for the cutter (G) to the hoop. The denied player immediately hustles to set a diagonal screen for the frontline player at the weakside block (S2).

Keys

See the following topics in "Man-to-Man Offensive Fine-Tuning" in chapter 1 (page 4): screening between post and perimeter players, setting a screen, slipping a screen, using a pick, throwing the ball inside, and passing into the low post.

A team will need to spend some time learning this offense before they can successfully use it in a game. My estimate is that approximately two hours of instructional time will be required. Several steps need to be completed to end a cycle of movement. I suggest the whole-part-whole method of instruction. Coaches should teach the entire pattern first. Initially, the team performs the offense without a defense. Defenders join the mix after players can execute the pattern at an acceptable level. As necessary, coaches can break down the offense into smaller parts (for example, the duck-in) in practice. Coaches should drill counters to defensive denials. On a dummy basis, they yell, "Overplay" whenever they want players to act as though the defense has denied the next pass option. Overplays may occur when the high post is popping out or at a wing when the ball is out front.

The timing involved with the pass to the top is critical. The passer down screens immediately. The opposite perimeter player quickly rushes out wide near the sideline. The frontline player at the far block starts sealing in the foul lane when the ball is on its way to the top. He or she executes the pivot portion of the duck-in once the player out front with the ball is in position to make an entry pass.

The player setting the screen on the ball does not need to hurry. He or she may choose to hesitate one or two seconds before moving. This delay enables the guard with the ball to observe the interior.

The team needs to demonstrate patience and understand that they are using the offense because three big players are in the lineup. The strength of the club is around the basket, not out on the perimeter. Players make a concerted effort to deliver the ball into the paint. Guards must not be too quick to pull the trigger on exterior shots. Coaches should define exactly what type and distance of shot they will permit their players to take early in the execution of the offense.

Personnel must be able to benefit from this offense. If the small forward lacks physical stature but is capable of shooting from the outside, this is not a suitable offense. If one of the two guards is not a quality shooter from the periphery, the offense will likely be less productive. The two guards need to shoot effectively from distance to keep the defense honest.

The coach who chooses to incorporate the offense into his or her system needs to be prepared to review it regularly throughout the season. Team members must memorize the continuity. The coach should test player recall. A mental mistake by one player can cause a breakdown in the offense.

Drilling five-on-none is an effective way to maintain mental sharpness. After the defense takes the floor, however, the pressure to run the offense correctly increases dramatically, as do the chances for mental errors. The team needs to be well trained through five-on-five practice to be ready to use the play during competition.

STRUCTURED OFFENSE

The structured offense is different from the others in this book. It is more organized than a passing-game offense yet provides more freedom of movement for players than a pattern offense does. Geography is the main factor guiding personnel motion. I devised the action as a way to put more discipline into a passing game. The structured offense is a way to place a harness on players while giving them more decision-making authority concerning their motion. I developed it to teach players how to create scoring opportunities while giving them control over their precise movements.

The coach must be confident in the ability of his or her team to understand the information. The offense requires a significant amount of teaching. Players must visually identify an existing formation of personnel and respond by executing a prescribed activity. Players make choices based on what they see, where they are located on the half-court, and where the ball is. Players have to process a considerable amount of information rapidly and react appropriately.

Personnel

Having two big players who possess strong scoring techniques around the basket is always welcome. If they (or at least one) also have the ability to shoot and handle the basketball from the perimeter, the offense gains a significant advantage. If perimeter skills are lacking, the coach needs to place some restrictions on the maneuvers that big players may use. For example, the coach does not want a perimeter player to establish a flare screen for a post player who is incapable of taking advantage of a potential scoring chance from outside. All five players ought to be proficient at putting the ball on the floor to head to the bucket. The quicker players are, the better. Strong outside-shooting skills by at least two or three of the players cause the defense to extend outward, giving offensive players more room to work. The coach must drill players on basic screening techniques and effective use of screens. Mental awareness and the ability to recognize surrounding events quickly are desirable traits if players are to perform this offense at a high level.

Scoring

All kinds of scoring chances are available, from layups and posting-up occasions to three-point shots. The ability to score off the dribble is important as isolations crop up and one-on-one prospects become apparent. Coaches should specify to players what shots each may attempt. Some players will be better than others are at taking advantage of one-on-one chances. Coaches should limit players who do not have the capacity to be productive when placing the ball on the court.

Execution

This man-to-man offense may best be called the three-and-two offense or the two-and-three offense. An imaginary line from half-court through the basket divides the court directly down the middle. Three offensive players operate on one half of the floor, and two players use the other half. The diagrams in this section do not identify personnel by position because any

of the five players can occupy a given site. If a spot requires a post player, the diagrams just use B. If a perimeter player is to fill the spot, then P is noted.

On each pass reception, players should catch the ball and face the hoop immediately. When a player possesses the ball on the exterior, he or she quickly pivots and squares to the bucket. Players watch for dribble-penetration opportunities while executing the offensive scheme. With proper spacing of personnel, unoccupied alleys to the hoop should open periodically.

First, I need to discuss player positioning within the offense. The side with two players regularly has one perimeter player and one big player. The two offensive players can occupy three general locations: top, wing, and post (figure 4.25). One of the two players must occupy the top or be about to occupy it; they do not leave it vacant for any length of time. On the side with three players, one post player operates with two exterior players. Players still move within the three basic areas (top, wing, and post), but the post region is slightly larger than the one shown in figure 4.25, extending up to include the high-post position. Only one of the three available post-up spots (low, mid, and high) is filled by one of the three players. Two players must not occupy the same area.

This offense emphasizes delivering the ball inside near the basket. Either a big player or an outside player can post; it makes no difference. When an entry pass goes from below the

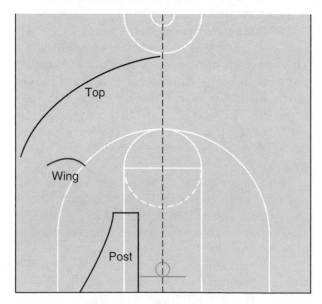

Figure 4.25   Court breakdown for the structured offense.

foul line extended into the midpost or low post (figure 4.26), certain motions are required. The passer cuts to the basket on either the foul line side or the baseline side of the pass receiver. If the cutter is an outside player, then the exterior player on the weakside will move to a ballside location. The nearest perimeter player to the top fills the vacancy created by the passer's cut. This player could even be the exterior player from the offside if an outside player is the cutter. Because the side of two must contain a post player and a perimeter player, the big player (B) fills the weakside elbow site (or the ballside elbow site if the cutter is a post player) and the exterior player (P) fills a ballside perimeter slot (or the weakside elbow site if the cutter is a big player).

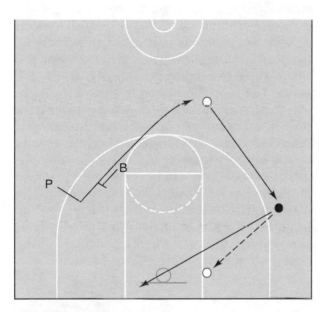

Figure 4.26   Pass thrown inside.

If by chance two post players happen to be on the same side of the half-court for some reason, players must immediately switch so that a big player is on each side. This rule holds true throughout the execution of the offense.

The next three scenarios are interconnected. Notice, however, that three players are present on one side of the court and two are on the other half of the court.

The players on the side of two (one big player and one perimeter player) are located in two of three possible areas—top, wing, or post. When the ball is on the opposite side, the players on the side of two have the following options.

• When a player is in the wing or post area, the player in the top area can execute a down screen (figure 4.27). The screener seals back toward the ball, anticipating a direct pass, and then darts to fill either the post or the wing spot.

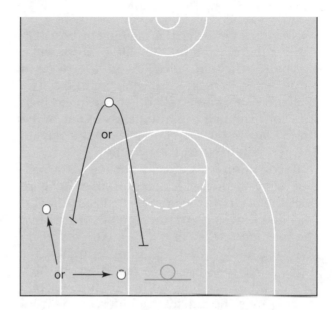

Figure 4.27   Top player executes a down screen.

• Another option is to fake coming off the down screen and back cut to the basket. The down screen should not be established too near the goal. Creating some room enables the fake and back cut to be executed. The screener reacts by returning to occupy the space on top. The player uses the maneuver whenever he or she sees the defender try to overplay the dash to the top. If the defender commits too early, a backdoor to an open spot near the basket is extremely effective.

• The rescreen option is another choice. Any screen can become a rescreen. Refer to the discussion of rescreening in "Man-to-Man Offensive Fine-Tuning" in chapter 1 on page 4. Of course, if the initial screen produces a desirable result, a rescreen is not required and is inappropriate.

• When the second player is in the post, a back screen can be established for the player in the top area. The back screen is especially effective when the player out front has just passed the ball to the other side of the floor. See the discussion of the back pick on page 5.

• When the second player is on a wing, a flare screen can be used. Refer to the discussion of the flare screen on page 6. The player in the top spot must be an effective shooter from at least 18 feet. Rescreening is a possibility if the motion does not achieve its initial goal. The second pick is a down screen, not a flare.

Now let's consider the movement possibilities for the players on the side of three when the ball is on that side. Players are to be in three general areas—top, wing, and post. The post area is expanded slightly to include a high location. The ball is in the hands of one of the three players on one side of the half-court on the perimeter (either top or wing).

Recognition of a defensive denial of the ballside wing mandates a countermove. In figure 4.28, the player in the post recognizes the overplay and moves up to the high post to receive the ball. On release of the pass, the player on the wing back cuts to the hoop, watching for a quick return toss for a layup. After the high post catches the ball, he or she immediately glances over the outside shoulder and delivers a bounce pass to the cutter, if open. If no pass is feasible, the cutter continues to the opposite side of the half-court. The passer out top hustles to fill the vacant wing site on the same side of the floor. The high post pivots to face the basket after looking over his or her shoulder to assess the motion taking place on both sides of the court. Once the players execute the option,

the side of two becomes the side of three and vice versa.

When the ball is on the wing of the side of three, the post player may be up high. A stationary screen by the high post allows the player on top to cut off a pick to the basket. If the player is in the low post when the ball heads to a wing, he or she could slide high to pick. To counter a defender who cheats over the screen too early to cover the basket cut, the cutter comes back to the top rather than to the hoop. The post player dives to the ballside low post if he or she feels that the opportunity exists.

On the side of three, down screening or back picking are possible when the ball is at the ballside top area (figure 4.29). Refer to the discussion of the down screen on page 4. If the down pick is far enough from the basket, the recipient can fake exploiting it and back cut to the hoop. If the curl move is employed as part of the down screen, the player cutting through the lane causes the side of three to become the side of two and vice versa. The rescreen option is always available whether the initial pick is a down screen or a back screen. If it becomes apparent that the action is not going to produce the desired result, players do not hesitate to rescreen.

The side of three can become the side of two in another way. If the ball is on the wing, the player in the post slides up all the way to the top area. The player at the top vacates his or her side by cutting to the opposite side of the floor near the weakside elbow. That side now

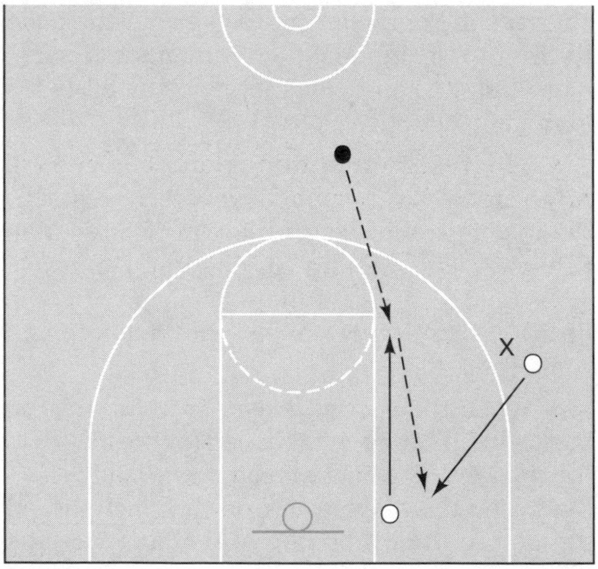

Figure 4.28   Wing denied when the ball is on the side of three.

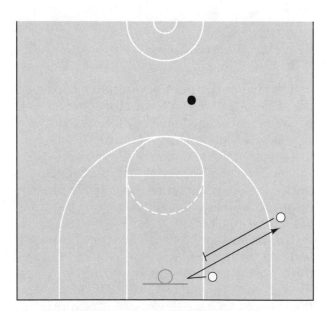

Figure 4.29   Down screen at the box on the side of three.

has three players, and they fill the top, wing, and post spots. The player with the ball considers a one-on-one opportunity when he or she realizes that the post is empty. Remember that if a post player runs from one side to the other, a big player must replace him or her. Perimeter players do not necessarily have to replace one another.

The next scenario deals with the motion possibilities when the ball is on the side of two, assuming that the ball is somewhere on the exterior. The ball in the post area obviously presents a scoring opportunity. Therefore, the concern is what motion is appropriate when the ball is in either the top area or the wing region.

Figure 4.30 illustrates player positions on the side of three players when the ball is at the top on the other side of the court (the side of two). The side of three has a player in each appropriate area—top, wing, and post. Remember, the post could be low, mid, or high along the lane. If no other movement is in progress, or as soon as it is concluded, the three come together off the foul lane below the offside elbow as the two players from the perimeter move inward to set the double screen. See the discussion of the double screen in chapter 1 (page 6).

Setting the double pick requires that players execute one of three alternatives. The first option for the three players is for the player in the post to use the double pick to slide over the double and curl into the foul lane. The player's

cut continues to the other side of the floor. This action changes the side of three to the side of two and vice versa. The player nearer the top in the double screen fades into the closer wing region after the curling player slices into the lane. The other player in the double pick races immediately to the nearby top region after both players dart by him or her in opposite directions.

The second option for the three occurs when the player in the post fakes coming around the double on the curl. Instead, he or she fades to the near corner. The players setting the double pick read the post player's move. The player nearer the baseline curls over the other player and cuts through the foul lane. The run across the foul lane causes a change of status (two to three and vice versa). The last player pops straight up to the top.

The final choice for the player in the post is to cut off the double pick to the top. The post player's destination is much closer to a sideline than normal. The player below closer to the baseline in the double pick curls over his or her teammate and sprints through the lane to the other side of the court. This movement changes the number of players on each side. The player in the high portion of the twin pick fades to the nearest corner and occupies the wing on the same side of half-court. Movement occurs after the team member curls around him or her into the foul lane.

Now let us review the final scenario that may arise during execution of the offense—action when the ball is in the hands of the wing player on the side of two. No other activity or cuts are present as the ball flies to the wing player or the motion has just concluded. As soon as the ball is on its way to the wing on the side of two, all four players without the ball rush to the weakside elbow area (figure 4.31). They do this quickly, without hesitation. The player in possession of the ball has an excellent opportunity to go one-on-one.

The four players in the group may do any kind of movement they desire, as long as they do not break the following rules. No more than two players may cut to the ballside, keeping in mind that only one big player can be on the strongside. Post and top areas are vacant and available. Players cannot bolt to the ballside post if a dribble penetration is in progress. If

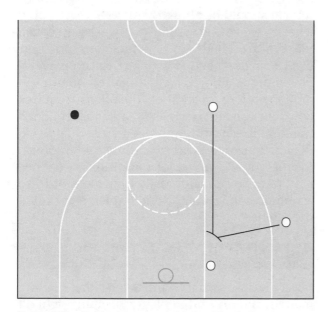

Figure 4.30 Ball in the top area on the side of two.

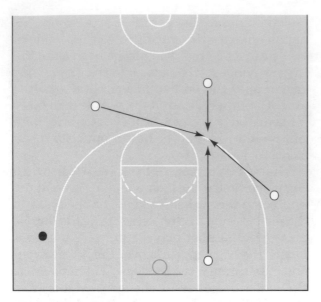

Figure 4.31 Ball goes to the wing on the side of two.

a dribble penetration is happening, the four other players scatter to appropriate locations to prepare for a dish. They are obliged to dash to spots that make coverage more arduous.

Keys

Refer to the following topics in "Man-to-Man Offensive Fine-Tuning" on page 4: screening between post and perimeter players, setting a screen, slipping a screen, using a pick, and throwing the ball inside.

This offense is not one that coaches teach on a whole basis at the beginning. I recommend breaking the team into smaller groups by position. Teams should practice two-on-a-side and three-on-a-side movement options. After players have learned what to do when on the side of two or the side of three, they can begin to move into five-player scenarios. The coach should review instances when the half-court sides switch from two players to three and vice versa. Teaching immediate recognition is important. Correct play becomes progressively harder when the numbers on the sides of the floor keep changing, sometimes rapidly. After players understand that floor spacing and balance are the concepts behind the three and two, they notice more easily which areas they are to occupy.

All players should be aware of any shooting or other restrictions (such as taking one-on-one chances) that the coach places on them individually. Big players and perimeter players can

be in any of the designated areas. The offense does not limit any players to specific regions.

Players need to maintain movement. They do not stand around waiting for someone else to move. The least they can do is go to a different area on their side of the floor.

Players do not hustle to areas too close to the basket when a dribble penetration is in progress or a teammate is cutting to an opening near the hoop. If they already occupy a post location when the dribbler begins the drive, players are ready to receive a pass when their defender goes to help with the ball handler. Players are aware of teammates' motion so that they do not interfere with potential scoring opportunities.

With this offense, players are not robots. They have options and rules. Their choices are limited, but they do not force players to execute a strict pattern of motion. Therefore, the coach has an element of control.

One of the most widely used and known man-to-man offenses is the flex (see chapter 3). The foundation for that offense is its ability to achieve a quick change of the weakside into the strongside and vice versa using a simple pass across the top out front. The number of players on each half of the court is either two or three. Moreover, they are constantly changing from a side of two to a side of three. The structured offense uses the same basic concepts but grants players more freedom of movement.

Teaching the entire offense takes some time, especially when using the part method initially. A team should be able to achieve a respectable level of execution within two weeks. Because players are making more decisions on their own, coaches need to be alert to the players' becoming enamored with a limited number of motion options. In addition, the offense requires constant use and review. A team must practice this offense more than once or twice a week. Players improve execution when they perform a substantial number of repetitions. Coaches may want to set aside daily time slots of 10 to 20 minutes for teaching and implementation of the offense.

WIDE OFFENSE

I was always partial to motion against man-to-man that incorporated players running right off the backside of a teammate while cutting to the basket. The initial alignment of the offense was 1-2-2. I devised movements that made the action continuous and maintained the formation. What evolved through my 13 years as a college head coach was the pattern called wide. The offense encompasses the same basic action but does not sustain the 1-2-2 shape. This rule-oriented offense does not restrict players to filling precise spots on the exterior regularly.

Because all activity takes place around the exterior, all players must be capable ball handlers. Each player operates under the same rules of motion. No player is restricted to specific positions. Every player carries out the same duties. If a team consists of players of roughly equal ability, the wide offense is a good choice. The offense stresses point distribution and places four players in motion every time the ball is passed.

Personnel

Post players should be able to function on the exterior of the half-court. Their ability to shoot effectively from 15 feet or beyond dictates the amount of respect the defense must show. High-quality outside shooting skills for all players are big positives. The greater the number of players who can drive to the basket, the greater the pressure put on the defense. The quicker the players are, the more likely they are to obtain shot openings. How well players understand the workings and concepts of the offense has great bearing on its effectiveness. Players must be able to recognize what is happening and respond with the appropriate move.

Scoring

Any player may receive a pass for a layup or short jump shot around the foul lane. All players get the chance to post up along the lane for a two-second count. Back-to-the-basket scoring situations can develop. Dribble penetrations can generate shots. Layups to 25-foot jump shots are possibilities. Anyone might gain an opportunity from any portion of the half-court. Layups through backdoor maneuvers are also conceivable.

Execution

This offense is different from others that have been reviewed. Although it is a continuity

offense, the pattern is not sequential. Player recognition of space after each pass dictates movements. All players take positions around the perimeter 12 to 15 feet apart. In the accompanying figures, the players are numbered 1 to 5 because the positions they play are irrelevant. The player circled in each figure is in possession of the basketball. Player movement begins after the playmaker is in position.

In figure 4.32, player 1 has the ball. He or she need not start at the same spot each time. Other players play off the point guard. Any of the four remaining players can initiate the offense. Players without the ball occupy spots on the periphery that adhere to spacing requirements (2, 3, 4, and 5 in figure 4.32). Notice that an imaginary line drawn from basket to basket through midcourt divides the half-court. The triangle symbol on the diagram shows the three players involved in the primary scoring action. In figure 4.32, players 3, 4, and 5 are involved.

When the ball is on the right side of the floor looking in, the first player to the left of the player with the ball (player 1) is the screener. In figure 4.33, player 4 initiates player movement by screening. Players 3 and 5 must immediately recognize their inclusion in the triangle with player 4. They are part of the scoring motion. Player 4 picks for the second player to his or her left (player 5). As soon as player 4 begins to go into motion, player 3 (the first player to the screener's left) cuts through the foul lane using player 4 as an obstacle by cutting directly

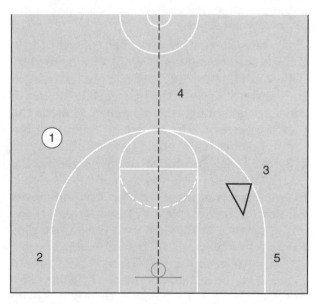

Figure 4.32 Sample starting alignment for the wide offense.

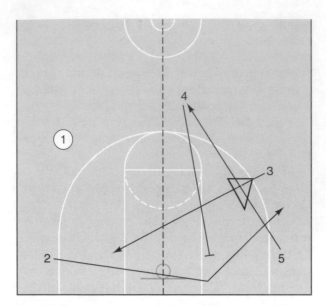

Figure 4.33   Standard motion when the ball is on the right side with a screener, cutter, player using the pick, and teammate replacing the cutter.

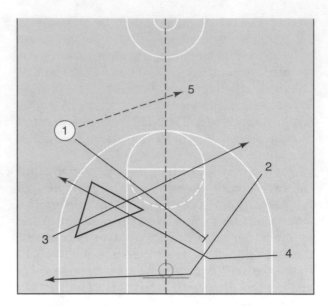

Figure 4.34   Same motion when the ball is on the left side.

off his or her rear. The two make some contact. Meanwhile, the nontriangle player without the ball (player 2 in figure 4.33) replaces the cutter (player 3). He or she commences movement at the same time as player 4 (the screener) and does not interfere with the cutter. The last player to move is the one receiving the screen (player 5). He or she exploits the pick to get open near the screener's original spot.

The four players in motion must follow one rule. A player not on the perimeter must go there quickly. Players hesitate only when they have a good chance of receiving an entry pass for a scoring opportunity.

The player catching the ball (player 5) is on the left side of half-court. Roles are defined by going to the right. The first player to the right on the outside (player 1, the passer) fills the role of the screener. In figure 4.34, player 1 plants the pick for player 4. The screener screens for the second player while going to the right. Players 1, 3, and 4 make up the triangle. Player 3 is the cutter (the first person to the screener's right). Player 2 is again the odd player out and moves when the screener (player 1) goes to replace the cutter (player 3). Player 4 uses the pick to slice to the region vacated by the screener.

The pattern continues. The next pass goes to player 3 on the left side of the floor (figure 4.35). Roles are defined by going to the right. Therefore, player 5 is the screener (the first player

to the right of the ball), player 4 is the cutter (the second person to the right), and player 2, who acquires the pick, is the third player in the triangle. Player 2 bolts to the area vacated by the screener. Player 1 is not in the triangle, so he or she replaces the cutter (player 4).

Figure 4.36 illustrates what happens if the ball is positioned straight out top. When the ball is in the center of the court (with player 2 in figure 4.36), roles are defined by heading to the right. The first player to the right of the ball (player 1) becomes the screener. Players 1, 5, and 4 make

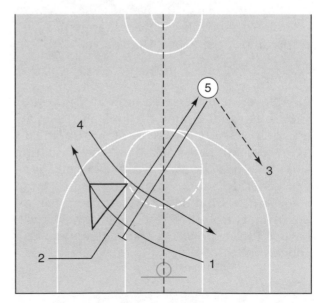

Figure 4.35   Motion continues with a pass to the player on the left side.

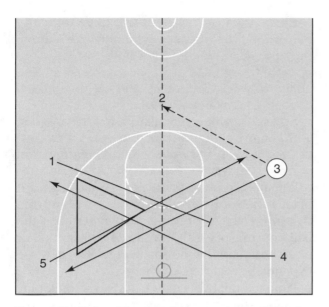

Figure 4.36 Ball positioned straight up top in the middle of the court.

up the triangle. Player 5 is the cutter, and player 4 uses the pick to head to the area vacated by the screener. Player 3 (the passer) is the one who replaces the cutter.

In figure 4.37, the pass goes to the right corner (player 5). Roles are defined by going left. The first player to the left starts the motion and is the screener (player 4). The first player to the left of the screener (player 1) cuts through the foul lane using player 4's tail to rub off the defender. Player 3 (the third member of the triangle and the second body to the left) receives the pick and moves last to the region vacated

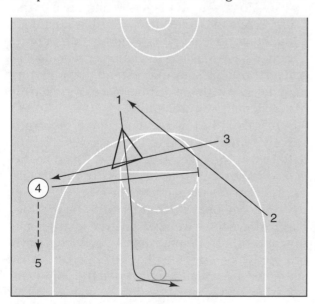

Figure 4.37 Ball on the right side of the court.

by the screener. The player out of the triangle (player 2) replaces the cutter (player 1). Player 4 (the screener) and player 2 (the replacer) embark at precisely the same moment. Player 1 (the cutter) moves next, a split-second after the screener begins (figure 4.37).

Keys

Refer to "Man-to-Man Offensive Fine-Tuning" in chapter 1 on page 4 for information on the following topics: setting a screen, slipping a screen, and using a pick.

Players must identify the location of the ball immediately. They do so as the ball is about to reach its destination.

When the ball is on the right side of the floor, players determine their roles by going to the left of the player with the ball. On the left side and straight up in the center, players determine roles by going right.

Players without the ball need to identify their roles immediately after ball possession is determined. The first person to the left or right (depends on exact location of ball) is the screener. The first body to left or right of the screener is the cutter. The player next to the cutter heading left or right is the receiver (uses the pick). The fourth player without ball (the one remaining player) is the replacer (replaces the cutter). The screener and replacer always move first. The cutter moves second, and the receiver moves last.

If the cutter is open going through the lane and does not gain the ball, he or she may post up for no more than two seconds. He or she stops only if an entry pass is likely. Otherwise, the player exits to the exterior and attains proper spacing with teammates.

The screener acts in a similar fashion. After a teammate partakes of the pick, he or she routinely steps back to the ball. The screener may possibly receive the ball. After realizing that no pass is coming, the player immediately scampers out beyond the three-point arc to a spot that maintains the required 12 to 15 feet between players.

The replacer must obey two rules. First, the replacer starts in motion precisely when the screener does. Second, the movement to replace cannot in any way interfere with the cutter. The route of choice must not allow the defense to offer help in covering the cutter.

The cutter must make physical contact with the screener. The cutter brushes the rear of the screener on his or her sprint through the foul lane. He or she is the primary target for the player who has the ball.

Coaches should clarify the types and lengths of shots that each player may attempt and any other restrictions placed on individual players. The squad operates at a disadvantage if players have to perform their weaknesses repeatedly.

A back cut to the hoop is the counter to defensive overplays. Players assume their perimeter positions at proper spacing (12 to 15 feet apart) as swiftly as possible if the backdoor move does not result in a scoring opportunity. Other players may need to adjust their perimeter positions to accommodate the return of the player who performed the back cut.

Because all five players are spread around the outer regions of the half-court, opportunities to penetrate the defense with the dribble may arise. Players are aware of potential dribble penetrations and take advantage of the opportunities whenever appropriate. Teammates react to the ball handler's drive and assume positions that make them difficult to defend if the ball comes in their direction.

Initial practice of the offense should be on a no-defense basis. Several 10- to 20-minute teaching sessions using this format are required. After players demonstrate an understanding of the motion, defenders take the floor and live competition commences. At least 7 to 10 competitive sessions are necessary to prepare a team to use the offense in game conditions. Five-on-five is probably the most effective teaching method. Breakdown drills are not particularly effective in teaching the offense. Four players move whenever a pass occurs, and players constantly repeat the motion.

Circumstances within a contest (the pace that the coach wants the team to establish, whether the squad is protecting a lead, and so on) dictate the shots that are permitted. The coach may want to consider a rule such as allowing shots only within 15 feet of the basket for the first so many passes. Alternatively, if the team is trailing late in a game, the first clear shot is approved.

Players are to be patient. This offense is designed to increase the likelihood of a defensive breakdown with time.

Elementary-age players will have difficulty performing the offense. By junior high school, they possess the cognitive skills necessary to operate the offense at an acceptable level. The ability to recognize, react, and identify spatial concepts improves with age.

Skip passes may be available, but they require a little more thought from everyone. A change of sides is likely to happen. Rapid identification of roles is essential.

A major advantage of this offense is that it places the four offensive players without the ball in motion. Moreover, as players pass the ball from one player to the next, no hesitation or interruption in the motion occurs. The defense expends a great deal of energy.

If mental mistakes occur, players should play through the errors. They space themselves properly on the exterior and make a pass.

PENETRATE OFFENSE

I designed this offense in response to current trends in the game. Today, especially in major college basketball and the professional leagues, the one-on-one initiative has gained significantly in popularity. Many programs have incorporated the dribble penetration against man-to-man defense. The concept is gradually drifting down to the other college squads and high schools. The dribble can be an extremely effective offensive weapon. In the 1950s and 1960s, coaches did not encourage its use. Most wanted players to limit use of the dribble. Against zone defenses, it was almost completely absent. Today's game is different. Coaches have learned the value of placing the ball on the floor. They understand that puncturing a defense with the dribble places a great deal of stress on the opponent.

A team that has two or more players who are effective when driving to the basket is a candidate to run the penetrate offense. Team speed is also important to the success of the attack. The quicker the players are, the more likely it is that they will beat a defender with the dribble. Players have to be well versed in jab-step execution and other offensive skills connected with productive one-on-one play. The offense is well suited for use late in a game when the opponent is leading and wary of fouling.

Personnel

All players are required to be proficient at handling the basketball on the periphery. Players should be able to go either right or left. The three exterior players ought to be capable of shooting successfully from beyond the three-point line. Big players may secure outside shots, but coaches should establish limitations based on the potent shooting ranges of their individual players. All players should be able to secure the ball while on the move. This offense could use four perimeter players with only one inside player. The offense is adaptable to different personnel configurations.

Scoring

Shots occur as a result of one-on-one situations. The ball handler can kick the ball out for an exterior shot or dish it off for a chance closer to the basket. Diagonal down screens create jump shots for perimeter players. Post players may land interior shots after receiving a screen across the lane. All players might attain scoring chances from pass receptions garnered during cuts to the hoop. Peripheral jump shots result from use of a horizontal pick. Back picks could produce direct tosses to players darting to the basket or lobs at the weakside of the rim. Big players gain outside shots from 15 to 19 feet.

Execution

The ball is on the perimeter below the foul line extended. Players without the ball fill four spots (figure 4.38). All positions are interchangeable, and there is no specific order. Players move in a triangular fashion. Three players are on the weakside—one at or just above the first hash mark above the box (B2) on the foul lane, the second at the elbow (S2), and the third (G) directly above the other two behind the three-point line. The fourth player participating in the triangular movement (B1) is on the ballside just past the lane line and three-point arc.

The four players in the triangular action keep their defenders occupied. The players moving in the triangle observe the following rules. The ballside elbow is the target for cutters in the triangle. The cut always occurs through the elbow and ends at the first hash mark above the offside block. The players away from the ball rotate one position as soon as the cutter (B1)

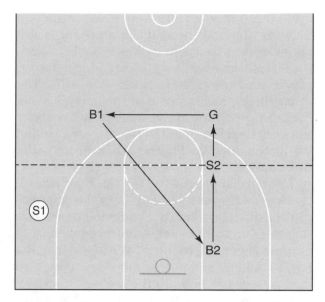

Figure 4.38 Motion when the ball is below the foul line extended.

hits the ballside elbow. The next player to go strongside is G in figure 4.38. The player coming toward the ball (G) does not stand stationary. If no pass comes, he or she sprints through the elbow and the process occurs again. The movements of the four players allow the player with the ball (S1) to go one-on-one.

The ball is above the foul line extended in figure 4.39. The diagram also shows the three vertical divisions of the half-court. When the ball is above the foul line extended, it is never within the lane area. With the basketball in either top

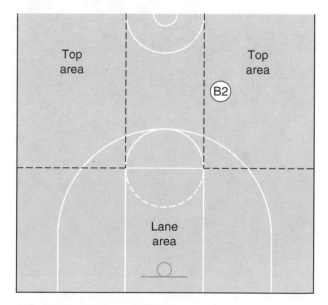

Figure 4.39 Divisions of the half-court.

area, the opponent must make a distinction between the ballside and the weakside, causing defenders to assume different roles. When the ball is above the foul line extended, only one player is on the ballside periphery below. The other three players position themselves along the offside lane line at the first hash mark above the box, the elbow, and in the top area behind the three-point line. Players can be in any of the three spots.

The normal motion for the three players on the weakside when the ball is in the opposite top area is an upward (back screening) rotation (figure 4.40). Immediately after recognizing that no pass is coming to the player in the top area (G), B1 and S2 slide up in an effort to set two back screens. G bolts to the hoop off picks on the side away from the ball. B1 and S2 move simultaneously before G dashes to the basket. The three players rotate one position and repeat the process. See the discussion of the back pick on page 5.

To create scoring chances, the offense gives the defense a consistent, repetitive pattern of motion and then suddenly reverses direction (figure 4.41). Periodically, the trio on the weakside varies its actions. The initial back screener, who must be one of the two post players, decides to deploy the option. In figure 4.41, B1 has already picked and stepped out. The player cutting off the back pick is one of the three perimeter players (in this case S1). B1

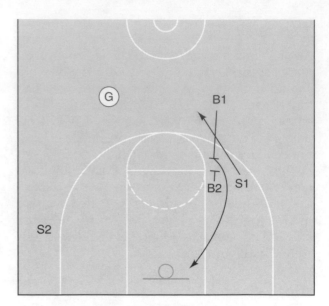

Figure 4.41 Variation of the back-picking action.

yells S1's name and quickly turns to rescreen. See the discussion of rescreening on page 4. S1 pops back up to the top area, using the pick. After rescreening, B1 exploits B2's pick and heads to the hoop.

To attain a strong shot, the team can deploy the same rapid backtrack from the normal triangle motion. When the ball is below the foul line, the four players without the ball break the usual triangle pattern. In figure 4.42, the player moving on the diagonal (S2) chooses to make the call. He or she yells the name of the player nearest the offside box along the lane (B2). An exterior player (G, S1, or S2) may make the call only when he or she views a big player close to the box. S2 yells the player's name before reaching the elbow. Teammates know that he or she is setting a screen for the big player (B2) instead of just cutting. B2 flashes over or under the pick to the ballside and anticipates a post feed for an interior shot (figure 4.42).

When a post player is the diagonal cutter and one of the three exterior players is closest to the weakside box, the action becomes a diagonal down screen. The outside player nearest the block gains freedom for a shot somewhere in the ballside top area. Refer to the sections about screening between post and perimeter players in "Man-to-Man Offensive Fine-Tuning" on page 4 in chapter 1.

Figure 4.43 shows what happens if the ball goes inside to B2 in the mid- to low post. After releasing the ball, the passer (B1) dashes to the

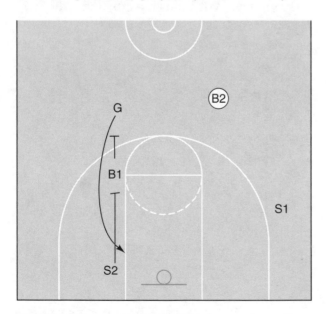

Figure 4.40 Back picks when the ball is in the top area on the other side.

In figure 4.44, B1 tosses the ball to the player in the strongside top area (S1). Because B2 did not catch the pass from B1, he or she races to assume a role in the three-person back screen. When the wing (B1) casts the ball to the top, he or she runs on the horizontal to pick for the middle player (S2) in the offside line. S2 darts to the ballside wing.

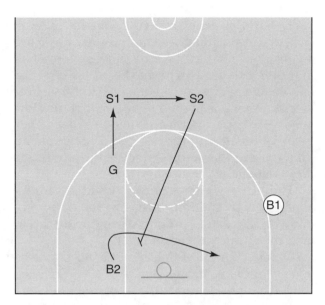

Figure 4.42 Variation of the triangular motion.

weakside box, heading to either the baseline or the foul line side of the pass receiver. The other three players race to fill three locations. A perimeter player (S1) always assumes the role of the replacer and fills the passer's spot. S2 and G fill the other two spots, the offside elbow and past the ballside elbow, respectively. When a big player is one of the other three players (not the passer or pass recipient), he or she sprints to the weakside elbow. If B2 does not receive the ball near the basket, he or she jumps back into the four-person triangle motion and players proceed with the cutting sequence.

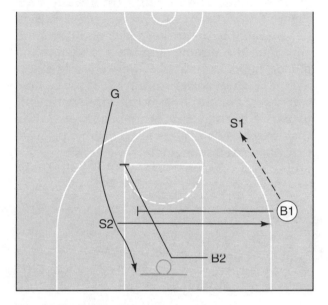

Figure 4.44 Ball passed outward to the top area.

When the ball goes from one top area to the other, players hustle to their appropriate locations (figure 4.45). The player nearest the block (G) races to the ballside periphery below the

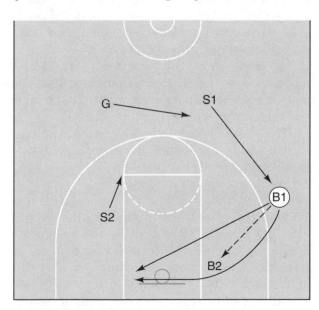

Figure 4.43 Ball passed inside.

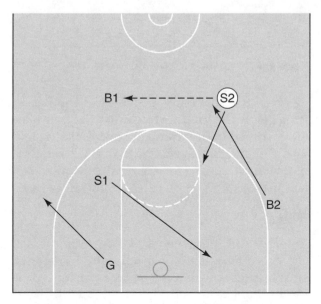

Figure 4.45 Pass from one top area to the other.

foul line extended. The passer (S2) heads to the offside elbow, the player on the strongside elbow (S1) slides toward the weakside box, and the other player (B2) fills the top area on the weakside. The three players away from the ball (B2, S2, and S1) are now aligned to start the back-screening action.

Players occupy the following sites when a dribble penetration occurs from a top area (figure 4.46). The exterior player on the ballside (G) is available to receive a kick-out for a jump shot. The three remaining players rush to the offside block (S1), above the weakside elbow (B2), and the vacated top area (S2). The final spot must contain one of the three perimeter players. A big player does not head there. When the three offside players see a dribble penetration, they react immediately.

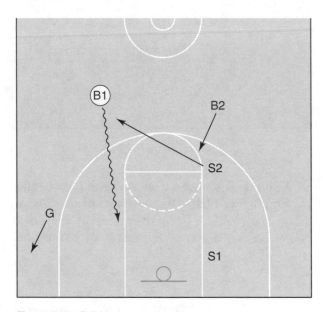

Figure 4.46 Dribble penetration from a top area.

When the ball handler drives to the basket from below the foul line extended, the four players involved in the triangle movements rush to fill the offside block, weakside elbow, strongside elbow, and the wing to replace the dribbler. The last player must be an exterior player.

Keys

Refer to the following topics in "Man-to-Man Offensive Fine-Tuning" in chapter 1 (page 4): setting a screen, slipping a screen, using a pick, low exchanges and cross screens, and throwing the ball inside.

The dribble penetration is key in this offense. The player positions and motions are designed to maximize the chance of success for a ball handler driving to the basket. Players take advantage of any one-on-one possibilities. Portions of practice should regularly include pairing players to work on one-on-one skills. Other players hustle to predetermined locations so that the dribbler knows precisely where his or her teammates are situated.

The other way the offense creates scoring chances is by suddenly breaking the pattern of motion. Movement progresses in one direction and then swiftly reverses itself.

Coaches should reinforce that no player is ever stationary in the lane area. Players slice through it but do not settle in the region.

The player moving to the ball in the four-player triangle does not hesitate to dart through the elbow if a pass does not come. The movement is automatic if the player is denied. After committing to the sprint, the player extends a target (the inside arm). This gesture tells the player with the ball that a cut is forthcoming.

If the ball is in a top area, one teammate must be on the ballside periphery below the foul line extended.

Transition into the three-player back-screen motion occurs when the ball goes to a top area from the wing directly below or the other top area. The player at the elbow initiates movement. The teammate at the first hash mark above the offside block moves up in conjunction with the player directly above. A scoring chance may develop from the movements executed immediately following the pass.

The player using the back picks may dart to either side of the screen. Usually, the track is away from the ball. An infrequent dash to the ballside might find freedom.

This offense is not difficult to teach. Motions are easy to comprehend. The four-player triangle movements and the three-player back-screen actions are the main ingredients.

Coaches should teach the jab-step series. When a player secures the ball on the perimeter, the possibility of a drive to the basket appears. Players have to learn how to break a defender down by using a short step directly at the opponent. The ability to maneuver left or right is critical for success at penetrating the defense.

Coaches must place restraints on some players. A big player incapable of handling the basketball should not have the green light to drive to the basket from the perimeter. Coaches should formulate shot restrictions as needed on an individual basis.

Players are not obligated to penetrate all the way to the hoop. They can stop a drive and look to throw the ball out to a teammate. Players are in assigned slots. Defenders will tend to help while collapsing toward the basket.

If a scoring wrinkle is used, players must know precisely how to resume normal movements. Coaches should review each specialized activity so that no undesirable hesitation is present.

Physical or mental breakdowns should be rare with this offense. The offense should be operational for game conditions after three to seven practice sessions. Coaches should educate players on a no-defense basis initially before engaging them in competition. If players exhibit sloppiness in execution, teaching on a dummy format should resume for a brief period.

Drills on driving to the basket are helpful. The coach should place the offense on the floor with the ball at specific exterior sites. The player with the ball goes to the hoop, and the other four players perform their designated tasks. Five defenders are used. After the dribbler completes the penetration, the drill ends and the process starts again. The ball should begin at varying points.

Sound reasoning is behind the demand that players never secure the ball in the lane area past the foul line. Ball possession is preferred within the two top areas. Having the basketball in a top area or below the foul line extended maximizes the distance between the player with the ball and the players remaining active. If the ball is straight out front, defenders have a tendency to pinch inward. When the ball is off center, the defense is concerned with the activities of the offense away from the ball. Drawing defenders' attention from the ball handler increases the odds of a productive dribble penetration.

Players give a clear signal when coming to the ball. The worst-case scenario occurs when the passer releases the ball and the player heading his or her way has already cut elsewhere. The potential pass receiver changes the target hand. The player coming to the ball in the four-player triangle places the outside arm up and out. After starting the slice through the elbow, he or she extends the inside arm and hand to the passer. When countering a defensive denial, the passer should give a ball fake, telling the cutter to start to back cut. The cutter therefore changes the target hand. If the cutter cleanly beats the defender, he or she executes the move more on a straight line to the hoop rather than through the ballside elbow.

PART II

Zone Offenses

CHAPTER 5

Tulsa Passing Game

Passing games are not used only against man-to-man defenses. The Tulsa offense was formulated to be successful against zone defenses. It combines the rule-oriented positioning and motion of a passing game with precise types of motion that players can execute to defeat a zone. Players have freedom to select from various movement alternatives. The coach retains some discretion and control to direct the team to perform specific actions.

Coaches have increasingly turned to this style of play when confronted with zone defenses. Players learn how to combat a zone and are not locked into a specific sequence of movements. Most major college programs use some form of conceptual assault, as opposed to sequential acts, to counter zone defenses.

Teams can use the Tulsa offense against all types of zone defenses. I prefer issuing specific direction to big players, but coaches can permit them the same freedom of choice enjoyed by exterior players. The Tulsa offense became my primary system for scoring against zones. Players learn to attack any type of zone.

The first and most important decision that coaches must make is which motion options to teach and which ones to use during the season. Coaches can install one piece at a time and add as the season progresses. They may select all or only a limited number.

The time required to teach the execution of Tulsa is not substantial. Players quickly comprehend the movements of perimeter and post players. Learning Tulsa consumes more time when big players and exterior players have to coordinate movements. Players must concentrate on proper timing of the various maneuvers when post and perimeter players are required to work together. Coaches should reinforce all motion objectives periodically to ensure sound execution. Players cannot become locked into only one or two maneuvers. Coaches may be required to teach players how to maintain a particular action for multiple tries within the offense.

When teaching Tulsa, a good approach is to educate perimeter players separately from big players. Later, both groups can come together to execute the total offense and learn any motion options that require interaction. A periodic return to split groups for review may be necessary. Coaches should initially teach concepts and offensive moves on a dummy basis. If players have difficulty with a particular portion, coaches can teach and drill that part alone before teaching the whole again. Breakdown drills correspond to each movement alternative.

The two post players should be able to score when facing the basket from 15 feet and must possess solid inside scoring skills. In some cases (such as Tulsa reversal), shots from three-point range may develop for big players. The Tulsa offense is more fruitful when exterior players are outside threats.

Scoring opportunities are widely scattered in the offense. The movements of the big players open chances inside, and perimeter players are able to generate shots through their own actions. Their shot opportunities are likely to happen near the three-point line.

The offense is based on teaching the three perimeter players numerous maneuvers that they are able to employ against zone defenses. The two post players learn other actions, which are effective at working inside zone defenses. The coach can give each group complete free-dom to select the exact motion to execute, or the coach can dictate the action to one or both groups. If perimeter players, post players, or all players are free to select their own motions, the coach must ensure that they execute the complete collection of moves. Players may even change the movements during the course of a single possession. Regardless, the basis of the offense is to attack the zone constantly. Several motion alternatives require coordination between the two groups. Players can repeat some for an entire possession, whereas others are designed to produce a quick scoring situation before players resume other motion options.

Zone Offensive Fine-Tuning

In zone offenses, certain principles hold true regardless of the precise motion displayed on the court. Coaches should emphasize the following topics when teaching players to combat zone defenses.

Proper Spacing

Proper spacing is essential. Offensive players must maintain a comfortable distance between each other to ensure that one defender is not able to guard two offensive players. The general rule is that players should be at least 12 to 15 feet apart, especially on the perimeter. Players working within the interior of the zone may decrease the distance to 10 feet.

Player Positioning

Player positioning against zones is important. Players dash to areas of borderline responsibility between two defenders. They attack the gaps in a zone to cause hesitancy in coverage or cause both defenders to move to cover the pass receiver. Either scenario is advantageous for the offense.

Player Patience

The team must exhibit patience. Players make the zone defenders work by forcing them to move and cover as much area as possible. Players usually throw five or more passes during each possession. Sometimes long-range shots that materialize early in a possession will need to be bypassed in order to make an effort to send the ball to the interior. The squad does not play tentatively. They are aggressive yet patient.

Attacking the Interior

Players attack the interior of the zone. This approach allows players on the perimeter to get open as the defense becomes more concerned with collapsing and shutting down the inside. Attacking the inside also creates greater risk of foul trouble for post defenders. Players on the periphery should look inside consistently. The high-post region is equally important as the area immediately in the vicinity of the basket.

Moving the Ball

Players move the basketball. They change sides quickly and frequently. They do not hold the ball too long, and they keep their eyes on the interior. When a player receives the ball on the periphery, he or she takes a quick glance toward the basket. Passing around the perimeter of the zone forces the zone to move.

Using Skip Passes

Players should not hesitate to use skip passes. They do not fear throwing cross-court passes to change sides of the floor. Skip passes produce quick changes for the defense, switching players from helpside to ballside and vice versa. A low-post player on the side to which the skip pass is completed tries to seal the defender who has ballside low post or middle responsibility while the ball is in transit. The offensive post player initiates contact and seals the targeted defender by facing the foul lane and physically bumping the defender. The post player pivots on the foot that provides leverage against the defender (usually the baseline foot) and opens to the ball. The post player maintains a wide base while sitting on the defender's thighs and moves his or her feet to continue the position advantage. Players should throw the skip pass overhead with two hands. The passer must read the weakside defenders to make sure that they are not decoying and looking to intercept the toss. A good counter is the ball fake. See the following discussion of using ball fakes.

Using Ball Fakes

Players use ball fakes against zones. They fake a pass in one direction and then look to throw the opposite direction. All types of passes can be fakes. A ball fake is effective because it makes the zone move when it should not. Making a zone defender move to cover when he or she is not supposed to is a big plus for the offense. Coaches should emphasize this important concept.

Catch and Shoot

The pass receiver on the exterior sets his or her feet square to the basket just before the catch. He or she consistently slides into position so that a catch and shoot is possible. The player does not dribble. The player gets behind the ball with the body square to the hoop and the feet in optimal shooting position.

Using the Dribble

Players use the dribble against zone defenses to accomplish the following:

- In some cases, the offensive team wants a specific opponent to cover the ball handler. The dribble ensures that the desired matchup occurs.
- Players do not allow one defender to play two offensive players. The player who dribbles at the defender forces coverage.

- Players dribble into gaps in the zone, forcing two defenders to guard one offensive player. The nearest exterior teammates prepare for an immediate shot if the closest zone defender helps to shut down the gap, leaving an opening. This action gives the offense an edge.
- Players dribble to compel defenders to leave their normal coverage areas. One defender has to release responsibility to another defender. A different defender must cover the ball. The dribbler takes the defender to the edge of his or her zone coverage area. An effective play is for the dribbler to take the defender just to the brink of a release. If a release takes place, the ball handler may dribble back to force another release between the same two defenders. I call this "playing games with the defender."
- The dribble improves passing angles and helps a player get out of trouble.
- Players dribble once or twice in either direction after a shot fake to avoid the defender for a shot attempt.

Filling the Void

Teammates consistently attempt to fill the voids created when the ball handler dribbles to another exterior location. They follow the ball handler to the open area that just became vacant. For example, the player dribbles off the baseline and looks below to the area along the baseline for a team member filling the newly created void.

Crashing the Glass

Players consistently crash the offensive glass. The coach should choose how many players should head to the glass. Players want to force one zone defender to try to box out two offensive players. Players make a special effort to move to the weakside rebounding location, usually the best place to acquire a two-on-one rebounding edge. Players learn to hit spots in the zone that are most vulnerable to offensive rebounding.

Screening

Screening against zones differs from screening against man-to-man defense in two ways. First, the player using the pick does not wait for

(continued)

his or her teammate to plant the screen. The player's movement begins when the pass is on its way to the recipient. Second, the target of the screen is more difficult to identify. Rather than going after a defender assigned to a teammate, the screener pinpoints the defender with a specific zone coverage responsibility. Persistent teaching ensures correct identification of the defender in the various types of zones. The coach should emphasize that the screener must still come to a stop just prior to contact.

High-Low Formation

The high-low formation to attack the interior of the zone has one player in the high post (above the hash marks on the foul lane near the foul line) and the other low along the lane between the blocks and the first hash marks. The low post does not put the baseline foot below the box. When the ball goes to the low post, the high post dives to the basket.

Midpost and Baseline Alignment

The midpost and baseline alignment to attack inside a zone has one player between the first

and final hash marks on the lane (midpost) and the other along the baseline. When in baseline position, the player's back is to the baseline and he or she faces out toward midcourt. The player is three to eight feet outside the foul lane and usually no more than three feet from the baseline.

The ball is tossed to the high-post or midpost player. The player turns to face the goal. His or her first look is to the player below moving to the basket. Sometimes a touch pass is appropriate. The next option is to throw to a teammate on the perimeter away from where the post player received the ball. The player also has the option to shoot or drive to the hoop. The final choice is to pass to one of the other two team members.

Beating the Zone

The squad tries to beat the zone down the floor, especially when the opponent is using zone as a transition defense. Players attempt to convert an easy scoring opportunity before the zone has a chance to set up. Up-tempo teams are more likely to pursue this approach.

PLAYER MOVEMENT OPTIONS

This portion of the description of the play comprises three sections, each dealing with a different aspect of the offense. I have outlined five options for perimeter players, four options for big players, and five options that require involvement of both groups. Where necessary, I point out whether the option can prove particularly useful against a certain type of zone.

Perimeter Players

Perimeter players have five different movement options: middle, overload, dribble chase, screen point, and dribble follow and fill the void. I generally give perimeter players complete freedom to use any of the movements when executing Tulsa.

Figure 5.1 shows the middle exterior player passing to a teammate on the outside and then

cutting through the zone. He or she darts to either the ballside or the weakside. The perimeter player who does not receive the pass (S2 in

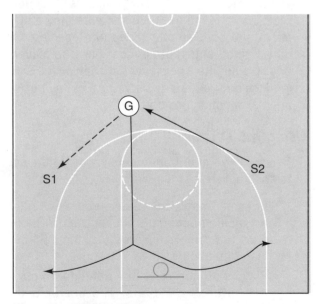

Figure 5.1   Middle option.

figure 5.1) moves to keep appropriate spacing with the ball. The players continually execute this option. When the player with the ball recognizes the perimeter players on each side, he or she passes and cuts through the zone. This option is especially useful against matchup zones because any time players run through a zone, defenders have to switch coverages. Players are not simply to change positions when using the middle option. This option is not an exchange. The middle player sprints into and then out of the zone.

The second option is for perimeter players to overload a side of the floor. The middle player does not cut, but the offside person hustles to a spot on the strongside below the ball. The player with the ball initiates the move by waving to his or her offside teammate to cut to the opposite corner before making pass to the other exterior teammate. In figure 5.1's setup, G would wave S2 through the zone to the corner below S1. All three perimeter players are on one (the right) side of half-court.

Figure 5.2 shows the dribble-chase option. A perimeter player (G) dribbles at an outside teammate (S1) and sends him or her through the zone. S2 (the third exterior player) moves with G to maintain proper spacing of roughly 15 feet. The players then rapidly reverse the basketball, from G to S2 to the cutter (S1) at his or her new peripheral location. Either S2 or G could garner a shot. The chased player may find that against a matchup zone it is often best

not to run all the way through the zone to the other side. Once the matchup defense begins to adjust player assignments, the cutter's most productive move may be to come back to the starting spot.

To initiate the screen-point option, the player with the ball sends one exterior teammate through the zone, putting all peripheral players on one side of the court. The other perimeter player then steps up to pick the zone defender guarding the ball handler. Accomplishing the overload just before the pick is actually set is usually best. The screener steps out after the ball handler uses the screen. The player with the ball *must* get the appropriate defender to guard him or her initially. For example, against a 1-2-2 zone, a wing, not the point, defends the ball. Thus, the back player in the zone has to choose between guarding the dribbler or guarding the player heading to the corner to overload the side. Matchup zones may not be as susceptible to the act because two defenders will likely just switch assignments.

Finally, the last option is the dribble follow and fill the void. Figure 5.3 shows S1 dribbling off the baseline while S2 races to occupy the vacated area. S1 draws out the back zone defender and is careful not to dribble too far and permit a defensive release. A post player can fill the void on the ballside baseline if no perimeter person is accessible. The dribbler off the baseline performs the only dribble follow move in which a big player may become involved. The

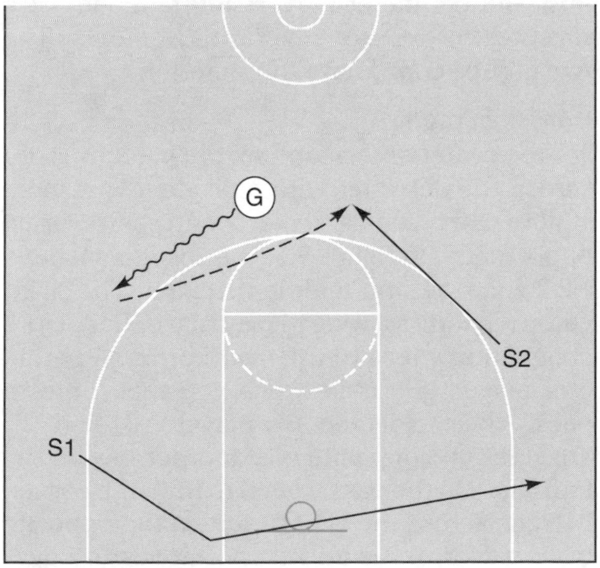

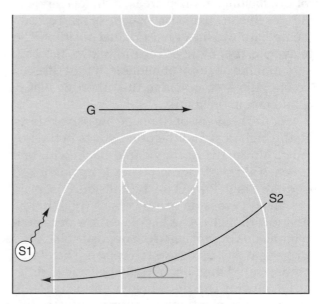

Figure 5.2 Dribble-chase option.

Figure 5.3 Dribble follow and fill the void.

other areas of the court are reserved solely for exterior players. When a perimeter player dribbles on the periphery of a zone, a teammate should follow. A shot may be available, especially if the dribbler takes a zone defender out of the normal coverage area.

Post Players

The two big players can choose from four movement options: over-under, man behind, high-low, and duck below. Post players can be on their own to execute the options, or the coach can direct the implementation of particular acts.

For the over-under option, the big players move in what is known as a wheel. One player begins high, the other low. Their movement is always in the direction of the ball. If the ball is on the left side of the court looking out, posts move counterclockwise. If the ball is on the right, the big players move clockwise. Players keep moving, attempting to find gaps inside the zone. If the player nearer the high post receives the ball, he or she immediately searches for the other big player low. The second consideration is to toss to the exterior player away from the spot where the ball was received. If the low-post player gains possession, the other post player cuts to the basket.

For the man-behind option, the two players work in two areas: along the baseline and in the midpost area. The player along the baseline operates from behind the zone and contemplates flashing to open areas. If the player does not receive the ball on a flash, he or she retreats immediately to his or her original position. The player in the midpost region follows the ball, maintaining position at midlane. If the ball goes to one, the first look is to the other big player sliding to an open area.

For the high-low option, one big player starts in the high post and the other starts in the low post. Alternatively, they could begin with one on each side, low or high. They keep moving to acquire a high-low set on the ballside. Post players always cross on ball reversals (high to low and low to high). The big player low occasionally vacates by moving to the opposite block. His or her partner dives low to replace. The player who vacated then bolts to the ballside high.

Finally, for the duck-below option, the big players take positions as shown in figure 5.4,

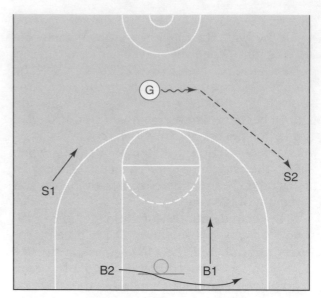

Figure 5.4 Duck-below option.

with one on each side of the foul lane low. The ballside post player steps up to midlane when the ball is out front or passed to the same-side wing. On the toss to the wing, the other big player cuts baseline below his or her partner to the strongside. He or she assumes baseline position (three to eight feet off the lane facing out). After the ball goes near the top of the key, the big players resume their positions on each side of the lane.

Movements for Both Post and Perimeter Players

Post and perimeter players interact and work together to execute several movements. The two groups coordinate their motion.

Center Screen

For the center-screen option, the objective is to screen the defender with ballside low responsibility to free a post player for an easy scoring opportunity. In figure 5.5, the team is facing a 1-2-2 zone with no middle defender. The point guard (G) forces a wing to play him or her before completing a toss to the near corner. A perimeter player (S1) is in a position that forces a back player to defend. Big players (B1 and B2) are stationed opposite one another low on the foul lane. On the pass from G to S1 in the corner, B1 runs across the lane to screen the opposite back player in the zone, who moves to cover ballside low. B2 cuts to the ball on release of

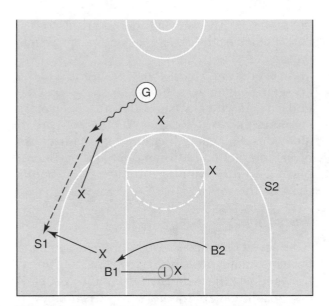

Figure 5.5   Center-screen option against a 1-2-2 zone.

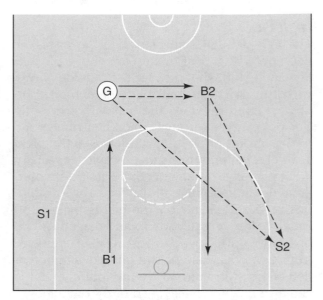

Figure 5.6   Reversal option.

the pass. B2 does not wait for the screen when confronting a zone. He or she moves after the ball leaves the passer's hands.

The alignment differs slightly when confronting a zone with a defender in the middle. For example, when the defense is a 2-3 or 1-3-1, which have a defender in the lane, big players are stationed high and low. The point guard forces a guard or wing to defend before throwing ball toward the corner. A back player in the zone comes out to cover the pass receiver. On the pass (not when it is caught), the ballside low post slides up to screen the middle defender. The high post races to the basket. The lead guard must toss the ball to the side occupied by the low post. If no scoring payoff occurs, the team enacts another Tulsa motion. With the center-screen option, players take specific alignments based on the zone formation and whether or not a defender is located in the middle.

Reversal

For the reversal option, one of the big players hustles to a perimeter position to reverse the ball (figure 5.6). This offensive call is most effective against odd-front zones. Each of two shooters (S1 and S2) is in a corner, and the strongside big player (B1) is low. The goal is to spread the zone defense and force it to cover the entire half-court. Players use skip passes and quick ball movement. If the ball goes to an exterior player in the corner below the reversal player (to S2), the big player out front (B2) dives to the ballside low position. The point guard (G)

slides over to replace the cutter while the other big player (B1) bolts up the lane line to reversal position away from the ball. Players resume the 2-3 alignment.

Weak

One of the big players remains along the offside lane. He or she sets a screen on the weakside defender in a zone. As team members overload one side of the court, a perimeter player sneaks behind the zone by dropping toward the weakside corner from the top area directly above. The pick is affixed on the weakside defender with coverage responsibility. Perimeter players on the ballside throw skip passes across the zone to the opposite shooter. The exterior players always send the ball to one side of the half-court in this option. The player closest to the weakside corner drops there. A strong ball fake of the skip pass might enable the screener to catch a toss inside. He or she flashes to the ball when the defender cheats early over the pick. After securing the skip pass, the player is prepared to shoot or dump the ball inside. The post player screening the backside of the zone always seals his or her opponent, who is providing low coverage, once the ball is grasped in the near corner. The screener initiates contact and gains a position advantage so that the ball can go inside. The weak option is most productive when a defender is isolated on the weakside. The targeted defender for the pick is easier to identify, and no other defenders are in the immediate area to provide assistance.

High Pick

The high-pick call simply instructs the big player nearer the high post to step out above the foul line and establish a pick for the outside player with the ball. The ball handler exploits the obstacle and reverses the ball with a dribble. The post player setting the screen usually rolls to the basket after the dribbler uses the pick. The screener may step out, however, especially if the big player is an effective outside shooter. Zone defenders must adjust their responsibilities as the defender on the ball is picked off. Quick ball reversal leads to an open shot. The high-pick option works best against an even-front zone because of the limited number of defenders stationed above the foul line, but it can also be effective against odd-front zones.

Off Base

The off-base alternative is similar to dribble follow and fill the void (page 87). The only difference is that the off-base call involves both post and exterior players. The perimeter player with the ball in the corner dribbles out to the closest wing while making the back-line defender cover. No defensive release is to occur. As the ball handler leads the defender away from the baseline, the closest big player fills the space along the baseline, about three to eight feet off the lane on the ballside. The dribbler contemplates tossing the ball to the teammate below.

Because Tulsa was my primary zone offense while at King's College, I became enamored with a few of the motion options because of their effectiveness. I devised the following three zone offenses (high, color, and combo) to take advantage of their ability to produce shots. I wanted to conjoin several movements from Tulsa into three distinct patterns. Unlike the Tulsa offense, the three offenses follow prearranged sequences. They are not passing games. Players do not have choices about what to execute. Instead, Tulsa motions are combined to form a series of movements that are effective versus zone defenses.

HIGH

The high-pick option in Tulsa is the primary component of the high offense. I incorporated other action to form a continuity offense. Repetition of the high-post screen is the focal point,

but other effective scoring actions are also present. Offensive motion imposes coverage issues on the defense.

An even-front zone is most susceptible to the screening maneuvers that take place above the foul lane. As with any zone offense, having more shooters makes it tougher for the zone. High also is useful against matchup zones because of the interaction between post and perimeter players and the number of cutters that move through the zone.

Personnel

A proficient distance shooter should assume the baseline runner position. A strong scoring threat draws substantial defensive attention. Post players must be capable scorers near the hoop with the ability to score in traffic. When the other two perimeter players (the point guard is one) possess effective shots from three-point range, the offense can do substantial damage.

Scoring

Inside scoring opportunities for big players are feasible. The primary shooter may acquire openings in either corner. The other two exterior players will see shots develop from the foul line extended in an arc around the top of the key.

Execution

The team executes the high offense throughout a possession until a good scoring chance presents itself. The starting set is a two-out front with the point guard (G) and one of the shooters (S2 in figure 5.7) filling spots. The other perimeter player (S1) takes a position toward the baseline on the same side as the lead guard. One post player is positioned high (B1), and the other is out toward the periphery just shy of the three-point line on the weakside (B2).

The offense begins with a pass to S1 and a return pass to G (it has already taken place in figure 5.7). The high post (B1) steps out to screen for the ball handler and rolls down the middle of the foul lane. At the same time, S1 runs along the baseline to the other side of the court. He or she may need to hesitate at the lane. B2 times his or her screen of the back player in the zone as S1 reaches the lane and G tosses the ball to S2. B2 steps directly up the lane line to

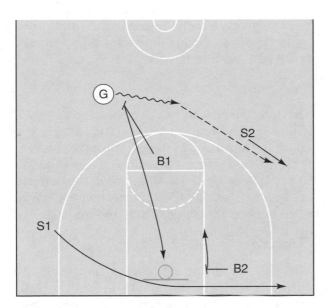

Figure 5.7 High offense starting set.

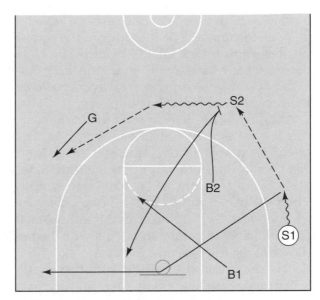

Figure 5.8 S1 dribbles off the baseline.

midpost after S1 uses the pick. The point guard (G) looks to puncture the defense and passes to S2, stepping into an open area for a possible shot. The squad overloads one side of the floor. S2 also has the option to toss to B1, who is cutting through the lane, to B2 at midpost, or to S1 in the near corner.

When the shooter (S1) receives the ball in the strongside corner, a shot is feasible. The player rolling down the foul lane (B1) continues and fills the baseline spot, three to eight feet off the lane facing out. The other two exterior players (S2 and G) resume the two-out front. The shooter (S1) may pass to B1 on the baseline or to the midpost player (B2). See "Zone Offensive Fine-Tuning" on page 84 for the discussion of midpost and baseline alignment.

S1 dribbles off the baseline (figure 5.8), again focusing inside. After the ball goes out to S2, the team changes sides. B2 screens so that S2 can dribble to the middle. B2 rolls down the lane, eventually reaching the ballside low position. The other post player (B1) crosses off B2's move to a spot mid to high on the strongside. S1 races along the baseline to the other corner immediately after throwing the ball to S2. S2 passes to G, who steps to an open area for a scoring chance.

The pattern continues. G passes down to S1 in the corner, the low post (B2) steps to the baseline, and the other big player (B1) occupies position at midpost. G and S2 fill the two-out front.

After S1 throws the ball out from the corner, the receiver initiates a change in sides by using a high-post screen. Players keep repeating actions and changing sides.

Keys

Refer to "Zone Offensive Fine-Tuning" on page 84.

Players should not have difficulty understanding the pattern, but they should not become robots just filling spaces. Players need to understand that they perform the movements to produce scoring chances. The coach should tell them why they are doing what he or she is asking of them. The offense combines the high-pick option and the dribble-off-the-baseline maneuver, with post players filling midpost and baseline positions from the Tulsa offense.

Players need to force defenders to cover as much area as possible. They take the ball from corner to corner. The squad cannot be tentative. They are to be aggressive yet patient.

When deploying a dribble off the baseline, the ball handler wants the back-line defender to maintain coverage. The dribbler watches for openings to the interior.

The high-post screen is the most important aspect to execute. If the pass recipient is a strong perimeter shooter and the defender is satisfactorily picked, another defender must slide over to cover. If the defense reacts too slowly, a quality shot is available. Quick coverage indicates that a rapid pass to complete ball reversal will find an open teammate. The toss toward the corner creates more issues for the defense if a back defender has rotated out to guard the ball reversal. For that reason, the corner player should be the best shooter from the periphery.

Although a big player rolls to the hoop, a direct shot is not likely. Remember that the offense is most effective against an even-front zone. A shot develops only if the middle defender steps out to cover the ball handler temporarily. The post player rolling to the hoop could see an open lane to the basket. Swift ball reversal is more likely to create an opening for the big player along the baseline.

The point guard uses the initial pass and return pass sequence only as a prelude to a high-post pick and ball reversal. When the ball is tossed from a corner, the post player at mid-post hustles up to establish a screen for the pass recipient. A momentary delay can occur if the midpost player is open and wants the ball.

For a breakdown drill that can be used in practice, big players set a pick for the perimeter player with the ball. The drill uses only two exterior defenders. The second exterior player is in the other slot out front. The dribbler off the screen can kick the ball out to a teammate for a shot when the second defender above the foul line races over to guard him or her.

COLOR

The color offense is another offshoot from Tulsa. The continuous deployment of the weakside screen enables a team to concentrate on getting the ball into the hands of one of its better distance shooters. Defenses today are so insistent on providing weakside help in the foul lane that they are vulnerable to action on the ballside while someone sneaks behind on the other side of the floor for completion of a skip pass. Not too long ago, coaches frowned on throwing cross-court passes. Now, most consider the cross-court pass a valuable weapon.

Teams that are drilled to sag into the foul lane defensively are prone to this offense. Some squads are not well drilled on defending screens applied to a zone defense. Weakside defenders can be caught looking toward the ball and subsequently be picked off. Although the color offense is applicable to all zone defenses, it can

be particularly effective against odd-front zones that sometimes leave a lone weakside defender (such as a 1-3-1 or 1-2-2).

Personnel

The team needs several convincing distance shooters. The more perimeter threats on the court, the more deadly the offense is. Big players must be capable screeners and have soft hands to catch balls zipped to them when the defense is caught cheating on ball fakes. Inside players must engage in proper sealing techniques.

Scoring

The shooter dropping toward the weakside corner is the primary target. He or she might be any of the three perimeter players. Most shot attempts will come at or just beyond the three-point line. Big players garner inside scores by flashing to the ball or making solid seals of interior defenders.

Execution

The coach can call the offense by yelling, "Red" or any other color. This continuity offense can be used against any type of zone but is particularly effective versus odd fronts. Players are set in a two-out formation. The lead guard (G) and a shooter (S2) fill both spots (figure 5.9). The big players (B1 and B2) are positioned low opposite one another, and the other shooter (S1) is on the same side as the playmaker (G).

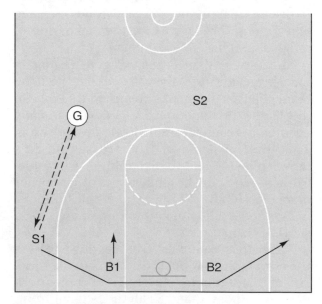

Figure 5.9 Starting set for color.

The pass and return pass between G and S1, shown in figure 5.9, starts the offense. S1 sprints to the other side of the half-court along the baseline after returning the ball to G. After S1 motors past, B1 steps up the foul lane.

The point guard (G) reverses the ball by passing to S2 out front or by skipping it to S1 (figure 5.10). After passing, the playmaker drops toward the corner on his or her side of the court. B1 tries to screen the weakside defender of the zone. The ballside post (B2) steps up to midlane. Basic movements in the offense are to send the corner player (S1) through the zone, reverse the ball with a pass, and drop the player out front opposite to the weakside corner behind the screen. Skip pass to G can come from S1 or S2. If not shot materializes S1 and S2 face to form a two-out-front.

Once the ball is reversed, the pass receiver immediately strives to skip the ball to the weakside exterior player. The pass across can come from either perimeter player (S1 or S2) on the ballside. After the cross-court pass is made, the two exterior players without the ball race to two-out spots straddling the top of the key. The weakside screener (B1) must be aware of two things. First, on the skip pass, he or she seals the defender who has ballside low coverage. (See the discussion of using skip passes on page 84.) Second, if the screener notices that the defender being screened is cheating, trying to intercept the skip pass, a flash to the ball or an open area might be available. Players read what

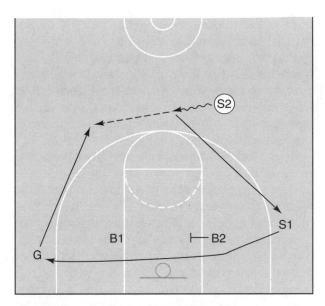

Figure 5.11   Send corner player through and drop.

the defense is doing and react accordingly. They do not force skip passes.

When the skip pass is not accessible from either perimeter player, the one nearer the top of the key (S2 in figure 5.10) may change sides with the dribble while his or her partner (S1) slides up to replace. Once the team reaches this stage, it returns to screening the weakside. The corner player (G) runs along the baseline to the other side, the team reverses the ball, and the nearer exterior player (S2) drops to the offside corner behind a screen by the weakside post (B1).

An alternative to the dribble is for the player out top with the ball (S2) to send the ballside corner (S1 in figure 5.11) through along the baseline. This action tells the point guard (G) to motor back up to a two-out position with S2. The team uses this option when the skip pass is not open or when the players are unable to dribble across the top to switch sides. This option will likely prove most useful against odd-front zones. S2 reverses the ball to G and drops. B2 screens the weakside of the zone. The team runs the play continuously until a good scoring moment develops.

Keys

Refer to "Zone Offensive Fine-Tuning" on page 84.

The ballside big player always steps up to a midlane location along the lane line. The weakside post player picks the offside of the zone. He or she may flash to the ball. If the player

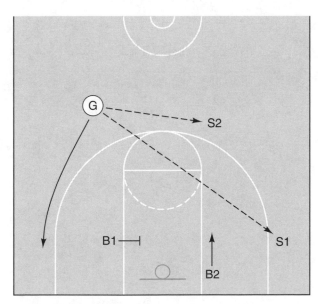

Figure 5.10   G sends the ball opposite and drops.

does not gain possession of the ball, he or she returns to the original position.

Players change sides quickly. They do not hold the ball too long. At the same time, however, they keep their eyes on the interior. Ball fakes, especially of the skip pass, can create openings for big players inside as the zone responds to the fake.

The general spacing rule is that players are roughly 12 to 15 feet apart. Although the player using the weakside screen will exceed that limit with relation to perimeter players, he or she maintains spacing with the nearest big player.

A team should not use the offense exclusively, but with judicious use it is very effective. An offensive team cannot defeat zones with just the weakside screen. On some occasions, however, it will produce a key shot. I regularly used the maneuver at critical junctions of a game, especially if I had one, or maybe two, exceptional distance shooters.

The color offense takes one Tulsa option (weak) and runs it repeatedly during a possession. The movement enables the weakside screen to be deployed constantly against a zone defense. If players already know the weak option, the amount of time required to teach the offense will be minimal. They should acquire an acceptable level of execution within 30 minutes. Players must be well versed in attacking a variety of zone defenses. Coaches can teach the basic player rotation on a dummy basis, but the team must learn the screening intricacies against live zone defenses.

COMBO

The combo offense is more complicated. It combines the actions of the high and color zone offenses. Multiple motions incorporated into the offense increase its success rate. Coaches can teach the combo offense independent of high and color, but the teaching is considerably easier if the team has learned and practiced high and color before instruction of combo begins. Combo is a continuity offense executed until the conclusion of the possession. This offense developed from my repeated use of the high-post pick and weakside screen within the Tulsa offense.

The combo offense is most effective against even-front and matchup zones but could also be used against odd fronts. Although the high-

post screen for ball reversal is still set, the player with the ball may not have much room to maneuver, especially if the screen is set on a defensive wing and the opponent at the top picks up the coverage. The exterior players must take advantage of picks on offside defenders for shots from distance. The combo offense is a good choice for the coach who prefers an offense with multiple actions.

Personnel

This offense requires two big players capable of affixing strong screens and scoring around the basket. The three perimeter players must be solid shooters from near or behind the arc. Their shooting ability is a major element in determining the success of the offensive attack. Exterior players must be proficient at delivering skip passes to designated targets and be able to read the defense so as to make sound choices.

Scoring

The offense gives players two main ways to secure acceptable shots: the high-post screen and the weakside pick. The two big players procure shots in the 15-foot range. Most shot attempts from outside players arise at or past the three-point line.

Execution

The team begins as shown in figure 5.12. They are actually executing the high offense. The

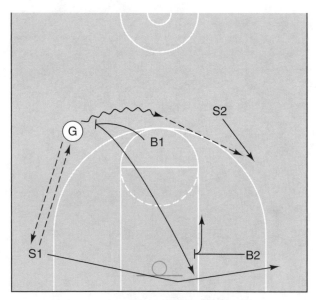

Figure 5.12 Start is the same as for the high offense.

sequence starts with a pass and return pass between the point guard (G) and the shooter (S1) in the ballside corner. S1 runs along the baseline to the other corner after sending the ball out to G. The high post (B1) screens for the player with the ball (G), and the reversal commences. The other post player (B2) steps in to pick the back player in the zone and then steps up the near foul-lane line after S1 uses the screen. G passes to the other perimeter player (S2) after dribbling off the screen. The screener (B1) rolls down the lane to the basket. The squad has overloaded one side of the court.

If the next pass goes to the person in the corner (S2 to S1), the screener (B1) continues movement and lands at the ballside baseline location. S1 could pass inside to B1 or B2. Whoever receives the ball looks for the other player to cut to the hoop.

S1 dribbles off the baseline (figure 5.13) and glances inside first before throwing the ball out to S2. After releasing the pass, S1 runs to the other corner. S2 reverses the ball to G as B2 dashes to a position high at the foul line. The player on the baseline (B1) steps up to screen the weakside zone defender when the ball is reversed to G. S2 slides down to the near corner behind the pick after passing. Players are now executing the color offense. Remember that the basic steps are sending the corner player through (S1), reversing the ball to G, and dropping toward the corner (S2).

If the skip pass reaches S2 on the offside, B2 darts to the ballside high post while the other two perimeter players (S1 and G) head opposite one another out front. The screener (B1) seals the defender with low coverage after the skip pass is completed.

Figure 5.14 illustrates the movements that occur if the skip pass is not possible. The player with the ball in the corner (S1) throws the ball to G, and the team begins to execute the high offense. G dribbles off the screen from the high post (B2). S1 takes off to the other corner as S2 steps up on the exterior and B1 moves off the foul lane. B1 goes back in to pick the back player of the zone and slides up the lane line after S1 (the cutter) has passed. If no good scoring chance develops during the execution of high, the team reverses the ball and runs color again (send through, reverse ball, and drop). In combo, the sequence always runs the same—high, color, high, color, and so on—without calling each stage.

Keys

See "Zone Offensive Fine-Tuning" on page 84.

If the coach teaches high and color before teaching combo, instruction of the offense is much easier. If the squad has not previously learned high and color, they should practice the high-post screen and weakside pick as separate entities. Breakdown drills are effective teaching tools. Combo easily breaks down

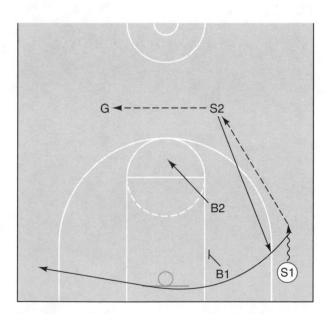

Figure 5.13 Dribble off the baseline and execute the color offense.

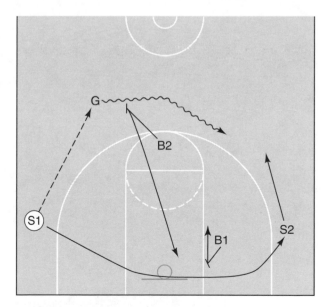

Figure 5.14 Running high after executing color.

into smaller parts that are eventually blended together. During the season the coach can either concentrate on executing only one portion of the offense or practice it as a whole. The team's performance under game conditions dictates which method is appropriate.

Any items listed in the keys section for high

and color earlier in the chapter are pertinent tips in the instruction of combo.

The offense may be difficult for some players to grasp. Breaking it into two distinct segments can greatly aid player retention of the desired movements.

CHAPTER 6

Popular Zone Offenses

Some of the best coaches in the game developed most of the offenses in this chapter. The sequences have been active for decades. Teams throughout the country use these familiar ways to counter half-court zone defenses. In some instances, coaches have slightly altered the basic pattern to fit their team's talents to the play. My presentation of each offense is based on what I have found produces quality scoring opportunities. The offenses use a variety of ways to defeat a zone.

I composed other offenses with particular objectives in mind. I actively pursued offenses that could disrupt matchup zone defenses because early in my head-coaching career I had found them difficult to solve at times. Therefore, many of the following offenses are useful against opponents who play man-to-man within a zone structure. Moreover, they are extremely effective against standard zones.

BASELINE AND BASELINE SPECIAL

The following basic offense comprises two sections. The first, baseline, is a standard 2-3 zone formation fabricated to defeat odd-front zone defenses. It specifically focuses on overpowering the back-line defender or defenders of the zone. The second section, baseline special, is a more recent development. Most major col-

lege programs have a zone play that is alike in structure to baseline special. I first saw a similar action during a University of North Carolina game under Coach Dean Smith.

Baseline is designed to counter odd-front zone defenses such as a 1-3-1 or 1-2-2. The simplicity of the play is appealing. The play creates multiple scoring opportunities for an outstanding shooter from deep. Opponents who might be overmatched along the baseline are superb targets for this offense.

Baseline special is called against any type of zone defense. The offense lasts only a short time, and coaches should use it sparingly. Prudent use ensures potency. At least one team member will be able to secure a lob pass at the hoop.

Personnel

The team needs two post players who are capable of setting solid screens to help free the excellent perimeter shooter for scoring chances in the baseline offense. Big players must be able to score around the basket. The other two exterior players must be strong outside (three-point) shooters.

The baseline special offense requires a big player who has good leaping ability. He or she attempts to score on a possible lob pass at the basket. The lead guard must be intelligent and a sound decision maker. He or she must be able to throw a precise lob near the rim.

Scoring

In baseline, scoring opportunities appear inside the zone for the two big players as they step to the ball after screening. Exterior players obtain perimeter chances from either corner or out front on each side of the key.

A variety of scoring chances may develop during execution of baseline special. The lob pass to the player heading to the basket is the main feature. Other players may find opportunities off a direct feed to the interior, a skip toss to a shooter for a jumper, or a pass to another shooter who is stepping out to ballside.

Baseline Execution

The best perimeter shooter should take a position along the baseline on the ballside behind the three-point arc (S1 in figure 6.1). Each of the other two perimeter players (G and S2) is above an elbow. These players remain in a two-out set and attack the wings in an odd-front zone. They use the dribble to induce the wing defenders to guard the ball. When the ball is reversed across the top, the shooter (S1) may choose to run the baseline while exploiting screens by the two post players. The big players try to screen the back players in the zone. In a 1-2-2 zone, they screen one of the two back defenders on their side of the court. Against a 1-3-1 zone, they screen the lone back-line defensive runner.

The first screener (B1 in figure 6.1) sets the pick and then flashes to the ball in the lane

against a 1-2-2 zone after S1 uses the screen. Against a 1-3-1, instead of flashing, he or she seals the offside wing as the drop is made to protect the basket on the ball reversal out front. After S1 uses the pick, B1 actively seeks out the wing to make contact. After the seal is complete, the offensive player (B1) points toward the basket to indicate to the ball handler (S2 in figure 6.1) that a lob toss to the weakside of the hoop is open.

The second screener (B2 in figure 6.1) always picks and steps up the lane to the ball. He or she may receive a direct pass from S2. The passer (S2) is ready to take advantage of the situation if the defender being screened cheats out early to cover the shooter (S1). S2 uses the ball fake to the corner to deceive the defender and cause him or her to move prematurely toward the shooter.

The shooter (S1) also has the option to fake running the baseline and then step back to the same-side corner. When the ball is reversed out top, S1 fakes the move along the baseline by heading into the lane and then racing back to his or her original position. The first screener reads the fake and tries to rescreen the backside of the zone. This action creates an opportunity for a skip pass to S1. The second screener sees what is happening and steps off the foul lane (5 to 10 feet), looking for a direct pass from G.

The pattern continues for the duration of the possession. Players prepare for an opponent who decides to double-team the corner receiver. If the defense traps, players counter by flashing the offside post player to the high post on the ballside.

Baseline Special Execution

Baseline special is a quick-hitting play designed to provide scoring chances with a limited number of movements. Because it is not a continuity offense, teams should use another offense if no good scoring chance arises. The element of surprise is essential to the success of the play. Normally, teams use the play judiciously, making it more difficult for the defense to handle. Certainly, if an opponent is not defending it well, there is nothing wrong with repeating it.

The initial setup of the offense (figure 6.2) is the same as that of the baseline offense except that the shooter (S1) moves to the block opposite the ball and one of the big players (B1)

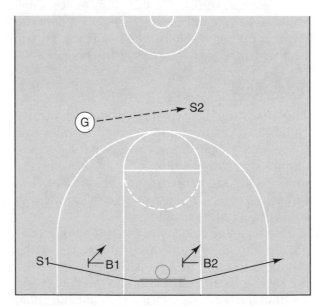

Figure 6.1 Shooter using baseline screens in the baseline offense.

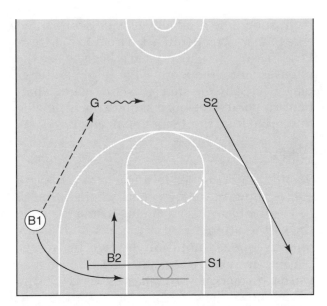

Figure 6.2 Back screen against zone in baseline special.

is positioned in the ballside corner. B1 is the featured player. He or she should be one of the team's biggest players and an excellent jumper. B1 must be able to catch a lob at the hoop. A perimeter player could possibly fill this position if he or she meets the criteria. The other post player (B2) is at the ballside box.

The initial pass goes to B1 in the strong-side corner (figure 6.2). This action invites a back defender to come out to guard the pass receiver. The type of zone that the opposition plays is irrelevant. After B1 secures the ball, he or she returns it to the point guard (G). When B1 releases the ball, these actions occur simultaneously:

- B2 steps up the lane line, anticipating an entry pass from G. He or she is careful not to slide up too high. B2's goal is to draw the attention of any middle defender.

- S1 races across the foul lane to pick the back player of the zone who had been guarding B1. S1 steps out to the exterior after setting the screen.

- B1 cuts off S1's back screen to the basket. B1 does not wait for the pick and anticipates a lob at the basket.

- S2 moves swiftly to the exterior near the offside baseline.

The point guard (G) might need to use one or two dribbles to the other side of the floor before deciding who should receive the next pass. To complete the lob to B1, G may need to improve the passing angle. The lob is not the only pass option. G views the basket for a potential toss to B2 inside, a pass to S1 popping out to the perimeter after screening, or a skip pass to S2 at the weakside baseline.

Keys

Refer to "Zone Offensive Fine-Tuning" on page 84 for pertinent information on attacking zone defenses.

The baseline offense is not especially time consuming to teach. Baseline special takes even less time. Several 20-minute teaching sessions should suffice for execution of the baseline offense. Players should rotate into the shooter's spot along the baseline. Anyone who may perform that role must practice the position. Big players should receive ample repetitions. I recommend teaching the offense using the whole-part-whole method, instructing the entire offense first and then breaking down the movements periodically to attain a sound level of execution along the baseline between the big players and the shooter.

In baseline special, players must learn to execute various positions. Any player who may receive the lob must practice that role vigorously. The perimeter player who sets the pick must practice timing and technique. The coach should teach the whole play first and review smaller pieces, such as execution of the lob, as required.

In the baseline offense, the shooter must learn when to run the baseline to the other side of the court and when to fake the move and head back to his or her original location for a possible skip pass. Big players may have a tendency to forget to pick and look for the ball out front. They need to work with the player running the baseline. Post players learn to pick appropriate defenders consistently. The first baseline screener must understand how and when to seal a weakside defender in the zone. He or she might be open for a toss to the weakside of the hoop. The team cannot ignore this critical scoring alternative. Perimeter players out front force the wings of the zone to guard them. The two players at the top are ready to be scoring threats if situations arise. They use ball fakes frequently in response to the screening action along the baseline. They fake the toss inside and then pass to the exterior or vice versa. All peripheral players observe the post players inside for conceivable scoring chances. The opposite big player learns to recognize a defensive double team in the far corner and responds immediately by flashing to the strongside high post.

In baseline special, the highlighted player and the point guard must work together to perfect execution of the lob pass. The point guard reads the defense by observing the entire half-court. The playmaker's evaluation determines where he or she will distribute the ball. Players must regularly rehearse the coordination and timing of the four movements triggered by the pass out of the corner. The big player does not step too high up the foul lane. He or she heads slightly into the foul lane. The team practices transition into another zone offense if baseline special does not provide a sound scoring chance. The action of the play takes only seconds to conclude.

PENN STATE: THE WHEEL

The Penn State offense, commonly known as the wheel, has existed for many years. In the offense, the frontline players rotate constantly through the opponent's zone defense. Coaches have found this a rewarding offense on countless occasions. The second portion of the offensive set (Penn State base) contains a subtle wrinkle in the motion that surprises the zone defense by breaking a pattern.

Although teams can use the Penn State offense against any type of zone defense, it is especially fruitful against matchup zones. The frontline players carry out the bulk of the motion. A team with three strong big players is an ideal candidate to run the offense.

Penn State base presents a slight variation in the movement of the offense. Its productivity increases with sporadic deployment. Players have freedom of choice to employ it.

Personnel

The offenses are most effective when the two perimeter players (one being the point guard) shoot well from three-point range. Their proficiency from deep stretches the defense and opens chances for the three frontline players. The three players performing the wheel move-

ment should be productive inside scorers and able to score facing the basket from 15 to 18 feet. Physical size is a plus. A team is likely to use the offenses more frequently if the third perimeter player (usually the small forward) is not a particularly good three-point shooter but is capable of scoring from the 18-foot mark and in.

Scoring

Scoring opportunities for the frontline players evolve above the elbows or anywhere within 15 feet of the basket. The motion inside the zone draws the attention of defenders and subsequently opens shots for the two perimeter players (lead guard and shooter). The defense will have a tendency to collapse toward the lane to shut down the wheel motion.

Penn State Execution

Penn State is a continuous half-court zone offense. In figure 6.3, S1 is on the right-hand side of the court facing the offensive basket. Therefore, the point guard (G) also selects that side to begin the offense. The frontline players (S2, B1, and B2) move in a wheel motion, searching for gaps in the zone defense in which to receive a pass. G and S1 toss the ball back and forth while looking for interior teammates. Frontline players adhere to these rules:

- They always move in the direction of the ball. The side of the floor dictates the way

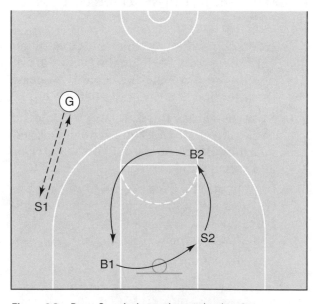

Figure 6.3 Penn State's three-player wheel action.

the frontline players travel. If the action is on the right looking in, they go counterclockwise. On the left, they move clockwise.

- Frontline players never stay in one spot for more than two seconds. They keep moving.
- They look for seams or gaps in the zone in which to cut for possible pass receptions.
- The weakside low player always moves up the near lane line to a location above the elbow before continuing the circular movement.
- The three players maintain 6 to 10 feet between each other.
- When one of the three receives the ball in the high post, he or she immediately turns and faces the basket. The player looks at the other two players in the wheel for a potential pass, considers creating a scoring chance, or tosses the ball to an exterior player.
- Players vary their initial starting points. B2, B1, and S2 positions are interchangeable.

Perimeter players (G and S1) also could be located on the other side of the court (to the left looking in). The three frontline players then move in a clockwise fashion. The three wheel players observe the same rules described earlier.

During the execution of the Penn State offense, the team must change sides periodically. When the ball is passed to the frontline player popping up above the weakside elbow (S2 in figure 6.3), the shooter (S1) has the prerogative to cut along the baseline to the other side of the court. Once the next pass is thrown, the lead guard (G) races to join S1 on the other side unless G has received the pass. In that case, S1 runs back to his or her original side. Another method of changing sides is for the point guard (G) to wave the shooter (S1) through the zone. If he or she feels the offense is too stagnant, G creates motion by having S1 switch sides. The playmaker (G) then simply reverses the ball with a pass, dribble, or combination and joins his or her teammate on the opposite side. Players do not permit the wheel motion to continue in the same direction for long periods.

Penn State Base Execution

Penn State base (figure 6.4) is simply a slight variation of movement in Penn State. As the three frontline players rotate in the wheel, one (S2 in figure 6.4) steps to the ballside baseline position. S2 is three to eight feet off the lane with his or her back to the baseline. The other two players (B1 and B2) continue to move in the wheel. If S2 receives the ball, he or she immediately glances to the interior as one player cuts to the basket and the other moves toward the high post. The offense operates in the same manner as Penn State except that occasionally any one of the three frontline players decides to step to the ballside baseline spot. Not designating the individual seems to work best. When squad members randomly decide who slides to the baseline, the element of surprise increases.

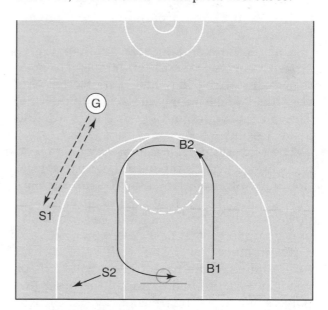

Figure 6.4 Penn State base.

Keys

See "Zone Offensive Fine-Tuning" in chapter 5 (page 84).

Penn State is not a difficult offense to teach. Several 15- to 20-minute instructional sessions are sufficient to teach players to execute the offense effectively. Periodic practice and reinforcement of appropriate movements will ensure that the level of execution remains high. Penn State base takes only minutes to incorporate because the variance between the two offenses is minor.

The teaching process begins by drilling frontline players on carrying out the wheel movement. Any player who may take part in the three-player motion must learn it, including the step-to-the-baseline variation. To drill players, a coach and one or two players can simulate the exterior roles. Adding another outside player enhances practicing a side change. Frontline players work on reversing the direction of their motion. Initially, the squad performs the three-player movement without defense. Later, the point guard and shooter join the mix to practice the offense as a whole. The team should execute the offense against a variety of defenses, including even-front, odd-front, and matchup zones.

The point guard always begins the offense on the same side of the half-court as the shooter. The shooter varies the starting site. He or she chooses the side. The choice dictates the motion of the three frontline players around the foul lane.

The playmaker and shooter constantly observe the interior and send the ball to open teammates. By hitting outside shots, they prevent the defense from collapsing into the lane. The more productive they are, the more the inside opens up.

The player involved in the wheel action on the weakside block regularly heads to a location above the offside elbow before continuing motion to the ballside. When on the move upward, the player looks for a pass. He or she may go up to six feet past the elbow.

The frontline player who catches the ball high turns and faces the basket immediately. He or she may toss the ball to one of the other two players moving in the wheel, deliver the ball to either exterior player for an outside shot, or create a personal scoring payoff with either a jump shot or a drive to the hoop.

Changing sides in the offense is important. The point guard and shooter control the start of the switch. The team cannot lock themselves into one side of the court. The shooter knows that when the ball goes to the player near the weakside elbow, he or she has the option of running the baseline and changing sides. The team never passes the ball to the reversal player three consecutive times without switching sides. Another means of switching is for the playmaker to motion the shooter through the zone and then join him or her.

In Penn State base, any of the frontline players can fill the strongside baseline site. They must not be overeager. The move is much more productive when it surprises the defense. The player who steps to the baseline may return to the three-player wheel rotation at any time during the execution of the offense.

IOWA

Iowa is an all-purpose zone offense. I first saw it used in the early 1980s. Dr. Tom Davis effectively used the pattern in his programs at Boston College, Stanford, and Iowa. Although he strongly advocated using bounce passes in his offenses, I never set controls on the types of passes my teams used. The offense is flexible in respect to the placement of the primary three-point shooter.

Iowa can be used against any zone defense. It is effective against matchup zones because of the horizontal and diagonal movement of players through the defenders. Defenses employing standard zone principles are also susceptible. The formation and action demand a power forward who has perimeter skills. The offense stretches the zone defense from corner to corner.

Personnel

The offense is more potent if the point guard is an effective perimeter shooter. The team's main three-point threat is able to move between two positions in the formation. The offense mandates that the team have one big, productive inside scorer who is capable of scoring with his or her back to the basket. The other big player must be a solid shooter from the periphery. The offense also provides the flexibility to play four perimeter players and only one big player instead of the normal three and two.

Scoring

The best inside-scoring post player receives shots around the basket. The primary shooter has the opportunity to discover open areas out front or in the corners for scoring chances. The playmaker and second exterior shooter earn shots close to the three-point line at the foul line extended, near the top of the key, or in the corner. The big player working on the perimeter acquires chances from 15 to 20 feet on either wing or could receive the ball in the foul lane for an interior shot. Second-chance opportunities develop because team members are in excellent offensive-rebounding positions.

Execution

Iowa is a continuity offense that requires players to learn a basic pattern. In some instances, players choose movements. Reading the defense is the key to making strong choices.

Figure 6.5 shows the basic set of the offense and its primary movements. The alignment could form on the other side of the floor. Players should vary the starting side during the game. The point guard (G) begins near the foul line extended. One shooter (S2) is in the ballside corner, and the other (S1) is at the top of the key. These two positions are interchangeable, and all shooters should know the actions from both spots in the offense. If the coach desires, they can change locations from one possession to the next. The center (B2), the premier inside scorer, is just above the ballside block on the lane. He or she works to gain position in anticipation of an entry pass from an exterior teammate. The other post player (B1) is opposite the basketball along the lane line. He or she is farther from the baseline than B2 is. B1 should be a good perimeter shooter.

When the lead guard (G) or shooter in the corner (S2) has the ball, the weakside big player

(B1) moves up the lane and looks to flash to the ballside high post. If he or she does not receive the ball, a swift return to the offside position is mandatory. B1 observes the defense and evaluates the value of the flash cut. S2 delivers ball inside to B2 if possible. Another option is for S2 to send the ball to S1 either via the point guard (G) or by using a skip pass (figure 6.5). On the toss to the top, S2 sprints baseline and heads to the opposite corner. At the same time, the weakside big player (B1) pops out to the perimeter near the foul line extended. The center (B2) contemplates a flash into the lane for a possible entry pass from S1. The team has begun to change sides. They endeavor to stretch the defense from one corner to the other.

Players continue to reverse the ball as S1 throws to B1 on the wing. Sending the next pass to S2 in the corner fully extends the defense. The toss from B1 to S2 in the corner initiates several movements (figure 6.6). B1 cuts through the foul lane at a point roughly between the first and second hash marks above the box. B1 begins the action on the release of the pass and always anticipates a return pass on completing the cut. Once B1 is certain that the ball is not coming his or her way, he or she tries to create an obstacle for the defender with ballside low responsibility. Alternatively, B1 stops the cut short and finds an opening along the ballside lane for a direct pass from S2. If B1 does not receive the ball on the cut, he or she continues through the foul lane to the weakside.

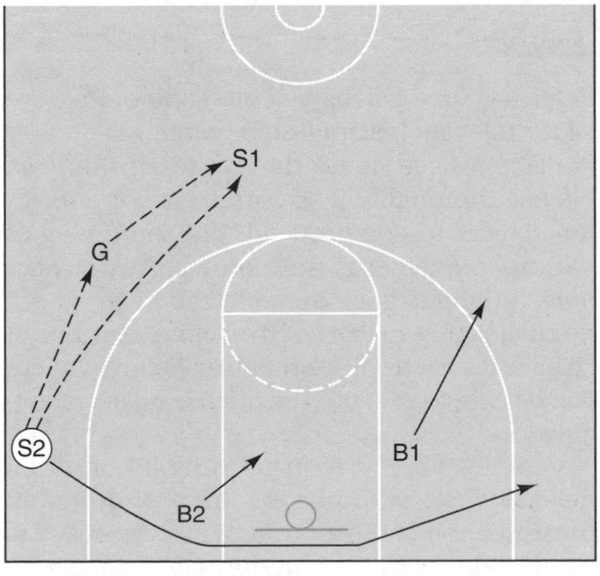

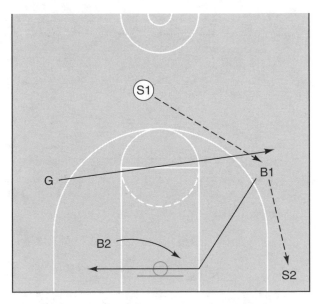

Figure 6.5 Iowa setup and basic movement.

Figure 6.6 Ball completely reversed by the post player on the exterior.

As soon as B1 steps toward the lane, the lead guard (G) sprints to the ballside wing, replacing B1. B2 comes across the foul lane to an open area on the strongside, timing his or her dash with B1's cut. They are not to interfere with one another. Ideally, B2 uses B1's movement to gain an advantage. S2 delivers the ball to B2 whenever possible. After executing their motions, all players have returned to the original set (figure 6.5) except they are on the other side of the half-court. The squad executes the movements illustrated in figures 6.5 and 6.6 until a quality-scoring situation arises.

In figure 6.7, S1 has the ball at the top of the key. Notice that S2 has already run baseline. In this case, S1 does not reverse the ball to B1. Instead, S1 returns the ball to the playmaker (G). On the pass to G, B1 sprints in toward the foul lane to screen the weakside of the zone. G throws a skip pass to S2 (figure 6.7) if open. When the pass is completed, the team returns to normal continuity as B1 continues across the lane after planting the pick. B2 slices to a ballside low opening, and the lead guard (G) hustles to the strongside foul line extended. If the skip pass to S2 on the offside is not available, the ball goes back to S1. B1 bolts back out to the wing after his or her weakside screen fails to create a scoring chance. The team is still in position for normal continuity.

The weakside post player (B1) constantly reads the defense and evaluates the likelihood of being open if he or she executes a cut baseline toward the ball (figure 6.8). S2 has possession in the corner. B1 yells, "Me" as he or she races to the ballside. Upon hearing the me call, the other post player (B2) slides up the lane a few steps. S2 glances inside when the me option is called. If B1 catches the post feed, B2 darts to the basket. If B2 is the pass receiver, B1 gets open along the baseline. B1's original move to the strongside baseline is a flash. If he or she does not receive a pass, a return to the original position is mandatory. This wrinkle is effective if used sporadically. B1 may be alone under the basket. After the defense has seen B1 flashing high several times, the call is primed for use.

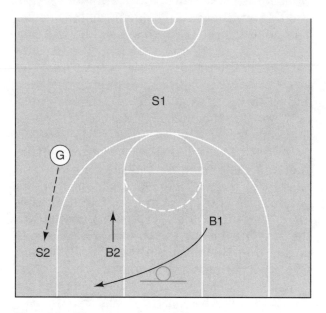

Figure 6.8   B1 executes the me option.

Keys

Refer to "Zone Offensive Fine-Tuning" on page 84 for relevant instructional points.

Players need some time to learn the Iowa offense thoroughly. The pattern is not difficult for players to comprehend, but the timing of various movements and knowing what happens if the ball goes here instead of there can be challenging. Seven to 10 teaching sessions of 20 minutes each will be required before players will be able to execute the offense at an acceptable level.

Coaches should instruct initially on a no-defense basis until players are well drilled in the execution of the motion. When the coach is comfortable with their performance, he or she can add defense. Players should learn to attack a

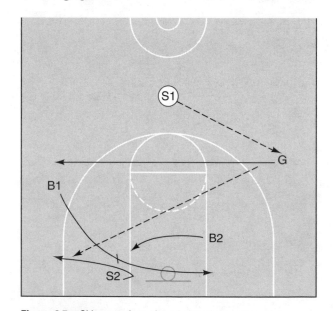

Figure 6.7   Skip pass from the wing to the corner.

variety of zone defenses. At first, the coach may need to halt instruction often to make corrections and remind players of available options, especially for B1. Personnel should take their places in all appropriate positions within the offense. The team must review the offense regularly throughout the season to avoid slippage in execution. Constant reinforcement is required. Iowa cannot be put on the shelf for long periods without loss in productivity.

The center (B2) must be an inside force. The center finds openings, obtains position, and scores when teammates deliver the ball.

The post player working on the perimeter (B1) is a key element in the success of the play. He or she has several movement options that can determine the development of scoring chances. B1 has the following maneuvers at his or her disposal: call the me option periodically when the ball goes to the shooter in the opposite corner, flash into a high-post opening when the point guard or corner player has the ball on the other side of the half-court, immediately cut to the hoop while awaiting a return pass after flinging the ball to the ballside corner, act as an obstacle to the defender with low-post coverage, or set a weakside screen when the player at the top of the key throws the ball back to the point guard. In addition, the player could secure shots near the three-point line at either wing.

When the player at top top of the key catches the ball, several movements occur simultaneously: The shooter in the corner sprints the baseline to the other side of the floor, the center flashes to the ball, and the other post player pops out to the closest foul line extended.

When teaching offensive rebounding from the Iowa offense, the coach has choices about which player or players should retreat defensively on shots. The coach may instruct only the point guard to sprint back and tell the player out top and the one running the baseline to crash the offensive boards. Alternatively, the coach may request one or both of those two players to hustle back after a shot is launched. Obviously, if the baseline player is near the basket at the time of a shot, forcing him or her to go back is foolish. The two post players consistently hit the offensive glass. The coach informs the players at each position precisely what they should do when a shot is launched.

The center delays slightly on the sprint to the strongside when the other post player tosses the ball to the corner and hustles through the zone. The center looks for gaps in the zone.

Players take the ball from one corner to the other and repeat. These actions force the defense to cover a large territory.

RIDER FOR NAME AND OREGON FOR NAME

Rider for name and Oregon for name are specific plays invented to deliver the ball to a preferred shooter. They are designed to confront the two general types of half-court zone defenses, even front or odd front. The number of players at the top of the zone (even or odd) is not always the key to zone identification. The slides can also characterize a zone as one or the other. For example, a tandem zone (1-1-3) is actually an even front because it acts like a 2-3 or 2-1-2 zone. A horseshoe zone (3-2) is an even front because the middle front player slides like the middle defender in a 2-1-2 zone. Correct visual identification by players is essential when selecting which offense will have the best chance for success.

Rider for name is used against even-front zones; Oregon for name is used versus odd-front zones. These offenses enable a team to create lapses in coverage, producing shot opportunities for the team's exceptional distance shooter. Coaches must instruct the other four players that the highlighted player will garner the bulk of the shots. The other players attempt to get the ball into his or her hands.

Personnel

In both Rider for name and Oregon for name, the primary prerequisite is an outstanding perimeter shooter. Both offenses revolve around this player. If a coach has the good fortune of having two excellent outside threats, these offenses allow him or her to set up one and then the other. The coach also could vary the featured player from possession to possession. In Oregon for name, one post player must have the ability to score around the basket and another should be adept at establishing strong, solid screens. To increase the productivity of Rider for name, both big players should be able to score from 15 feet and closer.

Scoring

In Rider for name, a big player at the high post who catches a pass from the lead guard may have a potential score. The other post player automatically dives to the basket. Perimeter shot possibilities are designed primarily to come from the player whose name was called (the highlighted shooter). Nevertheless, the other two exterior players may see some chances develop from outside.

In Oregon for name, players make a concerted effort to attack the back players of an odd-front zone. Baseline scoring possibilities are a fundamental result of the offense. All players are potential scorers, but only one is the featured shooter.

Rider for Name Execution

The coach yells, "Rider" and then the name of the player who is the featured shooter. In the illustrations that follow, N signifies the highlighted player and S is the other perimeter shooter. Teams use this offense against even-front zone defenses such as 2-1-2, tandem and three, horseshoe zone, and 2-3 zone.

Figure 6.9 shows the starting set of the offense and its main motion. Players are in a 1-4 high formation with the big players (B1 and B2) at the elbows and the perimeter shooter (S) and designated shooter (N) at the wings. The point guard (G) dribbles to the wing away from the designated shooter. S races toward the lane and

gains an angle to set the screen on the nearest back player. In the meantime, N begins to cut to the ballside corner. He or she is free to shoot the ball if open. After setting the pick, the screener (S) hustles to the opposite exterior.

When the ball goes to the main shooter (N), post players slide to ballside low and high-post spots. If N does not have a shot, the next option is to toss the ball inside to either the high or low post. See the discussion of the high-low formation and midpost and baseline alignment in "Zone Offensive Fine-Tuning" on page 86 in chapter 5.

The team executes the offense repeatedly (figure 6.10). N throws the ball out to the lead guard (G), who immediately dribbles opposite to change sides. On the pass out, post players return to their original high positions. As the point guard dribbles, S steps in toward the foul lane to screen the back player of the zone for N. N sprints along the baseline, uses the pick, and gains freedom for a shot attempt.

The playmaker has other passing options besides N. While team members are in 1-4 high alignment, the playmaker casts the ball to one of the big players. Regardless of which post player receives the ball, the other one cuts to the goal. The perimeter player away from the origination point of the pass is the next potential target. Another possibility for the lead guard is to skip the ball to the secondary shooter (S), who is hustling to the periphery after screening the back player of the zone. On the pass, the big

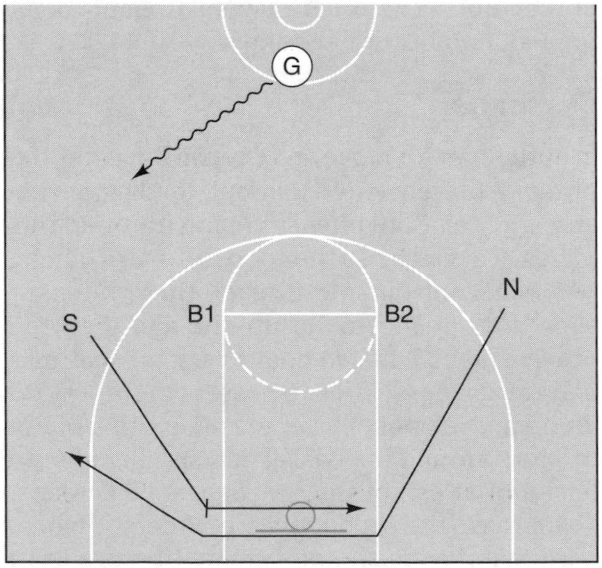

Figure 6.9   Rider for name alignment and movements.

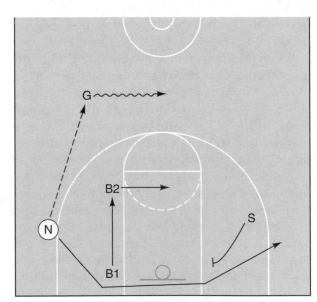

Figure 6.10   Main shooter tosses the ball out from the corner and action moves to other side.

players dart to ballside high-post and low-post spots. If no scoring chance develops, the pattern continues.

Oregon for Name Execution

This zone offense is formulated to attack odd-front zones such as 1-2-2, 3-2, and 1-3-1. The coach calls the offense by hollering, "Oregon" and then the name of the featured shooter. In the following illustrations, N indicates the featured shooter.

Figure 6.11 shows the initial set and motions. The two perimeter players (G and S) are above the key, more than a lane-width apart. N is on one wing (in this case ballside), and the power forward (B1) occupies the opposite wing. The center (B2) roams the high post, ready for entry passes from out front. If the center receives the ball, he or she immediately turns and faces the basket. The center contemplates a toss below and then to the exterior, opposite the side from where he or she received the ball. The high post may also take a shot or drive to the hoop.

The team undertakes the motion so that the highlighted shooter (N) can gain freedom for a shot. The point guard (G) reverses the ball across the top, and B1 immediately slides toward the near block on the lane to screen the back defender of the zone. On the pass, N runs the baseline to the opposite corner or wing while employing B1's pick (figure 6.11). The two players at the top (S and G) must make the defensive wings guard them. They dribble if

necessary. This activity leaves the back player of the zone exposed to the screen. Notice that B2 stays high and follows the ball. If the back defender cheats over the pick too soon to guard N, B1 steps to the ball and catches it directly from out front.

After the pass is delivered to the featured shooter (N), the screener (B1) posts low or slips to the ballside baseline three to eight feet off the lane facing out. He or she occupies one spot for two seconds only. If after two seconds B1 does not get the ball, he or she leaves the strongside and sprints baseline to the offside wing. The center (B2) slides down to fill the vacant area created by B1's movement. If B1 occupies the baseline spot, B2 stops at midpost but may glide lower once B1 races opposite. If no scoring opportunity develops, N passes the ball back to S. The center (B2) heads back to the high post. The team is in position to repeat the motion on the other side of the court.

If N controls the ball at a wing or corner, he or she may be able to zip a skip pass to G, the weakside player at the top. The main activity commences just as if ball had been cast across the top of the key. As soon as N releases the pass, he or she motors along the baseline and uses B1's pick on the back player in the zone. The team executes the play constantly until a quality scoring chance arises.

Keys

See "Zone Offensive Fine-Tuning" in chapter 5 (page 84).

The two offensive plays are not difficult to teach and do not consume much time. Each is likely to require no more than two 15- to 20-minute instructional sessions for players to comprehend the pattern. Coaches begin instruction on a dummy basis and work with any players who may perform the main shooter's role. All players who may perform the screener's job in each offense are also a focus. These are the two most important positions in each play.

In both Rider for name and Oregon for name, coaches should stress these points. Timing between the designated shooter and the screener is crucial. If the screener is too early or too late, the back-line defender's task is much easier. If the defender cheats over the pick too early to maintain coverage on the shooter, the

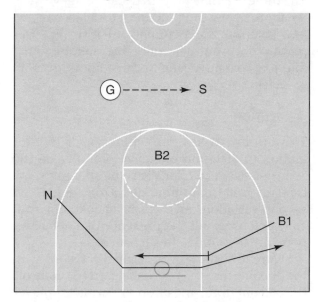

Figure 6.11   Oregon for name set and motion.

screener could be open when stepping toward the ball. In Rider for name, the likelihood of a score off an interior pass to the screener decreases significantly because the screener is a perimeter player. Both the passer and screener are prepared to take advantage of the situation. Players out top (the lead guard in Rider for name and the two exterior players in Oregon for name) must force the "right" defender to guard the ball. Accomplishing this goal permits the pick to be planted on a back defender in the zone.

In Rider for name, the perimeter player used as a screener must practice setting strong, wide-based picks on back players of even-front zones in a breakdown drill. The focus is solely on the screening action, particularly recognition of the targeted defender.

In Oregon for name, because the power forward establishes the pick, there is a chance that slipping the screen could lead to shots. The post player on the periphery must still adhere to the two-second restriction. The high post (center) is always prepared to receive the ball.

NORTH CAROLINA: T GAME

When I first learned of this offense, Coach Dean Smith at the University of North Carolina was advocating it. High school and college teams have used the North Carolina T game since the late 1960s. Over the years, others have put their touches into the play. It was part of the program at the University of Arizona when I was there as an assistant coach in the early 1980s. Several squads that I coached against at King's College formulated their own versions. The North Carolina T is a timeless zone attack.

North Carolina is a continuity offense that features a three-person rotation. The frontline players engage in a pattern that requires them to occupy selected spots, but it is possible to replace the small forward in the three-player exchange with the shooting guard. Two post players have no choice but to be part of the motion. The center must be competent on the periphery. If he or she is not, the three-person sequence is not appropriate. If the primary big player is strong only around the hoop, the coach can make an adjustment (see the keys section on page 111). The point guard and one other perimeter player take up locations out front above the foul line extended.

In North Carolina, motion develops through the interior of the zone defense while providing places for perimeter shot attempts. Perimeter players observe team members consistently filling high- and low-post positions. The team needs to make a concerted effort to send the ball inside the foul lane if possible. Players are patient and move the ball and themselves to generate an assortment of scoring opportunities. Perimeter players must exercise self-discipline and avoid putting up shots from deep too early in the operation of the offense.

Personnel

Two big players must be able to handle the ball on the perimeter and complete accurate interior passes. The potency of the offense increases if at least one, if not both, is able to score from at least 17 feet and in. Either the small forward or the shooting guard can be part of the three-person pattern. One player may have to learn two positions—a more stationary spot out front and a spot in the three-person rotation. The point guard and one perimeter player are out top above the foul line extended. They should be adequate shooters and have the capacity to use the dribble to penetrate the zone. Their jobs are not difficult. Players in the three-person rotation have tougher assignments, and their actions are the heart of the offense.

Scoring

The three frontline players usually achieve quality shots below the foul line extended, ranging from layups to 25-foot jumpers. The two exterior players out front generally operate above the foul line extended and receive shots from 15 to 25 feet.

Execution

The offense relies on a pattern of regular motion to maintain offensive pressure on the zone defense. The offense can be altered to confront an even-front or matchup zone defense. A second variation can be used against odd-front zone defenses, but the presence of a defensive point greatly diminishes its success.

Figure 6.12 shows the original set along with the opening moves. The lead guard (G) controls the ball out front, and another perimeter player (S2) occupies the position above the foul line.

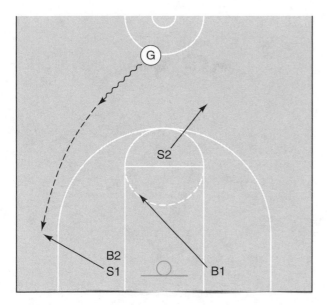

Figure 6.12 Starting set and motion in North Carolina.

The big players (B1 and B2) assume locations near each block along the lane. The final perimeter player (S1) is stationed behind either post player. S1 and S2 may switch assignments if doing so is advantageous.

Before getting into the normal action, the point guard (G) might be able to make an initial pass directly to S2 in the high post. The team exploits this alternative if it is attainable. S2 immediately turns and faces the basket. Once G passes the ball to S2, the post player (B2) on the same side as the perimeter player (S1) ducks into the middle of the lane. At the same time, S1 and B1 step off the lane, each toward a corner. Three offensive players are then in position across the baseline, possibly outnumbering the defense. S2 tosses the ball to the open player.

Once the lead guard (G) recognizes that an initial toss to S2 is not possible, he or she chooses a side of the floor. Against an odd-front zone, the defensive point may dictate the side. The low perimeter player (S1) pops out to the ballside wing. It makes no difference from which side he or she originates; S1 always assumes a strongside perimeter spot. The big players (B1 and B2) set screens on the back-line defenders of the zone for S1 if possible. The high-post player (S2) steps to an area opposite the point guard out front in figure 6.12.

If the ball goes to the wing (S1), the weakside post player (B1) cuts to the ballside high slot while the strongside big player (B2) establishes

position low. S2 heads to an offside area that may be open. If the coach desires, instead of filling ballside high and low spots the players can occupy a baseline slot three to eight feet off the lane facing out and the midpost. This setup makes it slightly more difficult to execute the alternative move for ball reversals when facing an even-front or matchup zone. The coach also may elect to have players at the top (G and S2) exchange positions each time a pass goes to a wing (S1 in figure 6.12).

S1, B2, and B1 begin the three-player rotation (figure 6.13). When the wing tosses the ball out front, the low-post player (B2) vacates and sprints to the weakside. The other perimeter player out top (S2) makes himself or herself available for the next pass.

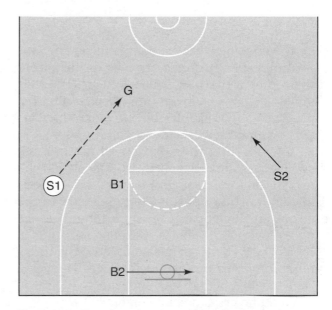

Figure 6.13 Pass from the wing to the top starts the three-player rotation.

Players can use two methods to change sides in the offense. The one used more against odd-front zone defenses is for G to complete a pass to S2. B2 continues to cut and ends up at the ballside wing. Simultaneously, B1 comes across the foul lane, searching for the ball, and the wing (S1) hustles to a space near the offside block.

The second method is shown in figure 6.14. Teams use this motion against even-front and matchup zone defenses. The player in the high post (B1) steps up to set a screen for the player with the ball (G). The other perimeter player out front (S2) adjusts his or her position based

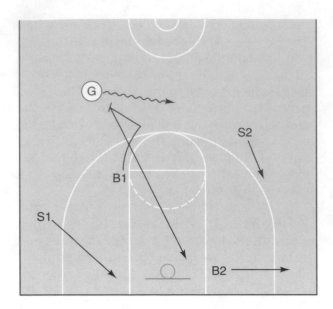

Figure 6.14　Ball reversed by using a high-post screen.

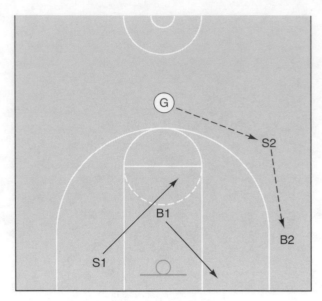

Figure 6.15　Ball thrown to the corner.

on the spacing with the ball handler. The low-post player (B2) runs more toward the corner than toward the wing. The screener (B1) rolls down the lane in anticipation of a pass after the playmaker (G) dribbles off the pick. The wing (S1) occupies a weakside low spot.

In figure 6.15, the point guard (G) has just dribbled off the high pick by B1. The player who was in the high post (B1) motors to a ballside low spot. The opposite wing (S1) cuts to the strongside high post at the same time. The low-post player (B2) runs the baseline and ends in the corner. The team has completed the three-person pattern on the side change. The verse "low to wing, high to low, and wing to high" will remind players of the movements.

S2 sends the ball to B2 in the corner in figure 6.15. After receiving the ball, B2 dribbles off the baseline while keeping the same defender occupied. The low post (B1) slides to the baseline, facing out, to fill the void left by the dribbler. The high post (S1) adjusts by moving to a midpost location, and S2 and G keep adequate spacing in relation to the ball and each other.

The three-player rotation begins again as B2 below sends the ball to S2. The low post (B1) races to the weakside on the toss to S2. The ball is reversed with a pass or a high-post pick on the ball. When the dribble-off-the-baseline maneuver is performed, executing the high-post screen is more difficult because the screener is lower on the lane (midpost). Changing sides

creates the same progression described previously. The low post becomes the opposite wing, the high post bolts to the low post, and the wing cuts to the high post.

Where the ball is sent on the floor determines player motions. The pass to the high post could come from the wing or one of the two players out top. The high post immediately pivots to look at the basket and evaluate three possible pass opportunities: to a teammate near the hoop, to the wing dropping to the closer corner, or to the perimeter player out front on the side away from the pass-origination point. The high post also may formulate a shot or drive to the hoop.

When the pass is completed to the low post, the high post slices to the basket, the wing spots up to look for a shot opening, and the weakside perimeter player out top flashes to the vacant space produced when the high post slices to the hoop. If the flasher does not touch the ball, he or she quickly returns to his or her original location.

If the person out front with the ball does not reverse the ball with a pass or dribble, the exterior player near the key passes the ball back to the ballside wing. The high post (B2) dives to the low position as the passer releases the ball. The low-post player who fled to the weakside comes back to the ballside, this time to the high post. The return pass to the wing is viable because the wing does not motor to the near block until the ball is reversed.

The skip pass from the wing (B1) to a teammate away out top (S2) causes an interchange of three personnel (B1, S1, and B2) (figure 6.16). The ball changes sides of the floor. The rules are consistent—low (B2) to wing, high (S1) to low, and wing (B1) to high. The passer (B1) dives to the near block before bolting high.

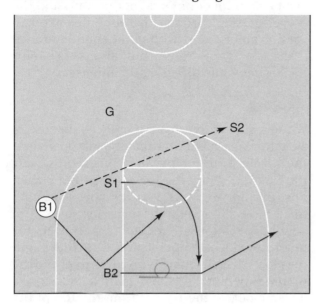

Figure 6.16 Skip pass from the wing to the top.

Figure 6.17 shows the areas occupied by the three players involved in the movement. Notice that the wing locations extend to the corners because a player could end there instead of at a true wing. Low-post spaces expand to include the baseline spot. Remember, the high

Figure 6.17 Spots filled during three-player rotation.

post or midpost is prepared to screen the ball for reversals with the dribble against even-front and matchup zones. The pass across the top to change sides is the best scenario against odd-front zones. Post players (B1 and B2) are obliged to be part of the rotation. Which of the perimeter shooters (S1 or S2) is the final piece in the three-player pattern is the coach's decision.

Keys

Refer to "Zone Offensive Fine-Tuning" in chapter 5 (page 84).

North Carolina takes some time to teach because of the player rotation and special circumstances that can arise. The three-player pattern consumes two to four 20-minute teaching sessions to ensure that all necessary personnel learn it. An additional 30 to 60 minutes of instruction time is necessary to teach the various movements required during specific circumstances, such as when and when not to set the high-post screen, use of the dribble-off-the-baseline maneuver, and the starting toss to the perimeter player at the foul line. Approximately two hours of total teaching and practice time are needed to instill enough knowledge to achieve a satisfactory level of performance and comprehension.

The coach should begin by teaching the offense using a no-defense system. Players must practice performing the three-person rotation on each side change. The coach should teach the pass reversal before getting into the high-post screen on the ball to trigger a side change. The next topic is directing certain passes or motion. The teaching process is not complete if the offense breaks down because of mental mistakes when a player tosses an out-of-the-ordinary pass. Mental lapses can occur if the team goes for significant periods without thorough review of the offense. Teams must revisit North Carolina regularly if they are to work all options and carry them to a successful finish.

When in the initial set of the offense, the lead guard is obliged to look at the perimeter player in the high post. The ball heads there if a teammate is open. In addition, coordination between the point guard and the shooter along the baseline is essential. The shooter reads the ball handler and sprints to the same-side wing. Big players may or may not have opportunities to screen the back players of the zone.

The two post players are always part of the three-person rotation. The coach decides whether the small forward or the shooting guard joins the rotation.

The dribbler off the baseline cannot extend too far from it. He or she does not allow the defender to release coverage. The low post regularly fills the void forged along the baseline, while the high post drops to midlane level.

North Carolina provides ample chances to employ breakdown drills to improve technique. The three-player rotation, high-post pick, and delivery of the ball to the low-post or baseline are just a few of the situations that may require extra attention.

Each player should practice in the position or positions that he or she will play. Some players may find it necessary to know the activity from every spot on the court.

The coach decides what shots each player is allowed to take. A center who has a 15-foot range should not be shooting three-pointers. The coach must communicate shot restrictions to players.

If the center is shaky handling the ball on the perimeter, a subtle alteration is possible. He or she works only in the low post and on the baseline or only fills the high post and low post. The other two players in the three-person rotation adjust and deploy what amounts to a two-player sequence. They occupy the two spots left vacant by the center.

DOUBLE STACK

The double stack offense was created to confuse defenders using a matchup zone defense. The offense expanded to confront any type of zone defense. Player actions cause the defense to adjust coverages frequently. I developed this offense to secure shot attempts for an extremely productive three-point shooter I coached.

Although the double stack can be used against any zone defense, it is especially effective against matchup zones. Squads with an exceptional shooter from the arc will find success with the double stack. The offense also provides opportunities for inside players. The offense is more difficult to defend when used sporadically. Because the activity is not complicated, the opponent may become accustomed to it. Overloading a side of the zone defense is desired.

Personnel

The double stack requires big players who can score around the basket. The offense becomes more effective if they are consistent shooters from 12 to 15 feet while facing the basket. With two excellent perimeter shooters, the offense can begin from either side of the court and the player cutting through the zone defense can vary. A point guard with good shooting range is an asset because opportunities may occur for him or her while directing the offense.

Scoring

When a side is overloaded and the defense is slow to react, a shooter may be left open near the corner. Exterior players consistently view the interior, searching for an open big player. Post players step into vacated spaces around the lane and along the baseline for shots. The second perimeter shooter is prepared for potential shot attempts near the arc that might develop if the defense overreacts to cover the premier shooter. The point guard could acquire a clean look at the basket from the top of the key. The point guard and the second perimeter player are less likely to garner chances than is the shooter running the baseline.

Execution

The movements associated with the double stack are not particularly complex. Players should be able to understand and learn the required movements without making mental mistakes for an extended period.

Figure 6.18 shows the initial set of the offense and opening motion. The two best perimeter shooters (S1 and S2) are stacked below the post players (B2 and B1, respectively) on each side of the lane. The lead guard (G) picks a side of the floor by faking in one direction and then coming back to the other. Once the point guard chooses a side, the two shooters race to their required sites on the strongside. The ballside perimeter player (S2 in figure 6.18) pops out behind the arc slightly lower than the foul line extended. S1 bolts to a spot behind the three-point line on the same side. The team has overloaded the zone. If the squad has only one good exterior shooter, he or she should be in S1's position. The point guard starts the offense by dribbling to the side opposite the primary shooter. The

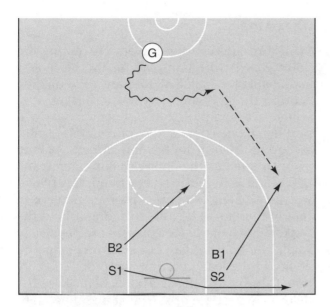

Figure 6.18   Double stack starting set and motion.

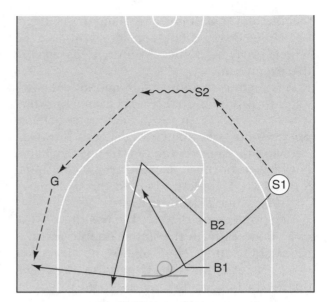

Figure 6.19   Ball sent to the other side in double stack.

playmaker wants a wing in an odd-front zone or a specific-side guard in an even-front zone to defend the initial dribble.

The first pass goes to the perimeter player on the wing (S2). If the lead guard has enticed the proper defender a back player in the zone must move out to defend S2. After S2 receives the ball, the opposite post player (B2) flashes to the ballside high post. S2 may toss the ball inside or to the player in the near corner (S1). S2 and S1 must look inside to the big players as the ballside post player (B1) works hard to obtain position in the low post. If the ball heads low, the high player cuts to the hoop. If the ball goes to the high post, he or she first considers a toss to the low post and then to the perimeter away. Once the ball goes to a corner, the playmaker (G) starts to drift to the weakside. S1 dribbles off the baseline, and the low post (B1) fills the void created along the baseline. S1 does not go too far up the sideline. At the same time, B2 slides down to the midpost and S2 heads away from the ball on the perimeter.

Figure 6.19 pictures player positioning after S1 has dribbled the ball off the baseline. S1 passes to S2 and cuts through the zone to the other corner. S2 uses a dribble (as shown in figure 6.19), a pass to G, or a dribble and pass to reverse the ball. S2 and G induce the preferred defenders to guard them. A pass followed by a return pass between the two may be necessary to get both players on the same side of the

floor and, therefore, into their "right" matchups. The primary shooter (S1) might have to hesitate near the low post before churning out toward the corner. This pause allows G and S2 to adjust their locations.

The high post (B2) follows the ball as it moves across the top and dives to the ballside low post once the ball is sent to the corner. The low post (B1) crosses off B2 to fill the opening in the ballside high post. The squad is in the same five positions as they were initially but on the other side. They run the play continuously from this point forward. The squad overloads a side, dribbles off the baseline and fills the void, and then reverses the ball, repeating as necessary.

Keys

Refer to "Zone Offensive Fine-Tuning" on page 84.

To teach the double stack effectively, the coach should set aside several 15- to 25-minute teaching slots. The team must review the offense periodically to prevent slippage in learning and comprehension.

The coach may wish to teach the offense on a dummy basis at first and eventually move into teaching against a live defense to point out the particular defenders to attack. Instruction must include different types of zones. The coach may need to break down the overload portion of the offense just to practice attacking the vulnerable people in a variety of defenses. Drilling the dribble off the baseline and filling the void can be helpful. By practicing specific portions of the offense, players increase productivity against live execution.

A team must acquire a fair amount of knowledge to produce quality execution. Knowing which players to attack in each zone defense provides the best chance for success. The team is trying to cause defenders to cover players out of their normal coverage areas. The squad forces two defenders to guard three offensive players on one side of the court.

The point guard dictates the positions of the two shooters from the initial double stack. If the shooters are of equal ability, the playmaker can begin at either side. Otherwise, the coach directs the ball handler to head to the side away from the primary shooter from deep.

Against odd-front zones, changing sides with the dribble will likely be tough. The defensive point will stop the ball handler. Therefore, the two players out front must use a pass, dribble away, and return pass to achieve the overload. The main shooter running to the corner might need to pause near the lane before completing the cut. Under certain circumstances, a rapid sprint to the corner might lead to a shot opening. The corner player makes the call.

STANFORD OFFENSE

In my early days as a college head coach, I liked the North Carolina T game and its three-person cycle. I began to think that a zone offense with a four-player rotation could prove worthwhile, so I sat down and created one. In my first year at King's College, that offense carried us to the conference championship game with a stunning upset of a ranked opponent in the semifinals. Our foe used a matchup zone and had difficulty keeping track of all movements into and through the zone from several outside locations in the zone offense.

The Stanford offense is effective against any type of zone defense, especially matchup zones because of the abundance of player movements. The team makes a serious effort to attack the zone on the interior by using a player in the baseline position (three to eight feet off the foul lane facing out) and consistently sending players into the high-post to midpost areas.

Personnel

Stanford requires four players (excepting the point guard) who can play on the perimeter and handle the ball. If all four are good outside scoring threats when facing the basket, it is a major plus, although it is not necessarily a problem if one (the center, for example) is not a scoring threat from beyond 15 feet. As long as he or she has the ability to find open teammates and deliver the ball to them, this player will be a valuable asset. The four players in the rotation must be able to score around the basket. If two of the four players are physically small, the offense may not suit the team. The ability of the lead guard to score occasionally from three-point range certainly helps keep the defense honest. He or she must be prepared to shoot if the opportunity arises.

Scoring

The only player who does not make a concerted effort to move to areas within the zone is the lead guard. Any shots from him or her come solely off slow defensive coverage on an exterior spot from the top of the key. Other players could have openings along the baseline, at the basket, near the high-post region, above either elbow close to the three-point line, and on the periphery along the arc below the foul line extended. Players make a concentrated effort to look inside, but opportunities will crop up for players on the perimeter, especially if the defense collapses to protect the basket.

Execution

The point guard (G) is not involved in the four-person rotation of Stanford. Two shooters and two post players need to understand their responsibilities if they are to execute the offense without any breakdowns.

Figure 6.20 shows the beginning formation and opening movements. The point guard (G) has the ball out front, and the two shooters (S1 and S2) occupy the wings. Post players (B1 and B2) station themselves on the blocks along the foul lane. If the team is attacking an odd-front zone with a defender at the point, it is unlikely that the lead guard will stay exactly in the center of half-court. The defense will probably force him or her to one side or the other. This is not a problem. The routing by the defense only dictates on which side of the floor the offense starts.

G1 sends the first pass to either wing (S1 or S2). In figure 6.20, the pass goes to S1. On the pass release, the opposite wing (S2) flashes to the ballside high-post to midpost region, and the player on the strongside block (B2) steps to the baseline position (three to eight feet off the lane, facing out). After the wing (S2) hits the lane, the player low on the weakside (B1) usually moves up the lane line to ball-reversal position opposite the point guard out top. He or she can either remain up top or flash back to the basket. B1 dashes to the hoop if he or she recognizes an opportunity for a lob pass from S1. If no lob is coming, the sprint to the top is mandatory.

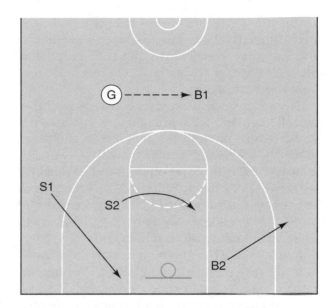

Figure 6.21 Ball thrown to the reversal player (B1).

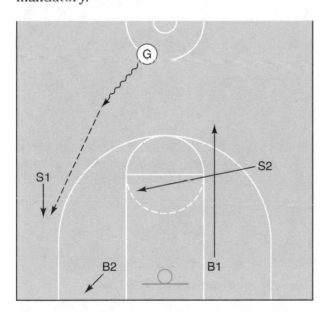

Figure 6.20 Stanford opening formation and movements.

If the pass to the interior of the zone is not available, S1 tosses the ball out to the point guard (G). On the release of the ball, the player on the baseline (B2) immediately hustles to the weakside block. Whenever a wing throws the ball to the lead guard, the player low darts to the offside box.

Figure 6.21 illustrates the next stage of the rotation. The lead guard throws the ball to the reversal player (B1) opposite him or her. With this pass, the player who ran the baseline (B2) continues moving and ends as the ballside wing. The high-post or midpost player (S2) follows the

ball and slices across the foul lane. He or she ends more near the ballside low post. The new weakside wing (S1) dashes to the basket and could have a possible pass reception. But S1 is not required to cut toward the block. He or she may elect to stay in the weakside wing area.

The ball is reversed to the ballside wing (B2), which completes the rotation of personnel (figure 6.22). The passer (B1) immediately slides down to a spot at the ballside high post to midpost, while the low post (S2) rushes to the baseline and faces out. The playmaker (G)

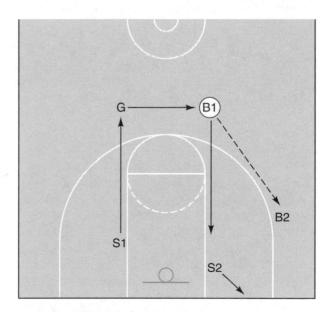

Figure 6.22 Reversal player tosses to the near wing.

hustles to replace B1, who has dropped to a place along the lane. The weakside wing (S1) is the only player away from the ball. S1 hustles above the closer elbow. He or she becomes the next reversal player.

The pattern continues as the wing with the ball (B2 in figure 6.22) first glances inside to B1 or S2 before passing the ball out to the playmaker (G). When B2 tosses the ball to the lead guard (G), S2 (the player on the baseline) dashes to the weakside block. When the ball is delivered to the reversal player (S1), S2 continues to run along the baseline to become the ballside wing. The player in the high post to midpost (B1) goes across the lane to a position low on the strongside. B2 (the weakside wing) has the option to remain in that area or cut to the basket. Players maintain the motion sequence until the conclusion of the possession.

Special circumstances may arise during the execution of the offense. When the ball is thrown to the baseline position, the movements illustrated in figure 6.23 take place. S2 flips the ball to B1. After the pass is released, the player in the high-post to midpost position (S1) cuts to the hoop, ending at the offside block. The player in reversal position (B2) immediately bolts to the post spot vacated by S1. S1 and B2 have changed positions. S1 is now in the reversal position. The squad remains in the regular offensive pattern.

When the high-post to midpost player receives the ball from a wing, he or she imme-

diately turns to face the basket. The following options are available: toss to the player on the baseline who is moving across the foul lane, pass to the wing (the initial passer) as the wing slides closer to the baseline for a possible scoring attempt, cast the ball to the reversal player opposite, initiate a scoring maneuver, or throw the ball out to the playmaker. Figure 6.24 illustrates the movements that occur if the high-post to midpost player (S1) passes the ball back out to the near wing (S2). Team members refill designated spots. S1 darts to the ballside baseline position. The player in the reversal spot (B2) swiftly fills the void created by S1's cut. B1, who is on the weakside box, becomes the player to fill the reversal role.

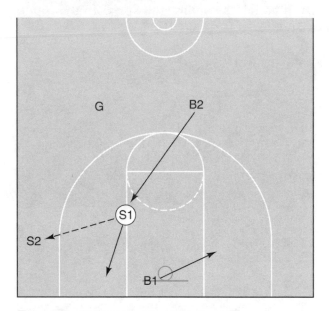

Figure 6.24   High post passes to the near wing.

Instead of swinging the ball to B1 on the other side of the court, the point guard (G) may send it back to a wing (S2) (figure 6.25). The three remaining players initiate the following motions: the high-post to midpost player (B2) darts to a baseline spot, the reversal player (B1) rushes to the high-post to midpost region on the ballside, and the weakside player (S1) scurries up to a location above the near elbow.

If a wing sends a skip pass to the player out front on the weakside, players execute the primary rotation and act as if the ball had been passed from the playmaker to the reversal player. The player on the baseline motors to the ballside wing. The high-post to midpost player flashes across the lane to a strongside low-post

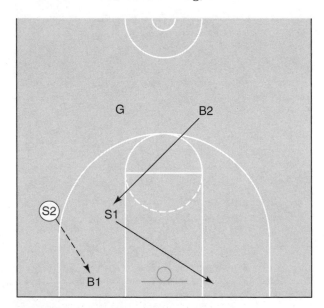

Figure 6.23   Pass to the baseline.

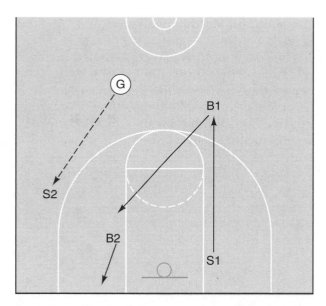

Figure 6.25 Ball passed back to the wing instead of reversed.

position. The passer slides toward the basket or remains near the current wing location. He or she makes the choice.

When the reversal player throws the ball back to the playmaker, squad members simply reverse their previous movements. They reoccupy spots at the ballside wing, high post to midpost, and offside block.

Figure 6.26 shows that S2 did not cut to the basket on the pass across the front, remaining wide instead. S1 hurls the ball cross-court to S2. The passer (S1) immediately hustles to fill the ballside high-post to midpost position. B1

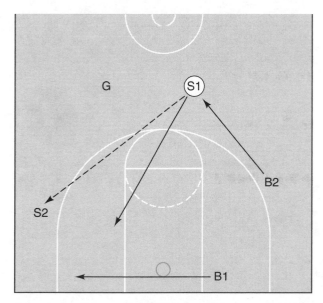

Figure 6.26 Skip pass from the reversal spot to the far wing.

sprints to the strongside baseline spot. The opposite wing (B2) becomes the player at the top on the weakside.

Keys

Refer to "Zone Offensive Fine-Tuning" in chapter 5 (page 84).

Close to two hours of practice time is needed to complete the instruction of Stanford to a quality level consistent enough to use in a game. Obviously, older, more savvy players require less time. The coach should unquestionably teach Stanford initially on a no-defense basis. He or she should finish the normal four-player rotation instruction before getting into pass-specific options. Players will need two or three 15- to 20-minute segments to comprehend the normal pattern thoroughly. Additional time is required to review the movements dictated when a pass goes to a specific site. Players will learn more quickly if they understand the concept of filling slots. The coach consistently reinforces the movements to ensure that players do not forget the required motions. The squad must review and practice this offense often.

The teaching process focuses on the four-player rotation. All four positions are interchangeable, so each player must have the same knowledge of the offense. Point guards are the only players not involved in the normal rotations. Because they are the quarterbacks of the club, however, they must understand the offense if they are to be effective leaders. Point guards dictate movements and corrections to teammates when necessary.

The team must be able to complete regular player rotations. Changing sides of the half-court at least six times with no mental breakdowns is an achievable goal. The team should begin by practicing the pattern with no defense. After the squad is comfortable with the pattern, they can go live against a defense. The coach should vary the zone (odd-front, even-front, or matchup) so that players become accustomed to attacking each. Progress may initially be slow but should pick up momentum as the amount of instruction time increases.

If execution problems or breakdowns begin to occur, the team should return to practicing on a dummy basis or take a specific action and cover it as a breakdown drill. The offense is easily broken into smaller portions to review in drill format periodically throughout the season. The coach does not want players to forget what they have learned. Players are not to execute the offense like robots, concerned only with running the pattern. They must grasp the reasons behind the movements.

Players attack the offensive glass. Usually, three players (all but the playmaker and ball-side wing) go to the boards, and the coach may choose to crash four people (all but the lead guard).

The coach informs players of their individual roles and what shots they may pursue. The center must not be shooting three-pointers if he or she cannot make them. If the off-guard is physically small, shots within the foul lane may be unrealistic for him or her.

CHAPTER 7

Offenses Versus a Box-and-One

The three offenses discussed in this chapter are designed to attack a junk defense, a defense that teams rarely encounter. In this kind of defensive scheme, either the box-and-one or the diamond-and-one, four defenders play zone and one player guards man-to-man. Although a coach may choose to deploy a normal zone or man-to-man offense after recognizing a combination defense, I have found it beneficial to use an attack designed exclusively to counter the opponent's move.

Two of the main advantages of deploying a junk defense are to surprise the offense and to use something that the opposition is not normally prepared to confront. A team that has in its offensive repertoire these special offenses can negate those advantages and feel comfortable facing a combination defense. Players are not caught off guard. They know how to attack the defense.

BOX SPECIAL

Any coach who has faced a junk defense knows that there is strong potential for difficulty. The opponent tries to take the primary scorer out of the offense. The opposing coach has decided that one player on the squad carries the offense. Box special can offset that defensive philosophy by providing an exceptional outside shooter a way to cope with the extra attention.

Personnel

The opponent has already decided that the team has one outstanding outside shooter. They guard that player man-to-man. Obviously, it is beneficial if the other two perimeter players can stick the jumper from the periphery. The two post players ought to be convincing scorers in the paint. The more offensive firepower a team can put on the floor with the player being defended man-to-man, the more difficult the job becomes for the defense. Coaches always have the option to substitute players to put better shooters and scorers on the hardwood.

Scoring

For the player being defended man-to-man, shots come on the perimeter from the second hash mark above the block on the foul lane down to the baseline. Most shot attempts are at or just beyond the three-point arc. Big players obtain scoring payoffs around and within the lane. The point guard and third perimeter player are not actively engaged in scoring. Their shots occur because the defense focuses elsewhere and they are left open.

Execution

Figure 7.1 shows the starting set and movements of the play. The player being defended man-to-man (S1) regularly begins at the foul line. The

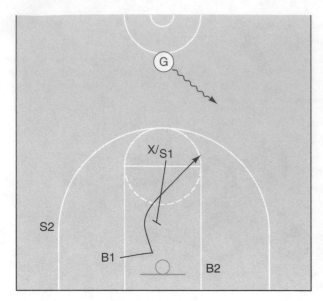

Figure 7.1 Box special opening action.

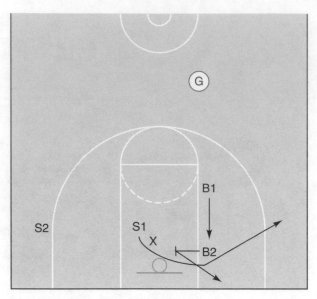

Figure 7.2 Motion continues as the targeted shooter uses a baseline screen.

best ball handler on the perimeter, in this case the lead guard (G), plays the point position out front. The other perimeter player (S2) is stationed past the three-point line below the foul line extended. He or she is free to choose the side. Post players (B2 and B1) begin at the blocks on the lane.

The first move of the offense is opposite S2. G dribbles to the side of half-court away from S2, while S1 sets a diagonal down screen (the direction may vary) for B1 on the nearest zone defender. S1 picks the defender expected to cover the area where his or her teammate will cut. A pass to B1 coming high to the ballside is possible.

S1 uses a screen by B2 (ballside low post) to sprint to the strongside corner (figure 7.2). The screener (B2) steps to the baseline three to eight feet off the lane facing out after S1 uses the pick. The high post (B1) slides down to a midpost location after his or her partner begins to move to the baseline. Four players (G, S1, B2, and B1) form a diamond on the ballside. G can deliver the ball to S1 for a possible score. If S1 receives the ball and no shot is available, he or she tries to send the ball inside to B2 on the baseline. If this happens, the midpost player (B1) cuts to the basket. S1 could also toss the ball to B1 at midpost. After B1 catches the ball, he or she turns and faces the hoop immediately. B2 slides to the bucket, while S1 glides down toward the corner when B1 receives the ball.

Figure 7.3 shows the four players in the diamond formation. No shot or interior pass materi-

alizes for S1. S1 throws the ball to G to start the ball reversal. G uses the dribble to head to the other side of the court. After G places the ball on the floor, the two big players (B1 and B2) come together to set a double screen for S1. S1 hustles to the other corner, employing the double pick by B2 and B1. S2 also sets a single down screen near the other box. After S1 slices off the double pick, the player on top in the screen (B1) flashes high to a point above the foul line. S1 continues to run and rubs off S2's pick.

The lead guard (G) casts the ball to S1 (figure 7.4). On the pass, S2 screens away, picking the

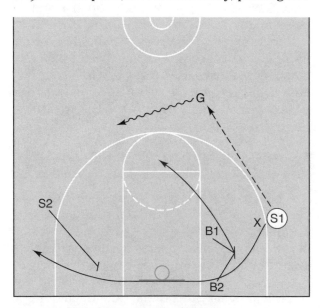

Figure 7.3 Ball thrown out top and reversed.

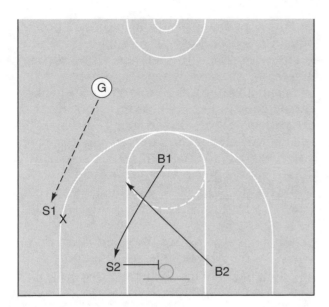

Figure 7.4 Pass from G to S1.

defender in the zone who has ballside low-post coverage. The pick allows the high post (B1) to dive to the ballside low position, which may be void of a defender. He or she slides to the baseline after recognizing that no pass is forthcoming. The player with the ball (S1) looks inside to B1 and delivers the ball if B1 is open. B2 flashes high to the ballside off B1's tail. Big players perform an X move. The high post (B2) slides down to midpost as B1 motors to the baseline. They move simultaneously. S1 may be able to shoot or throw the ball inside to B1 or B2. If S1 throws the ball out to G, it is reversed with the dribble. The team runs the play continuously until an open scoring outcome arises.

Keys

Refer to "Zone Offensive Fine-Tuning" in chapter 5 (page 84) for relevant topics.

In the initial set, when the player being guarded man-to-man deploys the original screen for the big player at the block away from the ball, the exterior player farthest from the ball may be open for a skip pass if he or she slides toward the weakside corner. The defense may be focusing on the high post. Players throw the skip pass only if the pass receiver is open for a quality shot.

If by some chance the ball goes to the other shooter at a wing or corner (not the player guarded man-to-man) and he or she has no shot, then that player tosses the ball out to the lead guard and races toward the near box to

pick for the targeted shooter. A second screen across the lane follows shortly.

The squad makes a concerted effort to free the player being defended man-to-man for a shot in the wing or corner. Post players regularly fill baseline and midpost positions when the ball is in the hands of the primary shooter in the wing or corner. Three players have picking responsibilities when the player being defended man-to-man runs the baseline. The point guard wants to get the ball into the hands of the targeted shooter.

The player defended man-to-man always begins at the foul line. Once movements commence, however, he or she never returns to that location.

The ball goes to the midpost or high-post player. He or she consistently turns and looks at the hoop. A shot attempt or dribble penetration for the mid- or high-post player is a possibility. The team stretches three players along the baseline when the high post has possession.

Post players come together to establish a double screen as soon as the player out front places the ball on the floor. The big player nearest the foul line flashes high once the primary shooter uses the double pick. The dribbler is aware of the action and flings the ball inside whenever possible.

The perimeter player on the weakside consistently sets two screens whenever the ball is reversed. The first one is at the block for the main shooter; the second is applied to the defender with strongside low-post coverage. The second pick commences when the ball leaves the passer's hands on its way to the premier shooter at the wing. After the screen is exploited, the screener races to a spot near the baseline on the other side of the floor.

When the ball is thrown to the main shooter, the high-post player dives low and could be open because of the pick planted on the zone defender covering the ballside low post. The featured shooter delivers the ball inside if a teammate is unguarded.

The players repeat the reversal action as many times as necessary to produce a quality shot, especially if they are playing without a shot clock.

Players should headhunt on screens and target the defender assigned to play the main shooter one-on-one. If executed properly, the offense will force another defender in the zone to provide temporary coverage, creating an opening for a teammate because two defenders are concentrating on one offensive player.

Teams use this offense against a box-and-one or diamond-and-one. Coaches should review defensive coverages of both zones so that players know which defender is responsible for what coverage. There are subtle differences between the two. Diamond is more vulnerable in the middle of the lane.

Although the offense does not eliminate shots for the four players guarded by the zone, their shots could be limited. The coach must have confidence in the big players, the most likely recipients. Coaches should use this offense when they feel it is necessary to acquire points from their best shooter even when he or she is drawing individual attention.

Instruction should be complete after two or three 15- to 20-minute sessions. Teaching should begin without using a defense. After players are able to comprehend their movements, the defense can be added. Within a week, the offense should be ready for use in a game. Teams must review box special periodically throughout the season to prevent slippage in execution.

BOX

If the opponent chooses to guard the main shooter with man-to-man and provide zone help, a coach can opt to let the other four players furnish the bulk of the scoring. The coach can use a player defended in one manner to disrupt the defensive execution of the rest of the opposing team. This concept is at the heart of the box offense. Facing a junk defense compels a coach to become equally creative to defeat it.

After the team recognizes that the opponent is using a combination defense that has only one person defending man-to-man, the play is called. The coach is confident that at least one other perimeter player has the ability to score when the defense is giving the team's primary shooter special consideration. The team sacrifices points from the best scorer in anticipation that others will pick up the slack.

Personnel

The two perimeter players not defended man-to-man must be capable exterior scorers. At least one of them needs to be a competent outside shooter. Post players should be proficient scorers on the interior. They receive increased chances when the defense takes the main shooter out of the offense. Coaches should substitute as necessary to ensure that the right people are on the floor. Some coaches even substitute for the targeted shooter when faced with the four-person zone. Personally, I do not subscribe to the idea of removing one of the team's more effective offensive players. Coaches who do so end up doing precisely what their adversary desires—taking an outstanding exterior shooter out of the game. Instead of removing the player, coaches should use the targeted player to help teammates score.

Scoring

Both post players receive openings within 15 feet of the basket. The two exterior players covered by the zone can garner scoring opportunities at the top of the key or in either corner. The player guarded man-to-man is not likely to secure open shots.

Execution

In figure 7.5, the defense guards the point guard (G) man-to-man. The other four players line up across the foul line, with post players (B2 and B1) at the elbows and the other two perimeter players (S1 and S2) on the wings. The lead guard

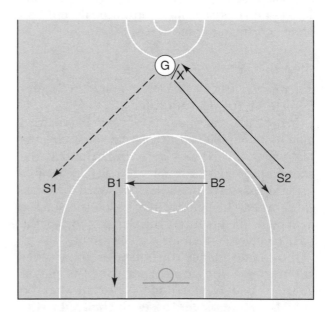

Figure 7.5   Starting set and movements in the box offense.

(G) can make the initial pass to either wing (S1 in this case). If the coach wants a particular shooter to have scoring chances, the playmaker directs the initial pass to that player. B1 slides down to the low post. B2 flashes ballside high, while G exchanges with S2.

The starting pass can go to one of the high posts (B1 or B2) in the 1-4 set (figure 7.5). The other big player slices to the hoop. The player with the ball turns and faces the basket. He or she considers a toss to the player cutting or to a teammate on the weakside exterior; thinks about taking a shot or driving to the basket; sends the ball to the strongside wing, who is dropping toward the corner; or tosses the ball back out to the point guard.

The player being guarded man-to-man could be S1 or S2 rather than G. If so, dribbling to the contested player's side of the floor starts the offense. A pass to a wing is not necessary.

S1 watches the inside action with B1 or B2 before tossing the ball out top to S2 (figure 7.6). Once S1 releases the ball, he or she runs the baseline and uses a screen on the back defender of the zone provided by G, the perimeter player being guarded man-to-man. The pass to the top signals a change of sides. S2 dribbles the ball to the other side of the half-court. As S2 dribbles the ball away from the vacated wing, he or she keeps an eye on the high post (B2).

S2 completes the pass to S1 (figure 7.7). On the pass, G cross screens and attacks the defender in the zone who has ballside low-post

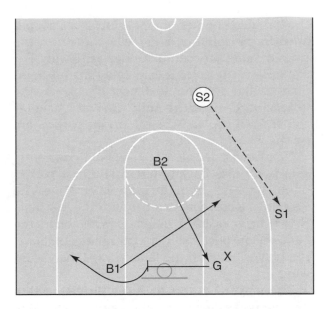

Figure 7.7   Pass to the wing after a pick by the targeted player.

coverage. It is his or her second consecutive pick. The high post (B2) slices to a spot low, and the low post (B1) bolts high. S1 could have a shot or pass inside to B1 or B2. If the ball goes to B2 in the low post, B1 slides to the bucket. If the ball heads to B1 high, the low post (B2) darts to the basket and S1 slides down toward the baseline. The high post is not likely to toss the ball to a weakside perimeter player because G is being guarded man-to-man. If no shot develops for S1 or the defense denies the pass to a post player, S1 throws the ball out to S2 and play proceeds. S2 dribbles away while S1 runs the baseline.

Keys

See "Zone Offensive Fine-Tuning" on page 84.

Usually, the defense targets one of the three perimeter players for man-to-man coverage. The team begins the offense based on who is receiving the added attention. Regardless, the subject becomes a wing and the initial screener. The other wing becomes the primary outside shooter.

The offense is not difficult to teach. Several 15- to 20-minute sessions should suffice. Coaches should teach it on a dummy basis initially and add defenders after players can run the pattern consistently. The toughest part of the instruction is for players to learn precisely how to start the play. The objective is to place

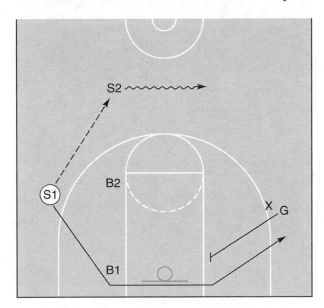

Figure 7.6   Pass to the top and run to the other side.

the targeted shooter on one wing as a screener and the perimeter player who becomes the main outside shooter at the opposite wing. For example, if the defense is playing the off-guard man-to-man and the next best shooter is the point guard, then the small forward handles the ball out top and the other two players are on the wings.

The player guarded man-to-man constantly sets two picks back-to-back. The first pick is on the back player of the four-player zone. The second is a cross screen through the foul lane. He or she goes at the defender who covers the ballside low post. Once the picks are complete, the player bolts off the lane toward the vacant wing.

The player out top reverses the ball with a dribble whenever he or she gains possession. The player glances at the high post during the dribble. The ball handler sends the ball there if possible.

The coach should identify the zone defenders assigned to the best shooter. They could be different for diamond and box zones. With a diamond zone, the coach wants the back player to guard the ball on the exterior so that the defense has to rotate in the four-player zone to guard the ballside low post. Therefore, the player with the ball up top tries to dribble at a defensive wing. In a box zone, a top defender guards the dribbler and a back player defends the pass to a wing.

DIAMOND OFFENSE

The diamond offense was developed to incorporate concepts from box and box special. To provide a well-rounded approach, the team needs to secure shots for the leading scorer and his or her teammates. The diamond offense enabled my outstanding shooter to score in the low 30s when our chief rival made him the target after he put 47 points on the board in our first meeting. We won convincingly because the remaining players also contributed significant numbers.

Coaches use this offense to attack a diamond-and-one or box-and-one defense. The prime shooter does not function strictly as a screener. He or she secures scoring chances. The coach is not willing to sacrifice the heavily defended shooter but also has faith in the ability of other players to contribute.

Personnel

One exterior player is an outstanding shooter from the periphery. The other two perimeter players, especially the one not handling the playmaker duties, need to be outside-scoring threats. One post player operates strictly in the high post and has a penchant for playing from inside the 15-foot mark. The other big player is able to score around the basket and should be an effective shooter from at least 18 feet.

Scoring

The primary perimeter scorer attains shots from 15 to 20 feet in either corner. The other two players on the periphery obtain opportunities in the corners and around the key. The high-post player acquires shots within 15 feet of the hoop. The other big player shoots from at least 18 feet and in.

Execution

The point guard (G) is out past the top of the key with the ball (figure 7.8). The perimeter player being defended one-on-one (S1) is stacked along the foul lane with the low post (B1). B2 is at the foul line. The other perimeter player (S2) is at the wing away from the stack.

If the man-to-man defender is on the point guard (G) instead of one of the shooters, the team makes a simple adjustment. The playmaker and either S1 or S2 switch roles. The player out front must be an adequate ball

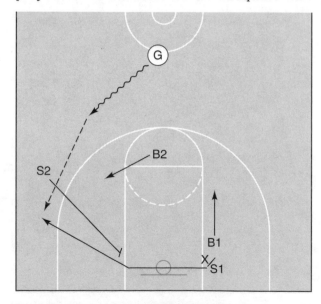

Figure 7.8 Diamond starting alignment and motion.

handler. The one on the wing gets set up for perimeter shots.

Motion begins when the player at the top (G) dribbles to the side away from the stack (figure 7.8). S2 hustles to the nearby block to establish a pick for S1 as he or she sprints to the ballside. The pass goes to S1. S2 posts low, B2 stays high, and the weakside player (B1) slides up the lane line toward, but not to, the foul line. S1 may have a shot or pass to S2 low, to B2 high, or across to B1.

S1 has the ball in the corner and tosses it out to the ball handler (G) (figure 7.9). The players switch sides with the dribble. S2 and B1 set picks close to each box on the lane for S1 as he or she runs the baseline. G looks to cast the ball to the high post (B2) as the dribble progresses. If S1 (the player guarded man-to-man) is not open to receive the toss from G, he or she immediately heads back to the closer block and picks the back player of the zone. S2 uses the screen and pops out for a potential score. S2 and S1 just exchange spots.

Subsequently, if S2 does not have a clear shot or pass inside, he or she flings the ball to the lead guard (G), who dribbles opposite. Once G is in position, S1 exploits the screen provided by the low post (B1) and bolts to the perimeter spot directly below the ball. S2 moves in to the block after passing to G. Therefore, when S2 is on a wing and a change of sides takes place, S1 uses only one screen along the baseline instead of two. When the main shooter passes the ball

out to the top, he or she must run the baseline and employ two picks.

Action proceeds as before except on the other half of the court. The pass goes to the player being played one-on-one (S1), or he or she hustles back toward the block to pick the back zone defender for the nearest teammate low (B1). The big player pops out to the wing instead of a perimeter player (S2). The team keeps repeating the pattern until an acceptable shot develops. The player guarded man-to-man rubs off one or two screens along the baseline to get open at either corner or wing. If he or she is covered, the targeted shooter runs to the near block to pick the ballside back player of the zone. The small forward (S2) or power forward (B1) pops out off the screen for a potential pass reception and shot.

Keys

Refer to "Zone Offensive Fine-Tuning" in chapter 5 on page 84.

Because teams usually play a perimeter player man-to-man in a box-and-one or diamond-and-one, the three offensive exterior players fill assigned spots at the start. The one guarded man-to-man is stacked with a post player at one block. The best shooter of the remaining two takes a position at the opposite wing, and the third player acts as the playmaker out top.

Although the diamond offense uses screens to free the player defended man-to-man for shots, it also uses the same player to screen zone defenders to aid teammates' effort to secure shots from the periphery. Unlike box and box special, the diamond offense does not contain the interior-screening action that increases the chances for shots around the basket. Even so, players can throw the ball inside, high or low, whenever feasible.

The coach should begin instruction on a no-defense basis and add defenders after players understand the basic motion of the play. Two or three sessions should suffice before practicing live. When a defense is on the floor, the coach points out the defenders to attack in both a box and a diamond zone.

The high post remains active and fills any openings that arise in the opponent's zone. He or she uses the top half of the lane. Players should glance in the direction of the high post regularly and send the ball there when appropriate.

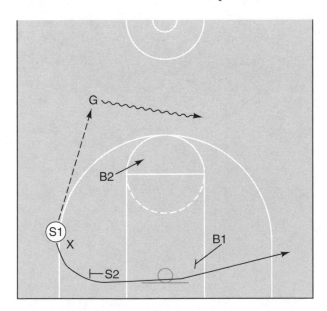

Figure 7.9 Ball thrown out from the corner and reversed.

When a player has the ball on the exterior below the foul line extended, he or she consistently views the interior, including the player along the offside lane line. The weakside player slides vertically to find an opening but does not venture above the elbow. Once the ball goes to the player out front, it is no longer possible for the weakside player to acquire the ball. Therefore, he or she rushes toward the box and screens for the primary shooter running the baseline.

When the high post catches the ball, he or she is obliged to turn and face the basket. Teammates on each side below the foul line extended may be accessible for pass receptions. The third player underneath is likely to be covered man-to-man. The high post also can shoot or place the ball on the floor and head to the hoop.

If the ball goes inside to the player in the low post, he or she strives to score. The low post also may toss the ball to the high post cutting to the hoop. The player on the weakside block circles up and replaces the high post. He or she fills the void created by the high post's cut and is another potential pass recipient.

CHAPTER 8

Offenses Versus a Triangle-and-Two

An opponent may decide to guard two offensive players man-to-man and play the remaining three defenders in a zone. This defense creates a completely different set of circumstances for the offense to counter. The specialized offenses outlined in chapter 7 are no longer appropriate. Coaches must unveil alternative weapons.

This chapter presents three distinctly different ways to beat a triangle-and-two defense. Each offense produces good scoring opportunities. The differences lie in which players obtain shots and the types of shots available. The three offenses vary in how they use the players who are guarded man-to-man (whether they act as screeners or are recipients of picks). Teams that deploy a junk defense are counting on the element of surprise. Preparation negates the advantage.

TRIPS

When an opposing coach tries to disrupt an offense by having defenders guard two offensive players man-to-man while keeping the other three defenders in a triangle zone, an unprepared offense usually reacts by being tentative. Timing within the offense is off and confusion erupts. The trips offense provides an organized counter to the defensive action. Anticipation is a huge part of being a successful coach. When

a club is ready to face whatever the defense tries, it takes a gigantic step toward a positive conclusion.

The triangle-and-two defense usually defends two of three perimeter players one-on-one. Rarely will a defense guard a big player man-to-man because doing so leaves the three-player zone to cover two outside shooters over a considerable amount of territory. Coaches call for the trips offense when they want to acquire shots for the two players the defense is trying to defend man-to-man rather than use them as screeners.

Personnel

The opposition has already determined that the team has two exceptional shooters. The opponent obviously feels that if they can restrict the two players offensively, they will limit the team's ability to score. The offense benefits if the two post players can score around the basket, and it is a real plus if the third perimeter player is able to stick jumpers from the periphery. The coach can always substitute to place another exterior shooter on the court. I do not recommend replacing one or both of the targeted players, but coaches may use that ploy if they wish to gauge the opponent's reaction. As far as I am concerned, following that path does precisely what the adversary wants—taking one or two shooters out of the game.

Scoring

Shots develop for the two players who are guarded man-to-man in the three-point line area below the foul line extended and the baseline. Post players receive inside scoring chances around the basket. The remaining exterior player could see shots out front from the foul line out.

Execution

In figure 8.1, the defense is playing the point guard (G) and one of the shooters (S1) one-on-one. Post players (B2 and B1) stack low on one side of the foul lane. The other perimeter player (S2) begins on the same side of the court as the post players. S1 occupies the opposite wing.

The point guard (G), who is out front, dribbles at S1 (figure 8.1). He or she throws the ball across to S2, who is moving to a position opposite G. S1 begins to move toward the baseline and same-side block as the dribbler heads toward him or her. After G passes to S2, S1 employs the twin screen established by B2 and B1 opposite and fills the corner. Big players face inward when they set the double pick. S2 tosses the ball to S1 if he or she is open. If S1 is not open, the post players recognize that and execute a twist move. One big player steps down and into the lane so that his or her partner can slide over the top toward the ball. The ball handler (S2) could throw the ball inside at this point.

In figure 8.2, S2 cannot deliver the ball to S1 or to B2 or B1 on the interior, so he or she dribbles at the lead guard (G). As the dribble occurs, B1 and B2 move directly across the lane, face inward, and establish a double screen for G. G cuts down the middle of the lane as S2 dribbles at him or her. G then uses the double pick to gain freedom on the ballside perimeter for the pass from S2. S1 slides up to replace S2 as the ball reversal occurs. If G receives the pass on the wing, he or she first considers a shot. The point guard does not force a shot but is thinking about scoring. The big players split apart. B2 inhabits the ballside baseline position, and B1 is at midpost. G tries to send the ball inside to B2 or B1. If one catches the ball, the other cuts to the hoop. If no interior pass is possible, G flings the ball out front to S2 so that the team can repeat the pattern. On the release of the ball, the midpost steps down to permit his or her baseline partner to swing over the top toward the ball. The player with the ball consistently looks inside. If neither big player is open, he or she dribbles to the other side and the process continues. Post players hustle across the lane to fix double screens as soon as the first dribble hits the floor.

If the defense is guarding the two shooters (S1 and S2) man-to-man, they each start at a wing location. The playmaker dribbles at the player away from the stack, who heads to the closer block. The ball handler maintains the dribble

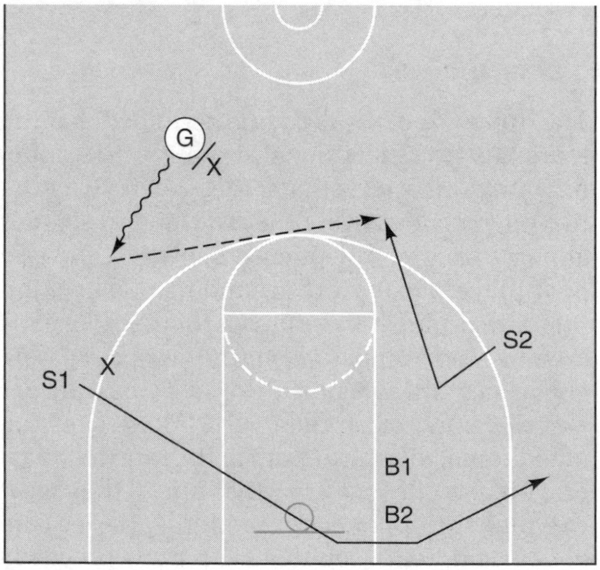

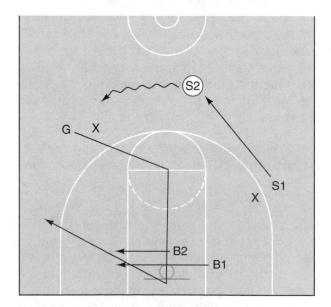

Figure 8.1 Opening set and pass in trips.

Figure 8.2 Dribble at a targeted player.

and returns to the side of the double pick. The shooter on the side of the big players loops below the ball handler and takes up a location opposite out front. The shooter at the box uses the double pick.

Keys

See "Zone Offensive Fine-Tuning" in chapter 5 on page 84.

The two players defended one-on-one must understand that the team completes the activity in this offense for their benefit. They must shoot whenever possible.

Players can begin the motion of the offense in two ways. The method they use depends on which exterior players the defense is covering man-to-man. Regardless, the action heads to the side of the big players as a shooter employs their double screen.

The offense is not difficult to teach. Several 15- to 20-minute sessions are all that are required. Within 10 minutes, players should have a good grasp of the offense without defenders. Once live competition begins, the offense should be ready to use in a game in just a few practices. If necessary, the big players can work on the twist maneuver as part of a breakdown drill. Otherwise, players best learn the offense as a whole.

Once the recipient of the double pick determines that no shot is available, he or she focuses inside on the big players. Post players are either splitting or twisting.

After the player out top places the ball on the floor to initiate the ball reversal, the big players slide across the lane to establish a low twin pick. The player at whom the ball handler dribbles hustles down the center of the lane by first cutting to the middle point of the foul line. He or she awaits the establishment of the double screen and times rubbing off the pick with the positioning of the ball handler.

When the ball goes inside to one of the big players, the other post player dashes to the basket. The post player with the ball tries to direct the next pass to his or her partner. An interior shot is the other alternative.

Players constantly observe the interior when confronted with a triangle zone. Post players need to know that how well they play has great bearing on how long the opposition sticks with their defense. The more the inside players score, the more quickly the defense changes.

BACK TRIANGLE

The two players defended man-to-man do not have to receive scoring opportunities. Although the opponent feels that shutting down those two players is advantageous, that theory may not be correct. The back triangle offense generates excellent shot chances for the three players being guarded by the zone. The offense focuses on forcing the three-player zone to change shape continually.

Coaches use the back triangle offense when they recognize the triangle-and-two defense and know that the three players guarded by the zone are capable of handling the scoring duties. The two players receiving extra attention are more useful as screeners than they are as scorers.

Personnel

The opponent has decided that the offensive team has two shooters who need extra defensive attention. The one remaining perimeter player should be an effective shooter out to about 20 feet. The two post players ought to be well prepared to take advantage of scoring situations around the basket. The offense benefits if they are satisfactory shooters from 15 to 18 feet.

Scoring

Any of the three players who confront the triangle zone gain shot chances around the basket or near the elbows. The two players defended man-to-man are not actively set up for shots, but they could see shot chances if their defenders help in the zone.

Execution

The defense covers the point guard (G) and a shooter (S1) man-to-man. The shooter receiving extra attention (S1) is stationed on one block. The lone perimeter player who is not guarded man-to-man (S2) begins at the wing opposite S1. One big player (B2) starts at the block away from S1. The other post player (B1) is at the elbow directly above S1.

The offense commences with the playmaker (G) dribbling toward the exterior player at a wing (S2). S2 then loops to a position above the ballside elbow. The players guarded one-on-one are now on opposite sides of the half-court.

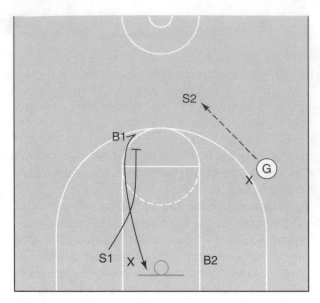

Figure 8.3 Back pick from a two-out set.

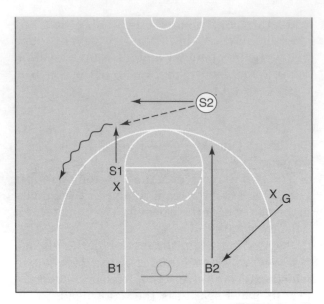

Figure 8.4 Pass to the back screener stepping out.

The lead guard (G) tosses the ball out to S2 (figure 8.3). Notice that S2 and B1 have established a two-out front to attack the triangle zone. B1 will likely have to be several steps above the closer elbow. As a way to encourage a second defender to head up in the triangle zone, S2 may have to toss the ball across to B1. This pass forces the defense to invert the triangle. B1 returns the ball to S2. If only one defender covers both B1 and S2, one of the two should be open for a 15-foot jumper. After a second defender attaches to B1, S1 races up to back pick while the ball is traveling from B1 to S2. S2 throws a lob to B1, who is racing to the hoop, or fakes it and hurls the ball directly into B2, stationed at the ballside box.

S2 sends the pass across to S1, who steps out after screening (figure 8.4). A shot attempt may be possible. If no shot is forthcoming, S1 dribbles to the same-side wing. Remember that the defense is playing S1 one-on-one. S2 moves over to replace S1 above the ballside elbow. B2 slides up to a spot just beyond the weakside elbow, and the lead guard (G) heads to the offside block on the lane. Players have returned to attack formation, the same alignment described previously except on the other side of the floor. S1 delivers the ball to S2. S2 may have to pass to B2 and secure a return pass to entice the zone to the two-out formation. When the defense inverts the triangle zone, the offense proceeds as the playmaker (G) sets the back pick for B2.

The offense keeps repeating the pattern until a desired shot outcome arises.

When the pass is not available to the back screener who is stepping out (S1 in figure 8.5), the player with the ball (S2) simply dribbles at the player denied by the defense (S1), pushing him or her to the near wing. After S2 puts the ball on the floor, B2 rushes to a spot above the closer elbow as G races to the near block. Players simply use the dribble to change the formation from one side to other. The offense continues.

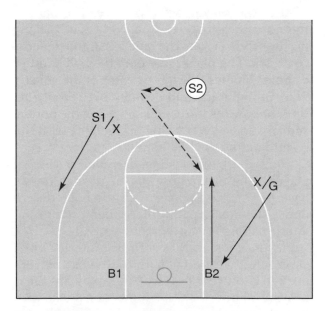

Figure 8.5 Defense overplays the back screener.

If the opponent decides to guard both shooters man-to-man and leaves the point guard free to operate against the triangle zone, the team starts the offense by stationing one shooter on a wing and the other at the block on the other side of the court. This setup produces the attack formation.

Keys

See "Zone Offensive Fine-Tuning" on page 84.

Coaches can easily teach the offense within a few practice sessions, teaching the basic pattern on a dummy basis. After 10 to 15 minutes, defenders join the action. Breakdown drills are not relevant for the offense. Players secure a two-on-one advantage against the triangle zone by learning the offense as a whole.

One player guarded man-to-man dictates initial player alignment. He or she heads to a box on the foul lane. Players then fill their required spots. The team establishes a two-out formation with one perimeter player who is not guarded man-to-man and a big player.

The team forces members of the triangle zone to invert it with two defenders at the top. Two players out front pass between them so that one zone defender cannot guard both. After the defense sends a second defender up, the back screen is engaged. The objective of the offense is to gain a two-on-one edge either high or low against a triangle zone.

The player with the ball out top can throw a lob pass to the player cutting off the back pick or feed the ball to the post player stationed near the ballside block. The passer may have to fake the lob to secure the other option. Regardless, he or she makes a concerted effort to send the ball inside because only one zone defender is likely to be low.

Whether the back screener receives a pass is irrelevant. He or she continually makes the next movement to the same-side wing with a dribble or by sliding there when the dribbler comes at him or her.

Defenders in the triangle zone may attempt to guard the two offensive players out front with one defender. If that happens, the two offensive players at the top have to make the defense pay. They must stick the 15-foot jumper. If they are unable to do so, the opponent has selected the right defense.

The coach should tell players exactly what perimeter shots are permitted and by whom. The coach can decide to allow a shot early in the possession or require the team to make an effort to deliver the ball inside first.

TRIANGLE SPECIAL FOR NAME

A method that encourages a team to exploit a well-rounded approach to defeating a triangle-and-two defense is the next logical step. The triangle special offense uses the two players defended man-to-man to garner shots for their teammates and vice versa. Triangle special takes advantage of a weakness in the three-player zone, which is vulnerable to activity along the baseline. This specialized offensive weapon was created to conclude the series of offenses that incorporate sufficient diversity against the triangle-and-two defense.

Coaches use the triangle special offense when they recognize that the opponent is using a triangle-and-two defense. In triangle special, all players are potential scorers. The coach is not content with allowing only a portion of the personnel on the floor to garner scoring chances.

Personnel

The defense determines that the offense has two strong perimeter shooters, so they defend them one-on-one. The quality of the countermoves improves exponentially when the other three players (two post players and a perimeter player) are offensive minded and can score. The offense still produces opportunities for the two players being guarded man-to-man.

Scoring

The players given individual defensive attention could attain shots above each elbow. Post players acquire openings in the lane and along the baseline. The third perimeter player achieves shot attempts from 15 feet and beyond.

Execution

The play consistently starts to the side of the player whose name has been called (N). N is one of the two players defended man-to-man. The point guard (G) is in possession of the ball above the top of the key (figure 8.6). The named player (N) assumes a position on the block along the lane. The one big player is right above N just

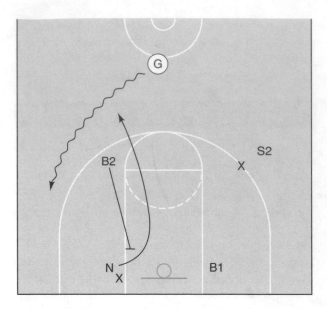

Figure 8.6   Triangle special opening set and motion.

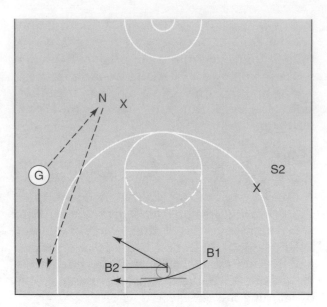

Figure 8.7   Pass to the player above the elbow.

past the elbow. The other post player starts at the opposite box. The other player defended man-to-man (S2) is at the wing away from N.

The lead guard (G) dribbles to the foul line extended on N's side of the court (figure 8.6). When G gets near his or her destination, B2 down screens for N so that N can hustle to a spot above the ballside elbow. He or she wants to come straight up the lane line for a possible opening and a shot.

G throws the ball out to N. N looks for a scoring chance. If one is not available, N tosses the ball back to G, who has drifted toward the same-side corner. On the pass, B2 screens across for B1. B1 darts to the ball, staying low (figure 8.7).

The pick can be highly effective if a back player in the triangle zone zips out to guard G. Therefore, as the ball is in the air to G, B2 dashes across the foul lane to cross screen and B1 hustles to ballside low. The screener (B2) steps back toward the ball opposite B1. B1 runs along the baseline as B2 bolts to midlane.

If the lead guard (G) is unable to complete the pass to N at the top, he or she maintains the dribble and drifts down to the same-side corner. The dribbler tries to force a back player in the triangle zone to come out and cover. After B2 notes the defense's move, he or she screens across the lane. This is the same action as if the pass had been thrown to G in the corner.

Figure 8.8 shows the team reversing the ball to the new side of half-court. N hustles to

screen on the ball for G, who dribbles out to the top of the key. The pick serves to cancel any possible five-second violation. The mid-post player (B2) comes to the foul line, and the baseline player (B1) occupies the closest block. S2 (the other targeted player) sprints to the nearest box.

The team runs the same motion on the second side of the court. The lead guard (G) continues to dribble, ending at the vacant wing. The high post (B2) picks down for the player immediately below (S2) like in figure 8.6. The players repeat their activities until a solid shot at the hoop develops.

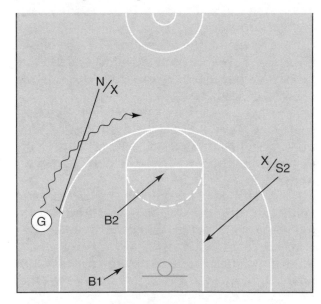

Figure 8.8   Screen for the ball handler to change sides.

If the defense covers the point guard one-on-one, he or she dribbles at the perimeter player guarded by the zone, who is stationed on a wing. The wing loops up to the top of the key and catches a toss from the ball handler as the two exchange places. The outside player is now operating the offense from the top spot.

Keys

Refer to "Zone Offensive Fine-Tuning" in chapter 5 on page 84.

At the beginning, the coach teaches the offense without defense. Because the number of movements is limited, the instruction should wrap up within 10 minutes. Breakdown drills are not necessary. The coach focuses on teaching triangle special as a whole.

This play does not require an excessive amount of time before an acceptable shot appears. Teams can operate the play as a continuity offense, but a scoring chance will likely develop after the team completes the motion to both sides of the floor, often even sooner. The dribble reversal of the ball is slow so the ball handler must avoid a five-second closely guarded violation. If the dribbler is in trouble, he or she picks up the ball to gain an extra four seconds. The nearest teammates scramble to receive a pass and quickly return the ball to the passer. The offense proceeds again. The dribbler to the wing maintains the dribble as long as possible.

The named player who is racing upward off the down screen initially might be able to shoot a jumper after receiving the pass. Because shots develop swiftly in the offense, naming the player ensures that he or she gets the first crack at a jump shot. The coach can eliminate the forname portion of the play if it makes no difference which of the two targeted shooters obtains the first chance to score.

After the ball reaches a spot on the periphery below the foul line extended, players look for a defensive release among the defenders in the triangle zone. When it occurs, the strongside big player picks across the lane for the other post player, who cuts along the baseline to the ball. The players execute the screen and the slice to the baseline simultaneously.

When an inside pass goes to one of the big players, he or she always watches for the other post player darting to the hoop. An interior shot is another desirable outcome.

The back defender of the three-person zone may not go out to guard the player with the ball who is below the extended foul line. In that case, the cross-screening action takes on more of a man-to-man feeling. The player receiving the pick may dash high or low. The screener always seals back opposite. If the ballside low defender stays or switches, the cutter goes high because of the cross screen and the screener seals low. They continue to slide simultaneously to the baseline and midpost regions if they do not receive the ball immediately.

The reversal of the ball in the offense is time consuming and slightly awkward, but at least a screen on the ball initiates it. The pick should give the ball handler a few extra seconds. He or she may also be open for a jumper near the foul line.

PART III

Quick Scoring and Delay Offenses

CHAPTER 9

Fast Breaks

This chapter describes in depth a number of fast break systems. Almost all teams operate some kind of fast break during the course of a game. Even teams like Princeton, that like to maintain a slow, steady pace, run a fast break several times in a contest. At the other extreme are squads like Loyola Marymount during the tenure of Coach Paul Westhead. The fast break was the entire offense. Scoring 150 points became almost routine. Most clubs fall somewhere between the two. Each coach has to address the fast break and prepare the team to execute what he or she desires.

If coaches were to ask players their preference, most would advocate running as much as possible. They like being involved in a fast break. Players will say that running is fun, and on a break they are excited when anticipating an opportunity to finish it with a bucket. The breakaway dunk is the most desired play in a game. The break also generates fan excitement. The faster the tempo, the more entertaining a contest is from the fans' viewpoint.

But a coach cannot pick a fast break style just because it might be more enjoyable for players and fans. Another factor influences fans and players—winning. Therefore, the coach must decide which type of fast break gives his or her personnel the best chance to win.

Selection of a fast break style is also closely associated with a thing called tempo. Squads who want to play at a faster pace will engage in more fast breaks. They are also more likely to use a five-player fast break system. With a five-player fast break the coach knows precisely what lanes are to be filled and by whom. He or she knows exactly where each person finishes. The five-player system is a consistent method of running the floor. Players get into the habit of running. Teams that are more deliberate gravitate away from the five-player system. They are not interested in sending all five players down the court in a hurry. Breaks center more on gaining a numbers advantage. Coaches establish a slower tempo by emphasizing the half-court game. What they do on the half-court is not tied into running the full court.

The first decision the coach must make concerning the fast break is when the team should use a specific method to run the floor. Three choices are available: Players run only off an opponent's turnover that remains in play; the fast break commences as a result of turnovers or defensive rebounds; or players sprint the floor off turnovers, defensive rebounds, or made field goals and free throws. Of course, the coach could instruct the team never to run, but that strategy is not practical.

The next step is to determine who is permitted to handle the ball on the fast break. Is it only the point guard? One or both of the other perimeter players? Which squad members possess the necessary ballhandling skills? This player or players will control and dribble the ball from the backcourt to the forecourt. He or she maintains possession unless a teammate is open in front of the basketball. The ball handler heads to a specific area whenever three or more teammates are along on the break. The coach designates one of the following as the ending points: the center of the foul line, above either elbow on the lane, or at either side foul line extended. The player with the ball will throw a bounce pass to players cutting to the hoop in most cases.

In a two-on-one opportunity, the offensive players split the defender and try to take the ball to the basket. The ball handler forces the defender to guard the ball before passing to teammate.

Regardless of the type of fast break, players always look to throw the ball ahead if possible, especially if a teammate is in front of the defense. The pass is the fastest way to send the ball down court. The player with the ball keeps eyes fixed for any teammate ahead. The team constantly tries to gain a numbers advantage. A fast break is more productive when it is three-on-two or two-on-one.

Whatever fast break the team uses, players must commit to it. They hustle to directed sites each time the circumstances are right. If racing down court after securing a defensive rebound, players need to outlet the ball as far as possible. The closer the pass goes to the half-court line, the better. Long rebounds (usually resulting from a missed shot from a distance of 18 feet or greater) provide excellent opportunities to secure productive fast breaks. The coach designates which players will serve as outlet personnel and where each will be located. Generally, players fill no more than two sites: the lane area in the middle of the floor and the ballside sideline. Players on a fast break try to maintain a spacing of roughly 12 to 18 feet.

Wing players on the break fill lanes quickly and stay wide out toward the sidelines. They plant the outside foot and V-cut to the hoop at the foul line extended if instructed to do so. If the ball handler is required to head to a foul line extended, the coach needs to adjust the lanes run by teammates out first with the dribbler. They keep their eyes on the basketball and are prepared to receive a pass from their teammate.

A five-player fast break forces the defense to guard the maximum amount of space. The coach encourages players to run the break to both sides of the floor. Players will tend to favor one side over the other. Trailers (usually two) should remain at ball level or behind and run specific lanes. They do not run ahead of the ball. The coach may ask one or more to race to another site below the ball after the ball handler reaches a particular spot. All five players must hustle down the court during each offensive possession.

What I refer to as the fly call is another fast break option. Players execute the action whenever the opponent shoots the ball behind the three-point line above the foul line extended. The player guarding the shooter (who can be in a zone or man-to-man) contests the shot and then immediately races to the offensive end of the court. He or she does not block out or worry about rebounding. As soon as a team member secures the ball, he or she looks to throw a baseball pass deep to the player at the opposite end. The passer is either the rebounder or a designated big player whose job it is to inbound the ball quickly on a successful shot. The coach should establish parameters for the fly call, such as determining which players are permitted to fly. The coach may not want the point guard to go if he or she is the team's best ball handler, because the opponent might press. The post player who inbounds the ball after a made shot is another potential exception. The player may be allowed to fly if the coach is confident that the second big player will adjust and assume the inbounding role. If a team uses the fly call sporadically, the nearest player could snatch the ball from the net, step out of bounds, and then look to throw long. A quick-inbounding formation may be unnecessary. The coach resolves the particulars after incorporating the call into the offensive system.

The objective of the fly call is to get the basketball into the hands of a player who has raced ahead of the opposing team. When successful, the fly call translates into a layup. If the ball does not drop into the net and the defense does not secure the rebound, the player on the fly may have to race to rejoin teammates on defense. The coach decides what players are to do if there is a quick put-back for a score. The fly call may have a negative psychological effect on the opponent's shooter. Used successfully near the beginning of the game, the fly call may cause shooters from behind the line to start worrying about the defender taking off down the floor rather than giving full concentration to the shot. Teams can use the fly call with or without any of the fast break options discussed in this chapter.

Whichever method a coach uses to fast break, the choice is tied to the tempo he or she wants to establish. The faster the tempo, the more the club is going to run.

TRADITIONAL FAST BREAK

The traditional fast break has been around for a long time, probably as long as the game itself. It was the dominant method for fast breaks in the 1950s, 1960s, and 1970s. Many teams still use it to manufacture scoring opportunities. The traditional fast break is the preferred means of running when the team wants to play at a slower tempo. The traditional break is not linked to any kind of rapid-inbounding method. Players run only because of turnovers by the opponent or when they snare defensive rebounds.

Teams can use the traditional fast break any time during a game, although it is most efficient when used after a defensive rebound or an opponent's turnover. The traditional fast break is a good fit for a team that wants a selective running game. Squads that enjoy a slower tempo will find it beneficial. Teams score by gaining a numbers advantage.

Personnel

All three perimeter players must be capable of handling the ball in the middle of the court to lead the fast break. If necessary, the ball handling can be restricted to one or two players. The fast break is more effective if the team is quick overall. The better the offensive posts are at shooting the ball from the periphery (especially corners, wings, and in the funnel area on each side of the basket), the greater the flexibility of personnel. Any player can fill lanes and receive possible scoring opportunities. If one or more players are not skilled at shooting the ball from the exterior, the wing's cut on the break is limited to heading directly at the hoop or to spots within his or her shooting range. The wing who cannot shoot well from outside should not fade to a corner, pop back out to the corner, or stop near the foul line extended for a shot.

Scoring

Players on each wing acquire layups, bank shots from 5 to 10 feet, or jump shots from the wing or corner. The ball handler sees shots from 15 to 18 feet within the width of the foul lane. A fourth teammate could receive short jumpers or layups within the lane.

Execution

In the traditional fast break, a player brings the ball up court in the middle of the floor (figure 9.1). The ball handler remains roughly within the lane area that extends between the lane lines over the length of the court. The ball handler (G in figure 9.1) heads to either elbow on the foul

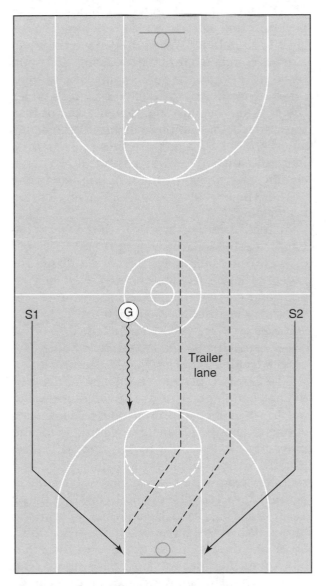

Figure 9.1 Traditional fast break with a trailer lane.

lane. Alternatively, the dribbler could race to the middle of the foul line and slide over to the ballside elbow once he or she throws a pass to a wing. The coach chooses one method. The ball handler regularly occupies an elbow location to create a lane for a fourth teammate to hustle to the hoop as a trailer.

The wings (S2 and S1) stay wide toward the sidelines and execute V-cuts to the bucket at the foul line extended. In this instance, wings slash directly at each box along the lane. The player in the middle could be anyone the coach deems capable of handling the ball on the fast break. The wings can be perimeter or post players or a combination of the two. The trailer is the first of the remaining two players down the court. The wings (S1 and S2 in figure 9.1) can perform other actions on the break based on the slice to each block. When they reach the hoop players could do one of the following: They pop back out beyond the three-point line on their respective sides of the half-court, cross under the goal and head to the opposite arc, or fake the cross before bolting outside to the same-side periphery. Players use these alternatives more often when the wings sprint down court significantly ahead of the ball handler in the center. The coach decides which, if any, option is available.

Instead of cutting directly to the basket at the foul line extended, the wings (S1 and S2) could drift to their respective corners, looking for potential perimeter jump shots by spreading the floor and making the defense cover more real estate. A wing uses this method more frequently when he or she is slow to fill a lane and is not out ahead of the ball handler in the middle. The coach decides if this is a viable alternative.

The first two players on the fast break with the ball handler may be on the same side of the full court. The coach can handle this scenario in one of two ways. The first method is for the player behind to loop to the opposite side, usually by going behind the ball handler. The second means is for the one farther back (S2 in figure 9.2) to yell, "Through!" to instruct his or her partner (S1) to make a normal V-cut to the basket. When the cutter reaches the near box, he or she moves across the lane to the other block and then beyond the opposite arc. The player behind (S2) motors to the block on his or her side of the lane at the foul line extended.

Keys

With the traditional fast break, the coach must make choices. He or she controls the action. The objective of the fast break is to secure a numbers advantage. Teams use break opportunities in the hope of scoring. Additional exploits from the wings may not set the desired tempo.

The players allowed to handle the ball in the middle assume outlet positions at the start of the fast break. Players need to know who can dribble and where they can find them on shots missed by the opponent.

The coach determines whether the ball handler in the middle dribbles directly to either elbow or to the center of the free-throw line. Regardless, he or she consistently slides to the elbow on the side of the pass. The coach should teach one way or the other and not give players the choice.

Wings must run hard up the court whenever a running opportunity presents itself. Wings need to bust ahead of the ball handler in the middle as often as possible. They are looking to secure shots in the funnel (the region between the foul line extended and the basket at an angle favorable for bank shots) or layups at the hoop.

The two players who do not fill wing roles recognize that fact, and the one nearest the offensive basket heads into the trailer lane. The player watches spacing with relation to his or her three teammates in the lead. The trailer does not draw defenders into the area, which could disrupt a scoring opportunity. The trailer is patient and not overeager. He or she exhibits enough self-discipline to hang in the ball handler's wake. The trailer could be open for a scoring opportunity, either a jumper or a layup using the trailer lane.

With the traditional fast break, players need to recognize when fast break scoring chances have ceased. The squad puts the ball into the floor general's hands to begin execution of a desired offense. No quick, smooth transition to a set offense or a particular play occurs, as it does with some five-player fast breaks.

The coach should put considerable time into two-on-one, three-on-two, and four-on-three practice. A large number of fast break drills are available to help teach the traditional break. Teams should practice the scenarios in which the offense has an edge. Adding a defensive trailer forces the offense to make quick decisions. Players learn to take advantage of the extra person during the fast break.

The traditional break is recommended for squads that choose to run the floor only off turnovers or defensive rebounds or both. This style of fast break is consistent with the play of teams that prefer to operate at a slower pace. The coach regulates when the club runs, who controls the ball, and how the players accomplish the fast break.

Just because a coach has decided that the team will not attempt a fast break after the opponent scores does not mean that the team cannot use a quick-inbounding system. The focus of such a system, however, is to defeat a full-court press, not start an offensive attack.

During scrimmage sessions in practice, the coach must reinforce to players that they are to take advantage of the fast break whenever circumstances are favorable. When the coach's criteria are present, the team attempts to fast break while adhering to the established guidelines.

TWO-OUT BREAK

The two-out break is probably the most popular of the five-player fast break systems. This break is a highly organized way for players to run the court. Each player has a specific slot to fill. Each has an assigned sprinting lane. The two-out fast break is interwoven with a quick-inbounds play after a successful field goal by the opponent. The team that uses this form of fast break has committed to running on makes, misses, and turnovers.

Teams can use the two-out fast break throughout a game. Players fill specific spots on the half-court and therefore can use the system under any game circumstance, except an underneath out-of-bounds situation. Teams can use the two-out fast break after a made basket (free throw or field goal) by the opponent, after a defensive rebound, following an opponent's turnover, and during any dead-ball inbounding situation from a sideline or the end line. (Although this last situation does not really qualify as a fast break chance, the system remains intact.) If players are going to fill lanes and slots, they should do so consistently.

A feasible plan is for a team to execute the break system only when trailing by a significant number of points. When time is running out, increasing the game's pace is an appropriate maneuver for the trailing team. When a team needs to catch up by scoring many points in a short time, the two-out fast break can help.

Personnel

The squad needs at least one solid perimeter player who is capable of handling the ball and making good decisions on the break. Having more than one such player provides more flexibility when choosing who will receive the ball to start the fast break. Having two big players is helpful. One should have good ball skills and be able to serve as the inbounder and primary trailer and shoot consistently from 18 to 20 feet. The other post player should be the team's best inside scorer. Exterior shooters fill the other two positions on the break. These perimeter players should be able to score from just beyond the three-point line. The team needs decent speed and quickness.

Scoring

One of the two post players will see an interior shot materialize. If appropriate, the other big players could acquire an 18-foot shot from the key. The two wings might receive layups or shots near the three-point lines below the foul line extended. The ball handler could see shots develop above either elbow. A number of shooting opportunities may arise because of offensive maneuvers at the conclusion of the actual break.

Execution

Figure 9.2 shows the basic lanes and spots that players will fill during the fast break. G, the ball handler, takes the ball at either elbow to just past the three-point arc. Although figure 9.3 shows G heading to the right elbow, he or she could go left.

The ball handler selects a side and hangs there. The ball handler should not change sides, especially after crossing half-court. The other two perimeter players (S1 and S2) run to locations opposite one another behind the three-point line below the foul line extended. It makes no difference who is on which side.

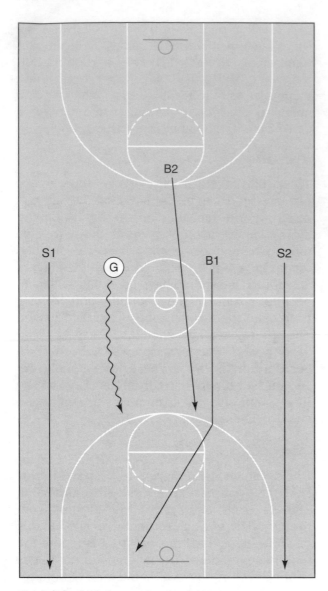

Figure 9.2 Basic two-out fast break lanes.

The post players (B1 and B2) fill two spots. First, the one to get out on the break first (B1 in figure 9.2) goes to a position directly opposite the ball handler (G). He or she does not get ahead of the ball handler. After the ball is just above the three-point arc, B1 heads to the near elbow and then bolts to the ballside block on the foul lane, awaiting an entry pass. Second, the other big player (B2) acts as the trailer and remains at the heels of B1. He or she stops at the periphery directly across from the ball handler. The roles of the big players are interchangeable.

The three perimeter players occupy predetermined sites. If the point guard must handle the ball, only two perimeter players are able to change positions. Using four exterior players and only one interior player is possible, but then the big player must fill the ballside box (no trailer option). The outside players rush to the four locations on the periphery.

Figure 9.3 shows the first two players on the fast break with the ball handler on the same side of the court. S1 and S2 are both caught on the right side. The player behind (S2) yells, "Through" to S1. S1 runs to the other side of the floor after hitting the near foul line extended and bolting to the closest block. The big players (B1 and B2) do their usual routines. B1 sprints to the ballside box, and B2 acts as the trailer.

If a big player is one of the first two players out on the break with the dribbler, several

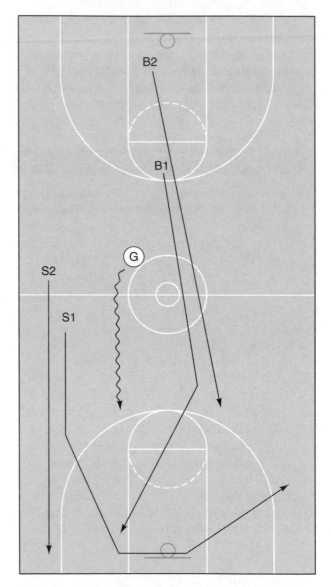

Figure 9.3 Two perimeter players out first are on the same side.

options are available. When the two are on alternate sides, the big player bolts to the ballside block (regular job). The other exterior player fills the lane the big player ran. If the post player is on the same side of the floor and behind the lead player, he or she yells, "Through" to send the perimeter player to the other side of the half-court. The post player executes his or her primary role and heads to the ballside box. The other outside player must adjust and fill the open territory in front of the internal player on the block. If the big player is leading, there is no through call. The post player just cuts to the ballside box on the lane (normal action), and the player behind stays on the outside. The other perimeter player occupies a vacant spot on the exterior away from the others. If players are doing their duty on the defensive glass, a circumstance should never develop in which both inside players are the first two out on the fast break.

When the first two players out on the fast break are perimeter players opposite each other and they are well ahead of the ball handler, they can cross at the basket or fake it before racing to locations on the periphery. Players communicate with each other when performing this option, which is available only under these circumstances.

When motion is complete to the other end of the floor, the team could enact a man-to-man or zone offense. The team needs to be able to start execution of the offense out of a two-out set with perimeters and posts situated as described. A number of actions are available to create scoring opportunities. For example, players start the motions associated with a passing game. Because passing-game offenses are rule oriented, players can begin execution from any positioning.

Another option is to run specific, quick-hitting maneuvers, such as the following:

• The squad reverses the ball using the trailer to the weakside, and the lead guard and trailer plant staggered screens for the shooter in the far corner to come to the top of the key. The big player in the low post follows the ball and posts up vigorously in anticipation of an entry pass.

• The shooter in the corner bolts off a baseline screen set by the low post as soon as the ball handler tosses the ball to the trailer. The shooter sprints over or below the screen to the opposite box. The screener steps to the ball after the shooter exploits the pick. The cutter can execute a fade back to the same corner for a skip-pass reception if his or her defender cheats over the screen too early.

• The trailer reverses the ball to the wing and moves to fix a screen for the pass recipient. They execute a two-player game. The remaining three players stay on the other side of the floor.

• The trailer sets a down screen for the shooter away from the ball handler. The pass goes to the player using the pick, who is darting to the top. On the pass across the key, the shooter in the corner runs the baseline to the opposite corner, using screens by each interior player. He or she can fade to return to the original corner or curl into the lane around the second screener.

• The weakside shooter establishes a back screen for the trailer who is being overplayed defensively. The ball handler attempts a lob or skip pass to the trailer. The screener steps out following his or her pick.

• The trailer transfers the ball on the reversal and then receives a back pick by either the ball handler or the shooter in the weakside corner. The player with the ball looks to lob to the weakside of the basket. The low post follows the ball and posts up strong on the ballside. The screener steps out after the screen is used.

Keys

Coaches must insist that players hustle to spots quickly. They have to pay a price by running the court hard. The leading big player always races to the ballside box on the foul lane. If he or she is not one of the first two players on the break, the post player lingers directly opposite the ball handler until they reach the three-point arc. Once at the three-point arc, the big player completes a diagonal cut to the far block. He or she is strong in the low post and works to gain position for an entry pass.

Peripheral players remain wide beyond the three-point line to create space. Perimeter players should glance inside. They deliver the ball to the low post whenever possible.

If a coach is committed to running the two-out break, he or she is obligated to equip the club with some type of scoring mechanism at its conclusion. A smooth transition into the chosen motion is required. Three possibilities are available: Execute a specific offense, start a passing game, or implement a precise sequence of movements designed to produce an acceptable shot.

The ball handler must understand that the team runs the break to either side of the court. He or she cannot lock into using only one side. Once the lead guard picks a side, he or she must stay there, but the player is not to choose the same side repeatedly.

Teams use the two-out break after turnovers, rebounds, and successful goals, which means they deploy it almost constantly. When used in conjunction with some kind of scoring action at the conclusion of the break, the resulting tempo is likely to be rather fast. If the coach deploys the two-out fast break, he or she has to be ready to commit to playing the game at a fast pace.

Initial instruction should use a five-on-none format. Players should begin in different places so that they can practice a variety of circumstances that could unfold when filling their break lanes and locations. The coach uses the no-defense method until he or she feels comfortable introducing defenders. The coach gradually adds defenders until the team is in a drill with four defenders and a chaser. Teaching the break in step fashion and within drill settings is the best way to develop correct execution of the play.

SIDELINE BREAK

An extensively used break similar to the two-out break is the sideline break. The major difference is that with the sideline break players favor one side of the floor. Players make a more determined effort to deliver the ball to the big player heading to the ballside block on the foul lane. The spots that players fill force the opposition to leave a lone defender on the weakside. Passes to the trailer are right at the center of the half-court, providing better access to teammates.

A team may use the sideline fast break as their primary method of running the floor or only if they need to play catch-up near the end of a game. A team does not deploy it periodically; they need to execute it consistently for an extended period. The team must be able to play at a fast pace. If the team overall lacks speed, the sideline break is not a good fit.

Personnel

The sideline fast break is designed to use three perimeter players and two big players, although it is possible to go with four exterior players and one inside player. The one interior player heading to the ballside low post needs to have strong scoring skills around the hoop. The trailer frequently must display sound passing and ballhandling skills and shoot effectively from outside. The sideline break is more productive if all three perimeter players are capable of shooting from distance. The break requires at least one solid ball handler.

Scoring

One big player may see scoring chances around the ballside block along the foul lane. The other post player might realize shooting opportunities near the top of the key. The ball handler attains shots from three-point range at the extended foul line or closer if part of a dribble penetration. The remaining two perimeter players acquire chances in the ballside corner or from various spots on the weakside of the court. Using additional motion at the end of the fast break creates an abundance of shot opportunities.

Execution

The sideline fast break is almost identical to the two-out break. The major differences are that the point guard dribbles to the foul line extended area instead of above the elbow and the trailer hustles to the top of the key instead of staying parallel with the ball handler. The player with the ball (G) heads to a starting position on either side of the court. One shooter (S1) runs to the corner below the ball. The other shooter (S2) sprints to the offside near the foul line extended behind the three-point arc. The three peripheral sites are interchangeable. Post players (B1 and B2) motor to the ballside box and trailer spots. The one in the lead occupies the block region (figure 9.4).

When the two lead people with the dribbler, both perimeter players, are on the same half of the court, the one behind yells, "Through" and the lead player races to the opposite perimeter location. The teammate behind assumes the

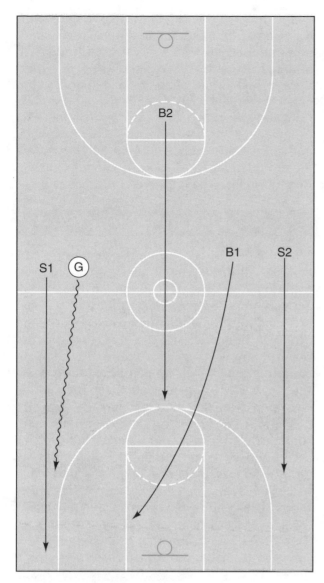

Figure 9.4 Sideline fast break lanes.

After players fill the five finishing spots, they must engage in motions that give them ways to score. For example, players initiate a man-to-man or zone offense that starts from the final set of the break. Actions should be limited so that transition is easy. A passing game offense is ideal because player motion is rule dictated and a precise starting formation is not necessary.

Another option is to initiate abbreviated, rapid movements designed to create specific shot attempts for certain players. The possibilities are more abundant against man-to-man defense than against zone. Here are some suggestions:

• The trailer sends the ball to an isolated wing. Players set staggered screens for the shooter in the weakside corner. The shooter bolts to the top of the key for a possible shot. The low-post player moves with the ball and pins the defender in the hope of receiving a post feed. A double screen could replace the staggered picks.

• The trailer reverses the ball to a wing and follows the pass to set a screen on the ball. Two-player game payoffs are in effect. The shooter with the ball dribbles toward the top of the key or baseline, based on the reaction of the defense. The big player has several choices after his or her screen is used. The big player can roll to the basket, roll early if appropriate, step back for a peripheral shot attempt, slip the screen, or yell, "Hot" to signal that the defense has switched and he or she has a mismatch. The defense dictates the selection. The low-post player does not move across the foul lane to follow the ball. This area must be void of people to allow enough room for the two-player game. After the screener moves to set the pick, the three players away from the action must work to draw the defenders' attention.

• The ball is passed to the trailer. The player in the corner cuts along the baseline, using a pick from the low post. He or she runs from corner to corner. The low post steps toward the ball after the cutter uses the screen. If no inside pass is available, the trailer rotates the ball. The big player low hustles to ballside at about midlane, anticipating an entry pass. The ball handler then back screens for the trailer (passer). The wing with the ball looks to throw a lob pass to the trailer on the weakside or to

last outlying position (either weakside wing or ballside corner). If the first two players on the same side of the court are a big player and a perimeter player, the post player must end at the strongside box. If the big player is in the background, he or she yells "Through," sending the perimeter player to the other side of the court. If the big player is in lead, the exterior player behind does not call, "Through" but simply fills the nearest external location. The second big player regularly hustles to the trailer location. The three perimeter players occupy three exterior slots. Whenever a big player is one of the first two out on a break, a perimeter player will lag behind. He or she races to the vacant slot on the periphery.

the screener stepping out. The ball handler must attain a proper angle for the back screen. His or her back points to the place where the teammate will be open. The timing of the back pick is important—it closely follows the reversal of the ball.

• The trailer tries to send the ball to an isolated wing. The wing executes a backdoor maneuver to the basket if the defense overplays him or her. The trailer completes a bounce pass for a layup if it is available. If the wing receives the pass from the trailer on the periphery, he or she can take a one-on-one chance. The low post does not flow across the lane to follow the ball.

Keys

The point guard (the ball handler) should use both sides of half-court. He or she mixes the starting point between right and left foul lines extended.

The first post player down the floor sprinting to the ballside block puts his or her baseline foot on or above the box. He or she is physical and actively tries to gain a position advantage. Staying above the block makes him or her more difficult to defend. The ball should go to the interior whenever viable.

This style of fast break is good after turnovers, defensive rebounds, and made baskets. Usually, use of a five-player fast break means that the team is dedicated to running whenever possible. Players need to realize that consistency of effort is important if they are to be an effective up-tempo team. A five-player fast break also provides a way to catch up, a way to score in a hurry when trailing late in a game. But allotting sufficient practice to the sideline break is difficult, though not impossible, if a squad uses it only when losing in the second half.

When choosing the action that the team will use at the conclusion of the break, the coach should consider the following. Will players become overloaded mentally if they have to learn too many variables combined with the break? Are all the defensive overplays that might occur accounted for? Is this break the most effective way to use the team's talents? Are the right personnel in the right positions to take advantage of the team's strengths? Is a smooth transition in place from the fast break to subsequent motions?

Teaching of the sideline break begins with a five-on-none format. The coach reviews all personnel combinations that could occur to initiate the fast break. When players can operate the fast break against no defenders, the coach gradually adds defense during practice, ultimately reaching a five-on-five situation. The progression starts by using two defenders back and one defensive chaser. Eventually, four players are on defense with one defender chasing. Repetition leads to improved performance.

ONE-OUT BREAK

The one-out break, a five-player method to achieve shots, is really an extension of the traditional fast break. The one-out fast break actively pursues screening situations as part of its action. Because numerous man-to-man offenses begin from a 1-2-2 formation, the one-out break enables a team to transform smoothly into a man-to-man offense. Because the playmaker brings the ball down the middle, weakside defensive help is minimal.

The one-out fast break is best versus man-to-man defense but also can be adapted to attack zones. Teams can use the one-out break after turnovers, defensive rebounds, and made baskets. Players must execute this break consistently. The coach who employs this particular five-player fast break wishes to play up-tempo. This break is not one that teams should use to come from behind. Good team speed is a necessity.

Personnel

To operate this break successfully, the team should have at least two solid outside scoring threats. The two interior players should be capable screeners, have some size and strength to post up, and be able to score around the hoop. The ball handler sees the entire floor so that he or she can make the best pass decisions. Personnel flexibility increases if all three perimeter players are good ball handlers, passers, and distance shooters. A team with only one decent outside shooter should not use the one-out fast break. This break is not conducive to using four perimeter players and only one big player. The three-out, two-in combination is mandatory.

Scoring

Two perimeter players catch bounce passes during their cuts to the goal, leading to layups. The big players seal their defenders and secure inside position to collect post feeds and subsequent scoring opportunities. Wings earn jump shots near three-point distance below the foul line extended. Shots within the foul lane develop after the curl around a down screen. The point guard shoots directly off the dribble as he or she breaks down the defender near the key. Several scoring alternatives develop from whatever action the coach decides to use after the fast break is over.

Execution

The point guard (G) dribbles at one of the elbows (the right one in figure 9.5). The coach decides whether the lead guard heads to either elbow or toward the center of the foul line. The lead guard should not have a choice. Regardless, he or she slides to the same-side elbow after making a pass to a wing.

The other two perimeter players (S1 and S2) are out wide toward the sidelines. At the foul line extended, they cut to their respective blocks and use the screens set by the big players (B1 and B2) to dart to beyond the three-point arc. S1 and S2 cross or fake it before coming off the screens. The post players (B1 and B2) also run their lanes wide to each sideline. Players who are not in possession of the ball never run in lanes anywhere near the center of the court. They are always wide and close to the sidelines.

Big players start to slash to the bucket at the foul line extended. Their focus is to establish screens by the boxes on the lane. In figure 9.5, two shooters (S1 and S2) cross low in the foul lane before using screens from B1 and B2. Timing is critical. Shooters cannot come off screens too early. When they see a big player at each sideline heading downward to the block, they must maintain their patience.

If a big player is out ahead of a peripheral player in the same lane, the big player V-cuts at the foul line extended and slices to the hoop. He or she works to gain an advantage over the defender along the lane. The trailing perimeter player runs to the near wing outside the three-point line. The ending spots are the same as those following the down screen.

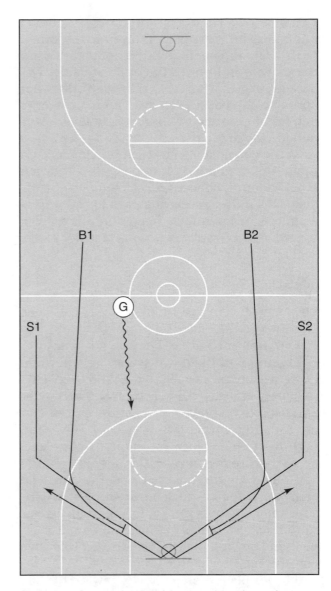

Figure 9.5 One-out fast break lanes and starting action.

When both perimeter players are on the same side of the floor, the one trailing yells, "Through" and sends a teammate to the other-side block on the lane. An identical scenario applies to two big players in the same running lane.

Three players could possibly be running the same alley of the full court. Therefore, someone yells, "Through," depending on whether there are two posts or two perimeter players. With two big players, the lone exterior player on the other side does not cut to the basket but remains on the wing. If a perimeter player is ahead of two post players, he or she races to the block on the other side of the lane. This enables him or her to use staggered screens set by the big players to fill the original-side wing.

When two shooters are scurrying down one side and post players are on the other, both trailing players yell, "Through" to send the players in front to the opposite side. The outside player who yells, "Through" does not sprint to the basket. Because no big player is behind him or her, the perimeter player stays outside the arc.

At the conclusion of the fast break, the team is in a 1-2-2 formation with a post player at each block. Scoring chances, because of the break, occur if a cutter receives a pass for a layup, if a shooter is open for a jump shot off a down screen, or if a big player is open at a block after sealing a defender.

Keys

Because players are running the same lanes (wide to each sideline), they must be at least 8 to 10 feet from each other. They do not tailgate.

Execution of the down screen is important. Players using picks need to wait and use V-cuts to set up screens. They rub off the pick tight and head to an open wing past the three-point arc, fade to a corner if the defender moves too high over the screen to maintain coverage, or curl around and over the screen into the lane when the defender is below the pick. The screener steps off the lane, creating space for a teammate to operate. For further details refer to the discussions of setting a screen, using a pick, and down screen in "Man-to-Man Offensive Fine-Tuning" in chapter 1 on page 4.

Interior players step directly toward the ball after their teammates use the screen, usually by pivoting on the foot nearest the foul line. They attempt to seal the defender on the tail or hip in anticipation of an entry pass. See the discussion of pinning the defender in "Man-to-Man Offensive Fine-Tuning" on page 7.

The point guard sees the entire half-court by keeping his or her head up. A pass could go to any of four teammates. Sound decision making is essential. The screening action near the boxes may also provide enough room for a dribble penetration and a potential shot.

Once the fast break is finished, the team must flow into some kind of scoring activity.

The coach has several choices. First, any offense or pattern performed from a 1-2-2 alignment or a 1-4 formation (post players simply go high once screens have been exploited) is a possibility. Another option is a passing game. There is no set sequence of motion. Players have freedom to decide their precise moves. Passing games are excellent complements to a fast break. Finally, the coach could devise some type of quick-hitting action that produces quality shots in a short period. For example, the point guard calls a post player up to the near elbow. The point guard passes to the post player whenever the defense aggressively denies the shooter on the same side of the court. The big player bounces a pass to the shooter, who executes a backdoor cut on the playmaker's release of the ball. Coaches can devise other types of quick hitters.

If the point guard (ball handler) is having difficulty with defensive pressure and the other four players are well in advance, the team must be patient. They wait for the lead guard to reach a delivery position before setting picks. The four players should coordinate their actions so that the ball handler initially has four pass alternatives. After the ball handler is in position, however, at least one side should be involved with the down screen.

Just because a team is running does not mean that they have to rush. Players remain under control and do not hurry through the down-screening action or any other motion.

To execute it persistently, the one-out fast break requires commitment from the coach and players. Breakdown drills centered on the down screen at the box are worthwhile. Initially, the team practices the fast break without defenders. The coach sets up scenarios, such as three players on one sideline, so that players know how to adjust to different personnel combinations and positioning. When the coach is confident in players' comprehension, he or she adds the defenders. With the one-out break it is best to work on defensive chasers only by using five-on-four. The coach selects which defender is to trail. This break has no separate trailer lane. Therefore, taking advantage of numbers happens only in three-on-two and two-on-one situations.

CHAPTER 10

Quick Hitters

Quick-hitting plays against man-to-man defense are an integral part of a well-rounded offensive arsenal. They enable a team to secure quality shots with a limited number of movements. Quick hitters also allow the team to garner specific types of shots and make it possible for the coach to control which team members receive chances. With the advent of the shot clock in the college game (and some high schools), swift-moving plays became a necessity. Although such plays usually manufacture shots quickly, at times they may reach a conclusion without producing a shot. I strongly encourage the use of a passing-game offense (chapter 1, page 3) in conjunction with quick hitters because no matter where personnel are positioned at the end of the play, an easy transition into a passing game is possible. Offenses that provide freedom of movement are significantly easier to get into than are those that require a precise formation before the start of any offensive movement.

The first section covers quick-hitting offenses designed for use against man-to-man defenses. Each offense in this section begins from a unique formation. The four plays have no common links. In contrast, the plays in the letter series all begin from a box set, and the plays in the motion series start from a 2-1-2 or 2-3 alignment. The major advantage of using multiple plays that start from a common set is that the

opponent has more difficulty recognizing what play the offensive team is going to execute. The initial formation itself reveals nothing about the pending movements.

With quick hitters I prefer to assign a number from 0 to 9 to each play. The coach can then call the offensive action using the two- or three-digit numbers. For example, play A is assigned the number 9 in two-digit format. Therefore, when the coach calls the number 19, 29, 39, and so forth, the players know to execute play A. The calling system makes it more difficult for opponents to know which play is coming. Letters are another effective calling method for quick hitters. Each play is named using a letter of the alphabet. For example, if play 1 is assigned the letter *M,* the coach calls out, "Montana," "Miami," or "Moravian" to instruct the squad to execute play 1. The coach can use any state, city, college, or university that begins with *M.* Quick hitters are limited movements designed to score quickly. Therefore, the opponent must not be able to gauge which play is coming just by the call. Although the plays in this chapter are given names, coaches should feel free to change the names as they wish or use the number or alphabet system to identify each play. (Although the alphabet system could conceivably use all 26 letters, realistically only 24 are possible—X and Z are tough!)

STARTING ALIGNMENTS

The offensive plays in this section do not use a common formation to initiate each play. Each play has a unique primary formation. Although the opponent will likely recognize each quick hitter by the set, the plays in this section have proved fruitful. The activities of the plays are difficult to defend. Sporadic deployment helps maintain their effectiveness. Each play features scoring opportunities for different players. An honest evaluation of a team's strengths and weaknesses helps determine which quick hitters a squad should use in its man-to-man attack. The coach should select plays that maximize the players' skills.

KENTUCKY

Kentucky was inspired by a play used by Rick Pitino at the University of Kentucky against man-to-man defense. Players begin away from the basket so that more room is available to thwart defensive pressure. The movements are not part of a continuous motion sequence. The team uses the play at the beginning of a possession and then employs a passing game for the remainder. Therefore, a coach must teach a freelance or rule-oriented offense so that a smooth transition into additional activity with a focus on scoring can occur after the Kentucky motion ends. The dynamics are complex compared with those of most of the other quick hitters in the chapter.

Personnel

Both post and perimeter players rely on basic basketball skills such as ballhandling, passing, and screening. The offense incorporates a variety of moves. All players must be able to score in the paint. Outside players, including the point guard, should be proficient exterior shooters because this play will produce shots.

Scoring

Although shots might arrive promptly, a good opportunity may take 15 seconds or longer. An abundance of shots may become available including perimeter jump shots, back-to-the-basket shots, layups off cuts to the basket, or jumpers off a dribble.

Execution

Kentucky is not a continuity offense. At the conclusion of the movements, the team executes a passing-game offense (see chapter 1, page 3). In many instances the passing game will be unnecessary. Quality shots may arise solely from the execution of Kentucky. Nevertheless, the team should be prepared to make a transition into a passing game.

The action begins from a 1-4 set. The lead guard begins at the top, one shooter is on each wing, and the big players are slightly above the elbows. The point guard (G) must communicate with teammates as he or she approaches position out front. The playmaker tells them which side should begin moving. One post player starts by setting a screen for his or her side wing, who is several feet above the foul line extended. The pick recipient cuts into the foul lane, anticipating a pass directly from the point guard. The ball handler delivers the ball if the cutter is open.

If the opening pass is not available to the shooter (S1) on the cut to the hoop, the point guard's second option is to throw the ball to B1, who steps out after screening (G to B1 in figure 10.1). The other three players (S1, B2, and S2) read the toss. On the pass, S1 pops out to a spot beyond the three-point line directly below the ball. The offside post player (B2) screens away for the near wing (S2), who cuts to the hoop. At same moment, the lead guard (G) begins to

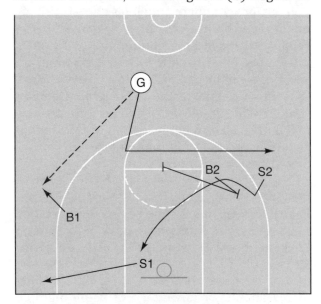

Figure 10.1   Pass to a post player at the start of Kentucky.

move straight down the lane. B2 sets a second pick for G as part of a flare maneuver.

B1 looks into S2 near the basket first (figure 10.2). If S2 is not open, the ball goes to either B2, who steps out after the pick, or to G as a result of the fade. Regardless, the ball should end up in the hands of the lead guard. Once the ball heads to G, S2 back screens for B1 to cut to the hoop and establish low-post position. B2 screens the screener (S2), who comes toward the top of the key for a shot attempt. After movements conclude, players begin executing a passing-game offense.

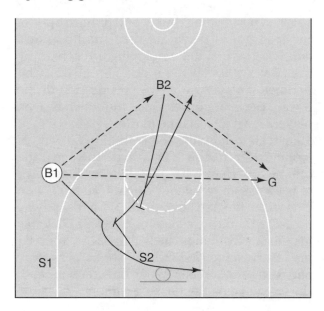

Figure 10.2 Post player reverses the ball to the point guard.

The next starting option out of the 1-4 set occurs when B1 does not catch the first pass. He or she quickly bolts to rescreen for S1. S1 gets free in the wing region by using B1's pick. After B2 sees S1 move out of the foul lane, he or she immediately goes to screen for S2 to cut into the lane.

When the post player throws the initial pass to the perimeter player who has exploited the rescreen, the big player posts strong along the ballside foul lane. Players make a concerted effort to get the ball inside. S2 stays near the offside block, while the point guard (G) bolts down the middle of the lane before receiving a flare screen by the other big player (B2).

The team again gets the ball to the playmaker (G) (figure 10.3), either with a skip pass or by tossing to B2 as B2 steps out above the top of

the key. B2 quickly reverses the ball to G. After the pass heads to the point guard (G), S1 drops to the same-side corner to clear away defensive help from the area above the foul line. S2 screens across for B1 to come to the ball. B1 can go over or under the pick. G checks out B1 on the interior. B2 moves down to screen the screener (S2). The toss to S2 may produce a score. Again, after completing these movements, the team begins to execute a passing game.

On one side of the floor, the post player picks for the near wing and pops out after screening. If the toss does not go to the post player stepping out, the big player initiates a rescreen. Players on the other side of the court perform the same steps but a half step behind. When a rescreen commences on one side, the back screen for the wing happens on the other. Therefore, the starting pass could go to a perimeter player who has used the rescreen or to an opposite post player who steps out after back screening. If neither player is open, then the rescreen on one side has yet to be completed. Figure 10.3 shows the action when the beginning pass heads to a perimeter player who just used the rescreen.

The playmaker might also throw the first pass to a post player who steps out before moving to screen for the wing. The playmaker uses this option if the defense aggressively denies the same-side wing. The playmaker delivers the ball to the post player nearest the defensive denial. The pass receiver looks over his or her outside

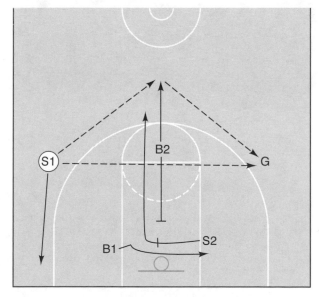

Figure 10.3 Perimeter player on one wing sends the ball to the point guard on the other wing.

shoulder to consider sending a bounce pass to the closest wing, who is performing a backdoor cut to the hoop. The wing ends on the opposite box. After tossing the ball to the high post, the point guard gradually moves straight down the middle of the lane to a spot low on the ballside. The lead guard must not be so quick that he or she interferes with the back cut by the wing and a potential layup, nor can the lead guard be too slow because he or she needs to vacate the area out front. The weakside wing (S2) receives a pick from the same-side post player (B2) and heads past the top of the key to a location above the player with the ball (B1).

S2 continues to cut over the top and receives a handoff from B1 (figure 10.4). S2 has the option to go one-on-one for a scoring chance. If S2 does not exercise the option, he or she becomes a passer. After the ball heads to S2, G establishes a back pick so that B1 can cut to the ballside low spot. At the same moment, B2 lands in the foul lane to achieve a proper screening angle for S1. S1 bolts off the screen to a region above the elbow opposite G. B2 sprints up to the foul line after screening.

If the wing (S2) sees that the inside big player (B1) is not open, S2 throws to the point guard (G), who pops back after the pick. B2, who is in the high post, moves to establish a screen for the ball handler (G). G dribbles off the screen away from the direction in which the pass was received. The offside shooter

(S1) reads G coming at him or her and tries to maintain proper spacing while staying toward the sideline. B1 slides across the lane to post up strong.

The lead guard can do one of the following:

1. Penetrate to the basket. B1 (the player low) adjusts position to give G an alley to drive.

2. Dribble penetrate and kick the ball out to the same-side shooter (S1).

3. Reverse the ball quickly to the exterior player (S1) directly in front.

When performing the second or third option, the lead guard fakes a cut to the hoop and fades to the offside, employing a rescreen by the player who set the pick-and-roll (B2). The perimeter player on the weakside (S2) drops toward the near corner. Once the action is over, players start a freelance motion.

Instead of handing the ball off to S2, who is looping over the top, B1 may pass to S1 near the other elbow (figure 10.5). S1 then dribbles down to get a passing angle for a post feed to B2 who cuts to the block. The passer (B1) screens away for S2, who did not receive the ball. S1 looks inside for B2 or flings the ball to S2 out front. B1 may also rescreen for S2. He or she screens away and then back screens. When these actions end, the team begins the passing game.

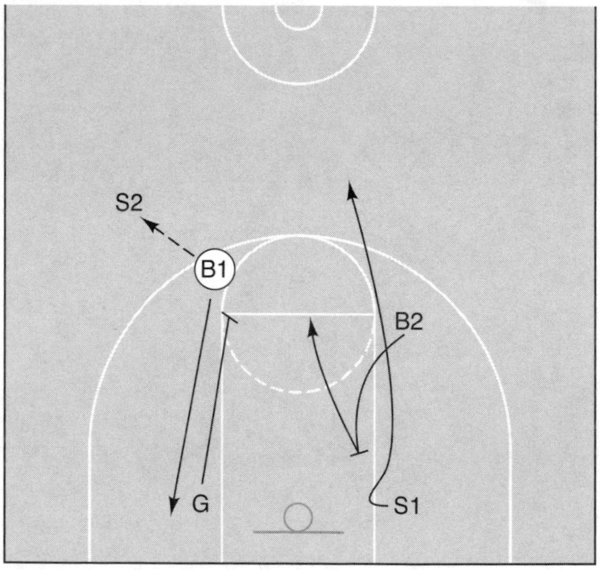

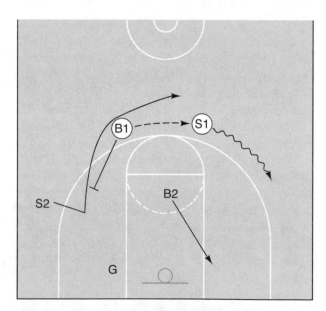

Figure 10.4   Big player hands off the ball to the perimeter player sliding over the top.

Figure 10.5   Big player passes across the top instead of handing off.

Keys

Refer to "Man-to-Man Offensive Fine-Tuning" on page 4 and these topics: screening between post and perimeter players, setting a screen, using a pick, rescreening, back pick, down screen, flare screen, and throwing the ball inside.

This offensive action takes a considerable amount of time to teach. As with any quick hitter, the coach must teach the passing game used in concert with Kentucky before teaching Kentucky. The coach may want to teach one step at a time. For example, the squad can practice what happens when the first pass goes to the post player who steps out after screening for a wing. Then they focus on the next step, when the initial pass heads to an exterior player at a wing after he or she receives a rescreen. This way the team learns each part before performing the whole. I highly recommend that the coach teach the whole set of options on a dummy (no defense) basis before placing the team live against a defense.

The point guard's first pass can go to the big player on either side who is stepping out before the main action begins to counter a denial of a wing, to the wing cutting to the hoop off a back pick, to the post player after the first screen is used, or to the wing after a rescreen. Team members must know the sequence triggered by each previous pass. The coach does not want mental breakdowns to materialize during execution of the offense.

Coordination of starting movements is essential. One post player screens for the wing on one side of the half-court. A rescreen occurs on that side concurrently with the other post screening for the wing on his or her side. Finally, a rescreen occurs on the second side. Action alternates.

The point guard must communicate with teammates (usually not orally) to designate a beginning side. The starting side can change each possession. The playmaker should visually relay the choice to the squad.

Proper spacing is vital. Wings in the 1-4 set are to be several feet above the foul line extended to create room for the initial screening progression.

The lead guard and nearer big player must be able to recognize an aggressive overplay on the wing when the team is in the 1-4 set. Players want to take advantage of any denial. If a post defender plays too aggressively while the team is in the 1-4 formation, a cut to the basket could result in a layup.

When the first pass connects with a post player in the 1-4 formation, the pass receiver looks for the backdoor cut by the same-side wing first, a handoff to the opposite wing moving out front above the ball second, and the perimeter player coming off a pick above the opposite elbow third.

The ball can be reversed with a skip pass or a quick pass to the top and then opposite. The faster the reversal occurs, the better.

When executing the two-player game at the top of the key, the post player does not roll to the basket. He or she steps back and focuses on a rescreen.

The coach should teach players all positions he or she may ask them to assume during competition. They need to practice those spots before the game. Any player who must know both post and perimeter positions has to concentrate on absorbing the offense as a whole. The point guard should know what everyone is doing. One of the point guard's roles is to take charge and get people to do what is expected of them.

OPEN

The open play was designed to have an extremely easy transition into the set and to provide a player with a chance to dribble penetrate to the hoop. Especially when a shot clock is in use, the coach must be able to isolate a player with the ball for a one-on-one opportunity when time is dwindling. Almost all coaches have some form of isolation play in their offensive arsenal against man-to-man defense. The open play is geared to an exceptional ball handler, but anyone who has the ability to go one-on-one can be effective using it. The coach can isolate a particular player for a one-on-one.

Personnel

The main ingredient is a player who is able to score off the dribble or create a scoring chance for a teammate. He or she needs strong one-on-one skills, the ability to penetrate with the dribble, and the knack of being able to read the defensive help. Completion of appropriate passes as the dribble penetration progresses is essential.

Scoring

The one-on-one action leads directly to a shot for the ball handler. Players create a variety of scoring chances using dribble penetration, which causes the defense to help. The ball handler kicks the ball out for a perimeter shot or dumps it off to a nearby teammate for a scoring chance close to the basket.

Execution

In figure 10.6, the half-court has been broken vertically into two sideline areas and one lane area. The horizontal division creates a region above the foul line extended and one below it. The four players without the ball use these divisions to get into position. In figure 10.6, the lead guard (G) with the ball is above the foul line and in the lane area. (Any of five players could be out front with the ball.) The other four players assume positions along the baseline, with the two biggest (B1 and B2 in figure 10.6) just off the boxes and the two perimeter shooters (S1 and S2) behind the three-point line about halfway between the baseline and the foul line extended on the sides.

When the play is called and the ball is above the foul line extended and in a sideline area, players without the ball move quickly to these locations: One shooter goes to the nearest

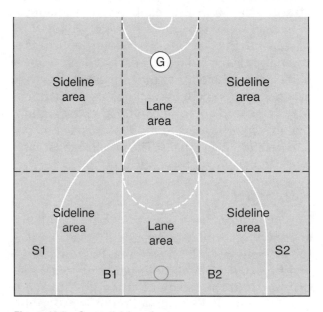

Figure 10.6 Court divisions for open.

corner; the second perimeter player hustles to the opposite sideline area behind the three-point arc and above the foul line extended; one post player sprints to the weakside block; and the fourth player (who could be post or perimeter) goes to the other sideline area inside the arc but still higher than the foul line. The ball handler now goes one-on-one.

If the ball is below the foul line extended on the perimeter in a sideline area when the play is called, the four players without the ball hurry to positions above the foul line extended in the ballside sideline region and the lane region. They create space for the ball handler to go one-on-one. They are not to occupy the weakside sideline region or any place below the foul line extended. Remember that any player could be in possession of the ball. The other four players follow the appropriate rules based on ball location.

Keys

The open play is a positive way to combat a shot clock close to expiring. Teams use it when the shot clock has fewer than 12 seconds remaining. Players should not panic when they notice the shot clock winding down. They must stay in control and should not force or rush shots. If it appears that a violation could happen, the coach yells, "Open!" The open call works best if it comes immediately after the desired ball handler receives a pass. The player with the ball when the coach makes the call gains a one-on-one chance. The player exhibits patience and waits for his or her teammates to clear to their assigned locations. The call is also helpful if a man-to-man offense has broken down and the team needs to establish order to gain a shot attempt.

Although most games at the high school level and in the lower grades do not use the shot clock, the open play is still a valuable aid. The play permits an outstanding individual player to showcase his or her skills. The coach calls the play when he or she wants a particular player to receive a one-on-one opportunity. Besides, the play is easy to teach, and players comprehend the rules rapidly.

Players must abide by the rules, which ensure maximum space for the ball handler. The four players without the ball move swiftly as soon as they hear the open call. The ball handler lets his or her teammates reach or draw near their designated sites before going one-on-one with the defender.

The coach chooses whether to allow the ball handler to give the open signal. The coach also can restrict the call option to selected players.

OPEN SPECIAL

Open special is a popular play that has seen widespread use in high schools and colleges. The motion is simple and rapidly executed. If the point guard is strong and one of the two big players is a solid inside scorer, those two players should carry out the pick-and-roll. Players assume their starting sites in a hurry. The play is useful when the coach has confidence in the two-player game and wants to produce a quality shot within 10 seconds.

Personnel

The play requires at least one post player who has the ability to screen and score around the hoop. The play works more effectively if the lead guard is a convincing external scoring threat and the other two perimeter players have expanded shooting ranges.

Scoring

The point guard might secure a 15- to 20-foot jump shot or possibly a layup. A perimeter scorer might get a chance at a three-point shot near a corner. A post player could become open while rolling to the basket for an inside shot. Another outside shooter may gain an opening around the top of the key for a jump shot.

Execution

Play begins with the point guard (G) handling the basketball above the top of the key. Post players (B1 and B2) are along the lane lines and above the elbows around the three-point arc. The other two perimeter players (S1 and S2) are in the corners (figure 10.7).

The playmaker (G) dribbles off the pick by either post player (B1 or B2). The playmaker pretends to go in one direction and then comes back in the other. The lead guard seeks to set up the defender to make the screen on the ball more potent. In figure 10.7, the ball handler (G) uses B1's pick. B1 rolls to the basket after G uses

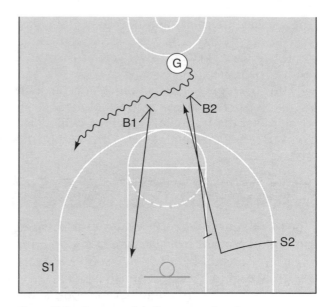

Figure 10.7 Open special alignment and motion.

the screen. The playmaker considers taking an outside shot, tossing to B1 as he or she rolls to the hoop, or instituting a dribble penetration and possibly flinging the ball to the shooter in the ballside corner (S1). After B1 begins to roll, the other post player (B2) bolts to establish a down screen for the shooter in the weakside corner (S2). This is the lead guard's final pass option—a peg to S2 for a distance jumper at the top of the key.

Keys

See "Man-to-Man Offensive Fine-Tuning" and the following topics: screening between post and perimeter players, setting a screen, slipping a screen, using a pick, and two-player game on page 4.

Both big players must remember that they are to act initially as screeners. They have to watch their spacing. Players cannot be too close to the foul lane or to one another. The lead guard convinces the defense that he or she is employing one pick but then uses the other. The guard must run the defender into a screener to start the two-player game.

The ballside shooter is prepared to receive a pass for a jump shot. He or she may have to move upward slightly from the corner.

The weakside post player times the down screen to coincide with his or her partner's roll to the hoop. The big player heads directly at the intended target (the defender on the shooter in the weakside corner) and becomes stationary just before contact. The weakside shooter waits for the down screen and discovers an open area above the foul line.

The coach may choose to instruct the point guard to use the pick of a specific post player. Otherwise, the lead guard decides which pick to use. He or she might need to dribble with the strong hand.

MINNESOTA

The few simple motions in Minnesota are based on one important premise: the point guard is an excellent ball handler and scorer. Players learn to react to specific defensive actions. The minimal movements manufacture good shots quickly. Minnesota creates scoring chances for the playmaker, a big player, or an outside shooter. The coach should situate personnel so that certain players receive opportunities to score.

Personnel

The lead guard should be a scorer. He or she needs to have an affinity for shooting the ball off the dribble and from 15 to 20 feet. A post player should be a potent interior scorer. The play also requires a shooter capable of hitting jump shots from near the top of the key.

Scoring

The point guard may have the chance for a dribble penetration on a cleared side of the floor, which could lead to a shot anywhere from 20 feet to as close as a layup. The post player rolling to the basket has inside scoring chances after screening for the player with the ball. A perimeter shooter may acquire a shot from the top of the key.

Execution

The team starts in a 1-4 high set with the point guard (G) out front and the other four players in a line across the free throw line extended. The big players (B1 and B2) are near the elbows, and the shooters (S1 and S2) occupy the wings (figure 10.8).

The play begins with one wing (S1 in figure 10.8) running to the offside block region. The lead

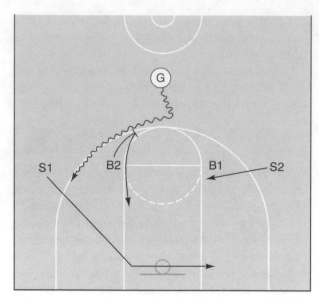

Figure 10.8 Minnesota set and beginning movements.

guard (G) uses a screen set by the post player (B2) on the side that the wing (S1) vacated. Players clear a side of the half-court to give the playmaker room to work. The weakside wing (S2) slides in next to B1 after the ball handler dribbles to the opposite side. The lead guard (G) considers taking a shot before looking to toss the ball to the big player (B2) rolling to the goal. If no defensive switch develops from the two-player game between G and B2, the two players at the weakside elbow race down to establish a double screen for the shooter who went through initially (S1). S1 heads to an open area near the top of the key. S1 is the third option for the playmaker.

When the defense switches during the two-player game, players want to take advantage of any mismatch. B2 wants the opposing point guard as his or her defender. Because offside defensive help should not be readily available, the two players (B1 and S2) near the weakside elbow plant a stationary double screen for S1 to use. B1 and S2 control the decision. They read what the defense did to counter the pick-and-roll and either set a stationary double pick or physically move down to double screen for the shooter directly below.

Keys

Refer to "Man-to-Man Offensive Fine-Tuning" and the following items: setting a screen, slipping a screen, using a pick, double screen, and two-player game on page 4.

The coach may want to place the most productive post player on the same side as the premier perimeter shooter in the initial 1-4 formation. The playmaker runs the play to their side. Alternatively, the coach may permit the lead guard to make the choice of sides.

The point guard communicates (nonverbally is best) with the wing in the 1-4, who is sent through to the box on the other side. The ball handler then fakes toward the big player away from the wing who vacated and then uses a screen by the other big player. The playmaker uses the pick to manufacture a shot on the cleared side of the floor.

The play features the point guard, who should be a strong one-on-one scorer.

The offside post and wing read the defense on the pick-and-roll and exercise a decision. They either remain stationary (if the defense switched the two-player game) or move downward (if they did not switch) to set a double screen for the perimeter player below.

LETTER SERIES

The quick-hitting plays included in the letter series start from a box set. Usually, post players arc positioned above the elbows on the foul lane not far from the three-point line and a perimeter shooter is positioned on each block. The point guard has the ball directly above the top of the key. Individual plays may feature a few exceptions to these positions, but movement into the starting formation begins from the box set. For the purpose of discussion, I have given all plays a name, which coaches are free to change. Recall that two- or three-digit numbers or letters are the preferred calling methods. The chapter contains a far greater number of plays than a team could possibly use in a season. Coaches should select the ones that best suit their personnel, accent their teams' strengths, and set up the appropriate players for scoring opportunities.

A considerable number of plays in this section show the play being initiated in one direction (normally to the right). Movement may also begin by going to the other side of the half-court. Of course, action that heads toward the opposite side will highlight different players. The diagrams may imply that N (the player whose name is called) can only be S1, but that is not so. The coach can call the name of the other shooter (S2). The lead guard (G) could also assume a shooter's role if one of the other perimeter players takes over the ballhandling chores. If the play is for a big player, the coach calls either B1 or B2.

LETTER

Coaches use the letter play to take advantage of a post player who has good jumping ability. The play can provide a large psychological lift by highlighting the athletic prowess of a big player.

Personnel

The post player in B1's position should have size and good jumping ability. He or she has to be able to take advantage of a lob. The point guard throws an effective lob pass toward the weakside corner of the backboard. The play is more effective if the perimeter player setting the back pick is a scoring threat from the outside. The big player coming to the ballside post needs to score inside.

Scoring

If the on-the-ball screen is effective, the lead guard will be open for a shot. The post player cutting to the basket on the weakside grabs the lob for a layup or dunk. The other big player gains an interior shot with a post-up. The player setting the back screen shoots an exterior jumper.

Execution

Players begin in box formation with big players high and shooters low. The point guard (G) dribbles off the screen set by the post player (B1), who will be set up for a lob pass (figure 10.9). If the defense switches or traps, there is no pick on the ball. On the ball handler's dribble, the shooter on the ballside block (S1) pops out to the near corner while the opposite post player (B2) slices hard to attain inside position just off the lane on the ballside. The point guard must read the defense and make the proper decision. After B2 crosses the middle of the foul lane on his or her cut, S2 races up to plant a

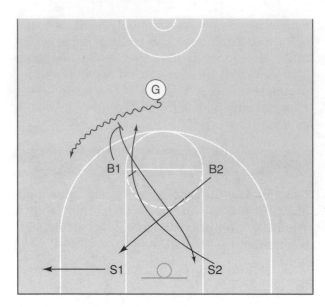

Figure 10.9 Letter play beginning.

back screen for B1. B1 bolts to the weakside of the hoop. S2 pops out after screening. The lead guard can throw a lob to B1, toss directly to B2 if the defender cheats to provide help against the lob, or cast the ball to the screener (S2) who is stepping out.

Keys

See the sections about setting a screen, using a pick, two-player game, and back pick in "Man-to-Man Offensive Fine-Tuning" in chapter 1 on page 4.

One post player hustles to the ballside low post as the lead guard dribbles off the other big player. The cutter gives a target and actively calls for the ball. He or she works to gain an advantage inside.

The coach can elect to drill the back pick execution separately as a breakdown drill.

The point guard can shoot, pass to the ballside interior, toss a lob at the weakside of the basket, or pass to the back screener for a trey attempt. The lead guard must be capable of throwing a weakside lob pass and should practice its execution. The methodology is similar to that used for a shot—hit a target with some arc.

LETTER FOR NAME

Letter for name is a popular quick hitter widely employed throughout the country. It was one of the first that I regularly included in my offensive program. The focus of the play is the exterior shooter whose name is called. The coach must be confident in the named player's ability to knock down a shot from beyond 17 feet.

Personnel

The featured player must be an excellent perimeter shooter. The play works more profitably if the other perimeter player is effective at obtaining position along the ballside foul lane and can score with his or her back to the basket.

Scoring

The perimeter player low along the foul lane posts up and could receive an interior shot. The designated shooter breaks free around the top of the key for a jump shot.

Execution

The team begins in a box set with post players on top and shooters low. The lead guard dribbles to the side of the floor where the named person (N) is situated (figure 10.10). When the ball handler reaches the foul line extended, N screens away for the player on the opposite box (S2). S2 darts high or low to move to a strongside low location. The playmaker's first choice is to toss the ball to S2. After picking for S2, N uses the double screen set by B1 and B2 to get free at the top of the key.

The point guard may dribble to the side away from the named player. The only adjustment is

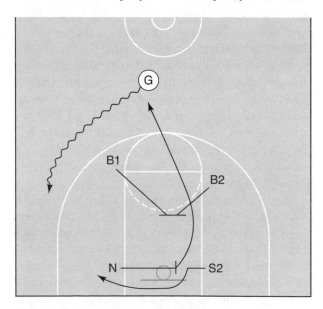

Figure 10.10 Letter for name action.

that S2 fakes the low exchange with N and slides back ballside low looking for a post feed. N acts as though he or she will use the low exchange but sprints to the top while using the twin pick set by the big players. B1 and B2 screen for the named player (N) regardless of which side the ball handler goes.

Keys

Refer to "Man-to-Man Offensive Fine-Tuning" on page 4 and these topics: setting a screen, using a pick, and double screen.

The point guard views the interior first, keeping his or her head up to see if a pass to the player coming to the ballside block on the lane is possible.

The low exchange move by N and S2 does not involve any seal back by the screener. The player coming off the screen steps high and goes low or vice versa but always ends just above the strongside block. Players must pay attention to details. The perimeter player at ballside low knows how to gain a position advantage. He or she supplies a target to the player with the ball, maintains a wide base, and uses his or her body to shield the defender.

The big players stay together and do not allow a defender to split them. They go right at the targeted defender, becoming still just before contact. Post players pick the appropriate defender. The defense may switch the low exchange.

The point guard starts play by dribbling toward either wing. Other team members react to the lead guard's actions.

CORNER FOR NAME

The corner for name action is a variation of the letter for name play. The activity is best when coupled with the letter for name call. The coach wants the ball in the hands of the main outside shooter or a particular big player near the hoop. The coach calls the play by yelling, "Corner" and then the highlighted player's first name or nickname.

Personnel

The primary shooter must be an excellent perimeter scorer. An effective inside-scoring post player is also desirable. Having a secondary shooter who is a three-point threat is a plus.

Scoring

The secondary shooter could possibly gain shot attempts along the baseline. The primary shooter receives chances near the top of the key. One post player secures shots low along the foul lane.

Execution

The called player is in position N (figure 10.10, page 158). The team performs the same movements that they do in letter for name with one notable exception. In figure 10.10, S2 rubs off the cross screen and does not stop at the ballside block. He or she sprints to the strongside corner. The point guard dribbles to the wing on the same side as N. N still comes up top after using the double screen set by B1 and B2. The lead guard first looks to S2 to see if he or she is open for a quality shot. The lead guard then looks to N close to the top of the key. One action added to the play is not shown in figure 10.10. After N uses the double pick set by the big players, the one nearer the ball (B1) steps down and in to screen so that B2 can glide over the top toward the ball. The interior pass to B2 could come directly from the lead guard or via S2, who is stationed in the corner. S2 and N are considered for shots if they become significantly free from their defenders. Otherwise, attention turns to the post players. Even if the point guard passes to N at the top, the big players execute the twist. The only difference might be that B2 picks for B1. N's position when he or she receives the pass determines the screener. The big players always perform the action so that the one using the screen is able to dart over the top toward the ball.

Keys

See the following topics in "Man-to-Man Offensive Fine-Tuning" in chapter 1 (page 4): setting a screen, using a pick, cross screen, throwing the ball inside, and twist move.

The player coming off the cross screen bolts to the corner. He or she is ready to shoot a jumper from the baseline if the maneuver hangs up the defender.

The point guard makes appropriate decisions and stays patient. He or she often waits for an inside scoring opportunity to develop through the twist of the big players. Perimeter players send the ball inside whenever possible, but two potential long distance shots—from the corner and from the top of the key—can develop before the twist move by the post players. The coach needs to let players know if they are cleared to take the shots.

The two people being highlighted (N and B2) are diagonal to each other in the beginning box alignment. If the playmaker dribbles to the other side of the floor, S2 and B1 are the featured players. If the team's personnel is roughly equal in skills, then going in either direction is beneficial. When the coach wants to feature one particular shooter and one big player, the lead guard heads to N's side nearly 100 percent of the time.

POST

The simple motion in the post play sends the ball inside to a specific post player. I used the post play regularly throughout my coaching career. This quick hitter is a good choice if the coach desires to involve the best interior scorer in the point production. The post play is a fast and easy way to get the ball inside against man-to-man defense.

Personnel

The play is designed primarily for an effective inside scoring post player. The play produces better results if the shooter running out top is a serious three-point threat.

Scoring

The ball handler looks inside to a big player first. The shooter coming to the top for a possible shot is the second target. If a screen is set on the ball, a scoring chance for the point guard may arise off the dribble.

Execution

The lead guard (G) dribbles to either wing to begin the play (figure 10.11). Just before reaching the foul line extended, the ballside low shooter (S1) screens on the diagonal for the post player (B2). The first pass option is to the big player (B2) posting up low. The other big player (B1) must time the screen of the screener (S1) to avoid interfering with B2's cut. The point guard's next choice is a pass to the shooter (S1) dashing up toward the top of the

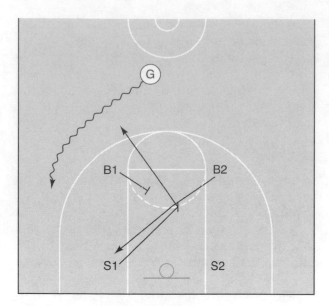

Figure 10.11 Post play alignment and motion.

key. If the coach elects to do so, the ballside post (B1) can set a pick for the ball handler at the beginning of the offense. The coach may prefer this alternative if the point guard is a quality scorer. The screen on the ball is not used when the defense is trapping the two-player game or if they are switching it.

Keys

Refer to "Man-to-Man Offensive Fine-Tuning" on page 4 and the discussions of setting a screen, using a pick, and throwing the ball inside.

Players know that the big player hustling to the ballside box on the lane is the primary target.

When the team runs the play to the other side of the half-court, the other perimeter shooter (S2) and big player (B1) are the featured players. The coach tells the point guard which side of the floor is likely to be the most productive. The ball handler heads that way on crucial possessions.

The timing of the screen for the screener demands that the ballside post player does not move until after the other post player slices to the basket off the initial diagonal pick.

POST CORNER

Combining certain quick hitters will often raise the effectiveness of both patterns. Post and post corner are complementary plays. After a team learns one, they can learn the other within minutes.

Personnel

A big player needs to be a potent inside scorer. One outstanding perimeter shooter is necessary, and a second one is a major plus.

Scoring

The big player shoots from a block on the foul lane. The exterior shooter acquires jumpers close to the top of the key. Another shooter receives chances in the strongside corner.

Execution

The play adds one motion to what is shown in figure 10.11 (page 160). The shooter on the weakside box (S2) races to the ballside corner. He or she reads the point guard's direction and moves immediately. When S2 reaches a spot near S1, S1 bolts to set a diagonal pick for B2. B1 (the ballside post player) properly times the pick of the screener (S1). The lead guard reads the defense. B2 is the primary target. The playmaker may pass to S2 in the corner for a shot, or S2 can deliver the ball inside to B2. The shooter (S1) hustles out front for a three-pointer as a final scoring option.

Keys

All keys associated with the post play are relevant for post corner.

Coaches will find it easier to teach this play to go only one direction. Otherwise, players have to key off the point guard's direction. The point guard can help the situation by identifying which shooter is to run to the opposite corner. Nonverbal communication is preferred. The designation should occur while the ball is straight up top. The runner starts as the ball handler begins to dribble to the wing. The lead guard learns to read defenders, especially the defender on the player coming to the strongside corner. If the defender sloughs toward the lane, the pass should go to the corner.

LETTER TWO-DIGIT NUMBER

In my last few years at King's College, I put together the movements for the letter two-digit

number play and used it frequently. The play produced some critical scores. In many cases, my team performed only the initial actions to secure a quality scoring chance near the hoop. Whenever the coach wishes to get the ball to the premier big player by the basket, this quick hitter is an appropriate choice. The action of the play continues so that other scoring moments might develop if the activity at the beginning does not fulfill its goal. To call the play, the coach yells, "Letter" and then any two-digit number.

Personnel

A go-to type of shooter is a necessity. At least one of the big players should be an excellent inside scorer. Ideally, both post players are equally effective.

Scoring

The big player cutting to the basket gains inside shots. The primary shooter receives shots near the basket or from the wing. Either post player may score from the low post.

Execution

Play begins with the big player (B1) popping out on a 45-degree angle to receive a pass from the lead guard. Immediately after making the pass, the point guard (G) sprints to the weakside block through the center of the foul lane (figure

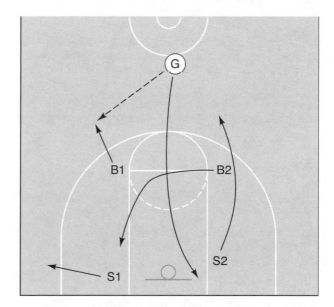

Figure 10.12 Letter two-digit number setup and starting movements.

10.12). The opposite post player (B2) dives to the hoop on the ballside by rubbing off G's tail. Some contact between the two may occur. When the play is called, the shooter (S1) on the same side as the big player who catches the initial pass hustles to the near corner to open the lane for B2's cut. B1 delivers the ball to B2 if possible. As the playmaker dives, S2 heads to a position opposite the ball handler (B1) to clear the area around the hoop further.

The playmaker (G) moves to the weakside periphery beyond the three-point line (figure 10.13). If B1 cannot complete a pass to B2, he or she throws the ball across to S2. S2 must get open to receive the ball. The pass to S2 signals S1 to use B2's baseline screen to motor into the lane. S2 may toss the ball to the interior if S1 is open. If S1 does not get the ball in the lane, he or she quickly reverses direction and uses the double screen set by the post players (B1 and B2). The passer (B1) fixes a screen with B2 after flinging the ball to S2. If S2 cannot send the ball to S1, S2 looks into the lane and the big players, who are performing a twist. The player nearer the ball handler (B1) steps down to pick for B2 so that B2 can race over the top of the screen toward the ball handler. If the pass goes to S1 but no scoring chance is available, the big players still execute a twist except that B2 screens in for B1 so that B1 can glide over the top to the ball. Therefore, regardless of who possesses the ball, the post players execute a twist.

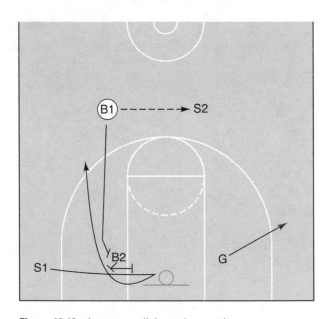

Figure 10.13   Letter two-digit number continues.

Keys

See the segments on screening between post and perimeter players, setting a screen, slipping a screen, using a pick, rescreening, double screen, throwing the ball inside, and twist move in "Man-to-Man Offensive Fine-Tuning" in chapter 1 on page 4.

The coach may want to restrict the initial toss by designating a big player to catch the first pass from the playmaker rather than letting the point guard decide which of the two receives the ball. If the lead guard can throw the first pass to either big player, he or she has to communicate effectively with teammates, especially the intended receiver. The shooter below pops out to the corner at the same time the big player steps out to receive the toss from the playmaker. When the play heads to the other side, it features different post and perimeter players.

When positioning posts and choosing sides, the coach should take into account the dominant hand of the post player cutting off the lead guard's tail. For example, in the previous diagrams B2 is right-handed. If the play goes to the other side, it is beneficial if B2 is a lefty.

The main shooter sells the baseline cut into the foul lane before coming back out for a perimeter shot set up by the double screen of the big players. The play creates sound scoring chances for an excellent outside shooter if the big player initially going to the hoop is not open.

The twist by the post players is an effective means of producing a score. Either big player can slide over his or her teammate to the ball, based on ball location. Big players adjust to the position of the ball so that the teammate sliding over is always heading toward the ball.

ISO

One of the teams in the Middle Atlantic Conference (of which King's College was a member) used the iso play with positive results against its opponents, including my squads at King's. I liked it so much that I soon began to use it with my players.

The coach has to have great confidence in the lead guard's ability to drive to the hoop and create a shot for him- or herself or for a teammate. The quickness of the lead guard is a definite factor when determining whether the play fits a team. Other players must have the ability to score as a result of specific motion alternatives.

Personnel

The iso play demands a quick point guard who has the ability to penetrate to the basket. The lead guard who can use either hand successfully increases the productivity of the play. An outstanding three-point shooter is placed at the ballside corner. The other exterior player also should be a productive outside scorer. At least one of the two post players needs to be an inside-scoring threat.

Scoring

The point guard penetrates to the basket with the dribble. He or she kicks the ball out to the primary shooter for a three-point shot. The secondary shooter may receive shots near the basket or on the perimeter. One big player scores from a post-up situation.

Execution

As soon as the iso play is called, players motor to their spots from the normal box set (figure 10.14). The ballside big player (B1) slides over to stack with a partner (B2). The primary shooter (S1) pops out to the strongside wing, while the other exterior player (S2) sprints to a site behind the two big players. (In this case, I am assuming that the point guard is right-handed.)

Players clear the lane for the lead guard to dribble penetrate with his or her strong hand. If the playmaker can take the ball all the way to the hoop, he or she does so. The lead guard (G) could also penetrate and then pass the ball to the nearest shooter (S1) on the exterior (figure 10.14). If S1's defender moves to help stop the penetration, S1 may have an opening for a three-point shot. If S1 does not shoot the basketball, the point guard (G) continues to move through the foul lane to the periphery near the weakside corner. S2 has been hiding behind the two big players (B2 and B1) above the weakside elbow. After the lead guard releases the pass, S2 curls around the two post players to look for an opening. The open area might be near the basket or on the strongside periphery. The next scoring alternative is for S1 to toss to S2 for a shot.

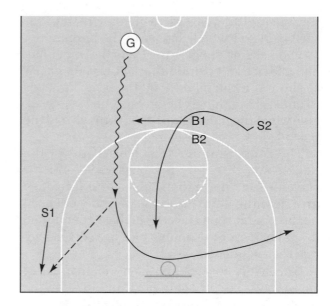

Figure 10.14   Iso play formation and one movement option.

Iso offers a second motion choice. The lead guard (G) can choose not to run through the lane to the offside but instead fake the action and pop upward to screen for the big player who is closer to the hoop (B2). B2 dives to the basket and establishes position at the ballside low post in anticipation of a post feed from S1. The screener (G) heads to the offside wing after B2 uses the pick. The other post player (B1) sets a single screen for the offside player (S2) to use to gain an opening near the ballside elbow for a possible shot.

Keys

Refer to "Man-to-Man Offensive Fine-Tuning" on page 4 and these topics: screening between post and perimeter players, setting a screen, slipping a screen, using a pick, rescreening, double screen, and throwing the ball inside.

The point guard's dominant hand dictates which post player evacuates his or her position. If the point guard is right-handed, the player to the playmaker's right slides over. If the point guard is a lefty, the player on the left darts to the other side. One outside shooter is always behind the arc and directly below the big player who moves. The team clears an alley for the ball handler.

The lead guard must recognize the desirability of penetrating to create a scoring chance. If the point guard kicks a pass out to the shooter, he or she mixes movements, either cutting through the lane to the weakside wing or screening for the big player who is closer to the hoop.

The ballside shooter (S1) sets his or her feet and slides to a position that allows him or her to shoot the ball directly off the pass. S1 needs to understand that a one-on-one chance is available when the point guard goes through and the ballside low post is vacant.

The other shooter (S2) learns to use the double screen set by the post players. He or she hides and darts to the ballside and an open area near the hoop or on the periphery. If need be, he or she runs toward the basket and then loops back over the double pick in a screen-and-rescreen sequence.

Big players must establish an effective double screen and adjust their positions to free the hidden shooter. One big player is ready to exploit a screen from the lead guard if it materializes.

LETTER SPREAD

The main formation is an expanded box. I simply put together a few scoring methods that I found fruitful over the years and created the letter spread play. Generally, the exterior players gain the bulk of the shots. The emphasis is on executing a trio of screening activities.

Personnel

Big players need to be effective screeners as well as inside-scoring threats with a posting action. The lead guard is obliged to have quickness and an ability to penetrate. Having two good outside shooters is also beneficial.

Scoring

The point guard's dribble penetration may lead to a score. Two shooters may get free for perimeter shots from a wing or corner region or for shots from the top of the key. A big player uses back-to-the-basket actions for scores.

Execution

Players begin in normal box alignment. When the letter spread play is called, they stretch out the box set. Big players hustle out past the top of the key and establish picks on each side of the floor for the playmaker. The two exterior shooters race out to the corners. The point guard (G)

exploits a screen provided by either big player (G has already used B1 in figure 10.15). G tries to dribble penetrate to the basket if possible. The playmaker might also see a kick-out opportunity to the near shooter if S1's or S2's defenders come off to help stop the drive. The post player (B1) setting the pick on the ball always steps back after the pick is used. He or she does not roll to the hoop. The point guard (G) sends the pass back to the screener (B1) (figure 10.15). The opposite shooter (S2) immediately moves into the lane. After B1 grasps the ball, he or she dribbles to the other side of the court at B2. B2 and S2 execute a down pick, and then B2 posts up by the lane. Remember that the screener (B2) steps to the ball after the pick is used. S2 does an outstanding job of setting up and exploiting the down pick.

After B1 throws the ball to the shooter coming off the down screen (S2), B1 establishes staggered screens with the point guard (G) for the shooter below (S1). G picks first. The big player (B1) screens last. S2 may have a shot as a result of the down screen, a post feed into the big player posting low (B2), or a toss to the shooter (S1) darting toward the top of the key as a result of the staggered picks.

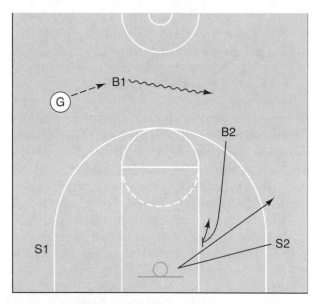

Figure 10.15 Letter spread play.

Keys

The point guard heads to the basket off the initial screen on the ball whenever possible. He or she needs to recognize when an opening exists while coming off the big player's screen. The big players must remember that they are not to roll to the hoop in this particular play. They always step out after the dribbler rubs off the pick.

The weakside shooter may find it difficult to sprint into the foul lane consistently when the lead guard throws the ball back to the opposite big player. The player may have a tendency to forget or may try to shortcut the action. The coach should insist that the player move into the lane every time. The player places both feet in the foul lane and waits for the approaching down screen.

The execution of the down screen is important. See the discussion of the down screen in "Man-to-Man Offensive Fine-Tuning" in chapter 1 (page 4). Other topics of interest are screening between post and perimeter players, setting a screen, slipping a screen, using a pick, two-player game, and throwing the ball inside.

Staggered screens are an effective way to secure shots for an outstanding outside shooter. The second screener (a big player) targets the proper defender. He or she is aware that the defense may switch during pick number one.

The point guard exhibits some patience. He or she allows other players to reach their starting locations. The floor is spread before beginning the motion.

HIGH

To isolate the best big player for potential scoring close to the hoop, the movements in the high play work well. The high play quickly became one of my favorite ways to deliver the ball to the premier post player.

Personnel

The play requires a strong inside-scoring threat, who will receive the ball on the interior. Ideally, the other post player can shoot effectively from 15 to 20 feet. Players in shooting positions should be three-point shooters.

Scoring

A big player receives the ball 5 to 10 feet from the hoop for a shot. The other post player may have 15- to 20-foot jump shots. Either outside shooter may attempt corner jumpers.

Execution

Players start in box formation. The point guard (G) dribbles to the side opposite the highlighted post player. (In figure 10.16, G dribbles to B1's side.) At the same time, the two shooters (S1 and S2) dart out beyond the three-point line in their respective corners. B2 screens so that B1 can get into position opposite the lead guard to receive the first pass. The pass goes to B1 out front (the toss has already taken place in figure 10.16). B2 takes the defender down into the foul lane and pins the defender on his or her back. B2 looks for a pass from B1. B1 could throw directly into B2 or could cast the ball to either shooter if their defenders are sagging too far into the lane. The shooters are ready for three-point shots or post feeds to B2.

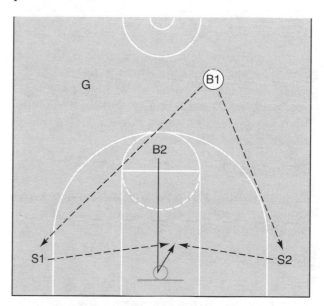

Figure 10.16 High play basic motion.

Keys

Big players should learn the art of sealing a defender. The player looking to gain possession of the ball inside walks the defender down into the foul lane. See the discussion of pinning the defender in "Man-to-Man Offensive Fine-Tuning" on page 7. The segment on page 6 about throwing the ball inside is also relevant.

The other post player must be adept at feeding the ball to the interior. He or she cannot let the defender back off and clog the passing lane. The player is prepared to take and make shots if the opposition gives little respect. At the least, the player dribbles at the defender to force the defender to play the ball and abandon giving help.

Big players with the ball out front must read the defense and respond appropriately. Big players need to recognize where the shooters' defenders are stationed and how the opponent is playing the other big player. They pass away from the defense, not to the offense.

The point guard needs to know if the coach wants one particular post player to work down low. The lead guard's dribble determines the featured player. The lead guard heads away from the preferred big player. If the two big players are of equal talent and skills, the lead guard should be free to choose who the featured player will be.

HIGH OVERLOAD

The high overload play is a variation of the high play. The same basic premise is behind both. When complemented with the high play, high overload supplies alternative action to accomplish the same goal—a toss inside. In this case, players clear half of the court.

Personnel

An outstanding inside scorer is a requirement. The other post player should be an effective shooter from at least 15 feet.

Scoring

One big player receives the ball 5 to 10 feet from the basket for inside scoring chances. The other post player shoots the ball from 15 to 20 feet away.

Execution

The starting method is the same as that used for the high play, but both shooters (S1 and S2) motor to the same side of the court instead of opposite corners. One is at the foul line extended (S1), and the other is in the corner (S2). They move in the same direction as the point guard (G). B2 is the featured player around the basket (in figure 10.16, S2 would be on the same side as S1). One side is cleared; B2 uses the space to pin the defender. The post player away from the dribbler (B2) picks for B1. G passes the ball to B1 out top (already accomplished in figure 10.16).

B1 cannot hesitate to dribble to the open side to improve the passing angle into B2.

Keys

The same keys that were outlined in the high play are in effect for high overload.

The other post player must be able to feed the ball to the interior effectively as well as keep the defense honest by sticking 15-foot jumpers. He or she dribbles at the defender if the defender is sagging into the passing lanes low. The player puts the ball on the floor to achieve a better angle for the inside pass.

Two shooters are on the same side of the floor to remove defensive help from the lane. If one or both of their defenders sloughs into the lane, the ball handler flings the ball to an open teammate for a shot. The two shooters make the defense pay for ignoring them. The coach may instruct the three peripheral players without the ball to engage in some type of activity to keep the defense occupied.

LOW

The low motion was devised solely to incorporate the duck-in action into the box alignment series. Low is a good way to begin the execution of a passing game offense. The movements conclude swiftly. The motion is useful if the coach wants to get the ball to a specific post player or a primary distance shooter.

Personnel

One good three-point shooter is preferred. One post player should be a productive scorer around the basket. The lead guard must be able to shoot the ball from the outside.

Scoring

The down screen movement allows one perimeter player to pop open for a jump shot. Both big players engage in post-up situations. The other shooter may have an exterior jump shot.

Execution

Players begin in a box set. The point guard (G in figure 10.17) passes to the big player (B1) who popped out to the wing. G then races to the basket, ending at the weakside block on the

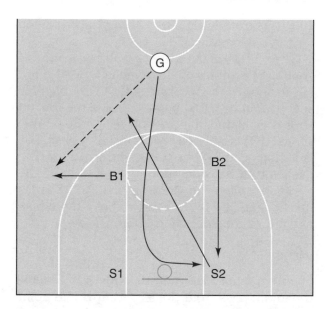

Figure 10.17 Low play alignment and beginning motion.

lane. At the same time, S2 moves toward the top of the key to receive the next pass. S2 is careful not to run too close to G. The two defenders are encouraged not to switch. The opposite post player (B2) drops toward the weakside box.

B1 passes the ball to S2 above the key. S2 dribbles opposite. On the pass, B1 screens down for S1. S1 should be a solid perimeter shooter. Simultaneously, the point guard (G) moves to position near the foul line extended behind the three-point arc on the other side of the court. Meanwhile, B2 ducks into the foul lane to receive an entry pass. S2 can toss the ball to S1 for a jump shot or to B1 on the interior. B1 steps to the ball after S1 uses the screen. S2 may also pass directly into B2 or to G, who would then look inside to B2.

Keys

The point guard knows which post player is to receive the duck-in opportunity. He or she initiates the play by tossing the ball to the other big player.

Refer to the section on the down screen in "Man-to-Man Offensive Fine-Tuning" in chapter 1 (page 4) for important tips. In this case, no curl option is available. Other relevant topics are setting a screen, using a pick, throwing the ball inside, and duck-in.

The weakside shooter must get open near the top of the key to receive the second pass. The player maintains enough space with the lead guard so that a defensive switch cannot take place. The point guard races to the weakside periphery behind the three-point line when the second pass heads out top.

The perimeter player out front with the ball reads the defense as the down screen and duck-in happen. If the defender on the big player who is ducking in is on the topside, the ball may need to be reversed to the point guard for the post feed. Players use the dribble to achieve proper passing angles. The ball handler at the top also views the down-pick action for a potential pass recipient.

WING

I developed the wing play to include one of my favorite scoring motions with the box formation. Coaches at all levels of play use the movements. This quick hitter provides a format to put a two-player game into effect rapidly. The play is especially useful if the coach wants specific big and exterior players to perform the pick-and-roll.

Personnel

The point guard must be an outside-scoring threat. One shooter, especially one who can effectively work off the dribble, is required. Big players must be capable of scoring around the basket.

Scoring

The point guard darts to the basket and may receive the ball for a layup. When the two-player game begins, the ball handler may see shots off the dribble or the big player may catch the ball while rolling to the hoop. Exterior jump shots for the point guard may occur because of a double pick. Big players may secure shots with post-up opportunities.

Execution

The team begins in the normal box formation (figure 10.18). To start the play, both shooters (S1 and S2) move to their respective wings. The pass goes to one of them (S1 in figure 10.18). The lead guard (G) slices to the basket off a high double screen set by B1 and B2. The lead guard reads the defenders. He or she may fake the cut to the basket and then step back behind the double pick for an exterior shot if the defender

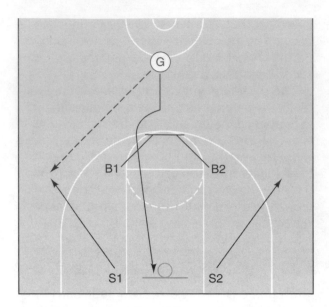

Figure 10.18 Wing play formation and start.

cheats over the double too early. Another option is for the playmaker to dart off the double screen but, instead of going to the hoop, to come back and pick for the big player farthest from the ball (B2 in figure 10.18).

Immediately after the point guard (G) heads to the basket, the big players (B1 and B2) make their moves after a one-second pause. This delay allows the lead guard to execute the pick for B2, if appropriate. The big player closer to the ball (B1) races to the weakside block to set a double pick with the opposite wing (S2 in figure

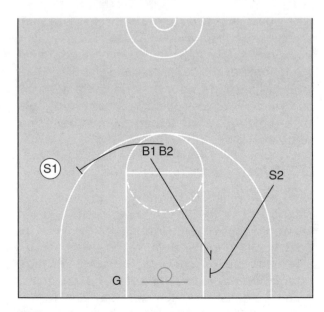

Figure 10.19 Motion continues in the wing play.

10.19). The other big player (B2) plants a screen for the ball handler (S1).

S1 and B2 execute the two-player game. As soon as S1 dribbles off the screen, the lead guard (G) dashes to the weakside off the double pick set by S2 and B1. If S1 passes the ball to G but no shot is available, the post player in the double screen (B1) is isolated low for an entry pass. The isolation occurs when the other big player (B2) flashes to a ballside spot at the foul line. The perimeter player in the twin pick (S2) hustles up the lane line to a position above the elbow and arc. G considers a toss into B1 low.

Keys

Shooters must lose their defenders to receive the initial pass from the lead guard. The point guard has three options when making the cut off the double pick at the foul line. He or she employs the appropriate alternative based on the defenders' reactions.

The starting pass goes to either side of the half-court. The post player away and the pass receiver engage in the two-player game. The coach may dictate which players are to be involved. If the coach has no preference, the opening pass can head to either wing.

Players must pay attention to the techniques used in the two-player game. See the discussion of the two-player game in "Man-to-Man Offensive Fine-Tuning" on page 5. Other relevant topics include screening between post and perimeter players, setting a screen, slipping a screen, using a pick, double screen, and throwing the ball inside.

The playmaker motors off the double pick along the foul lane as soon as the perimeter player with the ball dribbles once or twice toward the top of the key as part of the pick-and-roll or initiates a dribble toward the baseline.

LETTER FOR LAST NAME

Letter for last name is another play that will deliver the ball to the low post for a shot attempt. The motion is similar to the post play (page 160) but adds a second screener for the player heading low. A team uses this play when an interior shot is required against man-to-man defense and the coach wants a particular player to take the shot. Using the featured interior player's last name in the call informs the team where the ball is to go.

Personnel

The featured post player should be a productive scorer in the paint. One strong perimeter shooter should be on the same side of the half-court as the named post player.

Scoring

A selected big player earns chances in or around the basket. An exterior shooter obtains jumpers near the top of the key.

Execution

When the name of the featured big player (N) is called, the lead guard (G) dribbles to the wing away from N (figure 10.20). As G nears the wing, the other post player (B1) and the ballside shooter (S1) set screens for N. G's first and primary option is a toss inside to N at the ballside block along the lane. Subsequently, the screening shooter (S1) moves to a spot outside the three-point line on the weakside by going around the other shooter (S2). The playmaker's second choice is a pass to S2 at the top of the key after S2 rubs off B1's second pick. B1 seals back to the ball following the use of the second pick.

Keys

Refer to "Man-to-Man Offensive Fine-Tuning" on page 4 and the following topics: setting a screen,

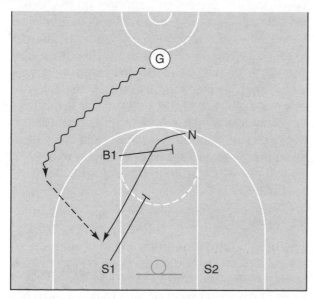

Figure 10.20 Letter for last name play.

slipping a screen, using a pick, throwing the ball inside, and pinning the defender.

The shooter setting the second of the starting staggered picks is aware of a possible defensive switch on the primary screen (when B1 picks for N). The shooter must target the right defender. The timing of the initial staggered screens is important. Players must not begin too early. The designated big player moves to the hoop as the playmaker nears the wing away.

The shooter who set the second pick for the featured post player loops to the sideline away from the ball by going around the other shooter. He or she tries to avoid a defensive switch by the defenders guarding the two shooters.

If the ball goes to the shooter out front, there is a chance the ball can be delivered to the player who just screened for the shooter. The screener seals and keeps the defender on his or her rear if possible.

LETTER COLOR FOR NAME

I was so fond of the specific scoring action in the letter color for name play that I created a quick hitter out of it. The letter color for name play manufactures quality shots. It was derived from one of the man-to-man continuous offenses (baseline shooter) reviewed on page 51. The play secures inside shots for one of the post players. An outstanding exterior shooter (the named player) serves as a decoy. The other big player plays facing the hoop. Any color and the first name or nickname of the shooter acting as a decoy is used to call the play, for example, "Letter Blue for Bob."

Personnel

One post player who can score in the paint is a necessity. More scoring options arise if the two perimeter players other than the point guard can shoot from 18 to 20 feet. A big player who can hit shots when facing the basket from at least 15 feet is beneficial.

Scoring

A shooter gains jump shots from the elbow or baseline. A big player in or around the low post may secure inside shots. The other post player can attempt 15- to 18-foot jumpers.

Execution

The team begins in normal box alignment with big players high and shooters low. The coach calls out the name of a shooter (N). He or she begins at a box on the lane. The point guard (G) dribbles above the elbow on the same side of the court as N. Both post players (B1 and B2) down screen for the shooters below. N pops out to an open area on the ballside wing or the baseline, while S2 hustles up the lane line to a spot across from G out front. Players end up in spots shown in figure 10.21. If the main shooter (N) is open as a result of the initial screening action, G sends him or her the ball for a quick shot. Otherwise, G completes the pass across the top to S2. The designated player (N) bolts off the baseline picks set by B1 and B2. N curls around the second screener (B2) and cross picks for the other post player (B1). B2 reacts to the curl by running to the nearest spot behind the three-point line. He or she may be able to get away with going out only to 15 to 18 feet. This movement clears the area low for B1 to catch the pass after exploiting the cross screen. Depending on the position of the defenders, the pass inside to B1 comes from either S2 or B2 (figure 10.21).

Keys

See the following topics in "Man-to-Man Offensive Fine-Tuning" in chapter 1 on page 4: screen-

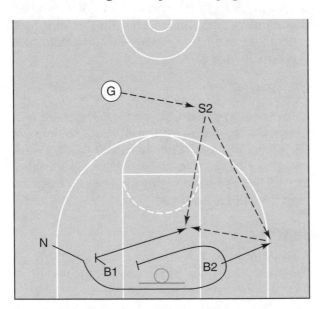

Figure 10.21   Letter color for name primary scoring motion.

ing between post and perimeter players, setting a screen, slipping a screen, using a pick, down screen, low exchanges and cross screens, and throwing the ball inside.

The coach should emphasize to the point guard that the initial pass goes to the named player only if he or she is wide open for a shot. A pass across the top to the other shooter is the main way to begin the play. The lead guard always heads to the area above the elbow on the named player's side.

The coach should stress to the main shooter that he or she could continue to cut off the baseline screens to the opposite corner. He or she chooses the option if 100 percent sure that a shot will be available. Otherwise, the shooter curls and then cross screens. He or she may also get open as a result of the curl. If a shot is probable, the passer can deliver the ball to the shooter heading into the lane. The main shooter must be ready for the pass. The cross pick is the most likely activity to produce a shot.

The shooter out front with the ball reads the defense and throws the appropriate pass. An easier play may be to fling the ball to the post player on the periphery and let him or her direct the ball to the interior player who is using the cross screen. The ball handler knows that if the shooter runs to the corner, he or she is asking for the ball and a subsequent shot.

SCREEN FOR NAME

Throwing a skip pass to a shooter on the weakside of the court is an excellent way to generate a shot. I link the maneuver with a pick-and-roll to increase the potency of the screen for name play. If the coach notices that the opponent has a tendency to sag significantly on the offside, this quick hitter could exploit the situation. The coach wants the ball to go to the team's best exterior shooter for a shot near the three-point line. The call includes the main shooter's first name or nickname, for example, "Screen for Bob."

Personnel

The point guard should be a scorer, and one of the post players should be a good shooter when facing the basket from 15 to 20 feet. Regardless, he or she must at least be able to score with his or her back to the basket. A legitimate three-point shooter is also a necessity.

Scoring

The point guard attains a jump shot or a penetration to the goal as a result of a screen on the ball. A post player rolls to the hoop or possibly obtains 15- to 20-foot jump shots. A designated perimeter shooter achieves distance shots.

Execution

Players begin in a box set with big players on top and perimeter players at the boxes. When the play is called, the point guard (G) uses a pick set by a post player (B1) on the same side as the named shooter (N). At the same time, the weakside players (B2 and S2) establish a twin pick at midlane (figure 10.22). N hustles to a weakside spot behind the three-point arc by using the double pick. If necessary, B2 and S2 can set staggered picks for N rather than the double. The lead guard (G) pursues his or her own shot, passes to B1 as B1 rolls to the hoop, tosses to B1 after he or she steps out after setting the screen, or throws a skip pass to N on the offside.

Keys

Players react quickly to the name that is called. The post player on the same side as the named player moves out to screen for the point guard. The post player and lead guard execute the two-

player game at the same time the weakside players set the double screen. The named player starts to cut to the offside while using the double pick as the playmaker reaches the screen.

The coach can allow the big player in the pick-and-roll to step back after screening (no roll) if he or she is a respectable shooter from 15 to 20 feet. If the player's shooting range is limited, he or she should roll to the hoop. See the discussion of the two-player game in chapter 1 (page 5) in "Man-to-Man Offensive Fine-Tuning." Other appropriate topics include setting a screen, slipping a screen, using a pick, double screen, and throwing the ball inside.

The point guard could create problems for the defense if he or she has the ability to score when operating on the cleared side of the court. The lead guard may have to dribble in the opposite direction to set up the screen before executing the pick-and-roll with the appropriate big player. The playmaker also has to be capable of throwing a strong two-handed overhead pass across the court to the named teammate.

HOFSTRA

The Hofstra play was developed to highlight a specific type of offensive movement. I have had great success with staggered screens for an outside shooter. My experience with the maneuver is overwhelmingly positive. The focus is putting the ball in the hands of the best shooter. Other players are secondary considerations.

Personnel

At least one post player should be able to score around the basket. An excellent outside shooter is also essential.

Scoring

A big player who posts in the midlane region may have a shot off a back-to-the-basket move. The point guard may have a layup when he or she cuts to the basket. The primary shooter may secure a jump shot near the top of the key. The other perimeter player may garner a layup from a backdoor move.

Execution

Players begin in the regular box alignment with big players at the elbows and shooters on the

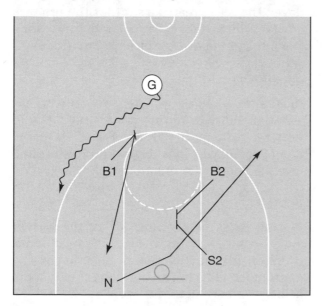

Figure 10.22   Screen for name setup and action.

boxes. The point guard (G) dribbles toward either post player (B1 or B2). The ballside big player (in this case B1) pops up and opposite the playmaker (G) to receive the pass. Simultaneously, the ballside shooter (S1) hustles to a position in the near corner behind the three-point line, and the other big player (B2) bolts to the strongside midlane location. The lead guard takes a quick look at B2, who is posting along the lane, before reversing the ball to B1 out front.

The playmaker (G) sends the ball to B1 (figure 10.23). At that precise moment, the weakside shooter (S2) executes an L-cut to gain freedom on the wing to catch the pass from B1. S2 may have a backdoor opportunity at this point if the defense remains in strong denial position. On the pass to S2, G races to the hoop using B2's screen. After G rubs off, B2 turns and moves to set a pick so that S1 can move above the top of the key. S1 also uses a pick by B1 (staggered screens). B1 goes to screen immediately after passing to S2. S2 looks to pass to G at the hoop or S1 at the top.

Keys

The coach should drill the team on the required initial movements to transform from the box set to the scoring alignment of the play. The ball handler dribbles to the main shooter's side. That way the best shooter gets a chance to employ the staggered picks set by the big players for a shot near the three-point line.

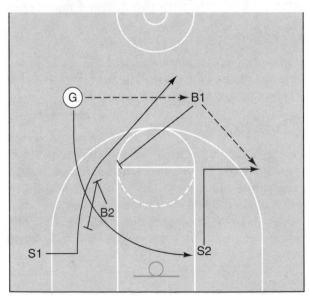

Figure 10.23 Scoring motion in Hofstra play.

Quick reversal of the ball increases the effectiveness of the play. The post player moving out top and the offside shooter must get free for the next two passes.

The point guard must not ignore the big player rushing to the ballside midlane spot.

The weakside wing repeats the L-cut if he or she does not secure the ball for a layup off a back cut. The lead guard must not cut to the basket until the ball is passed from the big player at top to the isolated wing. If the lead guard cuts too early, the action can interfere with a backdoor layup.

When the ball is reversed to the opposite wing, the post player in the midlane area needs to set two solid screens back to back, one to spring the lead guard for a dash to the basket and one for the shooter in the same-side corner.

Big players must head directly at the defender on the shooter in the offside corner to force the defender to deal with two obstacles in succession. Refer to "Man-to-Man Offensive Fine-Tuning" on page 4 for information on these topics: screening between post and perimeter players, setting a screen, slipping a screen, using a pick, throwing the ball inside, and L-cut.

ROANOKE

I began to use this play frequently in my latter years at King's College. The motion has been around for years but instead of using it for a big player, the play creates a shot for the primary shooter. The Roanoke play is another way for a coach to get the ball to the key shooter.

Personnel

The play features a perimeter shooter who has both the ability to score from the outside and the size and capacity to receive a lob to the hoop. Post players must be good screeners and have the talent to score around the basket.

Scoring

The lob pass to the weakside of the basket could lead to a layup or dunk. The skip pass to the offside may lead to an outside shot by a perimeter player. The big player may score inside after cutting to the hoop.

Execution

The play starts with players in a box set. The big players (B1 and B2) are above perimeter players (S1 and S2, respectively). The team can run the play to either side of the floor. The initial pass goes to an exterior player racing out past the arc and above the foul line extended. In this case, S1 is the highlighted player. On the point guard's pass to S1, the other shooter (S2) sprints to a spot just below S1 on the ballside periphery. The lead guard (G) runs through the foul lane to the strongside corner. The weakside post player (B2) races to a location near B1 above the ballside elbow. The team has cleared the offside. Personnel end in positions shown in figure 10.24.

S1 passes down to S2 (figure 10.24). The passer (S1) uses double or staggered screens set by the big players (B1 and B2) to dart to an open area on the weakside. S1 could cut toward the hoop, looking for a lob pass from S2, or to an area on the offside exterior for a skip pass. No matter which method is used, after planting the screen for the shooter (S1), the post players (B1 and B2) perform a twist maneuver. The player closer to the ball (B2) steps in to pick for B1, who heads toward the basket.

Keys

The point guard knows that whichever shooter receives the first pass is the featured player.

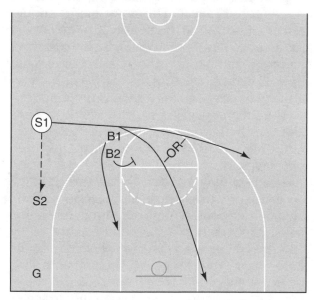

Figure 10.24 Roanoke scoring formation.

The coach can dictate which player receives the initial toss or can give the playmaker the choice. The designated shooter comes hard to the ball. The player does not receive the toss until he or she is above the foul line extended.

The motion of the passer, weakside shooter, and offside big player occur simultaneously. The two weakside players may hesitate briefly and wait until the point guard takes two or three steps on his or her cut to the ballside corner.

The post players have the option to establish a double screen or staggered screens. They mix the two choices randomly. When executing the twist, the post player farther from the ball races over the pick established by the other post player. See the discussion of the twist move on page 7 in "Man-to-Man Offensive Fine-Tuning." Other relevant items are setting a screen, slipping a screen, using a pick, back pick, double screen, and throwing the ball inside.

The shooter going to the offside must read the defense and get to a position void of defenders for a scoring chance.

SAN DIEGO

The motion in San Diego is another way to exploit the flare screen. The play simply couples the flare screen with other maneuvers and uses different personnel. A club uses this quick hitter only if they have a big player who is especially productive from the outside. The objective is to supply him or her with a chance to create a shot.

Personnel

The play is designed to take advantage of a good outside-shooting big player. San Diego works best if he or she also possesses good quickness in a one-on-one situation. An excellent perimeter shooter and an effective inside-scoring post player create more alternatives.

Scoring

The perimeter shooter attains jump shots from the corner or wing or receives layups. A post player gains 15- to 20-foot shots or possibly one-on-one chances. The other big player takes possession of the ball in the paint for a low-post scoring move.

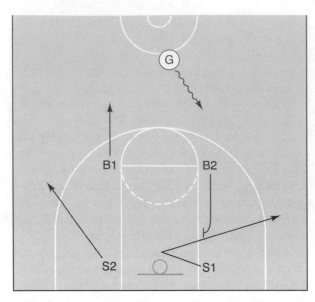

Figure 10.25   San Diego starting set and movements.

Execution

The squad starts in normal box formation with shooters on the blocks. The point guard (G) dribbles away from the featured big body (B1 in figure 10.25). B1 slides out past the three-point line above the elbow. At the same time, the other post player (B2) down screens for the shooter (S1) below on the box, and the other shooter (S2) pops to the wing away from the ball.

B1 races directly down the lane line and receives a pick from S2 coming in toward the lane (figure 10.26). B1 flares to secure a possible

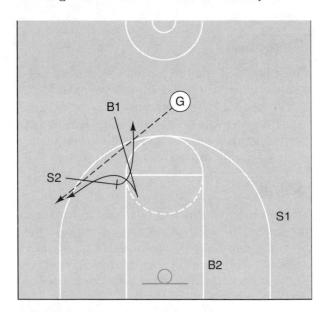

Figure 10.26   San Diego movements continue.

pass from the lead guard (G) on the offside wing. If there is no shot, he or she could go one-on-one. G could also throw the first pass to S1 if S1 is wide open. A shot is expected from S1.

If the pass does not go to B1 off the flare screen, one prerogative for the point guard (G) is to toss the ball to S2, who steps out after planting the flare pick. On the release of the ball, S1 runs off the baseline screen set by B2 to the basket. B2 heads toward the ball after screening. S2 considers passing to S1 near the hoop on the ballside or to B2, who is flashing to the ball. S1 could also fake a run off B2's baseline screen and instead fade back to the corner. If the skip pass goes to S1, he or she considers a shot or feed to B2.

Keys

The lead guard executes the initial movement away from the big player who is the main alternative. The playmaker makes a concerted effort to deliver the ball to the designated post player with the skip pass. The flare move is the heart of the play. Review the associated material in chapter 1 on page 6 under "Man-to-Man Offensive Fine-Tuning." Other topics of interest are screening between post and perimeter players, setting a screen, slipping a screen, using a pick, down screen, throwing the ball inside, and pinning the defender.

Although the play includes several options, the coach should stress sending the ball to the featured player. The point guard should also look to the same side of the half-court for a shooter popping out off a down screen. Although the shooter is not the primary target, the ball handler can toss the ball his or her way if the player is open for a shot attempt.

The shooter who pops to the offside foul line extended must be an effective screener. After all, his or her pick is what will free the highlighted big player.

The two players involved in the baseline screen work to ensure that a good scoring chance develops. They read the defense and use the motion that will generate a shot.

If the ball goes to the post player using the flare screen, the shooter on the opposite wing does not cut off the baseline screen. He or she remains on the periphery. This positioning gives the featured player enough space to go one-on-one for a scoring opportunity.

The featured big player must pop out front opposite the playmaker at the very start of the play. The player cannot shortcut the movements; he or she must go out top and then down the lane line before receiving the pick from the wing. He or she does not start the flare maneuver until the perimeter player has at least reached the wing on the same side.

UTICA

The movements for Utica again are taken from part of a pattern used against man-to-man defense. Refer to wing shooter on page 47. The player activity has proved rewarding, so it was just a matter of transforming it into the swift-hitting format. The coach uses this play when he or she wants to get the best outside shooter working with two big players to produce shots. Interior and exterior shots are possibilities.

Personnel

Both big players should be capable shooters from within 15 feet. The two perimeter players (not the ball handler) must possess decent outside-scoring skills.

Scoring

A wing shot arises for a perimeter player. A shot at the foul line occurs for one post player. Back-to-the-basket moves are available to the other big player. Shots at the foul line or the top of the key may develop for another perimeter player. The point guard is not likely to see a shot outcome.

Execution

Players begin in the regular box formation (figure 10.27). The play as diagrammed will set up S1 for shots. B2 down screens so that S2 can race out to the near wing. B1 slides down to the block directly below, and the highlighted shooter (S1) heads to the near corner. If the coach wants to highlight S2, then B1 down screens for S1. B2 then slides to the box underneath, and S2 runs out to the near corner. A scoring chance may develop because of the starting down pick. The coach has to clear the player to attempt the shot.

The point guard (G) must complete the pass to the player coming off the down screen (S2)

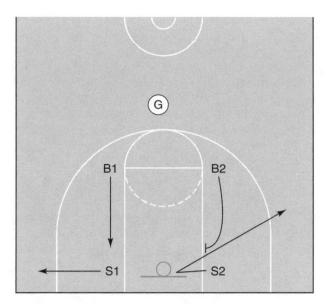

Figure 10.27 Utica starting action.

to the wing region. The lead guard (G) immediately hustles to pick for the player on the opposite block (B1). B1 may have a tendency to be anxious. He or she waits for the pick. B1 motors toward the opening near the foul line. S2 then passes the ball to B1. As soon as S2 makes the pass, the point guard (G) sprints to a spot on the closest wing. At the same time, the shooter in the corner (S1) replaces G on the box. B1 completes the reversal pass to G. If the coach chooses to get the lead guard into the main action, this is the time to do it. G stays at the block. S1 heads to the wing to catch the reversal pass.

After the playmaker (G) receives the ball on the reversal, the opposite wing (S2) slides to the nearer corner (figure 10.28). Clearing the defensive help from the key area is important. When G has the ball, S1 cross screens for B2. The point guard (G) considers a toss inside to B2, who is coming to the ball. As the action low develops, B1 comes down to pick the screener (S1). G's next pass option is to S1 near the foul line, top-of-the-key area. If S1 receives the ball and no shot is available, the screener (B1) heads down toward B2. B2 loops over the top of B1, looking for the ball from S1. The activity is similar to a twist maneuver.

Keys

The coach informs the ball handler which perimeter shooter should be highlighted. This decision determines which side executes the

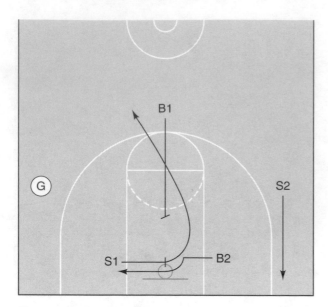

Figure 10.28 Motion continues in Utica.

down screen at the onset of the play. The featured shooter just pops out to the near corner. There is no screen. If the coach is so inclined, he or she can add the featured shooter's first name or nickname to the end of the call to tell the playmaker which shooter executes the beginning run to the closest corner, for example, "Utica for Bob." If the coach wants to highlight the point guard, it is best to do so at the point described previously in the execution section. That approach is much safer than asking another perimeter player to assume the playmaker's duties.

The initial down screen must get the perimeter player open to catch the first pass. A quality shot attempt is possible, but the coach should clear the pass receiver to shoot the ball.

Players should try to make post feeds to the big players at the ballside blocks on the lane.

The point guard sets a diagonal pick for the post player at the opposite box. The coach tells the big player exactly what shots are acceptable.

The reversal action requires that the lead guard and perimeter player in the corner move together. At that point, the point guard can assume the featured player's role if the coach desires.

The post player coming to the ball as a result of the cross screen usually steps high and goes low off the pick. This player is the first pass option for the player with the ball.

MOTION SERIES

The quick-hitting plays in the motion series start from a 2-1-2 or 2-3 alignment. This is another opening set from which a significant number of swift-hitting plays can begin. Each quick hitter is assigned a name, but the coach can change the names as desired. Two-digit numbers, three-digit numbers, and letters are other calling methods. An earlier section of the chapter reviewed those methods.

The plays initiated by a pass to a wing are shown heading to one side, the right, but the team can execute them heading to either side of the floor. To start at the wing to the left, the point guard completes the first pass across the top to the other guard. He or she then tosses the ball to the nearer wing to start the motion of the play. The pass across the top means that the play will feature different players from the ones illustrated in the diagrams.

BIG FOR NAME

I frequently used the big for name play to generate specific scoring opportunities. The motion has been around for a long time, and numerous coaches use it. Coaches can use the play when they feel it is important for an exceptional shooter to obtain a shot. He or she is the featured player. The play also isolates a big player in the low post for an inside scoring chance. A sample call is "Big for Bob."

Personnel

The chosen shooter must be an effective outside threat. The better inside-scoring big player is at the ballside wing. The better jump shooter of the two post players fills the high post.

Scoring

The play highlights the designated perimeter shooter. He or she receives 15- to 20-foot jump shots on either side of the court from wing to baseline. One big player obtains shots near the basket after setting a screen or performing a backdoor cut. The other post player could be open at the foul line for a jumper. The highlighted shooter earns shots with a cut to the basket.

Execution

The highlighted player (N) must be a quality exterior shooter. Post players (B1 and B2) begin on the blocks along the foul lane (figure 10.29). B1 executes an L-cut and receives the first pass from the point guard (G) at the ballside wing. B1 uses a backdoor move if he or she is overplayed on the wing. After B1 receives the ball, G sets a diagonal down pick for the other big player (B2). N cuts off G's tail to the strongside box. At the same time, S2 hustles to replace B2 along the lane.

N has a chance to use B1's single screen (figure 10.30) or the double pick set by G and S2. B1 passes to B2 out front and sprints to establish a solitary down screen for N. B1 picks N's defender and then steps to the ball. He or she may pop open if B1's defender tries to help the defender guarding N, leaving an opening for B1 to secure the ball from B2. The delivery to B1 inside normally occurs if a defensive switch takes place on the down pick. B1 yells, "Hot!" when a mismatch is present. The lead guard (G) always bolts to the wing opposite N when N uses the lone down screen. N employs B1's pick the majority of the time. If N chooses to rub off the twin pick set by G and S2 on the other side of the foul lane, then either G or S2 head opposite using B1's obstacle to finish at the far wing. G and S2 communicate with one another to decide who runs opposite. If B2 cannot deliver the ball to N off the double screen, B2 immediately looks

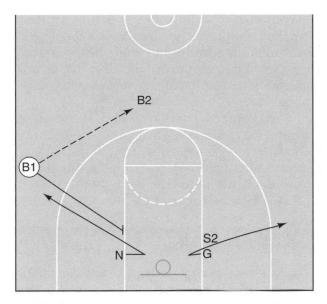

Figure 10.30 Big for name action continues. N uses the single screen.

to send the ball to the other wing. B2 is also aware of the fact that the one player remaining near the block after N uses the twin screen (G or S2) could pop open for a direct pass inside.

Keys

The offense is effective in freeing an excellent perimeter scorer. The defense will have difficulty switching the single screen. The opponent is leery of the subsequent mismatch. Therefore, the highlighted player should use the lone pick more frequently than he or she does the double screen.

The post player executing the L-cut must get open for the first pass. See L-cut in "Man-to-Man Offensive Fine-Tuning" on page 7. Other relevant items are screening between post and perimeter players, setting a screen, slipping a screen, using a pick, down screen, double screen, throwing the ball inside, and pinning the defender.

The play can start to the other side; the team simply flips personnel. Otherwise, the small forward is the lone screener, which is not a favorable situation for the offense. The coach wants the lone screener to be a post player.

The big player coming to the foul line should know exactly what shots the coach permits him or her to attempt. The post player could get open with the early diagonal pick by the lead guard.

The coach can highlight the lead guard if desired simply by eliminating the crossing action between N and the ball handler. The

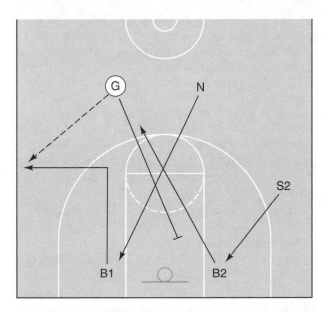

Figure 10.29 Big for name setup and starting movements.

player in N's position becomes the screener for the post player darting above the foul line. N attains an appropriate angle before setting the pick. The point guard performs a give-and-go and bolts to the ballside box as soon as the pass is released to the near wing.

The featured shooter makes the defense believe that he or she is heading in one direction and then comes back opposite. If the defender tries to slide over the top of the pick, the shooter does not hesitate to fade toward the corner to create distance between the two.

SMALL FOR NAME

This pattern was designed to take advantage of an excellent shooter with range. My teams used the play to create numerous crucial shots. Coaches use small for name primarily to acquire a shot (usually a three-pointer) for the squad's best exterior shooter. A sample call is "Small for Bob."

Personnel

The play sets up a perimeter player for a long-range shot attempt. Post players must be potent screeners and be able to score around the hoop. If one is a noteworthy medium-range shooter, the offensive team gains a further advantage.

Scoring

The post player's backdoor cut might lead to a shot around the goal. The point guard's cut to the basket may end with a layup. The other big player may secure a 15- to 18-foot jumper. The highlighted player acquires shots near the three-point arc. A pass can go inside to either big player in the lane area for a shot.

Execution

The team uses the same basic formation shown in figure 10.29 (page 177), except that no cross occurs between N and the playmaker (G). They cut to the blocks, with N gaining an angle to screen for B2, who heads to an area above the foul line. In addition, S2 moves cautiously toward the basket. One post player (B1) executes an L-cut to receive the first pass on a wing. When the beginning motion is complete, personnel are located in the spots indicated in figure 10.31.

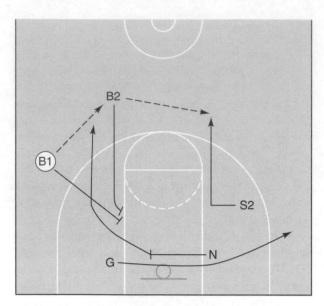

Figure 10.31   Scoring motion of small for name.

B1 throws the ball to B2, who quickly reverses the ball to S2. S2 is bolting out opposite (figure 10.31). He or she times the action with B2's gaining possession of the ball. On the toss to S2, the point guard (G) uses N's pick to rush to position outside the three-point arc on the ballside below the foul line extended. The big players (B1 and B2) move down together to plant a double screen for N. The designated shooter (N) uses the twin screen to break free on the periphery to catch a pass from S2. The post players always twist whether the pass goes to N or not. The player nearer the ball steps down and in to pick for the other big player so that he or she can glide over the top, heading for the player with the ball. If S2 or N does not have a clean shot, the ball goes in to the big player who is getting open with the twist.

Keys

Refer to "Man-to-Man Offensive Fine-Tuning" in chapter 1 on page 4 and these topics: setting a screen, slipping a screen, using a pick, double screen, throwing the ball inside, L-cut, and twist move.

The coach stresses to the highlighted player that he or she needs to achieve the proper angle when establishing the initial screen for the post player on the weakside block. The highlighted player heads into the lane and picks on an angle so that the player using the screen gains freedom above the foul line on the strongside.

The weakside wing gets open to secure the third pass, the one from the big player above the foul line. He or she darts toward the lane and then above the closest elbow opposite the post player with the ball. The timing is crucial. He or she scampers upward as soon as the post player grabs the ball out front. The players execute a swift ball reversal.

The team is not looking for the lead guard off the baseline screen to gain control of the ball. He or she acts only as a decoy. The major emphasis of the play is getting the ball into the hands of the squad's main outside shooting threat.

For the double down screen, the big players cruise together and do not permit a defender to race between them. They go right at targeted defender. The featured shooter uses the double screen to get open for an exterior jump shot. If the defender on the shooter scurries over the top, the shooter fades off the double pick to an open spot on the periphery closer to the baseline.

The big players' execution of the twist move ends the movement of the play. The post players read their location in relation to the ball to ensure that the screener steps down or in toward the lane. One player always swoops over the top of the pick, heading to the ball.

The lead guard should know that there is a possibility of a return pass for a layup if the give-and-go at the start is well done. The point guard passes, steps away, and cuts hard to the hoop.

MOTION SPREAD

Coaches have used the motion spread action from a 2-3 formation for decades to secure shots around the basket or on the exterior. I added the last few movements to create scoring opportunities for additional personnel. Coaches may select the play if they have an outstanding big player who they would like to isolate along the foul lane. The play spreads the floor offensively, enabling players to cut to the hoop.

Personnel

The center should be a capable passer and sound scorer around the hoop. The guards and forwards should be able to shoot the basketball from 12 to 20 feet.

Scoring

The guards obtain jump shots in the corners. The best inside scorer (usually the center) gains possession of the ball on a return pass while heading to the basket or while posting up. A forward receives a layup after dashing to the hoop. Forwards see 12- to 18-foot jump shots develop near the ballside elbow.

Execution

Players start in the 2-3 formation. The guards (G and S1) are out front, each of the forwards (B1 and S2) is on a wing (at the foul line extended), and the center (B2) is at the foul line (figure 10.32). The action begins when the center (B2) bolts out to catch the first pass. As soon as G releases the ball, the forwards (B1 and S2) back pick for the guards (G and S1, respectively). The guards use the back screens to storm to open areas at the corners.

B2's first pass choice is to either guard (G or S1) close to a corner. A guard may possibly find a clear alley to the basket off the back pick and secure a pass for a layup. In most cases, the guards sprint to vacant areas in the corners. After releasing the ball, B2 dives to the basket and establishes position low along the lane. The guard either shoots or tosses the ball to B2 inside.

If B2 cannot pass to a guard, he or she chucks the ball to either of the forwards (B1 or S2), who

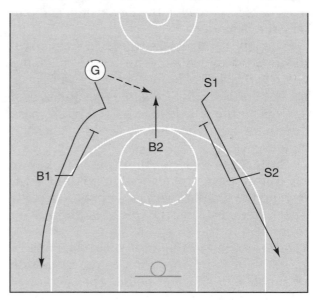

Figure 10.32 Motion spread alignment and beginning movements.

are stepping out after the guards have used their picks. The forward receiving the ball immediately tosses it to the guard (G) in the same-side corner. The passer zips to the hoop and goes through to the weakside if a return pass does not come. The guard in the offside corner rotates up to take the defender away from the basket. As soon as the forward catches the ball, the center slowly begins a pick-away action for the opposite forward. The actual screen is not planted until the passer starts to cut to the hoop. The pick recipient races to an open area on the ballside. He or she could go all the way to the basket or to a spot off the ballside elbow for a jump shot. If no pass comes, he or she sprints to the basket and out to the offside. The center is the third cutter to the basket and establishes position at the ballside low post to await an entry pass. Other players are rotating up from the weakside and heading toward the ball.

Keys

Without exception, the center must get open to snag the initial pass from the point guard.

The coach should stress setting solid back screens. The center must understand that a pass to either guard off a back pick is desirable. Any pass to a guard causes the center to burst to the hoop in hope of securing a return pass. See the discussion of the back pick in "Man-to-Man Offensive Fine-Tuning" on page 5. Other relevant topics are setting a screen, slipping a screen, using a pick, throwing the ball inside, and pinning the defender.

When the center passes the ball to a forward, the forward immediately throws the ball to the guard in the closest corner. After the ball leaves his or her hands, the forward races to the goal and out to the offside exterior if a return pass does not come. The forward accomplishes the actions swiftly.

The forward receiving the center's pick away invariably pops open for a jump shot from beyond the foul line with or without a dribble. The player must have the coach's authorization to shoot.

After bolting to the hoop off a back pick, a guard immediately pops out to the same-side corner if he or she does not gain possession of the ball for a layup.

The center is the only player who stops to post up in the low post. Therefore, if the coach wants a particular player to post up, he or she should start in the high post.

EASTERN

The movements in eastern are years old. Numerous college and high school teams use the motion. I first began using it while an assistant high school coach as a prelude to a passing-game offense against man-to-man defense. Eastern is a good way to use a few simple movements to get players moving.

Personnel

The ball handler should be an effective outside shooter. One other perimeter player needs to be a potent exterior jump shooter. Players occupying wing positions should be able to set convincing down screens as well as catch and score around the basket.

Scoring

The point guard and one perimeter shooter take advantage of the down screens to garner 15- to 20-foot jump shots close to the wings. The two screeners may be open near the blocks when they step toward the ball after their teammates use their picks. Post-up situations occur when the ball goes to the exterior directly in front of the player near a block.

Execution

Players start in a 2-3 formation as shown in figure 10.32 (page 179). The point guard (G) and best outside shooter (S1) are out front. B1 and S2 are the wings, and B2 starts at the high post. The coach has the option to switch S2 and B2. If he or she makes the adjustment, the two post players (B1 and B2) will screen for the two perimeter players (G and S1).

The first pass goes to the high post (B2 in figure 10.32, page 179) as he or she moves outward. On the release of the pass, the two players out front (G and S1) sprint to the basket. They may execute straight cuts down their respective lane lines. They cross near the baseline inside the foul lane (or fake it) before using the down picks set by B1 and S2. If B2 catches the initial pass near the top of the key, it may be possible for the shooters to cross immediately on the midcourt side of the pass receiver (B2) before racing to the boxes. The timing of the down screens is critical. B1 and S2 move toward the lane just before the cutters reach the blocks. The screeners step to the ball after the screening action. One of the cutters (G or S1) could be open for a layup on the initial move to the hoop by means of a give-and-go with the high post (B2).

Keys

See "Man-to-Man Offensive Fine-Tuning" on page 4 and these topics: setting a screen, slipping a screen, using a pick, down screen, throwing the ball inside, and pinning the defender.

The perimeter shooters out front vary their cuts to the basket. The lead guard dictates the type of cut. He or she motors straight to the hoop or starts a crossing motion over the top of the pass receiver. The two cutters communicate once they reach the baseline. They cross or fake it before taking advantage of the down picks.

The cutters make eye contact with the high post. They are ready for a direct pass for a layup. The high post views the entire half-court. He or she completes a pass to an open player. If a shooter catches the next pass and no shot is possible, he or she looks inside to the screener posting up.

The call includes the name of the player who begins as the high post, for example, "Eastern for Bob." The coach can give the high post the opportunity to go one-on-one if the toss to a teammate does not occur.

MOTION COLOR FOR NAME

The motion color for name play incorporates common scoring movements into a sequence that allows multiple players to become involved in scoring. Coaches use this offensive scheme when they are looking for offensive balance. The motion supplies inside and outside scoring chances. A sample call is "Motion green for Bob."

Personnel

The play is called for an excellent outside shooter. One post player must be able to catch a lob to the weakside of the hoop and should possess strong inside-scoring skills. The other big player should be a capable screener. If he or she shoots well from 15 to 18 feet, it is a huge plus. The other two perimeter players must be outside scoring threats.

Scoring

The point guard and one shooter may be open on a cut to the basket off a high-post screen. The designated shooter acquires a jump shot from 15 to 20 feet, and the post player serving as a screener steps to the ball for a possible interior score. The big player denied the introductory pass receives a layup as a result of a backdoor cut. A post player grabs the lob toss to the hoop. A seal of an interior defender is possible. The featured player receives a shot near the bucket with a back screen. The players setting the back picks step out after the picks are used to secure perimeter jump shots.

Execution

The offense begins with big players (B1 and B2) on the blocks along the lane, two perimeter players (G and N) out front, and the other exterior player (S2) on the weakside wing. B1 executes an L-cut to get open for the initial pass from the point guard (G). B1 performs a backdoor move if overplayed. The action is identical to that in figure 10.29 (page 177) with two exceptions. First, the post player at the offside block (B2) comes up to the high post to fix a pick simultaneously with the L-cut. After G sends the first pass to B1, the two players out front (G and N) cross off the high post to the basket. Second, the weakside wing (S2) remains stationary.

Another method by which to begin the offense is for the two players out front (G and N) to cut directly to the hoop using the high-post screen instead of crossing. Both players cut on the ballside, one after the other. The lead guard (G) decides which method to use. The ball handler always ends on the offside box, and the featured player settles on the strongside block on the lane.

The next stage is for B1 to toss the ball to the high post (B2), who steps out after picking. The wings, B1 and S2, execute down screens with N and G, respectively. The down screeners (B1 and S2) seal the defenders and head slightly toward B2 following their down picks. B2 may send the ball inside to either screener.

B2 has the ball near the top of the key and tries to complete the pass to N on the wing (figure 10.33). The ball *must* go to N. Once the ball leaves B2's hands, the perimeter player on the weakside box (S2) plants a back screen for the passer (B2). At the same time, the lead guard (G) slides above the top of the key. B2 sprints to the hoop in anticipation of a lob from N. N is aware that B1 is posting on the ballside block.

If N does not have a pass to either post player (B1 or B2), he or she sends the ball to S2, who steps out after screening. On the pass to S2, B1 sets a back pick so that N can race to the basket while B2 ducks into the lane, trying to gain position for a possible post feed from S2 or G. G has moved back to vacant wing.

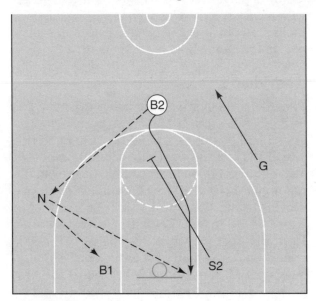

Figure 10.33 Motion color for name scoring motion.

Keys

The point guard decides whether to execute a straight cut to the basket or cross with the named player off the high-post screen. The big player setting the screen at the high post must get open to receive the ball from the wing. The wing must get the ball to the big player.

The designated shooter needs to get free off the initial down screen. The next pass goes in his or her direction. The screeners plant the foot closer to the foul line and swing open to the ball in an attempt to receive the ball from the high post.

The big player with the ball above the foul line may need to dribble to pull the defender closer. The back pick is more effective if the defense is close to the passer. If the big player allows the

defender to slough off, the chances for success decrease dramatically.

The highlighted player must be capable of throwing a lob pass to the basket. The post player receiving the pass needs to possess the athletic ability to catch and score.

The coach should teach big players how to perform a duck-in. See the discussion of the duck-in in "Man-to-Man Offensive Fine-Tuning" on page 7. Other pertinent items include setting a screen, slipping a screen, using a pick, down screen, back pick, throwing the ball inside, and pinning the defender.

The player popping out after setting the back pick for the high post could gain a shot. If it does not happen, he or she will probably need to dribble away from the side from which he or she received the ball to create a better passing angle for a feed into the post. When the screener does not have a shot, he or she views the entire half-court. The defense dictates the pass decision. The option selected should lead to a shot.

Players engage in action on one side of the court (back pick) while giving the big player inside a chance to seal the defender in the lane. The lead guard is on the same side as the duck-in and stays behind the three-point line above the foul line extended. Spacing is important.

MOTION INVERT FOR NAME

This call combines two of my favorite movements. I have always found that two-player games and staggered screens for an exterior shooter produce sound shots. Motion invert for name is helpful when a three-point shot is preferred. Although some inside chances may arise, the bulk of the activity centers on outside shooters. A sample call is "Motion Invert for Bob."

Personnel

One post player should be a persuasive screener on the ball and be able to produce when catching the ball in or near the foul lane. Having two excellent outside shooters is important. Each is likely to see opportunities.

Scoring

The point guard and one perimeter player may gain layups after cutting to the basket off a high-post screen. The other perimeter player may create layup chances by using a back cut to the hoop against a defensive denial. The two-player game occurs between a big player and a perimeter player. The shooter acquires jumpers directly off the dribble, and the post player rolls to the bucket for a possible catch and inside shot. The named player lands 15- to 20-foot jump shots by using staggered screens.

Execution

The team is in the normal motion set except that a shooter (S2) rather than a post player is on the ballside box (figure 10.34). The featured shooter assumes N's position. S2 executes an L-cut to break free for the first pass. On a defensive overplay, he or she performs a backdoor move for a possible layup. As S2 begins to move, B2 races to the high post. The initial pass goes to S2 on the wing. The point guard (G) and N execute a scissors maneuver or consecutive ballside cuts while using the high-post pick. Regardless, the lead guard (G) ends at the offside block along the lane.

After the two players out top have used the pick from the high post (B2), B2 hustles to plant a screen for the ball handler (S2 in figure 10.35). S2 and B2 perform the pick-and-roll. As soon as S2 dribbles off the screen, N darts toward the weakside wing while using the staggered down screens set by G and B1. S2 may be open for a shot, may toss the ball to B2, who is rolling to

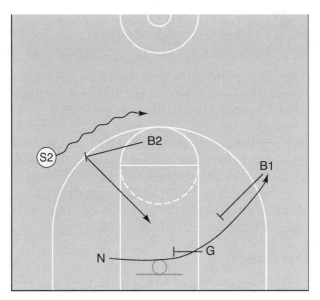

Figure 10.35 Motion invert for name action continues.

the hoop in the area vacated by N, or may throw directly to N for a jump shot.

Keys

The point guard chooses whether or not to scissors off the high post after releasing the initial pass. His or her first move is always a step away.

The big player rushing to the high post starts to move simultaneously with the player executing the L-cut.

See the segment on the two-player game in "Man-to-Man Offensive Fine-Tuning" in chapter 1 on page 5. Other relevant items are screening between post and perimeter players, setting a screen, slipping a screen, using a pick, and throwing the ball inside.

When executing staggered screens, the lead guard must not go too far into the lane to plant a pick. He or she is not to interfere with a possible scoring chance for the big player rolling to the hoop. The big player who establishes the second pick heads directly at the intended target and becomes stationary just before contact. He or she must screen the correct defender because a defensive switch might take place on the first pick. The big player plants the second down screen outside the lane approximately halfway between the lane and the three-point line. The last screen is similar to down screen discussed in "Man-to-Man Offensive Fine-Tuning" on page 4.

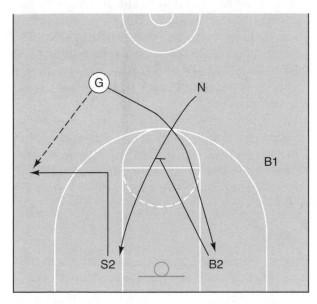

Figure 10.34 Motion invert for name set and opening motion.

MOTION TWO-DIGIT NUMBER

The action in this play is designed to take advantage of today's man-to-man defense. Squads have become proficient at supplying help in the foul lane. Why not exploit it? The motion two-digit number play gets the ball into the hands of the premier outside shooter. The play sends action in one direction and then quickly reverses it. Players take advantage of the desire of the defense to slough into the lane to provide help. A sample call is "Motion 32."

Personnel

One post player needs to be a good screener and have the ability to score off a post-up. An excellent perimeter shooter is the featured shooter. Ideally, the lead guard is a scoring threat.

Scoring

A big player can use a backdoor maneuver for a layup. The highlighted shooter obtains a 15- to 20-foot jump shot. A perimeter player secures a post-up situation. The other post player may have position along the lane for a back-to-the-basket scoring chance. The point guard may have a layup or jump shot from a skip pass. The highlighted shooter receives a jump shot on either wing.

Execution

The play begins in the normal motion formation with two perimeter players, the point guard (G) and the highlighted shooter (S1), out front. The other perimeter player (S2) starts on the offside at the foul line extended. Each of the big players (B1 and B2) is on a box along the lane (figure 10.36). B1 performs an L-cut to catch the first pass from G. B1 knows a backdoor chance may present itself if the defense tries to overplay. At the same time, B2 rushes to the high post. When B1 receives the pass from G, the weakside wing (S2) sprints to the ballside low post and establishes position. The high post (B2) picks so that S1 can head to the basket on the strongside of the screen. B2 rescreens for S1. S1 uses the back screen to get open on the offside above the foul line extended. S1's first cut is just a decoy. S1 sells the defense on the idea that he or she is heading to the hoop.

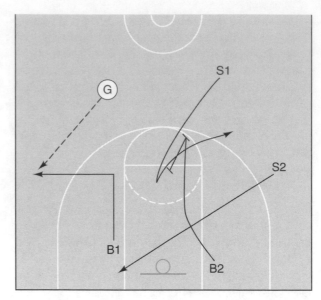

Figure 10.36   Main scoring motion used in motion two-digit number.

S1's first choice is to receive a skip pass from B1. B1 must be aware of the screener (B2). If the defense becomes confused, they may leave B2 open. S1's first thought is to shoot the ball if open. When the ball is skipped, B2 races to the ballside low location, S2 crosses off B2 (he or she moves second) to a spot above the strongside elbow, and B1 back picks for the lead guard (G). The playmaker hustles to the empty area in the weakside corner and could receive a skip pass from S1. If it is available, the point guard may dash to the hoop instead of the near corner.

B1 may pass the ball to the point guard (G) instead of S1. As soon as the pass is released, B1 and B2 move to ballside position along the lane to plant a double screen. In addition, S2 rushes to set a back pick for S1, who continues moving off the double pick to the other side of the half-court.

Another option for S1 is to fake the move toward the double screen and instead exploit S2's rescreen to the open spot on the offside. S2 may then use the double pick set by B1 and B2. S2 darts to the strongside after S1 uses the rescreen.

Keys

The post player works free to catch the first pass by using the L-cut. See the discussion of L-cut in "Man-to-Man Offensive Fine-Tuning" in chapter 1 (page 7). The subsequent items may also be useful: screening between post and perimeter players, setting a screen, slipping a screen, using a pick, rescreening, double screen, throwing the ball inside, and pinning the defender.

The other perimeter shooter (not the primary shooter) must sprint to the ballside box to clear the weakside. He or she moves quickly on the initial pass to the opposite wing.

The rescreen between the high post and the highlighted shooter is critical. The shooter makes the defense believe that his or her primary goal is to cut to the hoop.

The team must practice skip passes. In this play, several players might use skip passes—a big player to send the ball to a shooter, a shooter to pass to the point guard, or the lead guard to deliver the ball to a shooter. If a skip pass comes to the featured shooter off the primary rescreen, he or she immediately looks for a shot. If no shot is available, the shooter's next option is to feed the ball to the big player running to the ballside low site. The next alternative is to throw the ball across to the playmaker on the weakside. Throwing accurate passes is mandatory if players expect to succeed.

As soon as the big player on the wing passes the ball to the lead guard, both post players move together to establish a double screen along the foul lane. The perimeter player low on the strongside reacts rapidly and plants a back pick for the designated shooter as soon as the big player on the wing throws the ball to the point guard above.

OVER

This was the first action I learned that used a lob pass at the basket. The player movements have been used for decades. Coaches use this quick hitter to take advantage of a post player with sound athletic and basketball skills.

Personnel

The play demands a potent inside scoring big player. The player using the back screen for the lob at the hoop should have the size and athletic ability to make it work. The play works better if he or she is a strong perimeter shooter in the 15- to 20-foot range.

Scoring

The post player grabs the ball low along the lane for an inside scoring possibility. Shots occur as a result of a lob toss to the weakside of the basket or a skip pass to the desired player in the open portion of the court. The player back screening secures a perimeter jump shot.

Execution

The play begins in the regular motion set (figure 10.29, page 177) except that the weakside low player (B2) motors across the lane and the offside wing (S2) races to the strongside high post after the first pass is delivered to the big player on the strongside wing (B1) after an L-cut. The player receiving the back pick for a lob assumes B1's position. The weakside wing (S2) is the back screener. The lead guard (G) and other perimeter player (S1) are in a two-out front. Play starts with B1 grabbing the ball after an L-cut. A back cut is possible if the defense denies B1 at the ballside wing.

As soon as the point guard passes to B1, G races to the pass receiver. S1 leaves to replace G to clear one side of the court. The player in the low post (B2) may step off the lane slightly to bring the defender toward the ballside. B1 hands the ball to G and uses S2's back pick. B1 can either traverse to the basket in anticipation of a lob or drift to an open space on the weakside to grab a skip pass. The screener (S2) steps out after back picking for a quick jump shot (figure 10.37). The lead guard (G) looks to throw a lob at the weakside corner of the backboard so that the cutter (B1) can snatch the ball near the rim. Other options are to pass to the screener (S2) or inside to B2 working down low.

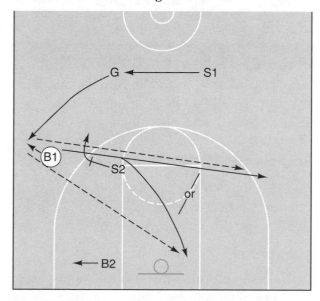

Figure 10.37 Main scoring movements in the over play.

Keys

If the team does not have a player capable of securing the lob pass at the offside of the basket, the coach can change the starting locations of three players. The best exterior shooter is in B1's spot to secure the first pass from the playmaker. The other perimeter shooter becomes part of the two-out front, and the big player (B1) assumes the role of the weakside wing. The primary shooter has a chance to capitalize on the high post's screen to move to a favorable spot on the side that the team has cleared for a cross-court pass reception.

The better inside-scoring big player begins on the offside block on the lane. A player in possession of the ball on the periphery must consider tossing the ball to the interior. The defender may cheat to offer help on a suspected lob. A ball fake helps. Passers always read the defense and make the appropriate toss.

Refer to "Man-to-Man Offensive Fine-Tuning" on page 4 and these items: screening between post and perimeter players, setting a screen, slipping a screen, using a pick, back pick, throwing the ball inside, and L-cut.

Players on the weakside originally must hustle toward the ballside once the pass is on its way from the playmaker to the opposite wing. The play requires the weakside to be vacant.

The lead guard must break free from his or her defender and secure the handoff from the wing. The lead guard regularly practices the lob pass, concentrating on timing, arc, and accuracy. The lob can determine the success or failure of the play.

FRISCO

The components of this play are widely used. Under legendary coach John Wooden, the UCLA Bruins performed numerous offensive movements from a 2-1-2 or 2-3 alignment. The motion in Frisco was part of UCLA's offensive package. The coach does not hesitate to call this play when he or she wants the ball inside but also has outside shooters who will keep the defense honest.

Personnel

An excellent perimeter shooter occupies a spot opposite the point guard out front. The big player who receives the introductory pass should be able to score around the basket. Ideally, the high post is a scoring threat from beyond 15 feet. The player beginning on the weakside wing should be a capable interior scorer. The play is more effective if the playmaker is a solid perimeter shooter.

Scoring

The backdoor maneuver used by the big player to get open for the initial pass may produce a layup. The perimeter shooter secures a layup with a dash to the ballside box off a high-post screen. The high post steps back for a jump shot after picking. The perimeter shooter on the wing garners a distance shot. A big player attains a shot in the lane after down screening and stepping to the ball. The other post player can use a duck-in maneuver to net a post feed and back-to-the-basket scoring payoff.

Execution

One post player (B1) begins at the ballside box and executes an L-cut to catch the first pass from the point guard (G) (figure 10.38). S2 commences motion from the weakside block and heads to the high post as B1 starts to move. On the pass to B1, the opposite wing (B2) motors toward the nearest box on the lane while the two players out top (G and S1) cross off the high post (S2). Although not shown in figure 10.38, the lead guard (G) could sprint on a straight line to the basket but still finish on the offside block.

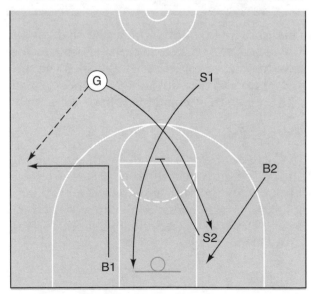

Figure 10.38   Frisco opening set and actions.

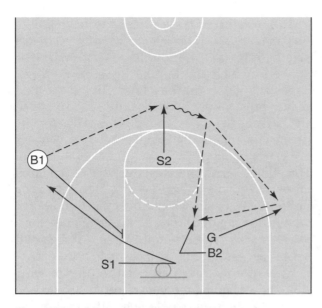

Figure 10.39 Frisco movements continue.

Therefore, G and S1 would conduct their cuts to the hoop one right after the other.

The high post (S2) pops out after the screen to retrieve the next pass from B1 (figure 10.39). On the pass to S2 near the top of the key, B1 immediately hustles to down pick for S1. The playmaker (G) races to the near foul line extended past the three-point arc. B2 ducks into the lane to post up. S2 may need to dribble toward G's side to achieve a proper angle for an entry pass to B2. The pass inside to B2 could come from S2 or G. S2 reads the defense before delivering the next pass. He or she glances into B2 as the primary target, but sees the entire floor, including the results of the down-screening activity.

Keys

See the discussions of setting a screen, slipping a screen, using a pick, down screen, throwing the ball inside, L-cut, duck-in, and pinning the defender in "Man-to-Man Offensive Fine-Tuning" on page 4.

The point guard decides whether to cross or cut straight to the basket off the high-post screen. The teammate alongside reacts to the playmaker's lead.

The player who is to acquire the duck-in opportunity is on the weakside wing initially. The coach may change the play call by using this person's name, for example, "Frisco for Bob."

The high post must get open to grab the second pass. No excuses are accepted.

MOTION FOR NAME

One of the hottest trends in college basketball is to provide players with one-on-one chances. The dribble penetration is the primary offensive action. Sometimes, when a team is struggling on the offensive end of the court, it is best to use this most basic method to secure a shot. The dribble penetration is the oldest and most popular form of motion to generate shots. The play is especially useful if the squad has a strong one-on-one player. A sample call is "Motion for Bob."

Personnel

The featured player should possess good athletic ability, have solid skills when facing the basket, and be able to put the ball on the floor to create a scoring chance. The player beginning at the weakside wing must be capable of hitting a jumper from approximately 20 feet.

Scoring

Motion for name provides a one-on-one chance for a specific player. A distant jump shot by a perimeter shooter is also viable.

Execution

The highlighted player (N) starts on the ballside block (figure 10.40). A post player (B2) begins at the weakside block. He or she motors to the high post at the same time that N begins execution

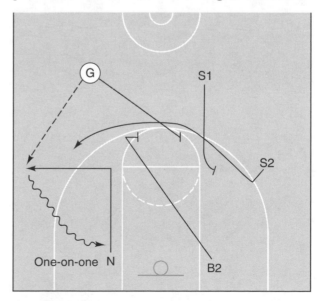

Figure 10.40 Motion for name play.

of an L-cut. An effective outside shooter (S2) occupies the weakside wing. The point guard (G) is in two-out formation with S1 and sends the introductory pass to N. After the ball leaves G's hands, G and S1 fix staggered screens for the opposite wing (S2). The high post (B2) plants a third pick for S2. The high post's screen is always the last one. S2 scampers to an open site near the opposite wing above the player with the ball. N controls the ball and immediately turns to face the basket. N drives to the hoop. If defensive help is impeding the dribble penetration, N shoots or flings the ball to S2 out in the area N just vacated or to one of the other three teammates.

Keys

See L-cut, setting a screen, and using a pick in "Man-to-Man Offensive Fine-Tuning" in chapter 1 on page 4.

Any player, except the point guard, can be the featured player. The lead guard can assume the highlighted player's spot only if a teammate can assume the playmaker's duties. The player whose name is called begins at the ballside block and gets the first pass. He or she has the chance to go one-on-one. The team's most potent perimeter shooter should start at the offside wing. He or she is the secondary scoring option. The remaining exterior player fills the slot opposite the point guard.

The designated player needs to have strong one-on-one skills. The team is clearing all defensive help toward the foul line to maximize the space in which the featured player operates, especially along the baseline. The highlighted player breaks down the defender and heads to the basket. If a quality shot does not develop, he or she immediately looks out to the near wing for the player coming off the three screens at the top. Sometimes, when the player driving to the hoop stops and pivots 180 degrees to face out to the periphery, he or she will discover that the shooter, who is coming off the three picks, is open for a long-distance shot attempt. When a three-point shot is necessary, this is one way to secure it.

The shooter originally at the offside wing times his or her movement off the three consecutive picks out front to coincide with the featured player's dribble penetration. The big player in the high post always sets the final screen. The pick is somewhere above the ballside elbow. The first two screeners actively target the defender on the shooter. All three screeners are ready to adjust to defensive switches.

After they have completed their jobs, the three screeners look to adjust their positions based on the reactions of their defenders to the dribble penetration. Two of the three cannot head to the same location. They watch their spacing so that the defenders cannot easily supply assistance to the defender on the dribbler.

CHAPTER 11

Delay Games

A stall can be a useful tool. Even if the offense is operating under the restrictions of a shot clock, a delay game can be an effective offensive weapon. It slows the tempo of a game, decreases the number of possessions, helps a club protect a lead late in a game when time is the enemy, and may cause a defense to extend outward farther than it likes and thus become more vulnerable.

When the game does not use a shot clock, stalling actually becomes an offense. Spreading the floor after gaining the lead is sometimes the preferred strategy. Coaches can choose to use a delay game regardless of the exact time on the game clock. Perhaps the offense is overmatched. To achieve the upset, the team needs to turn the game into a low-scoring affair. A club that is a serious underdog may want to shorten the game, running time off the clock to keep the game close until the final few minutes. A stall slows the rhythm of the game dramatically. Each offensive possession increases in value.

The five delay games in this chapter are designed to keep the ball away from the defense. Whatever the motive for using the delay, the five delay plays reviewed here will furnish the coach with enough variety to find one to match his or her needs.

DELAY

Rules for defending a ball handler have changed frequently over the years, ranging from no restrictions whatsoever to regulations based on where the dribbler is in relation to a sideline hash mark in the forecourt. When college basketball instituted the shot clock in the 1980s, the five-second closely guarded rule was soon eliminated, mostly because game officials did not want to count. With no threat of a five-second violation, a team could hand the ball to a player who would dribble for as long as he or she wanted. The delay offense was born.

Coaches use the delay offense any time they want to run time off the clock. A coach might use it early in a game to create a slower tempo or at the end of a game to protect a lead. The play is ideal if the five-second closely guarded rule is not in play. If the rule is in force, the ball should be in the hands of an excellent ball handler who is quick. If a shot clock is active, teams should use additional motion to manufacture shots at the 10- to 12-second mark. The coach must be confident that one of the players can dominate the ball to take advantage of the play.

Personnel

Ideally, the ball handler out front is the point guard. He or she must have the ability to dribble penetrate, handle the ball confidently, and be quick. The ball handler should be an excellent foul shooter if the play is used when protecting a lead late in a game against an opponent who is forced to foul. Two post players need inside-scoring capabilities, and two perimeter players must be able to shoot the ball convincingly from distance. Any player can be isolated up top if he or she has the required attributes.

Scoring

The ball handler creates all shots by passing and scoring off the dribble. Another section in this chapter, beginning on page 195, reviews the actual movements designed to produce scoring chances.

Execution

In the initial set, G, the point guard, has possession of the ball (figure 11.1). The other four players are stretched along the baseline. Two shooters (S1 and S2) occupy positions on each block along the foul lane. Post players (B1 and B2) are set in each corner.

The point guard (G) dribbles to keep control of the ball as the shot clock or game clock runs down. He or she may need to lose the defender periodically if a closely guarded violation is possible. The squad must be ready to handle

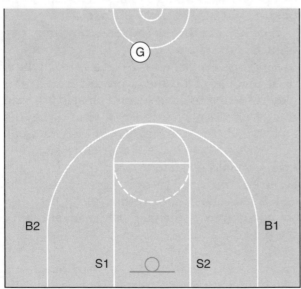

Figure 11.1   Initial set for delay.

any attempt to double-team the dribbler. If the defense double-teams the ball handler, one offensive player will be free of a defender. The player whose defender leaves to trap hooks up in front of the ball. As defenders rotate, the unguarded player fills a vacant spot in front of the ball. The ball handler reacts calmly to any defensive pressure.

Keys

The delay game is practical only if the five-second closely guarded rule is not in play or if the ball handler has exceptional quickness that would make it hard for a defender to guard him or her closely. Coaches use the offense any time they want to run time off the clock. They inform the ball handler precisely how much time is to disappear.

The ball handler out front dominates the ball as the shot or game clock winds down. He or she holds the ball until fouled or instructed to initiate a scoring movement. Scoring action commences at the 10- to 12-second mark on the shot clock. The coach decides whether to allow the ball handler to shoot before the designated time if he or she is able to lose the defender.

When protecting a lead, the best foul shooter should be out top with the ball, especially if the defense is likely to foul. This player should be at the foul line during crunch time.

The coach's confidence in the offense goes a long way in resolving when the team will execute it. Players must also be confident in the effectiveness of the play. Confidence is infectious. The higher the level of confidence, the earlier in the game a team can use the play.

Coaches should drill players on handling double-team pressure. Players hook up in open areas in front of the ball. The coach tells the team whether to attack and try to score or to continue to play keep-away. He or she instructs players concerning the types of shots permitted. Can they shoot layups or other shots under specific circumstances? If the squad does a good job of countering pressure, they are likely to see scoring chances.

FOUR CORNERS

Dean Smith, former coach of the University of North Carolina at Chapel Hill, made the four corners offense famous. To protect a lead in the always tough Atlantic Coast Conference, North Carolina simply placed a player in each corner to spread the offense on the half-court. The formation left the middle of the court vacant for the ball handler to use. Teams later used the play to slow the tempo of the game. Soon squads deemed heavy underdogs were using the offense to keep games within reach. Some final scores in 40-minute college games were in the teens and 20s. Fewer possessions increase the offensive pressure. Squads viewed as favorites want more possessions to take advantage of their perceived edge.

Teams use the four corners offense at any time during a game to slow the tempo. The offense can be used with or without a shot clock. With a shot clock, the team must be ready to use a scoring movement when the clock runs down. Four corners also is a good play to use to protect a lead. The team tries to hold the ball for as long as possible to knock off a given amount of time before trying to score. If no shot clock is active, an underdog team can use four corners as a half-court offense. Under those circumstances, having a lead is not necessary. Sometimes, a team just wants to keep the score close and have a chance to pull out a victory in the closing minutes or seconds.

Personnel

Three good ball handlers are out front near half-court. One could be a post player if he or she is one of the squad's best offensive players. These three players need to be quality foul shooters. The two big players or the weakest ball handlers and foul shooters assume positions in the corners. When using the play to score, three perimeter players should be out front to ensure a smooth transition into scoring movements. Big players must be fully capable of handling passes while still or on the move.

Scoring

The dribbler manufactures most shots in the four corners offense. Shots for the ball handler could include 20-foot shots, layups, or anything in between. Other players gain openings for layups, short jumpers, or shots from behind the three-point line as a direct result of the dribbler's ability to puncture the defense. The

dribbler's drive causes one or more defenders to leave their assignments, thus opening players to receive passes.

The go option creates a layup for one exterior player. Another perimeter player may see shots behind the arc in the wing or corner. The final perimeter player may get shots 5 to 20 feet from the basket. A big player acquires one-on-one opportunities.

Execution

In the starting set, two perimeter players (the best ball handlers and foul shooters) are in the corners near the half-court (S1 and S2), and the third, usually the playmaker (G), has the ball (figure 11.2). A big player (B1 or B2) is in each corner. The team spreads the offense as much as possible on the half-court. The ball handler looks to dribble penetrate. He or she is aware of the five-second closely guarded rule. The ball handler can hold the ball for four seconds, dribble for four seconds, and then hold it for four more seconds before a violation occurs. The dribbler might lose the defender far enough to cancel the closely guarded status and cause a new count to begin. The point guard (G) controls the ball in the middle of the floor as long as possible.

Often the defenders on the two players near midcourt will move away from their assignments to help on the ball handler in the middle. After the middle player gives up the ball to either teammate near half-court, he or

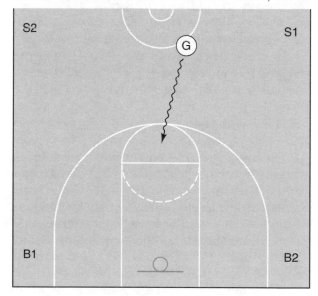

Figure 11.2 Four corners formation.

she moves horizontally to that sideline as soon as the receiver puts the ball on the floor. The passer replaces his or her corner teammate as a new player takes over in the middle. The pass receiver may hold the ball for several seconds before placing it on the floor and heading to the middle. If so, the passer hangs in the middle until the ball hits the court.

If the ball handler has a path to the basket, he or she might attempt a layup or dump the ball to either big player pinching to the hoop as defenders help on the penetration. Generally, the dribbler throws a bounce pass to the post player slicing to the goal. Short jump shots may develop for any of the three players.

Usually, the coach does not want to send the ball to a corner because the players there are the team's weakest foul shooters and ball handlers. But when circumstances require doing so, the coach wants to get the ball out of their hands as quickly as possible. If the ball goes to a big player in a corner, the middle player moves quickly to retrieve it. He or she must lose the defender. Otherwise, the remaining players in the midcourt corners engage in a scramble to regain the ball from the big player's control. Once they retrieve the ball, players immediately gain control of the situation by taking the ball to the middle and reacquiring the four corners alignment.

To run any of the scoring motions reviewed later in the chapter (page 195), players simply race to predetermined locations before initiating the actions of the scoring play.

Another alternative a team can use when executing four corners is the go option (figure 11.3). When the play is called, the big players (B1 and B2) move near the elbows. G delivers the ball to one of them (B1 in figure 11.3). On the pass, the player in the same-side upper corner (S2) back cuts to the basket. B1's first choice is to bounce a pass to S2, who is racing for a layup. At the same time, the player in the middle (G, who made the original pass to B1) picks for S1 in the other corner near the half-court. G and S2 make their moves simultaneously. S1 loops around the ball handler toward the strongside corner; S1 is the second pass option for B1. B2 back picks for the screener (G). G fades to the same-side corner. B1's third choice is a skip pass to G. If none of the three possibilities is available, B1 tries to go one-on-one.

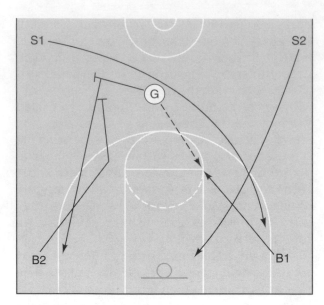

Figure 11.3 Go option.

Keys

The middle player with the ball is aware of the closely guarded rule. He or she completes a pass to a teammate to avoid a five-second violation. The middle player hesitates after completing the pass to the player in the corner near half-court. When the pass receiver places the ball on the floor and heads to the middle, the passer moves to the appropriate sideline. The middle player breaks to the same-side sideline in a line parallel with the midcourt stripe. An opponent may be able to prevent the dribble to the middle. In that case, the ball handler dribbles down the near sideline. As soon he or she does that, the player in the middle sprints up to the center circle and then over to the vacant corner.

The player with the ball in the middle looks to drive to the hoop. Players know exactly what types and lengths of shots each is allowed to pursue. The coach informs players what he or she wants to do. Some coaches give signs to the squad to indicate if they should take no shots, attempt only layups, or observe other restrictions.

If the shot clock is active, players attempt to score at the 10- to 12-second mark. Several scoring movements are reviewed later in the chapter on page 195. Players practice smooth transitions into each required set. The coach realizes that the point guard may not have the ball in the middle every time he or she wants a particular play executed. Other players may have to assume the playmaker's duties. Therefore, the lead guard also needs to know a shooter's role for each option. The inclusion of a shot clock requires more instructional time on transition to and execution of the scoring calls. Certainly, the coach is not obligated to teach every option. Whatever the coach decides, he or she must set aside sufficient practice time to drill movements.

If there is no shot clock, the timing of a scoring action is strictly at the coach's discretion. Four corners can be an extremely productive offense when a shot clock is not in use. Players must value and protect the ball. They must be patient and shoot only under clearly defined circumstances. Four corners negates a personnel or size advantage. Slowing the tempo of the game and spreading the floor is a good way for a mismatched team to compete on more even terms.

The go option is most effective when used with four corners and four to score (see the next section). The go option begins with post players in the baseline corners sprinting to the near elbows. The middle player passes the ball to either post player. The coach can direct the passer to deliver the ball to a particular big player. The go option could also be used with the delay, but players must assume the four corners formation before starting any scoring movements.

FOUR TO SCORE

Four to score uses the delay game as an offensive weapon. This offense became well known in the 1980s when St. Joseph's University in Philadelphia upset then number one DePaul University in the NCAA Tournament. The spread offense was used to control tempo and place the defense into a more vulnerable form. Rather than holding the basketball strictly to shorten the game, the four to score offense encourages shots other than layups. The play is appropriate with or without a shot clock.

The four to score offense, designed for a team that is a decided underdog, slows the tempo of the game. The play is most feasible when there is no shot clock, but it is certainly useful when there is one. The team is not playing keep-away; they use the offense to attack and score. The goal is to run time off the clock and decrease the number of offensive possessions in the game. Still, teams can use it to hold the ball. The coach just dictates the exact shots that players can attempt, if any.

Personnel

All three perimeter people should be proficient ball handlers, possess good quickness, and have the ability to dribble penetrate. Scoring opportunities develop through their capacity to use the dribble. The two post players must be potent scorers from 15 to 18 feet and in. The better they are at scoring when facing the hoop, the more productive the offense.

Scoring

Big players attain opportunities in the low-post regions after their teammates deliver entry passes inside. The second post player could gain freedom from the defender in the high post. Potential one-on-one situations may occur for the high post. Big players may earn layups or jump shots of 15 to 18 feet along the baseline because of a teammate's dribble penetration. Perimeter players shoot off the dribble or release jumpers if defenders leave to help on the ball handler. All scoring payoffs connected with the scoring movements described on page 195 and the go option discussed under the four corners offense are also feasible.

Execution

The starting set is identical to four corners (see figure 11.2, page 191). The main activity is from the middle player with the ball. He or she usually is the playmaker (G). Players are aware of the five-second closely guarded rule, if it applies. While in the holding-ball phase, maintaining possession is paramount. The other four players remain in their positions. Two perimeter players are near midcourt, and two big players are in the corners.

As in four corners, the middle player penetrates to the basket. This move is the backbone of the offense. All three perimeter players need to be proficient at dribble penetration and able to make sound decisions with the ball. As the defense supplies assistance, the middle player or either big player along the baseline may earn scoring payoffs, either layups or 15- to 18-foot jump shots. If the middle player (G) completes the toss to a player in a high corner, the passer waits in the middle until the pass receiver dribbles the ball. If the ball handler heads toward the lane, the middle player races on a path parallel with the midcourt line to the same sideline to which the ball was passed. The player then slides to the near high corner to replace the dribbler.

The offense differs from four corners when the middle player completes a pass to a player in the high corner and the defender sits on the pass receiver's inside shoulder. This circumstance forces the recipient to dribble down the sideline instead of to the middle. The passer (G in figure 11.4) hangs out in the lane until the ball is put on the floor. After the pass receiver begins to dribble down the sideline, the middle player screens away for the player in the opposite high corner. The screen recipient (S2) replaces the ball handler in the opposite corner near midcourt. When the dribbler (S1) reaches the foul line extended, the ballside big player (B2) hustles across the lane to set a pick for B1. The low-exchange recipient (B1) steps high and heads low off B2's pick. The screener (B2) seals back to the ball, rushing to the high post. The ball handler tosses to either big player for a shot attempt. The player exploiting the screen has a second alternative—step low and cut high. The screener (B2) seals back to a position low on the strongside. The big players use this prerogative every time their defenders switch the

low exchange. The screener (B2) is most likely open to catch the entry pass.

Keys

Players stay spread and give the middle player as much room to operate as possible. The ball handler tries to beat the defender by dribbling. A dribble penetration maximizes the opponent's defensive problems.

The offense is designed to stretch the defense. Defenders chase offensive players. Player alignment forces the opposing coach to decide how hard to come after the offense. Passive man-to-man pressure makes it easier for the offense to hold the ball and run time off the clock.

The middle player gives up the ball to a teammate to ensure that no five-second closely guarded violation occurs. After passing the ball to a teammate near half-court, the ball handler remains stationary in the lane area until the direction of the next dribble is determined. The penetrating player may need to toss the ball to one of the big players in a corner. If so, he or she looks to secure a quick return pass. Preferably, big players will not dribble the ball unless required. If needed, the other two perimeter players become involved in a scramble to retrieve the ball from the big player.

A player with the ball in the high corner may choose to dribble along the sideline instead of to the middle. He or she may choose that option without being forced there by the defense.

Additional motion occurs when a player drives down a sideline. He or she never reaches a corner. The pick across the lane commences after the ball hits the foul line extended. The big player receiving the pick waits for it. He or she steps one way and goes the other. The player using the screen regularly cuts high if the defense switches. The screener invariably heads opposite.

All three perimeter players have to be well versed in driving to the hoop. Their decision-making skills will be tested. Exterior players need to know that how well they dribble penetrate goes a long way in determining the success of the offense.

The coach should review with players exactly what types of shots are permitted. Because the offense has a scoring aspect, the coach must establish parameters so that players know what

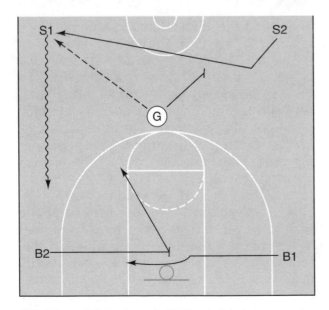

Figure 11.4 Dribble down the sideline in four to score.

to do. Theoretically, the coach could assign each player on the court a different distance, matching restrictions to player capabilities.

With four to score, the team has not abandoned all thoughts of shooting. In fact, more scoring may occur. The coach just does not want squad members to shoot too quickly. If using the offense to hold the ball to protect a lead, players know to keep the ball in the hands of the team's better free-throw shooters. Following this instruction is especially important if the opponent must foul to save time.

The coach has the prerogative to use one of the other scoring plays reviewed in the next section. The go option is also available (page 192). If there is a shot clock, the team must use one of the other scoring actions with no less than 10 seconds on the clock. If no shot clock is in use (more likely in high school and below), it is strictly the coach's choice about when to use a scoring motion. Teams must extensively practice transition into one of the scoring motions. The location of personnel when the play is called can vary greatly. Players must obtain enough repetitions to complete the transition successfully. Once players are in proper alignment for each play, the movements are not complicated and players should be able to execute them easily.

SCORING MOVEMENTS

The three delay games reviewed in this chapter so far—delay, four corners, and four to score—spread four players on the half-court. Either four players are stretched across the baseline, or they readily transform into the formation. When a shot clock is part of the game, the team wishing to slow the pace or hold the ball must know ways to score as time is about to expire. Without a scoring motion, delay games only run time off the clock. The ability to score is integral to any attempt to hold the basketball. Consuming time and scoring is the best delay game a team can use.

A team holding the ball with the shot clock running down needs to perform scoring movements at the 10- to 12-second point. If the goal is to slow the tempo of the game, the coach directs players to use a prescribed amount of time before employing one of the scoring

options described in this section: cross, distance, post, big name, open special, or open. Each play emphasizes different actions and creates different types of shots. Shots are spread among various players. Transition into the scoring motion must be easy, and the players must be able to manufacture a shot outcome in a short time.

Perimeter players must be capable ball handlers and shooters. Shots occur either directly off a pass reception or off a dribble. Players should be able to take the ball to the hoop. Big players can corral post feeds and must be able to score around the basket. If a step-back maneuver is allowed after screening for a ball handler, players must shoot well from 18 to 20 feet in front of the hoop.

Both perimeter shooters and the playmaker receive shot attempts from 15 to 20 feet at a variety of peripheral locations. Shots in or near the foul lane may develop for any of the five players. Shots may result from dribble drives for exterior players. Big players obtain scoring chances around the hoop. One of the post players can shoot from the key if the coach permits him or her to step out after setting the screen for the ball handler.

A number of calls are possible. The first one is *cross* (figure 11.5). The cross call dictates action along the baseline with post players screening for the two shooters. Two big players (B2 and B1) hustle toward the lane to screen for the

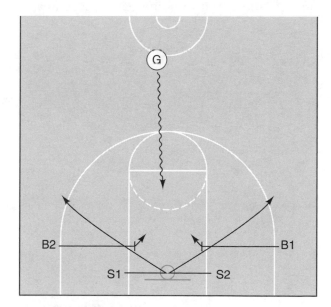

Figure 11.5 Cross call.

shooters (S1 and S2, respectively) to start the play. The shooters may cross near the center of the lane or fake it and use the pick on the same side of the floor. The point guard (G) passes to either shooter for an outside shot attempt. The screeners (B1 and B2) step to the ball after their teammates have exploited the picks. The lead guard considers an entry pass to either big player if the defender is sealed on the back. The playmaker uses a dribble drive to create a scoring chance for him- or herself or for a teammate. Between the screening action and dribble drive, an acceptable shot is likely to appear.

The next call is *distance,* which is discussed in depth in chapter 12. Distance emphasizes a dribble penetration by the ball handler. Perimeter players realize the bulk of the shooting opportunities. Players assume starting positions (figure 11.6). Two big players (B1 and B2) slide up to a location near the sideline at about the foul line extended. At the same time, the shooters (S1 and S2) bolt to the corners. The playmaker (G) dribbles into the lane. When the team needs only two points, the ball handler could go to the basket to create a shot. If this is not feasible, the point guard picks up the dribble just inside the foul line, pivots, and faces out toward half-court. Once the ball handler (G) dribbles across the foul line, the post players (B1 and B2) hustle to set screens for the shooters (S2 and S1, respectively) in each corner (figure 11.6). The shooters rub off the picks and go above the foul line extended on each

side of the floor. They anticipate a toss from the lead guard and a shot from behind the arc. Big players rescreen if necessary.

The third possible call is *post-up.* Post-up (figure 11.7) creates a corner shot for an exterior player who rubs off a double-screen established along the lane, produces an inside-scoring chance for one of the two post players, or creates a shot for the ball handler off the dribble. Post players (B2 and B1) move toward the lane to pick for teammates at the blocks. The shooter on the same side as B2 cuts opposite off S2 and B1's double screen. S1 heads to the ballside corner. If he or she is free for a shot attempt, the ball handler (G) delivers the ball. If S1 is not open for a shot, G uses a reverse dribble to return to the other side of the half-court. G casts the ball into B2, who is posting strong along the lane. B2 should be the most proficient interior scorer. He or she moves into the lane from the corner and walks the defender in while facing him or her. The player pivots on the foul-line foot to pin the defender on his or her back. For proper timing, the pinning action occurs as the lead guard dribbles back to the post's side. The playmaker executes a one-on-one if teammates are covered. The coach can call the play for a particular player by including in the call the name of the post player to be isolated inside.

The fourth call option is *big name* (figure 11.8). Big name is designed to set up a strong outside shooter for a peripheral shot. Other players may receive the ball for scoring oppor-

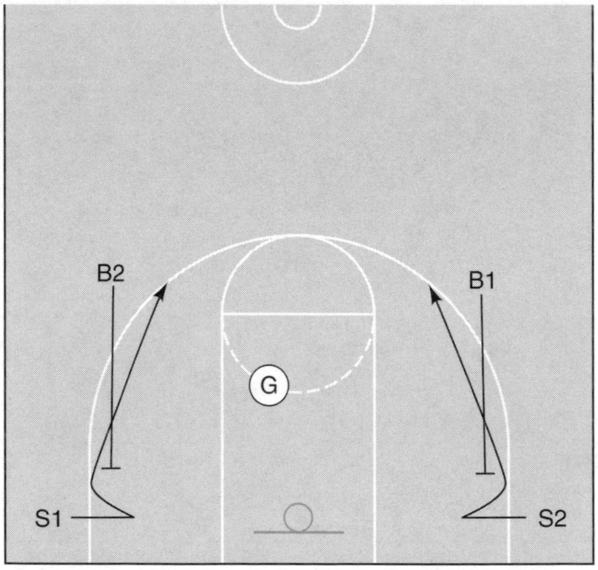

Figure 11.6 Distance option.

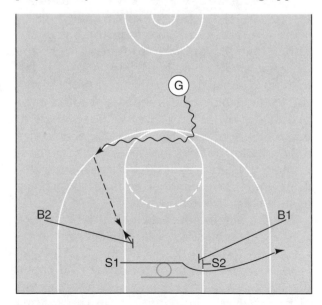

Figure 11.7 Post-up.

tunities if they pop open because of a defensive error or if the defense overextends while guarding the primary shooter. Post players (B2 and B1) move toward the lane to set screens on each side. In this case, S1's name was called (N in figure 11.8). N chooses to use the double pick set by S2 and B1 or the single screen set by B2. N usually uses the single screen. He or she sells the defender one way and sprints the other. The ball handler is ready to deliver the ball to the screener if the defender steps out to help on the shooter. The point guard casts the ball to the open player. B2 seals his or her defender and steps to the ball after N uses the screen. If N rubs off the lone pick, it is possible for the ball to be thrown directly to B2. If N exploits the double pick, S2 or B1 could spring open if either defender moves to help. Refer to chapter 10 for a more detailed review of a similar play, big for name (page 176).

Another choice is *open special*. In open special, four players may receive shot chances. The point guard uses a screen on the ball. One perimeter shooter is open by means of a kickout to a corner. The other shooter attains shot chances near the top of the key. A post player rolling to the hoop after setting the pick for the ball handler is another potential target. Some movements are necessary before players actually perform the play. The shooters (S1 and S2) pop out to their respective corners, while post players (B1 and B2) go above the elbows at the three-point arc. Refer to figure 11.9. The lead

guard (G) controls the ball above the key and waits for teammates to reach their destinations. After everyone is in place, the playmaker (G) dribbles off either B1 or B2's screen. G initially heads toward one and zips back off the other. In figure 11.9, G exploits B2's screen. B2 rolls to the basket as B1 screens down for S2 on the same side. The ball handler can penetrate to the basket, launch an open shot, drive to the hoop and kick the ball out to the shooter in the same-side corner (S1), bounce pass to B2 rolling to the hoop, or pass to S2, who is coming to the top of the key for an outside shot.

One key to open special is for the playmaker to convince the defense that he or she will exploit a big player's screen but then swiftly reverse the dribble to use the other big player's screen. The point guard becomes the creator and decision maker with regard to scoring chances. The coach may decide to allow the screener to step back after the lead guard uses the pick if the big body is an effective distance shooter and feels that stepping back will result in a shot. If by some chance the post player does not acquire the ball promptly, he or she moves to plant a second pick for the shooter heading to the top.

Another possible call is *open*. Open can be called wherever on the periphery the ball is controlled. Four players rapidly fill predetermined slots based solely on placement of the ball. They hustle to positions that enable the ball handler to go one-on-one, keeping defensive help away

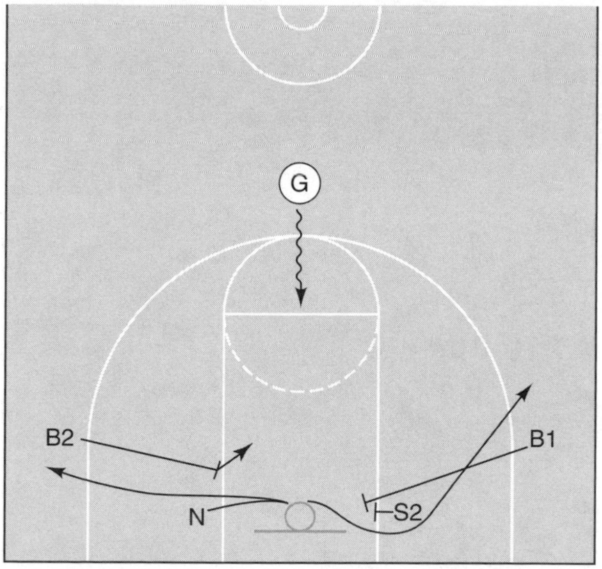

Figure 11.8   Big name call.

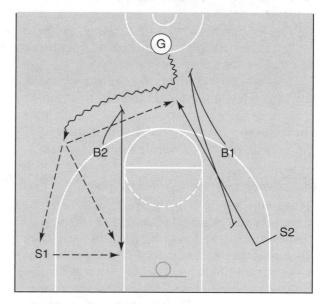

Figure 11.9   Open special option.

from the dribbler. Normally, the ball is above the foul line extended within the lane region (the area running the length of the court between the lane lines). Therefore, players space themselves evenly along the baseline. Ball location determines player positioning. The court is divided horizontally into sections below and above the foul line extended and vertically into three sections (two sideline areas and one lane region). A full description of the play is in chapter 10, beginning on page 153.

Chapter 10 reviews many quick-hitting plays (page 149). Any play that produces a shot in a short period is a potential scoring action that teams can use at the end of a delay game. But players must be able to perform a smooth transition into the play, and the motion should secure shots for the preferred team members.

Review the following topics in "Man-to-Man Offensive Fine-Tuning" in chapter 1 on page 4: screening between post and perimeter players, setting a screen, slipping a screen, using a pick, rescreening, down screen, two-player game, double screen, low exchanges and cross screens, and pinning the defender.

FREEZE

Ever since coaches began to slow the tempo or play keep-away at the end of a game, they have used the freeze play. Teams from junior high through college have used the play. The University of Scranton used the freeze alignment and motion for years while enjoying status as an NCAA Division III powerhouse. Teams use freeze to hold the ball while emphasizing counters to aggressive defensive procedures.

Teams will most likely use freeze when they are in the lead and decide to hold the ball. The goal is to slow the pace of the game, giving an underdog a shot at an upset. The primary function of the play is to run time off the clock.

Personnel

The team needs at least three proficient ball handlers who are strong foul shooters and can make sound decisions with the ball. One should be a post player if possible. The freeze offense works more effectively if all three are strong one-on-one players. The offense differs from those discussed previously because it has a big player out front handling the basketball.

Scoring

Any player may acquire layup chances. The player at the foul line can drive to the basket after catching the ball. Unlike delay, four corners, and four to score, the scoring movements discussed previously are not appropriate from this offense.

Execution

In the initial set, the three highlighted players (B1, S1, and G in figure 11.10) assume their positions (two out front and one at the foul line). In this case, the lead guard (G) has the basketball. B2 and S2 are on the wings at the foul line extended. These two players are last resorts for pass receptions. Because they are the weakest ball handlers and free-throw shooters, they are not part of the offensive motion. G tosses the ball out front to B1 and then immediately hustles to screen for S1 at the foul line. S1 waits for the pick. The wings (B2 and S2) remain close to their sidelines at foul-line level.

Periodically, the player at the foul line swiftly back picks for the passer, who darts to the hoop. Back picking is most effective on a passer because he or she is the only player on the floor who can score before the moment the ball leaves his or her hands. The back screen must be legal; the player must give the defender one step. The player at the foul line decides whether or not to back pick. He or she places a fist in the air and calls the passer's name as soon

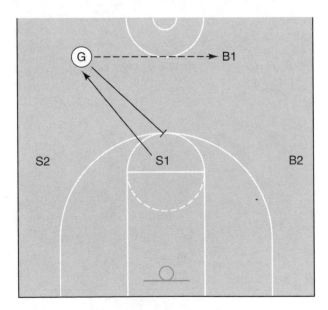

Figure 11.10   Freeze opening set and motion.

as the ball is released. Otherwise, the passer heads down to pick for the player at the foul line. Players mix in the back screen about 30 percent of the time.

When the defense aggressively overplays the ballside wing, a backdoor opportunity can arise. The player out front bounces a pass to the cutter for a layup. If a teammate is not open on the dash to the hoop, the cutter swiftly returns to the original position at the wing. The wing should handle the ball only on a back cut for a layup or as a last resort for the player with the ball directly above.

Figure 11.11 illustrates a back cut to the hoop for a layup by the down screener (G). The lead guard (G) delivers the ball across to B1. G sets a down pick. S1 moves opposite the ball. G (the screener) slips the screen by cutting hard to the basket before actually setting the screen. This action confuses the defense and leaves an opening for the screener bolting to the goal. B1 zips the ball to G. The pass may be sent to the high post whenever viable. The pass receiver is empowered to take the defender one-on-one to score. The team runs the play continuously, with the triangular motion occurring in the lane area and two players filling sites at the wings.

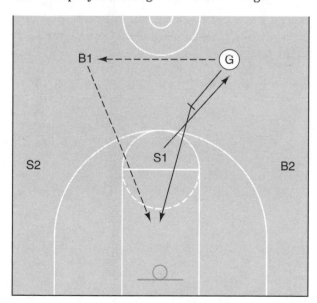

Figure 11.11 Slipping the screen for a layup.

Keys

Three players with appropriate skills must be out top and at the foul line. They do the bulk of the ballhandling and shoot most of the free

throws. The offense works best if one of the three is a big player because then the defense has more difficulty switching screens. They will be reluctant to allow a physical mismatch. See the discussion of screening between post and perimeter players in chapter 1 (page 4).

The sign for a back pick must be relayed as the passing motion across the top begins, as soon as the ball leaves the passer's hands. Otherwise, the down pick will have already begun.

The wing regularly looks for a backdoor opportunity when the player directly above catches the ball. The wing sets it up by stepping out while giving a target. The passer's ball fake tells the player to plant the outside foot (the one furthest from the basket), pivot, and dash to the hoop. If no pass comes, he or she rapidly returns to the same wing. The player does not back cut repeatedly. He or she reads the defender, watching for a head turn and determining if the location is too far on the high side.

The player out front tosses the ball to the wing only if a pass across or to the foul line is not available. Once the wing has the ball, the three primary players scramble to get open. The player with the ball dribbles when necessary. He or she can hold the ball for four seconds, dribble for four, and hold again for four before a five-second closely guarded violation occurs. Players do not put the ball on the floor immediately after the catch.

The player receiving the down screen at the foul line may be able to back cut to the hoop instead of using the screen to slide up toward half-court. The screener reads the act and comes back to his or her original location opposite the ball. Players look to score if instructed to do so. They need to know what shots they can attempt.

The one-on-one option at the foul line is not mandatory. The coach must authorize it. He or she may give the choice only to a selected one or two players. The coach decides who is permitted to go one-on-one.

See the following items in "Man-to-Man Offensive Fine-Tuning" on page 4: setting a screen, using a pick, rescreening, and back pick.

If a shot clock is active, the team needs some kind of quick-hitting play that allows a smooth transition at the 10- to 12-second mark. Another alternative is to allow the ball handler to go one-on-one. I highly recommend the one-on-

one scenario. An easy way to signal the option is to yell, "Open!" (Open is described in chapter 10). Whoever has the ball when the call is made executes the one-on-one.

GEORGETOWN

Coach John Thompson of Georgetown University used the Georgetown play as his delay action to win games. His success with the offense increased its popularity. Coaches at all levels of play have used it extensively. Teams can use the play at any time during a game to slow its pace, or they can use it to hold the ball for a last shot near the end of a quarter or half. Georgetown is extremely effective when a team uses it to sit on the ball to protect a lead.

Personnel

The three perimeter players must be effective ball handlers and sound free-throw shooters. They will probably have to make charity tosses under pressure. Exterior players must make sound decisions with the ball. The two post players should be capable scorers near the basket when asked to shoot. Physical size increases their potency as stationary screeners.

Scoring

Drives to the basket can lead to scores. Backdoor moves may create chances for layups. Big players could see back-to-the-basket situations develop.

Execution

In the starting set, the point guard (G) has the ball above the top of the key (figure 11.12). Post players (B2 and B1) are at the side elbows with a shooter (S1 and S2) stacked below each. The lead guard (G) dribbles wide off either stack. When he or she nears the foul line, the closest perimeter player (S1) pops out top using a big player (B2) as a stationary screener.

G passes to S1 out top and immediately moves to replace S1 in the stack with B2. S1 dribbles the ball to the wing on the other side. When he or she reaches the foul line extended, the players repeat the action.

Instead of reversing the ball after catching it, the pass receiver could dribble back to the side

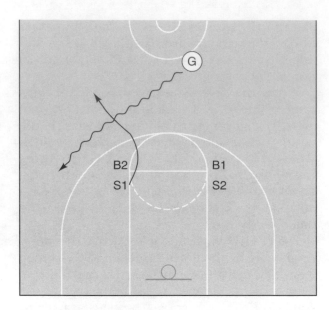

Figure 11.12 Dribble to the wing in Georgetown.

where the toss originated. The passer heads into the stack and then loops around the stationary pick, bursting out top.

S2 dribbles to the opposite wing after gaining the ball from S1 (figure 11.13). S1 returns to the stack with B1. As G moves around B2 to the top, he or she notices the defense cheating in that direction. The lead guard (G) recognizes that a back cut to the hoop may be open and executes it. S2 passes (likely a bounce pass) to G for a layup.

If the ball is on a wing and the defense overplays a perimeter player, making it difficult to

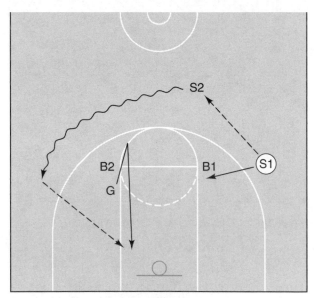

Figure 11.13 G back cuts to basket for a layup.

pass the ball to the top, the same-side big player dives to the basket for a post-up opportunity. The post feed inside to ballside low is possible. The big player's back cut to the hoop can occur not only when the player at the top is denied. The back cut can also surprise the defense, especially if the defender on the post player is not paying attention. If the wing does not have a pass to the big player low or the player out top, he or she dribbles back to position above the key. The other two players return to form a stack at the elbow. The wing is aware of the five-second closely guarded violation; it could come into play at this point. If other players recognize that the ball handler is in trouble, they respond by scrambling, losing defenders to get open.

Another movement option begins with S2 dribbling to the wing (figure 11.14). Players use the normal action of the play. When S2 nears the foul line, the nearest outside player (S1) races to screen away for the big player on the other side of the floor (B2). The post player (B2) cuts to the basket, and the screener (S1) bolts up to the strongside top region. The exterior player ends up in the same place; he or she just takes a slightly different route. S2 tosses either to B2 in the paint or S1 above.

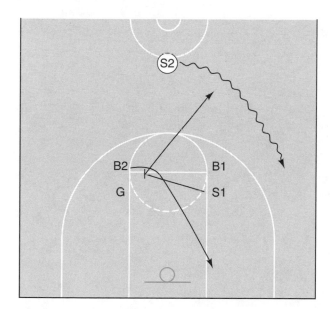

Figure 11.14 Screen away option in Georgetown.

Keys

Refer to the discussions of setting a screen, slipping a screen, using a pick, and throwing

the ball inside in "Man-to-Man Offensive Fine-Tuning" on page 4.

The beginning positions of the two stacks are along the foul lane, not in it. Perimeter players are below the post person (nearest the basket) in each stack. The perimeter player in the ball-side stack moves to the top off either side of the big player directly above.

The player dribbling to a wing may be able to drive to the basket for a shot. The dribbler goes less than full speed and then kicks it up a notch near the foul line extended to blow by the defender. If no drive is available, the ball handler maintains the dribble until a teammate is open for a pass.

The perimeter player busting out top may have a chance for a backdoor cut. If the defender cheats over the stationary screen too soon, a dart to the hoop may produce a layup. If no pass is forthcoming for a layup, then one of two moves occurs. The perimeter player in the other stack bolts to a spot above the ballside elbow to receive the next pass. The player who back cut races to join the post player in the stack away from the ball. The other alternative is for the backdoor cutter to bolt up the lane line off the big player to a site above the strongside elbow. The exterior player in the opposite stack remains there. The coach decides which way to teach the countermove.

Occasionally, the perimeter player in the ballside stack screens away for the post player on the other side of the lane before racing to the top of the key. If the coach has chosen to try to score, he or she encourages the wing to throw the entry pass to the big player low.

The perimeter player with the ball out top dribbles to either wing. He or she dribbles away most of the time.

Georgetown is a good offense to run to slow down the pace of a game when there is a shot clock. The team holds the ball while looking for possible shots. If nothing develops by the time the shot clock reaches 10 to 12 seconds, the coach calls, "Open." The ball handler goes one-on-one to produce a shot. (See chapter 10 for more on open.) Open is the most desirable way to generate a scoring chance from this offense. The transition is swift and easy for players to accomplish. If there is no shot clock, the coach determines how long the offense continues before the team attempts a shot.

As with any delay game, the coach must clearly establish shot criteria for each player: Who is allowed to take a shot? What type of shot is acceptable? From where on the court can players shoot? When is an attempt permissible?

PART IV

Situational Plays

Three-Point Shot Offenses

The seven specific offenses described in this chapter were designed to free players for three-point shots. Although a team can use these offenses at any time in a game, using these plays too early may enable the opponent to learn to defend a play that might be critical late in a game.

A three-point shot can lift a team mentally. It can put away an opponent, topping off a string of points. It creates a psychological advantage. It makes a lead more comfortable. Coaches might want to use the three-point shot after a time-out. I prefer to pull out these plays only when compelled to do so, but each coach determines the exact definition of *compelled*. My personal criteria for use has a need factor attached.

The three-point line has had a substantial effect on the game. Therefore, coaches need to address it. The three-pointer allows a losing team to narrow the point differential rapidly. Leads can evaporate in a hurry. Benches are not cleared as early. The outside shooter has more value.

ARC

I created the arc offense to use at any time during a game. Originally, it was not strictly a three-point offense. Although three-pointers are distinct possibilities, the concept behind the offense was to spread the team on the exterior

just past the three-point line to create drives to the basket. The action is reminiscent of the old weave offense, popular in the 1950s and 1960s. Many coaches no longer use the handoff. Therefore, its use can catch a defense unprepared.

The offense is designed to manufacture shots behind the line. Because big players are included in the motion, the coach must feel comfortable with their pursuit of a shot from beyond the arc. Teams can use the play at any time in a game, but it is especially effective when the offense has a quickness advantage over the defense. The offense is appropriate when either a two-point basket or a three-pointer is acceptable. Players take the ball to the hoop. The strategy is feasible when a team is trailing but the trey is not yet an absolute necessity.

Personnel

All players must be able to handle the ball with either hand. Perimeter players increase the effectiveness of the offense if they possess strong outside shooting skills. Big players ought to be good screeners and well versed in the pick-and-roll. They may shoot a trey.

Scoring

Perimeter players acquire jump shots near the three-point arc and beyond. Big players could obtain inside scoring chances with a cut to the basket following a screen on the ball or a handoff. Post players could also attempt three-pointers. Exterior players garner shots through their cuts to the hoop. Dribble penetrations are likely to occur.

Execution

Play starts as the point guard (G) brings the ball up court and heads for an elbow. One post player (B2) takes up position opposite the lead guard. The other big player (B1) is stationed at the box on the same side as the playmaker. The two shooters (S1 and S2) are beyond the three-point line at approximately the extended midline on each side of the court.

Offensive movement can start in three ways. In the first method, the ball handler (G) passes to a teammate at the ballside wing (S1). The pass receiver peers into the low post (B1) as the remaining three players (B2, G, and S2) assemble at a site directly above the offside elbow. If the low post (B1) does not catch the ball within two to three seconds, he or she moves to screen for the player with the ball (S1). The other three players clear the defensive help away from the screening action.

In the second way, the point guard (G) passes across to the opposite post player (B2) (figure 12.1). As soon as the passer (G) releases the ball, he or she cuts through the middle of the lane, searching for a return pass. G's final destination is the ballside corner if no return pass

comes. Meanwhile, the low post (B1) slides up to replace the passer (G). B2 dribbles the ball at the near wing (S2) and hands the ball to a teammate. B2 sprints to the hoop immediately after S2 receives the ball and could receive a pass during the cut. The handoff recipient (S2) may have a shot opportunity or a chance at a dribble penetration.

In the final method, the big player (B2) opposite the ball handler (G) sets a screen on the ball. B2 does not roll. He or she steps back beyond the three-point arc after his or her teammate uses the pick. At the same time, the low player (B1) slides to the other block. The lead guard (G) can shoot, pass back to the screener (B2), toss to the ballside wing (S2), or dribble penetrate to the hoop. Teams use this means whenever the defense overplays passes to the ballside wing (S1) and the big player opposite (B2).

If the pass is completed to the perimeter player at the wing (S1), the nearest big player (B1) steps out to pick for the pass recipient (figure 12.2). They execute the pick-and-roll. The three players (G, B2, and S2) above the weakside elbow move only when it is becomes clear that B1 will not be open rolling to the goal. Once that determination is made, the two exterior players (G and S2) cross and sprint to opposite corners. The big player (B2) stays out above the elbow.

Figure 12.3 illustrates the continuation of the action that began in figure 12.1. S2 dribbles

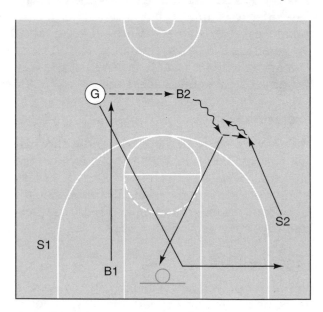

Figure 12.1 Pass across the top starts the arc offense.

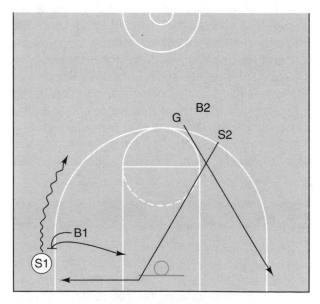

Figure 12.2 Pass delivered to exterior player near corner.

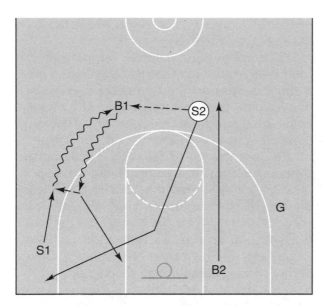

Figure 12.3 Perimeter player dribbling to the top passes to the closest post player.

toward the top of the key and passes the ball to the opposite post player (B1). After releasing the pass, S2 cuts down the middle of the lane to the strongside corner as the offside big player (B2) simultaneously heads up to a spot above the near elbow. B1 catches the ball and immediately looks for the cutter (S2). If no pass is available, he or she dribbles at the perimeter player (S1) below. S1 hustles around to secure a handoff from the post player and heads to the key. B1 sprints to the basket after exchanging the ball with S1.

Figure 12.4 illustrates the continuing standard action. S1 passes to B2 across the top. The pass signals the other post player (B1) to hustle out past the closest elbow. The passer (S1) cuts down the center, anticipating a return pass, and ends in the ballside corner. The big player (B2) dribbles at the perimeter player below (G) and hands the ball to him or her. B2 bolts to the hoop. This motion is actually the same as that shown in figure 12.3.

Figure 12.5 shows the play continuing and the start of a wrinkle in the action. G throws across to B1. The passer (G) sprints down the lane and finishes in the strongside corner, while the other post player (B2) dashes to a site above the offside elbow. B1 dribbles at the perimeter player below (S2). The only difference is that this time B1 does not give the ball to S2 on route around the outside. Because B1 does not execute the handoff, he or she throws the ball to G in the nearby corner. B1 follows the pass to establish a pick for the player with the ball. After the two-player game forms, the other three players (S2, S1, and B2) dart to locations above the offside elbow. This movement is the same as that shown in figure 12.2.

An exterior player with the basketball out top may face defensive overplays of the perimeter player below and the big player directly across. This circumstance prevents S2 from completing a pass in either direction. When players recognize the situation, the opposite post player glides over to screen for the ball handler while the low post heads to the other block.

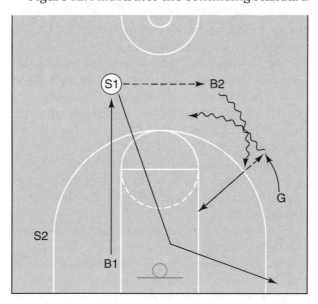

Figure 12.4 Motion on the other side of the court.

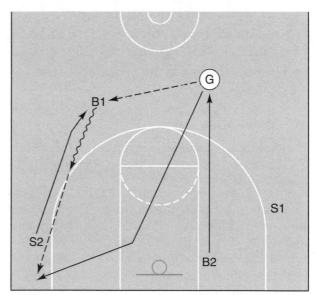

Figure 12.5 Big player does not hand off the ball.

Keys

See the discussions of the following topics in "Man-to-Man Offensive Fine-Tuning" in chapter 1 (page 4): screening between post and perimeter players, setting a screen, slipping a screen, using a pick, and two-player game.

The offense can be satisfactorily taught within one hour. Players will need some time before they catch on to the pattern. The coach must be patient. After sufficient repetition, players will be capable of executing the offense against a defense. Instruction should begin on a no-defense basis. Teaching the offense as a whole is best. Breakdown drills should not be necessary.

Although the offense includes a great deal of motion, it involves only three fundamental types of offensive movements: the dribble handoff, the two-player game, and the cut to the basket without the ball. The educational process is not conducive to breaking down play to specific components in practice. Teaching (dummy and live) is best accomplished by treating the offense as one unit involving all five players.

One big player begins high opposite the ball, and the other is low on the ballside. Shooters start on either side. The point guard must take the ball into the alley directly above the low post.

After a perimeter player receives the handoff from a post player, he or she dribbles and does one of the following:

- dribble penetrates to the hoop,
- tosses to the big player if the big player is open and cutting to the basket,
- throws the ball to the opposite post player out front,
- passes to the perimeter player below on the ballside, or
- takes advantage of an opening for a shot near or behind the three-point line.

If none of these options are available, the overplay option automatically kicks in. The opposite big player identifies the dilemma and reacts swiftly by picking for the ball.

Post players mix handing off the ball to the perimeter player sliding outside and continuing to dribble past the handoff point. When no handoff occurs, the ball goes to the player in the near corner. A screen is set for the pass receiver. Variety keeps the defense on its toes.

When executing a handoff, big players use their bodies not only to shield but also to pick. If the defender on the perimeter player goes underneath, the player obtaining the handoff could be open for an exterior shot. The post player may need to pick up the dribble and pivot on the foot nearest the basket, swinging the other leg around 180 degrees before the handoff. This method disrupts the defender heading below. The big player could also pivot on the foot furthest from the hoop if the defender is lying right on top of the handoff recipient. Regardless, the big players become stationary before making contact with defenders.

Perimeter players should drive to the basket, although if a three-point shot is necessary they should ignore dribble-penetration opportunities.

The coach should prepare the team for the trap possibility of the pick-and-roll, especially when it takes place close to a corner. The screener and remaining three players should know precisely what to do when this scenario occurs.

Dribblers must handle the ball with the proper hand. If the player goes to the right, he or she dribbles with the right hand and vice versa.

The perimeter player sprints down the center of the lane whenever he or she flips the ball to the big player across the top. The cutter lifts the inside arm as a target and prepares to catch the return pass if open. If no pass comes, he or she races to the ballside corner.

The motion generates three-point shots in several ways. The exterior player grabbing the handoff might see an opening. The perimeter player using the screen on the ball is another possibility. An outside player in the corner might acquire a shot as soon as the big player bypassing the handoff sends the pass in his or her direction. Post players above the elbows may achieve deep chances from the kick-out of a dribble drive.

Players with the ball contemplate delivering it to cutters and players rolling to the basket. When the situation calls for it, players should attack the hoop if possible. If the coach wants players to attempt only three-pointers, he or she must communicate that desire. Players do not loaf through their cuts but complete them with exemplary effort.

The two big players are interchangeable, as are the three perimeter players, but one or more players may need to learn both roles. They must practice both. Learning is much easier if they concentrate on understanding the pattern as a whole.

TREY

The trey play was born when the three-point line came into existence. Usually, the team that is behind on the scoreboard with time running out uses the trey play. This team needs offensive movement that can accomplish two tasks at once—develop a three-point chance for someone capable of putting the ball through the net and accomplish it without expending too much time. The motion produces a shot within 10 seconds. Shots from beyond the arc appear consistently. The coach should use the play whenever a trey is necessary, usually when his or her squad is in catch-up mode late in a game. Trey frees the two best distance shooters on the team for possible three-point shots.

Personnel

Two perimeter players other than the point guard should be proficient outside shooters. It helps if one of the two post players is able to hit a shot from beyond the three-point arc.

Scoring

One shooter garners a three-pointer in the ballside corner as a result of the screening activity at the box on the foul lane. The second outside player attains shots on the weakside in the area beyond the arc from the top of the key to the near wing. This player is the primary option because he or she is the one who employs the double screen set by the big players. A post player in the weakside corner is another alternative for a trey. Any shot the point guard achieves is strictly of his or her own creation. One big player is not included in potential scoring from behind the three-point line.

Execution

The play opens in a 1-3-1 alignment (figure 12.6). The lead guard (G) is above the top of the key

with the ball after crossing half-court. The ball handler commences action by dribbling at the wing player (S1) away from the low post (S2). The two best perimeter shooters fill these two spots. One big player (B1), the one who is more effective shooting from the periphery, begins at the foul line. B2 is at the wing on the same side as the low post (S2). After G dribbles toward S1, S1 moves to the near block to set a screen. In the first movement option, the low post (S2) uses the pick in anticipation of a three-point shot at the ballside corner. The lead guard (G) delivers the ball to S2 only if a good shot will develop. As S2 heads by S1's pick, the post players (B1 and B2) travel down together on the diagonal to establish a double screen for S1 (the screener). S1 uses the twin pick to gain freedom for a three-point attempt on the offside between the foul line extended and the top of the key. S1 is the point guard's second pass possibility. After S1 uses the double pick, B1 hustles behind the arc in the corner below S1. He or she is the final option for a trey and receives the ball with a skip pass from G or a toss from S1.

Players can execute a wrinkle in the offense. The subtle adjustment occurs only between S1 and S2; no other players are affected. Instead of sprinting off S1's screen to the ballside corner, the low post (S2) fakes it and uses the post players' double pick. The screener (S1) simply pops out to the corner below the playmaker (G). The toss goes to the ballside corner only if an open trey appears likely. The second option is

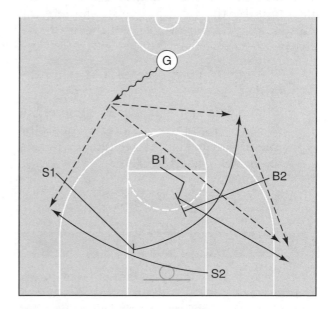

Figure 12.6 Trey starting set and motion.

to S2 out front on the weakside. B1 remains the final target in the offside corner. The low post (S2) uses the maneuver if he or she recognizes the defender cheating over S1's pick or if the defense switches too early. S2 is responsible for making the decision.

Keys

The perimeter shooter starting in the low post makes a sound decision in terms of using the single or double screen. He or she sells the defense on the single pick first. Reading the defense is critical. He or she selects the option that is most difficult for the defense to guard. The player cannot let desire for a shot dictate the movement.

The big players anchoring the double screen move together and time their moves to coincide with the low post's arrival at the screen set at the opposite block on the lane. The angle of the double pick, a diagonal in the lane, is crucial. See the discussions of using a pick, setting a screen, the double screen, and screening between post and perimeter players in "Man-to-Man Offensive Fine-Tuning" on page 4.

The shooter takes advantage of a cleared weakside. He or she finds a vacant space beyond the three-point line.

The play is run to either side of the floor. Players assume starting positions accordingly. The wings flip-flop sides, and the low post starts at the other box.

The offense has a definitive end. If no trey develops by the time players complete the motion, players perform one of these alternatives:

- The point guard creates a shot off the dribble.

- If the ball is in the hands of a shooter but there is no shot, the shooter assumes the role of playmaker and teammates race to the initial formation. They run the play a second time.

- Another offense is called.

DISTANCE

The distance play is my personal favorite. My teams were successful on many occasions and hit three-pointers at critical times. This offense manufactures shots from behind the arc. Although not every shot goes through the net, the right players procure good looks at three-pointers. The distance play also has a two-point element. The offense uses dribble penetration to set up shooters for treys.

A team behind late in a game and needing a three-point shot uses this play. The offense is also viable when either a two-point shot or a three-point shot is acceptable. The play is especially useful for teams that possess one or more shooters who are outstanding from beyond the line.

Personnel

The point guard needs the ability to penetrate the defense with the dribble. The offense benefits if he or she is a solid exterior shooter and able to score in a one-on-one situation. The other two perimeter players need to be able to shoot from distance. Big players must be effective screeners. They possibly could be called on to shoot threes but are more likely to acquire chances closer to the basket.

Scoring

The two exterior shooters gain opportunities past the three-point line on each side of the court. The area extends from above an elbow to the foul line extended. Once a rescreen is initiated, the same players end in the corners, where the ball is delivered for a shot at a trey. At the same time, the big players are potential shooters as they slide out past the arc after back picking. The lead guard could score with a drive to the hoop. Post players are more likely to receive shots in tight after a dish-off by the playmaker.

Execution

The lead guard (G) has the ball above the top of the key (figure 12.7). The post players (B1 and B2) are stationed at each foul line extended or slightly beyond the three-point line. The two shooters (S2 and S1) begin in the corners. If the team is interested only in shooting the three-pointer, the lead guard (G) dribbles to a spot just inside the foul line, picks up the dribble, pivots, and faces out, watching for shooters S1 and S2. As the playmaker reaches the foul line, the big players (B2 and B1) dart down to screen

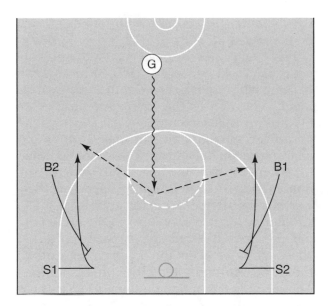

Figure 12.7   Distance formation and action.

for the shooters (S1 and S2). G tosses the ball to S1 or S2 for a three-point shot.

If the team wants to shoot either a two- or three-point shot, the point guard dribble penetrates and creates a scoring opportunity for him- or herself or for a teammate. The post players still screen down for the shooters when the lead guard hits the foul line. The playmaker could toss the ball out to a shooter or dump it off to a big player who is stepping to the basket after the pick. Once the big players pick, they immediately become potential pass receivers.

If the shooters (S1 and S2) are not open initially for a three-point shot, post players (B2 and B1) rescreen, this time setting back picks. The shooters (S1 and S2) fade off the screens to the corners. The screeners bolt out after their teammates rub off the picks. If either a two-point shot or a three-point shot is acceptable, shooters may slice to the basket off the back picks rather than fading.

The team performs the play continuously until a good scoring opportunity develops. Post players constantly screen for shooters. The coach determines whether shot attempts must be three-pointers or whether either a two-point shot or a three-point shot is OK. If the team completes the back screen but no shot develops, the lead guard passes to one of the big players dashing out following the back pick. The playmaker hustles to grasp the return pass. The offensive activities begin again.

When the pass goes to a shooter at the top and no three-point shot exists, the offense continues with a new perimeter player handling the ball in the middle. The shooter penetrates down the lane. The point guard simply replaces the pass receiver without hesitation after his or her teammate puts the ball on the floor. Big players pick and rescreen if necessary.

Keys

Refer to the following topics in "Man-to-Man Offensive Fine-Tuning" in chapter 1 (page 4): screening between post and perimeter players, setting a screen, slipping a screen, using a pick, rescreening, and the back pick.

The coach must clearly instruct squad members about the type of shot he or she wants. Visual or oral signals tell players to shoot only three pointers or to shoot either three-pointers or two-pointers.

The player in the middle sells the defense on a penetration to the basket. If the ball handler is having difficulty shaking the defender or must shoot a three-pointer, he or she picks up the dribble when the ball reaches approximately the second hash mark on the lane above the block.

The player in the middle (usually the point guard) must dribble penetrate to the hoop. If a trey is desired, the player in the lane dribbles to a spot just a few feet below the foul line and stops. He or she turns swiftly and faces the top of the key. The player in the center acts in a one-on-one mode when shots inside and outside the arc are acceptable. When the ball reaches the foul line, post players begin screening.

If a three-point shot is mandatory, the player in the middle could launch one from a one-on-one maneuver. I suggest that coaches not encourage this option until one full screening cycle has transpired.

BINGO

Bingo movements consume no more than 10 seconds but invariably produce a quality three-point shot. The action centers on sending the attention of the defense one direction and then hitting it with picks for the main shooting option the other way. A team that is losing late in a contest wants to get the ball in the hands of a solid outside shooter for an attempt at a trey using minimal time. The creation of the play coincided with the advent of the three-point line.

This play is specifically designed to create three-point shots. Bingo is useful late in a game when a team is down on the scoreboard and has to catch up by making treys. If the coach is not restricting the squad to three-pointers, a play such as distance is a better selection.

Personnel

Two perimeter players should be outstanding shooters from the outer regions. The ball handler is not one of the featured shooters. One of the two big players must be able to hit a shot from behind the three-point arc.

Scoring

One exterior player obtains a shot from beyond the arc in the weakside area above the foul line extended and outside the key. A second shooter is open in the corner for a shot from behind the three-point line. One big player could receive a shooting chance in the opposite corner.

Execution

The lead guard (G) is above the top of the key with the ball (figure 12.8). B1 starts at the high post, and B2 starts on either wing (in this case the right). Of the two post players, B1 is the more competent shooter from the periphery.

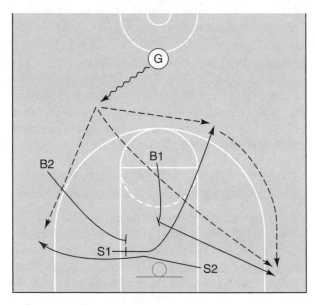

Figure 12.8 Bingo beginning set and movements.

Each shooter (S1 and S2) is stationed at a box on the foul lane.

Play begins with the point guard (G) dribbling at the big player on the wing (B2). B2 races down to establish a double screen with S1 at the near block. After they fix the double screen, S2 cuts off it to the ballside corner. A pass to S2 is the playmaker's first option. If he or she thinks that S2 will have an open chance at a three-pointer, G delivers the ball. As S2 begins to move off the double pick, B1 rushes from the high post to fix a screen for the shooter in the double (S1). The shooter heads to a spot beyond the arc on the offside above the foul line extended. After S1 slices off B1's screen, the big player sprints to the offside corner behind the three-point line. The second pass option for the lead guard is to fling the ball to S1 on the opposite side. A chance for B1 comes directly from the point guard with a skip pass or from S1 above.

The two shooters (S1 and S2) can choose to perform an alternative maneuver. Instead of employing the double screen, S2 fakes the action and uses B1's pick to dart to offside out front. B1 still hustles to the weakside corner. S1 notices S2 moving opposite so he or she pops out to the ballside corner, exploiting a single screen by the other big player (B2). S1 and S2 have exchanged roles.

Keys

See "Man-to-Man Offensive Fine-Tuning" in chapter 1 (page 4) for more information on these topics: screening between post and perimeter players, setting a screen, using a pick, and the double screen.

The best outside shooter of the two big players is stationed at the high post to start. The point guard always initiates the movement of the play by dribbling at the player on the wing. The big player in the wing position can be on either side of the floor. He or she is free to mix it up. The wing's location determines the direction of the play. When they run the play to the other side, players operate in the same fashion except that the other shooter has the choice of which screen to exploit. The shooter on the block away from the point guard's dribble always makes the decision.

The shooter with the choice reads the defense. If the defender is cheating over the double pick too early or the defense is switching assignments, the shooter reverses, capitalizing on the single pick. The other shooter reacts to the first shooter's motion and races opposite. The two shooters need to learn to communicate with each other. The big player at the high post moves to establish a screen as soon as the decision-making shooter reaches the double pick. The point guard passes to the shooter in the ballside corner only if a three-point shot is likely.

This play has a definite end. If no open three-point shot develops before the conclusion, players redo the play, begin a new one, or permit the lead guard to create a three-pointer off the dribble. The coach makes the choice before execution of the play.

The angle of the high post's screen is important. He or she slides down into the lane and sets the pick so that a teammate gains an opening on the offside above the foul line extended. The screener's back points in the direction where his or her teammate will catch the ball.

THREE SPECIAL

The three special offense has become the closest thing to a standardized means of player motion leading to a three-point shot. Probably half the squads I faced while at King's College used some form of the three special action to manufacture three-pointers at the close of a game. The philosophy behind the movement is that to produce a three-pointer, players should move along the arc.

Teams use this offense when losing late in a game. They need three-point shots to close the gap. If a two-pointer is still acceptable, coaches should consider using a different play, such as arc. A drive to the basket that begins outside the arc is a method that players can use to attempt two-point shots from the three special offense. The coach decides whether to put the two-point portion into the play.

Personnel

Ideally, three perimeter players are capable of hitting the trey. Two big players should be effective screeners, and they may acquire chances to shoot the ball from deep.

Scoring

Any of the three exterior players could acquire shots past the three-point line. Shots are likely to take place on the arc from the location of one foul line extended to the other. Post players garner scoring possibilities from three-point land after screening on the ball and stepping out. Any player may have an opening to drive to the hoop.

Execution

The point guard (G) is above the top of the key with the ball (figure 12.9). The post players (B1 and B2) are just above the elbows. The two shooters (S1 and S2) begin in the corners behind the three-point arc.

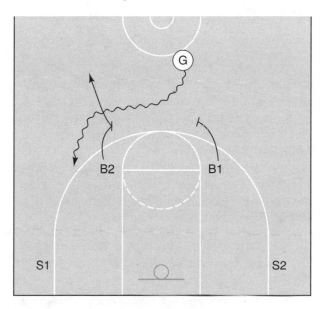

Figure 12.9   Starting set and motion in three special.

The lead guard (G) dribbles over either screen set by a big player. In this case, G dribbles off B2. If G is open for a shot, he or she may take it. The screener (B2) steps back following G's use of the pick.

When G does not have a clear shot, an alternative is a pass back to the screener (B2) who popped out. G immediately picks for the nearest perimeter player (S1) to race toward the ball (figure 12.10). Instead of tossing the ball to a big player, the playmaker may either execute a dribble and a handoff with the shooter below or pass from there and set a pick for the pass recipient. In either case, the shooter coming out of the

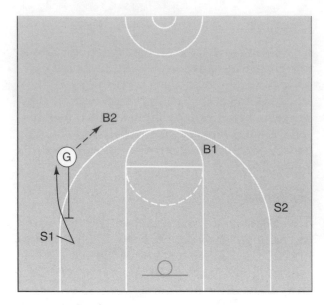

Figure 12.10 Pass to a big player and screen away in three special.

corner might attain a distant shot. The screener or the player handing the ball to a teammate steps out after the maneuver is complete.

Whenever a big player possesses the ball but does not have a viable shot, he or she looks to pass to an outside player and immediately screens for the receiver. The post player's other choice is to dribble at the perimeter player and execute a handoff. If no shot presents itself, exterior players have these options:

- toss the ball to a big player who is stepping out after screening and pick for another shooter below,
- pass to a teammate below and go to screen, or
- dribble at a team member below and initiate a handoff.

If coming toward the top of the key, the shooter usually tries to take the ball to the other side of the court and gain a screen from the second big player. The team runs the play continually until a shot appears.

Keys

Big players never roll to the basket after setting the pick for the ball handler. By stepping out they might secure a chance at a trey. The coach lets post players know if they are at liberty to release a three-point shot. Players square to the basket after exploiting the screen to attempt

a three-point shot. Exterior players also step out whenever they set a pick and a teammate uses it.

When a player launches a shot, teammates crash the boards. They have spread the defense around the perimeter, so they may be able to snatch an offensive rebound if they react quickly and rush to the glass. Considering that the team is desperate for points, at least four players (all but the shooter) should go to the glass.

Coaches may possibly choose to use the offense when trying to gain two- or three-point shots. Because all players are spread at least 20 feet from the hoop, they can dribble penetrate to the hoop when two-pointers are permissible. If the defense is concerned with the three-pointer, defenders may be unable to help on a drive to the basket. Another possible two-point scoring move is the back cut to the bucket to counter defensive overplays. A ball fake initiates the backdoor cut, and a bounce pass to the cutter follows shortly thereafter. The coach informs players exactly what they are to do.

DOWNTOWN

When formulating the offensive action, I sought to discover the optimum manner to achieve a shot opening from a site on the far side of the arc. Coaches today thoroughly train defenders to put more space between the offense and defense whenever the guarded player is away from the ball. The farther the assignment is from the ball, the farther the defender can be from the player. Therefore, offensive players on the weakside exterior normally enjoy the greatest distance from defenders. To take full advantage of the defensive setup, picking from behind is important.

The score or the coach's interpretation of the flow of the game dictates whether a team needs a three-pointer. The team may be running out of time and need to put a dent in the point differential. Perimeter players are the featured three-point shooters. The coach may call on them whenever he or she feels the trey can give the club a lift.

Personnel

Ideally, at least four of the five players have an aptitude for hitting three-point shots. If one big player is not a potential shooter, his or her starting spot is at the top of the key. Because the club is focusing on three-pointers, interior-scoring skills and the ability to drive to the hoop are not necessary.

Scoring

One outside shooter looks to shoot the three-pointer from the offside of the court between the key and the foul line extended. A second exterior player garners shots for three near the top of the key. The point guard receives three-point shots close to a wing. One big player might procure a three-pointer from the weakside corner.

Execution

Play starts in a box set with the shooters (S1 and S2) at the blocks and the post players (B1 and B2) just above the elbows. The point guard starts with the ball above the top of the key. He or she fakes using the pick in one direction and exploits the screen of the other big player. In this case, assume that the lead guard (G) has gone to the right off B1's pick. The point guard earns the first crack at a trey. The screener (B1) slides out after the dribbler goes past.

Action continues as shown in figure 12.11. As the playmaker heads off the screen, the shooter at the offside block (S2) picks across for S1, the other shooter. The big player at the weakside elbow (B2) screens down on a diagonal. S1 uses picks by S2 and then B2 to gain freedom in the offside area above the foul line extended. Fol-

lowing the pick, S2 sprints to the ballside corner. B2 races to the weakside corner after S1 uses the screen. G's first pass option is to S1. The point guard (G) passes to S2 in the near corner only if he or she is open for a three-point shot. Otherwise, the playmaker tosses the ball to B1, who is stepping out after picking. The ball also can go to B2 in the far corner via S1.

B1 has a couple of options after securing the pass from the lead guard (G). He or she may send the ball to S2 in the ballside corner or to S1 across the front on the weakside. B1 should not throw a skip pass to B2 in the distant corner unless he or she is open for a quality three attempt.

The ball is passed to S1 on the offside. If no shot is available, the toss goes to B2 in the same-side corner, but only if the receiver is open for a trey. S2 is the other potential pass recipient as he or she hustles toward the top of the key after employing the staggered picks. G and B1 rush to set screens as soon as the pass is released to S1 (figure 12.12).

If the ball goes to S2 and there is no shot, each post player screens for the closest perimeter player. B1 down picks for G, and B2 back screens for the passer (S1). B2 pops out past the arc after his or her teammate rubs off.

Keys

Refer to the following topics in "Man-to-Man Offensive Fine-Tuning" on page 4: screening

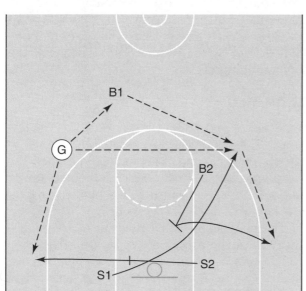

Figure 12.11 Point guard has already used B1's high pick.

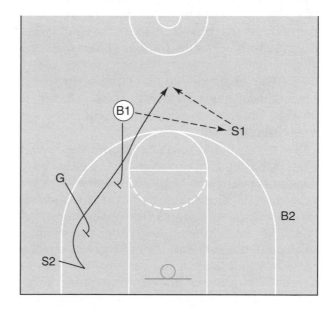

Figure 12.12 Shooter at the weakside top does not have a shot.

between post and perimeter players, setting a screen, slipping a screen, using a pick, back pick, two-player game, and low exchanges and cross screens .

The point guard uses either post player to initiate play. He or she fakes one way and goes the other. The screen is set right at the arc. This move sets up the defender to be run into a pick. The playmaker shoots the three-pointer if open. If no shot is viable, he or she passes to the shooter heading to the ballside corner only if a clean look from behind the arc is there. A skip pass across to the main shooter on the weakside is feasible. Finally, the toss goes to the screener (big player), who is stepping out after the pick is used.

Once the ball is in the screener's hands, he or she shoots only if open and cleared to do so. The likelihood that both conditions will be present is not great. Remember that he or she is one of the weaker three-point shooters on the floor. A pass to the shooter in the ballside corner is permissible if he or she is open for a trey. A throw across the top to the shooter opposite is the best option.

When the ball goes to the shooter moving to the weakside above the foul line extended, the other big player immediately sets staggered screens with the playmaker for the shooter in the offside corner. The ball could come from the playmaker or the big player who set the initial screen on the ball.

The timing and angle of the initial set of staggered screens are important. The weakside shooter on the box plants the screen across first. He or she moves to do so when the lead guard is just about to use the pick on the ball out front. The weakside big player fixes the down screen at an angle that allows the shooter to head to an area above the foul line extended away from the ball.

Shooters should take positions at the boxes. The roles they fill depend on the side to which the point guard dribbles off the initial pick by a big player. The coach can give the shooter on the ballside block a choice. When the initial cross screen happens, he or she can choose to exploit the two screens as normal or fake the move and dart straight out to the ballside corner. The cross screener uses the single diagonal screen by the big player above to run to the weakside top. The two shooters just exchange finishing spots.

After the final back pick and down screen are complete, a three-pointer should develop. The play will often not reach that stage. The offense is likely to produce a trey before its conclusion. If two-point shots are still in the mix, this offense is not practical because it does not contain such a component. Distance and arc are better offenses where two-pointers are acceptable.

QUICK THREE

The quick three play was developed to open up three-point shots for a premier shooter from distance. In addition, the play develops in a hurry. The three-point arc forced coaches to find ways to secure the extra point. The best way to separate a proficient three-point shooter from a defender is to screen with the big players. Quick three is useful whenever a team needs to complete a successful three-point shot. The play sets up a particular shooter to make the attempt in minimal time.

Personnel

The two post players should be formidable screeners. At least one strong outside shooter is needed. Quick three does not set up the point guard for a distant shot.

Scoring

A perimeter player sees a three-point shot develop in either corner. The play focuses on one outside player shooting the trey. The point guard could be the featured player only if one of the other two perimeter players assumes the ballhandling role.

Execution

One post player (B2) is at the foul line. The low post (B1) is stationed on either block. Each of the shooters (S1 and S2) is located at a wing. The wing opposite the low post (S1) is the featured shooter. The lead guard (G) is past the top of the key with the ball (figure 12.13).

The playmaker (G) dribbles at the wing (S1) away from the low post (B1). The other wing (S2) V-cuts to get open for a pass from the playmaker (G). As the pass receiver moves to get free, the high post glides down to form a double pick with his or her partner. S1 uses the double screen and ends in the strongside corner for

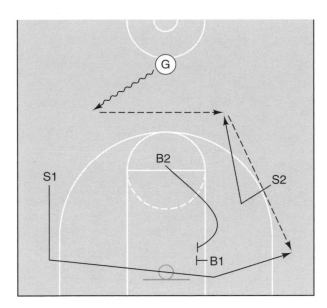

Figure 12.13 Quick three set and action.

a possible three-point shot. Post players position the screen so that they are in line with the shooter's defender. They become stationary just before any contact. If no three-pointer arises, the team must either reset and try again or run another play. The play concludes swiftly.

Another twist on the action is possible. After the ball handler (G in figure 12.13) releases the ball across the top, the low post (B1) slides across the lane to set staggered picks along the baseline with B2 (the high post), instead of the double. This maneuver also enables the primary shooter (S1) to fake running off the baseline picks. S1 fades back to corner nearer the first screen by B1. A skip pass from S2 to S1 should be open for a three-point shot.

Keys

Go to "Man-to-Man Offensive Fine-Tuning" in chapter 1 on page 4 to review the following topics: screening between post and perimeter players, setting a screen, using a pick, and double screen.

The low post player along the foul lane changes location each time the play is called.

He or she dictates which shooter is set up for a three. Obviously, if one of the wings is not proficient from distance, the low post begins on the same-side block.

After the playmaker dribbles to a side, the high post scampers opposite to establish a double screen with the other big player (or a single pick as part of staggered screens). Meanwhile, the shooter casually drops toward the nearest baseline.

The V-cut by the opposite wing is important. If he or she cannot pop free of the defender, the play bogs down. He or she takes the defender toward the basket, plants the foot closer to the hoop, and pivots to move to a site out top next to the ball. The outside hand is the target. The pass is mandatory.

The timing of the run off the double screen is critical. The highlighted shooter races to use the double pick as soon as the point guard releases the ball. The main shooter may need to vary speed in order to rub the defender into the screen. The same is true if staggered screens are in place.

The featured shooter changes at random, requiring a solid distance shooter to occupy each wing. If a team has only one, the defense will be able to zero in on the team's main weapon. Running the play repeatedly for the same player severely limits its effectiveness. The coach must not call the play too frequently. Its productivity will likely peak at only two to five possessions.

The play is easy to teach. Movements are few and simple.

The coach can teach one other option that will increase the chances of scoring. The point guard must be a potent shooter from the exterior. The ball goes back to the playmaker instead of going to the shooter who is capitalizing on the double pick. The alternative is not present if staggered screens are employed. The lead guard has an entire side of the half-court in which to use his or her one-on-one skills. If a trey is necessary, the player loses the defender and gains a three-point shot.

CHAPTER 13

Buzzer Beaters

Every team must be ready to confront special circumstances at the end of a game. Although the objectives of all the buzzer beaters in this chapter are similar, the actions have subtle differences. The following buzzer-beating plays have been tested under game conditions and have successfully met their objectives. Most have produced game-winning scores or were integral in their creation. When it comes to winning and losing, the defining moments are likely to occur in the waning seconds of play. The plays in this chapter are specifically designed to use during these times.

Each play assumes that the offense must travel the length of the floor to score. All diagrams show the ball being inbounded at the far end line, but the plays are also appropriate when the ball is thrown in from a sideline position in the half of the backcourt nearer the defensive basket. When the ball is located near midcourt, sideline out-of-bounds plays (chapter 16, page 275) are relevant.

GET BALL TO HALF

This play has a success rate of 100 percent. Every time I used it, we were able to achieve the desired result. Teams use the play with at least two seconds on the game clock, when they have at least one time-out remaining, and when the game is either tied or the offensive team is behind by one score. The ball is inbounded near the far end line.

Personnel

The inbounder is the key player. He or she must be able to throw the ball from the baseline at high speed to a teammate at half-court. The receiver must catch the ball cleanly.

Scoring

None.

Execution

In figure 13.1, the point guard (G) is the inbounder, but any of the perimeter players or even a post player could inbound the ball. Whomever the coach selects must have a strong arm and be able to whip the ball to a teammate at the half-court line without a problem. Someone who must arch the ball to get it to travel that distance would be a poor choice. The other four players line up across the court at top-of-the-key level on the end of the court away from the inbounder. The post players (B1 and B2) begin at outside locations. The two perimeter players (S1 and S2) are above the ballside and weakside elbows. All four players fake going deep to shake loose from their defenders and then sprint toward half-court. Players stay in their lanes. G may toss the ball into any player.

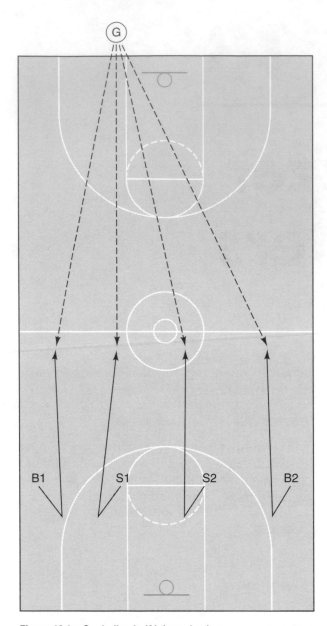

Figure 13.1 Get ball to half inbounds play.

The pass reception should occur close to midcourt. He or she targets the player who is open and closest to the opposite hoop. G throws the inbounds pass as deep as possible. The pass receiver calls time-out immediately after catching the ball.

The four deep players have another option. Instead of just racing to the ball, the big players (B1 and B2) burst inward to screen for the closer perimeter player. The perimeter players (S1 and S2) run along the sidelines to the ball. The screeners seal straight back to the inbounder after their teammates use the picks. The pass goes to an open player near midcourt. When the

pass receiver gains control of the basketball, he or she immediately calls time-out.

Keys

See the discussions of setting a screen and using a pick in "Man-to-Man Offensive Fine-Tuning" found on page 4. In "Breaking Presses Offensive Fine-Tuning," see the discussions of throwing the ball deep and receiving a pass (page 305).

The inbounder should be a perimeter player. That way, the two post players can screen for the other two perimeter players if necessary. This combination is most effective because defenders are less likely to switch. The inbounder should remember that he or she may run the baseline if the inbound follows an opponent's score.

The four deep players communicate with each other before the throw-in and decide whether the big players should pick for the perimeter players. Certainly, the coach may dictate which selection to execute. The four players must stay in their lanes as they approach midcourt. They maintain spacing so that the passer has four distinct alternatives heading to the ball.

When the team does not use screens, each player is responsible for breaking free from his or her defender. Players fake deep and sprint toward the opposite baseline. Big players also could fake screening across before everyone runs in their assigned lanes to midcourt.

As soon as the receiver catches the pass, he or she calls time-out to give the team an opportunity to set up a sidelines out-of-bounds play for the critical final possession. The team will be able to generate a better shot by using a sidelines out-of-bounds play rather than by launching a shot after traversing the length of the floor. No more than one second should tick off the game clock if the play is executed correctly.

CAROLINA

I first saw this play while watching a North Carolina team coached by Dean Smith. The success of the play depends on an official's call. Ideally, the team should have a time-out remaining, but the coach could decide to use the play even if one is not available. Teams use the play when only a few seconds remain, they are losing by one or two points or are tied, and the opposing team is over the foul limit. They attempt the play only if an aggressive defender is on the inbounder. The play follows a successful field goal or free throw by the opponent when the team has to move the ball the length of the court.

Personnel

The inbounder should be a post player who has decent quickness. One of the team's physically smaller players needs to be an excellent foul shooter.

Scoring

A designated perimeter player secures foul shots.

Execution

The inbounder (B1) runs the baseline (figure 13.2). He or she first heads to the near sideline and then comes back toward the basket. Remember that the inbounder can run the baseline after the basketball has successfully dropped through the net. G, one of the physically smallest players on the team, may or may not be the point guard.

G begins at the middle of the foul lane in the backcourt. G moves up and to the sideline, trying to entice the inbounder's defender to barrel over him or her. G is stationary when the defender makes contact. S2 (a perimeter player) begins at the top of the key closer to the inbounder and darts to the ballside sideline at approximately the foul line extended. On the other end of the floor, the other post player (B2) is above the top of the key, and the team's premier exterior shooter (S1) is under the hoop. B2 down screens for S1 as soon as the inbounder (B1) heads back in the direction of the hoop. S1 rushes off either side of B2, heading for midcourt. B2 seals back to the ball opposite S1's dash.

The team is trying to elicit a foul call that will send G to the charity stripe for two critical foul shots. If a foul is not called, B1 calls time-out immediately. The coach may give B1 the option not to take a time-out if he or she notices B2 or S1 open deep down the floor. The coach also decides whether to use the play with no time-outs remaining. If the defense does not foul, the inbounder (B1) sends the ball to either S1 or B2 deep or to S2 in the backcourt. The pass

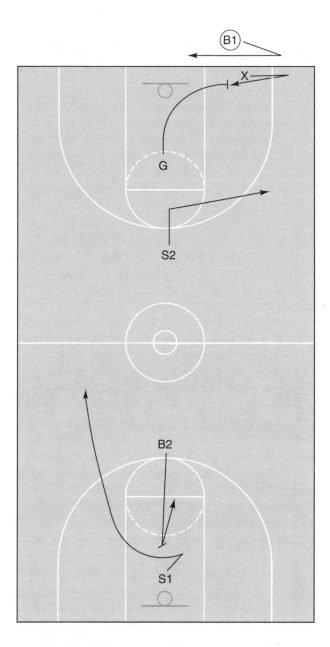

Figure 13.2 Carolina formation and motion.

recipient tries to score to tie or win the contest before the clock expires.

Keys

Refer to the sections on setting a screen and using a pick in "Man-to-Man Offensive Fine-Tuning" in chapter 1 on page 4. In "Breaking Presses Offensive Fine-Tuning" on page 305, see the discussions of throwing the ball deep and receiving a pass.

The inbounder should be one of the team's quicker big players. The inbounder runs toward the near sideline not quite at top speed. He or she reverses direction and goes full steam. The inbounder acts as if he or she is looking to toss the ball deep the entire time. This ploy gets the defender on the ball moving.

The player in the center of the closer lane times his or her movements to attain a position in a direct line with the inbounder's defender. He or she sneaks up by waiting until the last second to intersect the targeted defender's path. The defender will likely be motoring at a rate of speed that makes it difficult to stop and avoid running into the screener. The action deep does not commence until the inbounder reverses back toward the basket. The official may or may not call the foul. Players may execute the play to perfection, but the referee may not blow the whistle.

The right player must be heading to the foul line. The player must be able to sink critical free throws under pressure.

I prefer to execute the play with at least one time-out left. If the official does not call the foul, the time-out allows the team to run another offensive play for a crucial full-court possession. With one time-out left, the coach must choose to run this play or cast the ball to half-court and call time-out. If two time-outs remain, the team can perform this play first. If it does not work, they call a time-out, get the ball to half-court, and then use the second time-out.

The action near the inbounder could also serve as a decoy. The inbounder throws the inbounds pass deep. Teams can use this option when they do not have a time-out remaining. If the squad does not get the foul call, the inbounder throws the ball long.

Under no circumstances should the player trying to draw the foul commit one by setting an illegal screen. Remember, though, that the coach and players have zero control over the referees.

Obviously, the play is not practical if the team is not in the bonus. Without the bonus, a foul shot is impossible. If the opponent is still able to take one or more fouls, the team must use other plays for remaining possessions.

LONG

The long play was designed to provide several players with the possibility of taking the final shot. The long play is useful when time is nearly up and a team needs to score after running the length of the court. The long play has supplied game winners from several positions. The play gives a team a chance to snatch victory from the jaws of defeat. Teams use the play when down by one to three points with only one to five seconds on the clock. The inbounder throws the ball from the baseline opposite their basket. The squad must score.

Personnel

A big player who is capable of hurling the ball deep is the inbounder. The squad needs an outstanding outside shooter. The other post player must be adept at catching a deep throw-in and immediately scoring. The other two perimeter players must be effective ball handlers.

Scoring

The team's main distance shooter may secure a three-point shot. The key big player could grab the long inbounds toss for an opportunity inside 15 feet. The other two outside players could see shots form because of their ballhandling abilities.

Execution

Players set up just as they did for Carolina (figure 13.3). One post player (B1) is the inbounder. The best outside shooter (S1) begins under the hoop at the other end of the floor. The second big player (B2) starts above S1 near the top of the key. The point guard (G) is in the center of the foul lane closer to the ball. The other exterior player (S2) is stacked above G near the top of the key.

The players at the top of each key (S2 and B2) set picks for their teammates below (G and S1, respectively). G flies down the ballside sideline, while the screener (S2) heads down the other side after G uses the pick. The inbounder (B1) can pass to a teammate on either sideline (G or S2) as deep as possible. If the receiver catches the toss, he or she dribbles the length of the court to produce a shot. B1 also has the option to cast the ball deep to either S1 or B2. The big player (B2) steps back to the ball after S1 uses his or her screen. S1 fakes a move up the sideline away from the inbounder and uses B2's pick on an angle that enables him or her to break free near the strongside sideline.

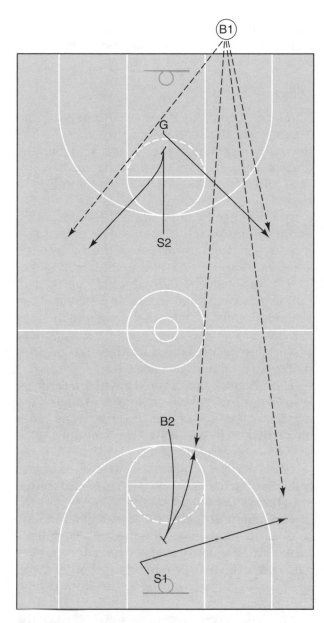

Figure 13.3 Long play.

Keys

See the discussions of setting a screen and using a pick in "Man-to-Man Offensive Fine-Tuning" on page 4. In "Breaking Presses Offensive Fine-Tuning" on page 305, see the discussions of the throwing the ball deep and receiving a pass.

The coach calls the play when one to five seconds remain on the game clock and the team needs to score. No time-outs remain. If the team still has a time-out left with two to five seconds to play, I suggest calling a play to deliver the ball to midcourt and using a time-out. I would hesitate to use the long play in a tie game because of the risk of the inbounds pass being intercepted or going out of bounds. Either result gives the opponent the last offensive possession and a chance to win the game.

If the team needs a three-point shot, all players are aware that they need to be beyond the arc before taking the shot.

The two perimeter players in the backcourt use a back pick to get free. The player using the screen cuts ballside or weakside up a sideline. The screener heads the opposite way. The ball goes to either player as far down the sideline as possible. The inbounder cannot commit a turnover. He or she must be conservative to ensure that a teammate catches the throw-in. The player who catches the inbounds pass most likely will have the opportunity for the final shot taken off the dribble.

The inbounder passes to any open teammate. He or she selects the one most likely to catch the throw-in. The squad cannot score unless a player catches the inbounds toss.

FULL

Every team needs a play geared for desperate times. The full play works. It helped my teams, and I have seen other coaches use it successfully. The ball must go the length of the floor with only one to three seconds on the game clock. The team is down one to three points, and they need a quality scoring chance. No time-outs remain.

Personnel

The inbounder is a post player who is able to toss the ball deep. The other big player must be capable of jumping and grabbing the ball in traffic. He or she has to be able to score after catching the ball. In addition, the team should have on the floor two productive peripheral shooters who can hit from 20 to 25 feet.

Scoring

The two outside shooters may have chances from behind the three-point line, perhaps out past 25 feet. The big player at the offensive end might have a shot opportunity from 5 to 20 feet.

Execution

B1, a post player, acts as the inbounder (figure 13.4). The point guard (G) is in the center circle.

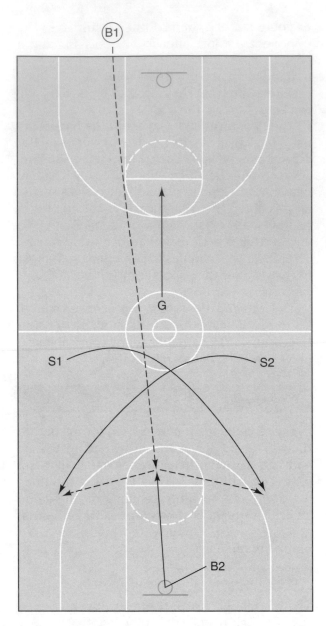

Figure 13.4 Full play.

If he or she is one of the team's best outside shooters, the perimeter players may have to adjust their positioning. Each of the two shooters (S1 and S2) is on one side of half-court. The other big player (B2) starts at the weakside block on the lane furthest from the inbounder.

The action begins when the lead guard (G) runs straight to the ball as the two shooters (S1 and S2) cross (or fake it) near the center circle at midcourt. The shooters race to spots near the sidelines and above the three-point line opposite each other. Meanwhile, B2 seals off the defender so that a direct pass can go to a site near the foul line. B2 leaps to grab the inbounds

pass. B2 may have time to tip the ball to S1 or S2 if either is open for the final shot. B2, S1, or S2 attempts the critical shot.

Keys

Refer to "Breaking Presses Offensive Fine-Tuning" and the sections on throwing the ball deep and receiving a pass (page 305). See the discussion of pinning the defender in "Man-to-Man Offensive Fine-Tuning" in chapter 1 on page 4.

The play can be used when the score is tied and only one second remains. The ball can be inbounded from anywhere in the backcourt, whether from an end line or either sideline. The team must not foul while trying to gain possession of the entry pass. In a tie game the inbounder must be sure that someone touches the ball. He or she cannot give the opponent possession of the ball under their basket with one second left in a tie game.

The inbounds pass should have some arch on it so that the target has to jump and snatch the ball to secure possession. The receiver's other alternative is to tip or slap the ball out to one of the two nearby shooters.

Three perimeter players are stretched across midcourt, with the two strongest distance shooters in the outside slots.

The action at half-court is designed mainly to occupy the defense and prevent them from providing adequate defensive help deep. At the same time, the play provides two shooters with the possibility of acquiring a shot from behind the arc.

The post player deep moves directly into the nearest defender and initiates physical contact. He or she heads up to the near foul line in anticipation of an entry pass. If either nearby shooter is open, the big player can slap the ball out to the open player. If the shooters are not open and the big player catches the ball, he or she may use one or two dribbles, depending on the amount of time remaining, before taking the crucial shot.

If two to three seconds remain on the game clock and the team has a time-out, the coach should call for a play that delivers the ball to half-court and then call time-out. If the team is down three points, the deep big player must know that any pass reception has to occur near the three-point line instead of the foul line. The inbounder also needs to know that the target area has changed.

FULL SCREEN

Coaches will discover that they cannot use the same desperation play too often. Having a few different ways to accomplish the same task is helpful. The full-screen play is a slight variation on the full play. The ball is put in play from the end line or deep on the sideline in the backcourt. Only one to three seconds remain in the game, and the club is behind by one to three points. The play is also feasible if the score is tied with only one second remaining.

Personnel

A post player is the inbounder and must be able to throw long and accurately. The big player receiving the deep pass ought to have the size and skill to go in the air to secure control of the ball in traffic. The two perimeter players must be strong outside shooters. The other perimeter player is one of the smallest players on the team.

Scoring

The big player at the offensive basket can gain a shot in or around the lane from 10 to 20 feet. The smallest player could get a layup. The two exterior shooters might see three-point chances develop.

Execution

The full-screen play is identical to the full play in its setup and movements with two exceptions. First, the player in the middle of the three perimeter players (G) does not run to the ball. Instead, he or she screens down for the big player near the weakside block (B2) (figure 13.5). The screener should be small in stature compared with his or her teammates to ensure that a smaller defender will match up. That way a defensive switch gives an edge to the offensive post player. Second, the two shooters (S1 and S2) do not cross or fake the cross. They simply slide down to sites near each sideline about five feet behind the three-point line. They move after the initial pass is in the air. B2 uses G's pick to sprint toward the foul line at the top of the key to snare the inbounds pass from B1. B2 also has

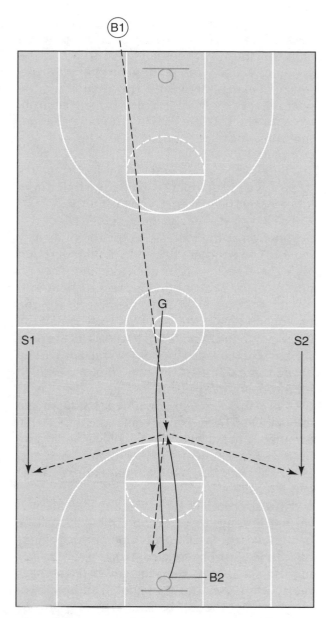

Figure 13.5 Full-screen play.

the option to tip the ball to S1, S2, or G under the hoop.

Keys

Refer to "Breaking Presses Offensive Fine-Tuning" on page 305. The relevant topics are throwing the ball deep and receiving a pass. See "Man-to-Man Offensive Fine-Tuning" in chapter 1 on page 4 to review the discussions of setting a screen and using a pick.

The big player inbounding the ball is able to fling it deep and throws the ball with an arc, forcing the deep big player to jump to make the catch.

The perimeter player who produces the best mismatch if the defense decides to switch is in the middle of the half-court to act as the screener. Usually the point guard fills this role. A size disparity between the screener and the post player receiving the pick can cause problems for the defense. Having the big player be the primary target enhances the odds of a pass completion.

The player in the center at midcourt moves to pick when the referee hands the ball to the inbounder. The screener must set a legal pick.

The big player receiving the screen heads to a destination at the foul line to the top-of-the-key region. The shooters are wide at midcourt and glide down to sites near each sideline. They do not move until the inbounder releases the ball.

The pass receiver might be able to tap the ball out to one of the two shooters behind the three-point line. A back tap to the screener near the basket might also be viable. A tap goes to any of the three if it can lead to a shot and enough time remains on the clock. The screener near the hoop may have to announce that he or she is available. The screener's defender might have a tendency to help with the big player and ignore his or her assignment. If a three-point shot is necessary, a back tap to a teammate at the basket is not feasible.

The pass receiver is prepared to leap to catch the ball in congestion. After grabbing the ball, he or she takes the last shot attempt. The player may have time to dribble once or twice before releasing the shot. After securing the ball, the pass receiver releases the final shot. The big player never catches the ball, lands, and throws it to one of the three teammates nearby. The ball goes to one of the three only with a tap or touch pass.

If losing by three points, the final shot has to be from beyond the arc. The big player must catch the ball above the top of the key or tap it to one of the shooters near a sideline.

If two to three seconds remain and one time-out is available, a more prudent play is to zip the ball to half-court and call time-out. The team then uses a sideline out-of-bounds play for the last shot.

LENGTH

When a team has to travel the length of the floor and score within seconds, specialty plays are required. Having only one specialty play in the offensive arsenal is not a good idea. Adding the length play provides a choice, another way to accomplish the task. The team is inbounding the ball at the baseline opposite their basket. Three to eight seconds remain on the clock. The score is tied, or the team is down by one to three points. The action created allows the team to achieve a quality final shot.

Personnel

The play works better if the point guard is an effective scorer off the dribble. Two other excellent shooters from outside are valuable. One big player should be a strong inside-scoring threat. The other post player delivers the entry pass.

Scoring

The lead guard attains a shot off the dribble near the three-point line. The primary shooter acquires a shot from a corner. The best interior player may catch the ball in the low post. The third perimeter player looks for a shot near the top of the key.

Execution

One post player (B1) serves as the inbounder. The other big player (B2), who should be the best interior player, is at midlane on the ballside at the offensive end. The preeminent outside shooter (S1) starts at the block opposite B2. The point guard (G) begins weakside at the level of the top of the key in the backcourt. The other perimeter player (S2) is ballside directly across from G (figure 13.6).

Initially, S2 screens across for the lead guard (G). G races to the strongside. B1 throws the ball to G as deep along the sideline as possible. The ball must go to the ball handler (G). The playmaker immediately puts the ball on the floor, heading up the nearest sideline. When he or she reaches the offensive side of half-court, B2 moves to screen for S1. S1 uses the pick to hustle to the ballside corner. B2 seals the defender and heads to the ball after S1 uses the screen. G looks to send the ball to S1 in the corner or low to B2. After screening for G in the backcourt, S2 hustles to a site below the foul line extended and outside the three-point line at the offside on the far end. After G catches the inbounds pass, B1 runs the floor and moves to

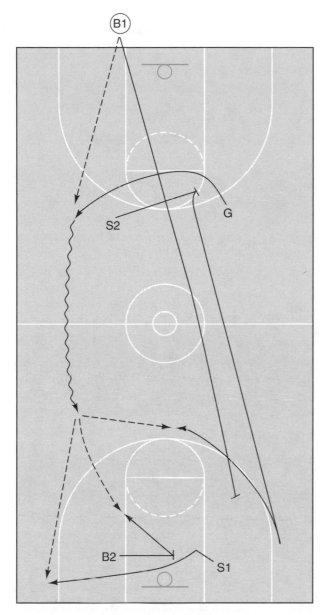

Figure 13.6 Length play formation and movements.

down pick on the weakside for S2. S2 motors to the top of the key for a potential shot. The point guard (G) considers tossing to either shooter (S1 or S2) or inside to the big player (B2). His or her last choice is to shoot.

Keys

Refer to the discussions of throwing the ball deep and receiving a pass in "Breaking Presses Offensive Fine-Tuning" on page 305. See "Man-to-Man Offensive Fine-Tuning" in chapter 1 on page 4 and the discussions of setting a screen, using a pick, slipping a screen, low exchanges and cross screens, throwing the ball inside, and pinning the defender.

The play is designed to be used with three to eight seconds remaining. If the team has a time-out left, a better choice may be to cast the ball to half-court, call time-out, and then use a sideline out-of-bounds play. With no time-outs, this play produces an acceptable shot. A team can use the play when the score is tied, but it is somewhat of a gamble because the first pass must go to a particular player. A turnover is possible.

The two perimeter players in the backcourt begin opposite one another near the top of the key. They must put ample space between them to give the lead guard room to get open on the strongside to receive the inbounds toss.

The inbounder and backcourt screener hustle to the offside while staying wide. The big player sets a solid screen for the shooter below. Both players must go at full speed. Otherwise, the screen will lag well behind the other action.

The point guard produces a respectable shot if his or her teammates are not open for a pass reception and clean shot.

Another option for the initial personnel placement is possible. The big player who is inbounding can change with the exterior player who picks for the point guard. The main advantage of this variation is that the screening action for the playmaker is likely to be more effective. See the discussion of screening between post and perimeter players on page 4. The drawback is that a perimeter player is picking for a post player on the down screen at the offensive end. Therefore, the post player must be able to shoot the ball well from the periphery. If the down screen is not a viable alternative, another possibility is replacing it with a back pick.

LAST

The last play emphasizes activity on the offensive half of the court. The team inbounds the ball along the baseline away from their basket. This play is an option when losing by one to three points with three to eight seconds remaining on the clock. The action makes it possible to attempt a shot in a short period when taking the ball the length of the court.

Personnel

The point guard must be fairly quick and able to break free from a defender. In addition, he or she should be able to score off the dribble. One post player should be adept at shooting the ball in the paint. The other two perimeter players must be proficient distance shooters.

Scoring

The lead guard may receive a shot off the dribble near the three-point line. One perimeter player shoots from a corner. The other exterior player acquires scoring opportunities at the key. The better inside scorer of the two post players garners shots in the foul lane.

Execution

One post player (B1) is the inbounder (figure 13.7). The point guard (G) starts in the backcourt at the weakside sideline above the top of the key. The other big player (B2) begins at the top of the key at the offensive end of the court. One shooter (S1) starts on the ballside block below B2, while the other shooter (S2) is at the offside box. Both must be quality scorers from around the arc. S1 should be a slightly better shooter than S2.

The lead guard (G) breaks free to receive the throw-in by swinging toward the strongside and dribbles quickly up the ballside sideline. After the ball handler crosses midcourt, the shooter on the strongside box (S1) sets a screen for the player opposite (S2). S2 hustles to the strongside corner for a scoring chance. After the screener (S1) heads across the lane, B2 dashes down to complete a screen on the screener. S1 races to an open area near the top of the key off B2's pick. The lead guard (G) passes to S2 in the ballside corner, to S1 at the key, or to B2, who is posting inside after S1 uses the pick. G also may create a shot off the dribble.

Keys

Refer to "Man-to-Man Offensive Fine-Tuning" on page 4 and these topics: screening between post and perimeter players, setting a screen, using a pick, low exchanges and cross screens, pinning the defender, and throwing the ball inside. See the discussion of throwing the ball deep in "Breaking Presses Offensive Fine-Tuning" on page 305.

The point guard must absolutely get open to receive the inbounds pass. He or she catches the ball as deep as possible down the ballside sideline. The starting position is designed to

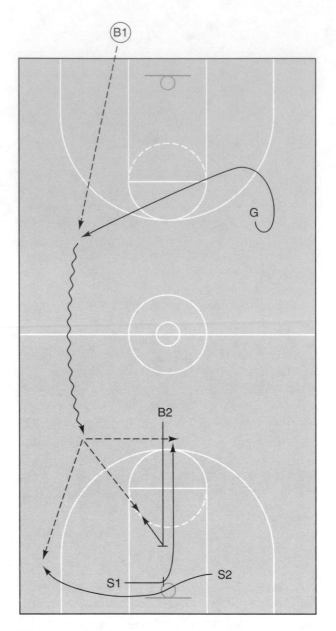

Figure 13.7 Last play.

provide a maximum amount of room in which to work.

The lead guard should be a good decision maker. After crossing the half-court line, he or she looks to one of three teammates located in the offensive half of the court. If the prospects do not appear likely, he or she uses the dribble to score.

Teams can use the last play when down one to three points. Players take the best available shot, although if a team is down by three, the shot must be a trey. In that case, the pass should not go to the big player in the lane. If the score is tied, calling this play is a gamble. Having only one inbounds pass option (to the point guard) is a calculated risk. If the opponent shuts down the throw-in, a turnover may occur at a critical time. Having one time-out left ensures that a turnover will not occur, but the time-out may be put to better use if it is called after the ball is sent to half-court. The team would then use a sideline out-of-bounds play to create the final shot.

END

The end play uses three players in the backcourt with a lone body on the offensive half of the floor. This play is another way to create a quick score. The end play is especially effective if the center possesses good leaping ability. The play is designed for use when only one to three seconds are left on the game clock and the squad is down by one to three points. The ball is inbounded at the deep sideline or end line. The team attains a suitable shot opportunity in only a few seconds.

Personnel

The inbounder is a post player who is capable of throwing the ball long with accuracy. The other big player should be able to jump, catch the ball in traffic, and score after catching the pass. Perimeter players must be able to dribble quickly and release a shot before time expires.

Scoring

Any exterior player may acquire a shot off the dribble. The big player at the offensive basket is the primary target and shoots from inside 20 feet.

Execution

Three players begin in the backcourt (figure 13.8). Two shooters (S2 and S1) are even with the top of the key, five to eight feet outside the lane on each side. The point guard (G) begins near the half-court line on the weakside. S2 and S1 cross or fake the cross and sprint down the sidelines. After they move to the sidelines, the lead guard (G) rushes to the center of the floor straight at the inbounder (B1). Only one player (B2) is on the offensive half of the court. He or she starts on the weakside block. B2 takes the defender into the lane, makes contact, puts the defender on his or her rear, and heads to an

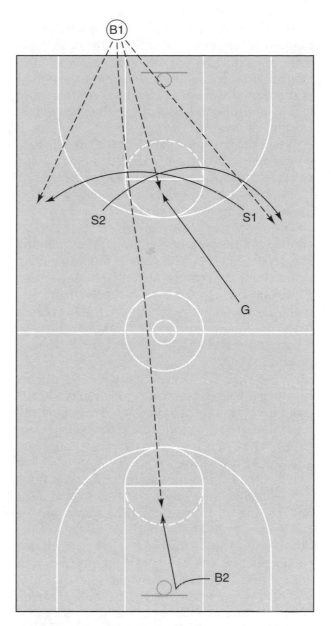

Figure 13.8 End play setup and options.

open area near the foul line to receive the pass from B1. The exact amount of time left on the clock determines whether one or two dribbles are possible. The ball could also go to one of the players in the backcourt as deep as possible. The player catching the ball dribbles and shoots just before the horn sounds. The three perimeter players are secondary pass preferences for the inbounder. B2 is the primary receiver.

Keys

Refer to the discussion of throwing the ball deep in "Breaking Presses Offensive Fine-Tuning" on page 305.

Most of the time the inbounder hurls the ball long to the lone teammate at the other end, especially with only one or two seconds left on the clock. With three seconds remaining, the option of throwing to players in the backcourt is more viable. The inbounder passes to the player most capable of scoring.

When the ball goes to one of the three perimeter players, he or she speed dribbles up the court and shoots before the clock expires. The player balances himself or herself before shooting and focuses on the rim.

The big player at the low block on the offensive end must do a respectable job of pinning the defender. He or she gains a favorable position to jump and catch the long inbounds pass. The receiver shields the defender from the ball. After making the reception, the big player lands on balance and looks to shoot. The time remaining determines if one or two dribbles are possible.

When down by three points, the player receives the deep catch at or beyond the three-point arc. The long pass needs to have some arc on it. When the inbounder casts the ball upward, the receiver can seal the defender, jump, and snatch the ball in the air.

If two to three seconds remain and a time-out is available, sending the ball to midcourt and calling an immediate time-out might be the best option. The team then uses a sideline out-of-bounds play for the final shot. With one second left on the clock, the inbounder looks almost exclusively at the big player at the other end of the court. The lead guard is likely to be the last inbounding alternative. The lead guard is a viable option only if at least two seconds (preferably three or more) remain because he or she is headed to the inbounder and must turn and change direction 180 degrees. The lead guard needs one or two seconds longer to reach a position to launch an acceptable shot.

The play is feasible when the score is even and only one or two seconds are left. The inbounder must understand that a turnover is not to occur under any circumstances. He or she delivers the ball to the open player. The deep big player cannot foul going for the ball.

Teams can use the play with four to eight seconds on the clock if the inbounder knows that the three perimeter players are now primary targets. The pass to the post player deep becomes a secondary option. When a perimeter player catches the inbounds pass, he or she watches the time on the clock. Through practice, the player gets a feel for the amount of time used. He or she should not release the final shot too early.

DOWN COURT

This time players are evenly split between backcourt and forecourt. The down court play gives the deep big player another option when a long inbounds pass comes to him or her. The play is viable when only one to six seconds remain on the game clock and a team is losing by one to three points. The team puts the ball in play from the baseline away from their hoop. The team needs to score as time runs out.

Personnel

The point guard should be an effective ball handler who can use the dribble to create a score. One excellent outside shooter is required, as well as a post player who is proficient at scoring around the basket. The big player inbounds the ball and should be capable of hurling it deep. The last perimeter player screens and is not likely to score.

Scoring

The primary post player could gain a shot 5 to 20 feet from the hoop. The main shooter acquires a three-point chance from a corner. The point guard shoots off the dribble behind or inside the arc.

Execution

The inbounder (B1) is a big player (figure 13.9). The amount of time left on the game clock dictates the pass recipient. The best distance shooter on the squad (S1) starts on the offensive side of midcourt near the ballside sideline. The other big player (B2) is stationed deep on the offside block. The other two perimeter players (S2 and G) begin in the backcourt near the top of the key, with the lead guard (G) on the weakside and S2 on the strongside, slightly more than lane-width apart. The third perimeter player (S2) and the inbounder (B1) can switch positions if the coach desires.

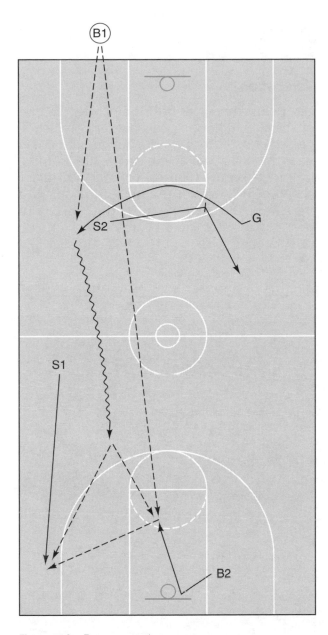

Figure 13.9 Down court play.

S2 screens across for the playmaker (G) to start the action. The lead guard (G) at the ballside sideline may obtain the pass from B1. If so, he or she dribbles quickly down the floor. The playmaker shoots or passes to either S1 or B2 for the critical shot. B1 may deliver the ball deep to B2. B2 steps into the lane, makes contact with the defender, and heads toward the foul line, keeping the defender on his or her back. B2 jumps, catches the ball, lands in a balanced stance, and shoots. He or she may dribble once or twice before shooting if time permits. B2 has the option to tap the ball out to the shooter (S1),

who has moved beyond the three-point arc near the ballside corner.

Keys

Refer to the segments on setting a screen, using a pick, and pinning the defender in "Man-to-Man Offensive Fine-Tuning" found on page 4. In "Breaking Presses Offensive Fine-Tuning," see the discussions of throwing the ball deep and receiving a pass on page 305.

The perimeter player in backcourt installs a solid pick to free the playmaker so that he or she can catch the throw-in as far down the court on the ballside sideline as possible. If the point guard snares the inbounds pass, he or she bolts up the court. When approaching the three-point line at the offensive end, the point guard takes control and tries to score. The playmaker can shoot from distance, drive the ball to the basket for a shot, or dribble penetrate and dish to the big player near the hoop or kick the ball out to the shooter in the corner.

The primary shooter who begins near half-court moves behind the three-point arc near the offensive corner. He or she moves as soon as the inbounder starts a throw-in motion. If the inbounder tosses deep, the shooter slides to the strongside ready to shoot a trey after the big player taps the ball in his or her direction.

The screener in the backcourt and the inbounder run down the floor on the offside after the ball is in play. Generally, neither player is a scoring alternative. The inbounder can set a down pick for a teammate below the weakside foul line extended if time permits. The exterior player might be able to acquire a pass from the lead guard near the top of the key for a last-second shot, but all the weakside action is primarily to divert the attention of the defense.

The big player who starts on the weakside block must do a commendable job of pinning the defender on his or her rear. He or she aggressively bursts up to receive the pass. The big player may have to gain possession in traffic. If unable to grab the ball, he or she may have a chance to tap the ball to the shooter on the ballside periphery. The big player initiates the tap if the shooter is open as the defender moves toward the inbounds pass.

The inbounder heaves the ball long if only one to two seconds remain. Otherwise, the deep throw-in is not necessary, and the inbounder uses it only if the intended receiver is likely to catch it. The inbounder sets his or her shoulders perpendicular to the baseline when tossing the ball long. In addition, the pass should have some arc on it. The defense can more easily knock away a pass sent on a line.

If two to six seconds remain and the score is tied, this play is not practical. The inbounder does not have enough entry-pass options. With three to six seconds on the clock, the point guard becomes the main target to receive the initial pass. The ball handler breaks open in the ball-side sideline area of the backcourt. The throw-in goes as far down the sideline as is safe.

If the post player at the far end of the court does not receive the throw-in, he or she slides to the offside of the lane and awaits a dish from the penetrating lead guard.

If a time-out remains with two to six seconds on the clock, the coach may want to send the ball to midcourt and call time-out immediately.

If a team is down by three points, the deep entry pass is still a possibility. The big player coming to the ball secures possession just behind the three-point line. Any shot attempt must come from past the three-point line.

FINAL TO MID

Sometimes it is best to throw the ball to midcourt and call a time-out when faced with dwindling time. I designed the final to mid play to allow post players to establish screens to free a perimeter player. Teams use the play late in a game when down by one to three points or when the score is tied, when they have at least one time-out left, and when two to eight seconds remain in the game. After inbounding the ball from the baseline away from their basket, the team throws the ball to half-court and quickly calls a time-out.

Personnel

One of the perimeter players must be able to throw an accurate pass to half-court from the end line. The post players must be efficient screeners who can catch a ball thrown with significant velocity. Quickness is the primary feature the coach craves in the other two exterior players.

Scoring

None.

Execution

One perimeter player is the inbounder (S2). He or she should have a penchant for completing passes of some length. The point guard (G) is near the ballside sideline below the foul line in the backcourt (figure 13.10). The primary shooter (S1) starts at the weakside box along the lane on the offensive end of the court. Both post players (B2 and B1) are on the far side of midcourt. One is at the ballside foul line

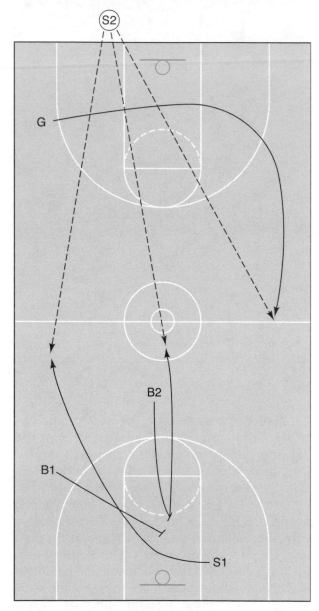

Figure 13.10 Final to mid setup and options.

extended behind the three-point arc (B1). The other is above the strongside elbow past the three-point line (B2).

The point guard (G) runs full speed to the opposite side of the court and then continues up the far sideline to await the pass near half-court. The post players (B2 and B1) come together to set a double screen on a diagonal in the lane for the main shooter (S1). S1 sprints to a spot on the strongside near midcourt at the sideline. B2 darts to the ball down the center of the floor after S1 uses the twin pick. The inbounder (S2) delivers the ball to S1 or B2. The playmaker (G) is the secondary choice. Immediately after catching the throw-in, the receiver calls time-out.

Keys

In "Breaking Presses Offensive Fine-Tuning," see the discussions of throwing the ball deep and receiving a pass on pages 305 and 306.

The inbounder considers tossing to the main shooter first and the big player second. The point guard who is swinging up the weakside sideline is the inbounder's last option. The inbounder must lead the playmaker so that he or she actually runs under the basketball. The receiver should get the ball on the offensive side of midcourt. If none of the alternatives pans out, the inbounder calls time-out and the coach plots a new strategy.

The big players establish the double pick to allow the shooter to get open near the ballside midcourt. See the discussion of the double screen in "Man-to-Man Offensive Fine-Tuning" in chapter 1 on page 6. After the shooter takes advantage of the double screen, the big player closer to midcourt sprints straight to the ball. As he or she approaches the center-jump circle, the big player may be open.

The pass receiver calls time-out immediately. If the ball is secured in the center of the court, the coach asks the referee from which side of the court his or her team will inbound the ball after the time-out. The coach must have this knowledge before huddling with the team. A sideline out-of-bounds play is forthcoming.

FINAL TO SCORE

The final to score play produces different motion options from the same alignment described in the previous play. A team that uses it can thus practice several plays at the same time. The play is feasible with one to three seconds left on the clock when trailing by one to three points. Final to score can be used in a tied ballgame, but only when one or possibly two seconds remain. The ball must go the length of the floor. The play creates scoring chances before the horn sounds.

Personnel

The perimeter player who inbounds must be capable of throwing the ball to a teammate at the other end of the court. One effective distance shooter is necessary. A post player must be able to leap to grab a pass thrown at the basket. Both big players must be convincing screeners. The ball handler is not a major contributor unless he or she assumes the shooter's position.

Scoring

The main shooter may see a shot from near the top of the key or at the ballside wing behind the three-point line. Either big player may have an opportunity to snatch the inbounds pass close to the basket. Although it is not likely, the lead guard could acquire a shot off the dribble.

Execution

The point guard (G) loops down the weakside sideline from the backcourt (figure 13.11). One post player (B2) starts above the ballside elbow past the three-point line on the offensive end. The other big player (B1) begins behind the arc at the foul line extended on the strongside, and the key shooter (S1) is at the offside block on the far foul lane. The post players move to set single down picks for the shooter (S1). B2 comes straight down the foul lane. B1 moves in to shield the defender near the ballside box. S1 uses either pick to race to an open spot to receive the throw-in.

The inbounder (S2) looks to the highlighted shooter (S1) as the first pass option. The shooter takes a shot after catching the pass. The time remaining determines how many dribbles are possible before the shooter releases the ball. A secondary target is the screener. He or she loops around the other post player to a spot at the top of the key or the ballside sideline left vacant by the primary shooter.

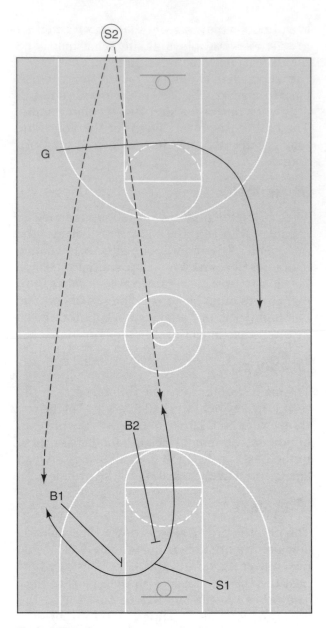

Figure 13.11 One movement option in final to score.

sideline. Meanwhile, S1 scampers to establish a back pick for B2 near the top of the key. S1 bolts up when he or she sees B1 approach the baseline. B2 races to the hoop while looking for a long entry pass. S2's first pass option is deep to B2. If B2 is not open, the inbounder may throw to B1 at the ballside sideline or to S1 who steps to the ball after B2 uses his or her pick. The toss to the lead guard racing down the offside sideline consistently remains the inbounder's final choice.

The fourth and final motion is for S1 to fix a back screen for the other post player (B1). The big player who starts at the foul line extended (B1) initially moves straight toward the baseline. Both B1 and S1 begin their actions when the official hands the ball to the inbounder. B1 dashes to the hoop and is the primary target for the entry pass. As S1 nears the point where the screen is planted, the second big player (B2) motors to screen the screener. S1 uses B2's pick after B1 has used the screen. S1 moves beyond the top of the key and is the second option for B1. B2 hustles to the closer sideline. The playmaker (G) is the last choice for the inbounder.

Keys

In "Breaking Presses Offensive Fine-Tuning," see the discussions of throwing the ball deep and receiving a pass on pages 305 and 306. Refer to "Man-to-Man Offensive Fine-Tuning" in chapter 1 (page 4) for the discussions of screening between post and perimeter players, setting a screen, using a pick, and the double screen.

The point guard jogs straight across the foul lane before picking up speed and racing up the weakside sideline. He or she starts to move as soon as the official hands the ball to the inbounder. When the lead guard catches the ball, he or she puts it on the floor and tries to score.

The three players on the offensive side of the court (two post players and the team's best shooter) have four motion choices. Although the coach can dictate which option the team executes, allowing players to choose enables the play to continue if no time-out is available before the critical final possession. If used, the double pick is set in the lane below the near elbow on a 45-degree angle. The shooter plants the back pick horizontally or vertically. As he or she is about to set the back pick, the other

Instead of setting two distinct down screens for the main shooter (S1 in figure 13.11), the big players (B1 and B2) can fix a double screen in the lane on an angle. S1 dashes off either side of the double screen to break free and grab the entry pass. The big player whose shoulder has been used by the shooter motors around the other big player to an area not selected by the shooter (S1).

A third alternative action is for the post player at the strongside foul line extended (B1) to run deep to the baseline. He or she pivots on the baseline foot to return to the original position. B1 stays within three to eight feet of the post player screens for the screener. In the first two movement options, the highlighted shooter must fake in one direction and exploit the screen in the other direction.

If post players set a double screen for the key shooter, one big player loops around the other after the shooter uses the double screen. When using this maneuver, it is extremely helpful if one or both big players are capable of scoring from the periphery. One post player steps down and in to set an obstacle for the other big player, who races over his or her teammate's back to the designated area.

This play is useful if the ball is inbounded from a sideline deep in the backcourt. With only one second left on the clock, any of the options reviewed are viable, but the inbounds pass must go at least to midcourt. With two to three seconds left, the coach deploys final to mid only if his or her team has one time-out left. With no time-outs, final to score is the preferred play. When down by three points, it is essential that the team attempt a three-point shot. The inbounder passes to a teammate outside the three-point line. This play is not a good choice when two or three seconds are left and the score is tied. The entry passes are too risky. The team cannot afford a turnover in this situation. Rolling the dice is OK with only one second remaining on the clock, but the inbounder must make sure that someone touches the entry pass.

BOMB TO MID

The bomb to mid play is the final action designed to deliver the ball to midcourt quickly. All players are in the forecourt. The probability of success is high because the big players pick for the exterior players. The team must go the length of the court to score. The coach calls this play when the score is tied or his or her team is trailing by one to three points, at least two seconds remain, and at least one time-out is available. The ball is inbounded from the end line directly to the half-court.

Personnel

A perimeter player inbounds the ball. He or she must be able to make a strong pass from the far baseline to a teammate at midcourt. The post players must be formidable screeners,

and at least one must be able to catch the ball consistently without fumbling. Quickness is a favorable attribute for players.

Scoring

None.

Execution

One perimeter player (S2) is the inbounder (figure 13.12). The point guard (G) is on the weakside block on the lane at the far end of the court. The final perimeter player (S1) is along the ballside sideline at top-of-the-key level in

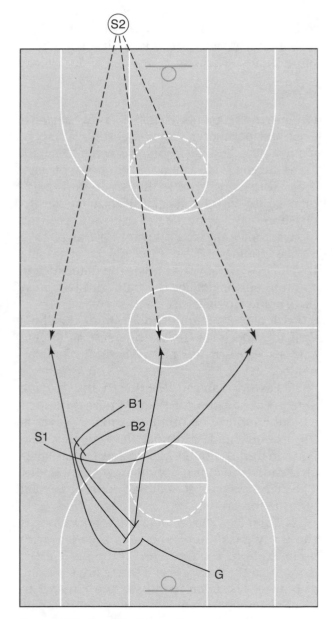

Figure 13.12 Bomb to mid.

the forecourt. The two post players (B1 and B2) are located near S1 in a stack directly above the ballside elbow beyond the three-point line.

The big players start the action by moving together to screen across for S1. S1 cuts under the double pick to the weakside near half-court and the sideline. As soon as S1 runs off the double screen, the big players turn and immediately head to plant a twin pick for the playmaker (G). The lead guard bolts under the double pick to the ballside sideline near mid-court. After G exploits the double screen, the post player closer to half-court (B2) sprints up the middle of the court for a possible pass reception at the center-jump circle. S2 throws to S1, G, or B2. The pass receiver immediately calls time-out. The game clock should not lose more than one second.

Keys

Refer to the segments about screening between post and perimeter players, setting a screen, using a pick, and the double screen in "Man-to-Man Offensive Fine-Tuning" in chapter 1 on page 4. See "Breaking Presses Offensive Fine-Tuning" on page 305 and give special attention to the discussions of throwing the ball deep and receiving a pass, topics that are relevant for this play.

The inbounder cannot be lazy when passing to midcourt. A lazy pass gives the defense time to intercept or deflect the ball. The ball must have some zip on it.

Post players should understand that how well they perform their jobs—setting double screens—determines how successful the play will be.

The exterior player sprinting to the weakside sideline at half-court is the first pass option for the inbounder. The other perimeter player is the second choice. The post player nearest mid-court in the last double pick rushes to the center circle and is the third option for the inbounder. The inbounds pass goes to half-court or beyond into the forecourt.

As soon as a player near half-court catches the entry pass, he or she calls time-out, with no hesitation. The time run off the game clock is minimal (probably less if the team is playing at home). The team then uses the time-out to discuss and review a sideline out-of-bounds play for the critical final possession.

Coaches normally call the play with two to

eight seconds showing on the game clock. The inbounder must avoid committing a turnover, which in all likelihood would seal a loss.

BOMB TO SCORE

Specialty plays used with only a few seconds left usually require the ball to travel some distance to reach certain players in specific sites where they can release quality shots. I feel that the best chance to accomplish that is with interactions between the big players and exterior players. The clock has run down to one to three seconds and the ball must be inbounded from the far baseline. The squad is down by one to three points. The team has no time-outs remaining. The bomb to score play may be used in a tie game, but only one second should remain on the clock. The play provides a quality scoring chance as the ball travels from one end of the floor to the other while consuming little time.

Personnel

The perimeter player inbounding the ball must be able to cast the ball deep. The best outside shooter is near the ballside sideline at top-of-the-key level in the forecourt. One post player must be capable of jumping in traffic to snatch a long toss at the hoop. The point guard, the physically smallest exterior player, plants a back screen and must be able to score from distance if necessary. One big player should possess at least decent jumping ability and substantial physical size. For the secondary action the most important player attribute is the effectiveness of the dribble penetration. Three players could potentially drive to the hoop in an attempt to score.

Scoring

The premier shooter receives a three-point chance from above the foul line extended. A big player snares a deep pass within 10 feet of the goal. The lead guard has a shot opportunity from above the top of the key. Alternative scoring maneuvers center on one-on-one ability.

Execution

The starting set in bomb to score (figure 13.13) is the same as that for bomb to mid. S2 is the perimeter player who inbounds the ball. The point guard (G) is at the offside box along the foul lane in the forecourt. Two post players (B1 and B2) are stacked above the three-point arc and the ballside elbow. S1 (the main shooter) begins at the offensive end near the strongside foul line extended.

The first motion option begins with the post player closer to the basket (B2) rushing to down screen for the key shooter (S1) at the ballside wing. S1 is the team's leading shooter from distance. As B2 begins the movement, S1 takes the defender to the baseline to set up the upcoming down pick. S1 races to the ball along the strongside sideline after using B2's screen.

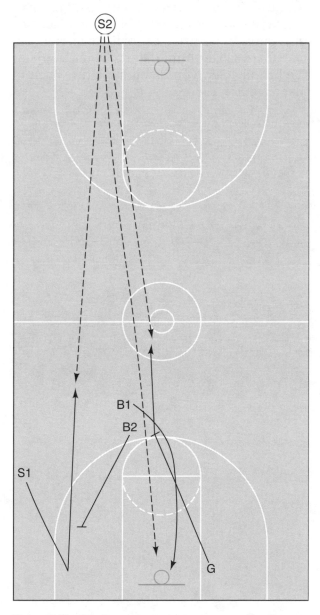

Figure 13.13   Bomb to score, one way to generate a shot.

Meanwhile, the lead guard (G) sprints up to establish a back pick for the other big player (B1). B1 slices to the basket. The back screener (G) darts toward the ball after B1 uses his or her pick. G is the third throw-in option for S2. The inbounder (S2) initially considers passing to the post player (B1) headed to the basket and then looks to either the primary shooter (S1) or the playmaker (G).

A secondary action that teams can use to create shots before time expires is to run the play identically to bomb to mid (see figure 13.12) except that when a player secures the throw-in, a time-out is *not* requested. Instead, the pass receiver immediately turns to face the hoop and execute a dribble drive to score. Teammates clear up toward midcourt. The big player from the double screen who does not race to the center-jump circle vacates the lane area. If the toss-in goes to one exterior player, the post player hustles to back pick for the other perimeter player at midcourt. If the throw-in goes to the big player at the center of midcourt, the other post player may choose either outside person to back screen.

Keys

Refer to "Breaking Presses Offensive Fine-Tuning on page 305." Two topics, throwing the ball deep and receiving a pass, are relevant to bomb to score. See "Man-to-Man Offensive Fine-Tuning" in chapter 1 on page 4 and review these topics: screening between post and perimeter players, setting a screen, using a pick, and back pick.

The play will not work if the inbounder cannot throw the ball long with some authority. The inbounder can back off the baseline some to increase space from the defender on the ball. When hurling the ball all the way to the far basket, the inbounder should arch the toss to allow a teammate to jump and catch the ball near the hoop.

The primary shooter runs to the baseline when the official hands the ball to the inbounder. The highlighted shooter steps toward the box on the lane before exploiting the down pick by the post player closer to the basket in the stack above the strongside elbow. The screener's back is parallel to the midcourt line.

The lead guard is in a starting position near the basket because if the defense switches the back screen an obvious size mismatch develops. The playmaker is usually the smallest player physically. The goal is to get the smallest defender to guard the back screener. The coach may have to place a different perimeter player at the weakside block to get the desired defender on the back screener.

With one second remaining, the inbounder focuses on throwing the ball long at the basket. Obviously, if the team is down three points, the deep entry pass is not used. The inbounds pass heads to another option so that the team has a chance to shoot a trey.

Remember that in a tie game the team with possession of the ball has a major advantage. The club with the ball is the only one who can score. In a tie game, the inbounder tosses the ball to any of the three potential receivers. Someone must touch the ball. Without a touch, the opposing team inbounds the ball under their own hoop. With two or three seconds left, any entry pass option is acceptable. If the team has a time-out, running bomb to mid is probably best.

The play is also appropriate if the throw-in takes place at a sideline well in the backcourt.

The defenders on the post players in the stack might play off them toward the basket. In that case, the post player whose defender is nearer the hoop fixes the down screen at the ballside baseline. The other big player acquires a back pick. The players read the situation, communicate, and adjust. The point guard targets the appropriate defender.

The second scoring motion is really bomb to mid. The difference is that the pass receiver creates a shot with the dribble by not calling a time-out after securing the ball. All other teammates are close to midcourt, which supplies the ball handler with ample room in which to maneuver for a score.

CHAPTER 14

Free-Throw Offenses

In general, the bulk of coaching attention concerning free throws is to teach players to put the shot through the hoop. Offensively, the coach wants players to take advantage of every opportunity from the charity stripe and score points without running any time off the clock. Defensively, the emphasis is on boxing out opponents to eliminate second-chance situations for the shooting team.

In this chapter, I discuss coaching the foul shot in directions that complement those objectives. When on offense, team members do not have as their sole purpose putting the ball in the basket. They also seek to retrieve any errant free throw. Therefore, the discussion covers both successful and unsuccessful foul shots. When defending a foul shot, the team learns to go on the offensive immediately after the ball drops through the net. When the opponent relaxes after making the free throw, the defense attacks for a quick, easy scoring chance.

WHEN SHOOTING A FOUL SHOT

Every coach wishes to see players successfully complete each free-throw attempt. A 100 percent rate, though desired, is not realistic. The percentages indicate that at least 3 of every 10 foul shots fail to drop through the net. Therefore, every coach needs to train his or her

players on techniques to retrieve missed shots. The following methods work. The team obtains critical possessions through these plays. Many games come down to the last few seconds when a player needs to make a free throw to tie the score. Does the coach simply tell players to get the rebound, or does he or she teach them a specific way to snatch misses?

X AND FX

The X and FX plays are conjoined. A team can use one of the plays regularly throughout the game and spring the other on the opponent periodically to keep the defense guessing. Using the plays in random order will prevent the opposition from knowing which action is coming. The coach makes the call whenever his or her team attempts a charity toss. These plays provide a way by which a team can rebound and possibly score following a missed foul shot.

Personnel

Players need no special skills. Obviously, having players who are tenacious rebounders and of good physical size helps.

Scoring

Three players stationed around the foul lane are potential offensive rebounders. Second-chance shots may happen within the foul lane.

Execution

The X call is shown in figure 14.1. In this case, the point guard (G) is attempting the free throw, but any player could be at the line. Regardless of who is shooting the foul shot, the two best rebounders (B1 and B2) are in the second slots on each side of the lane. The next best rebounder (S2) occupies the final space on either side of the lane. The fourth player (S1) is near half-court. When the shooter launches the shot, the player (B2) on the same side as S2 (on the side of two) cuts hard in front of the opposite defender. B1 crosses off B2's tail in an attempt to acquire an advantage on the defender in the number one space on the other side of the lane. S2 darts into the center of the lane, trying to beat the nearest defender.

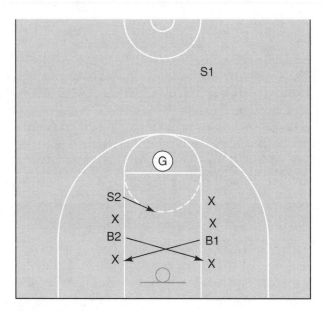

Figure 14.1   X play.

FX is another option. The personnel setup is the same as that in X. The player closer to the hoop on the side of two (B2) bolts to get inside the defender in the opposite first slot. But B1 does not cross off B2's rear. He or she fakes the cross and comes back to the same side for the rebound. S2 fakes a move into the middle of the foul lane and then loops outside to race to the basket. He or she is the likely candidate to grab the rebound.

Keys

Players must take the correct slots along the lane, which vary depending on who is shooting

the free throw. For example, if a post player is the shooter, the small forward likely will fill one of the two slots nearest the basket. The shooting guard is in the last spot on the lane. The three best rebounders of the four available players always assume spaces on the lane. In practice, the coach rotates the player shooting the free throw so that players know who should be on the lane and occupy which sites. One player, the weakest rebounder, always stays deep defensively.

The player low on the side with two players always moves first to gain inside position on the opponent in the first slot on the other side of the foul lane. The player in the opposite second slot executes the cross or fakes it. The crossing maneuver brushes his or her teammate's rear. When performing the FX option, the player closest to the foul line must carry out the fake inward before looping outside to head to the goal.

When the third player along the lane steps into the middle, no prior fake outside occurs. He or she tries to beat the defender with quickness. But in FX the third player fakes toward the middle before rushing outside to the basket.

The players in the slots along the foul lane step as far up in space as possible. Both feet are together at the top of the slot. This positioning creates space between the offensive rebounder and the defender responsible for boxing out. More space makes the block-out more difficult and gives the offense room to operate before running into defensive contact.

Players pursue the ball aggressively. They assume that each shot will miss. Consistency of effort and desire to gain possession of the ball have great bearing on how well players rebound.

If a squad is protecting a lead near the end of the game, the coach might consider removing the player closest to the foul line to place two people back defensively. The two players on the lane either cross or fake it. Before the shot, they communicate which one will initiate the action.

X SPECIAL AND FX SPECIAL

The X special and FX special plays are alternatives to the previous plays that require only slight changes in motion and personnel placement. Therefore, the coach may mix the four plays to keep the opponent off balance without taxing the players mentally. The coach should use a play each time the team takes a foul shot. Constant juggling of plays increases the effectiveness of each.

Personnel

No special skills are necessary. Players need to make sincere efforts to get offensive rebounds.

Scoring

Any of the three players around the foul lane may grab a missed shot and put the ball back up toward the hoop. In all likelihood, shots will not exceed 8 to 10 feet.

Execution

In figure 14.2, the point guard (G) is shooting the free throw, but any player could be shooting. Three players are on the lane, and one is long near midcourt (S1). In both X special and FX special, the best rebounder begins in the final slot on one side of the lane (B2). The other two players on the lane (B1 and S2) take the second spaces on each side. When the player at the line shoots, the players closest to the hoop (B1 and S2) swing outside to go for the rebound. They may fake inward before hustling out. The best rebounder (B2) fakes a move outside and crashes the boards by running straight down

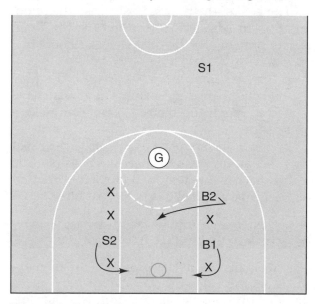

Figure 14.2   X special.

the lane. This creates a desirable matchup—the best rebounder against a smaller defender.

With FX special, players line up just as they did in X special. When the shot goes up, the player in the second slot (B1) on the same side as the best rebounder (B2) sprints across the lane to obtain inside position on the defender in the first space on the opposite side. The action is a speed move. S2 still fakes in and loops out for a rebound chance. The best rebounder (B2) fakes a slicing action down the lane and bolts to the outside. The motion is just like FX except that the best rebounder is in the slot nearest the foul line.

Keys

Rebounding is not all about size and jumping ability. Intensity, execution of footwork, and anticipation make a solid rebounder.

The coach varies the calls for X special, FX special, X, and FX. The schemes are more effective when used in conjunction with one another.

In practice, all team members should assume the role as foul shooter. The team then knows who should be in each slot along the lane. The weakest rebounder regularly takes a position near half-court. In X special and FX special, the best rebounder of the other three players starts in the space closest to the foul line on either side of the lane, whichever he or she chooses.

The lone player on one side of the lane always does the same maneuver in X special and FX special. He or she fakes in and zips out to the basket for a rebound opportunity. The actions of the other two players along the lane vary. In X special, the low player moves outside as the other player heads down the middle. In FX special, the low player darts across the lane, and the best rebounder fakes in and scampers out to the hoop.

The coach is counting on the best rebounder to grab an offensive rebound. He or she must slip away from any defensive box-out. Players start high in their slots. A gap increases the difficulty for defenders to block out.

DIVE

To prepare a team to execute the dive play, the coach must review the rules associated with free throws for their particular circumstances. When can players who are not in position around the foul lane break the three-point arc or foul line extended in pursuit of a missed foul shot—when the shooter releases the ball or when the ball hits the rim? In NBA games, teams often use the dive play (or something quite similar) on free throws. Coaches can use the play any time their squad is shooting a foul shot, especially if they perceive a weakness in the defense above the foul line. The opposing squad may ignore offensive players stationed above the foul line.

Personnel

Perimeter players have to be quick. They cannot be slow footed.

Scoring

Players procure shots within five to eight feet of the basket as a result of offensive put-backs.

Execution

The two best rebounders are in the second slots on each side of the foul lane (figure 14.3). In this case, the point guard (G) is shooting the free throw, though any player could be shooting. The other two perimeter players (S2 and S1) are stationed approximately five feet above the three-point arc just outside the lane line, one on each side of the court. These two are the quickest of the four available players. Before the shooter launches the foul shot, the play-

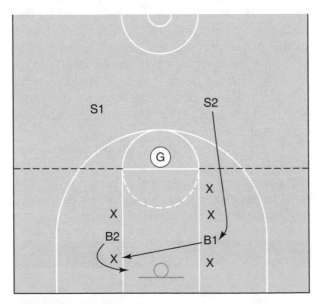

Figure 14.3 Dive left.

ers on the court determine whether the play is dive left or dive right. Figure 14.3 shows dive left. The player on the lane on the same side as the call (B1) slices across the lane and secures inside position on the defender in the first slot opposite. The player on the other side of the lane (B2) fakes inward and races outside to the basket. The player out front on the called (left) side (S2) times his or her sprint to the hoop. S2 needs to know when he or she can reach the three-point line or foul line extended without causing a violation—when the shooter releases the ball or when the ball hits the rim—based on the free-throw rules in the league or conference. The other player out front (S1) remains back defensively. S2 should be at a full sprint by the time he or she reaches the violation boundary.

Keys

In practice, all players shoot foul shots. Players need to become accustomed to positioning on and above the lane.

Players communicate with each other to decide if the call is dive left or dive right. All five players know the call. They do not make it easy for the opposition to overhear it.

The coach is responsible for reviewing with players the rules that apply when shooting a free throw. The player diving is to hit the point a split second after doing so becomes legal. The crashing player must not cause a successful free throw to be voided.

The goal of the play is to surprise the opponent as to whom and from where the team sends someone to the offensive glass on a free throw.

If the players out front are slow, the play is unlikely to be successful. They must have speed to reach the basket in time to make a difference.

The two players on the lane place their feet together as high in their spaces as possible. The extra space makes it more difficult for the nearest defenders to make contact and box out.

MISS

The miss play is not appropriate for the NBA because the rules do not allow the required number of offensive players along the foul lane.

As long as colleges and high schools do not limit the number of personnel around the lane, the miss play is viable. In the play, the free-throw shooter misses the free throw intentionally in an attempt to secure a two-point field goal with one to three seconds remaining in the game and his or her team behind by two points. A team trailing by one point can use the play, but the shooter tries to put ball through the hoop. The coach must then tell players to call a time-out as soon as the ball goes in the basket. The time-out is required because the opponent could inbound the ball quickly and go the length of the floor to beat the clock. If the foul shot is good, the time-out stops the clock to prevent a quick throw-in. If the free throw misses, players fabricate a two-point shot after securing an offensive rebound. When losing by three points, the squad uses the three-point field-goal option.

Personnel

Players are aggressive on the glass. Their ability to grab an offensive rebound determines whether an opportunity will arise for a two- or three-point field goal. When shooting the three pointer, the squad needs someone who is likely to hit the shot from beyond the arc. Coaches should substitute as needed because the outcome of the game is likely to come down to this play.

Scoring

Shots materialize within 10 feet of the basket when the team is going for two points. A quick shot for two points is feasible from any player. The team can achieve a three-pointer with execution of a specific wrinkle.

Execution

Figure 14.4 shows a team trying to obtain a two-point shot as a result of a missed free throw. In this case, the point guard (G) shoots the free throw, although any player could be the shooter. The two best rebounders (B1 and B2) are in the second slots along the lane. They cross, deciding who will cut first before execution. The first cutter races opposite to achieve inside position on the defender in the first slot. The other cutter busts off the first cutter's tail to the other side of the floor. The remaining two players (S1 and S2) take up positions on the

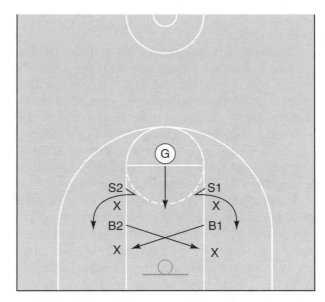

Figure 14.4 Miss play for two points.

lane opposite one another. These players fake a run into the lane and instead loop outside to the goal. All five players are around the lane; no one is back defensively. The shooter (G) heads down the middle following the shot in anticipation of grabbing a rebound. He or she makes sure not to cross the foul line early and cause a violation. He or she may see an open lane to the hoop. All five players try to secure a rebound and score a basket. The defense is outnumbered five to four.

For a three-point shot, players perform the same movements as described, but the foul shooter moves to a predetermined side behind the three-point line. Players choose a side before the free-throw attempt. If they decide to go right, the player in the top slot on the right is the screener. He or she sets the pick on the nearest defender, and the foul shooter races off the pick to a site near the right wing. The foul shooter and screener move as soon as the rules permit. Other players, including the screener, try to tap the ball out to the right wing for a trey. If the foul shooter is not a skilled three-point shooter, the player in the top slot opposite runs off the pick beyond the arc on the right wing. The foul shooter becomes one of the rebounders trying to tap the ball out to the wing.

Keys

The two best rebounders assume positions in the second slots on the lane. They determine who cuts first and who scrapes off the other's rear (X move).

Teams go for two points when down by one or two points with only one to three seconds left on the game clock. If losing by one, the free-throw shooter tries to make the shot. If he or she misses, players move as described to secure the rebound and shot. If the foul shot is good, the team calls a time-out if one remains, as soon as the ball goes through the net. Players need to know the time-out situation.

If the team has a time-out, the coach might also consider using it if the offensive rebound is converted. That way, the squad cannot get beat with a swift inbounds toss for a score after all five players have crashed the boards. Stopping the clock, however, allows the opponent to organize for one last offensive thrust. If the team does not use a time-out, they must sprint back quickly if they score a field goal after a successful offensive rebound.

When a team has no more time-outs, the coach can send a substitute to the scorer's table. The sub for the foul shooter must remind the timer to sound the horn when the foul shot is successful. The coach can also substitute for any other player as long as the official has handed the ball to the shooter. Both actions assure a stoppage in play when the free throw goes through the net. The coach must make sure that the official timer sounds the horn if the free throw is successful and a substitute is ready to go into the game.

When going for two points, the two players highest along the lane are opposite each other. They fake moves in then take outside routes to the basket. When the goal is a two-point shot, all five players go to the boards. Players must know the rules that apply to avoid a violation. Usually, the free throw must hit the rim before the shooter can move to the hoop.

When going for three points, players select right or left before the shot. The player in the high slot on the designated side is the screener. Either the foul shooter or the player in the high slot on the other side of the lane uses the pick to move behind the three-point line on the called side. Using the top player on the lane as the shooter has three advantages: The foul shooter is free of a defender as he or she heads to the hoop for the rebound, the top player on the lane probably has a clear path to use the screen, and

a skilled three-point shooter can take the top spot on the side away from the call. When the foul shooter is used, no defender is right with him or her so movement to the designated wing may be void of an opponent and therefore a clear shot at a trey could result. When going for three points, the coach needs to decide whether to allow an offensive rebounder by the hoop to shoot the ball if no tap-out is available. After all, a basket and a foul is another way to earn three points.

Coaches put the play into action when one foul shot remains before a change in possession, for example, a one-shot foul, the first or last shot of a one-and-one opportunity, the final shot of a two-shot foul, or the last shot of a three-shot foul. The foul shooter should miss if the team is down two or three points and only one shot remains with one to three seconds on the clock.

With three to six seconds on the clock, the coach must decide if it is best to order the miss. If the foul shot is successful and the team is still trailing, the squad must either foul quickly or force a turnover to gain possession and still have time to score. Does enough time remain to accomplish what needs to be done to secure a win?

AFTER THE OPPONENT MAKES A FREE THROW

A coach may at times wish to spring an offensive surprise on an adversary. An opponent often perceives a free-throw opportunity as a good time to change defenses or set up a full-court defense. Just before an opposing player shoots a foul shot, the coach can instruct players to prepare to execute a series of motions to send the basketball to the offensive end within seconds. The offense attacks before the opposition can set a defense.

Many teams apply a press immediately after a successful free throw. A strong counter is to use one of the plays covered in this section to beat the press before it is in place. If used occasionally, these plays can surprise the opponent. The plays also are useful at the end of the game when the team must foul. The squad needs to score in a hurry after the opponent shoots the last free throw.

HAND TO TOP OF HEAD

The free throw is an excellent setting to deploy a full-court press because the coach can direct players to execute a new defense, the defense has a chance to position personnel in appropriate locations, and odds are that the foul shot will be successful. Therefore, being ready for a press is prudent.

A team can use this play any time the opponent is shooting a foul shot. If the team is protecting a lead late in a game, the coach may not want to rush the ball up the floor. If the coach is attempting to play at a slower tempo, he or she will probably use the play sparingly. The play is appropriate when the team needs to attack the opponent quickly. The squad tries to score within a few seconds.

Personnel

The coach needs one, or possibly two, outstanding distance shooters. At least one post player must run the hardwood well and be a potent inside-scoring threat. The other post player should be a decent passer with the ability to hurl the ball deep down a sideline.

Scoring

A three-point shot develops in the right corner and possibly the right wing. The most proficient inside scorer on the team garners the ball while racing to the hoop or by a post feed to the right block.

Execution

Hand to top of head refers to the physical signal displayed to the team. The coach sends the sign as the opponent shoots a foul shot. The motion is down the right sideline. All five players are on the lane when the opponent shoots the charity shot. Post players B1 and B2 occupy the first slots (figure 14.5). The player in B2's spot (the first space on the left of the lane) is the team's best interior scorer and can run. B1, the big player in the first slot on the right, serves as the quick inbounder. The other three players (G, S1, and S2) take up positions around the lane. Although there is no set order, the player farthest up the lane (S1) should be the best exterior shooter on the club. He or she could be on either side of the foul lane.

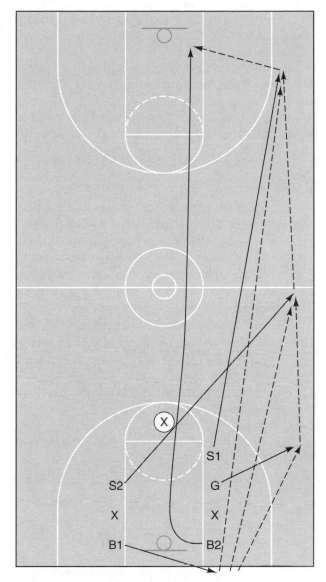

Figure 14.5 Hand to top of head inbounds play.

After the ball goes in the bucket, the point guard (G) races to the foul line extended on the right side of the floor (figure 14.5). The main shooter (S1) takes off to the right-side corner on the offensive end. The other perimeter player (S2) sprints to the half-court region near the right sideline. The inbounder (B1) grabs the ball out of the basket swiftly. He or she cannot let the ball hit the floor. The inbounder immediately bolts to the right side of the basket, facing down the court. The inbounds pass goes as deep as possible. The ball does not have to go to the lead guard first. B1 can throw it to S2 by midcourt or to S1 deep down the sideline.

The other big player (B2) darts down the middle of the court and looks for a bounce pass in the lane at the offensive end. Players rapidly pass the ball up the right sideline to S1 in the offensive corner.

B2 may find a shot by means of a post feed at the hoop. A jumper from the corner may develop for S1. Or the perimeter player (S2) may have a shot past midcourt from behind the arc. He or she fills the open area above the shooter in the corner.

Keys

The best inside-scoring post player is in the first slot on the left of the foul lane looking inward. He or she is the player who the coach envisions receiving the ball at the offensive hoop for a shot. The premier exterior shooter lines up on the lane close to the foul line on either side. These are the two highlighted players.

The big player who is not running snatches the ball out of the hoop. He or she moves rapidly to inbounding position. The inbounder looks straight down the right sideline to view multiple teammates and selects the deepest one to receive the throw-in.

All five players have jobs to perform as soon as the ball goes through the basket. Players and the ball should move down the court quickly. The ball travels faster with passes than it does with dribbles. Players use the dribble only if a teammate ahead is not open.

The player at midcourt may secure a shot from distance. He or she sprints to a spot above the player in the right corner, staying just behind the three-point arc. A toss out from the corner player may generate a shot. The player at half-court puts the ball on the floor to the same area if the defense denies a pass to the player in the corner.

HAND TO LEFT SHOULDER

The play varies the offensive action after an opponent makes a foul shot but does not use complicated changes to the previous play. The team simply changes sides of the full court. After opponents see the primary activity of the prior play, the switch might catch them off guard. Teams use the play whenever the opponent makes a free throw. The coach may not want to use it if the team is leading near the end of a game or if he or she wants to establish a slower pace.

Personnel

The play requires at least one post player who is a proficient scorer in the paint and possesses some quickness. One excellent shooter from the periphery and possibly a second are also mandatory. The other big player should be able to throw the ball deep with accuracy.

Scoring

The interior-scoring big player receives shots near the block on the lane. The two leading shooters from deep seize shots clear of the three-point arc on the left side of half-court at the wing or corner.

Execution

Hand to left shoulder is a physical signal that the coach gives to the team before the opponent shoots a foul shot. A sign is preferable to an oral call. The action is the same as that described for hand to top of head. The only difference is that the ball flows down the left side of the court rather than the right.

The post players occupy the first slots along the lane on each side. The remaining players fill sites on the lane, with the best exterior shooter nearest the foul line on either side. All five players are around the lane.

When the ball drops into the basket, players do not hesitate. The big player who starts in the first slot on the left of the lane facing the basket grabs the ball out of the net and hustles to the left side of the goal looking down the full court. He or she is the inbounder. The primary interior scorer is in the first spot opposite the inbounder. He or she races down the center of the court to the offensive hoop. The lead guard runs to the foul line extended area on the left side of the court in front of the inbounder. The third perimeter player sprints to a spot close to half-court near the left sideline. The main exterior shooter heads to the far left corner at the offensive end.

Players pass the ball rapidly down the left sideline. Ideally, they place the ball in the hands of the shooter in the corner quickly so that he or she can shoot the open jump shot or dump the ball inside with a bounce pass to the post player cutting to the hoop. The player at mid-court may pop open behind the three-point line at the wing above the corner player.

Keys

All points associated with the previous play are relevant here, substituting left for right.

If the coach has only one post player who is a solid scorer around the basket, he or she begins at the first slot on the right side of the foul lane. If both big players are approximately at the same skill level, their positioning on the lane is not important as long as they know the roles associated with each spot. Dictating the players' roles decreases the chance for confusion but also reduces the element of surprise.

Hand to left shoulder is better geared to a left-handed inbounder and an offensive post player whose left hand is the strong hand. Personally, I do not believe a player's strong hand is a factor. With enough repetitions in practice, a player can be equally effective on either side.

The players' goal is to send the ball from the baseline to the far corner within two seconds.

Players contemplate delivering the ball to the post player sprinting down the center. If no toss is forthcoming while in motion, the big player physically posts up along the lane while staying above the block. The bounce pass is usually the appropriate method of feeding.

If the two outside shooters are of roughly equal ability, the coach may allow them to decide which roles to fill. Their starting points on the lane become irrelevant. If the coach gives the two shooters the choice, it does not make sense to require the player running to the far corner to occupy the lane spot closer to the foul shooter. This way, players do not tip off the opponent about where they will sprint on a successful free throw.

The point guard stocks the backcourt because of the possibility of defensive pressure. The best ball handler is available to handle pressing defenses. If the playmaker is an excellent shooter, however, the coach must determine whether it is worthwhile for the lead guard to switch roles with one of the two shooters.

PART **V**

Inbound Plays

CHAPTER 15

Under Own Basket

This chapter is devoted entirely to plays that a team can perform when inbounding the ball from underneath its own basket. The chapter contains two distinct sections. The first section deals with plays for use against zone defenses. The second section discusses plays for attacking a man-to-man defense.

I use hand signals to call out-of-bounds plays underneath my team's basket. I want to make it easy to communicate my desires to the players. Vocal commands may be difficult for players to hear under noisy crowd conditions. Generally, I give two signals when an underneath out-of-bounds situation occurs, one to go against man-to-man defense and one to go against zone. For example, I may call number 2 and number 7. The inbounder calls number 2 if he or she recognizes man-to-man and number 7 if he or she sees a zone. The inbounder reads what the opponent is doing and calls the corresponding play.

Initially, it is best to teach underneath out-of-bounds plays as a whole on a dummy basis. Once the coach is confident in the players' comprehension of movements, he or she adds the defense. Teaching each play should take no longer than 15 minutes before the team is ready to use them in competition.

The inbounder must be aware of one movement option that can be effective against either man-to-man or zone defenses. He or she throws the ball off the back of the defender in front of

the ball (figure 15.1). The inbounder gets both feet inbounds and retrieves the ball for a layup. For this play to be successful, the inbounder must notice when the defender in front is directing attention elsewhere and has his or her back turned to the ball. The inbounder notes where the other four defenders are to prevent any interference with his or her collection of the basketball. The inbounder has the sole responsibility of choosing to make the play.

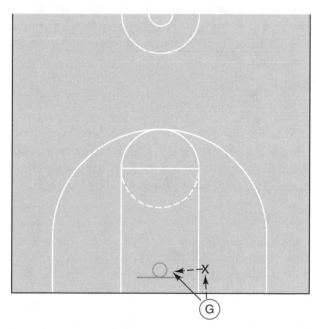

Figure 15.1　Throw-in off the defender's back.

Recognition keys execution of the play. A signal must start the players' movements on an out-of-bounds play from underneath the offensive basket. For some coaches the preference is for the inbounder to call out the play and then slap the ball to commence the motion. I prefer the signal to be the referee handing the ball to the inbounder.

PLAYS VERSUS ZONE DEFENSES

Coaches like to use zone defenses to guard an inbound under the opponent's basket. The zone allows easier protection of the area around the basket. In addition, with the zone there is less chance that defenders will be picked off and allow offensive players to get wide open. Because defenders cover areas, they are less likely to lose track of offensive players. The following plays attack the weaknesses of zone defenses.

NUMBER 6

The number 6 play includes two of my favorite actions against zone defenses: setting picks on weakside defenders and dribbling away from the baseline. The number 6 play is effective against any type of zone defense. The coach must be confident in the shooting ability of outside personnel. This play also has a version that a team can execute against man-to-man (see page 268).

Personnel

Post players must be productive screeners and able to score around the foul lane. The play works better if the point guard is a good exterior shooter. At least one perimeter player should be a talented distance shooter.

Scoring

The main perimeter shooter may have a shot in a corner near or behind the three-point line. The point guard may have a jump shot from the opposite corner after coming inbounds. The big players secure entry passes in the high- or low-post locations.

Execution

The point guard (G) is the inbounder (figure 15.2). S1 is the primary shooter, and S2 is the other perimeter player. B1 and B2 are the two post players. The initial set is a box with S2 and B1 on each block on the lane. S1 and B2 are just above the elbows. The big players are on the weakside, and the exterior players are on the ballside.

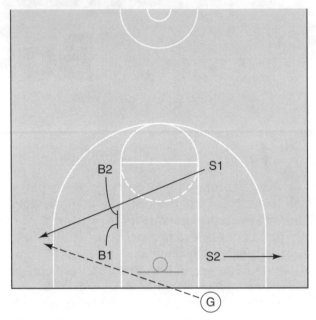

Figure 15.2 Number 6 versus zone defense.

After the referee hands the ball to the inbounder, the two big players move to establish screens on the two offside defenders in the zone. S1 moves around the screens to a place outside the three-point arc in or near the weakside corner. S1 is G's first pass option. As S1 begins to cut, S2 pops out to the strongside sideline.

The lead guard's second inbounds pass option is S2, who is on the strongside close to the corner. If S2 has no shot opportunity, he or she dribbles off the baseline with the intention of drawing the back defender in the zone with him or her. This action enables the playmaker (G) to step in play below S2 in the corner for a possible return pass and shot. When S2 receives the ball, the post players (B1 and B2) cross. B2 moves low, and B1 moves high. The post player closer to the foul line cuts first. The inside players are the last two scoring options.

Keys

See "Zone Offensive Fine-Tuning" in chapter 5 on page 84.

The inbounder must know the passing sequence. He or she looks to the weakside corner first before tossing to a teammate on the ballside periphery. The inbounder's final option is to pass to either post player cutting to the seams in the zone.

The coach should review the various types of zones that the team might face. The big players should know which defenders to screen on the weakside. The two big players set their picks at proper angles to free the player heading to the offside corner.

The primary shooter hustles to the opposite corner as soon as the referee hands the ball to the inbounder. He or she does not wait for the two big players to plant their screens.

The player in the ballside corner should understand that he or she dribbles off the baseline to draw the defender away from the area. He or she puts the ball on the floor with purpose. The player does not permit the defender to release coverage. The big players cross as soon as the throw-in is completed to a teammate in the ballside corner or if it looks as if no entry pass is available to either corner. Then post players cut to seams, looking to catch the toss-in.

When the ball goes inside to a post player, he or she immediately looks for the other post player. The other post player moves to an open area near the basket.

The inbounder could fling the ball to one of the post players who slips into the lane after picking on the offside if the defenders are more concerned about covering the main shooter.

NUMBER 7

Teams have used the line formation against zone defenses for as long as I can remember, even back to when I was in grade school. And you know what? It still works. The line formation is effective against any zone alignment. Using it against man-to-man is possible, but I do not recommend it.

Personnel

The team has a big advantage if one of the big players not only has good size but also gets off the floor well. The inbounder is the team's best outside shooter. Ideally, the other post player is a capable inside scorer and has the ability to obtain position around the bucket.

Scoring

The inbounder may have a shot from the near corner. One of the big players captures the ball while diving to the hoop. The other post player may score around the weakside block.

Execution

The inbounder (S1) is the squad's best outside shooter. The other four players are in a line along the ballside foul lane (figure 15.3). The line starts at the first hash mark above the block. The first player is one of the big players (B1). He or she cuts opposite to gain inside position on the defender near the offside box. He or she is active and physical. The next person in line (S2) pops out toward the ballside corner. The point guard (G) steps back deep on the strongside as a safety valve for the inbounder. B2 cuts to the hoop after the other three players have moved. He or she is the biggest post player and should possess some jumping ability. B1 and B2 are the first two options for the inbounder (S1). Either one can secure a good scoring opportunity around the basket.

If the inbounds pass goes to S2 in the ballside corner, S2 dribbles off the baseline if no shot

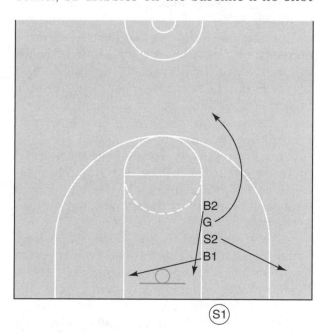

Figure 15.3 Number 7—the line.

is available. He or she takes the back defender of the zone with him or her. S2 does not intend to let the defense release coverage. This action ensures that the inbounder (S1), who steps in play to the ballside corner, is open for a return pass and possible shot. The post player at the weakside block (B1) flashes to a ballside high spot if he or she sees an opening. S1 and S2 also glance inside to B2.

S1 could complete a throw-in to the playmaker (G) out top. On the pass, S2 moves in toward the lane to pick the nearest back player of the zone. S1 fakes a run in the opposite direction and comes into play near the ballside corner. He or she anticipates receiving a pass and taking a shot. Again, B1 flashes to ballside high if an open area exists.

Another inbounding possibility occurs when players notice that a down screen set by S2 on the defender nearest the basket in the zone is likely to enable the inbounder to lob the ball at the hoop for B1 as he or she curls over S2's pick. When the movement happens, G pops out to the ballside corner instead of S2 and B2 steps back to act as a safety valve in place of G. If players recognize that the move could prove fruitful, they let each other know to execute the loop to the hoop. B1's physical traits (size and leaping ability) dictate whether this is a viable option.

Keys

Refer to "Zone Offensive Fine-Tuning" in chapter 5 on page 84.

The starting point at the first hash mark above the ballside block on the lane provides optimal space for players to move. The first player in line (a post player) goes hard to the offside box, initiates contact, and seals the nearest defender each time if he or she wishes to secure the throw-in.

A quality big player, someone who is tall and a strong jumper, is in the last slot. The best perimeter shooter inbounds the ball. These two players are the primary scoring options in the play.

All players have to be on the same page when they decide to curl the first player in the line over a screen from the teammate behind. Positioning of defenders keys the option. The coach should review with players how to recognize when the defense is vulnerable to the little screen down and move into the lane.

The perimeter player in the ballside corner wants the back defender of the zone to stay with him or her while dribbling out from the baseline. The inbounder breaks free for a shot after sprinting inbounds to the same-side corner.

The coach should drill the inbounder on throwing the lob to the basket. He or she may be able to flip it to either big player. The weakside big player should remember that he or she may flash to the high post if the ball is inbounded to the ballside perimeter. The player heads to an opening in the zone.

NUMBER 7 FOR NAME

I first saw this play performed by the University of North Carolina, led by Coach Dean Smith. The athletic prowess of Division I athletes certainly enhances execution of the play. Teams at the junior high and high school levels will have more difficulty executing it effectively. Teams can use the play at any point in the game, but because it must surprise the defense, it usually is useful only once or twice during a game.

Personnel

The highlighted player should have decent size and some jumping prowess. He or she must be able to catch the ball over the top of the defense. The point guard displays a command of the lob pass. All other players perform their assigned roles.

Scoring

The featured player grabs a lob pass directed at the basket. A big player may get the ball inside the lane for a shot. Other players along the baseline could see short jump shots arise.

Execution

The line formation is the same as that for number 7, with the named player in position N (figure 15.4). Normally N is a big player. Again, the line starts at the first hash mark above the ballside block on the lane. N pops out to the ballside corner. S2 cuts to the weakside box. The point guard circles out front to act as a safety net. All three players move at the same time. Once those three players initiate their movements, B2 slices straight down the lane line toward the ball.

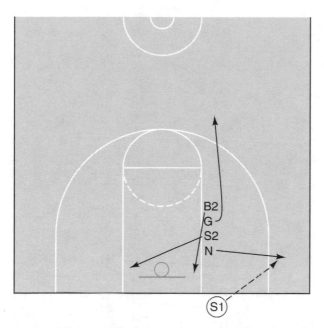

Figure 15.4   Number 7 for name initial movements.

The inbounder passes the ball to N. After throwing the pass, the inbounder (S1) moves near the offside box on the lane along with S2. If the defense stretches out to prevent a pass to N, S1 looks to throw the ball all the way out top to G. The pass also could go to S2 or B2 if they happen to spring open on their initial cuts. But S1 primarily tries to inbound the ball to N in the ballside corner.

The action shown in figure 15.5 is designed to produce a lob at the basket. N wants the back player of the zone to guard him or her. N might

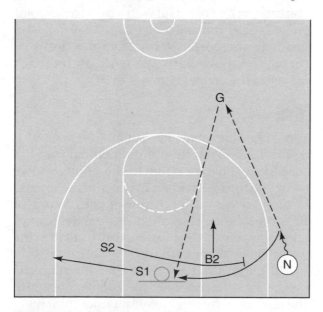

Figure 15.5   Back pick of the zone for a lob.

have to dribble once or twice outward to ensure that this takes place. The team clearly sees the desired defender on N. N tosses the ball to the point guard (G). On the release of the ball, B2 slides several feet up the lane line toward the ball as S2 hustles to the strongside to establish a pick on the back defender of the zone. Meanwhile, the inbounder (S1) speeds toward the weakside block and continues for several feet off the lane along the offside baseline. The playmaker (G) may have to dribble toward the top of the key to attain a proper passing angle for the lob. N slices off S2's back pick and catches the ball over the defense near the hoop. Depending on what actions the defense takes, B2 or S1 may be open to receive the ball directly from the lead guard (G). The ball handler reads the defense and makes the appropriate pass to an open teammate.

Keys

Refer to "Zone Offensive Fine-Tuning" in chapter 5 on page 84.

The inbounds pass goes to the highlighted player. The play is still operable if the defense extends and stops the initial pass to the corner. The throw-in just goes to the point guard out front. Players make their required movements immediately to set up the lob. The team treats a direct entry pass to the lead guard just as they would have handled it had N cast the ball out to the playmaker. The other two players (the big player stepping up the lane and the shooter moving to the weakside baseline) could pop open for a shot, although they are not the primary targets.

The playmaker must practice the lob. The pass is like a shot to the side of the hoop where the pass recipient is. The coach must select the proper player to catch the lob. Size and athletic ability are factors. The receiver of the lob decides what action to take off the lob: dunk the ball directly off the lob; catch the lob and shoot a layup before hitting the floor; or grab the ball, land on balance, and power the ball back up to the hoop for a shot. Players should drill regularly to establish proper timing within the play. Synchronization of motion enables the squad to execute the lob pass effectively.

The featured player watches how far he or she moves away from the baseline. He or she dribbles to draw the back defender with him or her but under no circumstances enables the defender to release coverage to a teammate. The featured player is prepared to grasp the toss directly from the lead guard.

The inbounder judges the distance off the lane required to keep the weakside defender occupied. He or she maintains status as a potential scoring threat. The playmaker must recognize the importance of reading the defense. The point guard makes the pass choice based on what the opponent is doing. He or she does not force the lob.

NUMBER 8

The number 8 play is a variation of the line plays previously described. Teams can use the action any time during a game when they are inbounding the ball under the offensive basket and the opposition is in a zone defense.

Personnel

The number 8 play requires an excellent outside shooter to inbound the ball. A post player who has some size and is able to jump fairly well is essential. The other three players are role players.

Scoring

The big player dives to the hoop for an inside score. The inbounder comes in play to a corner opposite the throw-in for a shot. The screener on the back-line defender of the zone could spring open for a score.

Execution

Players begin in the same starting set used for the number 7 play. The line begins at the first hash mark above the ballside block on the lane (figure 15.6). The second player (S2) pops to the strongside corner. The point guard (G) acts as the safety net, and the last player in line (B2) cuts to the ball after the others have moved. The only difference in the initial movements is that the first player (B1) does not dart to the offside box. Instead, he or she dashes to the offside corner.

If the ball goes to the player in the ballside corner (S2), the inbounder hustles opposite the pass, using the screen on the back weak-

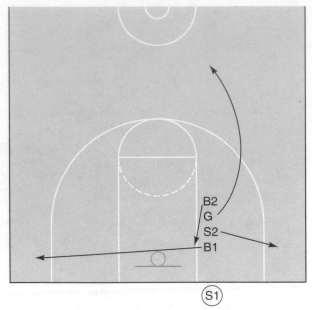

Figure 15.6 Number 8, a variation of the line.

side zone defender set by the player in the offside corner (B1). When S2 catches the ball, he or she glances inside to B2. If nothing is available, S2 must reverse the ball to the lead guard (G) out front. S1 could hurl the ball directly to G from out of bounds. Both S2 and G are likely to have to dribble. The lead guard sends the ball to S1 (the inbounder) for an exterior jumper. The playmaker is aware of a possible delivery to the screener (B1), who may slip the pick.

When the initial pass goes to B1 in the weakside corner, he or she dribbles off the baseline, starting the ball reversal with a toss to the point guard (G). S1 runs into the play at the lane and heads to the corner away from the throw-in, timing the move with S2's pick on the back player of the zone. G throws to S1.

Keys

See "Zone Offensive Fine-Tuning" on page 84.

The inbounder should understand that if a toss to a big player going to the hoop is open, he or she throws it. Players execute the motion of the play only if the throw-in goes to one of the other three players. The inbounder always comes in play to the corner away from the side where he or she inbounded the ball.

The players in the corners time their screens on the back defenders in the zone to maximize the chance of freeing the inbounder for a jump shot. Players regularly set the screen against the proper back-line defender. The coach reviews targets within varying zones.

The team reverses the ball swiftly around the exterior after the throw-in. The point guard may need to get a specific defender to guard him or her. The coach instructs players about who they are to attack in each type of zone defense.

If the defender cheats over the top of the pick too soon, the screener slips the pick to an exposed area so that he or she can receive a pass directly from the playmaker.

NUMBER 9

Number 9 is one of my favorite inbounds plays against zone defenses because of the freedom of movement provided to the two post players. Teams can use the play whenever they are inbounding the ball underneath their own basket and the opponent is playing a zone defense.

Personnel

The inbounder should be a talented perimeter shooter. The post players must be able to catch the ball in traffic and score in the paint.

Scoring

Either big player can gain a shot in the foul lane. The inbounder may acquire a jump shot from either corner.

Execution

The best shooter (S1) inbounds the basketball. The other two perimeter players (G and S2) are positioned in the corners. They stretch the coverage area of the zone as much as possible. One big player (B1) is at the foul line, and the other (B2) is at the top of the key. Their positions are interchangeable. Their job is to dive into the open lanes of the zone. Their moves do not have to mirror those in figure 15.7. The open spots in the zone may vary from possession to possession. B1 or B2 are the inbounder's first choices. If the ball goes to either player, the receiver engages in a scoring activity immediately after receiving the ball. When the toss-in goes to S2 or G in either corner, the pass receiver dribbles off the baseline and throws the ball back to the

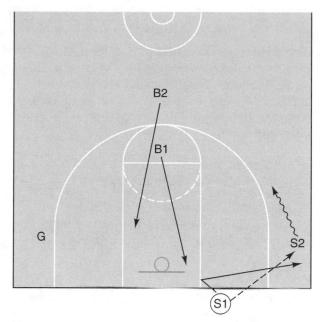

Figure 15.7   Number 9 play.

inbounder (S1), who steps into play near the same-side corner.

Keys

See "Zone Offensive Fine-Tuning" in chapter 5 on page 84 for any points that pertain to the play.

The best exterior shooter is the inbounder. The inbounder evaluates the position of the big players before flinging the ball to a corner. The inbounder always hustles to the same corner to which he or she threw the pass. He or she is the next potential scorer after each post player.

Here are the rules for the big players. The two big players must remain roughly within the lane width (up to two feet off each side) and start above the foul line. Big players have the freedom to cut to any vacant area in the zone. They must not interfere with each other's movement. Post players actively seek the ball with authority. If possible, teammates should place the ball into the hands of one of the big players for a shot opportunity.

Perimeter players in the corners do not dribble off the baseline too quickly or too far. The ball handler takes the defender with him or her to open an area along the baseline for the inbounder to step into without opposition. Defenders are not allowed to release coverage to defend the dribble off the baseline maneuver.

NUMBER 10

The number 10 inbound play relates closely to number 9. A few wrinkles in player movement make it unique. Teams can use the play any time the throw-in comes from the offensive baseline. Number 10 is a good play to use in conjunction with number 9.

Personnel

At least one big player should be a proficient scorer around the basket with the dexterity to catch the ball in a crowd inside the lane. The inbounder should be a strong outside shooter.

Scoring

The big player heading to the basket may have a shot within the foul lane. The inbounder may have a corner jump shot on the side away from the original pass.

Execution

The play begins with the same starting set used for number 9 (figure 15.8). The inbounder (S1) may have an opportunity for a perimeter shot and is a strong outside shooter. The other two perimeter players (S2 and G) start in each corner. Post players (B1 and B2) are stationed above the foul line and vertically stay inside

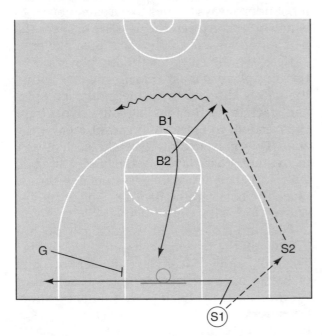

Figure 15.8   Number 10 play with the ball thrown to S2 in the ballside corner.

two feet outside each lane line. One big player (B1) cuts to an opening in the lane for a possible entry pass. He or she is S1's first choice to catch the toss-in. The post player (B1) looks to score. The other big player (B2) steps to a safety position out front above the top of the key. S1 throws the ball to a corner player (S2 in figure 15.8) as soon as he or she determines that the opponent is defending the big player heading to the hoop. The pass also could go to G. S2 immediately reverses the ball to B2 out top. B2 may need to dribble toward the other side of half-court. The inbounder (S1) hustles to the corner away from the throw-in and uses G's screen of the weakside back player of the zone. Even if the first pass goes to a big player (B2) out near the top of the key, S1 moves the same way.

Keys

Refer to "Zone Offensive Fine-Tuning" on page 84 for relevant topics.

The big players vary which of the two dives to the open space within the opponent's zone. One cuts into the lane while the other bolts out past the top of the key. The big player out front uses the dribble to reverse the ball and achieve a better passing angle toward the designated corner. The post players consistently exchange roles so that the defense never knows for sure who is diving.

The best outside shooter is in the inbounding position. The inbounder always glances initially at the post player diving into the heart of the zone. After the ball goes to one of the other three players, the inbounder becomes the primary target to receive a corner jumper. The other two exterior players may change starting spots.

The coach reviews with the team the various zone defenses so that players know which defenders they are to screen and at whom the post player out top should dribble. The team should practice the timing between the screener and the inbounder using the pick. The player using the screen along the baseline is prepared to catch the pass and get into position to shoot immediately after the reception.

Whenever the throw-in goes to a corner, the ball is reversed around the periphery and the shooter (the inbounder) comes into play at the opposite corner while using a pick on the back defender to get open.

NUMBER 10 FOR NAME

The second lob play for a featured player differs from the first (number 7 for name) only by which teammate plants the screen on the zone defender. The coach calls this play to battle an opponent's zone defense when inbounding the ball from underneath his or her team's own bucket. The coach should call the play sparingly. If a team performs the play too often, the opponent likely will recognize it and have a good chance of shutting it down.

Personnel

The coach calls the play for a team member with good jumping ability, some height, and the athletic skill to catch a ball thrown to the hoop. Usually this will be one of the post players. The point guard should be skilled at lobbing the ball at the basket. The play is more effective if another big player is an interior scoring threat and a perimeter player is an effective shooter. Both players can draw the attention of the defense.

Scoring

The featured player gets a chance for an alley-oop shot close to the rim. A big player may receive a toss in the lane for a shot. Two other players may see short jump shots develop on the baseline.

Execution

The inbounder (S1) should be an excellent outside shooter. The defense needs to be concerned that he or she could hurt it when coming inbounds after the throw-in. The named player (N) is at the ballside block in a stack with the lead guard (G) (figure 15.9). N pops to the ballside corner as G steps out above the foul line extended to a spot beyond the three-point line in front of the inbounder. The third perimeter player (S2) and one of the big players (B2) are stacked at the offside block. S1 throws the ball to N in the strongside corner if possible. Otherwise, he or she sends the ball all the way out to G.

The point guard ends up with the ball out front, either with a pass from N or directly from S1. Once G has the ball, S1 moves inbounds and

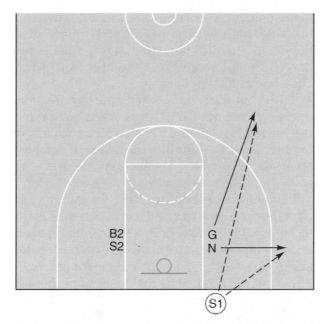

Figure 15.9   Starting motion for number 10 for name.

back screens the back-line player of the zone nearest N. At the same time, the two players stacked at the offside block (S2 and B2) begin their movements. B2 swings into the center of the lane, while S2 pops out to a position off the foul lane along the weakside baseline. N cuts off S1's pick to the basket, anticipating a lob from G. G may have to take one or two dribbles toward the top of the key to obtain a better passing angle. The primary scoring option is for G to toss to N. G may be able to throw the ball to B2 in the lane or to S2 at the weakside baseline for a jump shot.

Keys

All players who might assume the named player's spot should practice the position. The named player does not have to be a post player. The named player can be anyone who possesses the skills needed to catch a lob at the hoop. When a nonpost player fills the spot, both big players begin at a weakside box. The one who is a better shooter from distance pops to the baseline 15 feet or so from the lane.

The lead guard throws the ball on the receiver's side of the rim at basket level. The lob pass is similar to a shot.

If possible, the inbounder flings the ball to the named player in the ballside corner to ensure that a back zone player will guard the named player. The same effect occurs when the inbounder throws the ball directly out front if the defense denies the entry pass to the corner player. The inbounder sets a solid screen on the back-line zone defender.

The point guard makes the appropriate pass decision from out front. He or she tries first for the lob if it is available but also recognizes that the big player flashing into the lane or the player along the weakside baseline may be open for sound scoring chances.

Players should practice the timing of the lob pass. For the play to be successful, teams need to review it a number of times. Coaches cannot expect players to perform this play to perfection in a game situation without significant practice. Repetition is the key to the success of the lob pass.

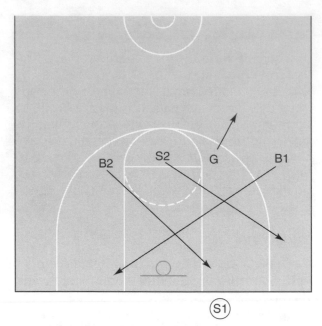

Figure 15.10   Number 12 setup and movements.

NUMBER 12

One of my opponents when I was at King's College performed an out-of-bounds play from the alignment used in this play. I added the motion to counter a zone defense. The play supplies chances to attack the interior of the zone while also generating opportunities from the periphery.

Personnel

The inbounder must be a quality distance shooter. Both big players attack the inside of the zone. One other perimeter player should be an effective outside shooter from the corners.

Scoring

Either post player could have a shot in the foul lane. The inbounder anticipates having a shot from either corner. An exterior player could secure a 15- to 20-foot jumper near the corner.

Execution

S1, the inbounder, is the squad's best shooter from distance. The point guard (G) is at the ballside elbow. The third perimeter player (S2) is at the center of the foul line (figure 15.10). G and S2 can flip-flop positions as much as they like, especially if the point guard (G) is a strong outside shooter. One post player (B1) begins at the foul line extended on the strongside. The

other post player (B2) is at the weakside elbow. These two also can switch starting positions.

The player at the ballside wing (B1) is the first to cut through the zone. He or she heads toward the offside block on the lane. The next two players in the line (G and S2) move simultaneously. G pops out high in front of the ball as an outlet. S2 cuts to the ballside exterior near the corner. He or she rubs off B1's tail. Finally, the player farthest to the weakside (B2) slices to the ballside block by also brushing B1's rear. S2 and B2 both brush B1's behind, about one second apart.

After receiving the inbounds pass in the ballside corner, S2 may have a shot chance. If not, S2 dribbles off the baseline and flings the ball back to the inbounder (S1), who has hustled inbounds directly below the ball. If B1 or B2 get open on their cuts through the zone, S1 sends the ball to one of them.

If S1 does not shoot, he or she throws the ball out to S2 or G. The ball is reversed around the perimeter. G will likely need to use one or two dribbles to head to the other side of half-court. The big player away from the inbounder (B1) establishes a screen on the weakside back defender in the zone. The original inbounder (S1) runs the baseline and uses the screen to get open in the weakside corner. The other post player (B2) flashes to the high-post region. G delivers the ball to the open player: S1 in the corner; B1, who steps to the ball after screening; or B2, who bolts to the high-post area.

Keys

Refer to "Zone Offensive Fine-Tuning" in chapter 5 on page 84 and review each pertinent topic.

The best perimeter shooter is the inbounder. The inbounder is aware that either big player may be open to receive the initial pass. They are the first two choices to receive the throw-in and have a chance to shoot. The inbounds pass keys specific actions. When the ball goes to the ballside corner, the play features the dribble off the baseline and the inbounder receives the shot. If the inbounds pass is to the player out front, the ball goes opposite the inbounder and the inbounder hustles to the opposite corner by using a screen.

Players can change roles periodically to keep the defense off balance. Big players switch starting spots, and exterior players may interchange positions.

Players attempt to cut to open sites against the zone defense. The timing of players' cuts through the zone is important. The player nearest the sideline is first, the next two players in line follow, and finally the player at the offside elbow cuts. Two players cut off the tail of the first cutter.

When dribbling off the baseline, the ball handler drags the defender out of his or her normal coverage area. The inbounder steps in play into an area void of defenders.

When the ball goes out top to be reversed, the big player on the offside block moves off the lane several steps before moving in to pick the baseline defender. Players time the screen and run off the pick correctly. Once the ball is in position out top for delivery to the weakside corner, the screener plants a pick and the player using it is right at the obstacle.

PLAYS VERSUS MAN-TO-MAN DEFENSES

Most coaches are eager to try to score when the defense plays man-to-man against an inbounding situation under the offensive basket. The plays reviewed in this section generate quality shots against man-to-man defense. The inbound play from under the offensive team's hoop is an opportunity to put points on the scoreboard.

NUMBER 1

The number 1 play is highly effective when a team is inbounding the ball from under the offensive basket and needs to attempt a three-point shot. The primary distance shooter usually gets open. The play is useful only against a man-to-man defense. Teams should use it when they need to attempt a three-pointer, whether down at the end of a game or in need of a trey to provide an added boost.

Personnel

The number 1 play requires one outstanding distance shooter. The play allows this player to pursue a field goal from beyond the arc. At least one big player sets an outstanding pick.

Scoring

A big player may have a shot near the basket. The secondary shooter could score along the baseline from 15 to 20 feet. The primary shooter seeks a three-point shot above the foul line extended.

Execution

The point guard (G) is the inbounder (figure 15.11). Post players (B1 and B2) are on the ballside, one at the box and the other at the elbow. The best perimeter shooter is at the weakside elbow (S1). The third exterior player (S2) starts at the offside block along the lane. If the point guard (G) is the team's best exterior shooter, he or she switches jobs with S1. The squad's foremost shooter from distance must occupy S1's spot.

B2 picks across for S2 so that S2 can head toward the strongside corner. B2 seals back to the ball after S2 uses the screen. Alternately, S2 may pick across for B2 before popping out to the closest corner. Meanwhile, S1 cuts off B1 to the ballside wing. Both players act as though B1 missed setting a screen for S1. After S1 is three to five feet past B1, B1 turns back and sets a screen for S1. S1 circles back out past the top of the key to catch the inbounds pass from G.

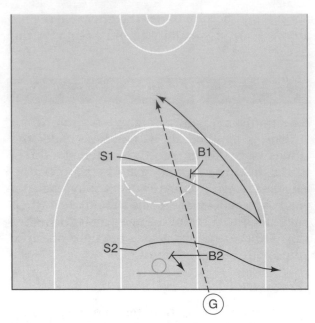

Figure 15.11   Number 1 player alignment and motion.

Keys

See "Man-to-Man Offensive Fine-Tuning" in chapter 1 on page 4 and review these topics: screening between post and perimeter players, setting a screen, slipping a screen, using a pick, rescreening, and pinning the defender.

At their discretion, the interior player and the perimeter player on the boxes along the foul lane can alter the screening action that takes place between them. The perimeter player could pick for the interior player or vice versa. They communicate and select a movement before the referee hands the ball to the inbounder. They make the choice, although the coach may direct a specific motion to take place.

If a defensive switch occurs when the big player picks, the screener plants the foot closest to the baseline, swings the other foot open to the ball, stays low, and secures the defender on his or her rear. He or she gives a target for the passer. If no switch happens, he or she establishes a position advantage by any legal means possible.

The inbounder glances at these two players and delivers the ball to the open player, especially if the big player obtains position at the weakside box. The only time a pass to the interior is not acceptable is if the game situation dictates that a three-point shot be attempted. If a trey is necessary, the only two viable outlets for the entry pass are to the perimeter player in the ballside corner or to the highlighted shooter out front. The inbounder must be capable of using a two-handed, overhead pass to throw the ball out top from underneath the hoop.

The best exterior shooter begins at the weakside elbow. The designated shooter's success in breaking free for a three-point shot above the top of the key depends on his or her theatrical performance and the acting of the screener. These two players must sell the defense on the fact that the post player missed setting a screen for the shooter heading to the ballside wing. The screener's actions and those of the shooter display disappointment. The angle of the second pick allows the shooter to gain freedom behind the arc above the ballside elbow. The screener must let the shooter go several steps past him or her before establishing the rescreen. When the shooter moves beyond the three-point line, he or she cannot be too far to the offside. The inbounder must have an unobstructed passing lane to complete the pass.

NUMBER 2

The number 2 play was my favorite against man-to-man defense. I do not recall precisely how I came to learn it, but I guarantee that it works. Its effectiveness is a direct result of the many movement variations. The number 2 play gives players the ability to choose which movement option to perform.

Personnel

At least one player must be an outstanding peripheral shooter. One post player, or preferably two, should be effective at scoring in the paint.

Scoring

The main shooter obtains shots from the ballside corner. Big players garner interior shots within five feet of the hoop. A second exterior player gets a shot from the offside corner. The inbounder does not secure any shots in this play.

Execution

When the coach calls, "Number 2," the following five options are available to the players on the floor. Players decide which action to execute before the referee gives the ball to the inbounder. The coach might want to dictate a movement in specific circumstances.

Figure 15.12 shows the first option. The point guard (G) is usually the inbounder, except if he or she is the club's best distance shooter. The big players (B1 and B2) begin stacked next to one another, facing the foul lane with the baseline foot of the player nearer the basket on the ballside box. The top player (B2) should be the more proficient inside scorer of the two big players. The best shooter (S1) begins on the offside block, and the other perimeter player (S2) starts at the foul line. When G receives the ball from the referee, S2 slices to the weakside corner to clear the defender away from the primary action. S1 exploits the double screen set by B1 and B2 and heads to the strongside corner. After he or she passes the double screen, one of the big players hustles to the weakside block while the other immediately seals the defender. They can vary who moves where. G's primary target is S1.

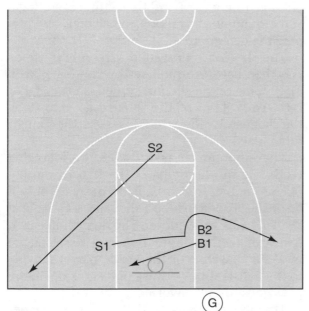

Figure 15.12   First option in number 2.

The second option is for the post players (B2 and B1) to plant staggered screens so that S1 can motor to an open area in the ballside corner. The player at the top of the stack (B2) always picks first, followed by B1. S2 still motors toward the weakside corner to occupy the defender. S1 is the inbounder's main target. Big players seal defenders after teammates use their picks.

In the third option, the two inside players in the stack move directly across the lane to set a double screen for S1. They initiate the action. After S1 sprints over the double screen toward the corner, the top big player (B2) curls back over B1 to the basketball. S2 still heads to the far corner.

For the fourth option, S1 picks across for the top player in the double stack (B2). B2 uses the pick to slide to the offside block. S1 uses the screen set by B1 to head to the strongside corner. This time, S2 (the player at the foul line) steps out toward midcourt for a long inbounds pass from G. G looks to B2 first, S1 second, B1 sealing back to the ball third, and finally to S2 near half-court.

In the fifth motion, S1 bolts up to pick for S2 at the foul line. S2 flees to the weakside corner and is the first throw-in option. The big players (B2 and B1) then establish a double screen for the screener (S1). After S1 races to the ballside corner, B2 glides over the top of B1 to the ball. This final maneuver is known as a twist.

Keys

See "Man-to-Man Offensive Fine-Tuning" on page 4 and the following topics: screening between post and perimeter players, setting a screen, slipping a screen, using a pick, double screen, pinning the defender, and twist move.

The coach should review all five options with his or her team periodically throughout the season and stress that mixing up the five options during a game is a necessity. The team should not allow the defense to become accustomed to only one or two of the options. The first three options are similar. The only difference among them is how the inside players screen (stationary double, staggered screens, or double screen across the lane). The team must communicate. Everyone has to be on the same page.

The inbounder looks at the interior players. They may be open. He or she cannot have tunnel vision and focus only on the shooter. The shooter who uses the screens set by the big players is prepared for a shot as soon as he or she catches the ball from the inbounder.

The key to the play is the post players' picks. The inside players are the main screeners. Their ability to plant convincing obstacles generates the bulk of the shots.

Shot payoffs are very probable. A club can rack up some serious points with this play.

NUMBER 3

The number 3 play uses the screen-the-screener move, increasing its chances for success. Often, the player movement begins from a box alignment, but I grew to prefer the triangle plus one formation. The number 3 play can be called at any time during a game, but it is best not to use it too often. I suggest using it not more than two or three times a game.

Personnel

The team needs to have a convincing inside scoring big player and an outstanding perimeter shooter. The play can produce better results if the other big player is a scoring threat from 15 to 18 feet.

Scoring

One post player gains a shot along the ballside baseline in the 10- to 20-foot range. The other big player secures a shot inside the lane. The primary shooter may have a 15- to 20-foot shot from the weakside corner.

Execution

The point guard (G) is the inbounder unless he or she is the best exterior shooter on the squad. The team's best shooter (S1) begins at the ballside block on the foul lane (figure 15.13). The better perimeter shooter of the two big players (B1) starts at the center of the foul line. The other post player (B2) is at the offside box. The remaining perimeter player (S2) heads out to a position directly in front of the inbounder, approximately five to eight feet from the half-court line.

The motion begins when S1 screens for B1. B1 is the first option for the entry pass only if he or she is open for a score. B2 picks for the screener (S1) and seals back to the ball. S1 cuts to the offside baseline. Either player could be open, and they are the primary targets for the inbounder (G). The last choice for the inbounds pass is to settle for a long outlet to S2, even into the backcourt if necessary and if the rules allow such a pass.

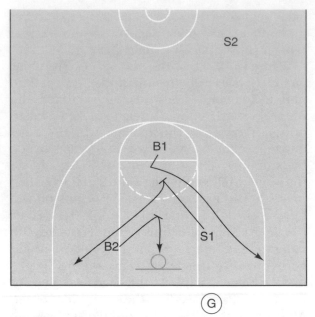

Figure 15.13 Number 3 play.

Keys

Refer to "Man-to-Man Offensive Fine-Tuning" in chapter 1 on page 4 and these topics: setting a screen, slipping a screen, using a pick, and pinning the defender.

The shooter sets a solid screen first. He or she then uses the pick set by the big player. The timing of the second screen is crucial. If it is too early, it tips off the defense. If it is too late, the defense is not as confused as they might otherwise be.

The inbounder has to make the following reads. He or she delivers the ball to the big player coming to the ballside baseline only if he or she is open to take a shot and is capable of stroking a 15- to 18-footer. The next choice is to toss to either the shooter breaking free along the weakside baseline or the inside player moving to the ball. If none of these players is open, the pass goes to the player near midcourt.

The inbounder is aware that his or her defender may be off in the lane trying to help defensively. The inbounder may be able to use the toss-off-the-back option to inbound the ball.

4 ACROSS

The action in 4 across takes advantage of the screens that the big players set for the primary shooter. Using an exterior player to pick later for a post player makes it tough for the defense to switch.

Personnel

One excellent exterior shooter is necessary. One post player should be a capable inside scorer, and the other should be a good outside shooter. The other perimeter player ought to be able to catch and score around the hoop.

Scoring

The primary shooter obtains a shot from the strongside wing or corner. One big player may have a shot from the weakside baseline. The other post player and perimeter player may score near the basket. The inbounder is not part of the scoring action.

Execution

Four players line up parallel to the foul line at approximately the midpoint of the lane (figure 15.14). The point guard (G) is the inbounder. The most productive outside-shooting big player (B1) is along the lane on the ballside. The best peripheral shooter (S1) starts in the middle of the lane. The third perimeter player (S2) is along the lane on the offside. The best interior-scoring big player (B2) begins outside the three-point arc on the strongside.

The post players (B1 and B2) start the action. They head in toward the player in the lane (S1)

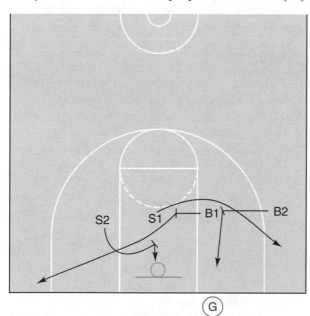

Figure 15.14 4 Across alignment and motion.

simultaneously to set staggered screens. S1 heads to a point beyond the three-point line near the ballside sideline. S2 moves next and picks for the first screener (B1). B1 motors to an open area on the weakside baseline about 15 feet from the goal. The action concludes as S2 and B2 seal back to the ball after their teammates use their screens.

Keys

Refer to "Man-to-Man Offensive Fine-Tuning" in chapter 1 (page 4) and these topics: setting a screen, slipping a screen, using a pick, and pinning the defender.

The team must recognize the importance of establishing a line away from the baseline. The line should be at least at midlane level, if not slightly beyond. This alignment creates space for players to roam. By spreading themselves across the width of the floor, players can employ the maximum amount of horizontal space.

All screeners seal back to the ball after teammates use their picks, with one exception. The big player who plants the first pick in the lane is the recipient of the final screen-the-screener maneuver. The screen-the-screener move is timed to create maximum confusion for the defense.

The inbounder reads the defender on the ball. The inbounder flings the ball off the defender's back if it is sufficiently exposed. Otherwise, he or she views the pass options from right to left if inbounding to the right of the hoop, left to right if inbounding from the left.

4 ACROSS SPECIAL

A team that is able to perform different motions from the same basic formation has greater likelihood of success. Spreading personnel across the half-court forces the defense to guard the maximum space.

Personnel

The play requires two strong exterior shooters and two interior players who are capable of setting solid screens and scoring in the paint.

Scoring

The two outside shooters may have scoring chances in the corners. Big players could acquire shots near or in the foul lane.

Execution

Four players line up across the court at least at midlane parallel to the baseline (figure 15.15). The inbounder should be the weakest outside shooter of the three perimeter players (G in figure 15.15). The other two exterior players (S1 and S2) take up positions along each side of the lane. The two post players (B1 and B2) are out wide near the sidelines, one on the ballside and the other on the weakside.

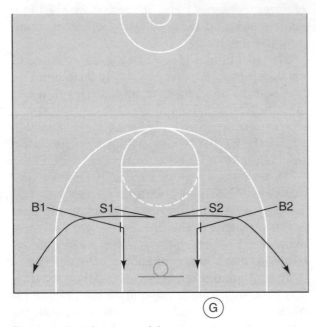

Figure 15.15   4 Across special.

The big players (B1 and B2) head in toward the lane to set picks on each side. The two shooters (S1 and S2) can cross or fake the crossing action before running off the picks set by the big players. The shooters contemplate possible three-point shots. The screeners (B1 and B2) step to the ball after their the shooters use their picks. The inbounder (G) observes the entire floor and delivers the ball to the open player for a score.

Keys

See the discussions of screening between post and perimeter players, setting a screen, slipping a screen, using a pick, and pinning the defender in "Man-to-Man Offensive Fine-Tuning" in chapter 1 on page 4.

Players extend across half-court at a minimum depth of midlane. They may be slightly beyond it but should never go past the foul line extended.

Shooters vary their movements. They cross or fake before using the picks set by the post players. The screeners (the big players) are viable targets for the inbounder. After their picks are used, the big players immediately seal their defenders and move toward the ball. The screeners must be aware of their screening angles. Ideally, both outside shooters receive scoring chances from the corners. The post players plant their picks so that their backs point toward the intended reception areas.

4 ACROSS DOUBLE

The 4 across double play provides more activity from stretching players across the court. In this play, the team tries to free one post player and two exterior players for inside and outside scoring possibilities.

Personnel

An interior player should have the ability to score in the paint, and two players should be effective outside shooters.

Scoring

The best outside scorer may have a shot from the ballside wing or corner. Shots develop above the ballside elbow for the other exterior shooter. One big player may have an interior shot near the strongside block.

Execution

The starting alignment is the same as that shown in figure 15.14 on page 265. The inbounder should be the least proficient distance shooter of the three perimeter players. In this case, it is G. One inside player starts along the foul lane on the ballside (B1). The other (B2) starts wide beyond the three-point line on the same side of the court. Of the two post players, B2 should be the better scorer in the paint. One shooter (S1) is in the center of the lane. The other shooter (S2) is just outside the lane on the offside. The line is at midlane or slightly farther from the baseline. Players should not line up too close to the free-throw line.

B2 initiates the movement of the play. B2 hustles toward the foul lane to set a double screen with B1. S1 manipulates the twin screen to secure an opening behind the three-point line at the foul line extended or below. S1 is the inbounder's first pass option. After S1 uses the double pick, B1 and B2 move simultaneously to establish a double screen for S2. Before using the twin screen, S2 slides down into the lane near the hoop. S2 heads to a strongside position off the double pick above the foul line and beyond the arc for a pass reception and shot. After S2 comes off the double pick, the big players execute a twist. B1 steps up and in, allowing B2 to slice over his or her backside to the ball. The ball goes inside to B2 either from the inbounder or from either shooter.

Keys

See "Man-to-Man Offensive Fine-Tuning" on page 4 and these topics: screening between post and perimeter players, setting a screen, slipping a screen, using a pick, double screen, pinning the defender, and twist move.

The coach should place players in the spots that best take advantage of their assets. The two best outside scorers assume shooter roles, and the better interior player begins past the three-point line on the ballside. The weakest perimeter shooter of the three exterior people is always the inbounder. The best shooter starts in the middle of the foul lane.

The post player at the strongside wing makes the first move to set a double pick with the other big player. He or she invariably darts above the other player. At exactly the same moment, the perimeter player on the offside heads to a spot in the lane near the basket. The first shooter cuts off the double pick to an area below the foul line extended, while the second shooter moves above the boundary, closer to the top of the key. After the first shooter uses the double pick, the two post players move together to set the next double screen. They go directly at the defender and become stationary just before making contact.

The twist move that the two post players perform can be extremely productive. The one nearer the baseline steps up and in toward the other's defender. The player above curls over his or her teammate's rear to the ball. The big players adjust the timing of the maneuver depending on who possesses the basketball.

The inbounder views the floor and sends the ball to an open teammate. After the ball is in play, the inbounder does not come to the ballside. He or she stays away from the big players who are executing the twist.

NUMBER 5

A coach can improve the chance for success by giving players the opportunity to decide the motion that they will perform. The number 5 play sets up shots for one big player and two shooters.

Personnel

Inside players should be adept at scoring around the hoop. Perimeter players should be potent shooters from the 15- to 20-foot range.

Scoring

The main shooter acquires shots near either corner. The other outside player gains shots in the opposite corner. One post player lands an inside shot.

Execution

The inbounder (G) should be the weakest distance shooter (the point guard in figure 15.16). One post player (B1) starts on the weakside box on the lane. The other post player (B2)

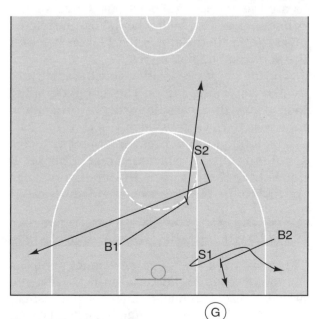

Figure 15.16   Number 5 play.

begins in the ballside corner. The perimeter shooters are at the strongside box (S1) and the ballside elbow (S2). Players communicate with each other which of the two movement options they will perform.

In the play shown in figure 15.16, the big player in the corner (B2) slides in to screen for the peripheral player on the block (S1). At the same time, the big player on the offside box (B1) moves up to set a diagonal pick for the perimeter player at the strongside elbow (S2). S2 cuts to the weakside baseline. The screener closer to the hoop (B2) steps to the ball after S1 uses the pick. The screener farther from the basket (B1) steps out to act as a safety net near half-court.

The other movement option encompasses a switch in roles for the interior players. Each big player screens for the opposite shooter from the first motion alternative. All other rules of execution remain the same as in the first option.

Keys

Refer to "Man-to-Man Offensive Fine-Tuning" in chapter 1 on page 4 and the discussions of screening between post and perimeter players, setting a screen, slipping a screen, and using a pick.

The weakest long-distance shooter of the three perimeter players is the inbounder. The starting positions for the shooters are interchangeable, as are the big players' positions. Players must communicate with each other before the referee gives the ball to the inbounder. Players agree on the screening combinations.

The initial player positions enable some productive screening angles. The inbounder must look toward the weakside corner before settling for a toss to the safety valve.

The inbounder focuses on either perimeter shooter or the post player nearer the bucket. If none of the three is open, the inbounder flings the ball to the big player near midcourt.

NUMBER 6 (MAN-TO-MAN)

This play uses the same personnel setup as number 6 (page 252) does, but the movements are geared against man-to-man defense instead of a zone. The action for number 6 focuses on the primary shooter and the tendency of the

defense to slough in to the foul lane from the weakside. Coaches use the number 6 play to free a particular shooter.

Personnel

One outstanding outside shooter assumes the primary shooter's role. Big players should be good screeners who have the ability to score inside. If one is a potent shooter from inside 18 feet, the squad will have more scoring flexibility.

Scoring

The team's best shooter shoots from either corner. Post players gain opportunities in the lane; one could secure a shot from the weakside baseline. The other exterior player and inbounder generally do not have scoring opportunities.

Execution

The point guard (G) acts as the inbounder unless he or she is the team's best outside shooter. If so, another exterior player would be the inbounder. S1, the best distance shooter, is at the ballside elbow (figure 15.17). The other perimeter player (S2) begins at the ballside block. The interior players (B1 and B2) start at the weakside box and offside elbow, respectively. B2 should be the better shooter from the periphery.

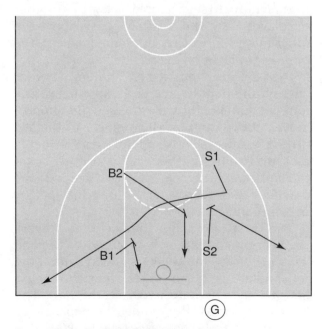

Figure 15.17 Number 6 against man-to-man.

S2 screens up in the direction of S1. If S1 does not use the screen, S2 sprints to the ballside corner. Simultaneously, B2 and B1 set staggered screens, allowing S1 to dart to a vacant spot along the offside baseline. S1 is the primary target for the inbounder (G). The shooter can chose to use the solo pick or the staggered screens. The screeners (B2 and B1) bolt toward the inbounder after S1 uses their picks. If the shooter rubs off the single pick, the first big player to screen (B2) uses his or her partner's (B1's) pick and moves to the offside baseline.

Keys

See the discussions of screening between post and perimeter players, setting a screen, slipping a screen, and using a pick in "Man-to-Man Offensive Fine-Tuning" on page 4.

The best outside shooter on the squad starts at the ballside elbow starting spot. He or she is the main target. The team tries to put the ball in the shooter's hands for a shot attempt.

To increase the effectiveness of the play, the main shooter mixes the two movement sequences. He or she should capitalize on the staggered screens more frequently, however, perhaps as often as four times out of five. The remaining players adjust to the shooter's decision. Although the second option involves an exterior player picking for another perimeter player and one big player screening for the other big player, when used sporadically the element of surprise negates any disadvantage of employing screens that are easily switched.

The screeners seal to the ball immediately after their picks are used. The inbounder glances in their direction because they may pop open if the defenders are overly concerned about the primary shooter.

The players who move to the outside shooting slots are ready to catch the ball, square their shoulders to the hoop, and shoot immediately. A shot fake and one dribble may also be useful.

This play is the same as the number 6 play against zones (see page 252) except that the screening targets differ. If the coach calls, "Number 6," players implement the proper option based on the defense the opposition is playing. Calling two plays, one for man-to-man and one for zone, is not necessary.

NUMBER 11

Delaware Valley College, one of our conference opponents at King's College, used the number 11 play to score on more than a few occasions. Of course, I had to incorporate it into my repertoire. The number 11 play is appropriate for teams that have a quality big player who can grab a lob pass at the basket and score.

Personnel

The team should have a big player with size who jumps well, is able to snatch the ball in traffic, and can score in the paint. Otherwise, any of the three outside players could have a 15- to 20-foot jumper.

Scoring

One perimeter player gets a shot from the ballside or weakside corner. The playmaker shoots from the strongside corner. The center scores within five feet of the basket. The other big player could have a shot around the hoop. The inbounder has a shot possibility from above the foul line.

Execution

A good exterior shooter (S1) inbounds the ball (figure 15.18). The secondary post player (B1) begins five to eight feet from the baseline out-

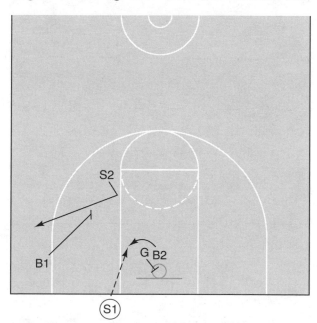

Figure 15.18 Number 11 formation and movement.

side the three-point line on the ballside. Another peripheral player (S2) begins on the strongside along the lane just below the elbow. The point guard (G) is usually the smallest player physically. He or she and the featured big player (B2) start beside one another in the middle of the lane just in front of the hoop. G is closer to the ball.

To start, B1 picks for S2 to keep their defenders occupied. G steps down, allowing B2 to slide over the top to receive a lob from the inbounder (S1). B2 is the primary target, especially if he or she has a height advantage on the defender.

An option is available if players foresee difficulty in lobbing the ball to the big player at the goal. Players determine which of the two movements to perform. B2 screens up so that S2 can hustle to the weakside corner for a possible pass reception and shot. B1 picks in for G at the same time. G heads to the ballside corner, while B1 steps to the ball after G uses the pick. The inbounder tosses the ball to either corner. In figure 15.19, the pass goes to G in the strongside corner. After the inbounder throws the ball to a corner, B2 and B1 come together to plant a double screen for the inbounder (S1). S1 sprints to an open area above the foul line, anticipating a shot chance.

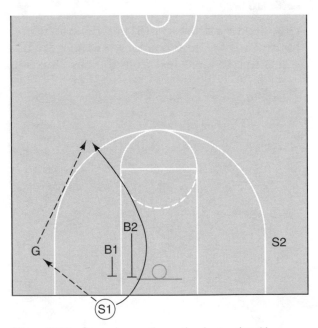

Figure 15.19 Secondary motion option for number 11.

Keys

Refer to "Man-to-Man Offensive Fine-Tuning" in chapter 1 (page 4) and these topics: setting a screen, slipping a screen, using a pick, double screen, and twist move.

The primary target is the big player at the basket. A physical, athletic post player will be able to take advantage of his or her ability around the hoop. The inbounder must know how to throw a lob pass in front of the basket. He or she places the lob where only the offensive big player can grab it. Players carry out the motion involving the lob most of the time.

The inbounder must be aware that his or her defender may back off and try to offer assistance. If the defender is facing the court, the inbounder is prepared to throw the ball off the defender's back.

The two players in the lane initially are right in front of the basket. They adjust their starting positions as needed to counter any defensive maneuvers when the lob is the desired result.

The players at the elbow and the corner must execute their screens quickly. They draw the defenders' attention to keep help away from the two players in the lane.

The second motion option is one of the rare plays in my repertoire against man-to-man in which the inbounder is the intended recipient of a scoring chance. Big players try to plant a double pick for the inbounder, but they may have to supply two distinct single screens to free a teammate at the foul line. The inbounder always motors around the screens by placing the picks between him or her and the ball. The team mixes this movement alternative into the main action and uses it more frequently if the big player in the lane has difficulty securing a lob in front of the basket from out of bounds. After the ball goes to the inbounder out top, the big players can twist. One steps down and the other slides over the top, looking for the ball.

When the coach places outside players in starting locations, the first consideration is that the physically smallest should be in the lane next to the biggest teammate. The next consideration is placing the better outside shooter of the remaining perimeter players as the inbounder.

TRIANGLE

I developed the triangle play so that all players (except the inbounder) would have a chance to score in sequence. The interaction between the post and perimeter players ensures that an opening occurs. The big players stay close to the hoop, and the outside players score from the exterior.

Personnel

The two big players should be effective screeners and have the capacity to score around the basket. The two peripheral players should be outside scoring threats.

Scoring

The best exterior player shoots from the ballside wing. Another perimeter player garners a jump shot along the ballside baseline. One post player secures an opportunity from 5 to 15 feet along the weakside baseline. The other big player catches the ball in front of the inbounder.

Execution

The lead guard (G) inbounds the basketball (figure 15.20). The best perimeter shooter (S1) is at the midlane spot on the offside along the foul lane. The other outside player (S2) is in the middle of the lane directly in front of the bucket and only a few feet away from it. One post player (B1) is on the ballside lane line across from the shooter. The other big player (B2) is in line with S1 and B1 beyond the three-point arc on the strongside. B2 should be the better inside-scoring big player.

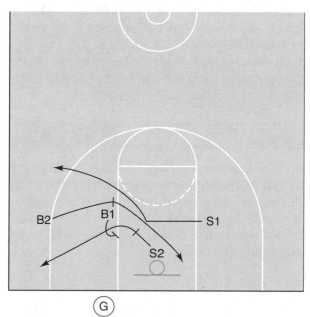

Figure 15.20　Triangle play setup and actions.

B2 makes the first move. B2 glides in next to B1 to anchor a double screen for S1 to manipulate. Once S1 moves around the double screen, S2 sets a diagonal pick, allowing B2 to dash to the weakside block or baseline. S2 then uses a pick set by B1 to twist over the top to the strongside baseline. B1 moves directly to the ball after S2 uses his or her pick.

Keys

See "Man-to-Man Offensive Fine-Tuning" in chapter 1 on page 4. The following sections are pertinent: screening between post and perimeter players, setting a screen, slipping a screen, using a pick, and double screen.

Movements occur sequentially. Therefore, the inbounder has a specific order of reads. Even if the first player is open for a three-point shot, the inbounder must be certain that a quality scoring chance is available. If the inbounder has any doubt, he or she looks to the next option, the big player close to the offside block on the baseline.

The primary shooter using the initial twin screen set by the big players cannot curl over it to a spot too close to the baseline. He or she heads to the general area above the foul line extended. The shooter watches spacing to avoid interfering with a teammate's later opportunity along the same-side baseline.

When setting the double pick, the big players may want to angle their screen slightly to send the shooter to a region above the foul line extended. The screeners' backs point to the desired destination. The angle makes it a little easier to prevent the shooter's defender from racing over the top of the double to continue coverage. If no pass for a shot is forthcoming, the shooter drifts out toward midcourt to increase the open space below.

The other perimeter player properly times the screen-the-screener maneuver when establishing the pick for the top interior player in the double screen. He or she sets the pick right after the shooter cuts off the double, being sure to target the proper defender within the twin pick.

The second successive screen-the-screener move and interaction between post and perimeter players enhance the productivity of the play. Back-to-back activities of this nature confuses the defense, and switching the picks is difficult.

SQUARE

The focus of the square play is on getting the ball to the inbounder for an outside shot. The big players inside the foul lane are potential shooters if the prime option is not open. The team makes a concerted effort to pass the ball to the inbounder for a perimeter shot.

Personnel

The play requires one excellent peripheral shooter and two inside players who are effective screeners and can score in the paint.

Scoring

The two exterior players not inbounding are likely to be sufficiently guarded in the corners, making a shot difficult. The inbounder acquires shots from beyond the foul line. Either big player could score in the lane.

Execution

The premier outside shooter (S1) is the inbounder (figure 15.21). The two post players (B1 and B2) are at the elbows in a box alignment. The other two perimeter players (G and S2) complete the box by settling at the blocks on the lane.

S2 and G cross or fake it to start the action. Each heads to a different corner. S1 flings the

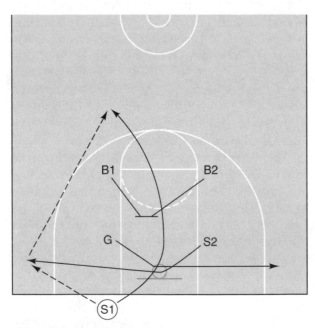

Figure 15.21   Square underneath out-of-bounds play.

ball to a corner, in this case to G. The big players (B2 and B1) hustle to plant a double screen for the inbounder (S1) as soon as a corner player touches the ball. S1 breaks free out front above the foul line for a shot. Once S1 has the ball, the big players (B2 and B1) execute a twist. If no immediate shot arises, S1 glances inside. If S1 cannot get open, the big players still twist even though the ball is in one of the corners.

Keys

Refer to the discussions of screening between post and perimeter players, setting a screen, using a pick, double screen, throwing the ball inside, and twist move in "Man-to-Man Offensive Fine-Tuning" on page 4.

The perimeter players who start at the boxes are required to get open in the corners. They do whatever it takes to get free for the entry pass.

The inbounder uses the double pick. He or she runs the defender smack into it. The inbounder cuts off the double while keeping the screen between him or her and the ball. The exact positioning of the twin screen varies depending on which corner player receives the throw-in. If the pass goes to the ballside, the big players establish the double screen near the strongside lane line. When the inbounds pass goes to the weakside corner, they plant the double pick closer to the middle of the foul lane.

The twist move concludes the play's actions. The twist move is a productive way to deliver the ball inside for a score. For the twist, one player steps down and in so that the other can curl over the top. If the player sliding over the top is moving away from the ball, then the wrong player twisted. Big players adjust roles depending on the location of the basketball.

SIDE SQUARE

For the side square play, I created a variety of activities that players can use from the same alignment. Players determine which action they will perform. The play gives team members some choice of actions to perform from a common set.

Personnel

The play requires two good outside players who can score around the hoop and from the exterior. At least one effective inside-scoring big player is a necessity.

Scoring

One shooter gets shots from the ballside corner. The other outside player gains jumpers in the weakside corner. One post player grabs the ball near the hoop after picking. Another movement option gives an outside player a shot near the ballside corner as the other perimeter player cuts in the lane. The big player collects the ball for a shot on the offside baseline. In the final motion, a shooter gains a shot from the offside periphery as the post and exterior players operate within the lane.

Execution

Players use the square formation, but they form it entirely on the strongside of the court (figure 15.22). Initially, no players are stationed on the weakside. One post player (B2) is in the ballside corner. The other big player (B1) is diagonal at a spot near the center of the foul line. The primary shooter (S1) is directly above B2 close to a sideline and approximately even with B1. The second peripheral player (S2) starts in the middle of the lane right in front of the basket.

The first option is for the post players (B1 and B2) to screen horizontally for the perimeter players (S1 and S2, respectively) as shown in figure 15.22. S1 sprints to an open area on the weakside near the baseline, while B1 steps back as a safety net following the screen. S2 slices to the ballside corner off B2's pick. At the conclusion of the screen, B2 seals the defender on his or her back and steps to the ball.

The second option is for the players closest to the baseline to screen upward. Players screen on the vertical. S2 picks for B1. B1 cuts off either side of the screen to the bucket. S2 seals back opposite. Simultaneously, B2 picks for S1. S1 heads to the ballside corner as B2 darts toward midcourt as the safety net.

The final option is a combination of the first two. B2 rushes up to screen for S1 as B1 hurries toward S1 to pick on the horizontal. S1 fakes exploiting B2's screen and uses B1's pick to fly to an open area on the weakside near the baseline. After S1 cuts opposite, B2 returns to the strongside corner. S2 then screens the screener (B1). B1 motors off either side of the screen to

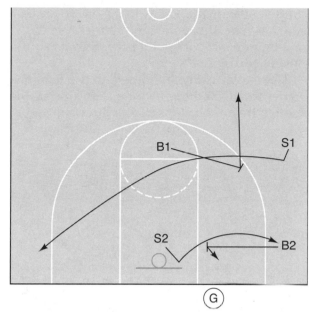

Figure 15.22 Side square set and first movement option.

the basket. S2 sprints opposite B1's move to the hoop. All four players finish stretched along the baseline.

Keys

See "Man-to-Man Offensive Fine-Tuning" in chapter 1 on page 4 and these topics: screening between post and perimeter players, setting a screen, slipping a screen, and using a pick.

The side square play always incorporates all four players on the ballside in a square formation. After the coach calls for the play, players decide which of the three movement options they will perform *before* the referee hands the ball to the inbounder. Letting the players decide places more pressure on the defense. Players usually have a good idea of what works.

On the horizontal screen closer to midcourt, the main shooter whisks to an open area on the weakside. He or she watches so that the backboard does not interfere with the throw-in coming in his or her direction.

The player using the up screen nearest the ballside sideline is aware of the distance between teammates performing the other screening actions. Players need to stay within their designated lanes during each play option.

Post players must remember which of them acts as the safety net in each of the first two movement options. The last option has no deep outlet. In the final option, the main shooter sells the defender on the action going toward the ball-side baseline. He or she then suddenly changes and employs a horizontal screen to go to the offside corner.

The player using an up pick in the foul lane can rush to the hoop from either side of the screen. He or she steps in one direction and V-cuts the opposite way. The screener seals the defender and heads opposite his or her teammate. If the player using the pick slices off the left shoulder, the screener turns over the right shoulder and steps with the right foot, coming back to the ball (or vice versa).

CHAPTER **16**

From a Sideline

At first glance, it may seem like this chapter has an overabundance of plays for inbounding the ball from a sideline. Typically, a team must inbound the ball from a sideline 6 to 15 times a game, and the inbounding opportunities generally increase at the end of a tight game. If the game comes down to the last few possessions, the outcome can depend on the success of a sideline inbounds play. Recall that in chapter 13, "Buzzer Beaters," we covered an entire group of player movements intended to send the ball from a distant baseline to midcourt as quickly as possible. Sometimes the outcome of a game hinges on a shot manufactured from a sideline inbounds play after a time-out. The job of the coach is to prepare his or her team for whatever circumstances might arise. Preparing players with some of the plays that follow may be just the key to securing a win.

This chapter covers two types of inbounding plays. The first type of motion is designed solely for inbounding the ball safely from a sideline. The team makes no attempt to score. For the second type of motion, I present movements that create scoring situations from a sideline inbounds play. Activities are further broken into motions to use against man-to-man defense and those that are most effective versus zones. I subdivide man-to-man plays by grouping certain plays based on the personnel alignment that they have in common.

PLAYS TO ATTACK MAN-TO-MAN DEFENSES

When inbounding the ball from a sideline against a man-to-man defense, the location of the ball is important. Most of the plays in this section begin with the inbounder in what I refer to as the midcourt region, defined as any place between the two foul lines. What I consider the deep region is the area bordered by the foul line and the closer baseline. Some motion is not workable from the deep areas.

SIDELINE

I do not recall the precise source of the sideline play, but I know I did not come up with the idea. I freely employed the play, however, throughout my head-coaching years at King's College. This play is appropriate for any inbound opportunity from a sideline. The main goal is to inbound the ball successfully without a turnover.

Personnel

The play includes no specific personnel requirements except that the inbounder should be a strong exterior shooter and one post player should be a solid inside-scoring threat with some physical size.

Scoring

The inbounder may toss the ball directly to the big player low near the hoop for a shot. If left unguarded, the inbounder may have a shot close to the three-point line.

Execution

The best perimeter shooter (S1) inbounds the ball. The bigger and better post player (B2) establishes position on the ballside block along the foul lane (figure 16.1). The other three players (G, S2, and B1) have two basic rules: They remain above the foul line extended, and they have complete freedom of movement. They begin moving just before the referee hands the ball to the inbounder. Their motion endeavors to free the point guard (G) to receive the throw-in.

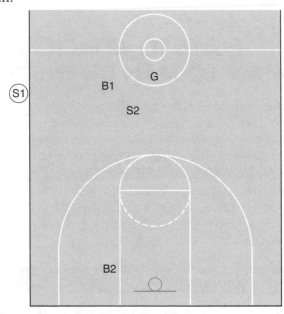

Figure 16.1   Sideline play alignment.

The inbounder's first choice is to B2 in the low post. If the defense is fronting B2, the inbounder may have a chance to lob a pass to B2 over the defender. If S1 cannot get the ball to B2, he or she concentrates on the action of the three players out front and delivers the ball to an open player. The point guard is the next desirable option to catch the inbounds pass.

Keys

Refer to "Man-to-Man Offensive Fine-Tuning" on page 4 and the discussions of setting a screen,

using a pick, throwing the ball inside, and pinning the defender.

The big player on the ballside box must be aggressive and physical as he or she tries to secure position to receive the inbounds pass. If fronted, the big player uses his or her legs and lower body to push the defender farther off the lane. He or she creates more space to increase the likelihood of a successful lob. The inbounder never tosses to the big player if he or she makes no effort to gain a position advantage. The inbounder throws the lob at the near corner of the backboard. The pass is similar to a shot; the player tries to hit a target with some loft. The post player seals the defender and jumps to grab the lob, being careful not to push off when going for the ball.

The three players out top improvise. They keep just one thing in mind: free the point guard to catch the throw-in. The best perimeter shooter is the inbounder so that if the opponent elects to play well off him or her, a quick return pass may produce a shot attempt.

The coach can call an offense or play for the team to execute immediately after successful completion of the throw-in. For example, the coach can tell the team, "Run sideline into the flex offense." Because the major goal of the sideline play is only to put the ball in play without a turnover, the team needs to have a play or offense to execute after they have accomplished that objective.

SIDELINE SPECIAL

The sideline special play is an easily taught, productive variation of the sideline play. The team uses the sideline special play only against man-to-man defense when a defender is harassing the inbounder. The ball is midcourt at a sideline. Scoring is a priority.

Personnel

The same player qualities are needed as with the sideline play. The best exterior shooter inbounds the ball.

Scoring

The ball is passed to the inbounder (the major exterior threat) either on a cut to the basket or a fade to the strongside corner.

Execution

Players begin in the sideline set (see figure 16.1, page 276) because it was the originally called play. If the players see that the defender on the ball is close to the inbounder, the players call sideline special. The inbounder tosses the ball to one of the players out front (G, S2, or B1). On the release of the throw-in, the low post (B2) hustles to set a back screen for the inbounder (S1). S1 uses the back pick and cuts directly to the hoop or fades toward the strongside corner, whichever is more difficult to defend. S1 races off either side of the screen to dart to the hoop. The next pass goes to S1 (the inbounder) for a shot.

Keys

See the discussions of setting a screen, using a pick, and back pick in "Man-to-Man Offensive Fine-Tuning" on page 4.

This play is simple to teach, requiring just a slight alteration of the sideline play. The coach should teach the sideline play first.

The inbounder should have a sight call. The inbounder makes the call (sideline special) based on how he or she is guarded. The coach only issues the order to run the sideline play. The inbounder reads that the closest defender is tight on the ball and calls the sideline special option when he or she is confident that the defender is positioned favorably. The screener plants the back pick for the inbounder as soon as the ball is released. The screener makes contact with the defender guarding the passer, allowing one step.

The throw-in goes to one of the players above the foul line extended. The three players are aware of the need to keep all potential passing lanes open for the next pass to the inbounder. The two players who do not receive the ball must not interfere with the back screen action.

SIDELINE INVERT

The sideline play described on page 276 can become a scoring play by stationing some personnel in different starting spots. The ball must be on a sideline on the offensive side of half-court and above the foul line extended. A team should use the sideline invert play only sporadically to maintain the element of surprise against an opponent who is defending man-to-man. The play provides a possible scoring outcome for a post player.

Personnel

One big player should possess good athletic ability. He or she must jump and catch the ball tossed in the direction of the hoop. A perimeter player needs to be able to cast an effective lob pass toward the goal from a corner.

Scoring

The inbounder grabs the ball near the weakside of the basket after cutting off a back screen. The second post player may possibly receive an inside scoring chance.

Execution

Players align as they did for the sideline play (see figure 16.1, page 276), except that a post player (B1) takes the ball out of bounds on the sideline instead of the main shooter (S1). In other words, the two players exchange starting locations. The inbounder should be the most athletic big player.

The movement rules are the same as those in sideline. The big player who is not inbounding (B2), low on the ballside block, is the first inbounding option. B2 works to gain a position advantage so that he or she can receive an entry pass. The players above the foul line (G, S1, and S2) have total freedom of movement but cannot go below the foul line extended. The ball goes to any of the three, whoever is open. Any of the three could attain a chance to throw a lob pass. Once B1 inbounds the ball, the receiver (in this case S2) dribbles away from the inbounder to the top of the key or higher. The other two players (G and S1) sprint to the corners. The only no-no is that they cannot both run to the same corner. The player at the top (S2) throws the ball back to the inbounder (B1), who has stepped into play (figure 16.2).

After passing, S2 follows the toss and moves to the ballside about 6 to 10 feet from half-court. He or she gets well above the pass receiver. B1 quickly sends the ball to the point guard (G) in the same-side corner. Remember that any of the three perimeter players could be in the ballside corner. G must break free from the defender to receive the ball. S1 starts to establish a back

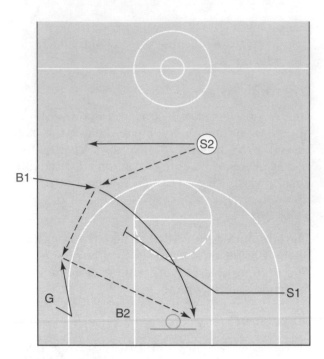

Figure 16.2 Sideline invert setup and movements.

screen near the ballside elbow as soon as S2 passes to B1. When B1 has the ball, the low post (B2) becomes very active and may slide up the lane slightly. S1 races from the offside corner and times the setting of the back screen to coincide with B1's release of the ball. B1 hustles off the back pick to the weakside of the hoop and anticipates a lob pass from G in the corner. During the entire play, B2 is posting up strong just above the strongside box on the lane. If open, he or she gets the ball from either B1 or G.

Keys

Refer to "Man-to-Man Offensive Fine-Tuning" in chapter 1 on page 4 and the segments about screening between post and perimeter players, setting a screen, using a pick, back pick, throwing the ball inside, and pinning the defender.

The inbounder is the most athletic big player. The play demands someone who is able to jump in traffic to snare a lob pass at the basket. The second big player always assumes the starting position near the ballside block.

The inbounder's first option is to toss the ball directly to the other post player at the ballside low post if he or she is open. The squad takes advantage of this option every time it is available.

Once the ball goes to one of the three perimeter players out top, the other two are in a full-out sprint to fill the corners, trying to reach their destinations as quickly as possible. They cannot loaf through their cuts. The pass receiver dribbles away from the inbounder and past the top of the key.

The ball is returned to the inbounder after he or she steps onto the court. The inbounder may need to fake a cut to the hoop to lose a defender. Without exception, the inbounder must reverse the ball to the perimeter player in the same-side corner. The player in the ballside corner is obliged to get open.

After the ball goes to the inbounder, the player in the weakside corner begins to move toward the ballside elbow. He or she times the back pick to coincide with the moment the inbounder releases the ball on the pass to the corner. The screener's back is to the hoop to ensure a proper screening angle. He or she becomes still just before making contact (gives one step) with the inbounder's defender.

The player catching the ball in the strongside corner considers throwing a lob pass to the post player who is cutting to the hoop off a back pick at the ballside elbow. The passer lofts the ball up to the front of the basket to give his or her teammate a chance at the catch. The pass is similar to a shot, arcing as it travels toward its target. The passer is aware that the defender on the ballside low post may try to help defend the lob. If that is the case, the toss goes directly to the post player just above the box.

The player catching the lob realizes that a shot (or even a dunk) while in the air may not be feasible. The recipient will more likely have to jump, catch, and land balanced before driving the ball back up for a shot.

SIDE IN

Using the big players to interact with the prime outside shooter is a good way to create scoring chances. The ball is inbounded from a midcourt sideline, and the team seeks to score. The opposition is defending man-to-man.

Personnel

The play demands one excellent peripheral shooter, one post player who is an outstanding scorer in the paint, and a second big player who is a capable shooter from 15 to 18 feet.

Scoring

The big player moving to the strongside corner shoots from 10 to 20 feet. The main shooter receives a chance near the top of the key. The other post player may have a shot in the paint.

Execution

The primary shooter (S1) starts about halfway between the foul-lane line and the three-point arc along the ballside baseline (figure 16.3). The better post player from the exterior (B1) begins at the weakside block. The other perimeter player (S2) and main inside scorer (B2) are together at the top of the key, with the big player closer to the inbounder (the point guard, G).

S1 moves across the lane to screen for B1 as S2 sprints toward the half-court line on the ballside. S2 heads into the backcourt if necessary. B2 hustles to set a down pick for the screener (S1) and seals back to the ball after the screen is used. S1 uses the pick to sprint to an open area around the top of the key. The lead guard (G) can inbound to S1 out top; directly to B2, who is sealing the defender; or to B1 in the strongside corner. If B1 catches the throw-in, he or she may shoot or dump the ball to B2, who is posting along the foul lane. S2 is the playmaker's last resort.

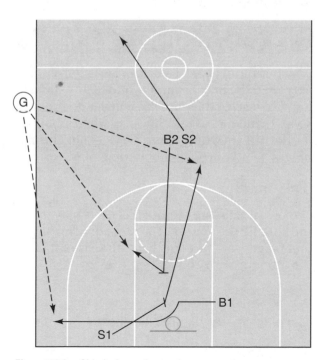

Figure 16.3 Side in formation and movements.

Keys

Refer to "Man-to-Man Offensive Fine-Tuning" in chapter 1 on page 4 and these topics: setting a screen, using a pick, throwing the ball inside, and pinning the defender.

The big player hustling to the ballside corner off a screen could have an outside shot so he or she should be able to stroke the ball from 15 to 18 feet. When he or she can score from the perimeter, the defense must play honestly.

The inbounder has to make a good decision with the ball. The inbounds pass should lead to a quality scoring attempt. The point guard takes the best shooter's spot when appropriate, and another perimeter player assumes the inbounding chores.

The perimeter player out front sprints toward half-court and continues past the midcourt line if possible. He or she acts as though a pass is coming. This maneuver clears the top of the key region for the main shooter.

The big player out front properly times the screen of the screener. He or she sets the pick a split second after the first screen has been used. The big player then consistently seals back to the ball after the teammate uses the down pick. He or she tries to keep the defender on his or her back. If the shooter coming to the top receives the throw-in but has no shot, he or she glances inside for the big player along the lane.

SIDE OUT

The side out inbounding motion was a favorite of an opposing coach during my tenure as a college head coach. When opponents' plays work well, coaches should not hesitate to use them themselves. The source of learning is irrelevant. What is important is being open to good ideas. A team can use the side out play any time during a game against man-to-man defense when inbounding the ball from a sideline at midcourt. The team is trying to score.

Personnel

The squad's outstanding inside and outside scorers work together on the baseline. The presence of another strong exterior shooter helps.

Scoring

The play manufactures a shot from the ballside corner for a shooter. The shooter can dump the ball inside to the better interior scorer, who is posting along the foul lane. An exterior player may have a shot from the offside of the floor.

Execution

The premier post player (B2) is on the ballside beyond the three-point line toward the corner. The highlighted shooter (S1) is at the ballside box on the lane. These are two of the team's better players. B1 is in the extended lane area near the top of the key, and S2 takes a position in the strongside sideline region; they are approximately 8 to 12 feet apart (figure 16.4).

The two post players (B2 and B1) screen for the shooters (S1 and S2, respectively). B2 plants a down or front screen, and B1 sets a back pick. The inbounder (G) throws to S1 for a shot; tosses directly to B2, who is sealing the defender on his or her back; or skips a pass to S2 on the weakside for a long-distance shot. S1 may elect to dump the ball to B2 instead of shooting. B1 is the last throw-in option.

Keys

See the segments about screening between post and perimeter players, setting a screen, using a pick, back pick, pinning the defender, and throwing the ball inside in "Man-to-Man Offensive Fine-Tuning" on page 4.

The two players on the baseline and the two players out front maintain sufficient spacing. Two distinct sets of action are taking place.

The post players establish solid screens for their shooting partners. They make contact with the defenders after becoming stationary.

The big player who screens down for the player at the block seals the defender and actively posts up after the shooter uses the pick. The coach wants the ball to go inside if the shooter does not have a clear shot.

The point guard reads the defense and primarily tries to deliver the ball to either shooter. The big players stepping to the ball after screening are secondary targets. The point guard tosses to the post player out front only as a last resort. The lead guard must be capable of hurling a skip pass to the offside. Because the weakside is vacant, the pass across to the shooter could lead to a score.

This play isolates two of the best players on the baseline. These two players are the primary targets. When a second quality outside shooter is out front, the likelihood increases that a skip pass to the offside will be productive. Passing to that player therefore becomes a higher priority for the inbounder.

LINE

Coaches dating back to before I was born probably used the line formation, and teams still use it today. If something works, it never goes out of style. Teams can use the line play when inbounding the ball anywhere along the sideline. The line play is an all-purpose inbounding play.

Personnel

No special skills are required. The five players on the floor fill the spaces. The more quickness the four players on the court have, the easier it is for the inbounder to complete the entry pass.

Scoring

The play creates no specific shots.

Execution

A perimeter shooter acts as the inbounder (in

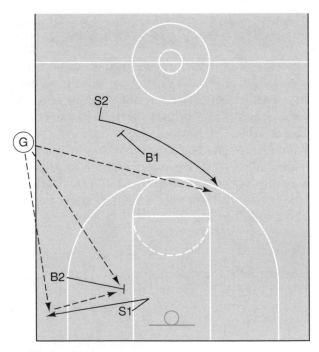

Figure 16.4 Side out setup and motion.

figure 16.5, it is S1). The other four players place themselves in a line directly in front of the ball handler. Each of the big players (B1 and B2) is on an end. They move vertically only. Their lanes are parallel to the sidelines. The point guard (G) is in the middle on the weakside of the court. The other perimeter player (S2) is in front of him or her on the ballside. These two have complete freedom of movement. S2 could even screen for G. Their only rule is that they cannot both cut to the same location.

S1 inbounds to whoever is open. One player can occasionally sprint directly to the offensive basket. The coach needs to let players know who has the chance. The team should use the action sporadically to surprise the defense.

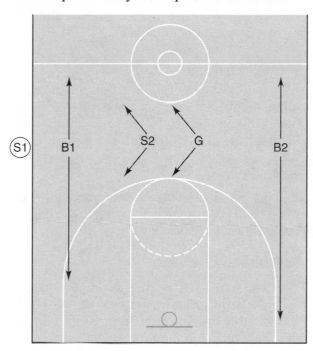

Figure 16.5 Line inbounds play.

Keys

Refer to "Man-to-Man Offensive Fine-Tuning" on page 4 and the discussions of setting a screen, using a pick, and double screen.

Line is an all-purpose sideline inbounds play that a team can also use against zone defense. The only objective is to put the ball in play without a turnover. The inbounder can toss the ball to any of the other four players.

Players move after the official hands the ball to the inbounder. They cannot expect to get open without any effort. Big players remain in their vertical alleys. The two perimeter play-

ers in the line move as they deem fit. They can move freely except that they do not run to the same location.

Players must initially space themselves properly across the width of the court, keeping roughly the same amount of space between each player. The line is always directly in front of the inbounder unless the ball is too close to either baseline. The line should never be closer to the baseline than the hash mark on the lane nearest the foul line. The coach can allow one player to run directly to the offensive basket. The runner communicates with his or her teammates so that no more than one player heads to the hoop at any given time.

If the team has a big player who is a solid ball handler, it is practical to switch a perimeter player to the ballside sideline area so that the big player can occupy one of the two center spots. The other post player is located in the offside sideline region. The adjustment increases the effectiveness of any screening action between the two people in the middle of the line.

FIVE ON A SIDE

I am certain that my high school coach used the actions for five on a side. Several of our opponents at King's College used the play. When something has been around that long, it is for a reason. The play is appropriate when inbounding the ball at midcourt from a sideline against man-to-man defense. Although the primary objective is to inbound the ball safely, a scoring chance could arise if the player heading to the hoop is open.

Personnel

A fairly athletic post player who is quick, a good jumper, and has good hand-eye coordination is a major asset. The inbounder ought to be able to throw a deep entry pass. Another excellent ball handler other than the point guard is helpful.

Scoring

The post player gets the ball while sprinting to the hoop.

Execution

The best perimeter shooter (S1) is the inbounder (figure 16.6). The other four players

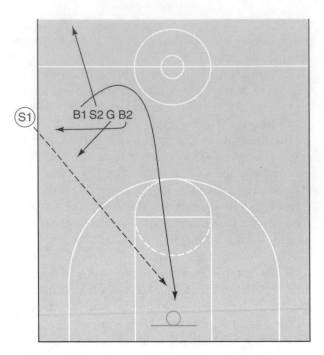

Figure 16.6   Five on a side formation and movements.

form a line directly in front of the inbounder. They are approximately 8 to 12 feet from the sideline, facing the inbounder. The most athletic big player (B1) is closest to the inbounder. The perimeter player (S2) is next, followed by the point guard (G). The other post player (B2) is last. Players are tight enough to prevent defenders from moving between them.

B1 is the first player to move. He or she races to the backcourt side of the line and then sprints off the other three players to the basket. These three turn to face the backcourt and form a triple screen. Obviously, if B1 comes open, S1 sends the ball to him or her. After B1 darts off the line, G and S2 move in opposite directions toward the ball as the big player (B2) flies directly to the ball. S1 inbounds the ball to any of the three players (G, S2, or B2).

Keys

Players assume their line positions quickly and do not give the defense the chance to wedge between them. The line starts 8 to 12 feet from the inbounder, with players facing the ball.

The first player in line initially hustles toward the opponent's basket. After the movement starts, the other three players in the line turn sideways, facing the defensive hoop. They now act as screeners. The player using the triple pick runs the defender into the screen. He or she can

rub off either side, but usually the end closer to the center of the floor is preferred.

The inbounder always considers a possible peg to a teammate sprinting to the hoop. The inbounder does not force it. If the toss is unavailable, he or she just waits to get the ball in play successfully to one of the other three players.

TWO STACKS

The two stacks action was designed to be used at critical moments late in a game. The play emphasizes scoring. I specifically included a skip pass to the primary shooter off a back pick because of its effectiveness. The inbounds pass is from the midcourt sideline. The objective is to produce a shot for the premier outside shooter or a strong inside post player.

Personnel

The two stacks play requires one outstanding distance shooter, one big player to keep the defense honest out to 18 feet, and another big player who is an effective interior scorer.

Scoring

The best outside shooter may have a shot from 16 to 22 feet. The big player diving to the basket may get the ball inside for a shot attempt.

Execution

The lead guard (G) is the inbounder (figure 16.7). S1 is the primary outside shooter, and S2 is the third perimeter player. S1 and S2 are stacked together just above the inbounder (G) at the ballside sideline. S2 is closer to the hoop. The two post players (B1 and B2) are together just above the weakside elbow. B1 should be the better exterior shooter. B2 may receive the ball on the interior.

The play begins with three movements, all taking place at the same time. S2 dashes over S1 and heads to the backcourt. B2 sets a back pick for S1, while B1 sprints to the ballside below the foul line extended behind the three-point arc. S1 uses B2's back screen to sprint to an open area on the offside for a possible entry pass and perimeter jumper. After S1 uses the pick, B2 runs straight down the near lane line to the basket. G can throw the ball directly to B2, or G can throw to B1, who throws to B2. The point guard (G) looks for S1,

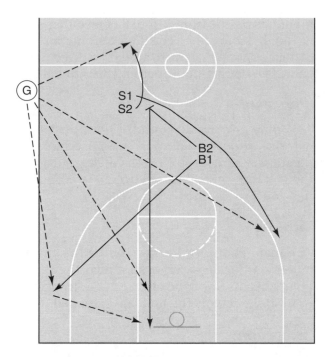

Figure 16.7 Two stacks.

B2, and B1 primarily. The inbounder throws the ball to S2 in the backcourt as a last option.

Keys

See "Man-to-Man Offensive Fine-Tuning" and the sections about setting a screen, slipping a screen, using a pick, back pick, and throwing the ball inside.

The positioning of the two stacks is crucial. The player closest to the inbounder is always above the ball. Big players are near the weakside elbow. The players stagger the stacks and space them slightly more than lane-width apart.

The point guard must be able to throw a strong skip pass. The pass to the big player, who is diving to the basket, is usually a bounce pass. The toss comes directly from the inbounder or by way of the other post player in the ballside corner. To draw the defense out, the post player in the corner needs to be a competent shooter from 15 to 18 feet. If he or she is not a shooting threat, the defense sags and prevents the pass to the big player heading to the basket.

The back screen is set between a post player and a perimeter player to decrease the likelihood of a defensive switch. If the defense does switch, the team finds a way to send the ball inside to the player with the mismatch. The screener sets a solid back pick for the primary shooter. The

screener targets the correct defender and gives one step before contact occurs.

DOUBLE STACK FOR NAME

I came across this play while scouting an upcoming opponent on film. They had used the play to secure a buzzer beater and a win. I recommend saving this play for a crucial inbound from the sideline when the clock is running out and a score is necessary. The throw-in is from midcourt.

Personnel

The featured player must have strong one-on-one skills and the ability to finish with a successful field goal. The player's name is called as part of the play.

Scoring

The highlighted person creates a shot with a dribble penetration.

Execution

The best one-on-one player on the club is the named player (N) (figure 16.8). He or she could be any player—a shooter, playmaker, or big player. In this case, the point guard (G) is inbounding the ball. If G is the named player, someone else inbounds the ball. N stacks below

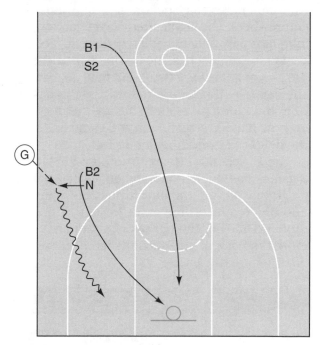

Figure 16.8 Double stack for name.

B2 at the foul line extended on the ballside about halfway between the lane line and the sideline. S2 stacks below B1 on the strongside at half-court. They are in line with N and B2.

B1 sprints to the bucket, looping to the weak-side of the floor. At the same time, B2 cuts in front of N to sprint to the hoop. N steps forward to catch the inbounds pass from G. N now goes one-on-one to create a score, while B1 and B2 go to the hoop in anticipation of securing an offensive rebound if needed.

Keys

When the ball begins on the offensive side of half-court above the foul line extended on a side-line, the two stacks are positioned as described. If the inbounding point is in the backcourt por-tion of midcourt, players adjust the starting locations of the two stacks. Players keep the stacks about 15 to 20 feet apart.

The featured player is a strong one-on-one player. The key player also could be the one who has a distinct advantage over his or her defender. The person highlighted has the ability to create a shot with the dribble and make it.

The two biggest players move at the same time. Both dart to the basket, ready to rebound. As soon as a big player loops in front of the featured player, the featured player jumps directly to the ball. Some contact between the teammates may occur. The ball must be entered here. The highlighted player catches the inbounds pass and immediately turns to face the basket, beginning the one-on-one play. Usually, the player looks for a two-point field goal. He or she can take the ball all the way to the basket or pull up for a jump shot, basing the decision on how much time is left in the game and how the defense is guarding him or her.

The coach should save the play for late in a game. The one-on-one maneuver can beat a clock that is running out. If possible, the ball handler leaves some time for an offensive rebound. Ideally, the opponent should have no more than one or two seconds left if the squad does secure the lead.

STACK HIGH

Players can quickly learn the simple movement of the stack high play. The play was designed to deliver the ball to a specific shooter. The inbounds pass is from 5 to 10 feet on either side of the midcourt line. The squad's outstanding distance shooter needs to attempt a three-point shot. The opponent is guarding man-to-man.

Personnel

The play revolves around one superlative exterior shooter. The post players must be persuasive screeners. The playmaker must fire the ball long on a diagonal from one corner of half-court to another.

Scoring

The main shooter receives the ball from the inbounder for an exterior shot near the three-point line. His or her position can be strongside or weakside below the foul line extended.

Execution

The point guard (G) is the inbounder (figure 16.9). Two post players (B2 and B1) begin close to the three-point line and above the foul line, one on the ballside and one on the weakside. The primary shooter (S1) is stacked with the other perimeter player (S2) in the center of the floor about halfway between the top of the key and the half-court line. S1 is closer to the basket.

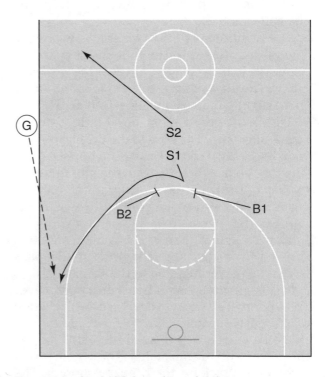

Figure 16.9 Stack high formation and actions.

S2 rushes to a ballside location near midcourt. He or she may head into the backcourt if necessary. S1 could use B2's screen to hustle toward the ballside corner or exploit B1's pick and fade to the offside corner. S1 needs to sell the defender on one direction and then move opposite. Post players establish their picks right at the three-point line. The point guard (G) contemplates a pass to S1 for a possible shot attempt from either the strongside or offside corner.

Keys

Refer to "Man-to-Man Offensive Fine-Tuning" on page 4 and these topics: screening between post and perimeter players, setting a screen, and using a pick.

A post player begins on each side of the foul lane just above foul-line level, three to six feet off the lane. The post players' job is to help the main shooter from deep get open for a pass reception and shot. They set picks close to the three-point arc. The other perimeter player out top is only a decoy. He or she darts to midcourt or beyond and receives the ball only as a last resort.

The prime shooter rubs off a single screen and heads to either the ballside or weakside corner. He or she remains behind the three-point line.

The point guard must be proficient at throwing an overhead pass across the court. The lead guard attempts to send the ball to the main shooter. If he or she cannot do so, any of the other three players will suffice, as long as the team inbounds the ball successfully. If the point guard is the best outside shooter on the squad, he or she assumes the main shooter's role and another perimeter player becomes the inbounder.

The stack high play is designed to create a three-point shot. The coach uses the play only if he or she deems it necessary for the premier exterior shooter to attempt a trey.

ATLANTA

The actions in the Atlanta play exploit the entire forecourt to produce quality shots. The player movement differs from that of many plays in that it relies heavily, though not completely, on the interaction of a post player with his or her part-

ner and the three perimeter players as a group. Normally, I prefer to mix the positions to secure scoring chances. The coach can call the Atlanta play any time the team is inbounding the ball from the midcourt sideline and the opponent is playing man-to-man defense. A number of players may obtain scoring opportunities.

Personnel

The play requires a post player who has the ability to shoot the ball from 18 to 20 feet. The other big player should be an effective inside scorer. The inbounder and another perimeter player should be strong peripheral shooters.

Scoring

The post player who sets the screen near the basket could have an interior shot off a direct pass from the inbounder or a shot from the periphery off a down pick. The exterior player who uses the diagonal down screen may have a shot close to the arc above the foul line. The inbounder may gain an outside shot close to the three-point line. The lead guard does not acquire a chance to score.

Execution

The best outside shooter (S1) is the inbounder (figure 16.10). The more effective post player

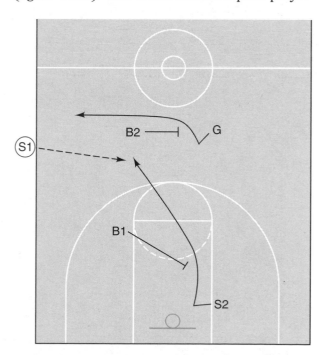

Figure 16.10 Starting motion for Atlanta.

from the perimeter (B1) starts at the ballside elbow. The other post player (B2), who should be productive in the paint, is just above the inbounder along the ballside lane line. The playmaker (G) is even with the weakside lane line, directly behind B2. The other perimeter player (S2) begins at the offside block.

The action begins as the big players (B1 and B2) screen for the nearer perimeter players (S2 and G, respectively). Both players dash toward the inbounding point. When S2 receives the entry pass, B2 sets a second pick, this time for B1 in the lane. B1 pops out to the weakside perimeter at the foul line extended or below for a possible jumper. B1 also could dump the ball inside to B2 (the screener) if he or she is open in the low post. The lead guard (G) picks for the inbounder (S1), allowing S1 to scurry over the top, awaiting a pass from S2. G plants a screen at the same time B2 picks for B1 on the weakside interior.

Figure 16.11 shows what happens when the inbounds pass goes to the playmaker (G) instead of to S2. The big players (B1 and B2) perform the same motion described previously. The inbounder (S1) uses S2's pick (not G's) to fade to the ballside corner. The ball handler delivers the next pass to S1 or B1 for a possible shot or maybe into B2, who is sealing the defender low.

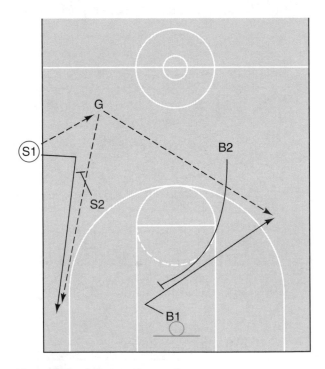

Figure 16.11 Atlanta action continues.

B1 and S1 also could send a post feed to B2 if shot attempts are not available.

Keys

Refer to "Man-to-Man Offensive Fine-Tuning" in chapter 1 page 4 and the segments about setting a screen, using a pick, back pick, pinning the defender, and throwing the ball inside.

The Atlanta play is a little more complex than many of the other plays. Players must commit more moves to memory. The coach may need to review the play a little more frequently to ensure retention.

A team uses the Atlanta play when the ball is between the foul lines on a sideline. If the throw-in point is toward the backcourt, two players out top adjust their starting positions. The best perimeter shooter is the inbounder. He or she is most likely to acquire a shot.

The two post players simultaneously set the initial picks. The throw-in goes to either the point guard or the other perimeter player. The prime shooter (the inbounder) rubs off a screen set by whichever player does not receive the entry pass. The shooter always fakes toward the pass recipient before using the pick set by the player who did not receive the pass.

The big player out front automatically sets a second screen for the other post player in the foul lane no matter who catches the entry pass. After the pick, he or she works to establish position in the low post for a possible feed from a teammate.

If the lead guard is the team's best shooter from distance, he or she handles the throw-in. Another perimeter player replaces the point guard out front in the initial formation.

HAWK

I am not 100 percent positive, but I believe that Hubie Brown, NBA head coach and broadcast analyst, was my source for this play many years ago. The hawk play is appropriate any time the team inbounds the ball from the midcourt sideline. Scoring is a primary objective.

Personnel

The featured player is the small forward. He or she should possess decent quickness and have the talent to score when receiving the ball en route to the hoop. One post player must be a capable passer from the periphery and an outside scoring threat out to at least 15 feet.

Scoring

The highlighted player secures a layup with a cut to the goal.

Execution

The team's main exterior shooter (S1) is the inbounder (figure 16.12). One post player (B2) starts on the weakside block. The other big player (B1) is on the ballside vertical extended lane line, directly in front of the ball. The point guard (G) lines up opposite B1 on the offside. Neither player takes a position below the midline between the top of the key and the half-court line. The key player (S2) is at the offside wing.

B1 screens for G and seals back to the ball opposite G's motion. This action is just a decoy. The ball heads here only if S1 cannot complete the entry pass to B2. B2 sprints to the ballside behind the three-point line below the foul line extended. He or she receives the pass from S1. In the meantime, S2 trots across the court at less than full speed. S2 picks up the pace and races to the basket as soon as B2 catches the inbounds pass. The cutter tries to catch the defender off stride. B2 tries to send the ball to S2 as S2 cuts to the hoop.

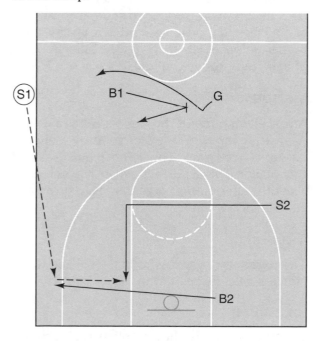

Figure 16.12 Hawk setup and motion.

Keys

See the discussions of setting a screen, using a pick, and throwing the ball inside in "Man-to-Man Offensive Fine-Tuning" in chapter 1 on page 4.

The big player in the strongside corner receives the throw-in near or beyond the three-point arc. A bounce pass is used to send the ball to the player running to the hoop.

The small forward must do a good job of timing the move to the strongside. He or she jogs and does not go into a full sprint until he or she plants the foot closest to the half-court line and heads to the hoop. The cutter knows when he or she will accelerate. The defender can only react.

Any player may replace the small forward in the featured starting spot. The coach makes the choice. Regardless, the player retrieving the inbounds pass in the corner should be a post player. He or she must get open. If the player is a shooting threat from at least 15 feet, the defender will be reluctant to slough off the pass receiver. A defender backing away from the player with the ball will likely interfere with passing lanes to the cutter. The big player securing the throw-in may be required to dribble at the defender if there is too much space between the two.

SIDE BOX PLAYS

The next eight plays begin from the same starting formation, a box around the foul lane; only the beginning locations of individual players and their actions differ. These plays are designed to attack man-to-man defense during an inbounds play from a sideline.

SIDE BOX FOR SHOOTER

A team can use the side box for shooter play any time to get a quality shot from distance for the primary outside shooter. The basketball needs to be between the foul lines. The opponent is guarding man-to-man.

Personnel

The side box for shooter play is designed for the best outside shooter. The two big players need to be strong screeners. The playmaker must be able to deliver the ball to the main shooter.

Scoring

The major shooting threat from the periphery could score from the ballside corner or the top of the key. The two post players step to the ball after their screens are used, and either could receive the ball for a scoring chance.

Execution

The point guard (G) is the inbounder. The highlighted shooter (S1) starts at the weakside box. The third perimeter player (S2) is at the offside elbow, and the two big players are at the ballside elbow (B1) and block (B2) (figure 16.13).

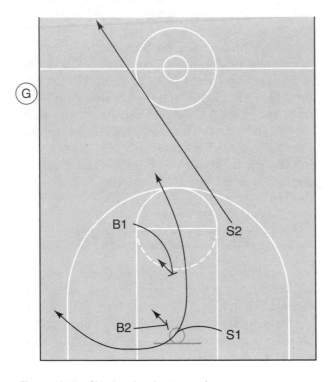

Figure 16.13 Side box for shooter motion.

S2 rushes to half-court and beyond if necessary, while B1 screens down and B2 picks across for S1. They establish their picks at the same time. S2 vacates the area to give S1 room to maneuver at the top of the key. S1 exploits either pick. He or she fakes one way and sprints the other. G looks solely for S1 initially. If S1 is not open, the throw-in may go to S2 or to one of the post players, who will be trying to help when they see that the inbounder is in trouble.

Keys

See "Man-to-Man Offensive Fine-Tuning" in chapter 1 (page 4) and the sections about screening between post and perimeter players, setting a screen, and using a pick.

The perimeter player at the weakside elbow hustles to midcourt and beyond. He or she is a decoy. The inbounder throws to him or her only if all else fails. But the player must act as though the team is interested in getting the basketball in his or her hands.

The lead guard searches for the primary shooter. He or she throws the ball elsewhere only if a toss to the shooter is not available. The shooter has to sell the move in one direction and then head the other way. The shooter runs the defender into one of the two picks.

Post players acquire proper angles for their screens. The screen at the ballside block is set so that the shooter can dart to the ballside corner. The post player at the ballside elbow loops into the lane and heads down to pick so that the shooter bolts out to the top-of-the-key vicinity. Both players plant picks at the same time.

SIDE BOX FOR PERIMETER

The side box series highlights different players. The secondary exterior shooter is the primary scoring target in side box for perimeter. Team uses the play when trying to score from an out-of-bounds situation along a sideline against man-to-man defense. The ball is on the offensive side of half-court above the foul line.

Personnel

An excellent outside shooter serves as a decoy. A post player who is effective away from the basket is necessary. The defense must respect this player. The other big player is a screener. The other perimeter player needs to be able to score inside 15 feet.

Scoring

The perimeter player who begins at the weakside elbow acquires a shot from about 15 feet.

Execution

The opening set is shown in figure 16.13 (page 287). The point guard (G) is the inbounder. The best exterior shooter (S1) starts at the weakside block. The other perimeter player (S2) is at the offside elbow. The better outside-shooting big player (B2) begins at the ballside box. The other post player (B1) is at the strongside elbow.

S1 moves first, sprinting to a position near half-court. He or she is a decoy; no pass heads his or her way. Once S1 hits the arc, B2 pops out to the ballside corner. The throw-in can go to B2 if he or she is open. At the same time, B1 turns and screens across, allowing S2 to slice to the ball. The pass to S2 may come directly from G (the inbounder) or via B2 in the ballside corner.

Keys

See "Man-to-Man Offensive Fine-Tuning" in chapter 1 on page 4 and the discussions of setting a screen, slipping a screen, and using a pick.

The prime shooter must make the defender believe that he or she is a threat and that the toss-in will be coming his or her way. Players at the elbows act as though they have missed setting a screen for the main shooter. The timing is critical. Big players cannot start their moves until the shooter reaches the three-point line on the sprint to midcourt.

The post player popping to the corner should be an exterior threat. Otherwise, the defender will just play off and prevent any inside pass. If the big player receives the toss-in, he or she may have to dribble at the defender to send the ball inside to the cutter. If the big player in the corner and the perimeter player slashing to the ball are not open, the inbounder delivers the ball to another player just to get it inbounds. The main objective is to put the ball in the hands of the secondary shooter.

A big player bumps the defender on the outside player receiving the screen near the foul line. The big player is stationary before contact. In most instances, the perimeter player steps low and goes over the top of the screen. If the defender cheats over it too soon, the exterior player can cut to the baseline side off the pick.

SIDE BOX FOR POST

This time one of the post players is the main character in the motion. The side box for post play must begin with a sideline toss-in on the forecourt side of midcourt.

Personnel

The big player who starts at the ballside elbow should possess some athletic prowess and have jumping ability sufficient to catch a lob pass. The other post player is a scoring threat from at least 15 feet. The inbounder must have the skill to lob a pass at the hoop from out of bounds on the sideline.

Scoring

The ball goes to a big player moving to the basket for a layup or dunk. The player planting the back pick may acquire a shot by stepping out after the featured player uses the screen.

Execution

The introductory set is the same as that shown in figure 16.13 (page 288). The point guard (G) is the inbounder. S1, the primary outside shooter, is at the weakside box. S2 is at the weakside elbow. The post player who is an outside scoring threat (B2) is on the ballside box. B1 is above B2 at the strongside elbow. B1 is the premier inside scorer and featured player.

Motion begins when S1 sprints out to half-court. He or she clears the defensive help from the foul lane. Once S1 reaches the foul line, B2 pops out to the ballside corner. When S1 crosses the three-point line, S2 hustles to set a back screen for B1. He or she acquires the proper angle on the pick. If the throw-in goes to B2, he or she tosses the ball inside to B1 at the bucket. The pass from B2 may or may not be a lob. The lead guard also could inbound the ball directly to B1 at the hoop.

Keys

See the sections on screening between post and perimeter players, setting a screen, using a pick, and back pick in "Man-to-Man Offensive Fine-Tuning" in chapter 1 (page 4).

The highlighted player begins at the ballside elbow. He or she should have decent size, be strong around the basket, and be able to rise up and snare a lob pass at the hoop.

The best peripheral shooter is a decoy. He or she cuts hard to midcourt and acts as if he or she is the primary pass receiver for the inbounder. To throw off the defense, the players at the elbows may simulate missing a screen for the main shooter.

The big player on the ballside block moves after the shooter touches the foul line on the way to midcourt. The perimeter player at the weakside elbow moves shortly thereafter. The perimeter player sets a back pick at an angle that enables the player at the opposite elbow to slice to the hoop. The screener steps out once the player using the screen rubs off. The screener could receive the toss-in for a shot.

The big player in the ballside corner and the point guard must be capable of throwing a lob pass. The lob, similar to a shot, puts the ball in front of the basket. The player receiving the lob pass may have to catch the ball and come down before bouncing back up for a shot. The player decides which kind of shot to take based on whether he or she is balanced for a shot (possibly a dunk) directly off the lob.

If the inbounder's only play is to the player heading to midcourt, the team no longer looks to score. The objective then is to inbound the ball without a turnover.

SIDE BOX FOR BIG PLAYER

The action in the side box for big player play is an alternative means to get the ball to one of the post players. This is another sideline play that uses the box alignment. The ball must begin on the offensive side of midcourt along a sideline. Defense is man-to-man.

Personnel

An effective outside shooter is vital. A big player who has the dexterity to catch a lob pass at the hoop is necessary. The other post player should be a proficient inside scorer. The ball handler must be able to throw a lob at the weakside of the goal.

Scoring

The toss goes to the main shooter in the strongside corner for a shot. The primary target is a big player who races to the basket off a back pick.

Execution

The starting set is shown in figure 16.13 (page 288). The point guard (G) is the inbounder. The best exterior shooter (S1) begins at the weakside box. The other perimeter player (S2) starts at the offside elbow. The big player who is most capable of scoring with his or her back to the basket (B2) is at the ballside block. The most athletic post player (B1) starts at the strongside elbow.

Play begins when B1 steps toward the inbounder to secure the inbounds pass. He or she is the only option. The action continues as the lead guard (G) steps in play and takes a handoff from B1. This exchange must take place. B2 immediately sets a stationary screen for S1 to use as he or she motors to the ballside corner. The screener (B2) seals the defender and steps to the ball after S1 uses the pick. At the same time, S2 darts to set a back pick for B1. B1 slashes to the basket, anticipating a lob pass from the player with the ball. The ball is tossed at a sufficient height, similar to a shot. The playmaker can pass to S1 in the corner. S1 then shoots or flips the ball inside to B2. Another option is for G to lob the ball to B1 in front of the hoop. The back screener (S2) steps out after B1 cuts off the pick. The point guard could toss to S2, but spacing between the two may be too close to make it worthwhile.

Keys

Refer to "Man-to-Man Offensive Fine-Tuning" on page 4 and the following topics: screening between post and perimeter players, setting a screen, using a pick, back pick, throwing the ball inside, and pinning the defender.

Any inbounding spot that is too deep toward the corner or past half-court does not provide sufficient room. Without exception, the first pass goes to the post player who moves out from the ballside elbow. The lead guard then races to receive the ball with a handoff from the post player. The activity is mandatory.

After the point guard has retrieved the ball, the big player on the baseline sets a stationary pick for the shooter on the weakside block, allowing the shooter to dash to the corner. The perimeter player at the weakside elbow sets a back pick for the player who handed the ball to the playmaker. The screener establishes the back pick so that his or her rear points in the direction where he or she wants the teammate to get open. The baseline screener stays put. He or she works to acquire position down low on or above the block.

SIDE BOX FOR TWO

Another play from the side box alignment gives the inbounder three potential pass recipients for scoring outcomes. The ball must be along a sideline in the offensive end of the midcourt region.

Personnel

One post player who is well versed in scoring around the bucket and an outstanding shooter from the periphery are the key individuals.

Scoring

The inbounder throws the ball inside to a big player who is heading to a low spot on the strongside of the lane. The primary shooter has a shot chance near the top of the key. The post player setting the final pick may have a shot as a result of sealing to the ball.

Execution

The point guard (G) is the inbounder. B2 and B1, the big players, are at the weakside block and elbow, respectively. B2 is the primary scorer in the paint. S1 and S2, the shooters, are on the ballside box and elbow, respectively. S1 is the primary shooter. The main targets start at the blocks (figure 16.14).

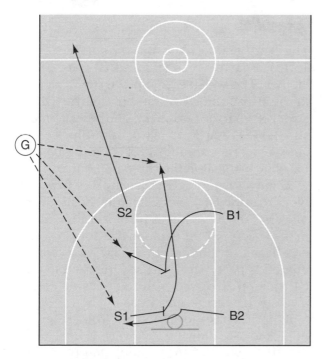

Figure 16.14   Movements in side box for two.

As S2 sprints to half-court and beyond, S1 screens across for B2. The first look is for a pass directly to B2, who is coming to the ballside low location. The other post player (B1) then picks down for the screener (S1). S1 heads to an open area near the top of the key. S1 is the next major target. B1 steps to the ball immediately after S1 uses the pick. The point guard tosses the ball to B2, S1, or B1.

Keys

Refer to these topics in "Man-to-Man Offensive Fine-Tuning" on page 4: screening between post and perimeter players, setting a screen, using a pick, cross screen, throwing the ball inside, and pinning the defender.

The perimeter player's sprint past midcourt occurs at the same time the screen across for the primary big player is taking place. The big player using the shooter's pick across the lane steps high and goes low or vice versa. The inbounder's first choice is for the ball to go directly inside.

The big player picking down for the screener (the primary shooter) acquires the proper screening angle. He or she moves toward the ballside before heading down to pick. Motion should free the shooter at the top of the key but could actually be more toward the weakside. The screener steps to the ball after the pick is used and heads toward the high post to avoid interfering with the player posting low.

The squad is primarily trying for a two-point field goal with a throw directly inside, but a three-point shot may develop for the shooter out front.

The inbounder (the lead guard) views the big player coming to the ballside low post first, to the shooter near the top of the key next, and finally to the down screener who steps to the ball in the high post. The ball goes to the player nearest half-court only as a last resort.

SIDE BOX FOR THREE

The next play of the side box series can be used when a three-point shot is needed.

Personnel

One effective deep shooter is required. Big players need to be quality screeners.

Scoring

An extraordinary shooter garners a shot from behind the three-point line on the side of the court away from the throw-in. The screeners head to the ball after the picks are used and could secure passes for shot chances.

Execution

As in figure 16.14, the lead guard (G) is the inbounder. S1 and S2, the shooters, are at the ballside block and elbow, respectively. The featured player is on the strongside box. B2 and B1, the post players, are on the weakside box and elbow. The personnel setup is the same as that used in side box for two.

S2 rushes past half-court as the big players (B1 and B2) set staggered screens from behind for the main shooter (S1). The staggered screens allow S1 to move beyond the arc on the offside of the floor. The screeners (B2 and B1) hustle toward the ball after S1 uses their picks. The point guard (G) uses an overhead pass to send the ball across the floor to S1 for an attempt at a trey.

Keys

Refer to the discussions of screening between post and perimeter players, setting a screen, using a pick, and pinning the defender in "Man-to-Man Offensive Fine-Tuning" on page 4.

The playmaker must be able to deliver a strong overhead toss across the court to the highlighted player. The highlighted player, the best exterior shooter, starts at the ballside low position. He or she will launch an important shot from beyond the arc.

Big players set solid, staggered screens for the highlighted shooter. They angle their picks to allow the shooter to break free on the weakside near the wing. The picks must be stationary, and players may need to allow one step for the targeted defender. The success of the screens set by the big players determines whether the team achieves the goal of the play. The throw-in goes to a big player if the inbounder cannot deliver it to the main shooter or if a three-pointer is not necessary.

PHILLY

No playbook of mine would be complete without a play named in honor of my hometown. I com-posed the motion to take advantage of the entire half-court. The play is most effective if the ball begins on the offensive side of midcourt above the foul line extended. Two- or three-point field goals may develop as a result of this play.

Personnel

One post player is the mainstay of the team's inside offensive attack, and the other must possess some skills on the perimeter. The post player playing on the periphery must be able to shoot the ball from 18 to 20 feet. The point guard must have the capacity to shoot the ball from distance. The other two perimeter players ought to be quality outside shooters.

Scoring

The main shooter may have a shot attempt either from the strongside corner or from above the top of the key. The inbounder (the playmaker) may secure a three-point jumper from the ballside corner or on the offside above the foul line extended. The other outside player could receive a skip pass for a jump shot on the weakside periphery. One big player is isolated low for a potential inside shot. The other post player might acquire a shot either from the strongside corner or from out front above the key.

Execution

The lead guard (G) is the inbounder (figure 16.15). Post players (B2 and B1) are at the elbows. The ballside post player (B2) is better in the paint; the weakside post player (B1) is stronger from the periphery. The best perimeter shooter (S1) starts at the weakside block on the lane. The other shooter (S2) is on the ballside baseline just inside the three-point arc.

S2 moves in toward the lane by the strongside block to establish a pick. Simultaneously, the big players come together to plant a double screen in the lane for S1. S1 exploits the double screen and heads to the top of the key, ready for the inbounds pass. After S1 uses the double pick, B1 runs off S2's screen to the ballside corner, awaiting a possible entry pass.

If the first pass goes to S1 out front, B2 moves to pick for S2, allowing S2 to race to an exterior location near the three-point line on the far side of the court. B1 moves up to screen for the inbounder (G). G fades to the same-side corner.

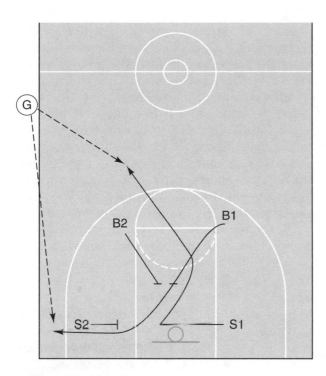

Figure 16.15 Philly.

S1 can shoot, pass to S2 or G on the perimeter for shots, toss directly to B2 as B2 steps to the ball, or fling the ball to B1, who is coming to the ball after setting the back pick.

When the inbounds pass goes to B1 in the ballside corner, B2 still screens for S2. S2 stays relatively close to the baseline as he or she races to the weakside periphery. At the same time, S1 picks for the inbounder (G), allowing G to dart to an area near the top of the key slightly to the weakside. B1 can shoot, dump the ball inside to B2 as B2 comes to the ball after setting a pick, throw a skip pass to G or S2 for an exterior shot, or toss to S1 as S1 heads to the ball after G uses his or her pick.

The play can begin in another way. Instead of coming up off the double screen set by the big players to the top of the key, S1 fakes the action and instead races off a single screen set by S2 to the ballside corner. B1 reacts by popping up to the top of the key using a single pick set by B2. Therefore, S1 and B1 exploit the screens just as before except that they switch destinations. The play continues as previously described.

Keys

See the segments about screening between post and perimeter players, setting a screen, using a pick, double screen, and pinning the de-fender in "Man-to-Man Offensive Fine-Tuning" on page 4.

Teams use the Philly play to score. The play begins from the offensive side of a sideline above the foul line.

The point guard can assume the role of the main shooter. Another perimeter teammate handles the throw-in.

The primary shooter determines the movements the other players will perform. He or she can fake running off the double screen set by the post players in the lane and instead use a single pick to head to the ballside corner or vice versa. The other players react to his or her choice.

The inbounder throws the ball to the player in the ballside corner or the player near the top of the key. The player who does not receive the pass always screens for the inbounder.

The two players who screen initially (one post player in the double pick and a perimeter player who sets a single screen) pick between them after the ball is in play. The big player always sets the screen. He or she then seals the defender and works to obtain a low-post position for a post feed and scoring chance.

When the inbounder sends the ball to the ballside corner, the two teammates heading to the offside by using the screens must keep sufficient space between them. The player with the ball in the corner uses a two-handed overhead pass to send the ball to either teammate on the weakside.

Players should not ignore the post player who remains in the foul-lane area. If he or she is open, the ball should go inside. The big player who goes out to the perimeter needs to know his or her exact shooting limits. The coach establishes the player's range and sets limits for other players as needed.

This play generates several shooting opportunities from deep on the periphery. Players realize that this means the big player inside is well isolated. A pass to the interior should provide a good scoring chance in the paint.

EIGHT PLAY

The eight play is a man-to-man play that can be effectively adjusted to attack zone defenses. For this reason, it was a favorite of mine when I was concerned about what defense my players would confront. The only difference between the two versions is the addition of one scoring movement against man-to-man. The coach can call the play whenever the team is inbounding the ball from a sideline in the midcourt region. Squad members recognize the defense and react accordingly. The team is trying to score.

Personnel

The play requires two strong outside shooters, a big player who is able to score in the paint, and a point guard who has the ability to hit a shot off the dribble.

Scoring

One outside player receives a shot in the offside corner. The primary shooter obtains a scoring opportunity from the same area. The point guard shoots off the dribble after using a pick set by a big player. The screener may have an interior shot by making a roll to the hoop after screening on the ball.

Execution

The best perimeter shooter is the inbounder (S1) (figure 16.16). The point guard (G) starts at the weakside elbow. The premier big player (B2) is at the ballside elbow. The other post player is at the offside block (B1). The other exterior

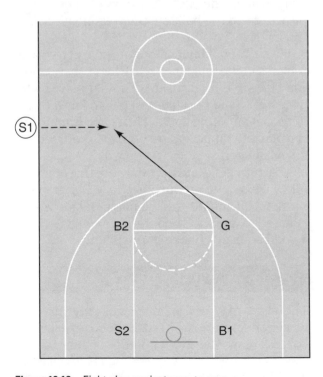

Figure 16.16   Eight play against man-to-man.

shooter (S2) starts at the strongside box. The point guard (G) gets free from the defender to catch the entry pass from S1. The inbounds pass must go to the lead guard (G).

After catching the inbounds pass, the point guard (G) dribbles away from the inbounder. B1 sets a baseline screen for S2 to use to get open in the ballside corner for a shot attempt. The secondary shooter (S2) times his or her move off the pick to coincide with the playmaker's arrival at the side. Meanwhile, the inbounder (S1) hurries to replace S2 at the near box on the foul lane. He or she moves there as quickly as possible. If S2 is not open for the pass from G for a shot, he or she moves in to set a double screen with B1. The ball goes to S2 only if a shot is possible. After S2 and B1 set the double pick, S1 uses it to gain an opening in the opposite corner. This is the playmaker's next pass option. The final option is for the point guard (G). If the ball handler recognizes that a pass to S1 is not possible, he or she reverse dribbles to use a screen set by a big player (B2) near the top of the key. G may have a shot off the dribble. He or she may also bounce a pass to B2 as B2 rolls to the basket.

Keys

See the segments about setting a screen, slipping a screen, using a pick, back pick, double screen, and pinning the defender in "Man-to-Man Offensive Fine-Tuning" on page 4.

The eight play takes 8 to 10 seconds to complete.

The point guard has to work to break free to catch the inbounds pass. The play comes to a standstill if the point guard does not receive the inbounds pass. After securing the ball, the lead guard dribbles away from the inbounder. He or she must make good decisions with the ball and deliver it to the teammate with the best chance of scoring. If the lead guard is the best outside shooter on the squad, switching him or her to the inbounder's position is not necessary.

Players using the single or double screens along the baseline have to wait for the right time to use them. The secondary shooter exploits the single pick as soon as the point guard is in position to make a pass. After realizing that a pass is not coming from the playmaker, the secondary shooter moves toward the lane to set a twin pick with the big player. After the two are in position, the main shooter runs off the double pick to the ballside corner. The players planting the double screen stay together while facing into the lane.

The playmaker keeps the dribble active as the two shooters hustle to the ballside corner. If neither shooter is open for a shot, the playmaker reverses the dribble and uses a screen set by the big player near the top of the key. The playmaker is aware of the five-second closely guarded rule. If he or she is not careful, a violation could occur. When the point guard uses the screen on the ball, an entire side of the floor is at his or her disposal. The point guard shoots or bounces a pass to the big player (screener) who is heading to the basket on a roll.

T FORMATION PLAYS

When I sat down to create some sideline inbounding plays, I first chose a formation—in this case, the T formation. The following two plays use the T formation as the initial set. These plays are effective against man-to-man defenses when inbounding the ball from a sideline at midcourt. I liked the options that were available from the alignment.

TEE NUMBER 1

I used the tee number 1 motion to score and clinch a major upset in overtime on the road when I was at King's College. The ball is inbounded near midcourt. A scoring payoff is possible.

Personnel

The inbounder should be a good scorer who has the ability to throw an effective skip pass. The other perimeter shooter should have some athletic ability and be capable of lifting off his or her feet to catch a pass sent to the basket.

Scoring

One outside player could receive an inbounds pass while heading to the hoop. The inbounder throws the ball to a big teammate and then races off him or her for a return pass and layup.

Execution

Players begin in a T set as shown in figure 16.17.

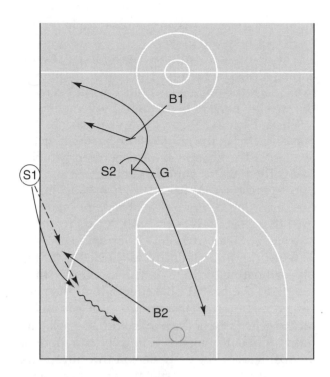

Figure 16.17 Tee number 1 play.

The best shooter or scorer on the squad is the inbounder (S1). Two big players (B1 and B2) and the point guard (G) form a line along the ballside foul-lane line. The lead guard (G) is directly in front of the inbounder (S1), B1 is toward half-court, and B2 is near the basket. Post players can be in either position. The other perimeter player (S2) also starts directly in front of the inbounder (S1) in the middle of the ballside sideline. Thus, S1 (the inbounder), S2, and G are also in a line, forming a *T*.

The lead guard (G) moves first to back pick for S2. S2 exploits the screen and loops to the basket. As soon as G sets the screen, B2 sprints to the ball in anticipation of an entry pass from S1. The inbounder tries to send the ball to S2 or B2 initially. B1 screens the screener (G) and steps to the ball. G and B1 are the last two options for the inbounds pass. If S1 directs the throw-in to B2, S1 immediately cuts off B2 to receive a return pass for a scoring attempt.

Keys

See the discussions of setting a screen and using a pick in "Man-to-Man Offensive Fine-Tuning" in chapter 1 on page 4.

Players check their starting positions to make sure that they form a T. They should maintain sufficient space between themselves, at least 8 to 10 feet between players.

The point guard initiates the action by establishing a back screen for the player directly in front. After the point guard sets the back screen, the two big players begin their movements.

The inbounder throws the skip pass to the player racing to the hoop off the back pick if it is available. The big player moving directly to the ball is the next inbounds preference; a scoring opportunity is present on toss to cutter. Finally, the throw-in goes to either the point guard or the other post player out front. A toss to either one will not lead to a scoring situation.

When the inbounder tosses the ball to the big player busting to the ball, the inbounder then bursts to the basket off either side of the pass receiver. The passer fakes one way before racing off the other side of the player with the ball. The pass recipient pivots, trying to create more of an obstacle for the defender on the cutter. The timing of the pivot is crucial; any contact with the defender must be legal. A pivot that occurs too early makes it easier for the defender to adjust coverage. After the inbounder receives the return pass, he or she heads to the goal for a score.

TEE NUMBER 2

This is the second play to use the T formation. I like the scoring movements that are possible. As long as the team is inbounding the ball from the midcourt region of a sideline, the play is useful. The play generates a scoring outcome.

Personnel

A big player with the athletic ability to catch a ball thrown near the basket is essential. One of the better exterior shooters must be able to throw a lob pass at the hoop from a sideline.

Scoring

The big player who starts the action is the main target as he or she heads to the basket.

Execution

Players begin in the T set, as shown in figure 16.18. The lead guard (G), another perimeter player (S2), and the featured big player (B1) are in a row even with the extended ballside foul

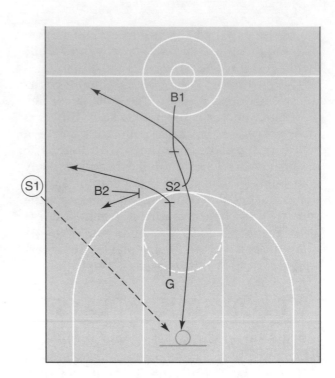

Figure 16.18 Tee number 2 motion.

lane line. S2 is directly in front of the inbounder (S1). The point guard (G) is near the hoop. B1 is closest to the opponent's basket. The other post player (B2) begins at the halfway mark between and in line with S2 and S1.

B1 makes the first move by screening for S2, allowing S2 to slice toward the backcourt. S1 does not want to throw to S2, at least not yet. He or she may do so later if the inbounder cannot get the ball to one of the other three players. The lead guard (G) screens the screener (B1). B1 cuts to the basket, anticipating a pass at the hoop from the inbounder (S1). S1 tosses the entry pass up toward the front of the rim, allowing B1 to jump and snatch it. B2 picks for the screener (G) and steps back to the ball opposite G's cut. S1's next two pass options are to G and to B2. One of them should be open so that the throw-in does not have to go to S2 in the backcourt.

Keys

Players align in a T formation with approximately 8 to 10 feet between them. The most athletic big player starts in the spot farthest from the offensive basket. He or she will use his or her size and athletic ability to catch the ball thrown at the hoop.

Players must recognize that they perform their movements sequentially. The big player nearest half-court screens first. Next, the point guard back screens for the screener. Finally, the big player in front of the ball picks for the playmaker.

The inbounder's first choice is to pass the ball to the post player racing toward the basket off the back pick. A dunk directly from the pass is possible, although it is more likely that the big player will jump to secure the pass and land before attempting a shot. When the ball is inbounded closer to midcourt or at a backcourt sideline location, any pass to the cutter is not going to be a lob. The throw-in will have to lead the cutter, who has raced ahead of a defender. The cutter makes the catch and completes the drive to the goal.

PLAYS TO ATTACK ZONES

Fewer options are available against teams defending in zones than against opponents who are guarding man-to-man. Safe plays to ensure that the team can throw the ball in play are not necessary. Zone defenses should not cause inbounding problems. Occasionally, the coach may elect to try to score. When time is running out and the throw-in is from a sideline, scoring quickly is necessary. To score against a zone defense on a sideline inbounds play, teams can use one of the five plays that follow. Of course, an alternative that is always available is to toss the ball in play and then run a zone offense. The throw-in should take place at a point no more than 10 feet into the backcourt. If the throw-in goes to any site beyond that, the play run should be a safe throw-in followed by execution of a zone offense.

SIDELINE WEAKSIDE

The sideline weakside play is my favorite movement against zone defenses. Players send the action in one direction and then throw across the court to a shooter. Skip passes are effective ways to combat zones. A team can use the play when they are inbounding the ball from a sideline near midcourt to the offensive foul line extended, the defense is in a zone, and the team needs to score quickly.

Personnel

The inbounder should be a strong outside scoring threat. A three-point opportunity is likely to develop. The other two perimeter players should be proficient at throwing skip passes.

Scoring

A toss to a big player who is diving low to the ballside is feasible. The main target is the inbounder, who moves to the offside corner for a shot of at least 18 feet. The weakside post player secures a pass if the defender he or she is screening cheats over the screen too soon in an attempt to guard the shooter in the corner. The weakside post may also gain a post feed from the recipient of the skip pass.

Execution

The main shooter (S1) inbounds the ball. The better big interior player (B2) is at the ballside block on the foul lane. The three remaining players (B1, S2, and G) operate above the foul line and carry out whatever motions they choose to free themselves for the toss in from the sideline (figure 16.19). Because of the zone defense, a direct pass to B2 is highly unlikely. If possible, the point guard (G) should receive the entry

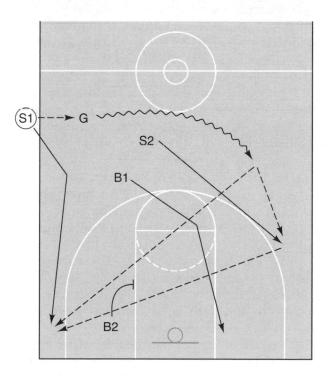

Figure 16.19   Sideline weakside motion.

pass, unless he or she is the best shooter on the squad and therefore the inbounder.

After S1 inbounds the ball, the action heads away from the original sideline. The point guard (G) dribbles to the other side of the floor. The post player out front (B1) dives to the vacant box on the lane as the other perimeter player (S2) races out wide below the foul line extended opposite the inbounder. After inbounding the ball, S1 slides down to the same-side corner. As the motion flows away, B2 sets a screen on the defender with weakside responsibility in the zone. S1 might receive a skip pass for a jumper from G or S2. The team is also prepared to send the ball inside to B2. The offside defender might cheat over the weakside screen to defend the skip pass and leave B2 open for a direct pass from G or S2. When the pass goes to S1, B2 reads the pass, moves to seal the zone defender with ballside low-post coverage, and anticipates a feed from S1.

Keys

See "Zone Offensive Fine-Tuning" in chapter 5 on page 84 for all relevant topics, especially using skip passes.

The coach should review the various types of zones and point out which player is the weakside defender in each. Big players must learn to recognize coverage responsibilities on the offside. Limited teaching time is required. The key to the play is to get the flow to go one way to suck the offside defender into the lane and then throw the ball across the court over the pick.

The point guard should handle the ball initially. The three players above the foul line motor to the side away from the inbounder to create a flow in that direction. The second perimeter player maintains 10- to 15-foot spacing on the periphery ahead of the lead guard. The playmaker looks to the inbounder, who is dropping to the offside corner. The point guard may need to toss the ball to the closest exterior player for the crosscourt pass to be effective.

The inbounder hustles to the same-side corner behind a pick set by a big player. The inbounder acts as if he or she is joining the flow opposite and then bolts down to the corner behind the weakside screen.

The main shooter receives the ball from one of two fellow perimeter players. Both perimeter players must be capable of throwing the two-handed overhead pass.

When the pick on the weakside defender is set and the defender is hung up in the lane, a crosscourt pass is appropriate. If the screener is able to spring open for a direct pass, the defender had probably gambled and raced over the offside pick early. The player with the ball may need to ball fake before seeing the post player pop open, especially if the passer thinks that the defender is decoying and looking to intercept the skip pass. The passer reads the weakside defenders. If they are fixated on the skip pass, the screener may be open.

The post player planting the weakside screen on a zone always steps in toward the lane as the ball heads to the same-side corner. He or she is preparing to pin a nearby zone defender. The post player contemplates a post feed from a teammate in the corner.

SIDELINE SCREEN

Instead of screening the weakside defender of a zone, another alternative is to pick a back-line defender. The sideline screen play is appropriate when the inbounding location is on a sideline above the offensive foul line extended and the backcourt cutoff point. The opponent is in a half-court zone defense. The coach has decided the team should make an effort to score.

Personnel

To take advantage of the motion of the play, an outstanding distance shooter is necessary.

Scoring

A toss might go to the high post for a shot or for a pass to one of three players along the baseline. The primary shooter (the inbounder) shoots from the corner away from the original inbounding spot after exploiting the pick set on the rear defender of the zone.

Execution

The better interior player (B2) is at the ballside block (figure 16.20). Because of the surrounding zone, a direct pass to B2 is not feasible. The other three players (G, S2, and B1) remain above the foul line extended and move as they desire. S1 is the inbounder and featured shooter. The inbounder (S1) should toss the ball to the lead guard (G) if possible, unless he or she is the

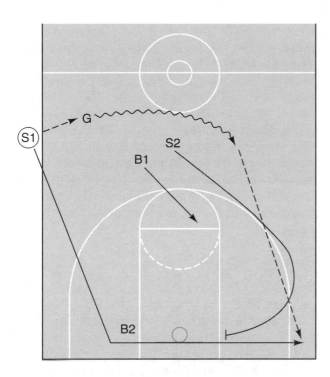

Figure 16.20 Sideline screen movements against an even-front zone.

best outside shooter on the team and thus the inbounder.

After S1 throws the ball in play, he or she darts to the baseline on the same side of the court. The point guard (G) dribbles to the opposite side. S2 runs ahead of G while staying wide. S2 eventually screens the back zone defender on his or her side. B1 fills the high post. S1 times the cut along the baseline with S2's screen. S1 races to the corner opposite the one where the inbounds pass originated. G passes to S1 for a quality shot attempt.

Keys

Refer to "Zone Offensive Fine-Tuning" in chapter 5 on page 84.

The inbounder sends the ball to the lead guard most of the time. Occasionally, the point guard and an exterior player may change roles to give the defense a different look.

The three players out front all move away from the inbounder. The big player scampers to the far elbow. The two perimeter players stay behind the arc, spaced about 15 feet apart. The one in the lead hesitates until the ball and inbounder are in position before screening the back zone defender. After completion of the

entry pass, the inbounder darts to the same-side baseline near the block. He or she times the move to the opposite corner with the pick on the back-line defender. The baseline run commences when the ball is almost in position. The back player of the zone is picked just after the baseline runner reaches the strongside block.

When a defensive point extends out on half-court (for example, in a 1-3-1 zone), the point guard may have difficulty dribbling to the side away from where he or she received the inbounds pass. The team recognizes the problem and makes a simple adjustment. The perimeter player does not loop to set a screen on the back zone player away from the ball. Instead, he or she hustles to a spot on the other side of the defensive point so that the point guard can reverse the ball with a pass. The screener is the high-post player. The high post runs through the elbow to the exterior below the perimeter player almost to the arc before heading downward to set the pick. Communication between players occurs before they put the ball in play. They identify the defense and adjust their movements if there is a defensive point.

The player with the ball on the side away from the throw-in must get a defensive wing in an odd-front zone to guard him or her. Doing so allows a teammate to continue downward to screen the appropriate back-line defender. Against an even-front zone, the guard on the side away from the inbounds pass is the target.

A second way to run the play against an even-front zone is to run the point guard and other perimeter player to the periphery away from the inbounds pass. The exterior player is at a site several feet below the foul line extended. The pass goes to this player while the high post moves to screen the next defender below, who would provide corner coverage. The ball is passed to the main shooter in the corner after he or she has used the obstacle.

ZONE SPECIAL

Another way to secure shots against a zone defense is to overload a side on the periphery. The objective is purely mathematical—to outnumber the defenders in a given area. Teams use the zone special play when inbounding the ball from a sideline near midcourt. Players must be proficient shooters from the periphery.

Personnel

Ideally, all three perimeter players are strong outside shooters. One post player is the inbounder. If the inbounder is also an effective shooter from near the arc, the play will be more effective. The more exterior firepower a team has, the tougher the job of the defense.

Scoring

Any of four players on one half of the court could acquire a shot of at least 17 feet. The big player at the offside high post may gain a 15-foot shot if ignored by the zone.

Execution

Figure 16.21 shows how to overload a side against a zone defense. The better interior big player (B2) starts at the weakside box on the lane. The other post player (B1) is the inbounder. The three perimeter players begin evenly spaced in a line along the ballside extended foul-lane line. One shooter (S1) is at the block, the other shooter (S2) is at the elbow (these two could exchange spots), and the point guard (G) is out front near half-court.

The inbounder tosses the ball to the lead guard (G), who immediately dribbles outside

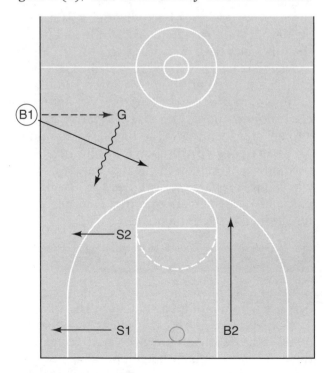

Figure 16.21   Zone special.

the three-point line and several feet above the foul line extended on the same side of the court. The inbounder (B1) loops around the pass receiver to a spot directly above the ballside elbow beyond the three-point arc. The big inside player (B2) darts to the weakside elbow. As the point guard dribbles, S2 pops out past the arc to a spot just below the foul line extended. S1 moves out to a deep-corner location. Four players are on the periphery on the same side of the half-court. They pass the basketball among themselves until one is open for a clear three-point shot.

Keys

See "Zone Offensive Fine-Tuning" in chapter 5 on page 84.

Ideally, the team has four good outside shooters. The more scoring threats a team has from the perimeter, the better. The four players on the exterior maintain enough space between one another to make it difficult for one defender to guard two offensive players. They pass the ball back and forth while looking for a shot. Players may have to put the ball on the floor to make a particular defensive player guard them. The amount of time allowed to pass the ball and create a shot is not unlimited. The coach should set a limit of 10 to 15 seconds before the squad begins executing a zone offense.

The shooters below the toss-in receiver scamper beyond the three-point line as the point guard puts the ball on the floor. The inbounder loops around the playmaker to a strongside position above the elbow.

The weakside post player slides up to the elbow to give the defense another player away from the hoop to defend. His or her main job is to rebound from the offside. But the defense could leave him or her open for a 15-foot shot if the zone tilts to the side of the court that contains the majority of the offensive players.

SIDE BOX FOR ZONE

The side box format can be used against man-to-man or zone defenses. I incorporated the picking action on a back defender with the outnumber approach to score against zones. The ball is inbounded within the appropriate throw-in area from a sideline. The opponent is in a half-court zone defense, and the coach wants to assault the zone immediately.

Personnel

The two big people must be productive scorers around the hoop, and one outstanding exterior shooter is mandatory. The other perimeter people are strong assets if they are capable shooters from the three-point line.

Scoring

Any of the three exterior shooters could gain a shot of at least 17 feet. Big players receive shots from the high-post to midpost area or the low-post to baseline area.

Execution

The point guard (G) is the inbounder (figure 16.22). The big players are at the ballside elbow (B1) and about two feet outside the strongside block (B2). They may switch positions. The main outside shooter (S1) begins at the weakside box. The other perimeter player (S2) is at the offside elbow.

Two players make the initial moves to receive the entry pass. B1 pops straight out to the foul line extended, and S2 sprints out top well above the top of the key and slightly

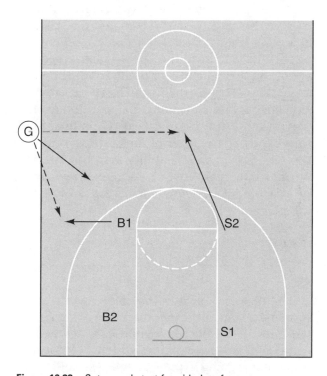

Figure 16.22 Setup and start for side box for zone.

to the ballside. The ball goes to either player. The point guard (G) then steps inbounds to a spot between the two. Regardless of which player catches the toss-in, the next pass goes to the point guard (G). The big player on the outside (B1) heads toward the same-side box to screen the back zone player as the other post player (B2) slides up the lane line to the halfway mark. The shooter at the offside box (S1) runs off B1's pick to the ballside corner for a possible deep shot. Either the lead guard or the shooter could toss the ball inside the zone to either post player. One big player is at midpost, and the screener steps toward the baseline after the pick is used. All five players are on one side of the court. The lead guard (G) and the shooter at the top (S2) are secondary scoring options.

Keys

Refer to "Zone Offensive Fine-Tuning" on page 84.

The team's best distance shooter is at the block on the foul lane away from the ball to start. If the point guard is the top shooter, he or she begins at the offside block and another perimeter player handles the throw-in. The starting positions of the post players are interchangeable.

The big player making the initial move out to the foul line extended to catch the first pass must watch that he or she does not move too near the corner. The offensive team wants the back-line defender to stay close to the other post player at the ballside block. That arrangement sets up the defender for the pick.

Timing of movements is critical. The ball is always returned to the inbounder. Once the return pass is on its way to the point guard (the inbounder), the post player at the ballside wing heads down to pick the back zone player. The other big player slides up to midpost at the same time. The shooter at the offside box times his or her move so that he or she is rubbing off the screen just as it is planted. The destination is the strongside corner. The screener dashes to the baseline (three to eight feet off the lane) and faces out immediately after the screened defender moves out toward the corner.

A ball fake from the lead guard to the shooter in the corner could cause one or more defenders to move when they are not supposed to and leave one of the inside players free. Players on the periphery look to either post player if no outside shot is available. Players look to toss the ball to take advantage of having all five players on one side of the floor if the main shooter using the screen does not take a shot.

If the coach is unsure whether the defending team is going to play a zone or man-to-man defense, this play is a good call because it provides numerous choices from the same side box format against man-to-man.

EIGHT PLAY FOR ZONE

This is the first sideline out-of-bounds play I ever used against zones. I believe I came across it in a coaching periodical when I first began coaching junior high basketball. The play was still helpful when I coached at King's College. The play is suitable when the team recognizes that they are facing a half-court zone defense, the throw-in is from an appropriate location on a sideline, and they want to score quickly.

Personnel

The play requires two productive exterior shooters, usually from three-point range.

Scoring

A pass to the high-post player could conceivably produce a shot. One perimeter player may have a shot from the corner opposite the inbounder. The inbounder (the primary outside threat) may secure a shot from the same location as the previous player. Screeners could receive passes inside if the zone defense leaves them open.

Execution

The squad's premier distance shooter (S1) takes the ball out of bounds. One post player (B2) is at the weakside box on the lane. The other (B1) is at the high post. The point guard (G) is above the top of the key. The other perimeter player (S2) begins at the ballside block.

The point guard (G) must break free to catch the entry pass. He or she has no choice. The playmaker dribbles to the other side of half-court. The first option is to pass to S2, who is racing to the corner away from the throw-in. S2 uses B2's pick on the back zone player. B2 may start by stepping off the lane several feet in the

initial alignment. He or she moves inward to set the screen as soon as G hits the top of the key with the dribble. After releasing the ball, the inbounder (S1) scurries to replace S2 at the closest box on the lane (figure 16.23).

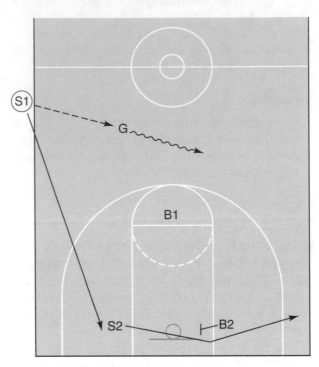

Figure 16.23   Start of eight play versus zones.

In the final stage of the play, S2 is not open to receive the pass from the lead guard (G). Once S2 knows that a pass is not going to come, he or she heads toward the lane to plant a second screen on the back player of the zone. S1 comes around two screeners (S2 and B2) to the strongside corner and is the next pass option for the playmaker. If the point guard (G) is unable to throw the ball to either of the first two options, then the last pass possibility is to the interior. A toss to the high post or a screener low could be feasible if the defense loses track of one of the players.

Keys

Refer to "Zone Offensive Fine-Tuning" on page 84.

The play is basically the same against zone or man-to-man, although there are some subtle variations. The play is a good call, however, if the coach does not know which defense the opponent is going to play. Coaches should teach players the different types of zones they could confront. The team should know the specifics associated with each defense and the particular defender or defenders who they will need to screen.

The point guard must get open to catch the entry pass. He or she immediately takes the ball to the opposite side of the floor. Problems can occur if a defensive point out top is trying to prevent a dribble reversal. Once the big player in the high post recognizes the problem, he or she pops out opposite the lead guard and the ball is reversed with a pass. The high post is then left vacant. If there is no defensive point, the dribble reversal should suffice. The offensive team wants the strongside defensive wing in an odd-front zone or the guard in an even-front zone to defend the player with the ball as the screening action ensues below. That way, the back-line player of the zone is exposed for the pick.

The first shooter comes to the ballside corner, using a big player's screen on the back defender of the zone. The pass goes to the first shooter only if he or she has an open shot. Otherwise, the ball handler out front holds the ball and waits for the first shooter to race back into the lane. The first shooter actually tries to lure the back defender in toward the lane. A pick may

not be necessary; getting the back-line defender to move inward may suffice. A slight bump by the first shooter or the big player setting the original screen may help create an obstacle for the back-line defender. The primary shooter rushes to the ballside corner in anticipation of a pass reception and jump shot as soon as the defender's position is most advantageous.

The ball would go to the high post only after the player out front with the ball determines that the second shooter is not open or that screeners are not available for a direct pass. The high post catches the ball and faces the basket. Three offensive players should be below, stretched on the same side of the court (just in the lane, midbaseline, and corner).

The timing of the shooters' movement to the ballside corner is critical. The first one goes as soon as the ball approaches the top of the key when the opponent is in an even-front zone. Versus an odd-front zone, the first shooter goes when the pass heads to the high post stepping out opposite the lead guard. The second player runs after the first shooter gets the back defender moving in toward the foul lane at least six to eight feet. Screeners step to the ball, looking for a possible pass from the player out top after the shooters race past on their way to the corner.

CHAPTER 17

Breaking Presses

I have used all of the worthy press-breaking offenses in this chapter at some point in my career as a basketball coach. Early in my career I looked at presses with trepidation. I felt that handling a full-court press was critical for success. Later, I felt so confident in my team's ability to counter a press that the press no longer generated much concern.

Teams can use five of the offenses to attack full- or three-quarter-court presses that are using zone or man-to-man defense. Four additional plays are specifically designed to attack man-to-man full-court pressure. Two offenses can be used against a half-court zone-trapping defense.

Breaking Presses Offensive Fine-Tuning

Several specific points are integral to attacking a press successfully. Coaches should address the following important techniques during the instruction of breaking pressure defenses.

Throwing the Ball Deep

The inbounder places his or her shoulders perpendicular to the baseline (parallel to the sideline) when heaving the ball deep from the end line. The back foot is on the same side as the throwing hand to provide a strong base from which to hurl the ball long with authority. This technique also permits the inbounder to step into the throw. The lead foot cannot touch the baseline or sideline. The inbounder may elect to run the baseline after the opponent completes a successful field goal or a free throw drops through the net. He or she might step slightly

back off the inbounding spot to put more room between the throw-in and the defender.

Clearing Out

Clearing out is an effective tactic whenever the defense applies man-to-man pressure. The other four players allow the player with the ball to use a maximum amount of space. They swiftly vacate the backcourt while watching to make sure that their defenders do not race to engage in a trap or run-and-jump action against the ball handler. The ball handler exhibits patience against a man-to-man press. The player waits for his or her teammates to clear before dribbling the ball up the court. The only exception is if the lane forward is clear after a pass reception. If the coach is not confident in a player's ability to handle the basketball against pressure, then he

(continued)

(continued)

or she instructs one or more players to secure possession of the ball in the backcourt. Teammates clear out after an acceptable ball handler gains control of the ball.

Executing Against Double Teams

Handling double teams or run-and-jump maneuvers from an opponent is critical to combating pressure defenses successfully. The player with the ball recognizes potential trouble spots such as down a sideline or turning back to the defense. The middle of the floor is the most difficult area for the defense to trap because the ball handler can make shorter passes and therefore has more options. The ball handler keeps his or her head up and the dribble alive if possible. The ball handler avoids turning his or her back to the defenders. The reverse dribble invites traps. Any player trapped by the defense regularly seeks to split defenders if possible. Players away from the ball hook up in open areas in front of the ball whenever their defenders leave to become involved in a trap, run-and-jump move, or defensive rotation. Players do not stand and wave their arms, waiting for the ball to come. Once the ball handler makes a successful pass out of the double team, the team has a numbers advantage. Players attack the basket unless they are holding the ball to protect a lead or the coach wants to keep the tempo slower.

Using the 2-1-2 Press-Break Formation

Teams employ the standard 2-1-2 press-break formation against any full-court or three-quarter-court zone press. The configuration has a built-in pressure release. The weakside deep player reads the amount of pressure on the ball handler and does one of two things. If the intensity of the trap is light, the weakside deep player is likely to remain on the long diagonal from the ball handler. If the pressure is high, he or she races down the sideline area to the gap between the safety player and the middle player. He or she gets open for the player under duress. The player in the middle is active. He or she seeks out the open area ahead of the ball, generally within the lane area. The player deep on the strongside sideline may sprint to the ball if the ball handler is in trouble. Otherwise, the two deep players remain ahead of the player in the center.

Receiving a Pass

When receiving a pass against pressure, coaches tell players to "run over the ball." This directive means that they come meet the pass from a teammate. Squad members do not wait for the ball to reach them. By decreasing the distance that a pass must travel, players reduce the likelihood that a defender will shoot the gap and intercept or deflect the ball.

Getting the Ball to the Middle of the Floor

Against zone presses, coaches stress getting the ball to the middle of the floor, where a trapping defense is most vulnerable. The player operating in the center of the floor in advance of the ball is a high-priority target. The team looks to send the ball to that location. The middle player remains active and finds an open spot. He or she "runs over the ball" to decrease the length of the toss and reduce the chance of interference by the defense. After the player secures the ball, he or she turns to face the offensive basket and looks to pass ahead (usually down either sideline) if possible. The player does not dribble until he or she has made a pass evaluation. If the pass is not available, the ball handler is free to advance with the dribble. The only time it is appropriate for the player to put the ball on the floor while making a quick turn is after a defender tries for an interception or deflection and misses. In that case, the player in the middle is able to dribble immediately while heading to the offensive basket. He or she attacks in anticipation of getting a quality shot.

REGULAR

The regular press-break offense was my number one weapon against teams that tried to apply full-court pressure. This offense uses a method of quick inbounding. Simply stated, the offense attempts to beat a press before it can get started. Quick inbounding is closely connected with running teams.

While at Loyola Marymount University, Coach Paul Westhead took the idea of the quick inbound to the extreme. He wanted the ball up court within seconds, and most shots were out of a shooter's hands within 10 to 12 seconds. Scores were in the 120s, 130s, and even higher. Regular employs the same basic methodology. The coach decides how much to push the envelope.

Teams can use the regular press-break offense in any full-court inbounding situation. There are three potential uses:

1. Strictly as a quick-inbounds play to beat the establishment of a full-court zone or man-to-man press. In using the offense to break a press, the squad need not become a "run at all costs" type of club, but they must get the ball out of the basket swiftly and put it back in play immediately.

2. As an integral part of any up-tempo fast-break system.

3. In the latter stages of a contest when the club is trailing and wants to use as little time as possible to score.

The idea is to put the ball in play immediately after the opponent scores a basket (last free throw or a field goal). The play includes a dead-ball set for use in appropriate circumstances.

Personnel

The most important personnel requirement is having a post player who is a capable passer (including having the ability to throw the ball deep) and possesses sound ballhandling skills. This player is the inbounder. He or she should be fast enough to keep the ball from hitting the floor. The point guard is the strongest ball handler. The play requires another perimeter player with good ballhandling skills. When the third exterior player is a potent outside-scoring threat, the stress on the defense increases. The final player is the second post player and the weakest ball handler. The quickness of a team's personnel is a factor in the potency of the offense (the faster, the better).

Scoring

By beating a press, a team creates a numbers advantage. This edge manufactures shots on the offensive end of the floor. Layups to three-point shots are possibilities.

Execution

When the ball goes through the hoop, players sprint to their positions (see figure 17.1). The inbounder (B2) snatches the ball out of the net and steps behind the end line to the left of the basket facing the hoop. This side is most conducive for right-handed players (the spot to the right of the goal is better for left-handed players). The inbounder always looks deep first. He or she looks for the best outside shooter (S1) long down the ballside sideline. The inbounder completes that pass if it is available. The point guard (G) runs directly in front of the inbounder. The playmaker never goes too near the baseline.

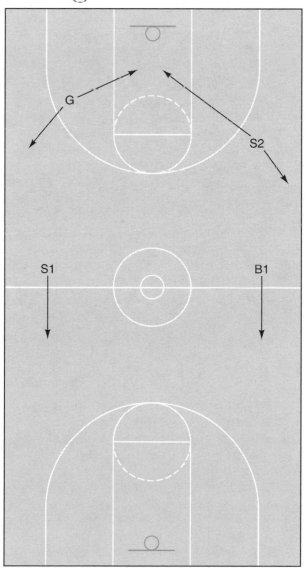

Figure 17.1 Positioning for the regular press-break offense.

He or she is the second target for the inbounder. The second-best ball handler on the team (S2) heads to a spot opposite the lead guard (G) on the weakside. He or she also keeps some distance from the baseline. The other inside player (B1) moves deep on the offside sideline. The inbounder's final two looks are short to the perimeter player (S2) and then long to the second post player (B1) away from the ball.

Figure 17.2 shows the initial pass being completed to the lead guard (G). Against a man-to-man press, players clear the backcourt and let the playmaker bring the ball up the court, standard practice against man-to-man pressure. Versus a zone press, S2 motors to a

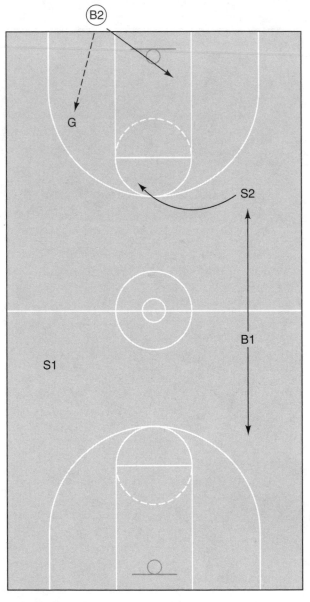

Figure 17.2 Throw-in to the point guard.

position in the middle of the floor in advance of the basketball. The inbounder (B2) steps across the baseline, staying behind G. He or she is the safety net. S1 remains ahead of the ball down the sideline. The deep player away from the ball (B1) must read the needs of the point guard. B1 can wait deep or may have to rotate straight up the sideline if G is under extreme pressure. B1 races to an open point between B2 and S2. The playmaker (G) can toss to B1 if necessary. The team stays in this basic 2-1-2 design when facing any zone press.

The starting pass may go to the weakside player (S2) instead of the point guard (G). Versus man-to-man pressure, the receiver (S2) focuses on delivering the ball to the lead guard if possible so that G can bring the ball up court. Players vacate the backcourt to give the ball handler room to operate. When opposed by a zone press, the playmaker establishes position in the middle of the court ahead of the ball, actively finding a vacant spot. The inbounder steps in play and lingers behind the ball handler (S2). The ballside deep player (B1) remains directly in front of the ball along the sideline past the player in the middle (G). The weakside deep player (S1) reads the defense and either stays ahead of the middle player on the weakside or runs between the inbounder and the player in the middle. Again, the squad is in the basic 2-1-2 set to attack zone pressure. Once either player nearest the inbounder (G or S2) receives the initial pass, the player who does not receive the ball becomes the player in the middle.

When the inbounder is having difficulty sending the ball to one of the closest players, the big player deep on the weakside (B1) recognizes the problem and yells, "Middle." The player nearest the offside baseline (S2) reacts by sliding to the center of the court. The weakside deep player sprints straight up the sideline to catch the inbounds pass. The player who slid to the middle sprints to a spot directly ahead of the ball along the sideline. The point guard (G) races to the vacant middle ahead of the basketball. The inbounder steps inbounds and acts as a safety net. The deep player opposite the pass receiver (S1) is in normal position to create the 2-1-2 press configuration.

The dead-ball set of regular is similar. Player positions stay the same except that the two players nearest the baseline stack in the center of the court. One begins just inside the three-point line, and the other (usually the lead guard) is about five to eight feet closer to half-court. Versus a zone press, one heads in one direction toward the baseline and the other moves opposite. The team is in normal regular set. If the defense is playing man-to-man, the player in front plants a screen for the playmaker directly above. The point guard cuts either left or right to the ball as the screener seals back opposite. The inbounder prefers to deliver the ball to the point guard. All other players clear out and let the ball handler dribble the ball up the court. The ball handler needs to be prepared for defenders to run and jump or blitz (trap). If one of these scenarios happens, any player whose defender leaves to become involved in a jump or blitz immediately goes to a vacant spot in front of the ball handler. Players recognize the situation and react swiftly. Against a man-to-man press, the two deep players are ready to fake long and sprint to the ball to catch the inbounds pass if necessary.

Keys

Refer to "Breaking Presses Offensive Fine-Tuning" earlier in the chapter on page 305. All six points are relevant.

The inbounder must grab the ball out of the net and quickly move to inbounding position every time the ball goes inside the rim. Regardless of why the team is using the quick inbounds, the inbounder is ready to pass within one or two seconds after the ball falls through the hoop. The ball does not hit the floor.

The inbounder's spot could depend on whether the player is left-handed or right-handed. The coach may want to determine the side according to the strength of the primary inbounder. My experience says that it is better to settle on one side, usually the right side, for inbounding. With practice, whether the inbounder is left-handed or right-handed becomes irrelevant. Players learn to use a reverse or inside pivot to set their feet parallel to the sideline. The inbounder's side affects the starting positions for the remainder of the squad. The point guard and main distance shooter are always on the ballside. The inbounder looks deep to the ballside first, then to the point guard directly in front, and finally to the weakside of the court (short then long).

Four players on the court dart to their starting spots every time the ball drops through the hoop, whether the opponent is pressing or not. This system prevents the adversary from using the element of surprise. No matter where the players are located on defense, once the ball drops through the rim they sprint to their assigned regions. Players find openings in their areas and anticipate securing the toss-in.

To attack zone presses, coaches and players must keep these points in mind:

- If the trap on the ball is aggressive, the ball handler may not be able to see the player long diagonally. Therefore, that player needs to move up the sideline to a more accessible location.
- The coach should drill players, especially the middle player, to catch the ball and turn immediately to view the court. Players cannot have tunnel vision. They dribble as necessary.
- Players must remember that it is faster to move the ball up court by passing it.
- A strong outside shooter should be at the offensive end. He or she secures quality scoring opportunities when the ball travels rapidly down the floor. Having a strong scoring threat at the offensive end may discourage an opponent from pressing.
- The inbounder always functions as the safety net. He or she stays relatively close and behind the player with the ball.

The inbounder must recognize a dead-ball situation. When appropriate, he or she communicates to teammates to start in the dead-ball set. Circumstances other than a dead-ball inbounding situation are possible. The ball may be knocked away or the inbounder may not get the ball to the inbounding spot swiftly enough. The inbounder recognizes when the formation organizes too slowly and the defense has time to apply the press. The inbounder responds by calling for the dead-ball set.

The two players nearest the baseline (the playmaker and the second-best ball handler) must not catch the inbounds pass too close to the end line. This locale is an excellent area for the opponent to use the trap, especially if it is near a corner.

The post player deep on the weakside knows when to call, "Middle." Rapid recognition is imperative. He or she cannot take long to react because a five-second violation against the inbounder is imminent.

DEEP

High school and college teams are best suited to using this radical approach to breaking full-court pressure. Physical maturity is necessary to deliver the basketball effectively from one end of the court to the other. I first came across the deep offensive set during my first year as head coach at King's College. Stonehill College used the deep offense when they confronted a full-court press. At first I did not embrace its unorthodox technique, but later I became a staunch advocate of the plan of attack because it worked. Teams can execute the play on any dead ball when they need to travel the length of the court against a pressing defense. Teams can also use it after a successful basket, but the inbounder does not rush to grab the ball out of the hoop. The inbounder should be able to complete a deep throw if necessary, and the offensive team wants to spread the defense to create more room for players to operate against a press.

Personnel

An interior player who is an effective passer should be the inbounder. He or she must be capable of throwing the ball long. An outstanding perimeter shooter is stationed deep and keeps the attention of defense in that vicinity. Two outside players should possess some quickness and sound ballhandling techniques. The final player is the other big player. He or she needs no special skills except the ability to catch a long pass.

Scoring

Shots are likely to crop up. The best perimeter shooter is near the offensive basket with one other teammate. The main shooter receives opportunities anywhere from behind the three-point line to five feet from the basket. The scoring abilities of the two deep players determine how long the opponent will press.

Execution

B2 is a post player with unequaled passing and ballhandling skills. B2's position in figure 17.3 is ideal for a right-hander. A left-handed player may want to go to the other side for the throw-in, although that is not necessary. If the inbounder's side changes, other personnel must flip sides as well. The two best ballhandling perimeter players (S2 and G) are positioned in a tandem, with S2 at the foul line and G approximately three to five feet beyond the top of the key. The ace outside shooter (S1) occupies the deep ballside slot. The other post player (B1) is opposite on the offside.

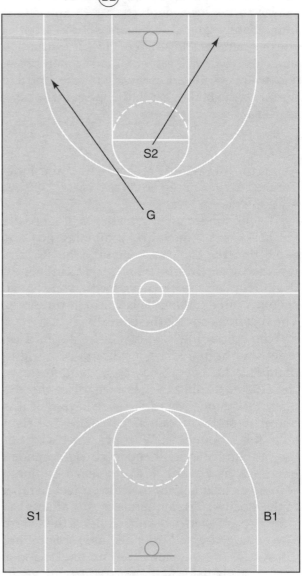

Figure 17.3   Starting set and movements for deep.

The inbounder (B2) initially looks long. If the defense is not covering sufficiently, he or she should throw the ball long. The inbounder may wish to fake to one player and then toss to another. G and S2 move to open areas to receive the initial pass (figure 17.3). They should not be too close to each other or move too near the baseline against a zone press. Against man-to-man pressure, S2 picks for G, who cuts to the ball. The deep players (S1 and B1) race to the inbounder only if B2 is having trouble inbounding the ball. The two long players are always prepared to get the ball whenever the pass comes in their direction. They do not wait for the ball to reach them.

If the ball goes to one of the two players near the baseline, the other player runs to an open area in the center of the court in advance of the ball. The inbounder steps in play opposite the pass receiver and remains slightly behind. Deep players stay long but are ready to race forward to help the ball handler if necessary. The pass receiver looks to throw deep if he or she can. Against a man-to-man press, other players clear the backcourt and allow the point guard (or any other designated player) to bring the ball up court.

Keys

See "Breaking Presses Offensive Fine-Tuning" on page 305.

When a coach first uses the offense, he or she may feel that the play is a high-risk gamble. All I can say is that coaches who try it, like it.

The offensive alignment gives players more room to work against a full-court press. More room means more holes to exploit. The team uses the added space to make it difficult for a pressing opponent.

The inbounder does not force a long pass, but the player needs to show the opponent that he or she is not afraid to throw long. A fruitful long toss keeps the opponent honest. If the inbounder ignores the long players, the opponent can cheat up and raise the productivity of its defensive press.

A shooter positioned long on the ballside gives the defense something to worry about. A scorer in this position can do some serious damage.

The players at the offensive end of the court make sound choices concerning shots. A press

is designed to increase the tempo of the game. They need to watch the flow of the game. The coach must not allow the tempo of the game to accelerate past his or her liking.

LOUISVILLE

I learned the Louisville plan of attack while I was an assistant coach at Widener University. It was my predominant press-break offense when I began my head-coaching career. One way to beat a full-court press is to outnumber the defense. After all, if the defense traps, one offensive player is unguarded. I like the four-on-three idea. Later in my coaching career, this press offense became a specialty piece. I would use it occasionally under certain circumstances. The methods described in regular and deep became my primary approaches to defeat pressure.

Teams use Louisville only in dead-ball inbounding situations. The squad must get into the set each time a press is present or expected. The coach may wish to save Louisville for a crucial full-court inbounding situation late in a game. Louisville is extremely effective when the defense is making it difficult to inbound the ball. Lining the team four across the width of the court improves the likelihood of a successful toss-in against intense defensive pressure.

Personnel

Two big players must be capable of handling the ball well. The three perimeter players should possess strong passing and ballhandling skills. Everyone is actively involved in the execution of the offense.

Scoring

Although an acceptable shot could appear on the offensive half of the court, the primary goal of the Louisville play is to bring the ball up the floor without committing a turnover. Success is judged by lack of turnovers, not points scored.

Execution

One peripheral player (S2) is the inbounder (figure 17.4). After the opponent scores, the inbounder can run the baseline if necessary. The inbounder cannot move along the baseline in other dead-ball inbounding situations.

The other four players are stretched across the court at approximately the top of the key. This starting point is crucial and helps create space for player movement. Big players (B2 and B1) are on each end of the line. The better ball handler (B2 in this case) is always on the ballside. Post players move on vertical planes as necessary. They can fake toward the ball and sprint long or vice versa. They hang in their respective lanes along the sidelines. The other two exterior players are lane-width apart in the middle of the floor. The ballside player (S1) screens for his or her partner (G, the point guard) and steps back to the ball. A pick may not be compulsory against zone presses. I have also put these two players in a tandem in the center of the court with about five to eight feet between them. G and S1 have the center of the floor in which to work.

Another motion option is available to the two players in the middle of the court against man-to-man defense. B1 and B2 do their normal jobs. As the ballside perimeter player goes to pick for a teammate, he or she cuts it short and hustles long, anticipating a pass from the inbounder. No more than one player heads deep before the throw-in. Two post players stay in their assigned lanes. Players must read the movements of their teammates.

When the inbounder completes the opening pass to a big player (B2 in figure 17.5), the

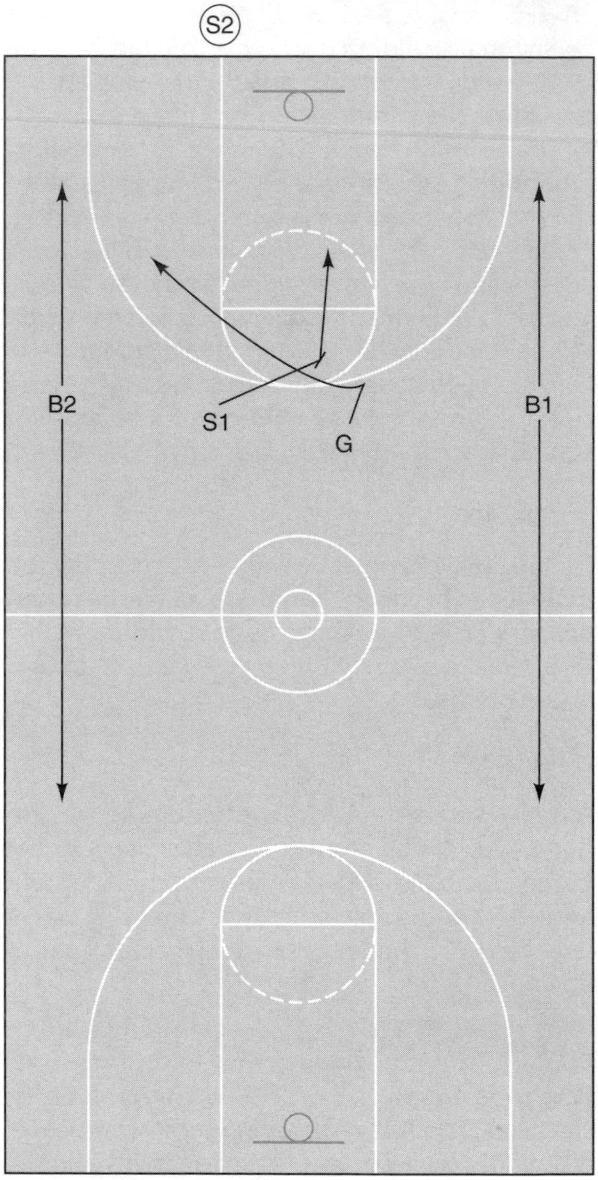

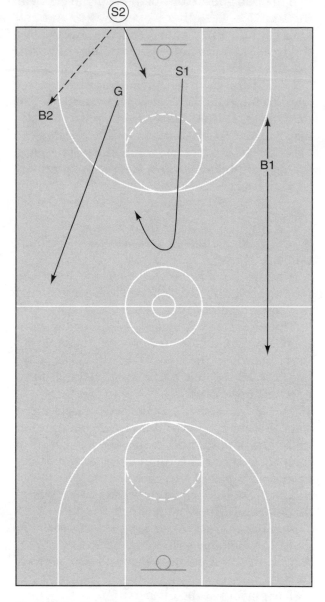

Figure 17.4 Louisville set and inbounding motion.

Figure 17.5 Throw-in goes to the ballside big player.

inbounder (S2) steps in play to act as a safety net. He or she stays close behind the ball handler. The player nearest the ballside sideline (G in figure 17.5) runs to a spot directly ahead of the basketball. The other exterior player (S1) finds a vacant area in the middle of the court in advance of the ball. The big player away from the ball (B1) moves up or down depending on the defensive pressure. If the defense applies a strong trap on B2, B1 races into the gap between S1 and S2. A long, diagonal pass would be difficult to see or complete because of the stress on the ball. By stepping toward the player being trapped, B1 helps the ball handler. If the double team on the ball handler is timid, B1 can stay at the long, diagonal position.

When the ball goes to a player in the center of the court, the passer and safety net stay behind the pass receiver. The player in the middle catches, turns, and looks down the floor. He or she looks to cast the ball to either outside player ahead of the ball. If the area is void of defenders, the player in the center can dribble up court, but he or she must be aware of the potential of the defense to sneak up from behind and tip the ball away. Teammates provide a warning if a defender is in hot pursuit.

Figure 17.6 illustrates movements that happen when the ball is hurled up a sideline. In this case, the ball travels from B2 to G. The middle player (S1) reacts quickly and sprints to a spot directly beyond the ball on the sideline. The safety net (S2) hustles to an open site in the center of the court ahead of the ball. The passer (B2) is the new safety net. His or her place is behind and opposite the pass receiver (G). The other deep player (B1) runs down the sideline. All the motion accomplishes the basic 2-1-2 press-break set.

Keys

Refer to "Breaking Presses Offensive Fine-Tuning" on page 305. All six points are applicable.

The offense looks to attack the defense and does not let the defense instill fear or hesitation. The coach informs the team precisely what he or she expects of them. Should they be aggressive and constantly looking to score, or should they just advance the ball to half-court without a turnover?

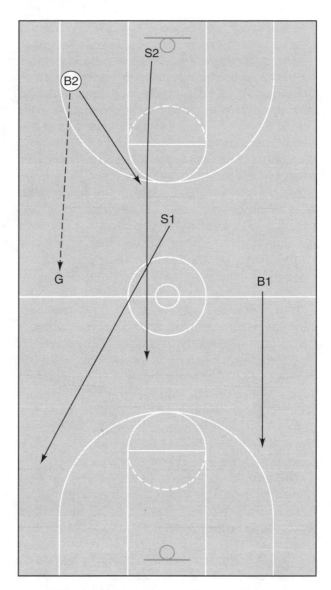

Figure 17.6 Ball thrown up the sideline in Louisville.

The inbounder must be aware of the possibility of running the baseline. He or she knows when it is mandatory to remain stationary. The weakest free-throw shooter should be the inbounder late in a game. The ballside big player should be the better foul shooter of the two post players.

Not all players can go deep at once. Players must work together to ensure that only one player sprints long initially. Breaking long is more effective against man-to-man pressure. Against man-to-man pressure, the team gets the ball into the hands of the point guard. The coach decides if any other teammates are permitted to handle the basketball. The other players clear the backcourt. Players are ready to combat defensive traps or run-and-jump maneuvers.

The four players lined up across the court have to stay in their respective lanes when getting open to catch the initial pass. They maintain discipline. The team establishes the four-across line at a level at least even with the top of the key nearest the inbounder.

Against zone presses, the ballside perimeter player in the center may not have to screen for the other player in the middle. The two may be able to cut opposite each other. The two external players in the middle can form a stack, with one just above the foul line and the other three to five feet past the top of the key, instead of spacing themselves parallel to the baseline.

The team must make sound decisions at the end of the press break. Shot selection is important. The club needs to know what types of shots are acceptable and who is allowed to shoot.

Whenever a player receives a pass with his or her back to the hoop, he or she immediately turns and faces the offensive goal. Throwing the ball to an open teammate up court is the preferred way to advance the ball. If no one is open, a dribble attack is viable.

When a pass goes down a sideline, the player in the middle sprints to a site directly in front of the ball on the same sideline. The player acting as a safety net hustles to fill the center. The passer is the new safety net.

LOUISVILLE SPECIAL

Every coach has seen or used a gimmick to beat a press at one time or another. Louisville special takes advantage of the rule that allows the inbounder to move after the opponent puts a shot through the hoop. Louisville special springs the unexpected on the pressing team and is an excellent change-up to Louisville. Teams can use it only after the opponent has made a field goal or a free throw; otherwise, it is not a legal maneuver because the inbounder must be able to run the baseline. This offense is productive when the zone pressure on the inbounder is intense and an effective defender is harassing the ball, or when the defense is using a centerfielder (player protecting deep as teammates full front defensively) late in a game as part of its man-to-man full-court pressure.

Personnel

The inside player who inbounds should have sufficient passing and ballhandling skills. If a team is using the offense at the end of a game to counter face guarding, the initial inbounder (an outside player) is likely to shoot free throws after gaining control of the ball. He or she should be an effective foul shooter.

Scoring

The probability of a shot is small, although one could evolve because of a numbers advantage when the ball crosses midcourt. Accurate prediction of the location and length of any shot attempt is impossible.

Execution

The team is in the standard Louisville set (figure 17.7). After S2 is in position for the throw-in, the big player on the weakside (B1) runs out of bounds opposite S2. He or she is 15 to 20 feet from the passer. S2 flings the ball to B1 as soon as he or she is fully out of bounds (both feet on the floor). Delivering the pass too early risks a violation. On the throw to B1, S2 steps inbounds. The point guard (G) cuts to a spot near the foul line extended in front of B1. S1 goes deep along the same sideline near half-court. The other inside player (B2) moves on a vertical plane to get open to receive the toss-in if necessary.

If the first pass goes to the lead guard (G in figure 17.7), the inbounder (B1) steps in play opposite and behind the pass receiver. The original inbounder (S2) hustles to the middle past the pass recipient as the big player on the offside (B2) motors to a site based on the intensity of the defensive pressure. He or she is up if pressure is intense and long diagonal if tension is low.

When the throw-in goes to the original inbounder, the point guard moves to a vacant spot in the center of the court ahead of the ball. The inbounder steps in play away from the pass receiver and acts as a safety net. The offside big player and deepest perimeter player are past the player in the middle, but they are ready to move up if needed.

The inbounder could toss the pass to the post player on the weakside. The inbounder still remains behind the ball. The exterior player in

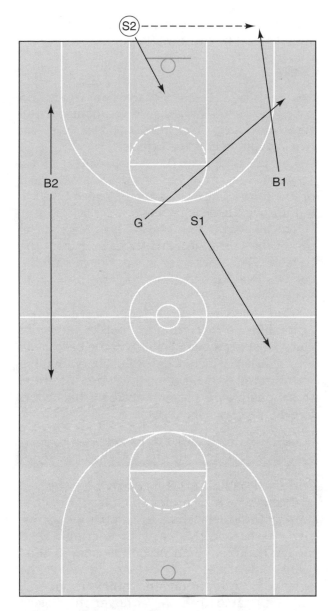

Figure 17.7 Formation and action in Louisville special.

The original inbounder must exhibit some patience. Both of the pass recipient's feet have to be out of bounds before he or she catches the ball. If his or her feet are in the air during the reception, it is a violation. All players, except the new inbounder, move as soon as the original inbounder throws the pass across the baseline.

Teams use the press attack primarily against zone presses when an extremely aggressive defender is working on the inbounder. When attacking a zone press, the offense transforms into a 2-1-2 alignment, the standard approach when facing zones.

When confronting a man-to-man press, teams use the play if no one is guarding the inbounder. Against man-to-man pressure, the other four players clear the backcourt to let the ball handler bring the ball up court. In some cases, the lead guard might find it necessary to go get the ball from a teammate. Players anticipate defensive traps or run-and-jump maneuvers.

When a player catches the ball in the middle, he or she is aware of defenders who follow the ball to tip it from behind. Teammates let the dribbler know if a threat is developing.

LOUISVILLE BIG PLAYER

The Louisville big player play was developed to beat full-court man-to-man pressure, especially at the end of a game. The play uses the same formation used in Louisville special. The defense will turn up the intensity a notch if their opponent is leading late, frequently by employing a man-to-man press. Louisville big player is a sound way to inbound the ball near the end of the game when protecting a lead. The play uses a movement variation from the Louisville formation.

Personnel

Because the team is protecting a lead, its best foul shooters should be in the game. Exact player positioning depends on their free-throw shooting abilities. Two post players and three perimeter players are on the floor.

Scoring

No shots are directly related to the activity of the play.

the lane cuts along the sideline to a spot directly beyond the pass receiver. The point guard fills the open space in the middle. When opposed by a zone press the team should send the ball to the middle if possible. The deep player on the offside adjusts position depending on the ferocity of the trap.

Keys

See "Breaking Presses Offensive Fine-Tuning" on page 305 for further relevant information.

Players must remember that they use the offense only after a successful basket by the opponent (free throw or field goal).

Execution

Players form the basic Louisville set. A peripheral player (S2) inbounds the ball, and the other four players make a line across the court, with the big players (B1 and B2) in the outside positions and the perimeter players (G and S1) in the interior positions. The finest free-throw shooters are on the ballside. G is the next best free-throw shooter. S2 is the weakest (figure 17.8). Interior players (B2 and B1) move in to set screens for the closest perimeter players (S1 and G, respectively). S1 and G use the screens to get open to catch the inbounds pass. The screeners (B2 and B1) seal back toward the ball after their teammates use the picks. S2 has

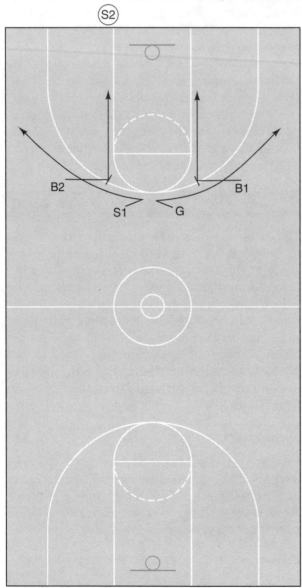

Figure 17.8   Motion in Louisville big player.

four inbounding options. Preference goes to the squad's best free-throw shooters.

Keys

See "Breaking Presses Offensive Fine-Tuning" on page 305. Also refer to the sections about setting a screen and using a pick in "Man-to-Man Offensive Fine-Tuning" in chapter 1 (page 4).

The inbounder can run the baseline if necessary after the opponent has made a field goal or free throw. The inbounder may need to move to improve the passing angle.

The line of the four players is at least at the top of the key, if not slightly farther from the baseline. The perimeter players in the middle can be closer to midcourt. Players crave room to operate.

If the defense does not foul quickly, the priority shifts to delivering the ball to the point guard. Placing the lead guard on the ballside in the initial setup increases the likelihood that the throw-in will go in his or her direction. After the toss is completed, players vacate the backcourt to give the playmaker space.

LOUISVILLE INVERT

Certain situations arise regularly near the end of a game, such as protecting a lead. Coaches must groom their teams to combat an aggressive defense. In this case, protecting a lead means completing an inbounds pass against a full-court man-to-man defense in which the defense is trying to create a quick turnover. If they are unable to get the turnover, the closest defender usually fouls. The Louisville invert approach was designed to combat this tactic. Teams execute the play late in a game when it is crucial to inbound the ball against an extensive man-to-man onslaught. Louisville invert is especially helpful when protecting a lead. The play uses a twist on the Louisville play to put the ball in the hands of specific players.

Personnel

Both big players should be effective screeners. At least one should be a potent free-throw shooter. It is helpful if the point guard is an excellent foul shooter. The inbounder should be the club's second-best ball handler and must be good at hitting free throws.

Scoring

A shot prospect results if the inbounder throws the ball deep to the player running to the other end of the court. The coach must decide if players can take advantage of this option.

Execution

The team establishes the same four-across line as in Louisville except that the big players and exterior players switch their starting assignments (figure 17.9). The perimeter players (S1 and G) are on the outside, and the post players (B2 and B1) are inside. The line forms at least at the top of the key. The weakest foul-shooting exterior player is the inbounder (S2) only if the coach intends to direct the outside player on the ballside (S1) to break free coming to the ball to catch the throw-in before any sprint deep. The most likely choice is to place the weakest foul shooter of the three exterior players in S1's spot.

S1 fakes heading toward the ball and runs long to clear out the area. The point guard (G or the best free-throw shooter) is wide on the offside and is the primary receiver. B2 and B1 are above the elbows. The better free-throw shooter of the two is on the ballside. The first option for the two big players is to set staggered picks for the lead guard (G). After the point guard uses each screen, the screeners seal back to the ball. B2 and B1 are the second and third choices, respectively, for the inbounder.

Another option for the post players (B2 and B1) is to establish a double pick for the point guard (G). After G uses it, B2 and B1 head to the baseline to receive a possible entry pass from S2. B2 is above (nearer half-court) in the double pick so that he or she is able to twist over B1 on the move toward the inbounder. B2 is the first to break to the ball. The second post player (B1) reads his or her partner's move and heads to an open spot.

Keys

See "Breaking Presses Offensive Fine-Tuning" on page 305. Also refer to "Man-to-Man Offensive Fine-Tuning" in chapter 1 (page 4) for details about setting a screen and using a pick.

The ballside big player is the ace foul shooter of the two post players. The perimeter player away from the inbounder is the strongest free-

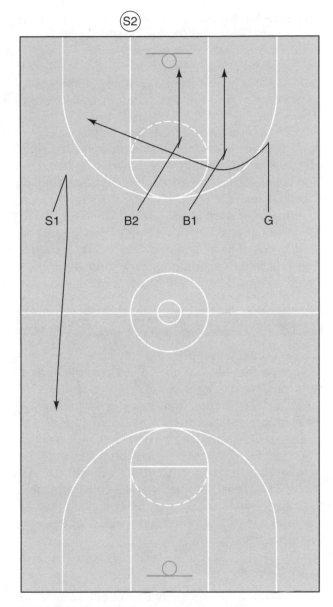

Figure 17.9 Louisville invert action.

throw shooter of the three exterior players and is an excellent ball handler. The second-best ball handler and foul shooter is the inbounder because a return pass might come quickly from one of the big players. After a made shot by the opponent, the inbounder can run the baseline if necessary to improve the passing angle.

The perimeter player on the ballside fakes toward the ball and takes off long. The inbounder sends the ball deep if the player is wide open for a layup and the coach has authorized such an action. The main reason the ballside perimeter player goes deep, however, is to clear the strongside zone in front of the inbounder. As a variation, the ballside exterior player can fake deep and race to the basketball for the entry pass. In that case, he or she should be the second-best foul shooter instead of the weakest.

Big players mix their actions. Sometimes they set a double pick; sometimes they set staggered picks for the point guard. I prefer to allow them to choose.

The play is an effective way to inbound the ball against intense man-to-man pressure. The defense will have difficulty switching because the big players screen for a much quicker player, the lead guard.

If the opponent is not fouling, the ball goes to the point guard. The other four players clear the backcourt. The playmaker may need to snatch the ball from certain players whom the coach does not want to handle the basketball.

LOUISVILLE MIX

The Louisville mix play operates from the Louisville alignment. Each item in the series has a different twist to keep the defense guessing. The alternatives prevent familiarity. When the clock is running out and a club is ahead, the coach wants to be able to throw something new at the defense. The offense can be used anytime a squad is having difficulty inbounding the ball because of intense man-to-man pressure. Usually, teams use it near the end of a game to protect a lead. Inbounding the ball successfully is of paramount importance.

Personnel

The two post players must be effective screeners. At least one of them should be a good foul shooter. Having two perimeter players who are solid free-throw shooters with good ballhandling skills is an advantage.

Scoring

A shot may arise when the inbounder casts the ball the length of the court to a streaking big player. The coach determines whether this kind of pass is allowed.

Execution

The team begins in the same four-across formation as Louisville except that player positions are switched (figure 17.10). The best ballhandling, foul-shooting perimeter player (prefer-

ably the point guard, G) starts out top on the ballside. The stronger foul-shooting big player (B2) is inside above the strongside elbow. The other interior player (B1) is outside on the weakside. The ballhandling and foul-shooting skills of the remaining two exterior players (S2 and S1) dictate their positioning. One perimeter player (S2) is the inbounder. The final exterior player (S1) uses the pick set by B1. S2 and S1 are interchangeable. The weakest foul shooter (in this case, B1) races deep. The post players (B1 and B2) screen for the exterior players (S1 and G, respectively). On the offside, one player sprints deep. On the ballside, the screener (B2) always seals back toward the ball after the pick is used.

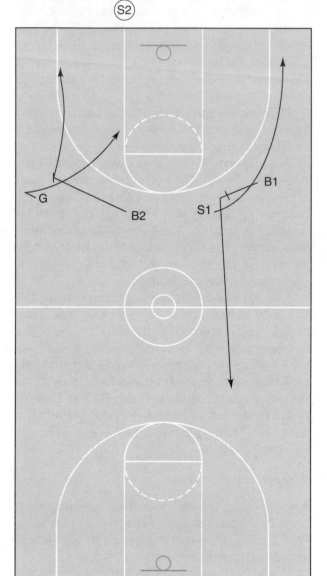

Figure 17.10 Louisville mix alignment and movements.

Keys

Refer to "Breaking Presses Offensive Fine-Tuning" on page 305. See also "Man-to-Man Offensive Fine-Tuning" in chapter 1 on page 4 for details about setting a screen and using a pick.

The inbounder throws the ball deep only if the deep player is wide open for a layup. The player going long should be the weakest foul shooter. The coach may opt not to permit the toss at all.

The line of four across is parallel to the baseline at least at top-of-the-key depth.

The primary action is the screen set by the big player closer to the inbounder for the nearest perimeter player. The picks set by the big players for the perimeter players make it difficult for the defenders to switch and therefore are more effective.

Players heading to the baseline to receive the inbounds pass remain in their lanes to keep sufficient space between them.

If the defense is not in a situation that requires a foul, players clear down court to enable the pass receiver to dribble up the floor. The point guard may need to get the ball from particular players if the coach does not permit them to handle the ball.

Players must make an effort to deliver the ball to the right players when the outcome of the game is in question.

CLEMSON

The final specialty play to counter full-court man-to-man pressure has a twist. Sometimes it is effective to let players decide precise movements. The coach concocts the basic formation, but players execute what they think will work. I have used the Clemson play since I first entered the coaching profession because it produced favorable results. The offense is appropriate during the final stages of a game when protecting a lead, although teams can use it throughout a game to counter full-court man-to-man pressure. The goal is to toss the ball in play without a turnover.

Personnel

The inbounder must be able to throw the ball deep. Players who pick must have a knack for

screening and understand how to seal back to the ball. The best foul shooters take positions where they are most likely to receive the throw-in.

Scoring

One big player races deep to await a long inbounds pass. The coach must decide if a resulting layup is an acceptable shot.

Execution

Clemson includes two ways to complete its motion. The inbounder raises his or her right or left fist, which gives the play two different movement sequences. The first appears in figure 17.11. The inbounder (S2) is normally the weak-

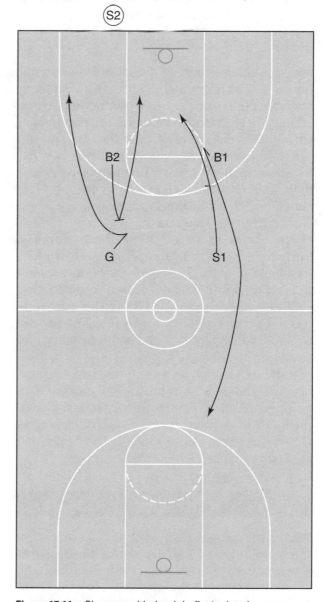

Figure 17.11   Clemson with the right fist in the air.

est foul shooter of the three perimeter players. He or she must be a decent ball handler. The big players (B2 and B1) start outside the elbows. The other two perimeter players (G and S1) line up directly behind the big players between the top of the key and the center-jump circle. The inbounder (S2) raises his or her right fist to signal the big player on the right side (B2) to move up to set a screen for the playmaker (G). The screener steps back to the ball opposite the teammate's cut. At the same time, S1 down picks for B1, allowing B1 to hustle long. S1 then steps directly to the ball. Whichever fist the inbounder raises signals the side on which the big player should move up toward midcourt to plant the screen. The other side has a screening action going in the opposite direction.

Keys

See "Breaking Presses Offensive Fine-Tuning" on page 305. Refer also to the discussions of screening between post and perimeter players, setting a screen, and using a pick in "Man-to-Man Offensive Fine-Tuning" in chapter 1 on page 4.

The inbounder signals with his or her fist before receiving the ball from the referee so that teammates know which option to execute. The coach decides the criteria under which players can attempt the deep pass.

Players must space themselves properly. Peripheral players are approximately 10 feet from post players. The coach places personnel in starting spots based on their foul-shooting skill and likelihood of catching the inbounds pass. The point guard always begins on the ballside. After all, he or she is the primary ball handler.

If the defense is not attempting to foul, players clear the backcourt for the ball handler. The point guard might need to secure possession of the ball from certain players. The coach chooses which players are not to handle the basketball against pressure.

YALE

What does a coach do if he or she has an exceptional point guard who can deal with pressure? A press-break offense that revolves around the playmaker ensures that the ball is in competent hands. Coaches regularly give the ball to the lead guard to beat a man-to-man press. Yale enables them to take a similar approach to defeating a zone press. Yale is useful any time during a game as a way to counter full-court defensive pressure, although it is not a practical quick-in press break. The play requires the club to create a fixed formation before inbounding the ball. A strong lead guard benefits from the play. The goal is to get the ball to the point guard in a favorable attack position. Yale is useful when the coach wants to generate a score directly from the press offense.

Personnel

Both inside players must be adequate ball handlers and have the capacity to pass the basketball effectively. The weaker free-throw shooter of the two inside players inbounds the ball. The point guard is the featured player. The rest of the team tries to send the ball to the point guard to allow him or her to infiltrate the defense. The lead guard must be a strong foul shooter. The better ball handler and foul shooter of the two remaining exterior players is on the ballside.

Scoring

The Yale offense puts perimeter players in position to attack the offensive basket, with the point guard leading the charge. Shooters run with the ball handler to the offensive end to expand the type and length of shots that the team can attempt. The fastest players could manufacture a numbers advantage.

Execution

B1 is the inbounder (figure 17.12). The other post player (B2) starts on the backcourt side of the center-jump circle. The playmaker (G) is at the foul line nearest the inbounder. The two shooters (S1 and S2) are at midcourt, each near a sideline. These two players initially move deep while the point guard (G) picks up for B2. The throw-in goes to B2. The inbounder (B1) steps in play opposite the pass receiver (B2). B1 is about 10 to 15 feet from and slightly behind the pass recipient. G remains active in the middle of the court ahead of the ball. He or she is the primary target for the next pass. In the meantime, S1 and S2 clear to the offensive end of the court, creating space for the playmaker. This movement creates a 2-1-2 formation. The

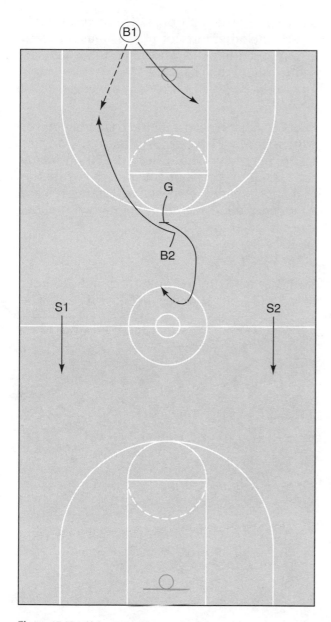

Figure 17.12 Yale starting set and motion.

player on the deep diagonal line from the ball adjusts position according to the extent of the defensive pressure.

A second inbounding alternative is available if the defense denies the entry pass to the big player coming to the ball (B2 in figure 17.12). Instead, the entry pass goes to the perimeter player on the weakside (S2), who is racing toward the baseline. The player at the offside sideline sees the inbounding trouble and reacts by sprinting straight to the baseline. The next pass goes to the lead guard (G) in the middle, if possible. If the pass to the lead guard cannot be accomplished against a zone defense, the player

with the ball passes back to either big player and swiftly runs ahead of the point guard down the weakside sideline. Against man-to-man pressure, the throw-in recipient can bring the ball up court if he or she is unable to get the ball to the lead guard and is a capable ball handler.

The final throw-in choice is to the ballside perimeter player (S1 in figure 17.12), who is sprinting to the baseline. He or she responds after seeing that the first two options (to B2 or S2) are not likely to happen. The point guard (G) is always the target to receive the second pass. If the ballside exterior player cannot deliver the ball to G when confronted with a zone press, he or she throws it back to either big player. Once the ball goes to a post player, the two outside players at the sidelines move promptly to spots ahead of the lead guard in the middle. The normal 2-1-2 zone press-break configuration is intact.

Keys

Refer to "Zone Offensive Fine-Tuning" on page 84 for six relevant topics.

The coach fits players to the roles performed at each position. The four players other than the playmaker operate from starting spots based on their strengths and weaknesses.

The team focuses its attention on the point guard. The preferred method of attack against a press is to place the ball in the playmaker's hands. The coach informs the team that they are making a concerted effort to score at the offensive end by attacking with the lead guard.

The big player cutting to the ball is the inbounder's first choice. The inbounder's next alternatives are to the perimeter player who is running toward the baseline along the weakside sideline and to the other outside player doing the same on the ballside.

The two exterior players at the sidelines may have difficulty recognizing the precise moment when they should sprint to the ball to secure the inbounds pass. If they wait too long, a five-second violation might occur. I would rather see them move too early than risk the five-second call.

Against man-to-man pressure, the point guard must be able to break free from the defender to receive the next pass. The coach should establish strict guidelines about who should handle the ball if players cannot get it to the playmaker. Players vacate the backcourt once the playmaker is in possession of the ball.

The post player who is not inbounding takes advantage of the point guard's screen to retrieve the ball against a man-to-man press. Against a zone, he or she cuts hard to an open area to catch the inbounds pass. The pick is a nonfactor unless the front of the press is face guarding.

Players create room for the point guard to operate in the middle ahead of the ball. He or she is the primary target and regularly receives the second pass. After the lead guard gets the ball, he or she immediately turns to view the two players running down the sidelines. He or she tosses the ball forward if a player is open. Alternatively, the point guard accelerates with the dribble. The three perimeter players attack the defense.

The team can make a subtle adjustment against man-to-man pressure, especially late in a game when the opponent may be forced to foul. If the point guard is one of the better free-throw shooters on the team, sending the throw-in directly to him or her is a good idea. The big player and lead guard switch starting positions. The post player sets the pick to free his or her teammate. The point guard has substantial room to get open to receive a pass from the inbounder.

HALF

At times an opponent does not extend pressure to full court. Trapping half-court defenses usually transpire from an odd-front formation. A defender at the point is normal. Double teaming takes place in the corners. Teams use the half play to counter an odd-front half-court or three-quarter-court zone-trapping defense such as 1-2-2, 1-3-1, or 1-2-1-1 formations. The defense intends to maintain the zone trap for the duration of the possession. The offense is flexible enough to succeed when pressure comes from a two-out alignment. The squad is looking to score. Half is easily adapted to be used as a quick-inbounds offense.

Personnel

The two perimeter players out front (one is the point guard) must be sound ball handlers. The team has an advantage if they are effective outside scorers. One big player must be a proficient

passer from the high post. The two forwards (one is the other interior player) must possess strong outside skills and have the ability to score around the basket.

Scoring

Shots are distinct possibilities. One big player works within 15 feet of the basket. Two forwards may have shots near the hoop, along the baseline, or from the periphery at the foul line extended or baseline. Guards release shots near the three-point line above the foul line extended.

Execution

Two guards (G and S1) split the point defender of an odd-front zone trap (figure 17.13). The

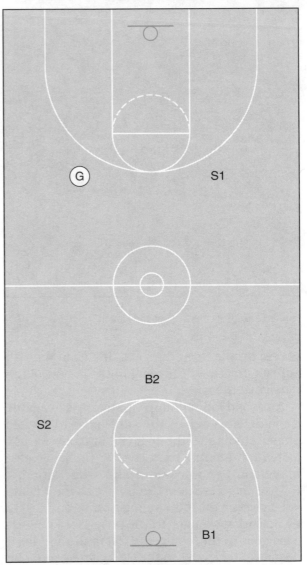

Figure 17.13 Half opening formation.

center (B2) sets up at the top of the key and works in the high post. He or she finds open space in the middle of the floor. The ballside forward (S2) is out on a wing near the foul line extended. The weakside forward (B1) is at the offside block on the foul lane.

When the ball is sent across the front between the two guards, the forward away from the ball darts to the weakside block. The ballside forward pops out to a wing. If the next toss goes to the high post, he or she turns and looks to pass to the offside forward low, then to the guard away from where the pass originated, and finally to the strongside wing, who is sliding toward the baseline.

A guard can also throw the ball to a wing (figure 17.14). In this case, S1 passes to B1. In the first movement option, the player at the weakside block (S2) runs the baseline to the ballside while B2 stays in the high post. If the pass goes to S2 on the baseline, his or her initial look is to the high post (B2) cutting to the bucket. The second choice is to the guard away from the ball (G), who is spotting up on the weakside behind the three-point arc. Therefore, B1's pass prospects are to S2 on the baseline, to B2 in the high post (he or she looks low to S2 and then opposite to G), to G with a skip pass, and to S1 above (S2 returns to the offside block from the baseline).

The second movement option when a guard (S1 in figure 17.14) passes the ball to a wing (B1) is for the high post (B2) to dive low and the

player at the weakside block (S2) to fill the open area in the high post. The high post can dive low and then drift toward the baseline position if the ball is not forthcoming on the cut.

If players recognize that the defense is trapping from a two-out alignment, the point guard takes control and assumes a point position while telling teammates to rotate. The squad creates a 1-3-1 formation. The other guard is a wing. The forward on the same side works the baseline. The high post continues in his or her role.

Keys

See the section on executing against double teams in "Breaking Presses Offensive Fine-Tuning" on page 305. Because the offense is attacking a zone trap that the defense will play for the duration of a half-court possession, refer to "Zone Offensive Fine-Tuning" found on page 84.

Against an odd-front defense, guards always split the lead defender of the odd-front trap. When a guard is in possession of the ball, he or she always notices the weakside forward at the block on the lane. A skip pass might be available. The player low must have a position advantage. If flinging the ball diagonally, the guard should put some arc on it and direct it at the weakside low corner of the backboard.

Transformation into the half offense from a quick-inbounds offense is easy. In the regular press-break offense, one of the big players inbounds the ball and trails opposite the point guard. The other exterior player is in the middle of the court when the ball is with the lead guard. To form the half set, the big player who is trailing and the perimeter player in the middle simply change places as quickly as they can.

Guards attack the defense by sending the ball to the high post. Any trapping zone defense is vulnerable if the offensive team consistently delivers the ball to the middle. When the ball is in the center, the defense will have difficulty executing a double team because so many passing opportunities are accessible.

When the wing gains possession of the ball, he or she can shoot, pass to the player along the baseline, chuck the ball to the high post, skip a pass to the guard on the other side of the court, or toss the ball back to the guard directly out front.

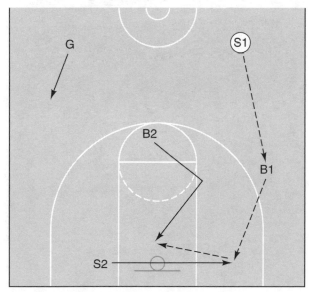

Figure 17.14 Pass to the wing in half.

When the ball is in the hands of the high post or a wing, the guard away spots up. Preferably, he or she stays behind the three-point line and is ready to catch and shoot. When the ball is at a wing, players decide whether the high post dives low or stays put. The high post communicates with the other forward. The play works best if the players make the choice.

Players move as directed as they throw the ball around the exterior. When the ball is at specific locations, players must occupy specific spots.

Against an even-front zone half-court trap (2-2-1 or 2-1-2), the transition is simple. The point guard takes charge to ensure that players occupy appropriate spaces. Players attack with a 1-3-1 alignment with the lead guard at the point. The coach may want to request that the small forward assume a wing position in the 1-3-1 with the shooting guard. The other post player (the power forward) runs the baseline. Players may need to change spots quickly during the transition. The high post and baseline player still have the two movement options that were available against odd-front traps when the ball goes to a wing.

WISCONSIN

My approach always included having an alternate play to use against half-court traps. Keeping the motion simple with both offenses enabled players to comprehend the action with minimal training. Coaches should groom players so that both options are available against a half-court trap. Keeping a player in close proximity to the hoop puts pressure on the defense to guard the basket. Wisconsin is used by design against odd-front zone traps (1-2-2, 1-3-1, or 1-2-1-1) maintained on the half-court. Wisconsin is especially useful if a coach wants to keep his or her center close to the hoop. The team is geared to score.

Personnel

Two perimeter players out front (one is the lead guard) must be effective passers. Ideally, they can score from the arc. The center stays around the foul lane. The two wings (one is the other post player) are proficient outside shooters and are able to score in the paint. They may obtain shots as far as 20 feet out.

Scoring

The main interior player is a primary target and secures shots close to the hoop. The guards remain above the foul line; their shots are likely to be of at least 18 feet. Forwards may have chances to score within 15 feet around the lane and deep at the wings or corners.

Execution

Two guards (G and S1) begin opposite one another, splitting the defensive point player (figure 17.15). The center (B2) is always at the weakside block when the ball is in the hands of one of the guards. One forward is on the ball-side wing, and the other occupies the high post

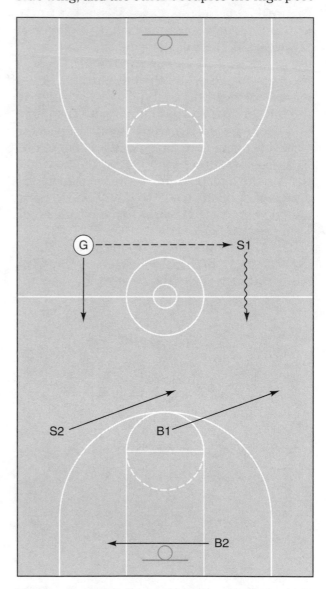

Figure 17.15 Wisconsin set and motion on a guard-to-guard pass.

(middle). In figure 17.15, G throws the ball to S1. The player in the middle (B1) sprints to the ball-side wing, and the other forward (S2) hustles to the vacated area. B2 runs to the offside box.

If the pass goes to the player in the middle or the high post, he or she immediately turns to face the hoop. The first glance is to the low-post player at the box for a possible pass. The next option is to toss the ball to the guard on the opposite side from where the ball was received. The high post also can shoot or drive to the basket. The high post's last choices are to pass to the lone wing or toss to the other guard, who may have sent the ball his or her way originally. The ball to the high post could also have originated at the wing. If the pass goes to the opposite guard, the passer races to the ballside wing and the other forward heads to the middle. The low post consistently slides to the offside block.

The pass can go to a wing (figure 17.16). In this case, the pass is from S1 to B1. The high post (S2) cuts to the basket low, while the center (B2) fills the vacant high post. S2 can move to a baseline location off the lane if he or she did not receive a pass on the cut low. The guard away from the ball (G) spots up behind the three-point arc for a possible skip-pass reception. Another option is for the big player low to yell, "Stay!" The high post (S2) remains in place, and the low player (B2) busts along the baseline to ballside. On B1's pass back to the guard (S1), players return to their original positions.

When a wing delivers a skip pass to the opposite guard, the passer quickly fills the high post. The center hustles to the weakside box. The other forward, who could be at the baseline or high post, sprints to the ballside wing below the pass receiver.

Keys

See the discussion of executing against double teams in "Breaking Presses Offensive Fine-Tuning" on page 305. Because the team is using the offense to attack a zone trap that the defense will play for the duration of a half-court possession, refer to "Zone Offensive Fine-Tuning" found on page 84.

The coach should drill the high-post player on his or her choices after receiving the pass. He or she immediately turns and faces the hoop.

A player who catches a pass along the baseline could be at the block or off the lane three to eight feet. The baseline player always has a chance to score with or without putting the ball on the floor.

On a pass to a wing, the coach should give the center control over the movements. If the center yells, "Stay," he or she races to the ballside along the baseline and the high post stays put. No call means that the high post zips low while the player on the weakside box flashes to the vacant high post.

Teams can make a smooth transition from the quick-in offense, regular, to Wisconsin. The big player who is trailing (the inbounder) switches spots with the perimeter player in the middle when the ball is in the hands of the lead guard. The other post player assumes position near the basket.

Players must not be afraid to throw skip passes. Their most important tasks are to read the defense and make the right pass decision.

Guards must be ready to shoot the ball immediately after receiving the pass. The ball may come from the high post, the low post on the ballside, or the opposite wing. Guards look to the center at the weakside block whenever they possess the ball. A lob may be permissible. The target is the offside, low corner of the backboard. The lob should have enough arc to enable the center to catch the pass. To gain a position advantage, the center initiates contact with the weakside low defender. The center places the defender on his or her hip or

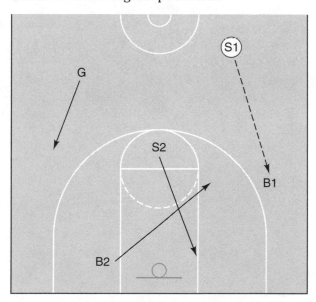

Figure 17.16 Pass from a guard to a wing in Wisconsin.

buttocks. A defensive wing who rotates down to cover the low weakside is susceptible to the action. To help the guards, the low player points to the basket to indicate that a lob is feasible.

Players are in attack mode. They do not let the defense dictate the action. The squad moves the ball and forces the defense to react. Players abide by movement guidelines. They hustle to designated locations each time the ball is passed.

One inside player in the wing or high post must be competent on the periphery. He or she is not to launch shots from distance if incapable of making them. The coach places shot restrictions on players as necessary.

Play and Offense Finder

About the Author

Ken Atkins has more than 20 years of experience coaching basketball, from junior high school to the collegiate level. In 13 years as head coach of the Monarchs at King's College in Wilkes-Barre, Pennsylvania, he took a struggling basketball program and turned it into a constant force in the Middle Atlantic Conference. Prior to his tenure at King's College, Coach Atkins served as an assistant coach at Wiedner University and the University of Arizona.

At King's College, Coach Atkins notched the school's second-most career wins, the most wins in a season, the longest winning streak, and the best career winning percentage. He led the Monarchs to their first conference championship and to three NCAA Division III Tournaments and was twice named Middle Atlantic Conference-Northern Division Coach of the Year. Atkins was a member of the National Association of Basketball Coaches for 17 years.

Coach Atkins enjoys writing, reading, and gardening. He resides in Larksville, Pennsylvania, with his wife, Betsy.

Tap into the tactical genius of Morgan Wootten

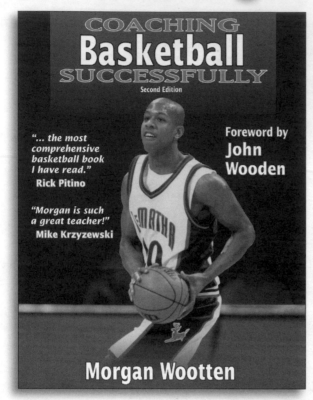

"... the most comprehensive basketball book I have read."
Rick Pitino

"Morgan is such a great teacher!"
Mike Krzyzewski

Foreword by **John Wooden**

Morgan Wootten

2003 • 240 pages • ISBN 0-7360-4790-5

With five national championships, Morgan Wootten retired in 2002 as the winningest—and one of the most respected—coaches ever. Now, in *Coaching Basketball Successfully,* Morgan Wootten shares his full arsenal of coaching wisdom on topics ranging from player communication and motivation to Xs and Os.

This latest edition includes new material on zone offense, quick-hitting plays off the secondary break, man-to-man and trapping defenses, and situational in-bounds plays. Wootten also provides guidelines for physical conditioning, recommendations for job interviewing, advice on conducting summer camps, and a master plan for handling game situations. Sprinkled throughout the book are many "thought for the day" phrases the coach has found especially effective in motivating and communicating important lessons to athletes.

To place your order, U.S. customers call
TOLL FREE 800-747-4457 or visit www.HumanKinetics.com
In Canada call 800-465-7301
In Australia call (08) 8277 1555
In New Zealand call (09) 448 1207
In Europe call +44 (0) 113 255 5665

HUMAN KINETICS
The Premier Publisher for Sports & Fitness
P.O. Box 5076, Champaign, IL 61825-5076
www.HumanKinetics.com

2335

Perform and perfect the fundamentals

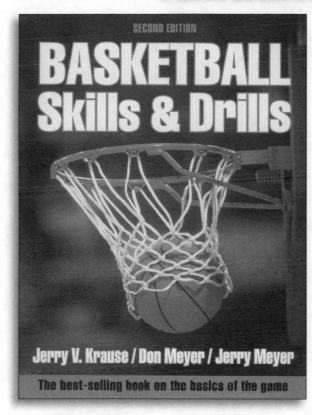

SECOND EDITION
BASKETBALL
Skills & Drills

Jerry V. Krause / Don Meyer / Jerry Meyer

The best-selling book on the basics of the game

1999 • 216 pages • ISBN 0-7360-0171-9

Basketball Skills & Drills provides a complete blueprint for building the foundation every well-rounded player needs. Perfect for both coaches of beginning players and for players themselves, this all-inclusive manual teaches and illustrates each key individual skill, including

• basic positioning,
• moving without the ball,
• ballhandling,
• shooting,
• passing,
• perimeter moves,
• post moves,
• defense, and
• rebounding.

The book includes 59 drills to reinforce the skill instruction and make every practice session more fun and effective. Coaching tips sprinkled throughout the book emphasize key points and explain how to correct common errors.

This book is also available with a CD ROM package that brings the book's instruction to life. The two-disk CD ROM set is compiled of high-quality video footage so you can view live demonstrations of the drills from the book.

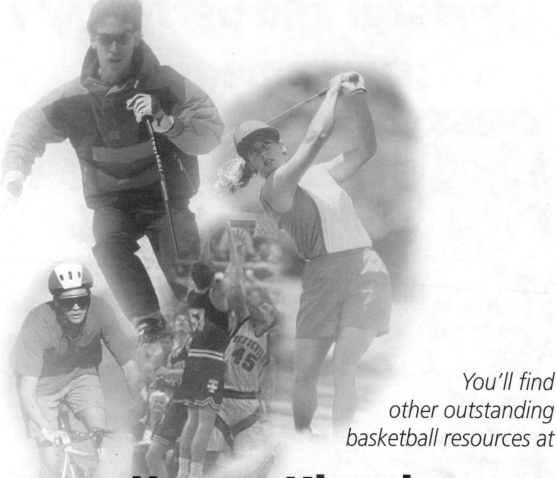

THE ESSENTIAL
appetizers
COOKBOOK

bay books

Published by Bay Books, an imprint of Murdoch Magazines Pty Ltd,
GPO Box 1203 Sydney, NSW Australia 1045

Series Editor: Wendy Stephen
Editorial Director: Diana Hill
Designer: Michèle Lichtenberger
Design Concept: Marylouise Brammer
Food Editor: Kathy Knudsen
Food Director: Jody Vassallo
Photographers (cover and special features): Chris Jones, Lindsay Ross
Stylist (cover and special features): Mary Harris
Stylist's Assistants (cover and special features): Kathy Knudsen, Michelle Lawton, Kerrie Mullins
Indexer: Russell Brooks
Picture Librarian: Annette Irish

CEO: Juliet Rogers
Publisher: Kay Scarlett
Production Manager: Kylie Kirkwood
International & Domestic Sales Director: Amanda Roberts

ISBN 1 74045 251 8

IMPORTANT: Those who might be at risk from the effects of salmonella food poisoning
(the elderly, pregnant women, young children and those suffering from immune deficiency
diseases) should consult their GP with any concerns about eating raw eggs.

OUR STAR RATING: When we test recipes, we rate them for ease of preparation.
The following cookery ratings are used in this book:
★ A single star indicates a recipe that is simple and generally quick to make—perfect for beginners.
★★ Two stars indicate the need for just a little more care, or perhaps a little more time.
★★★ Three stars indicate special dishes that need more investment in time,
care and patience—but the results are worth it. Even beginners can make these
dishes as long as the recipe is followed carefully.

APPETIZERS

There is something remarkably attractive and indulgent about appetizers. Maybe it's the wonderfully adult feeling of breaking all the rules we've grown up with: 'sit still while you're eating' and 'you can't leave the table until you've finished'. Appetizers, reckless and hedonistic, mean gliding around the room, usually with a drink in one hand and a tiny bite-sized treat in the other. The association is with parties—lots of people, new friends to be made and the freedom to flit, plateless, from one fabulous conversation to the next. Appetizers should always look good, colourful and fresh, piled high, with everyone taking from the communal platter, a meeting place where the food can lighten the mood and provide a topic of conversation. Appetizers can be exciting and sometimes a bit risky— even the most cautious will try a new taste sensation if it's only one bite. But, remember the golden rule: whether it's sophisticated miniature Peking duck, or party-sized potato rosti, there is one thing that every appetizer should be—utterly irresistible.

CONTENTS

SPECIAL FEATURES

PLANNING & PARTYING

What are appetizers? This is a question we've had to ponder quite carefully while devising the recipes for this book. We decided that ideally appetizers should be one or two bites at most, removing any real need to hold cutlery and a plate while you're chatting and moving about the room. If you decide not to provide plates, your appetizers shouldn't be messy and explosive, leaving your guests with food all over their hands and clothes, searching desperately for the nearest pot plant to hide the remains.

However, there are also some fabulous recipes that we didn't want to miss out on, for example for antipasto and marinated cheese or vegetables, where you might need to supply plates and cocktail sticks or small forks for your guests. And, obviously, some of our most popular appetizers are dips, where you'll need to provide bread or other 'dippers' to scoop up your delicious creation. So, as you can see, appetizers can be a fairly wide variety of dishes. It is also not restricted to savouries. Sweet appetizers have a place at many gatherings.

A NIBBLE OR A PARTY?

Appetizers are ideal for many occasions. You might invite a small group of friends round for hors d'oeuvres before an evening out, or a late supper after going out, or perhaps you are having a special dinner party and want to hand round some canapés with the drinks beforehand. Alternatively, you might be hosting a wild party for 50 people, a marquee wedding for 250 or a simple picnic or brunch in your back garden. Appetizers have their place at all these events.

HOW OUR CHAPTERS WORK

We have divided our appetizers into chapters based on flavours, dishes and styles of food from around the world. This means that you can easily put together a whole themed menu using a few dishes from one chapter. If you are choosing to serve Tex–Mex nibbles, for example, you probably wouldn't want to mix them with dishes from other chapters because of the rather unique and strong flavours. Having said that, many of the chapters can easily be combined with

RIGHT: Marinated trout and cucumber tarts (page 80)

others... you might choose to serve a couple of large antipasto platters, accompanied by a few Tapas or Meze dishes and give your guests a Mediterranean evening. Some of the Indian dishes will complement a careful selection of Eastern food, perhaps Thai or Malaysian. And, of course, our chapters of purely party food and sweet things can be mixed and matched with just about anything else. The choice is yours.

PLANNING A MENU

Many factors will affect your choice of menu. What type of gathering are you intending to have? How long will it go on for? What time of day? What time of year? How many people will be attending? What are their tastes in food? What are their ages and interests? Are there many vegetarians, or seafood-haters? How much time will you have to prepare? How well-equipped is your kitchen?

When serving appetizers it is best to keep it simple. Don't try to attempt too much. A few platters of well-chosen ideas will create more impact and give you more time and freedom than attempting 20 recipes with just small quantities of each. Simply double or treble the recipe quantities given, if necessary, and pile your platters high. If your guests are staying for the whole evening you might want to consider one or two sweet dishes to be brought out later on. The time of day and year will influence you in your choice of hot and cold dishes —in summer there is little need to serve hot dishes, so you'll immediately give yourself more time on the day if you don't need to be cooking and reheating right up until when your guests arrive.

Obviously your choice of guests will have a major bearing on your choice of menu. A gathering of the local football team is probably not going to be fully satisfied by a plate of party quiches and petits fours, while your Great Aunt Maud might be a little perplexed by a selection of Mexican corn dogs and stuffed chillies for her ninetieth birthday. You will have to make your own decisions here. However, a good rule of thumb with a mixed group is to serve a couple of conservative 'all-rounder' items such as quiches or tartlets, something more substantial and usually bread based (especially if you are serving alcohol) and perhaps one or two more innovative ideas. You will find with appetizers that people are much more adventurous in their tastes when only a couple of mouthfuls are involved (so perhaps Aunt Maud might enjoy that chilli anyway).

Think about the variety of dishes that you're offering. Try not to repeat ingredients—so don't

serve prawn dumplings *and* prawn tempura (unless you're having an evening for local fishermen with a prawn theme). Think about the colours and textures and try to get a good, show-stopping variety of both. Think about complementary flavours—sour, salty, spicy, subtle, savoury, sweet, as well as hot and cold—and try to create an interesting balance.

HOW MUCH TO SERVE

One of the biggest quandaries people have when preparing appetizers is how much to make. How do you know how many of those little pieces everyone will eat? How do you know which will be the most popular? And, horror of horrors, what happens if you run out of food?

You will find that most of our recipe serving quantities are given as 'makes 40' for single items such as tarts or pikelets, or 'makes about 20 pieces' to give you an idea of how generously something like a frittata or pizza should be cut.

ABOVE: Curried chicken pies (left); Lamb korma pies (page 104)

nibbles, not a full meal. If it's an all evening affair, let them know you'll be providing food equivalent to an evening meal. Obviously it's better to make too much food than have people leave feeling hungry.

BUFFET TABLE OR 'WAITER'?

Once you've decided what to serve, you need to decide how you are going to serve it. Once again you will be governed by how many people are attending and how much room and equipment you have available. If you are just having a few friends over, you will probably be quite happy to hand round the food yourself (or perhaps enlist a couple of friends to help). For a larger gathering you might decide to set up a buffet table, or even to hire waiting staff— either of these options obviously gives you much more freedom on the day.

If you are handing food round, whether you are providing plates or not, make sure to always have plenty of napkins handy. If you aren't providing plates, make sure there's somewhere for people to get rid of used cocktail sticks etc.

If you are using a buffet table, you will need to give its layout some thought. For a large gathering, if you have the space and tables, it is a good idea to set up two tables so that everyone isn't queuing together. If this isn't possible, set up your one table with duplicate dishes starting from each end so that people work from both sides. Have plates, forks, napkins etc. available at each end and, if you are serving sweet food, set it up on a separate table.

The whole idea is not to create a traffic jam. So don't set the buffet table right next to the drinks table or people will get under each other's feet. And, rather than making a general announcement that the food is served, you might want to gradually invite people over to the table in smaller groups. Once again, make sure there is somewhere for people to leave their dirty plates.

PRESENTATION

There is little point in creating wonderful food if you're then going to cram it messily on unsuitable plates or in baskets so that the whole impact is lost. Appetizers should always look fabulously tantalizing, so presentation is important. Decorate the platter before arranging the food on top. A beautiful folded napkin, banana leaves or even grape leaves and sprigs of various fresh herbs all make good 'beds' for appetizers. Linen napkins look better than paper doilies which can soak up grease and look off-putting when the plate is half empty.

However, some recipes (such as carpaccio or other antipasto dishes) are impossible to calculate in pieces and you will find the recipe states, say, 'serves 8'. By this we mean it will give 8 people one serving as part of a whole antipasto platter.

A rough idea for quantities for pre-dinner nibbles is to serve about 3–5 pieces per person, and for a short (say two to three hour) cocktail party you should allow about 4–6 pieces of food per hour for each person, for as long as the party is expected to continue. For a full-length party or occasion when appetizers are being served in place of a sit-down meal (such as a wedding or birthday party), allow 8–12 pieces per person.

Chips and nuts and other stand-bys are not included in this calculation.

As far as variety goes, as we stated earlier, it's best to keep it simple and concentrate on a few fabulous dishes than have a vast quantity of mediocre ones. We advise for 10–20 people, preparing about six different dishes and, for any number higher than that, about eight dishes.

For a whole evening occasion, you would move through light canapés, to more substantial bites (this is when you would serve any hot dishes) and finish with sweet nibbles.

It is always sensible to give your guests a rough idea of what to expect, food-wise, when you issue the invite. So if you're planning to have a two-hour cocktail party, it's a good idea to put start and (assumed) finish times on the invitation: that way people will be expecting

ABOVE: Ham and olive empanadillas (page 193)

You could also experiment with flat baskets, bowls, steel or glass platters, tiles and wooden boards. The ideas are endless, as long as they are clean and hygienic. Think about the theme of your food when choosing your platters—Tapas and Meze can look stunning served on Mediterranean-style tiles.

Don't mix more than two items on a platter. If you pile your platter high with just one recipe you'll give it great impact, as well as making it much easier to top up when supplies run low. Garnishes should be fresh and small enough not to overshadow the main item.

BEING PREPARED

Choose some foods that can be prepared well ahead and frozen, some that can be made a couple of days in advance and refrigerated, and one or two that need to be finished on the day. At the end of many of our recipes you'll find an 'in advance' note that lets you know what can be done. Limit those to be made on the day to simply frying or baking or to simple garnishing. Last minute cooking should be avoided wherever possible. Cook earlier in the day and reheat just before serving.

Write a detailed list of what you need to buy, what can be prepared in advance and when you should do it. Non-perishable foods can be

DRINKS

* There are 5 glasses of wine in a 750 ml bottle. For a two-hour wine and appetizers party, allow 1 bottle between two people.
* White wine is usually more popular than red so allow 1 bottle of red for every 2 white.
* There are 6 glasses in a 750 ml bottle of Champagne. Allow 2½ glasses per person for a two-hour drinks party. Allow 1½ glasses per person as a drink before dinner.
* Keep it simple. Serve drinks to fit your food 'theme', and not too many varieties.
* ALWAYS supply soft drinks. For a two-hour drinks party, allow 1 glass per person. If only soft drinks are to be served and no alcohol, allow about 3 glasses per person.
* If people are bringing their own drinks, provide 1 glass per person in addition.
* Buy ice. Chill the drinks well in advance.
* If making punch, freeze some in ice-cube trays to chill the punch without diluting it.
* Freeze berries or tiny wedges of fruit in ice-cubes for decoration.
* Provide twice as many glasses as there are guests—they are easily abandoned.

bought well ahead, while some foods such as fresh herbs and vegetables should be bought as close as possible to the day.

When freezing small items such as mini quiches, meatballs and pikelets, allow them to cool completely before placing on baking paper covered trays and freezing until firm. Then remove from the trays and transfer to freezer bags. Label and seal, pressing out as much air from the bag as possible. Alternatively, arrange in single layers between sheets of greaseproof paper in airtight containers, then seal and freeze. Marinated foods can be frozen in the marinade in plastic bags. Flatten the bag, excluding most of the air and freeze while flat—this will take less time to thaw out.

People often forget to to take a good look at the adequacy of their kitchen equipment. Check that your fridge and freezer are large enough to store all you have planned. Is your oven adequate to reheat large quantities of food? Do you have enough platters, plates, glasses and cutlery? If you don't, all is not lost. These can be easily hired or borrowed. Just don't forget to check beforehand and be prepared.

ABOVE: Lemon grass prawn satays (page 108)

ANTIPASTO

It is an understatement to say that food is important to the Italians. They love to eat and meals are prepared with great pride and affection as a daily highlight of family life. And what more delicious way to whet the appetite than with a colourful antipasto platter? The word translates literally as 'before the meal' and the tradition arose from the lengthy banquets of the Roman Empire. Today, antipasto doesn't have to mean 'before the meal', it can be the whole magnificent feast itself. So pour yourself (and your guests) a glass of vino and bring a little Italian passion into your kitchen. *Buon appetito.*

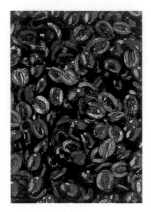

BLACK OLIVES

Olives are indispensable as a savoury nibble to accompany drinks and are an attractive addition to an antipasto platter. They also add a distinctive flavour to many Mediterranean dishes. Some varieties are larger, some rounder than others. When olives are unripe, they are green, hard and bitter. Black olives have been left on the tree to darken and mature. Olives can either be preserved in oil, sometimes flavoured with herbs, or in brine. Italian and Greek olives are considered the best.

ABOVE, FROM LEFT:
Carpaccio; Pasta frittata;
Stuffed cherry tomatoes

CARPACCIO

Preparation time: 15 minutes + freezing
Total cooking time: Nil
Serves 8

★

400 g (13 oz) beef eye fillet
1 tablespoon extra virgin olive oil
rocket leaves, torn
60 g (2 oz) Parmesan, shaved
black olives, cut into slivers

1 Remove all the visible fat and sinew from the beef, then freeze for 1–2 hours, until firm but not solid. This makes the meat easier to slice thinly.
2 Cut paper-thin slices of beef with a large, sharp knife. Arrange on a serving platter and allow to return to room temperature.
3 Just before serving, drizzle with oil, then scatter with rocket, Parmesan and olives.
IN ADVANCE: The beef can be cut into slices a few hours in advance, covered and refrigerated. Drizzle with oil and garnish with the other ingredients just before serving.

PASTA FRITTATA

Preparation time: 15 minutes
Total cooking time: 25 minutes
Makes 8 wedges

★

300 g (10 oz) spaghetti
4 eggs
50 g (1¾ oz) Parmesan, grated
2 tablespoons chopped fresh parsley
60 g (2 oz) butter

1 Cook the spaghetti in a large pan of boiling water for about 10 minutes, until just tender but still retaining a little bite, then drain well.
2 Whisk the eggs in a large bowl, then add the Parmesan, parsley and some salt and freshly ground black pepper. Toss with the spaghetti.
3 Melt half the butter in a 23 cm (9 inch) frying pan and add the spaghetti mixture. Cover and cook over low heat until the base is crisp and golden. Slide onto a plate, melt the remaining butter in the pan and flip the frittata back in to cook the other side (do not cover). Serve warm, cut into wedges.

STUFFED CHERRY TOMATOES

Preparation time: 15 minutes
Total cooking time: Nil
Makes 16

16 cherry tomatoes
50 g (1³/₄ oz) goats cheese
50 g (1³/₄ oz) ricotta
2 slices prosciutto, finely chopped

1 Slice the tops from the tomatoes, hollow out and discard the seeds. Turn them upside-down on paper towel and drain for a few minutes.
2 Beat together the goats cheese and ricotta until smooth. Mix in the prosciutto, then season. Spoon into the tomatoes and refrigerate until required.

PROSCIUTTO WITH MELON

Preparation time: 20 minutes
Total cooking time: Nil
Makes 16

1 rockmelon or honeydew melon
16 slices prosciutto
extra virgin olive oil

1 Remove the seeds from the melon, cut into thin wedges and wrap a slice of prosciutto around each. Drizzle with oil and grind black pepper over each. Refrigerate until required.

MARINATED EGGPLANT
(AUBERGINE)

Preparation time: 15 minutes + salting + marinating
Total cooking time: 15 minutes
Serves 6–8

750 g (1¹/₂ lb) slender eggplant (aubergine)
¹/₄ cup (60 ml/2 fl oz) olive oil
2 tablespoons balsamic vinegar
2 cloves garlic, crushed
1 anchovy fillet, finely chopped
2 tablespoons chopped fresh parsley

1 Cut the eggplant into thick diagonal slices, place in a colander and sprinkle well with salt. After 30 minutes, rinse and pat dry.
2 Whisk the oil, vinegar, garlic and anchovy until smooth. Season, to taste.
3 Heat a little oil in a frying pan and brown the eggplant in batches. Transfer to a bowl, toss with the dressing and parsley and marinate for 4 hours. Serve at room temperature.

CHERRY TOMATOES
There are many different types and sizes of cherry tomato, all low in acid and quite sweet. Most are an ideal size for stuffing with a filling, but some are as tiny as small grapes and are sold in clusters. Although these can't be stuffed, they can be used to add colour or to garnish a dish.

LEFT: Prosciutto with melon (left); Marinated eggplant

PROSCIUTTO

Prosciutto is an Italian ham that has been salted and dried in the air. It needs no cooking and is usually sold and served in wafer-thin slices. Its mellow flavour makes it ideal for eating as an antipasto with fruits such as sliced melons or fresh figs.

OPPOSITE PAGE:
Oregano and prosciutto pinwheels (top); Herbed goats cheese

OREGANO AND PROSCIUTTO PINWHEELS

Preparation time: 30 minutes + chilling
Total cooking time: 10 minutes
Makes about 40

★ ★

1 red pepper (capsicum)
1 green pepper (capsicum)
1 yellow pepper (capsicum)
125 g (4 oz) cream cheese, softened
25 g (3/4 oz) Parmesan, grated
2 spring onions, finely chopped
1/4 cup (7 g/1/4 oz) chopped fresh oregano
1 tablespoon bottled capers, drained and
    chopped
1 tablespoon pine nuts, chopped
12 thin slices prosciutto

1 Cut the peppers into quarters and remove the seeds and membrane. Cook, skin-side-up, under a hot grill until the skin blackens and blisters. Place in a plastic bag until cool, then peel.
2 Mix together the cream cheese, Parmesan, spring onion, oregano, capers and pine nuts.
3 Place the pepper pieces on the prosciutto slices and trim the prosciutto to the same size. Remove the pepper and spread some cheese mixture on the prosciutto. Top with the pepper and spread with a little more cheese mixture. Roll up tightly from the short end. Cover and refrigerate for 1 hour, or until firm. Slice into 1 cm (1/2 inch) rounds and serve on toothpicks.

PESTO-TOPPED CHERRY TOMATOES

Preparation time: 35 minutes
Total cooking time: Nil
Makes about 50

60 g (2 oz) fresh parsley, chopped
2 cloves garlic, roughly chopped
2 tablespoons pine nuts, toasted
1/4 cup (60 ml/2 fl oz) olive oil
60 g (2 oz) Parmesan, grated
15 g (1/2 oz) fresh basil leaves
15 g (1/2 oz) butter, at room temperature
500 g (1 lb) cherry tomatoes

1 Finely chop the parsley, garlic, pine nuts and oil together in a food processor or blender.
2 Add the Parmesan, basil leaves, butter and freshly ground pepper, to taste, and process until well combined.
3 Slice the tops from the cherry tomatoes (a small amount of tomato flesh can be scooped out of each tomato first so you can use a generous amount of filling). Spoon a little mound of the pesto mixture into the top of each tomato.
NOTE: The pesto can be made several days ahead. Spoon into a container and cover the surface of the pesto with a thin layer of olive oil to exclude air, thus preventing discoloration. Alternatively, the pesto can be frozen. Spoon into a shallow container and press plastic wrap onto the surface, again to eliminate air.
IN ADVANCE: The tomatoes can be cut and scooped up to 2 hours ahead, then refrigerated.

HERBED GOATS CHEESE

Preparation time: 20 minutes
Total cooking time: 6 minutes
Serves 6–8

200 g (6 1/2 oz) vine leaves in brine
3 teaspoons bottled green or pink peppercorns,
    drained and chopped
1 tablespoon chopped fresh marjoram
3 x 100 g (3 1/2 oz) rounds soft goats cheese
rye bread, for serving

1 Place the vine leaves in a heatproof bowl and cover with hot water to rinse away the brine. Drain well and pat dry with paper towels.
2 Combine the peppercorns and marjoram in a shallow bowl or on a plate. Toss the goats cheese in the mixture until the sides are well coated. Arrange a few vine leaves, shiny-side-down, on a work surface. Wrap each goats cheese round in a few layers of vine leaves. This will prevent the cheese from overcooking and losing its shape.
3 Cook the cheese on a barbecue hotplate or under a hot grill for 3 minutes each side, or until the outside leaves are charred. Transfer to a plate and cool to room temperature. (The cheese is too soft to serve when hot, but will firm as it cools.) Use scissors to cut away the vine leaves and serve the cheese with the sliced rye bread.
IN ADVANCE: The cheese can be wrapped in the vine leaves a few hours ahead.

BASIL

Sweet basil is the most widely used of the many varieties of this aromatic, pungent herb. Although most well-known for its affinity with tomato, it is also the basis of pesto sauce and is used in many dishes and salads. Basil leaves bruise easily so they should be shredded rather than chopped. Fresh basil can be refrigerated for up to three days with the stems standing in a bottle of water.

PIZZETTA SQUARES

Preparation time: 20 minutes
Total cooking time: 40 minutes
Makes about 50

2 tablespoons oil
4 onions, finely sliced
2 sheets frozen puff pastry, thawed
1/3 cup (90 g/3 oz) sun-dried tomato pesto
10 anchovies, finely chopped
15 g (1/2 oz) fresh basil leaves, finely shredded

1 Preheat the oven to moderately hot 200°C (400°F/Gas 6). Heat the oil in a large pan and cook the onion over medium heat for 20 minutes, or until soft and golden. Cool.
2 Lay each sheet of pastry on a lightly greased oven tray, then spread the tomato pesto evenly over the pastry. Scatter the onion over the top.
3 Sprinkle the anchovies and basil over the top and bake for 20 minutes, or until the squares are puffed and golden. Cool, then cut into squares. Serve warm or at room temperature.

ABOVE: Pizzetta squares

IN ADVANCE: Cook the onions 2 days ahead and refrigerate. Bake no earlier than 2 hours ahead.

PIZZA FRITTATA

Preparation time: 30 minutes
Total cooking time: 30 minutes
Makes 20 pieces

20 g (3/4 oz) butter
60 g (2 oz) button mushrooms, finely chopped
1 small tomato, peeled, seeded, finely chopped
1 small red pepper (capsicum), seeded, finely chopped
1 small onion, finely chopped
1 stick cabanossi, finely chopped
1 teaspoon dried basil leaves
4 eggs
2/3 cup (170 ml/5 1/2 fl oz) cream
100 g (3 1/2 oz) Parmesan, grated

1 Preheat the oven to moderate 180°C (350°F/ Gas 4). Heat the butter in a pan, add the mushrooms, tomato, pepper, onion, cabanossi and basil and cook until soft.

2 Mix the eggs, cream and Parmesan. Add the mushroom mixture and pour into a greased 20 cm (8 inch) pie plate. Bake for 30 minutes. Cool to room temperature and cut into small wedges to serve.

NOTE: You can use chopped ham or salami instead of the cabanossi.

ASPARAGUS AND PROSCIUTTO ROLLS

Preparation time: 20 minutes
Total cooking time: 8 minutes
Makes 24

☆

12 slices prosciutto
24 asparagus spears
100 g (3½ oz) butter, melted
60 g (2 oz) Parmesan, grated
fresh nutmeg, grated
1 lemon

1 Preheat the oven to moderate 180°C (350°F/ Gas 4). Cut each slice of prosciutto in half. Cut off the base of each asparagus stem so that the spear is about 9 cm (3½ inches) long. Bring a pan of lightly salted water to the boil, add the asparagus and cook for 1 minute, or until just tender.

2 Drain the asparagus and pat dry. Brush with the melted butter, then roll the spears in the grated Parmesan. Wrap each asparagus spear in half a slice of prosciutto.

3 Brush an ovenproof dish, large enough to hold the asparagus in a single layer, with melted butter. Place the asparagus bundles in the dish. Sprinkle with any remaining Parmesan, grated nutmeg and cracked black pepper, to taste. Bake for 7 minutes. Squeeze a little fresh lemon juice over the top and serve.

NOTE: Thinly sliced bacon can be substituted for the prosciutto.

IN ADVANCE: The rolls can be assembled up to 6 hours ahead, covered and refrigerated. Cook just before serving.

NUTMEG
Nutmegs are available whole or ground. However, freshly grated nutmeg has a fresher and much more fragrant flavour than ready-ground, so buy whole nutmeg and a grater and grate your own when required. The spice is used in both sweet and savoury dishes.

LEFT: Asparagus and prosciutto rolls

MEDITERRANEAN PANTRY

Anchovy fillets: small fish fillets that are salt cured, canned or bottled in oil. The strong flavour and saltiness can be reduced by soaking in milk or water for a short time.

Arborio rice: Italian-grown, short-grain rice, used for making risotto because of the high starch content.

Artichoke hearts: the edible buds from a large plant of the thistle family. Available canned or bottled in brine or oil.

Pine nuts: high-fat nuts from a variety of pine tree. One of the more expensive nuts, due to the labour required to separate the nuts from the cones. Toasting brings out the flavour.

Parmesan: a hard cheese with a crumbly texture and distinctive flavour. Made from skimmed or partly skimmed cow's milk and aged for 2–3 years in large 'wheels'.

Mozzarella: a smooth, mild, white soft cheese. Originally made from buffalo milk, but now made from cow's milk or a mixture. Available sealed in plastic, or loose in whey or water. Bocconcini are small individual mozzarella balls.

Goats cheese: varies in texture from smooth and creamy to soft and crumbly, depending on the age of the cheese. Available plain or rolled in a variety of coatings from herbs to ash. Has a distinctive sharp taste.

Ricotta: a fresh, white, moist curd cheese, usually made from the whey drained off when making mozzarella. Slightly grainy, but smoother than cottage cheese.

Balsamic vinegar: gets its sweet and syrupy intense flavour and dark colour from being aged in a variety of wooden barrels. Use sparingly as a flavouring as well as a vinegar.

Olive oils: extra virgin olive oil is made from the first pressing of the olives and used mainly in uncooked dishes or dressings. Use a basic olive oil for cooking.

Olives: are black or green and varying sizes. Some are stuffed with anchovies, almonds or pimientos, others are cured in salt or marinated in oil.

Capers: flower buds of a bush native to the Mediterranean and parts of Asia. Sun-dried, then pickled in vinegar or brine. Available in several sizes. Also sold salted in jars.

Sun-dried tomatoes/peppers (capsicums): chewy, intensely flavoured and dark in colour. Available packed in oil or dry. The dry ones must be soaked in oil or other liquid to reconstitute before use.

Rocket: also known as arugula. A bitter, aromatic salad leaf with a peppery mustard tang. Available in bunches, sometimes with roots attached.

Feta: Firm white cheese with a crumbly texture and mild salty flavour. Originally made from goat and sheep's milk, now often made with cow's milk. Pressed into cakes and preserved in brine.

Haloumi: a firm, yet creamy, salty cheese. It is made from sheep's milk and matured in a whey and salt mixture. Smooth and creamy when melted.

Vine leaves: Available in jars or plastic packs in brine. Wash before use to remove saltiness. Fresh vine leaves need to be simmered before use to soften.

Pastrami: a well-seasoned dry-cured, smoked, cooked lean cut of beef, rubbed with a mix which can contain salt, pepper, cumin, paprika and garlic.

Prosciutto: salted and air-dried hind leg of pork. The salt removes some of the moisture. Pancetta is a good substitute.

Roma tomatoes: also known as egg or plum tomatoes. Egg-shaped with thick walls yielding a high flesh to seed ratio, making them great for cooking.

21

ARTICHOKES

When you are in a hurry, as you are quite likely to be when entertaining, marinated bottled or canned artichokes can be used instead of fresh artichokes which are quite fiddly and time consuming to prepare.

CANNELLINI BEAN SALAD

Preparation time: 20 minutes
Total cooking time: Nil
Serves 6–8

425 g (13¹/₂ oz) can cannellini beans
1 tomato
3 anchovy fillets
1 tablespoon finely chopped red onion
2 teaspoons finely chopped fresh basil
2 teaspoons extra virgin olive oil
1 teaspoon balsamic vinegar
bread, for serving

1 Rinse and drain the cannellini beans. Finely chop the tomato and slice the anchovies.
2 Mix the cannellini beans, tomato and anchovies with the red onion, basil, olive oil and balsamic vinegar. This can be spooned onto crusty sliced bread or slices of French bread stick lightly brushed with oil, then toasted and rubbed with garlic.
IN ADVANCE: The salad can be prepared up to a day ahead, covered and refrigerated.

ARTICHOKE FRITTATA

Preparation time: 20 minutes
Total cooking time: 25 minutes
Makes 8 wedges

30 g (1 oz) butter
2 small leeks, sliced
1 clove garlic, sliced
6 eggs
100 g (3¹/₂ oz) bottled marinated artichoke hearts, sliced
1 teaspoon chopped fresh tarragon
lemon juice, for drizzling

1 Heat the butter in a 20 cm (8 inch) non-stick frying pan, add the leek and garlic and cook until soft. Spread evenly over the bottom of the pan.
2 Lightly beat the eggs and season with salt and black pepper. Pour the eggs into the pan and arrange the artichoke slices on top. Sprinkle with the tarragon and cook over low heat until set (this will take about 10 minutes), shaking the pan occasionally to evenly distribute the egg.
3 Place under a hot grill to lightly brown. Cut into wedges and drizzle with a little lemon juice.

ABOVE: Cannellini bean salad (top left); Artichoke frittata

SCALLOP FRITTERS

Preparation time: 20 minutes
Total cooking time: 4–5 minutes per batch
Makes 40

250 g (8 oz) scallops
6 eggs
25 g (³/₄ oz) Parmesan, grated
3 cloves garlic, crushed
I cup (125 g/4 oz) plain flour
2 tablespoons chopped fresh thyme
2 tablespoons chopped fresh oregano
oil, for shallow-frying
mayonnaise, for serving, optional

1 Clean and roughly chop the scallops. Lightly beat the eggs and combine with the Parmesan, garlic, flour and herbs. Stir in the scallops.
2 Heat 3 cm (1¼ inches) oil in a deep frying pan to 180°C (350°F). The oil is ready when a cube of bread browns in 15 seconds. Cook the fritters in batches. Using 1 tablespoon of batter for each fritter, pour into the oil and cook for 4–5 minutes, over moderate heat, until golden brown. Drain on crumpled paper towels and sprinkle lightly with salt. Can be served with mayonnaise for dipping.

SARDINES IN VINE LEAVES

Preparation time: 30 minutes + soaking
Total cooking time: 30 minutes
Makes 12

12 packaged or fresh vine leaves
3 tablespoons olive oil
I clove garlic, crushed
I spring onion, finely chopped
2 tablespoons pine nuts
3 tablespoons chopped fresh parsley
2 teaspoons finely grated lemon rind
3 tablespoons fresh white breadcrumbs
12 butterflied sardines

1 If using vine leaves in brine, soak in cold water for 30 minutes, drain and pat dry. For fresh leaves, place in a large heatproof bowl and cover with boiling water. Leave for 2–3 minutes,

rinse with cold water, drain and pat dry. Preheat the oven to moderate 180°C (350°F/Gas 4).
2 Heat 1 tablespoon of the oil in a frying pan and add the garlic, spring onion and pine nuts. Cook, stirring, over medium heat, until the pine nuts just begin to brown. Combine in a bowl with the parsley, lemon rind and breadcrumbs. Season with salt and freshly ground black pepper.
3 Fill the sardines with the breadcrumb mixture and wrap each in a vine leaf. Place in a single layer in a well greased baking dish. Drizzle with the remaining olive oil and bake for 30 minutes. Serve at room temperature.
IN ADVANCE: You can prepare and wrap the sardines the day before and store, covered, in the refrigerator. Remove, drizzle with the oil and bake a few hours ahead of time.

ABOVE: Scallop fritters (top); Sardines in vine leaves

23

SUPPLI

Preparation time: 40 minutes + chilling
Total cooking time: 1 hour
Makes about 30

★★

3 cups (750 ml/24 fl oz) chicken stock
60 g (2 oz) butter
1 small onion, finely chopped
1²/₃ cups (360 g/12 oz) arborio rice
¹/₂ cup (125 ml/4 fl oz) white wine
pinch of powdered saffron
50 g (1³/₄ oz) Parmesan, grated
2 eggs, lightly beaten
100 g (3¹/₂ oz) mozzarella cheese
1 cup (100 g/3¹/₂ oz) dry breadcrumbs
oil, for deep-frying

1 Put the stock in a pan, bring to the boil, reduce the heat and maintain at simmering point. Heat the butter in a large heavy-based

BELOW: Suppli

pan. Add the onion and cook for 2–3 minutes, until softened but not brown. Add the rice and stir for another 2–3 minutes, until well coated with butter and onion.

2 Add the combined wine and saffron and stir until all the wine is absorbed. Add ¹/₂ cup (125 ml/4 fl oz) stock to the rice and stir continuously until absorbed, then continue adding the stock a little at a time, stirring, until ¹/₂ cup stock remains (about 15 minutes). Add the remaining stock and stir, then cover with a tight-fitting lid. Reduce the heat to very low and cook for 10–15 minutes, until the rice is tender. Allow to cool.

3 Gently stir through the Parmesan, eggs and salt and pepper, to taste. Cut the mozzarella cheese into 30 small cubes. With wet hands, form the rice mixture into 30 walnut-sized balls. Push a cube of mozzarella into the centre of each ball and mould the rice around it.

4 Coat each ball with breadcrumbs. Chill for at least 1 hour to firm. Fill a deep heavy-based pan one third full of oil and heat the oil to 180°C (350°F). The oil is ready when a cube of bread turns golden brown in 15 seconds. Fry 3–4 balls at a time for 4–5 minutes, or until golden brown. Drain on crumpled paper towels. Serve hot.
NOTE: The full name is Suppli al Telefono. Serve hot, so that when bitten into, the cheese filling pulls out into long thin strands like telephone wires.
IN ADVANCE: Cover and refrigerate for up to 3 days. Reheat in a warm oven for 15 minutes.

CHEESE FRITTERS

Preparation time: 15 minutes + chilling
Total cooking time: 10 minutes
Makes about 35–40

★★

175 g (6 oz) block firm feta cheese
125 g (4 oz) mozzarella cheese
¹/₃ cup (40 g/1¹/₄ oz) plain flour
1 egg, lightly beaten
¹/₂ cup (50 g/1³/₄ oz) dry breadcrumbs
oil, for deep-frying

1 Cut the feta and mozzarella into 2 cm (³/₄ inch) cubes. Combine the flour and ¹/₄ teaspoon black pepper on a sheet of greaseproof paper. Toss the cheese lightly in the seasoned flour and shake off the excess.
2 Dip the cheese into the egg a few pieces at a

STUFFED SARDINES

Remove the head of the sardine, then cut through the gut to open the sardine out flat.

Carefully scrape the flesh away from the backbone, cut at either end and lift out the bone.

Spoon a little stuffing along the middle of each sardine and carefully lift onto a baking tray.

time. Coat with breadcrumbs and shake off the excess. Repeat the process with the remaining cheese and crumbs. Arrange on a foil-lined tray and refrigerate, covered, for 25 minutes.

3 Heat 3 cm (1¼ inches) oil in a deep frying pan to 180°C (350°F). The oil is ready when a cube of bread browns in 15 seconds. Cook a few pieces of cheese at a time over medium heat, for 2–3 minutes each batch, or until golden and crisp. Drain on crumpled paper towels. Serve.

NOTE: Serve cheese fritters with sweet chilli, plum or cranberry sauce or warmed mint jelly.

STUFFED SARDINES

Preparation time: 40 minutes
Total cooking time: 20 minutes
Makes 16

✷ ✷

16 large sardines
⅔ cup (65 g/2¼ oz) dry breadcrumbs
2 cloves garlic, crushed
2 tablespoons capers, drained and
    finely chopped

35 g (1¼ oz) Parmesan, grated
2 egg yolks, lightly beaten
juice of 2 lemons, to serve

1 Preheat the oven to moderately hot 200°C (400°F/Gas 6). Lightly grease a baking tray.
2 Remove the heads from the sardines, make a slit through the gut and open out flat. Remove the guts and carefully scrape the flesh away from the backbone; trim at the tail end, leaving the tail intact. Lift out the backbone; discard. Wash the sardines well and drain on paper towels.
3 Mix together the breadcrumbs, garlic, capers, Parmesan, freshly ground black pepper and enough egg yolk to bind the stuffing together. Spoon a little onto each open sardine, put on the baking tray and bake for 20 minutes, or until golden. Serve warm or cold, drizzled with lemon juice.

NOTE: You can buy sardines already filleted at some fishmongers. This makes the recipe quick and simple.

IN ADVANCE: The sardines and stuffing can be prepared a day ahead and refrigerated separately. Assemble several hours ahead.

ABOVE: Stuffed sardines

ITALIAN MEATBALLS

Preparation time: 25 minutes
Total cooking time: 20 minutes
Makes about 25

250 g (8 oz) lean beef mince
I small onion, grated
I clove garlic, crushed
1/2 cup (40 g/I 1/4 oz) fresh white breadcrumbs
40 g (I 1/4 oz) pitted black olives, chopped
I teaspoon dried oregano
I tablespoon finely chopped fresh parsley
oil, for cooking

I Combine the mince, onion, garlic, breadcrumbs, olives, oregano, parsley and salt and black pepper, to taste. Mix together thoroughly with your hands.
2 Form teaspoons of the mixture into balls. This is easier if you roll them with wet hands. Heat a little oil in a frying pan and cook the meatballs in batches until well browned and cooked through.
IN ADVANCE: You can prepare the meatballs, cover and refrigerate, then cook when you are ready, or cook them in advance and reheat them, lightly covered with foil, in a warm 160°C (315°F/Gas 2–3) oven. They can also be cooked and frozen, then reheated.

SMOKED COD FRITTATA

Preparation time: 20 minutes
Total cooking time: 20 minutes
Makes 12 slices

500 g (I lb) smoked cod
I cup (250 ml/8 fl oz) milk
8 eggs
60 g (2 oz) Parmesan, grated
60 g (2 oz) Cheddar, grated
2 tablespoons chopped fresh thyme
30 g (I oz) fresh basil leaves, torn
2 tablespoons olive oil

I Place the smoked cod in a pan with the milk mixed with enough water to cover. Bring to the boil, then reduce the heat and simmer for 3–4 minutes. Remove with a slotted spoon and flake the flesh.

2 Whisk the eggs in a bowl and add the Parmesan and Cheddar, thyme, basil leaves and the fish. Mix together well.
3 Heat the oil in a large 23–25 cm (9–10 inch) heavy-based frying pan. Pour in the mixture and cook over medium heat for 10 minutes, or until nearly cooked. Place under a hot grill for 3–4 minutes, or until just set and lightly golden. Cut into wedges for serving.

MUSSELS WITH CRISPY PROSCIUTTO

Preparation time: 20 minutes
Total cooking time: 15–20 minutes
Makes about 20

I tablespoon oil
I onion, finely chopped
6 thin slices prosciutto, chopped
4 cloves garlic, crushed
1.5 kg (3 lb) black mussels
60 g (2 oz) Parmesan, grated
60 g (2 oz) Cheddar, grated

I Heat the oil in a small frying pan and add the onion, prosciutto, and garlic. Cook over medium heat for 5–8 minutes, until the prosciutto is crispy and the onion softened, then set aside.
2 Scrub the mussels with a stiff brush and pull out the hairy beards. Discard any broken mussels, or open ones that don't close when tapped on the bench. Add to a large pan of boiling water and cook for 5 minutes. Stir occasionally and discard any mussels that don't open. Remove the mussels from their shells, keeping half of each shell. Place 2 mussels on each half-shell and top each with a little of the prosciutto mixture.
3 Combine the Parmesan and Cheddar and sprinkle over the prosciutto. Cook under a preheated grill until the cheese has melted and the mussels are warmed through.
IN ADVANCE: The mussels can be scrubbed and beards removed several hours ahead of time.

OPPOSITE PAGE, FROM TOP: Italian meatballs; Smoked cod frittata; Mussels with crispy prosciutto

27

BRUSCHETTA Crusty bread—whether

it's an Italian loaf, French stick or sourdough—lightly toasted and topped with

colourful fresh ingredients will satisfy the hungriest of guests.

SMOKED SALMON AND CAPERS

Cut 2 small French bread sticks into 1 cm (1/2 inch) slices and lightly grill until golden on both sides. Mix 250 g (8 oz) cream cheese with 2 tablespoons lemon juice and 15 g (1/2 oz) chopped chives. Spread over the toast and top with small slices of smoked salmon and a few baby capers. Garnish with sprigs of fresh dill before serving. Makes about 24.

GRILLED PEPPERS (CAPSICUMS)

Cut 2 yellow, 2 green and 2 red peppers (capsicums) in half lengthways. Remove the seeds and membrane, place skin-side-up under a hot grill and cook until the skins have blackened. Cool in a plastic bag, then peel off the skins. Thinly slice the peppers and place in a large bowl. Add 1 small red onion, sliced into thin wedges, 1½ tablespoons olive oil, 1½ tablespoons balsamic vinegar and

2 crushed cloves of garlic. Slice 2 small sourdough bread sticks into 1 cm (1/2 inch) slices. Lightly grill until golden on both sides. Top with the pepper mixture. Makes about 24.

ROCKET AND FETA

Cut a large French bread stick or an Italian loaf into 1 cm (1/2 inch) slices, brush with olive oil and grill until golden on both sides. Arrange rocket leaves over

each piece, using about 90 g (3 oz) altogether. Toss 200 g (6½ oz) crumbled feta with 2 teaspoons finely grated orange rind and 2 tablespoons olive oil. Spoon 2 teaspoons of the mixture over the rocket on each bruschetta. Grill 6 slices prosciutto until crispy, then crumble over the bruschetta. Makes about 30.

CAPRESSE

Mix 150 g (5 oz) finely diced bocconcini, with 3 tablespoons shredded fresh basil and 3 tablespoons warm extra virgin olive oil in a glass bowl. Season with salt and pepper, to taste. Cover and leave in a warm place for 1 hour to allow the flavours to develop. Cut a large French bread stick or an Italian loaf into 1 cm (½ inch) slices, brush with olive oil and grill until golden on both sides. Spread the bocconcini mixture over the toast. Makes about 30.

MUSHROOM AND PARSLEY

Cut a large French bread stick or Italian loaf into 1 cm (½ inch) slices, brush with olive oil and grill until golden on both sides. Heat 1 tablespoon of olive oil in a small frying pan, and fry 200 g (6½ oz) quartered small button mushrooms until just tender. Stir in 1 tablespoon lemon juice, 50 g (1¾ oz) crumbled goats cheese, a tablespoon of chopped fresh flat-leaf parsley and season, to taste. Spread over the toast. Makes about 30.

TOMATO AND BASIL

Cut a large French bread stick or Italian loaf into 1 cm (½ inch) slices, brush with olive oil and grill until golden on both sides. Finely chop 4 ripe tomatoes and mix with ½ cup (30 g/1 oz) finely shredded fresh basil and 2 tablespoons extra virgin olive oil. Spread over the toast. Makes about 30.

PASTRAMI AND HERBS

Cut a large French bread stick or Italian loaf into 1 cm (½ inch) slices, brush with olive oil and grill until golden on both sides. Combine 200 ml (6½ fl oz) of crème fraîche with 1 teaspoon each of chopped fresh parsley, chives and basil. Spread 1 teaspoon over each slice of toast. Halve 30 slices of pastrami, fold in half again and place 2 pieces over the crème fraîche. Mix 2 chopped tomatoes with ½ finely chopped red onion and 2 teaspoons each of balsamic vinegar and olive oil. Spoon over the top and garnish with small fresh basil leaves. Makes about 30.

FROM LEFT: Smoked salmon and capers; Grilled peppers; Rocket and feta; Capresse; Mushroom and parsley; Tomato and basil; Pastrami and herbs

29

CAPERS

Capers are the unopened flower buds of a small plant native to the Mediterranean. They are sold pickled and should be refrigerated after opening. The flavour is quite strong so they are used in small quantities. Smaller capers have a more subtle flavour and crunchier texture. Capers are also available coated and packed in salt. They should be rinsed before use.

ABOVE: Fritto misto di mare

FRITTO MISTO DI MARE

Preparation time: 30 minutes
Total cooking time: 12 minutes
Makes about 50 pieces

Tartare sauce

1 1/2 cups (375 ml/12 fl oz) mayonnaise
1 bottled gherkin, chopped
1 teaspoon bottled capers, drained and finely chopped
1 tablespoon chopped fresh chives
1 tablespoon chopped fresh parsley
1/4 teaspoon Dijon mustard
1/4 small onion, finely grated

Batter

1 cup (125 g/4 oz) self-raising flour
1/4 cup (30 g/1 oz) cornflour
1 tablespoon oil

500 g (1 lb) fish fillets, bones removed
12 sardines
8 raw medium king prawns, peeled

8 scallops, cleaned and deveined
1 calamari hood, cut into rings
flour, for coating
oil, for deep-frying
lemon wedges, for serving

1 For the tartare sauce, combine all the ingredients in a small bowl and mix well.
2 To make the batter, sift the flour and cornflour and a little salt and pepper into a large bowl. Make a well in the centre. Combine the oil and 1 cup (250 ml/8 fl oz) water and gradually whisk into the flour until a smooth batter is formed.
3 Cut the fish fillets into 5 cm (2 inch) strips. To prepare the fresh sardines, remove the heads and split them open down the belly, then clean with salted water. Ease the backbone out with your fingers and cut the backbone at the tail end with sharp scissors.
4 Dry the prepared seafood on paper towels, then coat in the flour and shake off the excess.
5 Heat the oil in a large deep pan to 180°C (350°F). The oil is ready when a cube of bread dropped into the oil turns golden brown in 15 seconds. Coat a few pieces of seafood at a time with batter and gently lower into the hot

oil with tongs or a slotted spoon. Cook for 2–3 minutes, or until crisp and golden brown. Drain on crumpled paper towels. Keep warm while cooking the remaining seafood. Serve with a bowl of tartare sauce and lemon wedges.
IN ADVANCE: The seafood for this dish can be prepared several hours ahead and kept covered in the refrigerator.

ROASTED BALSAMIC ONIONS

Preparation time: 15 minutes + overnight chilling
Total cooking time: 1 hour 30 minutes
Makes about 30

1 kg (2 lb) pickling onions, unpeeled (see Note)
¾ cup (185 ml/6 fl oz) balsamic vinegar
2 tablespoons soft brown sugar
¾ cup (185 ml/6 fl oz) olive oil

1 Preheat the oven to warm 160°C (315°F/ Gas 2–3). Bake the onions in a baking dish for 1½ hours. Leave until cool enough to handle.

Trim off the stems and peel away the skin (the outer part of the root should come away but the onions will remain intact). Rinse a 1-litre wide-necked jar with boiling water and dry in a warm oven (do not dry with a tea towel). Put the onions in the jar.
2 Combine the vinegar and sugar in a small screw-top jar and stir to dissolve the sugar. Add the oil, seal the jar and shake vigorously until combined—the mixture will be paler and may separate on standing.
3 Pour the vinegar mixture over the onions, seal, and turn upside down to coat. Marinate overnight in the refrigerator, turning occasionally. Return to room temperature and shake the jar to thoroughly combine the dressing before serving.
NOTE: Pickling onions are very small, usually packed in 1 kg (2 lb) bags. The ideal size is around 35 g (1¼ oz) each. The sizes in the bag will probably range from 20 g (¾ oz) up to 45 g (1½ oz). The cooking time given is suitable for this range and there is no need to cook the larger ones for any longer. The marinating time given is a minimum time and the onions may be marinated for up to 3 days in the refrigerator. The marinade may separate after a few hours, which is fine—simply stir occasionally.

ABOVE: Roasted balsamic onions

HAM AND PINEAPPLE PIZZA WHEELS

Rub the chopped butter into the flour with your fingertips until the mixture resembles breadcrumbs.

Roll the dough into a rectangle and use a flat-bladed knife to spread all over with tomato paste.

Use the baking paper as a guide as you roll up the dough from the long side.

HAM AND PINEAPPLE PIZZA WHEELS

Preparation time: 25 minutes
Total cooking time: 20 minutes
Makes 16

★ ★

2 cups (250 g/8 oz) self-raising flour
40 g (1¼ oz) butter, chopped
½ cup (125 ml/4 fl oz) milk
4 tablespoons tomato paste
  (tomato purée)
2 small onions, finely chopped
4 pineapple slices, finely chopped
200 g (6½ oz) sliced ham, shredded
80 g (2¾ oz) Cheddar, grated
2 tablespoons finely chopped fresh parsley

1 Preheat the oven to moderate 180°C (350°F/Gas 4). Brush 2 baking trays with oil. Sift the flour into a bowl, add the butter and rub into the flour with your fingertips until the mixture resembles fine breadcrumbs. Make a well and add almost all the milk. With a flat-bladed knife, mix with a cutting action until the mixture comes together in beads. Gather into a ball and turn onto a lightly floured surface. Divide the dough in half. Roll out each half on baking paper to a 20 x 30 cm (8 x 12 inch) rectangle, about 5 mm (¼ inch) thick. Spread the tomato paste over each rectangle, leaving a 1 cm (½ inch) border.

2 Mix the onion, pineapple, ham, Cheddar and parsley. Spread evenly over the tomato paste, leaving a 2 cm (¾ inch) border. Using the paper as a guide, roll up the dough from the long side.

3 Cut each roll into 8 even slices. Place on the tray and bake for 20 minutes, or until golden. Serve warm.

IN ADVANCE: The wheels can be made in advance and gently reheated.

ABOVE: Ham and pineapple pizza wheels

CAVIAR POTATOES

Cook some unpeeled baby potatoes (enough for your gathering) in a large pan of boiling water until tender. Allow to cool slightly. While still warm, carefully cut off the top and scoop out a little of the centre. Fill the hole with sour cream and top with caviar. You can mix finely chopped herbs or spring onion into the sour cream if you wish. Garnish with tiny sprigs of fresh dill. Serve warm.

PESTO AND TOMATO TOASTS

Preparation time: 15 minutes
Total cooking time: 5 minutes
Makes about 30

Pesto

1 cup (50 g/1 ¾ oz) fresh basil leaves
½ cup (50 g/1 ¾ oz) pecan nuts
¼ cup (60 ml/2 fl oz) olive oil
3 cloves garlic

1 French bread stick, thinly sliced
10 large sun-dried tomatoes, cut into thin strips
150 g (5 oz) Parmesan, thinly shaved

1 To make the pesto, mix the basil leaves, pecans, oil and garlic in a food processor until the mixture is smooth.
2 Toast the bread slices under a grill until brown on both sides.
3 Spread the pesto evenly over the pieces of toast. Top each slice with sun-dried tomatoes and some of the Parmesan.
IN ADVANCE: The pesto can be made several days ahead and stored in a jar. Pour a thin layer of olive oil over the top of the pesto to just cover. Pesto can also be frozen in ice cube trays and thawed when required.

MINI VEAL SALTIMBOCCA

Preparation time: 20 minutes + soaking
Total cooking time: 15 minutes
Makes about 40

40 small wooden skewers (about 10 cm/ 4 inches) long
500 g (1 lb) piece veal fillet
8–10 slices prosciutto
60 g (2 oz) fresh sage leaves
30 g (1 oz) butter
2 teaspoons oil
2 tablespoons dry sherry

1 Soak the wooden skewers in warm water for about 20 minutes to prevent them burning while the meat is cooking. Cut the veal fillet into 40 thin slices, each measuring roughly

3 x 6 cm (1 ¼ x 2 ½ inches). Cut the prosciutto slices slightly smaller than the veal. Top each piece of veal with a piece of prosciutto, then a fresh sage leaf. Weave a skewer through all the layers to secure.
2 Heat half the butter and oil in a large frying pan, add half the skewers and cook over high heat until the veal is brown, then turn and brown other side.
3 Drizzle half the dry sherry over the cooked meat and gently shake the pan. Remove the skewers from the pan, pouring any juices over the skewers. Keep warm while you repeat with the remaining skewers. Serve soon after cooking, drizzled with any juices.
IN ADVANCE: The skewers can be prepared a day ahead. Keep covered in the refrigerator.

ABOVE: Pesto and tomato toasts

1 Pat the feta cheese dry with paper towels and cut into 2 cm (¾ inch) cubes. Transfer to a bowl and sprinkle the oregano, coriander seeds and 1 tablespoon cracked black pepper all over the feta cheese.

2 Drain the sun-dried tomatoes over a bowl so that you retain all of the oil. Arrange the feta, chillies, rosemary and sun-dried tomatoes in a sterilized 3-cup (750 ml/24 fl oz) wide-necked jar with a clip-top lid. Cover with the reserved sun-dried tomato oil (you should have about 3 tablespoons) and top up with olive oil. Seal and refrigerate for 1 week before using. Serve at room temperature.

NOTES: To sterilize a storage jar, rinse with boiling water, then place in a very slow oven until completely dry.

The oil in the bottle will partly solidify when refrigerated, but will liquify when returned to room temperature.

IN ADVANCE: The marinated feta will keep in the refrigerator for 1–2 months. Use the oil to make salad dressings or to flavour pasta.

BLACK OLIVE AND PEPPER (CAPSICUM) TAPENADE

Preparation time: 15 minutes
Total cooking time: Nil
Makes about 1 cup (250 ml/8 fl oz)

75 g (2½ oz) pitted black olives, sliced
75 g (2½ oz) sun-dried peppers (capsicums) in oil, drained
1 tablespoon capers
1 large clove garlic
30 g (1 oz) flat-leaf parsley
1 tablespoon lime juice
90 ml (3 fl oz) extra virgin olive oil

1 Blend the olives, sun-dried peppers, capers, garlic and parsley together in a food processor or blender until finely minced. With the motor running, slowly add the lime juice and olive oil and process until just combined.

2 Transfer to a sterilized jar, seal and refrigerate for up to 2 weeks. Return to room temperature before serving.

3 Serve on bread or crackers, either as a spread by itself or spooned on top of ricotta cheese. It can also be served with pork and lamb skewers.

MARINATED FETA

Preparation time: 10 minutes
+ 1 week chilling
Total cooking time: Nil
Serves 6–8

350 g (11 oz) feta
1 tablespoon dried oregano
1 teaspoon coriander seeds
125 g (4 oz) sun-dried tomatoes in oil
4 small fresh red chillies
3–4 sprigs fresh rosemary
olive oil

ABOVE: Marinated feta

GARLIC AND HERB MARINATED ARTICHOKES

Preparation time: 20 minutes + overnight chilling
Total cooking time: Nil
Serves 8

2 cloves garlic, chopped
1/2 cup (125 ml/4 fl oz) olive oil
2 tablespoons finely chopped fresh dill
15 g (1/2 oz) finely chopped fresh parsley
2 tablespoons finely chopped fresh basil
2 tablespoons lemon juice
2 x 400 g (13 oz) cans artichoke hearts
3 tablespoons finely diced red pepper
  (capsicum)

1 To make the marinade, combine the garlic, oil, herbs and lemon juice in a bowl and whisk until well combined. Season with salt and cracked black pepper.
2 Drain the artichoke hearts and add to the marinade with the red pepper. Mix well to coat. Cover and marinate in the refrigerator overnight. Serve as part of an antipasto platter or use in salads. Return the artichokes to room temperature before serving.
IN ADVANCE: The artichokes will keep in an airtight container in the refrigerator for up to a week.

SMOKED TROUT PUFFS

Cut 36 small squares from a sheet of ready-rolled puff pastry. Brush the tops lightly with beaten egg and sprinkle with sesame seeds. Place on greased baking trays and bake in a hot 220°C (425°F/Gas 7) oven for about 8 minutes, until puffed and well browned. Allow to cool, then gently split in half. Soften 250 g (8 oz) light cream cheese and blend with some finely chopped capers, finely chopped spring onion and chopped fresh dill. Spread on the bases of the squares, top with a small roll of smoked trout, then replace the pastry tops at a slight angle. Makes 36.

ABOVE: Garlic and herb marinated artichokes

FLAT-LEAF PARSLEY
Also known as continental parsley, flat-leaf parsley has a slightly stronger flavour than curly-leafed parsley and is available all year round. Both the stems and leaves are used in French cooking, whereas in Italy they normally just use the leaves. Buy parsley with firm stems and bright leaves, not yellowing. To store, stand the stalks in a jar of water in the refrigerator or wrap in paper towels and keep in the vegetable crisper.

ABOVE: Whitebait fritters

WHITEBAIT FRITTERS

Preparation time: 20 minutes + resting
Total cooking time: 15 minutes
Makes 12–15

1/4 cup (30 g/1 oz) self-raising flour
1/4 cup (30 g/1 oz) plain flour
1/2 teaspoon bicarbonate of soda
1 egg, lightly beaten
3 tablespoons dry white wine
2 teaspoons chopped fresh flat-leaf parsley
1 clove garlic, crushed
1/2 small onion, grated
200 g (6 1/2 oz) Chinese or New Zealand whitebait
olive oil, for shallow-frying
lemon wedges, for serving

1 Sift the flours, bicarbonate of soda, 1/2 teaspoon salt and some freshly ground black pepper into a bowl. Stir in the egg and wine, whisk until smooth, then add the parsley, garlic, onion and whitebait. Cover and refrigerate for 20 minutes.

2 Heat about 2 cm (3/4 inch) of the oil in a deep frying pan to 180°C (350°F). The oil is ready when a cube of bread dropped into the oil turns golden brown in 15 seconds. Drop in level tablespoons of batter and, when the batter is puffed and bubbles appear on the surface, carefully turn to cook the other side.
3 Drain on paper towels and serve immediately with lemon wedges.
NOTE: The whitebait is very small and fine and is available fresh or frozen. There is no need to gut or scale them as they are so small.

WRAPPED PRAWNS WITH MANGO DIP

Blanch some snow peas (mangetout) and wrap around peeled cooked prawns. Secure each with a toothpick. Make a dip by mixing 1/2 cup (125 ml/4 fl oz) mayonnaise with 2 tablespoons mango chutney, 1 teaspoon curry paste and 1 tablespoon lime juice. Vary the amount of snow peas and prawns according to your needs and double the dip if you need more.

CHARGRILLED OCTOPUS

Preparation time: 15 minutes + marinating
Total cooking time: 10 minutes
Serves 6

2/3 cup (170 ml/5 1/2 fl oz) olive oil
1/3 cup (10 g/1/4 oz) chopped fresh oregano
1/3 cup (10 g/1/4 oz) chopped fresh parsley
1 tablespoon lemon juice
3 small red chillies, seeded, finely chopped
3 cloves garlic, crushed
1 kg (2 lb) baby octopus

1 Combine the oil, herbs, lemon juice, chilli and garlic in a large bowl and mix well.
2 Use a small sharp knife to remove the octopus heads. Grasp the bodies and push the beaks out from the centre with your index finger; remove and discard. Slit the heads and remove the gut. If the octopus are too large, cut them into smaller portions.
3 Mix the octopus with the herb marinade. Cover and refrigerate for 3–4 hours, or overnight. Drain, reserving the marinade. Cook on a very hot lightly oiled barbecue or in a very hot pan for 3–5 minutes, or until the flesh turns white. Turn frequently and brush generously with the marinade during cooking.

MARINATED SEAFOOD

Preparation time: 40 minutes + chilling
Total cooking time: 10 minutes
Serves 8

500 g (1 lb) mussels, scrubbed, beards removed
1/2 cup (125 ml/4 fl oz) white wine vinegar
3 bay leaves
500 g (1 lb) small squid hoods, sliced
500 g (1 lb) scallops
500 g (1 lb) raw prawns, peeled and deveined
2 cloves garlic, crushed
1/2 cup (125 ml/4 fl oz) extra virgin olive oil
3 tablespoons lemon juice
1 tablespoon white wine vinegar
1 teaspoon Dijon mustard
1 tablespoon chopped fresh parsley

1 Discard any mussels that are already open. Put the vinegar, bay leaves, 3 cups (750 ml/24 fl oz) water and 1/2 teaspoon of salt in a large pan and bring to the boil. Add the squid and scallops, then reduce the heat to low and simmer for 2–3 minutes, or until the seafood has turned white. Remove the squid and scallops with a slotted spoon and place in a bowl.
2 Repeat the process with the prawns, cooking until just pink, then removing with a slotted spoon. Return the liquid to the boil and add the mussels. Cover, reduce the heat and simmer for 3 minutes, or until all the shells are open. Stir occasionally and discard any unopened mussels. Cool, remove the meat and add to the bowl.
3 Whisk the garlic and oil together with the lemon juice, vinegar, mustard and parsley. Pour over the seafood and toss well. Refrigerate for 1–2 hours before serving.
NOTE: Seafood should never be overcooked or it will become tough.

ABOVE: Chargrilled octopus (top); Marinated seafood

37

MINI PIZZAS

Is there anyone who doesn't love pizza? Make the basic pizza bases as instructed, then top them off with one, or several, of the following ideas. Then watch them walk off the plate.

PIZZA BASES

Mix 7 g (¹/₄ oz) dried yeast, ¹/₂ teaspoon sugar and ³/₄ cup (185 ml/6 fl oz) warm water, cover and set aside for 10 minutes, or until frothy. Sift 2 cups (250 g/8 oz) plain flour and ¹/₂ teaspoon salt into a large bowl and make a well. Pour in the yeast mixture and add 1 tablespoon olive oil. Mix with a flat-bladed knife using a cutting action until the mixture forms a dough. Turn onto a lightly floured surface and knead for 10 minutes, or until

smooth. Place in a lightly oiled bowl, cover with plastic wrap and leave for 45 minutes, or until the dough has doubled. Punch down the dough (give it one firm punch with your fist to remove the air) and knead for 8 minutes. Roll to 1 cm (¹/₂ inch) thick. Cut out 7 cm (2³/₄ inch) rounds with a cutter. Place the rounds on a lightly greased baking tray, top with one of the following fillings and bake in a moderately hot 200°C (400°F/ Gas 6) oven for 15 minutes. Makes 25.

BEEF AND ROAST PEPPER (CAPSICUM)

Press 1¹/₂ tablespoons cracked black pepper onto a 250 g (8 oz) piece of rump steak. Heat a large frying pan, cook the steak for 5 minutes each side, then slice into thin strips. Cut a red pepper in half lengthways and remove the membrane and seeds. Grill skin-side-up until the skin is black and blistered. Place in a plastic bag until cool, then peel away the skin. Slice the flesh into thin strips.

Mix ⅓ cup (90 g/3 oz) tomato paste (tomato purée) with 2 teaspoons dried mixed herbs and spread the mixture over the pizza bases, leaving a small border. Sprinkle with ½ cup (75 g/2½ oz) grated mozzarella cheese, then top each one with a few beef and pepper strips and bake for 15 minutes, or until the bases are crisp and golden. Mix ⅓ cup (90 g/3 oz) sour cream with 2½ tablespoons seeded mustard, spoon over the pizzas and garnish with trimmed snow pea (mangetout) sprouts.

SPINACH AND BOCCONCINI
Spread 1 teaspoon tomato relish over each base (you will need ½ cup/125 ml/ 4 fl oz relish). Divide 60 g (2 oz) shredded English spinach leaves, 25 slices Roma (egg) tomato and 180 g (6 oz) sliced bocconcini among the pizza bases, then bake for 15 minutes, or until the bases are crisp.

PRAWN AND MANGO
Spread 1 teaspoon mango chutney over each base—you will need ½ cup (140 g/ 5 oz) chutney. Sprinkle with fresh coriander leaves and top each pizza with a peeled cooked prawn. Bake for 15 minutes, then top with thin slices of pepper brie cheese and allow to melt.

BRIE AND PEAR
Put 50 g (1¾ oz) brie, 1 tablespoon each of chopped fresh coriander, basil and parsley and 1 tablespoon each of cream, water and olive oil in a food processor and mix until smooth. Season, to taste, with a little salt. Core 2 small pears and cut each one into 14 thin slices. Spread half the brie mixture over the pizza bases, top each with a slice of pear and cover with the remaining cheese mixture. Bake for 15 minutes, or until the bases are golden and crisp. Serve immediately.

SUN-DRIED TOMATO PESTO AND CHICKEN
Fry 2 chicken breast fillets for 5–8 minutes on each side, or until golden. Cool slightly and slice into thin strips. Using 100 g (3½ oz) sun-dried tomato pesto, spread 1 teaspoon pesto over each base, leaving a small border. Mix together 35 g (1¼ oz) grated mozzarella cheese and 25 g (¾ oz) grated Parmesan, sprinkle over the bases and top with a few chicken strips. Bake for 15 minutes, or until the bases are golden and crisp. Garnish with small fresh basil leaves.

FROM LEFT: Beef and roast pepper; Spinach and bocconcini; Prawn and mango; Brie and pear; Sun-dried tomato pesto and chicken

BOCCONCINI

These small balls of fresh mozzarella cheese, found in some delicatessens and supermarkets, are often used in antipasto. Their creamy mild flavour combines well with tomato and basil. Smaller bocconcini are called ovolini, or sometimes cherry bocconcini. Store them in the refrigerator, fully covered in the whey in which they are sold, for up to three weeks. If you see any sign of yellowing, discard them.

RIGHT: Bocconcini tomato skewers

BOCCONCINI TOMATO SKEWERS

Preparation time: 20 minutes + chilling
Total cooking time: Nil
Makes 20

20 cherry bocconcini or ovolini, or 5 regular
    bocconcini, sliced into quarters
2 tablespoons olive oil
2 tablespoons chopped fresh parsley
1 tablespoon chopped fresh chives
20 small cherry tomatoes
40 small fresh basil leaves

1 Put the bocconcini in a bowl with the oil, parsley, chives, 1/4 teaspoon salt and 1/2 teaspoon ground black pepper. Cover and refrigerate for at least 1 hour, or preferably overnight.
2 Cut each cherry tomato in half and thread one half on a skewer or toothpick, followed by a basil leaf, then bocconcini, another basil leaf and then another tomato half. Repeat with more skewers and the remaining ingredients and serve.
IN ADVANCE: These can be served immediately, or covered and chilled for up to 8 hours.

MUSHROOM RISOTTO FRITTERS

Preparation time: 20 minutes + chilling
Total cooking time: 35 minutes
Makes 28

3 1/4 cups (810 ml/26 fl oz) vegetable stock
1 tablespoon olive oil
20 g (3/4 oz) butter
1 small onion, finely chopped
1 cup (220 g/7 oz) arborio or short-grain rice
150 g (5 oz) button mushrooms, thinly sliced
35 g (1 1/4 oz) Parmesan, grated
oil, for shallow-frying

1 Put the stock in a pan, bring to the boil, reduce the heat and keep at simmering point.
2 Heat the oil and butter in a heavy-based pan, add the onion and stir over medium heat for 3 minutes, or until softened. Add the rice and stir for 2 minutes. Add the mushrooms and cook for 3 minutes, or until soft.
3 Add 1/2 cup (125 ml/4 fl oz) stock to the rice and stir continuously until absorbed. Add more stock, stirring constantly, until all the stock is

absorbed and the rice is just tender and creamy. (This will take 15–20 minutes.) Stir in the Parmesan and remove from the heat. Transfer to a bowl. Cool, then refrigerate for at least 1 hour.
4 With wet hands, shape tablespoons of the mixture into flat rounds. Chill for 15 minutes.
5 Heat about 2 cm (³/4 inch) oil in a deep pan to 180°C (350°F). The oil is ready when a cube of bread dropped in the oil turns golden brown in 15 seconds. Cook the fritters in batches for 3 minutes each side, or until golden. Drain on crumpled paper towels. Can be served with relish.

HERB BAKED RICOTTA

Preparation time: 25 minutes + overnight marinating
Total cooking time: 30 minutes
Serves 4

1 kg (2 lb) wedge of ricotta (see Note)
2 tablespoons fresh thyme leaves
2 tablespoons chopped fresh rosemary
2 tablespoons chopped fresh oregano
3 tablespoons chopped fresh parsley
3 tablespoons chopped fresh chives
2 cloves garlic, crushed
¹/2 cup (125 ml/4 fl oz) olive oil
2 teaspoons cracked pepper

1 Pat the ricotta wedge dry with paper towels and place in a baking dish.
2 Mix the herbs, garlic, oil and cracked pepper in a bowl. Spoon onto the ricotta and press on with the back of a spoon. Cover and refrigerate overnight.
3 Preheat the oven to hot 220°C (425°F/Gas 7). Bake for 30 minutes, or until the ricotta is set. Delicious served with crusty bread.
NOTE: If you can only buy ricotta pieces, drain overnight in a colander over a bowl, in the refrigerator. Spread half the herb mixture in a 1.25 litre loaf tin. Spoon the ricotta in and spread with the remaining herbs before baking.

ABOVE: Herb baked ricotta

41

SEMI-DRIED TOMATOES

Preparation time: 10 minutes + overnight chilling
Total cooking time: 2 hours 30 minutes
Makes 64

16 Roma (egg) tomatoes
3 tablespoons fresh thyme, chopped
2 tablespoons olive oil

1 Preheat the oven to warm 160°C (315°F/ Gas 2–3). Quarter the tomatoes lengthways and lay skin-side-down on a rack in a baking tray.
2 Sprinkle with 1 teaspoon each of salt and cracked black pepper and the thyme and bake for 2½ hours. Check occasionally to make sure the tomatoes don't burn. Toss in the oil and cool before packing into sterilized jars and sealing. Refrigerate for 24 hours before using. Return to room temperature before serving. Suitable for an antipasto plate.
NOTE: To sterilize storage jars, rinse them thoroughly with boiling water, invert and drain, then place in a very slow oven to dry thoroughly. Don't dry with a tea towel.
IN ADVANCE: Can be kept in an airtight container in the fridge for up to 7 days.

ABOVE: Semi-dried tomatoes

ARTICHOKE PANZAROTTI

Preparation time: 35 minutes + resting + chilling
Total cooking time: 20 minutes
Makes 24

Oil and wine dough

2 cups (250 g/8 oz) plain flour
½ teaspoon baking powder
½ tablespoon caster sugar
1 egg, lightly beaten
⅓ cup (80 ml/2¾ fl oz) olive oil
¼ cup (60 ml/2 fl oz) dry white wine
beaten egg, to glaze

2 tablespoons olive oil
20 g (¾ oz) butter
100 g (3½ oz) lean bacon, diced
1 small red onion, sliced
2 cloves garlic, crushed
3 artichoke hearts, finely chopped
2 tablespoons finely chopped fresh parsley
150 g (5 oz) smoked mozzarella, diced
oil, for shallow-frying

1 Combine the flour, baking powder, sugar and ½ teaspoon salt in a bowl. Make a well in the centre of the dry ingredients, pour in the combined egg, oil and wine and mix with a flat-bladed knife to form a dough. Transfer to a floured surface and gather together into a ball.
2 Knead for 3–4 minutes, until smooth and elastic. Cover and set aside to rest at room temperature for at least 30 minutes.
3 Roll the dough out on a floured surface to 3 mm (⅛ inch) thickness. Rest for 10 minutes, then cut out twenty-four 8 cm (3 inch) circles. Brush around the edge with beaten egg.
4 While the dough is resting, heat the oil and butter in a frying pan, then add the bacon, onion, garlic and artichoke. Cook gently for 10 minutes, adding the parsley for the last 1–2 minutes. Remove from the heat, then drain.
5 Place 1 teaspoon bacon mixture in the centre of each circle of dough. Add some cheese, and salt and pepper, to taste. Fold one side of the dough over to meet the other, encasing the filling. Press firmly to seal, then press the edges with a fork. Place on a large plate or baking tray and refrigerate for 30 minutes.
6 Heat 2 cm (¾ inch) oil in a frying pan to 180°C (350°F). The oil is ready when a cube of bread dropped into the oil turns golden brown in 15 seconds. Fry the panzarotti, two or three at a time, until puffed and golden on both sides. Remove with a slotted spoon and drain on crumpled paper towels before serving.

MARINATED CHILLI MUSHROOMS

Preparation time: 20 minutes + marinating
Total cooking time: Nil
Makes 20–25

750 g (1½ lb) button mushrooms
2 cups (500 ml/16 fl oz) light olive oil
2 tablespoons lemon juice
1 clove garlic, finely chopped
¼ teaspoon caster sugar
1 red chilli, finely chopped
1 green chilli, finely chopped
1 tablespoon chopped fresh coriander
1 tablespoon chopped fresh parsley

1 Wipe the mushrooms with a damp paper towel to remove any dirt and place in a bowl.
2 Mix together the oil, lemon juice, garlic, sugar and chilli. Pour over the mushrooms and mix well so that the mushrooms are evenly coated. Cover with plastic wrap and marinate for at least 30 minutes. Just before serving, add the herbs, season and mix well.
NOTE: If you prefer a stronger flavour, add the herbs before marinating.
IN ADVANCE: The mushrooms can be marinated up to 1 week ahead and stored in the fridge.

BUTTON MUSHROOMS
Button mushrooms are commonly used for party dishes because of their uniform size and mild flavour. When buying them, make sure they are dry and firm. Refrigerate in a paper bag, not plastic, so they don't sweat. They don't need to be peeled but can be wiped over with damp paper towels if they need cleaning.

LEFT: Marinated chilli mushrooms

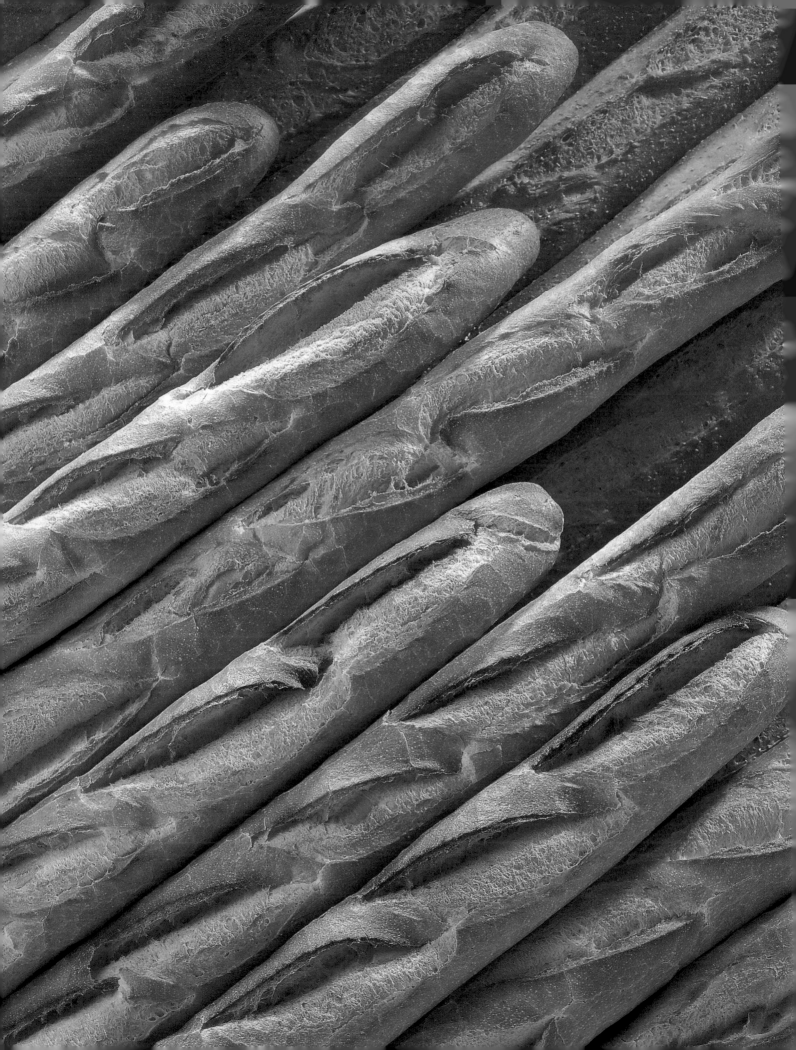

CANAPES

Canapés were originally small pieces of bread or toast spread with a savoury paste and served before the meal. The word 'canapé' comes from the French, meaning, surprisingly enough, 'couch'—the idea being that the toppings sit on the pieces of bread as if sitting on little sofas. Canapés have come a long way since then and, as well as bread, we now serve blinis, pikelets, polenta wedges, pastries and tartlets with an almost infinite variety of savoury toppings. The perfect canapé should be one, or at most two, dainty mouthfuls, requiring neither a fork nor a plate, thus allowing your guests to mingle at will, discussing what a fabulous chef you are.

the bread, flatten the slices well with a rolling pin and brush both sides with melted butter.
2 Spread the pepper mixture on each slice, leaving a 1 cm (½ inch) border. Roll up and secure with toothpicks. Cover and refrigerate for at least 2 hours.
3 Preheat the oven to moderate 180°C (350°F/ Gas 4). Cut each roll in half and secure with a toothpick. Bake on a baking tray for about 10–12 minutes, or until the rolls are crisp and pale golden. Sprinkle with paprika. Serve warm.
NOTE: The rolls can be served like mini rolled pizzas with different fillings. Brush bread slices with oil, then spread with tomato paste. Sprinkle with sliced olives, sun-dried tomatoes, grated Parmesan and chopped anchovies, mushrooms or other favourite fillings.
IN ADVANCE: These can be prepared and refrigerated up to a day in advance and baked just before serving.

HERB PANCAKES WITH AVOCADO BUTTER

Preparation time: 30 minutes
Total cooking time: 30 minutes
Makes about 50

½ cup (60 g /2 oz) plain flour
½ cup (60 g/2 oz) self-raising flour
1 egg, lightly beaten
½ cup (125 ml/4 fl oz) milk
20 g (¾ oz) chopped fresh mixed herbs
1 teaspoon cracked black pepper

Avocado butter
½ ripe avocado
60 g (2 oz) butter
1 tablespoon lemon or lime juice
½ teaspoon cracked black pepper

1 Sift the flours into a large bowl and make a well in the centre. Gradually add the combined egg, milk, herbs and pepper, whisking until the batter is smooth and free of lumps.
2 Heat a frying pan and brush with melted butter. Drop teaspoons of batter into the pan and cook until bubbles appear on top. Turn and cook until golden underneath. Keep warm.
3 Mix the avocado, butter, juice and pepper in a small bowl until smooth. Spread on top of the pancakes and serve.

PEPPER (CAPSICUM) ROLLS

Preparation time: 30 minutes + chilling
Total cooking time: 12 minutes
Makes 20

1 large red pepper (capsicum)
60 g (2 oz) Cheddar, grated
30 g (1 oz) Parmesan, grated
2 tablespoons whole egg mayonnaise
2 tablespoons finely chopped fresh parsley
1 teaspoon chopped fresh thyme
1 teaspoon chopped fresh oregano
2 drops Tabasco sauce
10 slices fresh bread
45 g (1½ oz) butter, melted
paprika

1 Halve the red pepper and remove the seeds and membrane. Cook skin-side-up under a hot grill until the skin is black and blistered. Place in a plastic bag and leave to cool, then peel. Finely chop the flesh and combine in a bowl with the Cheddar, Parmesan, mayonnaise, herbs, Tabasco and salt and pepper, to taste. Cut the crusts from

ABOVE: Pepper rolls

SMOKED SALMON PIKELETS

Preparation time: 15 minutes + standing
Total cooking time: 10–15 minutes
Makes about 50

Pikelets
1 cup (125 g/4 oz) self-raising flour
2 eggs, lightly beaten
1/2 cup (125 ml/4 fl oz) milk
1 tablespoon sour cream

Topping
1/2 cup (125 g/4 oz) sour cream
2 tablespoons mayonnaise
2 teaspoons lemon juice
1 tablespoon finely chopped fresh chives
1 tablespoon finely chopped fresh mint
125 g (4 oz) sliced smoked salmon
strips of lemon peel, to decorate

1 Sift the flour into a bowl and make a well in the centre. Mix the beaten egg, milk and sour cream and pour into the well. Stir into the flour until the batter is smooth and free of lumps. Set aside for 10 minutes.

2 Heat a large frying pan, brush with oil or melted butter, then drop teaspoons of mixture into the pan. When bubbles appear on the surface, turn the pikelets over and cook the other side. Remove and set aside. Repeat until all the batter has been used.

3 For the topping, stir the sour cream, mayonnaise, lemon juice, chives and mint together until well combined. Spoon a small amount onto each pikelet. Top with a piece of smoked salmon and decorate with strips of lemon peel.

IN ADVANCE: The pikelets can be made a day ahead, or frozen in single layers for up to a month. The sour cream mixture for the topping can be prepared a day ahead. You can assemble the pikelets up to an hour before you are going to serve them.

CHIVES
Although part of the onion family, fresh chives are used more like a herb. They impart a mild onion flavour to dips, vegetables and cheeses. If you grow some in a pot, you can just cut a little off when required. The grass-like stems are easy to snip with scissors.

LEFT: Smoked salmon pikelets

BACON

Lightly fried bacon is a vital ingredient in traditional quiche Lorraine. When covered with a creamy custard mixture and baked, the flavour of the bacon is enhanced. Bacon is fat and lean meat from the side and back of pigs. It has been preserved by dry salting (curing) and is usually smoked.

MINI QUICHE LORRAINES

Preparation time: 20 minutes
Total cooking time: 25 minutes
Makes 24

3 sheets ready-rolled shortcrust pastry, thawed
60 g (2 oz) Gruyère cheese, grated
30 g (1 oz) butter
2 rashers bacon, finely chopped
1 onion, finely chopped
2 eggs
³/4 cup (185 ml/6 fl oz) cream
¹/2 teaspoon ground nutmeg
fresh chives, cut into short strips, to garnish

1 Lightly grease two 12-hole round-based patty tins. Preheat the oven to moderately hot 190°C (375°F/Gas 5). Using a plain 8 cm (3 inch) cutter, cut rounds of pastry and fit in the tins. Divide the cheese evenly among the pastry bases. Cover and refrigerate while making the filling.

2 Heat the butter in a small pan and cook the bacon and onion for 2–3 minutes, until tender. Drain on paper towels. When cool, divide the mixture evenly among the bases. Whisk the eggs in a bowl with the cream, nutmeg and freshly ground black pepper. Pour or spoon carefully over the bacon mixture.

3 Place 2–3 strips of chive on top of each quiche to decorate. Bake for 20 minutes, or until lightly browned and set. Serve hot or warm.

IN ADVANCE: These quiches can be cooked up to 2 days ahead and stored in an airtight container in the refrigerator. They can be frozen in single layers for up to 2 months. Reheat in a moderate 180°C (350°F/Gas 4) oven.

ABOVE: Mini quiche Lorraines

CUCUMBER AND SALMON BITES

Preparation time: 20 minutes
Total cooking time: Nil
Makes about 40

250 g (8 oz) cream cheese or neufchatel
210 g (7 oz) can red or pink salmon, drained
1 tablespoon sour cream
1 tablespoon mayonnaise
1–2 teaspoons lemon juice
1 tablespoon finely chopped fresh coriander
1 tablespoon finely chopped fresh chives
2 teaspoons finely chopped fresh lemon thyme
4 Lebanese cucumbers, thickly sliced
sprigs of fresh dill or thinly shredded chilli or
    red pepper (capsicum), to decorate

1 Beat the cream cheese in a small bowl with electric beaters until soft and creamy. Add the salmon, sour cream, mayonnaise, lemon juice, coriander, chives, lemon thyme, and salt and pepper. Beat for 1 minute, or until combined.
2 Place a teaspoon of the cheese mixture on each cucumber round and decorate.
IN ADVANCE: The salmon mixture can be prepared a day ahead and refrigerated in an airtight container. Slice the cucumber into rounds and assemble just before serving.

PORT AND PEPPER PATE WITH MOON TOASTS

Preparation time: 40 minutes + overnight chilling
Total cooking time: 10 minutes
Makes about 30

450 g (14 oz) chicken livers, chopped
100 g (3½ oz) butter
1 onion, chopped
2 cloves garlic, crushed
⅓ cup (80 ml/2¾ fl oz) port
⅓ cup (80 ml/2¾ fl oz) cream
1 tablespoon chopped fresh chives
60 g (2 oz) can green peppercorns, drained
    and lightly crushed
10 slices bread
lemon pepper seasoning

1 Discard any green or discoloured parts from the livers. Heat the butter in a large, heavy-based pan. Add the liver, onion, garlic and port and stir over medium heat until the liver is almost cooked and the onion is soft. Bring to the boil and simmer for 5 minutes.
2 Remove from the heat and cool slightly. Combine in a food processor in short bursts until smooth. Press through a fine sieve into a bowl, then stir in the cream, chives and peppercorns. Spoon into a large dish, cover and refrigerate overnight, or until firm.
3 Preheat the oven to moderate 180°C (350°F/ Gas 4). Line a baking tray with foil. To make the moon toasts, using a moon-shaped cutter, cut shapes out of the bread. Place on the tray and sprinkle with pepper. Bake for 5 minutes, or until pale golden and crisp. Cool on a wire rack.
IN ADVANCE: The pâté can be made 2 days ahead, and refrigerated, covered. The toasts can be made a week ahead and stored in an airtight container.

ABOVE: Cucumber and salmon bites

SMOKED TROUT TARTLETS

Preparation time: 40 minutes
Total cooking time: 20 minutes
Makes 34

1 loaf sliced white bread, crusts removed
60 g (2 oz) butter, melted
1 smoked trout (about 300 g/10 oz), skinned
   and boned
1 tablespoon chopped fresh chives
¼ cup (60 g/2 oz) mayonnaise
2 spring onions, finely chopped
1 teaspoon horseradish cream
1 teaspoon seeded mustard
black olives, pitted and cut into strips,
   to garnish

1 Preheat the oven to very slow 120°C (250°F/ Gas ½). Flatten the bread slices with a rolling pin, cut 8 cm (3 inch) rounds with a cutter, then brush both sides with butter. Press into two 12-hole round-based patty tins. Bake for 10 minutes, or until crisp. Cool. Repeat to use all the bread.
2 Place the trout in a bowl and break the flesh into small pieces with a fork. Add the chives, mayonnaise, spring onion, horseradish cream and mustard. Season with salt and pepper; mix well.
3 Spoon the filling into the tartlet cases, garnish with strips of olives and serve immediately.
IN ADVANCE: The bread cases can be made 2 days ahead and stored in an airtight container.

SMOKED SALMON ROLLS

Preparation time: 30 minutes + chilling
Total cooking time: 5 minutes
Makes 36

6 eggs
3 teaspoons cornflour
125 g (4 oz) spreadable cream cheese
2 tablespoons chopped pickled ginger
2 tablespoons chopped fresh chives
200 g (6½ oz) sliced smoked salmon,
   chopped
sprigs of fresh parsley, to garnish

1 Beat 1 egg in a bowl with 1 teaspoon water and half a teaspoon of cornflour. Season.

2 Heat a frying pan and brush it lightly with oil. Add the egg and cook over medium heat, drawing the outside edges of the mixture into the centre with a spatula, until the mixture is lightly set. Cool in the pan for 2 minutes, then carefully slide out onto a clean, flat surface with the uncooked side upwards. Set aside to cool. Repeat with the remaining eggs, beaten with water and cornflour, to make five more omelettes.
3 Place each omelette on a sheet of baking paper on a flat surface. Divide the cream cheese among the omelettes, spreading over each. Sprinkle with pickled ginger, chives and salmon. Season with black pepper. Roll each gently but firmly, using the paper to help pull the roll towards you. Chill, wrapped in plastic wrap, for at least 3 hours.
4 Using a sharp knife, cut the rolls into 2 cm (½ inch) slices, discarding the uneven ends. Garnish with parsley sprigs.
IN ADVANCE: Can be made a day ahead, covered and refrigerated. Serve at room temperature.

CARAMELIZED APPLES ON PUMPERNICKEL

Preparation time: 30 minutes
Total cooking time: 15 minutes
Makes about 24

2 golden delicious or pink lady apples
2 tablespoons lemon juice
½ cup (60 g/2 oz) icing sugar
30 g (1 oz) butter
175 g (6 oz) blue cheese, crumbled
30 g (1 oz) walnuts, finely chopped
1 stick celery, finely chopped
250 g (8 oz) pumpernickel rounds

1 Peel and core the apples and slice each into twelve wedges. Brush with lemon juice and sprinkle generously with icing sugar. Heat the butter in a frying pan and, when foaming, add a few wedges and cook until brown and beginning to caramelize. Cool on a sheet of baking paper. Repeat with the remaining apple wedges, adding more butter to the pan as needed.
2 Combine the cheese, walnuts and celery in a bowl and spoon a little onto each pumpernickel round. Top with an apple wedge.
NOTE: Granny Smith apples are not suitable.
IN ADVANCE: Prepare a few hours ahead and refrigerate, covered with plastic wrap.

Cook the egg over medium heat until lightly set. Use a spatula to draw the outside edges into the centre during cooking.

Sprinkle pickled ginger, chives and salmon over the cream cheese.

Roll each omelette gently but firmly, using the paper to help pull the roll towards you as you roll.

OPPOSITE PAGE: Smoked salmon rolls (top); Caramelized apples on pumpernickel

HERBED CHEESE TARTLETS

Preparation time: 30 minutes + chilling
Total cooking time: 8–10 minutes
Makes 48

Pastry

4 cups (500 g/1 lb) plain flour
1 teaspoon paprika
250 g (8 oz) butter, chopped
1/3 cup (80 ml/2 3/4 fl oz) lemon juice
8–10 tablespoons iced water

Filling

500 g (1 lb) cottage cheese
2 tablespoons chopped fresh chervil, plus extra
   to garnish
2 tablespoons chopped fresh tarragon
2 teaspoons chopped fresh chives
1/2 cup (125 ml/4 fl oz) thick (double) cream
24 black olives, pitted and sliced

1 Sift the flour and paprika with a pinch of salt
into a large bowl. Add the butter and rub into
the flour with your fingertips, until the mixture
resembles fine breadcrumbs. Make a well in the
centre and stir in the lemon juice and up to
8–10 tablespoons iced water. Mix with a flat-
bladed knife until the mixture comes together in
beads. Gently gather together and lift out onto a
lightly floured surface. Flatten into a disc, wrap
in plastic wrap and refrigerate for 15 minutes.
2 Preheat the oven to moderately hot 200°C
(400°F/Gas 6). Grease two 12-hole round-based
patty tins. Roll the dough out on a lightly
floured surface to 3 mm (1/8 inch) thick and,
using an 8 cm (3 inch) cutter, cut 48 rounds
from the pastry and line the patty tins. Bake for
8–10 minutes, until golden brown. Repeat with
the remaining pastry and ingredients.
3 To make the filling, beat together the cottage
cheese, herbs and cream until smooth. Stir in the
olives with salt and black pepper. Spoon into the
cases and garnish each tart with a small sprig of
chervil. Grind black pepper over the top and
serve immediately.

CRAB AND LIME QUICHES

Preparation time: 15 minutes
Total cooking time: 20 minutes
Makes 18

2 sheets frozen puff pastry, thawed
2 eggs
3/4 cup (185 ml/6 fl oz) coconut cream
finely grated rind of 1 small lime
2 teaspoons lime juice
200 g (6 1/2 oz) can crab meat, drained
1 tablespoon chopped fresh chives

1 Preheat the oven to hot 210°C (415°F/
Gas 6–7). Using two 12-hole round-based patty
tins, lightly grease 18 of the holes. Cut 18 rounds
of pastry, using an 8 cm (3 inch) cutter.
2 Beat the eggs lightly in a small bowl and add
the remaining ingredients. Season with salt and
white pepper. Spoon about 1 tablespoon of
filling into each pastry case.
3 Bake for 20 minutes, or until golden. The
quiches will rise during cooking, then deflate
slightly. Serve warm.

*ABOVE: Crab and
lime quiches*

CROSTINI WITH (CAPSICUM) ROULADE

Preparation time: 30 minutes + chilling
Total cooking time: 10 minutes
Makes about 20

2 red peppers (capsicums)
2 yellow peppers (capsicums)
8 English spinach leaves
1 tablespoon chopped fresh flat-leaf parsley
1 small French bread stick
2 tablespoons olive oil
shaved Parmesan, to garnish

1 Cut each pepper in half and remove the seeds and membrane. Cook skin-side-up under a hot grill until the skin is black and blistered. Place in a plastic bag and leave to cool. Peel.
2 Remove the stalks from the spinach and put the leaves in a bowl. Cover with boiling water and set aside for a couple of minutes until the leaves have wilted. Drain and cool. Squeeze out the excess water and spread the leaves out. Pat dry with paper towels.
3 Place two sheets of overlapping plastic wrap on a flat surface. Flatten out the red pepper to form a rectangle, overlapping the ends. Lay the spinach leaves over the pepper to make a second layer. Place the flattened yellow pepper on top to make a third layer, making sure there are no gaps, and overlapping the ends. Sprinkle with the parsley. Using the plastic wrap to assist, roll up the pepper tightly lengthways, sealing the ends. Wrap tightly in foil, twist the ends firmly and chill for 3 hours.
4 Preheat the oven to moderately hot 200°C (400°F/Gas 6). Cut the bread stick into 1 cm (½ inch) slices. Place on a baking tray, lightly brush with olive oil, sprinkle with salt and bake for 5–10 minutes, until golden.
5 Remove the plastic wrap, cut the roulade into 1.5 cm (⅝ inch) thick slices and place on the crostini. Drizzle with oil. Garnish with Parmesan.
IN ADVANCE: The topping and the bread can be prepared separately up to 6 hours in advance. However, don't top the bread any earlier than 30 minutes before serving as it may go soft.

CROSTINI WITH PEPPER ROULADE

After grilling the peppers and allowing them to cool, peel away the skin.

Layer the pepper and the spinach leaves onto the plastic wrap.

Unwrap the chilled roulade and cut it into thin slices with a sharp knife.

LEFT: Crostini with pepper roulade

CHIVE CREPE CORNETS WITH SMOKED TROUT

Cover the base of the pan with batter, then sprinkle with chopped chives.

Place the smoked trout on a work surface and carefully peel away the skin.

Lift the flesh away from the bones, keeping the trout as intact as possible. Remove any stray bones.

ABOVE: Chive crepe cornets with smoked trout

CHIVE CREPE CORNETS WITH SMOKED TROUT

Preparation time: 45 minutes + standing
Total cooking time: 15–20 minutes
Makes 20

★ ★

3/4 cup (90 g/3 oz) plain flour
1 egg, plus 1 egg yolk, lightly beaten
1 cup (250 ml/8 fl oz) milk
20 g (3/4 oz) butter, melted
2 tablespoons chopped fresh chives

Filling
250 g (8 oz) smoked trout
125 g (4 oz) cream cheese, at room temperature
1/4 cup (60 g/2 oz) sour cream
1/4 cup (60 ml/2 fl oz) cream
Tabasco sauce
2 teaspoons lemon juice
1 tablespoon chopped fresh chives
1 tablespoon drained capers, chopped
2 small gherkins, finely chopped

1 carrot, cut into julienne strips
1 celery stalk, cut into julienne strips
strips of fresh chives

1 Sift the flour into a bowl, make a well and gradually add the combined egg, yolk, milk and butter, mixing until smooth and free of lumps. Pour into a jug, cover and leave for 30 minutes.
2 Heat a crepe or frying pan measuring 20 cm (8 inch) across the base and brush lightly with melted butter. Pour enough batter into the pan to thinly cover the base, pouring the excess back into the jug. (Add more milk if the batter is too thick.) Sprinkle some chopped chives over the batter and cook for about 30 seconds. Turn the crepe over and cook the other side until lightly brown. Transfer to a plate while cooking the remaining batter and chives.
3 Remove the skin from the trout. Carefully lift the flesh from the bones, keeping it as intact as possible and removing any stray bones. Divide into twenty even-sized pieces. Mix together the cream cheese, sour cream, cream, a few drops of Tabasco, lemon juice, chopped chives, capers and gherkins.
4 Blanch the carrot and celery in boiling water for 1 minute, then refresh in cold water. Drain and dry on crumpled paper towels.

5 Place a crepe on the work surface, chive-side-down. Spread with some of the filling mixture, then cut in half. Fold each half-crepe in half, so that the chives show decoratively. Repeat with the remaining crepes.

6 Arrange a piece of trout, a few sticks of carrot and celery, and 2–3 lengths of chives on each folded crepe, then roll up firmly like a cornet. The julienned vegetables should poke decoratively from the top of the crepe. Fold the top edge of each cornet over (you could use a little remaining filling to make them stick). Cover and refrigerate until ready to serve.

IN ADVANCE: Crepes and fillings can be made separately a day ahead and refrigerated. Alternatively, the crepes can be frozen in layers with greaseproof paper between them.

COCKTAIL TARTLETS

Preparation time: 30 minutes + chilling
Total cooking time: 10 minutes
Makes about 30

1 1/2 cups (185 g/6 oz) plain flour
100 g (3 1/2 oz) chilled butter, chopped
30 g (1 oz) Parmesan, grated
1 egg, lightly beaten

Fillings

pesto, sun-dried tomato and black olives
olive tapenade, hard-boiled quail eggs and fresh flat-leaf parsley
cream cheese, shredded sliced smoked salmon, thinly sliced Lebanese cucumber, and chopped fresh chives

1 Sift the flour and 1/4 teaspoon salt into a large bowl, add the butter and rub into the flour with your fingertips until the mixture resembles fine breadcrumbs. Stir in the Parmesan, then make a well in the centre. Add the egg and a little water and mix with a flat-bladed knife, using a cutting action, until the mixture comes together in beads. Gently gather together and lift out onto a lightly floured surface. Press together into a ball. Wrap in plastic wrap and refrigerate for 30 minutes.

2 Preheat the oven to hot 210°C (415°F/Gas 6–7). Lightly grease two 12-hole round-based patty tins. Roll the pastry out very thinly and using an 8 cm (3 inch) cutter, cut 30 rounds from the pastry. Press the pastry into the tins and prick lightly all over. Bake for 8–9 minutes, or until golden. Allow to cool in the tins. Remove and repeat with the remaining pastry.

3 Fill the cooled shells with the different fillings.

IN ADVANCE: The tartlet shells can be made up to a few days ahead and stored in an airtight container. If necessary, re-crisp briefly in a moderate 180°C (350°F/Gas 4) oven before use.

LEFT: Tartlets, from left: Olive tapenade, quail eggs and parsley; Pesto, sun-dried tomato and olives; Cream cheese, salmon, cucumber and chives

the pastry evenly with a fork and bake for 15 minutes, or until golden brown. Reduce the oven to moderate 180°C (350°F/Gas 4).

3 Heat the oil in a heavy-based pan. Add the mushrooms and stir over medium heat for 5 minutes, or until well browned. Remove from the heat and stir in the bacon, spring onion and parsley. Season with salt and pepper, to taste, and allow to cool.

4 Using electric beaters, beat the cream cheese and eggs in a small bowl for 5 minutes. Add the cooled mushrooms and stir to combine. Pour the mixture onto the cooked pastry base. Bake for 25 minutes, or until firm and lightly browned. Cool in the tin. Cut into triangles when cool.

NOTE: These bites are best eaten on the day they are made.

ROSEMARY AND CHEESE BISCUITS

Preparation time: 10 minutes + chilling
Total cooking time: 20 minutes
Makes about 50

1 cup (125 g/4 oz) plain flour
100 g (3 1/2 oz) butter, chopped
1 tablespoon sour cream
60 g (2 oz) Cheddar, grated
65 g (2 oz) Parmesan, grated
3 teaspoons chopped fresh rosemary
3 teaspoons chopped fresh chives

1 Preheat the oven to moderate 180°C (350°F/ Gas 4). Lightly grease 2 baking trays with melted butter or oil. Sift the flour and some salt and cracked black pepper into a large bowl and add the chopped butter. Rub the butter into the flour with your fingertips until the mixture resembles fine breadcrumbs.

2 Add the sour cream, cheeses and herbs and mix with a flat-bladed knife. Press the mixture together with your fingers until it forms a soft dough. Press into a ball, wrap in plastic wrap and refrigerate for 15 minutes.

3 Roll level teaspoons of the mixture into balls and place on the prepared trays, leaving a little room between the biscuits for spreading. Flatten slightly with a lightly floured fork.

4 Bake for 15–20 minutes, or until lightly golden. Transfer to a wire cake rack and leave until cool.

BACON AND MUSHROOM CREAM BITES

Preparation time: 15 minutes
Total cooking time: 45 minutes
Makes 18

1 egg yolk, lightly beaten
2 sheets ready-rolled shortcrust pastry
2 tablespoons oil
375 g (12 oz) mushrooms, finely chopped
4 bacon rashers, finely chopped
4 spring onions, finely chopped
15 g (1/2 oz) fresh parsley, finely chopped
250 g (8 oz) cream cheese, softened
4 eggs

1 Preheat the oven to hot 210°C (415°F/ Gas 6–7). Brush a shallow 23 cm (9 inch) square cake tin with melted butter or oil.

2 Brush egg yolk over one sheet of pastry. Place the other sheet over the top and gently press together. Trim the edges to fit the tin. Prick

ABOVE: Bacon and mushroom cream bites

HERBED MUSSEL TARTS

Preparation time: 30 minutes
Total cooking time: 15 minutes
Makes 24

Filling

2 kg (4 lb) black mussels

90 g (3 oz) butter, softened

2 cloves garlic, crushed

2 tablespoons chopped fresh chives

2 tablespoons chopped fresh flat-leaf
  parsley

24 slices white bread

60 g (2 oz) butter, melted

1 Scrub the mussels with a stiff brush and pull out the hairy beards. Discard any broken mussels, or open ones that don't close when tapped. Rinse well. Bring 2 cups (500 ml/16 fl oz) water to the boil in a large pan, then add half the mussels. Cover and cook for 3–5 minutes, until just opened. Discard any unopened mussels.

Repeat with the remaining mussels. Cover the mussels immediately with cold water and remove the flesh from the shells (if the mussels are very large, cut in half). Pat dry with paper towels. Beat the butter until smooth. Add the garlic, chives and parsley and season, to taste.

2 Preheat the oven to moderate 180°C (350°F/Gas 4). Flatten the bread slices with a rolling pin and, using an 8 cm (3 inch) biscuit cutter, cut a circle from each slice. Brush both sides of each circle with the melted butter, then press into two 12-hole round-based patty tins. Bake for 8 minutes, or until crisp and lightly golden.

3 Divide the mussels among the hot bread cases and carefully spread herb butter over the top. Bake for 5 minutes, or until the mussels are heated through. Serve at once.

IN ADVANCE: Bake the bread cases up to 6 hours ahead and store in an airtight container. Cook the mussels up to 2 hours ahead, cover and refrigerate. Assemble and reheat to serve.

BLACK MUSSELS
Black mussels are bivalve molluscs found on rocks and wharf piles or grown commercially. When you buy them, they should be firmly closed. Discard any broken mussels, or open ones that don't close when tapped on the bench. To prepare them for cooking, scrub the mussels with a stiff brush to remove all the dirt, then pull off the hairy beards. Rinse well. If the mussels are particularly gritty, soak them in salted water for 1 or 2 hours so they will expel sand and grit. Rinse and cook as per the instructions in your recipe. When they are all opened, they are cooked. At this stage, discard any unopened mussels and any with dried flesh.

*LEFT: Herbed
mussel tarts*

TWISTS

Quick and simple, using frozen ready-rolled puff pastry, twists can be made up to three days in advance and stored in an airtight container. Crisp in the oven if they soften. All recipes can be doubled or trebled.

THYME TWISTS

Lay 1 sheet of puff pastry on a work surface and, when thawed, brush lightly with beaten egg. Remove the hard stems from a bunch of fresh thyme and sprinkle the leaves over the pastry. Gently press onto the pastry and top with a second sheet of pastry. Cut the pastry into 2 cm (¾ inch) strips. Holding both ends, twist the strip in opposite directions twice. Place on a lightly greased baking tray and bake in a hot 210°C (415°F/Gas 6–7) oven for 10–15 minutes, or until puffed and golden. Makes 12.

CHEESE TWISTS

Lay 1 sheet of puff pastry on a work surface and, when thawed, brush lightly with beaten egg and cut into 1.5 cm (⅝ inch) strips. Holding both ends, twist the strip in opposite directions twice. Place on a lightly greased baking tray and sprinkle 3 tablespoons finely grated Parmesan over the flat part of the twists. Bake in a hot 210°C (415°F/Gas 6–7) oven for 10 minutes, or until puffed and golden. Makes 16.

SESAME AND POPPY SEED TWISTS

Lay 1 sheet of puff pastry on a work surface and, when thawed, brush lightly with beaten egg, then sprinkle with 1 tablespoon sesame or poppy seeds and gently press onto the pastry. Cut the pastry into 1.5 cm (5/8 inch) strips. Holding both ends, twist the strip in opposite directions twice. Bake on a lightly greased baking tray in a hot 210°C (415°F/Gas 6–7) oven for 10 minutes, or until puffed and golden. Makes 16.

PROSCIUTTO TWISTS

Lay 1 sheet of puff pastry on a work surface and, when thawed, brush lightly with beaten egg and cut into 1.5 cm (5/8 inch) strips. Holding both ends, twist the strips in opposite directions twice. Bake on a lightly greased baking tray in a hot 210°C (415°F/Gas 6–7) oven for 10 minutes, or until puffed and golden. Cut 8 slices of prosciutto in half lengthways. Wrap a slice around and down each twist. Makes 16.

ASPARAGUS SPEARS

Lay 1 sheet of puff pastry on a work surface and, when thawed, brush lightly with beaten egg and cut into 1.5 cm (5/8 inch) strips. Secure to one end of a blanched fresh asparagus spear (you will need 16). Wrap around and down the asparagus, brush the end of the pastry with egg and secure to the other end of the asparagus. Place on a lightly greased baking tray and bake in a hot 210°C (415°F/Gas 6–7) oven for 10–15 minutes, or until puffed and golden. Makes 16.

SUN-DRIED TOMATO PLAITS

Lay 1 sheet of puff pastry on a work surface and, when thawed, brush lightly with beaten egg and cut into 1 cm (1/2 inch) strips. Join 3 strips together at the top, by pressing. Plait them together, inserting slices of semi-dried tomato at intervals in the plait (you will need 40 g/1 1/2 oz tomatoes for this). Place on a lightly greased baking tray and bake in a hot 210°C (415°F/Gas 6–7) oven for 10–15 minutes, or until puffed and golden. Makes 8.

FROM LEFT: Thyme twists; Cheese twists; Sesame and poppy seed twists; Prosciutto twists; Asparagus spears; Sun-dried tomato plaits

TURKEY AND CRANBERRY PIKELETS

Preparation time: 25 minutes + standing
Total cooking time: 15 minutes
Makes about 30

1 cup (125 g/4 oz) self-raising flour

1 egg, plus 1 egg yolk

1¼ cups (315 ml/10 fl oz) milk

25 g (¾ oz) butter, melted

3 tablespoons mayonnaise

150 g (5 oz) cooked turkey, shredded

3 tablespoons cranberry sauce

60 g (2 oz) alfalfa sprouts

3 hard-boiled eggs, sliced

1 Sift the flour and a pinch of salt into a bowl and make a well in the centre. Lightly whisk together the egg, egg yolk, milk and melted butter in a jug and gradually add to the flour, whisking to make a smooth, lump-free batter. Cover and leave for 30 minutes.

2 Heat a frying pan and brush lightly with melted butter or oil. Drop tablespoons of the batter into the pan, allowing room for spreading. Cook over medium heat until small bubbles begin to appear on the surface and the undersides are golden. Turn the pikelets over and cook the other sides. Transfer to a plate, cover with a tea towel and leave to cool while cooking the remaining batter.

3 Spread mayonnaise over each pikelet and top with turkey, cranberry sauce, alfalfa sprouts and a slice of egg.

IN ADVANCE: Pikelets can be made a day ahead and stored, covered, in the refrigerator. They can be frozen if you prefer, in single layers, for up to 2 months.

ABOVE: Turkey and cranberry pikelets

MUSHROOMS EN CROUTE

Preparation time: 40 minutes
Total cooking time: 20 minutes
Makes 48

8 slices white bread, crust removed

80 g (2¾ oz) butter, melted

1 tablespoon olive oil

1 clove garlic, crushed

½ small onion, finely chopped

375 g (12 oz) small button mushrooms, finely sliced

1 tablespoon dry sherry

⅓ cup (80 g/2¾ oz) sour cream

2 teaspoons cornflour

1 tablespoon finely chopped fresh parsley

1 teaspoon finely chopped fresh thyme

30 g (1 oz) Parmesan, grated

1 Preheat the oven to moderate 180°C (350°F/ Gas 4). Brush both sides of the bread with the butter. Cut each slice in half vertically, then each half into three horizontally. Bake on a baking tray for 5–10 minutes, or until golden and crisp.
2 Heat the oil in a large frying pan, add the garlic and onion and cook, stirring, over low heat until the onion is soft. Add the mushrooms and cook over medium heat for 5 minutes, or until tender. Season with salt and pepper.
3 Pour the sherry into the pan. Blend the sour cream and cornflour, add to the mushrooms and stir until the mixture boils and thickens. Remove from the heat and stir in the herbs. Allow to cool.
4 Spread the mushroom mixture onto each croûte and sprinkle with the Parmesan. Place on a baking tray and bake for 5 minutes, or until heated through. Serve decorated with small sprigs of fresh herbs, if desired.
NOTE: To serve as a pâté, purée the mushroom mixture, spoon into small dishes, then chill.
IN ADVANCE: Bake the bread up to 4 days in advance and store in an airtight container. Make the topping and assemble just prior to serving.

ABOVE: Mushrooms en croûte

2 Melt the butter in a pan, add the onion and bacon and cook over medium heat for about 3 minutes, until softened but not browned. Stir in the flour and cook for 2 minutes. Remove from the heat and gradually stir in the reserved liquid. Return to the heat and stir until the sauce boils and thickens. Stir in the cream, juice and parsley, reserving a little parsley. Season.

3 Heat the vol-au-vent cases in the oven for 5 minutes. Reheat the sauce, stir in the seafood and warm through. Divide among the cases, garnish with parsley and serve.

GOATS CHEESE TARTLETS

Preparation time: 40 minutes + chilling
Total cooking time: 25 minutes
Makes 30

2 cups (250 g/8 oz) plain flour

150 g (5 oz) chilled butter, chopped

2–4 tablespoons milk

Filling

12 sun-dried tomatoes, sliced

200 g (6¹/₂ oz) goats cheese, chopped

2 tablespoons chopped fresh basil

20–30 pitted black olives, sliced

2 tablespoons chopped spring onion tops

4 eggs, lightly beaten

1 cup (250 ml/8 fl oz) cream

1 Sift the flour and a pinch of salt into a bowl. Add the butter and rub in until the mixture resembles fine breadcrumbs. Make a well and add enough milk to mix to a soft dough, using a knife. Lift onto a floured surface and gather into a ball. Chill in plastic wrap for 30 minutes.

2 Preheat the oven to moderate 180°C (350°F/ Gas 4). Roll out the pastry to 2 mm (¹/₈ inch) and cut 30 rounds with an 8 cm (3 inch) cutter. Line two lightly greased 12-hole patty tins, prick the pastry lightly and bake for 7 minutes, or until cooked but not coloured. Bake all the rounds.

3 Arrange the sun-dried tomatoes in the bases and cover with the cheese, basil, olives and spring onion. Combine the eggs and cream in a small bowl and season with salt and pepper. Spoon the mixture over the filling and bake, for 15 minutes, or until the filling is just set. Repeat with the remaining pastry and filling. Serve warm or at room temperature.

PRAWN AND SCALLOP VOL-AU-VENTS

Preparation time: 25 minutes
Total cooking time: 20 minutes
Makes 36

1 cup (250 ml/8 fl oz) fish stock

1 cup (250 ml/8 fl oz) white wine

250 g (8 oz) scallops

250 g (8 oz) raw prawns, peeled

60 g (2 oz) butter

4 spring onions, finely chopped

1 bacon rasher, finely chopped

¹/₄ cup (30 g/1 oz) plain flour

¹/₂ cup (125 ml/4 fl oz) cream

1 teaspoon lemon juice

¹/₂ cup (30 g/1 oz) finely chopped fresh parsley

36 small ready-made vol-au-vent cases

1 Heat the stock and wine in a pan until simmering. Add the scallops and prawns and cook gently for 2–3 minutes. Remove with a slotted spoon, cool and chop. Reserve 1 cup (250 ml/8 fl oz) of the cooking liquid. Refrigerate the seafood while making the sauce. Preheat the oven to warm 160°C (315°F/Gas 2–3).

ABOVE: Prawn and scallop vol-au-vents

Turn the bread slices over after about 5 minutes of baking and continue to bake until lightly browned.

Squeeze out the excess liquid from the softened spinach leaves and put on paper towels to dry.

Spread the pimiento evenly over the cheese mixture before rolling up, using the plastic as a guide.

CHEESE AND SPINACH
ROULADE BRUSCHETTA

Preparation time: 30 minutes
Total cooking time: 10 minutes
Makes about 24

★★

1 French bread stick

2 tablespoons oil

500 g (1 lb) English spinach

90 g (3 oz) spreadable cream cheese

90 g (3 oz) goats cheese

3 tablespoons canned pimiento, drained and
   finely chopped

 Preheat the oven to moderately hot 200°C (400°F/Gas 6). Cut the bread into 24 thin slices and lightly brush both sides with oil. Bake in a single layer on a baking tray for 10 minutes, or until lightly browned, turning once. Remove and allow to cool.

2 Remove the stalks from the spinach and place the leaves in a bowl. Cover with boiling water and leave for a couple of minutes, or until the leaves have wilted. Drain and leave to cool. Squeeze out the excess liquid and drain on crumpled paper towels.

3 Lay the spinach leaves flat, overlapping, on a piece of plastic wrap, to form a 25 x 20 cm (10 x 8 inch) rectangle. Beat the cheeses together until soft and smooth. Spread the cheese mixture evenly and carefully over the spinach. Top the cheese evenly with pimiento. Using the plastic wrap as a guide, carefully roll up the spinach to enclose the cheese. Remove the plastic wrap and cut the log into thin slices using a sharp knife. Serve on the toast.

NOTE: Be sure to thoroughly drain the spinach and pimiento to avoid a watery result.

IN ADVANCE: The bread slices can be baked several days ahead and stored in an airtight container. The roulade can be made a day ahead and stored, wrapped in plastic wrap, in the refrigerator. Assemble them together just before serving time.

*ABOVE: Cheese
and spinach
roulade bruschetta*

PARMESAN TUILE CONES

Place the cutter back over each circle and sprinkle with the Parmesan and paprika mix, spreading evenly to the edges.

Lift each round from the tray with a spatula and wrap around the end of a cream horn mould to form a cone.

OPPOSITE PAGE: Tuna tartlets with apple mousseline mayonnaise (left); Parmesan tuile cones

TUNA TARTLETS WITH APPLE MOUSSELINE MAYONNAISE

Preparation time: 1 hour + curing + freezing
Total cooking time: 10–15 minutes
Makes about 48

★★

375 g (12 oz) tuna, in one piece, skinned
24 hard-boiled quail eggs, halved lengthways, to garnish
45 g (1½ oz) fresh coriander leaves, to garnish

Cure
500 g (1 lb) rock salt
1½ cups (375 g/12 oz) sugar
½ teaspoon ground black peppercorns
1 teaspoon ground ginger

Filo tartlets
250 g (8 oz) filo pastry
250 g (8 oz) unsalted butter, melted

Apple mousseline mayonnaise
2 tablespoons smooth apple sauce
1 cup (250 ml/8 fl oz) whole egg mayonnaise
2 tablespoons cream, whipped

1 Choose a large flat glass dish for curing. Cut the tuna into 3 cm (1¼ inch) strips the length of the tuna, then cut the lengths to fit the dish.
2 Mix the cure ingredients and cover the base of the dish with a layer of the cure, then a layer of tuna. Continue layering, finishing with a layer of cure. Weigh down and refrigerate for 4 hours.
3 Remove the tuna from the cure. Wash the tuna under cold running water, then dry thoroughly. If not using right away, wrap in a lightly oiled cloth to prevent drying out. Refrigerate before slicing.
4 Preheat the oven to moderately hot 190°C (375°F/Gas 5). For the filo cups, layer 6 sheets of filo on top of one another, brushing each with butter. Keep the remainder under a damp cloth.
5 Cut 8 cm (3 inch) rounds of the layered filo with a cutter. Cut through with scissors if necessary. Line two 12-hole round-based patty tins with the rounds, butter-side-down. Press into the holes and prick with a fork. Arrange on baking trays and freeze for at least 10 minutes. (This can be done a day ahead.) While chilling, prepare the remaining filo rounds, but keep covered to prevent them drying out.

6 Bake the pastry cases for 4–5 minutes. Remove from the tins and cool on a wire rack. Repeat with the remaining filo rounds.
7 For the apple mousseline mayonnaise, fold the apple sauce into the mayonnaise, then fold in the cream. Taste and add salt and pepper if necessary.
8 Do not assemble until just before serving. Slice the tuna across the grain in paper-thin slices with a sharp knife. Spoon a teaspoonful of mayonnaise into each case. Top with a slice of tuna, half a quail egg and a coriander leaf. Serve at once.
NOTE: Cook quail eggs in boiling water for 5 minutes, then place in cold water to cool.

PARMESAN TUILE CONES

Preparation time: 40 minutes
Total cooking time: 30 minutes
Makes 36

★★

150 g (5 oz) Parmesan, finely grated
pinch of paprika
150 g (5 oz) ricotta cheese
2 teaspoons lemon juice
1½ tablespoons milk
2 teaspoons fresh chopped chives, plus extra, cut into short lengths, to garnish
3 slices prosciutto
2 fresh figs, cut into small pieces

1 Preheat the oven to hot 220°C (425°F/Gas 7). Line two baking trays with baking paper. Using a 7 cm (2¾ inch) cutter as a guide, draw circles on the paper. Invert the paper onto the trays. Place the cutter back over each round and sprinkle with 3 teaspoons of Parmesan combined with the paprika, spreading evenly to the edges.
2 Bake only 3–4 at a time for 3 minutes, or until melted and golden. Remove each round from the tray, using a spatula, and wrap around the end of a cream horn mould to form a cone shape. Cool. If they begin to harden too quickly, return to the oven for 10 seconds to soften again.
3 Beat the ricotta cheese, lemon juice and milk in a bowl until smooth. Stir in the chopped chives and salt and cracked black pepper, to taste.
4 Grill the prosciutto until crisp. Allow to cool, then break into pieces about 2 cm (¾ inch) long. Carefully spoon 2 teaspoons of the cheese mixture into each Parmesan tuile. Decorate the end of each tuile with a piece of fig, prosciutto and chives.

SUN-DRIED TOMATOES
Sun-dried tomatoes are usually halved, sprinkled with salt and left to dry in the sun. Sometimes they are dried in the oven. The salt preserves them, but makes them too salty to eat so they are soaked in water for a few hours to swell and rid them of salt. Sometimes they are soaked in vinegar and water, drained, dried, then stored in a mix of olive oil and flavourings such as herbs and garlic. They are readily available and add flavour to many dishes.

SESAME SHAPES

Preparation time: 35 minutes + standing
Total cooking time: 15–20 minutes
Makes about 30

1¹/₂ cups (185 g/6 oz) self-raising flour
4 tablespoons sesame seeds, toasted
2 teaspoons finely grated orange rind
2 eggs
2 teaspoons sesame oil
1 cup (250 ml/8 fl oz) milk
4 tablespoons orange juice
125 g (4 oz) sun-dried tomatoes, finely chopped

Filling
200 g (6¹/₂ oz) soft cream cheese
2 tablespoons chopped fresh coriander

1 Sift the flour and a pinch of salt into a bowl, stir in the sesame seeds and orange rind and make a well in the centre. With a fork, gradually whisk in the combined egg, sesame oil, milk and orange juice to make a smooth lump-free batter. Set aside for 15 minutes.
2 Heat a frying pan and brush lightly with melted butter or oil. Pour ¹/₃ cup (80 ml/2³/₄ fl oz) batter into the pan and cook over medium heat for 3–4 minutes, or until bubbles appear on the surface. Turn over and cook the other side. Transfer to a plate and cover with a tea towel while cooking the remaining batter.
3 Use biscuit cutters to cut out various shapes (you will be sandwiching 3 of each shape together so make sure you have the right number of each).
4 To make the filling, mix the cream cheese and coriander and use to sandwich together three pikelet shapes. Decorate with sun-dried tomato.
IN ADVANCE: Pikelets can be joined and cut into shapes a day ahead. Store in an airtight container in the refrigerator.

RIGHT: Sesame shapes

RED PEPPER (CAPSICUM) PIKELETS WITH PROSCIUTTO

Preparation time: 30 minutes + resting
Total cooking time: 25 minutes
Makes about 20

1 small red pepper (capsicum)
1 cup (125 g/4 oz) plain flour
1/2 teaspoon bicarbonate of soda
1 1/4 cups (315 ml/10 fl oz) buttermilk
1 egg
50 g (1 3/4 oz) butter, melted
130 g (4 1/4 oz) can corn kernels, drained
1 tablespoon finely chopped fresh chives,
  plus some for garnish
1 cup (250 ml/8 fl oz) crème fraîche
  or sour cream
5 slices prosciutto, cut into strips

1 Cut the red pepper into large flattish pieces and remove the seeds and membrane. Cook, skin-side-up, under a hot grill until black and blistered. Place in a plastic bag and leave to cool, then peel. Chop the flesh finely.
2 Sift the flour, bicarbonate of soda and a pinch of salt into a bowl and make a well in the centre. Gradually add the combined buttermilk, egg and melted butter and mix until just combined and lump-free. Stir in the pepper, corn and chives. Do not overmix.
3 Heat a frying pan and brush with melted butter or oil. Drop 2 teaspoons of batter into the pan for each pikelet, leaving a little room for spreading. Cook until bubbles begin to form on the surface. Turn over and cook the other side. Transfer to a plate and cover with a tea towel to keep warm while cooking the remaining batter.
4 Top each pikelet with a teaspoon of crème fraîche and a strip of prosciutto. Garnish with fresh chives.

ABOVE: Red pepper pikelets with prosciutto

MINI QUICHES

Make the pastry cases as directed, then fill with one of our quiche mixtures. Making two trays of quiches takes no extra time, as they can be baked side by side.

PASTRY CASES

Preheat the oven to moderately hot 200°C (400°F/Gas 6). Grease two round-based shallow 12-hole patty tins. Lay 2 sheets of ready-rolled shortcrust pastry on a work surface and cut 12 rounds from each with an 8 cm (3 inch) cutter. Line the tins with pastry, fill with one of the following suggestions and bake as instructed. Remove from the tins while warm and cool on wire racks. Makes 24.

CARAMELIZED ONION AND BACON

Heat 2 teaspoons oil in a large pan. Add 1 large, finely chopped onion, cover and cook over medium-low heat for 30 minutes, or until golden (caramelized onion is slow-cooked to bring out the sweetness, so don't rush this step). Transfer to a bowl to cool. Add 125 g (4 oz) finely chopped bacon to the pan and cook until crisp. Mix with the onion, add 3 teaspoons

wholegrain mustard and season with pepper. Place a small amount in each pastry case. Beat 2 eggs with ½ cup (125 ml/4 fl oz) milk and pour over the onion and bacon. Bake for 15–20 minutes, or until puffed and golden.

GOATS CHEESE AND SEMI-DRIED TOMATO

Mix together 60 g (2 oz) crumbled goats cheese and 60 g (2 oz) chopped semi-

dried tomatoes and place a small amount in the bottom of each pastry case. Beat 2 eggs with ½ cup (125 ml/4 fl oz) milk and 3 tablespoons chopped fresh basil. Season and pour into the cases. Bake for 15–20 minutes, or until puffed and golden.

CURRIED APPLE AND ONION

Heat a little oil in a pan. Lightly brown a small thinly sliced onion, then add a small peeled and grated green apple. Add ¼ teaspoon curry powder and stir for 1 minute. Cool slightly. Spoon heaped teaspoons into the pastry cases. Mix ½ cup (125 ml/4 fl oz) milk, 2 lightly beaten eggs and 2 tablespoons cream in a jug and pour enough into each pastry case to cover the onion. Sprinkle with a little grated Cheddar—you'll need about 20 g (¾ oz) altogether. Bake for 15–20 minutes, or until puffed and golden.

CREAMY HERB

Mix together 2 beaten eggs, 2 tablespoons milk, ½ cup (125 ml/ 4 fl oz) cream, 2 teaspoons chopped fresh chives and 1 teaspoon each of chopped fresh dill, thyme and parsley. Pour into the pastry cases and sprinkle with grated Parmesan, using only about 2 tablespoons altogether. Bake for 15–20 minutes, or until puffed and golden.

SMOKED SALMON

Put 100 g (3½ oz) cream cheese, ¼ cup (60 ml/2 fl oz) cream and 2 eggs in a food processor and mix together, then add some cracked black pepper, to taste. Sprinkle a little finely chopped smoked salmon into the pastry case—you will need about 100 g (3½ oz) smoked salmon. Pour the cream cheese mixture over the top and bake for 15–20 minutes, or until puffed and golden.

CORN AND RED PEPPER
(CAPSICUM)

Drain a 130 g (4 oz) can corn kernels and mix with ⅓ cup (40 g/1½ oz) grated Cheddar and half a finely chopped red pepper. Beat 2 eggs, ⅔ cup (170 ml/ 5½ fl oz) cream, 2 teaspoons Dijon mustard and a dash of Tabasco sauce in a jug and season with salt and pepper. Spoon the corn mixture into the pastry cases, dividing evenly among them, and top with the egg mixture until almost full. Bake for 15–20 minutes, or until puffed and golden.

QUICHES, FROM LEFT: Caramelized onion and bacon; Goats cheese and semi-dried tomato; Curried apple and onion; Creamy herb; Smoked salmon; Corn and red pepper

RED ONIONS
These onions are quite sweet and mild compared to other onions and are often finely chopped or sliced and used raw in salsas and salads. They are best kept in the vegetable crisper in the refrigerator.

CRAB CAKES WITH AVOCADO SALSA

Preparation time: 25 minutes + chilling
Total cooking time: about 15 minutes
Makes 20

2 eggs
340 g (11 oz) can crab meat, drained
2 spring onions, finely chopped
1 tablespoon mayonnaise
2 teaspoons sweet chilli sauce
1¼ cups (100 g/3 oz) fresh white breadcrumbs
oil, for shallow-frying

Avocado salsa
2 ripe Roma (egg) tomatoes, chopped
1 small red onion, finely chopped
1 large avocado, finely diced
3 tablespoons lime juice
2 tablespoons fresh chervil leaves
1 teaspoon caster sugar

1 Beat the eggs lightly in a bowl. Add the crab meat, spring onion, mayonnaise, sweet chilli sauce and breadcrumbs, and stir well. Season, then cover and refrigerate for 30 minutes.
2 To make the avocado salsa, combine all the ingredients in a bowl, season with salt and pepper, and toss gently to combine.
3 Using wet hands, form the crab mixture into 20 small flat cakes. Heat 3 cm (1¼ inches) oil in a large heavy-based pan and cook the crab cakes over medium heat for about 3 minutes each side, or until golden brown on both sides. Drain well on crumpled paper towels and serve immediately, with avocado salsa to spoon onto the top.
IN ADVANCE: The crab mixture can be made a day ahead, then covered and refrigerated. Prepare the salsa close to serving time.

ABOVE: Crab cakes with avocado salsa

PINE NUTS
Pine nuts have a sweet flavour and are an important ingredient in pesto. They are also used in salads, rice pilafs, pasta dishes and stuffings for vegetables and poultry. As pine nuts have a high fat content, they can go rancid quite quickly, so they are best stored in an airtight container in the freezer or the refrigerator.

MUSHROOMS IN BASIL PESTO ON SOURDOUGH

Preparation time: 20 minutes
Total cooking time: 20–25 minutes
Makes 24

Basil pesto

25 g (³/4 oz) fresh basil leaves
30 g (1 oz) Parmesan, grated
2 tablespoons pine nuts, toasted
2 tablespoons olive oil

1 small clove garlic, crushed
2¹/2 tablespoons olive oil
1 sourdough bread stick, cut into 24 x 1 cm
   (¹/2 inch) thick slices
500 g (1 lb) small flat mushrooms, thinly sliced
3 teaspoons balsamic vinegar
80 g (2³/4 oz) thinly sliced prosciutto

1 For the basil pesto, finely chop the basil leaves, Parmesan and pine nuts in a food processor. Gradually add the olive oil in a thin stream, with the motor running, and process until smooth. Season with salt and pepper.

2 Combine the garlic with 2 tablespoons of the olive oil in a small bowl and brush it over both sides of the bread slices. Place on baking trays and cook both sides under a medium-hot grill until golden brown.

3 Heat the remaining ¹/2 tablespoon of olive oil in a large frying pan. Add the mushrooms and cook over medium heat for 3–4 minutes, or until the mushrooms are heated through. Drain away any liquid. Add the pesto and the vinegar to the mushrooms, stir to combine, then cook over low heat for 1–2 minutes, or until heated through.

4 Preheat the oven to moderately hot 200°C (400°F/Gas 6). To assemble, top the toasts with mushroom, then torn and folded prosciutto. Bake on baking trays for 6 minutes, or until the prosciutto is crisp. Serve immediately.

IN ADVANCE: The basil pesto can be made up to 3 days ahead. Cover and refrigerate. Alternatively, it can be made well ahead and frozen in ice cube trays or a small container. Any other type of bread stick can be used if sourdough is not available.

ABOVE: Mushrooms in basil pesto on sourdough

SPRING ONIONS
Sometimes called scallions or green onions, spring onions are immature onions harvested before the bulb has formed. They are sold in bunches. Trim off the roots and tips and wash thoroughly before using. They do not need much cooking to soften them. Sometimes they are added to a dish just before serving and are often added raw to salads to give a mild onion flavour.

OPPOSITE PAGE:
Florentine scones with mortadella and artichoke (top left); Lamb on polenta

FLORENTINE SCONES WITH MORTADELLA AND ARTICHOKE

Preparation time: 30 minutes
Total cooking time: 15 minutes
Makes 60

100 g (3½ oz) English spinach leaves
20 g (¾ oz) butter
3 spring onions, finely sliced
1¼ cups (155 g/5 oz) self-raising flour
50 g (1¾ oz) Parmesan, grated
⅓ cup (80 ml/2¾ fl oz) milk, approximately
2 teaspoons milk, extra
200 g (6½ oz) artichokes in olive oil, drained
¼ cup (60 ml/2 fl oz) thick (double) cream
100 g (3½ oz) thinly sliced mortadella
1½ tablespoons finely chopped pistachio nuts

1 Preheat the oven to hot 220°C (425°F/Gas 7). Wash the spinach and cook, covered, in a saucepan over medium heat for 2 minutes, or until wilted. Drain and cool. Squeeze the spinach with your hands to remove as much liquid as possible, then chop finely.
2 Heat the butter in a small pan, add the onion and cook over medium heat for 2 minutes, or until very soft.
3 Sift the flour into a bowl and stir in the spinach, onion mixture and Parmesan. Make a well and use a flat-bladed knife to stir in enough milk to mix to a soft, sticky dough. Turn onto a lightly floured surface and knead lightly until just smooth. Roll out to about 1.5 cm (⅝ inch) thickness, then cut 30 rounds with a 4 cm (1½ inch) cutter. Lightly grease a baking tray and place the rounds on it so they are almost touching. Brush the tops lightly with the extra milk and bake on the middle shelf for 10–12 minutes, or until cooked and golden brown.
4 Meanwhile, chop the artichokes in a food processor until smooth. Add the cream and process quickly until combined. Do not overprocess or the mixture may curdle. Season with salt and pepper, to taste.
5 To assemble, split the scones horizontally in half, top each half with artichoke cream, then torn and folded pieces of mortadella. Sprinkle with pistachio nuts.
IN ADVANCE: The scones are best made on the day of serving. The artichoke cream can be prepared a day ahead and refrigerated.

LAMB ON POLENTA

Preparation time: 15 minutes
Total cooking time: 15 minutes
Makes 24

3 cups (750 ml/24 fl oz) chicken stock
¾ cup (110 g/3½ oz) instant polenta
2 tablespoons grated Parmesan
2 lamb fillets (150 g/5 oz)
oil, for frying
¼ small cucumber, thinly sliced
3 tablespoons natural yoghurt

1 Lightly grease a 20 x 30 cm (8 x 12 inch) shallow tray. Pour the stock into a saucepan and bring to the boil. Add the polenta and stir over medium heat for 5 minutes, or until thick. Remove from the heat. Stir in the Parmesan and salt and pepper, to taste. Spread into the tray; cool.
2 When cool, cut the polenta into rounds with a 4 cm (1½ inch) cutter. Trim the lamb of any excess fat and sinew.
3 Heat a little oil in a frying pan, add the lamb and cook until brown all over and cooked as desired, about 3 minutes each side for medium. Remove the lamb fillets from the pan and wipe the pan clean. Add more oil to the pan and fry the polenta rounds until lightly browned on both sides. Remove from the pan.
4 Cut the cucumber slices into quarters. Thinly slice the lamb and place on top of the polenta. Top with yoghurt and a piece of cucumber.
NOTE: For extra flavour, the lamb can be rolled in cracked black peppercorns prior to cooking.

ASPARAGUS BOATS

Cut 3 sheets ready-rolled shortcrust pastry into 25 cm (10 inch) squares. Cut at 6 cm (2½ inch) intervals to make rectangles. Cut in half. Use to line twenty-four 8 cm (3 inch) lightly greased metal boat-shaped tins; chill. Fry 2 crushed cloves garlic and a finely chopped small onion in 30 g (1 oz) butter until soft. Cool, then stir in 2 beaten eggs, ¾ cup (185 g/6 oz) sour cream and 4 tablespoons grated Parmesan. Season. Spoon into the boats and place on baking trays. Bake in a moderately hot 200°C (400°F/Gas 6) oven for 15 minutes, or until golden. Top with blanched asparagus spear tips (cut in half if too thick). Makes 24.

FIGS

There are hundreds of varieties of the fig, which has a history dating back to the leaves that are associated with Adam and Eve. It is thought figs originated in Syria, but they are now grown in many countries. A lot of today's varieties are cultivated in Italy. Some are round, others pear-shaped and the size varies considerably. When buying figs, avoid any with mould or broken skin. They should be plump and slightly soft. Dried figs are also available.

ABOVE: Mini scones with ham, leek and port figs

MINI SCONES WITH HAM, LEEK AND PORT FIGS

Preparation time: 40 minutes + chilling
Total cooking time: 45 minutes
Makes about 40

★★

2 cups (250 g/8 oz) plain flour
3 teaspoons baking powder
110 g (3½ oz) chilled butter
100 g (3½ oz) Stilton cheese
2 tablespoons chopped fresh chives
¾ cup (185 ml/6 fl oz) milk

Filling

1 cup (250 ml/8 fl oz) port
6 large dried figs, stems removed
1 teaspoon sugar
1 large leek
1 teaspoon Dijon mustard
2 teaspoons red wine vinegar
1 tablespoon olive oil
150 g (5 oz) shaved ham

1 Sift the flour, baking powder and ¾ teaspoon salt into a large bowl. Coarsely grate the butter and cheese into the flour and rub in with your fingertips until the pieces are the size of coarse breadcrumbs. Stir in the chives. Pour in the milk and combine with a fork until large clumps form. Turn onto a floured surface and press into a ball.
2 On a floured surface, roll the dough into a 15 x 25 cm (6 x 10 inch) rectangle. With the long edge of the dough facing you, fold in both ends so they meet in the centre, then fold the dough in half widthways. Roll again into a 15 x 25 cm (6 x 10 inch) rectangle, about 1 cm (½ inch) thick. Cut rounds close together with a 3 cm (1¼ inch) cutter. Push the scraps together and roll and cut as before. Place 2.5 cm (1 inch) apart on a baking tray and refrigerate for 20 minutes. Preheat the oven to hot 220°C (425°F/Gas 7) and bake for 10–12 minutes, or until lightly browned.
3 In a small pan, heat the port, figs and sugar. Bring to the boil, reduce the heat and simmer for 15 minutes. Remove the figs and, when cooled, roughly chop. Simmer the liquid for about 3 minutes, until reduced and syrupy. Put the figs back in and stir to combine. Set aside.
4 Discard any tough leaves from the leek, then rinse the leek. Trim off the dark green tops. Slit

the leek lengthways, almost to the bottom, roll a quarter turn and slit again. Wash well, drain and steam for about 10 minutes, or until very soft. Roughly chop, then combine with the mustard, vinegar and oil. Season with salt and pepper.
6 Cut the scones in half. Put a folded piece of ham on each bottom half, top with a teaspoon each of leek and fig mixture, then replace the tops.

GOATS CHEESE AND APPLE TARTS

Preparation time: 10 minutes
Total cooking time: 25 minutes
Makes 32

2 sheets frozen puff pastry
300 g (10 oz) goats cheese, sliced
2 cooking apples
2 tablespoons extra virgin olive oil
1 tablespoon chopped fresh lemon thyme

1 Preheat the oven to hot 210°C (415°F/ Gas 6–7). While the pastry is still frozen, cut each sheet into four squares and then each square into quarters. Place slightly apart on a lightly greased baking tray. Set aside for a few minutes to thaw and then lay the cheese over the centre of each square of pastry, leaving a small border.
2 Core the unpeeled apples and slice them thinly. Interleave several slices over the pastry, making sure the cheese is covered completely. Lightly brush the apples with oil and sprinkle with lemon thyme and a little salt and pepper, to taste.
3 Bake the tarts for 20–25 minutes, or until the pastry is cooked through and golden brown at the edges. The tarts are best served immediately.
IN ADVANCE: The pastry can be topped with cheese, covered and refrigerated overnight. Top with the apple just before cooking.

ABOVE: Goats cheese and apple tarts

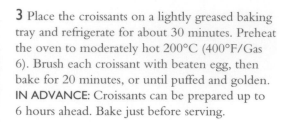

3 Place the croissants on a lightly greased baking tray and refrigerate for about 30 minutes. Preheat the oven to moderately hot 200°C (400°F/Gas 6). Brush each croissant with beaten egg, then bake for 20 minutes, or until puffed and golden.
IN ADVANCE: Croissants can be prepared up to 6 hours ahead. Bake just before serving.

GARLIC TOAST WITH SALMON MAYONNAISE

Preparation time: 35 minutes
Total cooking time: 30 minutes
Makes 32

I pepper (capsicum)

I tomato

8 slices of bread, crusts removed, cut into triangles, or French bread stick, sliced

1/3 cup (80 ml/2 3/4 fl oz) olive oil

2 cloves garlic, crushed

2 tablespoons olive oil, extra

I onion, finely chopped

Salmon mayonnaise

2 egg yolks

2 cloves garlic, crushed

2 teaspoons lemon juice

3/4 cup (185 ml/6 fl oz) olive oil

60 g (2 oz) sliced smoked salmon

I Remove the seeds and membrane from the pepper and finely chop the flesh. Peel the tomato by scoring a cross in the base, soaking in hot water for 30 seconds, then plunging in cold water. Peel the skin away from the cross. Scoop out the seeds and finely chop the flesh.
2 Preheat the oven to moderate 180°C (350°F/Gas 4). Brush both sides of the bread with the combined oil and garlic and bake on a baking tray for 10–15 minutes. Turn halfway through cooking. Set aside.
3 Heat the extra oil in a frying pan, add the pepper, tomato and onion and fry until the onion is soft. Remove from the heat.
4 For the salmon mayonnaise, whisk the egg yolks, garlic and lemon juice together in a small bowl. Beat the oil into the mixture, about a teaspoon at a time, ensuring all the oil is combined before adding more. The mixture will have the consistency of thick cream.

MINI CROISSANTS

Preparation time: 30 minutes + chilling
Total cooking time: 40 minutes
Makes 30

40 g (1 1/4 oz) butter

3 onions, finely chopped

12 pitted black olives, finely sliced

2 tablespoons chopped fresh parsley

3 sheets frozen puff pastry, thawed

I egg, beaten

I Melt the butter in a frying pan and cook the onions over medium-low heat for 20 minutes, or until golden and sweet tasting. Remove from the heat and stir in the olives, parsley, salt and cracked black pepper, to taste. Allow to cool.
2 Cut each sheet of pastry in half, then each half into 5 triangles with a base (shortest side) of 8 cm (3 inches). You will have a couple of odd shapes left at each end. Place a little onion mixture at the base of each triangle and roll up towards the point, enclosing the filling. Curl the ends around to form a croissant shape.

ABOVE: Mini croissants

5 Transfer the mayonnaise to a food processor, add the salmon and freshly ground pepper, to taste, then process until smooth.

6 Serve the garlic toasts topped with some pepper mixture, then salmon mayonnaise.

IN ADVANCE: The mayonnaise and garlic toast can both be made a day ahead. Cover, separately, and refrigerate. Assemble close to serving.

PUMPKIN AND HAZELNUT PESTO BITES

Preparation time: 20 minutes
Total cooking time: 35 minutes
Makes 48

750 g (1¹/₂ lb) butternut pumpkin
3 tablespoons oil
35 g (1¹/₄ oz) roasted hazelnuts
35 g (1¹/₄ oz) rocket
3 tablespoons grated Parmesan

1 Preheat the oven to moderately hot 200°C (400°F/Gas 6). Peel the pumpkin and cut into 2 cm (³/₄ inch) slices, then cut into rough triangular shapes about 3 cm (1¹/₄ inches) along the base. Toss with half the oil and some salt and cracked black pepper, until coated. Spread on a baking tray and bake for 35 minutes, or until cooked.

2 For the hazelnut pesto, process the hazelnuts, rocket, 1 tablespoon of the Parmesan and the remaining oil, until they form a paste. Season with salt and cracked black pepper.

3 Spoon a small amount of the hazelnut pesto onto each piece of pumpkin and sprinkle with the remaining Parmesan and black pepper if desired. Serve warm or cold.

IN ADVANCE: Pesto can be made several days ahead. Pour a film of oil over the surface to prevent discoloration. Tip the oil off before using the pesto.

BELOW: Pumpkin and hazelnut pesto bites

BEEF EN CROUTE WITH BEARNAISE

Preparation time: 20 minutes
Total cooking time: 30–35 minutes
Makes 40

500 g (1 lb) piece beef eye fillet, trimmed
2 teaspoons oil
60 g (2 oz) butter, melted
1 clove garlic, crushed
2 small bread sticks, cut into very thin slices
25 g (³⁄₄ oz) mustard cress, cut in short lengths

Béarnaise
200 g (6¹⁄₂ oz) butter, melted
¹⁄₃ cup (80 ml/2³⁄₄ fl oz) white wine vinegar
1 bay leaf
1 tablespoon chopped fresh tarragon
6 black peppercorns
3 parsley stalks
2 egg yolks
2 teaspoons chopped fresh tarragon, extra

1 Preheat the oven to moderate 180°C (350°F/Gas 4). Tie the beef with string at even intervals; season. Heat the oil in a pan and fry the beef to brown all over. Transfer to a small baking dish and bake for 20–25 minutes for medium to medium-rare. Remove and set aside.
2 Combine the butter and garlic in a bowl and brush over both sides of the bread. Bake on baking trays for 10 minutes, or until just golden.
3 For the Béarnaise, melt the butter slowly over low heat, remove from the heat and leave for 2–3 minutes to allow the milky mixture to separate to the bottom. Pour off the butter, leaving the milky sediment behind; discard the sediment. Combine the vinegar, bay leaf, tarragon, peppercorns and parsley in a pan and simmer briefly until reduced to 1 tablespoon; strain. Beat the egg yolks and the reduced sauce in a heatproof bowl over a pan of simmering water until slightly thickened. Remove from the heat and drizzle in the butter a few drops at a time, beating continuously until thick. Stir in the extra tarragon and season, to taste. If the mixture becomes too thick (it should be the consistency of mayonnaise), stir in a little water. If the butter is added too quickly, the mixture will separate.
4 Cut the beef into very thin slices, drape on each crouton and top with Béarnaise. Place the mustard cress on the Béarnaise.

SWEET ONION TARTS

Preparation time: 25 minutes + chilling
Total cooking time: 40 minutes
Makes 20

1 cup (125 g/4 oz) plain flour
75 g (2¹⁄₂ oz) butter, chopped
1 tablespoon bottled green peppercorns, drained
1 egg yolk
1 teaspoon Dijon mustard

Sweet onion filling
2 tablespoons olive oil
3 onions, sliced
1 clove garlic, sliced
2 teaspoons sugar
2 tablespoons balsamic vinegar
3 tablespoons raisins

1 tablespoon olive paste
75 g (2¹⁄₂ oz) feta cheese

1 Lightly grease 20 holes in two 12-hole round-based patty tins. Sift the flour and ¹⁄₄ teaspoon salt into a bowl and add the butter. Rub in with your fingertips until the mixture resembles fine breadcrumbs. Make a well in the centre. Crush the peppercorns with the back of a knife and chop finely. Add to the flour with the egg yolk, mustard and up to 2 teaspoons water. Mix with a flat-bladed knife until the mixture comes together in beads. Turn onto a lightly floured surface and press together into a ball. Wrap in plastic wrap and refrigerate for 20 minutes.
2 Preheat the oven to moderately hot 200°C (400°F/Gas 6). Roll the dough out on a lightly floured surface to 2–3 mm (about ¹⁄₈ inch). Cut 20 rounds with an 8 cm (3 inch) cutter. Put in the patty tins and prick with a fork. Bake for 8–10 minutes, or until golden.
3 For the filling, heat the oil in a heavy-based pan. Add the onion and garlic and cook, covered, over low heat for 30 minutes, or until the onion is very soft and beginning to brown. Increase the heat to moderate, add the sugar and vinegar and cook, stirring, until most of the liquid has evaporated and the onion is glossy. Stir in the raisins.
4 Spread a little olive paste into the base of each pastry case. Spoon the onion mixture over it and crumble the feta cheese on top. Serve warm or at room temperature.

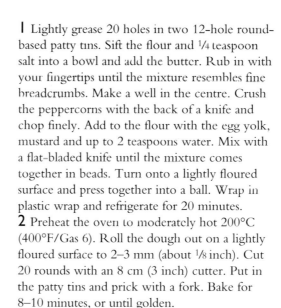

OPPOSITE PAGE: Beef en croute with Béarnaise (top); Sweet onion tarts

79

LEMONS

Lemons are probably the most versatile and useful citrus fruit to have in the kitchen. The juice and rind add flavour to a wide variety of dishes. A sprinkling with the juice preserves the colour and enhances the flavour in many fruits and vegetables such as bananas, avocados and apples. The juice is used in marinades to flavour and tenderise. And, of course, lemons are synonymous with fish. Lemons are available all year round. Choose fruit that is firm, brightly coloured and heavy for its size. Refrigerate if the weather is humid.

ABOVE: Marinated trout and cucumber tarts

MARINATED TROUT AND CUCUMBER TARTS

Preparation time: 30 minutes + standing
  + freezing
Total cooking time: 10 minutes
Makes 20

Filling

300 g (10 oz) ocean trout fillet

1/4 cup (60 ml/2 fl oz) lemon juice

2 tablespoons extra virgin olive oil

1/2 small Lebanese cucumber, finely chopped

2 spring onions, finely sliced

1 tablespoon chopped fresh dill or chervil

20 baby English spinach leaves

1 cup (125 g/4 oz) plain flour

2 tablespoons grated Parmesan

75 g (2 1/2 oz) chilled butter, cubed

1 egg, lightly beaten

1 Remove the skin from the trout, then, using kitchen tweezers, remove the bones. Freeze the fish in plastic wrap for 1 hour. Whisk the lemon juice and oil in a bowl. Cut the fish into strips about 3 x 1 cm (1 1/4 x 1/2 inch) and add to the lemon juice marinade. Cover and set aside at room temperature for 20 minutes, or until the fish turns opaque (in summer, refrigerate—the process will take a little longer). Drain off most of the marinade, leaving just enough to moisten the fish. Add the cucumber, spring onion, dill or chervil, and season with salt and black pepper.

2 While the fish is marinating, sift the flour and a pinch of salt into a large bowl and add the Parmesan and butter. Rub in with your fingertips until the mixture resembles fine breadcrumbs. Make a well, add the egg and stir in with a flat-bladed knife until the mixture comes together in beads. Turn onto a lightly floured surface and gather into a ball. Wrap in plastic wrap and refrigerate for 30 minutes.

3 Preheat the oven to hot 210°C (415°F/Gas 6–7). Lightly grease two 12-hole round-based patty tins. Roll out the pastry to about 2 mm (1/8 inch) thick and cut 8 cm (3 inch) rounds to line 20 holes. Prick the pastry lightly with a fork and

bake for 8–10 minutes, or until golden. Remove from the tins and set aside to cool. Place a spinach leaf in each tart case and top with 1 level tablespoon of filling. Serve at once.

IN ADVANCE: Prepare the tart cases up to 2 days ahead and store in an airtight container.

STILTON, PEAR AND WATERCRESS SHORTBREADS

Preparation time: 20 minutes
Total cooking time: 20–25 minutes
Makes 20

125 g (4 oz) Stilton cheese
100 g (3 1/2 oz) butter
2 cups (250 g/8 oz) plain flour
250 g (4 oz) walnuts, finely chopped
2 small ripe pears
1/2 cup (125 ml/4 fl oz) crème fraîche or light sour cream
watercress leaves, to garnish

1 Preheat the oven to moderate 180°C (350°F/Gas 4). In a small bowl, beat the cheese and butter with electric beaters for 2–3 minutes, until pale and creamy. Add the flour and walnuts and season with black pepper. Stir until the mixture forms a stiff paste, then turn out onto a lightly floured surface and gather together.

2 Press the mixture into a 30 x 20 cm (12 x 8 inch) shallow tin and score with a knife into 20 even pieces. Bake for 20–25 minutes, or until the shortbread begins to brown. While hot, cut into individual biscuits following the score lines. Cool in the tin.

3 Quarter, core and thinly slice the pears close to serving. To assemble, dot a small amount of crème fraîche in the centre of each biscuit to hold the pear in place. Top the biscuit with slices of pear. Spoon the remaining crème fraîche on top of the pear and garnish with watercress leaves.

IN ADVANCE: The shortbread biscuits can be made up to 3 days ahead and stored in an airtight container when cold. If you need to assemble the whole dish a while before serving, lightly brush all over the sliced pear with a little lemon juice to prevent the pear browning.

ABOVE: Stilton, pear and watercress shortbreads

FLAVOURS OF INDIA

If your friends enjoy the spice of life, why not give your finger food an Indian theme? Some of the dishes—samosas, pakoras, chicken tikka—are well-known and loved favourites. But spicy doesn't have to mean fiery and Indian food can also be delicate and amusing—lamb korma pies and bread bowls filled with dhal combine the flavours of the hot country but are hardly the robust fare we have come to expect. For a large and hungry gathering offer a selection of our miniature flatbreads to scoop up colourful side dishes and chutneys.

ABOVE: Chicken tikka

CHICKEN TIKKA

Preparation time: 30 minutes + overnight marinating
Total cooking time: 15 minutes
Makes 25–30 skewers

750 g (1 1/2 lb) chicken thigh fillets
1/4 onion, chopped
2 cloves garlic, crushed
1 tablespoon grated fresh ginger
2 tablespoons lemon juice
3 teaspoons ground coriander
3 teaspoons ground cumin
3 teaspoons garam masala
1/3 cup (90 g/3 oz) natural yoghurt

1 Cut the chicken into 3 cm (1 1/4 inch) cubes. Soak 30 wooden skewers in cold water for several hours.
2 Finely chop the onion, garlic, ginger, juice and spices together in a food processor. Transfer to a bowl and stir in the yoghurt and 1/2 teaspoon salt.

3 Thread 4 pieces of chicken onto each skewer and place in a large baking dish. Coat the chicken with the spice mixture. Cover and refrigerate for several hours, or overnight.
4 Barbecue, fry or grill the chicken skewers, turning frequently, until cooked through.
IN ADVANCE: Skewered chicken can be left to marinate in the refrigerator for 1–2 days.

TANDOORI CHICKEN

Preparation time: 40 minutes + overnight marinating
Total cooking time: 10 minutes
Makes about 60

1.5 kg (3 lb) chicken thigh fillets
2 cups (500 g/1 lb) natural yoghurt
1/3 cup (80 ml/2 3/4 fl oz) white wine vinegar
1 tablespoon lemon juice
1 tablespoon ground sweet paprika
1 tablespoon cayenne pepper

1 tablespoon ground coriander

1 tablespoon ground cumin

6 cloves garlic, crushed

1 tablespoon grated fresh ginger

2 bay leaves

3 green peppers (capsicum), seeded and cut
into small squares

1 Cut the chicken into bite-sized pieces and put in a large glass or ceramic bowl. Add the yoghurt, vinegar, juice, spices, garlic, ginger and bay leaves and mix well. Cover and refrigerate overnight. At the same time, soak 60 small wooden skewers in cold water overnight.
2 Thread the chicken onto the skewers, alternating with the pepper squares. Grill for 5–10 minutes, or until the chicken is tender and cooked through, turning often. Serve hot.

BEEF SAMOSAS WITH MINT CHUTNEY DIP

Preparation time: 50 minutes
Total cooking time: 15 minutes
Makes about 20

2 tablespoons oil

1 onion, finely chopped

2 teaspoons finely chopped fresh ginger

400 g (13 oz) beef mince

1 tablespoon curry powder

1 tomato, peeled and chopped

1 potato, cubed

1 tablespoon finely chopped fresh mint

6 sheets ready-rolled puff pastry

1 egg yolk, lightly beaten

1 tablespoon cream

Mint chutney dip

20 g (3/4 oz) fresh mint leaves

4 spring onions

1 red chilli, seeded

1/4 teaspoon salt

1 tablespoon lemon juice

2 teaspoons caster sugar

1/4 teaspoon garam masala

1 Heat the oil in a pan, add the onion and ginger and cook over medium heat for 3–5 minutes, or until the onion is soft.
2 Add the mince and curry powder and stir over high heat until the beef has browned. Add 1 teaspoon salt and the tomato and cook, covered, for 5 minutes. Add the potato and 3 tablespoons water and cook, stirring, for 5 minutes. Remove from the heat, then cool. Stir in the mint.
3 Preheat the oven to hot 210°C (415°F/ Gas 6–7). Cut the pastry into 13 cm (5¼ inch) circles using a cutter or small plate as a guide, then cut in half. Form cones by folding each in half and pinching the sides together.
4 Spoon 2 teaspoons of the mince into each cone. Pinch the top edges together to seal. Place on a lightly greased baking tray. Beat the egg yolk with the cream and brush over the pastry. Bake for 10–15 minutes, or until puffed and golden brown. Serve with mint chutney dip.
5 To make the dip, roughly chop the mint leaves, spring onion and chilli and place in a food processor or blender with 3 tablespoons water and the remaining ingredients. Mix thoroughly and serve with the hot samosas.
IN ADVANCE: Prepare the samosas up to a day ahead and refrigerate. Cook just before serving.

*ABOVE: Beef samosas
with mint chutney dip*

CORIANDER

Fresh coriander is an ancient plant. The leaves look like parsley but they are a lighter green and, when chopped, the aroma is quite distinctive. All parts of the plant, including the roots, leaves, stems and seeds (dried), are used in some cuisines, especially Thai. Sometimes coriander is called cilantro or Chinese parsley. Stand the roots, which are still attached when you buy a bunch, in a jar of water in the refrigerator and coriander will keep for several days.

OPPOSITE PAGE: Onion bhajis with tomato and chilli sauce (top left); Bread bowls filled with dhal

ONION BHAJIS WITH TOMATO AND CHILLI SAUCE

Preparation time: 30 minutes
Total cooking time: 40 minutes
Makes about 25

★ ★

Tomato and chilli sauce
2–3 red chillies, chopped
1 red pepper (capsicum), seeded, cut into small dice
425 g (14 oz) can chopped tomatoes
2 cloves garlic, finely chopped
2 tablespoons soft brown sugar
1 1/2 tablespoons cider vinegar

Bhajis
1 cup (125 g/4 oz) plain flour
2 teaspoons baking powder
1/2 teaspoon chilli powder
1/2 teaspoon ground turmeric
1 teaspoon ground cumin
2 eggs, beaten
4 onions, very thinly sliced
50 g (1 3/4 oz) fresh coriander leaves, chopped
oil, for deep-frying

1 To make the sauce, combine all the sauce ingredients with 3 tablespoons water in a saucepan. Bring to the boil, lower the heat and simmer for about 20 minutes, until it thickens. Remove from the heat. Season, to taste, with salt and freshly ground pepper.
2 For the bhajis, sift the flour, baking powder, chilli powder, turmeric, cumin and 1 teaspoon salt into a bowl and make a well in the centre. Gradually add the combined egg and 3 tablespoons water, whisking to make a smooth lump-free batter. Stir in the onion and chopped coriander.
3 Fill a deep, heavy-based pan one third full of oil and heat the oil to 180°C (350°F). The oil is ready when a cube of bread dropped into the oil turns golden brown in 15 seconds. Drop small rough balls of batter, about the size of a golf ball, into the oil and fry in batches for about 1 1/2 minutes each side, or until crisp and golden. Drain on crumpled paper towels. Serve hot with the tomato and chilli sauce.
IN ADVANCE: These are best served freshly fried, but can be made ahead of time and reheated in a moderately hot 200°C (400°F/Gas 6) oven for about 5 minutes.

BREAD BOWLS FILLED WITH DHAL

Preparation time: 25 minutes
Total cooking time: 35 minutes
Makes 24

★ ★

1/2 cup (125 g/4 oz) red lentils, rinsed and drained
1 cup (250 ml/8 fl oz) vegetable stock
24 slices white bread
60 g (2 oz) ghee or butter
1/2 teaspoon cumin seeds
1/2 teaspoon ground coriander
1/4 teaspoon yellow mustard seeds
2 cloves garlic, crushed
1/2 teaspoon chopped red chilli *pepper — Fresh*
2 tablespoons chopped fresh coriander leaves *(Cilantro)*

1 Preheat the oven to moderately hot 200°C (400°F/Gas 6). Combine the red lentils and stock in a heavy-based pan. Bring to the boil, reduce the heat and simmer, covered, for 10 minutes, or until tender. Stir occasionally and check that the mixture is not catching on the bottom of the pan. Remove from the heat.
2 Meanwhile, using an 8 cm (3 inch) cutter, cut 24 rounds of bread. Roll each to 1 mm (1/16 inch) thick with a rolling pin. Melt half the ghee or butter, brush on both sides of the bread, then push into two 12-hole mini muffin tins to form little bowls. Bake for 12–15 minutes, or until firm and golden.
3 Heat the remaining ghee or butter in a small frying pan and add the cumin, ground coriander and mustard seeds. Cook until the mustard seeds begin to pop, then add the garlic and chilli. Cook stirring, for 1 minute, or until fragrant. Stir the spice mixture into the cooked lentils, return to the heat and simmer over very low heat, stirring frequently until the dhal is thick and creamy. Season, to taste, with salt and set aside to cool a little before serving
4 Fill each bread bowl with 2–3 teaspoons of warm dhal, scatter with the chopped coriander and serve immediately.
IN ADVANCE: Bread bowls and dhal can be made 2 days ahead and stored separately. Store the bread bowls in an airtight container and the dhal, covered, in the refrigerator. Gently reheat the dhal and fill the bread bowls with warm dhal close to serving time.

AROMATIC PANTRY

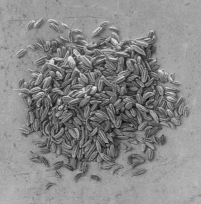

Besan flour: pale yellow, finely milled flour made from dried chickpeas (garbanzo beans). High in protein, it is used in many dishes, including doughs and sauces. Also known as gram flour.

Chilli powder: made by finely grinding whole dried red chillies. Flavour varies from mild to fiery hot, so add sparingly to dishes until the heat of the particular chilli powder has been ascertained. Sometimes available as a blend containing chilli, oregano, cumin and garlic.

Curry leaves: small shiny, bright green pointed leaves from a tree native to India. Fresh leaves are used in many Indian dishes. Much of the flavour is lost from dried leaves.

Fennel seeds: greenish brown seeds from the fennel plant. Have a light licorice taste, not overpowering if used sparingly. Also available ground. Used in both sweet and savoury dishes and to flavour some liqueurs.

Garam masala: a mixture of dry-roasted ground spices, usually including cinnamon, pepper, coriander, cumin, cardamom, cloves and either mace or nutmeg. Some variations contain up to 12 spices.

Kaffir lime leaves: dark, shiny, double leaves with a distinctive citrus flavour and strong perfume rich in aromatic oils. Remove the central thick vein and slice thinly. Dried leaves may need soaking before use.

Coriander seeds: small pale yellow/brown, slightly ridged round seeds with a mild fragrance. Also available ground. Often used in conjunction with fresh coriander. The flavours are completely different.

Lemon grass: The tough exterior leaves are removed and the white interior is used in cooking, sliced or pounded into a paste. The bruised stem can be used in soups or curries and removed before serving.

Red lentils: tiny round flat pulses. Can also be deep orange or yellow. Not necessary to soak before cooking. Widely available.

Fresh coriander: a pungent herb, also known as cilantro and Chinese parsley. All parts of the plant are edible. Whole dried seeds or ground coriander also available.

Curry powder: blend of up to 20 spices. Varies depending on the region, but ranges from mild to hot. Will lose flavour after two months and should be bought in small quantities.

Cumin seeds: small, pale brown aromatic seeds which have a warm pungent earthy flavour. Also available ground.

Brown mustard seeds: small golden brown seeds. Hotter and more aromatic than the yellow mustard seeds.

Kalonji/nigella seeds: small black seeds with a slight peppery onion flavour. Available in speciality stores.

Ghee: pure clarified butter with no milk solids, so it can be heated to a high temperature without burning. Available in tins or the refrigerated section of the supermarket.

Palm sugar: made from the boiled sap of palm trees. Sold in blocks or jars, it is thick and crumbly and is generally grated before use. Soft brown sugar makes a good substitute.

Ground turmeric: dried ground root of fresh turmeric, a member of the ginger family. Has a mild musky flavour and imparts a distinctive yellow colour to food.

SESAME PRAWNS WITH TANGY MINT CHUTNEY

Preparation time: 20 minutes
Total cooking time: 20 minutes
Makes 24

✹✹

1 kg (2 lb) raw king prawns (about 24)
¹/₄ cup (30 g/1 oz) plain flour
1 egg, lightly beaten
²/₃ cup (65 g/2¹/₄ oz) dried breadcrumbs
¹/₂ cup (80 g/2³/₄ oz) sesame seeds
oil, for deep-frying

Tangy mint chutney

50 g (1³/₄ oz) fresh mint leaves
¹/₂ cup (140 g/4¹/₂ oz) fruit chutney
2 tablespoons lemon juice

1 Peel the prawns, leaving the tails intact. Carefully cut the prawns down the back, devein and flatten slightly.
2 Toss the prawns in the flour and shake off the excess. Dip the floured prawns in the beaten egg and coat with the combined breadcrumbs and sesame seeds.
3 Fill a deep, heavy-based pan one third full of oil and heat the oil to 180°C (350°F). The oil is ready when a cube of bread dropped into the oil turns golden brown in 15 seconds. Deep-fry the prawns, in batches, for about 2 minutes each batch, until golden brown. Remove from the oil with tongs or a slotted spoon. Drain on crumpled paper towel.
4 To make the tangy mint chutney, combine the mint, chutney and lemon juice in a blender or food processor for 15 seconds, or until smooth. Serve as a dip.
IN ADVANCE: The prawns can be crumbed a day ahead. Place in a single layer on a tray, cover and refrigerate. Alternatively, freeze in a single layer and when frozen, place in a plastic bag and seal. Thaw in a single layer on a baking tray in the refrigerator. Prepare the mint chutney close to serving time.

ABOVE: Sesame prawns with tangy mint chutney

SPICY PUMPKIN PUFFS

Preparation time: 20 minutes
Total cooking time: 50 minutes
Makes 20

1 tablespoon vegetable oil
1 onion, finely chopped
3 fresh or dried curry leaves
1 tablespoon brown mustard seeds
2 teaspoons mild Madras curry powder
1/2 teaspoon chilli powder
1/2 teaspoon ground turmeric
350 g (11 oz) pumpkin, diced
1/2 cup (80 g/2³/4 oz) frozen peas
3/4 cup (185 ml/6 fl oz) chicken stock
5 sheets ready-rolled puff pastry
1 egg, lightly beaten

1 Heat the oil in a frying pan and cook the onion for 2–3 minutes over moderate heat.

Add the curry leaves and mustard seeds and fry for 1–2 minutes, or until the mustard seeds pop. Add the curry powder, chilli powder and turmeric to the pan and stir for about 30 seconds, or until combined.

2 Add the pumpkin to the pan and stir for 1–2 minutes, or until the pumpkin is well coated with spices. Add the peas and stock to the pan and simmer gently for 8–10 minutes, or until the pumpkin is tender and most of the liquid has evaporated. Remove from the heat and allow to cool completely.

3 Preheat the oven to hot 220°C (425°F/Gas 7). Lightly brush two baking trays lightly with oil. Cut four 10 cm (4 inch) circles from each of the pastry sheets and spoon 1 tablespoon of the mixture into the centre of each. Brush the edges with the beaten egg and fold over to enclose the filling. Seal the edges by rolling and folding, or pressing with a fork. Place the puffs on the trays and lightly brush with the remaining beaten egg. Bake for 25–30 minutes, or until puffed and golden.
IN ADVANCE: Can be made 2 days ahead or frozen for up to 2 months.

SPICY PUMPKIN PUFFS

Add the curry leaves and the mustard seeds to the onion in the pan and fry until the seeds pop.

To check whether the pumpkin is tender, gently insert the point of a knife into a piece.

Brush around the edges of each pastry circle with lightly beaten egg.

Seal the edges of the puffs by rolling and folding, or pressing lightly with a fork.

LEFT: Spicy pumpkin puffs

PALM SUGAR

Palm sugar is made by boiling the sap of either the sugar palm or the palmyra palm both of which grow wild in Malaysia and Indonesia. It is a thick, crumbly sugar with quite a rich flavour. The colour varies from pale caramel to dark brown. It is sold in Asian food speciality stores in block form, or in jars, and keeps for months in an airtight container.

ABOVE: Coconut-crusted lamb cutlets

COCONUT-CRUSTED LAMB CUTLETS

Preparation time: 10 minutes + marinating
Total cooking time: 10 minutes
Makes 24

24 thin, lean lamb cutlets
1 large onion, grated
2 cloves garlic, crushed
2 teaspoons ground turmeric
1 tablespoon soft dark brown or palm sugar
2/3 cup (60 g/2 oz) desiccated coconut
2 teaspoons soy sauce
2 tablespoons lemon juice

1 Trim the meat of excess fat and sinew. Combine all the remaining ingredients in a bowl with 1 teaspoon of salt and 1/2 teaspoon of freshly ground black pepper. Stir until the coconut is thoroughly moistened.
2 Add the lamb cutlets and press the coconut mixture onto the surface of each one. Cover with plastic wrap and marinate in the refrigerator for 2 hours.
3 Preheat and lightly oil the grill, then grill the cutlets for 3–5 minutes on each side, or until crisp and golden brown.
IN ADVANCE: This recipe can be prepared a day or two ahead and refrigerated, covered. Bring to room temperature before grilling.

CURRIED MINCE MEATBALLS

Preparation time: 40 minutes + chilling
Total cooking time: 40 minutes
Makes 25–30

2 tablespoons olive oil
1 large onion, finely chopped
1 clove garlic, finely chopped
45 g (1 1/2 oz) butter
1 tablespoon curry powder
2 tablespoons plain flour

³/₄ cup (185 ml/6 fl oz) milk

1 tablespoon mango or tomato chutney

400 g (13 oz) minced, cooked, cold lamb, beef
  or chicken

¹/₄ cup (30 g/1 oz) plain flour, extra, for coating

2 eggs

1¹/₄ cups (125 g/4 oz) dry breadcrumbs

oil, for deep-frying

mango or tomato chutney, extra, for serving

1 Heat the oil in a medium saucepan, add the
onion and cook over medium heat for about
5 minutes, or until soft and golden. Add the
garlic and cook for 30 seconds. Add the butter to
the pan and, when melted, stir in the curry
powder until aromatic. Add the flour and cook
for 1 minute, or until foaming. Remove from
the heat and gradually stir in the milk. Return to
the heat and stir constantly over medium heat
until the sauce boils and thickens. Reduce the
heat and simmer for 2 minutes. Add the chutney
and ¹/₄ teaspoon each of salt and black pepper.
Remove from the heat and add the meat, stirring
until the mixture is well combined. Cool, cover

with plastic wrap and refrigerate for at least 1 hour.
2 Using wet hands, form tablespoons of the
mixture into balls and place on greaseproof paper
covered trays.
3 Place the extra flour on a plate. Beat the eggs
in a shallow bowl. Put the breadcrumbs on a
sheet of greaseproof paper. Lightly coat the balls
in flour, shake off any excess, dip in egg and
then coat with breadcrumbs. Cover and
refrigerate on paper-covered trays for 1 hour,
or overnight.
4 Fill a deep heavy-based pan one third full of
oil and heat the oil to 180°C (350°F). The oil is
ready when a cube of bread dropped into the oil
turns golden brown in 15 seconds. Deep-fry the
meatballs in batches for about 2 minutes each
batch, or until golden brown all over. Remove
from the oil with a slotted spoon and drain on
crumpled paper towels. Serve with chutney.
NOTE: You can use any leftover roast meat.
Mince it in a food processor or cut finely with
a sharp knife.
IN ADVANCE: The meat mixture can be made
up to 2 days ahead. The crumbed balls can be
frozen for up to 2 months. Allow to thaw
thoroughly before frying.

*ABOVE: Curried mince
meatballs*

BREADS Traditionally used in India to accompany curries

and mop up the sauces, these wafer-thin or sometimes puffy flatbreads can also be

broken up and served with creamy vegetable- or yoghurt-based dips, or sambals.

GHEE

Ghee, or clarified butter, used in India, keeps longer than butter and can be heated to a higher temperature without burning. To make your own, melt unsalted butter over very low heat, without stirring, until frothy. Remove from the heat, scoop off the foam, then gently pour the liquid into a heatproof container, discarding the milky sediment in the pan. When set, discard any solids from the base, reheat and repeat the process, straining through muslin or cheesecloth.

CHAPATTIS

Sift 3 cups (450 g/14 oz) wholemeal plain flour and 1 teaspoon salt into a large bowl. Return the husks. Add 40 g (1¼ oz) ghee and rub with your fingertips until the mixture resembles fine breadcrumbs. Make a well and pour in 1 cup (250 ml/ 8 fl oz) warm water. Mix with a flat-bladed knife until the dough comes together. Turn onto a lightly floured surface and knead for 10 minutes. Place in a lightly oiled bowl, cover and leave for 1 hour. Knead again for 5 minutes, or

until smooth. Roll tablespoons of dough into thin circles. Heat a little oil in a large frying pan and cook 2 chapattis at a time for 1 minute each side. Remove and drain on paper towels. Makes 35.

PURIS

Sift 3 cups (450 g/14 oz) wholemeal plain flour and 1 teaspoon salt into a large bowl. Return the husks. Stir in 2 teaspoons cumin seeds. Add 40 g (1¼ oz) ghee and rub in with your fingertips until the mixture resembles fine breadcrumbs.

Make a well and pour in 1 cup (250 ml/ 8 fl oz) warm water. Mix with a flat-bladed knife until the dough comes together. Turn onto a lightly floured surface and knead for 10 minutes. Place in a lightly oiled bowl, cover and leave for 1 hour. Knead for 5 minutes, or until smooth. Roll tablespoons of dough out into thin circles. Heat 3 cm (1¼ inch) oil in a large frying pan. Cook 1 round of dough at a time, turning over until puffed and golden. Drain on paper towels. Makes 35.

GARLIC NAAN

Combine 2½ teaspoons dry yeast, 2 teaspoons sugar and ¾ cup (185 ml/ 6 fl oz) warm water in a small bowl, cover and leave in a warm place for 10 minutes, or until foamy. Sift 3 cups (375 g/12 oz) plain flour and 1 teaspoon salt into a bowl. Make a well and pour in 60 g (2 oz) melted ghee, 2 tablespoons yoghurt and the yeast mixture. Mix with

a flat-bladed knife to a soft dough, gather into a ball then turn out onto a lightly floured surface and knead for 15 minutes, or until smooth and elastic. Place in a large oiled bowl, cover loosely and leave in a warm place for 1 hour, or until it has doubled in size. Punch down the dough, then turn onto a lightly floured surface and knead for 1 minute. Divide into 4 and divide each portion into 8. Roll each piece of dough out to a 7 cm (2¾ inch) circle and place on a greased baking tray. Brush with melted ghee and sprinkle with crushed garlic and finely chopped fresh parsley. Bake in a moderate 180°C (350°F/Gas 4) oven for 5–8 minutes, or until lightly golden. Serve. Makes 32.

PARATHAS

Sift 1 cup (150 g/5 oz) wholemeal plain flour and 1 teaspoon salt into a large bowl. Return the husks to the bowl. Make a well and add 30 g (1 oz) melted

ghee and ⅔ cup (170 ml/5½ fl oz) water. Mix with a flat-bladed knife to a soft dough, gather into a ball, then turn onto a lightly floured surface and knead for 10 minutes. Place in an oiled bowl, cover loosely and leave in a warm place for 1 hour. Knead for 1 minute, divide into four, then cut each portion into four. Roll out each piece on a lightly floured surface until 2 mm (⅛ inch) thick. Melt an extra 90 g (3 oz) ghee and brush some over each circle. Fold the circle in half to make a semi-circle, brush with ghee and fold in half again to make a triangle. Roll to a thin triangle. Brush some ghee in a large frying pan and heat. Brush each triangle with ghee and cook for 1–2 minutes each side, or until puffed and golden brown. Serve. Makes 16.

FROM LEFT: Chapattis; Puris; Parathas; Garlic naan

SIDE DISHES

A spoonful of fruit chutney or vegetable pickle provides extra spice and flavour to Indian food. Alternatively, serve a selection as dips to have with flatbreads or pappadums.

SWEET MANGO CHUTNEY

Slice the flesh of 3 large mangoes and sprinkle with salt. Finely chop 2 seeded red chillies. Blend 1/2 teaspoon garam masala with 1 1/2 cups (330 g/11 oz) raw sugar and place in a large pan with 1 cup (250 ml/8 fl oz) white vinegar. Bring to the boil, reduce the heat and simmer for 5 minutes. Add the mango, chilli, a finely grated 5 cm (2 inch) piece of fresh ginger and 1/2 cup (95 g/3 1/4 oz) finely chopped pitted dates. Simmer for 1 hour, or until the mango is tender. Spoon into warm sterilized jars and seal. Store in the fridge for a week before using. Keeps for up to 1 month. Fills three 250 ml (8 fl oz) jars.

INDIAN LIME PICKLE

Cut 10 ripe yellowed limes into eight wedges each. Place in a large glass bowl, sprinkle with 2 tablespoons cooking salt and stir well. Cover with plastic wrap and leave for 48 hours in a cool dark place, stirring occasionally. Drain, rinse well and mix with 200 g (6 1/2 oz) raisins and 150 g (5 oz) sultanas. Process in batches in a food processor until coarsely chopped. Heat 3 tablespoons peanut oil in a large heavy-based pan, add 2 teaspoons ground cumin, 1 teaspoon ground coriander, 1 teaspoon black mustard seeds, 1/2 teaspoon ground chilli powder, 1/2 teaspoon ground black pepper, 5 finely

chopped cloves of garlic and a 5 cm (2½ inch) piece of fresh ginger, grated. Don't overcook the ginger or it will be bitter. Cook over medium heat for 2–3 minutes, or until very aromatic. Add the lime mixture, 1¼ cups (315 ml/10 fl oz) malt vinegar and 500 g (1 lb) soft brown sugar. Bring to the boil, stirring until the sugar dissolves. Reduce the heat and simmer for 1–1½ hours, stirring occasionally. Pour into warm, sterilized jars and seal. Refrigerate after opening. Makes about 2½ cups (600 ml/20 fl oz).

CUCUMBER WITH YOGHURT

Mix 1 finely diced small tomato, ½ finely chopped onion, ½ coarsely grated cucumber, 1 tablespoon cumin seeds and 1½ tablespoons plain yoghurt. Season, to taste. Cover and refrigerate until ready to use. Makes about ¾ cup (185 ml/6 fl oz).

BANANA WITH COCONUT

Finely dice 2 bananas, add ⅔ cup (35 g/1¼ oz) flaked coconut and ½ cup (125 ml/4 fl oz) lemon juice and stir well. Cover and refrigerate until ready to use. Makes about 1 cup (250 ml/8 fl oz).

CUCUMBER AND CORIANDER

Peel a telegraph cucumber, discard the seeds, then dice finely. Mix with 1 tablespoon lemon juice and 2 tablespoons chopped fresh coriander leaves. Season with salt, cover and refrigerate until ready to use. Makes about ¾ cup (185 ml/6 fl oz).

PAPAYA WITH MINT

Peel a papaya, slice thinly, then cut into small dice. Mix with 3 tablespoons fresh orange juice and 1 tablespoon chopped fresh mint. Cover and chill until ready to use. Makes about 1 cup (250 ml/8 fl oz).

CHILLI EGGPLANT
(AUBERGINE) PICKLE

Slice 3 eggplants (aubergines) into 1 cm (½ inch) thick slices, put in a colander and sprinkle with salt. Leave for 1 hour, then rinse and pat dry. Bring 2 cups (500 ml/16 fl oz) white wine vinegar to the boil, add a few slices of eggplant at a time and cook for 4 minutes each batch. Layer the eggplant, 10 peeled cloves garlic, 2 sliced red chillies, some fresh curry leaves and a sliced lemon, in sterilized jars. Pour in enough olive oil to cover the eggplant. Seal and leave for a week in the fridge before using. Fills five 250 ml (8 fl oz) jars.

CLOCKWISE, FROM TOP LEFT: Sweet mango chutney; Indian lime pickle; Banana with coconut; Cucumber and coriander; Chilli eggplant pickle (2 jars); Papaya with mint; Cucumber with yoghurt

CORN AND POTATO FRITTERS

Preparation time: 15 minutes
Total cooking time: 20 minutes
Makes about 40

2 large potatoes
260 g (8 oz) can corn kernels, drained
4 eggs, lightly beaten
6 spring onions, chopped
1/2 cup (50 g/1 3/4 oz) dry breadcrumbs
1 teaspoon garam masala
3 tablespoons oil

Dipping sauce
2/3 cup (160 g/5 1/2 oz) natural yoghurt
2 tablespoons chopped fresh mint leaves
2 teaspoons sweet chilli sauce

1 Peel and coarsely grate the potatoes. Drain on paper towel and squeeze out the excess moisture. Combine in a bowl with the corn, eggs, spring onion, breadcrumbs and garam masala. Mix well.
2 Heat 2 tablespoons of the oil in a heavy-based frying pan. Cook heaped tablespoons of mixture over medium heat for 2 minutes each side, or until golden. Drain on crumpled paper towel and keep warm. Repeat until all the mixture is used, adding extra oil to the pan if necessary.
3 For the dipping sauce, combine all the ingredients in a bowl.

CRISPY CHEESE AND CURRY LENTIL BALLS

Preparation time: 15 minutes
Total cooking time: 20 minutes
Makes about 30

1 cup (250 g/4 oz) red lentils
4 spring onions, chopped
2 cloves garlic, crushed
1 teaspoon ground cumin
1 cup (80 g/2 3/4 oz) fresh breadcrumbs
1 cup (125 g/4 oz) grated Cheddar
1 large zucchini (courgette), grated
1 cup (150 g/5 oz) cornmeal (polenta)
oil, for deep-frying

1 Place the lentils in a pan and cover with water. Bring to the boil, reduce the heat, cover and simmer for 10 minutes, or until tender. Drain.
2 Combine half the lentils in a food processor or blender with the spring onion and garlic. Process until smooth. Transfer to a large bowl, then stir in the remaining lentils, cumin, breadcrumbs, cheese and zucchini until well combined. Roll level teaspoons of mixture into balls and toss lightly in cornmeal to coat.
3 Fill a heavy-based pan one third full of oil and heat the oil to 180°C (350°F). The oil is ready when a cube of bread dropped into the oil turns golden brown in 15 seconds. Cook small batches of the lentil balls in the oil for 1 minute each batch, or until golden brown, crisp and heated through. Carefully remove with tongs or a slotted spoon and drain on crumpled paper towels. Serve hot.

TANDOORI LAMB CUTLETS

Preparation time: 25 minutes + overnight marinating
Total cooking time: 10–15 minutes
Makes 24

24 lamb cutlets
2 cups (500 g/16 oz) natural yoghurt
2/3 cup (30 g/1 oz) chopped fresh coriander leaves
2 tablespoons ground cumin
4 cloves garlic, crushed
2 tablespoons grated fresh ginger
1 teaspoon ground turmeric
1–2 red chillies, seeded and finely chopped

1 Clean the bones of the cutlets by scraping down the bone with sharp knife. Put the cutlets in a large shallow dish.
2 To make the marinade, combine the yoghurt, coriander leaves, cumin, garlic, ginger, turmeric and chilli in a bowl. Pour over the cutlets, mix to coat, then cover and refrigerate overnight.
3 Leave a coating of the marinade on the cutlets and barbecue on a hot barbecue plate, or grill, until tender.
IN ADVANCE: The cutlets can be marinated up to 2 days ahead. This marinade is also delicious with chicken.

ZUCCHINI
(COURGETTE)
The zucchini, a species of summer squash that originated in America, is now used in many cuisines. The most common zucchini is green, but there is also a yellow one. Zucchini don't need much preparation, just a trim on both ends and a rinse, nor do they take long to cook. They are delicious in salads, either grated or thinly sliced. Available all year, zucchini should be firm and evenly coloured when bought and should be kept in the crisper in the refrigerator.

OPPOSITE PAGE: Corn and potato fritters (top); Crispy cheese and curry lentil balls

2 Combine the yoghurt with the fresh coriander, mint and salt, to taste. Pour over the prawns, mix well and leave for 5 minutes.
3 Mix the ginger, garlic, chilli powder, turmeric, coriander, garam masala and food colouring in a large bowl, add the prawns and marinate for 10 minutes.
4 Thread the prawns onto metal skewers and barbecue or grill for about 5 minutes. Turn the skewers once, so the prawns cook evenly. They are ready when they start to curl and turn opaque. Serve on skewers or loose with lemon wedges and side dishes (see page 96).

HERBED NAAN BREAD

Preparation time: 35 minutes + rising
Total cooking time: 20 minutes
Makes 32

★ ★

2 packets naan bread mix
90 g (3 oz) sweet potato, finely diced
90 g (3 oz) pumpkin, finely diced
90 g (3 oz) frozen peas, thawed
30 g (1 oz) chopped fresh coriander
2 tablespoons mango chutney
1 teaspoon curry powder
1/2 teaspoon garam masala
1 teaspoon crushed fennel seeds
1/4 teaspoon chilli powder
1 egg, lightly beaten

1 Prepare each packet of naan bread, according to the instructions, up to the rising stage. Knead lightly. Be careful not to overwork the dough or it will be tough.
2 Boil or steam the sweet potato and pumpkin until just tender and combine with the peas, coriander, chutney, curry powder, garam masala, fennel seeds and chilli powder in a bowl. Preheat the oven to moderately hot 200°C (400°F/Gas 6).
3 Divide each quantity of dough into 4 portions, roll each out on a lightly floured surface and cut 4 circles from each with an 8 cm (3 inch) cutter.
4 Spoon a heaped teaspoon of the filling on half of each circle, brush the edges with beaten egg, fold over and seal. Place on lightly greased baking trays, brush the tops with the remaining egg and bake for 20 minutes, or until crisp and golden brown.
IN ADVANCE: Can be made 2 days ahead or frozen for up to 2 months.

TANDOORI PRAWNS

Preparation time: 20 minutes + marinating
Total cooking time: 5 minutes
Makes 24

★

1 kg (2 lb) raw king prawns (about 24)
1/2 cup (125 g/4 oz) natural yoghurt
1/3 cup (20 g/3/4 oz) finely chopped fresh coriander
2 tablespoons finely chopped fresh mint
1 tablespoon chopped fresh ginger
2 cloves garlic, crushed
1 teaspoon chilli powder
1 teaspoon ground turmeric
1 teaspoon ground coriander
1 teaspoon garam masala
few drops red food colouring, optional
2 lemons, cut into wedges, for serving

1 Peel and devein the prawns, leaving the tails intact. Rinse and pat dry with paper towels.

ABOVE: Tandoori prawns

SPICY KOFTAS

Preparation time: 25 minutes
Total cooking time: 25 minutes
Makes 45

500 g (1 lb) lamb mince
1 small onion, finely chopped
1 clove garlic, crushed
1 teaspoon ground coriander
1 teaspoon ground cumin
1/4 teaspoon ground cinnamon
1/2 teaspoon finely chopped red chilli
1 teaspoon tomato paste (tomato purée)
1 tablespoon chopped fresh mint
1 tablespoon chopped fresh coriander
oil, for frying

Yoghurt dip

1 small tomato, peeled, seeded and finely
  chopped
1/2 Lebanese cucumber, peeled and finely
  chopped

1 clove garlic, crushed
1 tablespoon chopped fresh mint
1/2 cup (125 g/4 oz) natural yoghurt

1 Combine the mince, onion, garlic, coriander, cumin, cinnamon, chilli, tomato paste and mint and coriander leaves in a large bowl and mix well with your hands. Season well, then roll into small balls (about 1 1/2 teaspoons each).
2 Place a large heavy-based frying pan over moderate heat and heat a little oil. Cook the koftas in batches until well browned all over and cooked through. Drain on crumpled paper towels.
3 Mix together the dip ingredients and place in a small bowl.
4 Skewer each kofta with a cocktail stick and serve with the dip.
IN ADVANCE: You can freeze the cooked koftas. When required, defrost, cover with foil and reheat in an ovenproof dish in a moderate 180°C (350°F/Gas 4) oven for 5–10 minutes. The dip can be made several hours ahead.

BELOW: Spicy koftas

POTATOES

Potatoes originated in South America and have been cultivated for centuries. In the 16th century, the Portuguese and Spanish transported potatoes to Europe, and probably India. They served as a staple for the poor as they contain protein, starch and vitamins. If they have to be peeled, peel thinly as the vitamins are just under the skin. There are many varieties, some versatile and suitable for all types of cooking, others best used for specific styles of cooking. There are also old and new potatoes. New ones, picked when immature, do not store well and should be refrigerated, but only for a few days. Old ones are best kept in a cool, dark place, away from onions which will make them deteriorate. If potatoes have green spots, cut them off thickly, and if very green, discard the potato.

ABOVE: Fresh herb pakoras

FRESH HERB PAKORAS

Preparation time: 30 minutes + standing
Total cooking time: 10 minutes
Makes 30

1 1/2 cups (165 g/5 1/2 oz) besan flour
1 teaspoon ground turmeric
1/2 teaspoon chilli powder
1 1/2 teaspoons garam masala
1 zucchini (courgette), diced
1 small orange sweet potato, diced
60 g (2 oz) cauliflower florets
50 g (1 3/4 oz) frozen peas, thawed
1 small onion, diced
2 tablespoons chopped fresh coriander
2 tablespoons chopped fresh basil
2 tablespoons chopped fresh parsley
2 cloves garlic, crushed
oil, for deep-frying
natural yoghurt and mango chutney, for serving

1 Sift the flour, turmeric, chilli powder, garam masala and 1 1/2 teaspoons salt into a large bowl. Make a well and gradually add 1/2 cup (125 ml/ 4 fl oz) water, whisking to make a stiff lump-free batter. Cover and set aside for 30 minutes.
2 Beat the mixture again and stir in the vegetables, herbs and garlic. Fill a deep heavy-based pan one third full of oil and heat the oil to 180°C (350°F). The oil is ready when a cube of bread dropped into the oil turns golden brown in 15 seconds. Drop heaped teaspoons of mixture, in batches, into the oil and cook until golden. Drain on crumpled paper towels. Serve with bowls of yoghurt and mango chutney for dipping.

POTATO AND CORIANDER SAMOSAS

Preparation time: 1 hour
Total cooking time: 45 minutes
Makes about 24

50 g (1 3/4 oz) butter
2 teaspoons grated fresh ginger
2 teaspoons cumin seeds
1 teaspoon Madras curry powder
1/2 teaspoon garam masala
500 g (1 lb) waxy potatoes, finely diced
30 g (1 oz) sultanas
80 g (2 3/4 oz) frozen baby peas

15 g (¹/₂ oz) fresh coriander leaves

3 spring onions, sliced

1 egg, lightly beaten

oil, for deep-frying

thick natural yoghurt, for serving

Samosa pastry

3³/₄ cups (465 g/15 oz) plain flour, sifted

1 teaspoon baking powder

110 g (3¹/₂ oz) butter, melted

¹/₂ cup (125 g/4 oz) thick natural yoghurt

1 Heat the butter in a large non-stick frying pan, add the ginger, cumin seeds, curry powder and garam masala and stir over medium heat for 1 minute. Add the potato and 3 tablespoons water and cook over low heat for 15–20 minutes, or until the potato is tender. Toss the sultanas, peas, coriander leaves and spring onion with the potato, remove from the heat and set aside to cool.

2 To make the samosa pastry, sift the flour, baking powder and 1¹/₂ teaspoons salt into a large bowl. Make a well in the centre, add the butter, yoghurt and ³/₄ cup (185 ml/6 fl oz) of water. Using a flat-bladed knife, bring the dough

together. Turn out onto a lightly floured surface and bring together to form a smooth ball. Divide the dough into four to make it easier to work with. Roll one piece out until very thin. Cover the rest until you are ready to use it.

3 Using a 12 cm (5 inch) diameter bowl or plate as a guide, cut out six circles. Place a generous tablespoon of potato filling in the centre of each circle, brush the edges of the pastry with egg and fold over to form a semi-circle. Make repeated folds on the rounded edge by folding a little piece of the pastry over as you move around the edge. Continue with the remaining pastry and filling.

4 Fill a deep heavy-based pan one third full of oil and heat the oil to 180°C (350°F). The oil is ready when a cube of bread dropped into the oil turns golden brown in 15 seconds. It is important not to have the oil too hot or the samosas will burn. Add the samosas two or three at a time and cook until golden. If they rise to the surface as they puff up, you may need to use a large, long-handled slotted spoon to hold them in the oil to cook the other side. Drain on crumpled paper towels. Serve with yoghurt.

NOTE: The samosa pastry becomes very tough if overworked. Use lightly floured hands when working the dough to prevent it sticking.

POTATO AND CORIANDER SAMOSAS

Cut six circles from each sheet of pastry, using a bowl or plate as a guide.

Measure a generous tablespoon of potato mixture onto the centre of each circle of pastry.

To secure the samosas, make folds on the edge, folding a piece over as you move along.

When the samosas are cooked, remove from the oil with a slotted spoon.

LEFT: Potato and coriander samosas

CURRIED CHICKEN PIES

Preparation time: 45 minutes + chilling
Total cooking time: 50 minutes
Makes 24

3 cups (375 g/12 oz) plain flour
1 teaspoon ground cumin
1 teaspoon ground turmeric
200 g (6½ oz) butter, chopped
2 egg yolks, lightly beaten
50 g (1¾ oz) butter, extra
1 onion, chopped
350 g (12 oz) chicken tenderloins, trimmed and cut into small dice
1 tablespoon curry powder
1 teaspoon cumin seeds
1 tablespoon plain flour, extra
1 cup (250 ml/8 fl oz) chicken stock
2 tablespoons mango chutney (mango chopped)
3 tablespoons chopped fresh coriander
milk, for glazing

1 Sift the flour, cumin and turmeric into a bowl. Rub in the butter using just your fingertips, until the mixture resembles fine breadcrumbs. Make a well and add the egg yolks and 5–6 tablespoons water. Mix with a flat-bladed knife using a cutting action, until the mixture comes together. Lift onto a floured surface and gather into a ball. Wrap in plastic wrap and chill for 30 minutes.
2 Lightly grease two deep 12-hole patty tins. Roll out two-thirds of the pastry to 2 mm (⅛ inch) thick, and cut 8 cm (3 inch) rounds to fit the tins. Roll out the remaining pastry and cut 24 tops with a 5.5 cm (2¼ inch) cutter. Chill.
3 Heat the extra butter in a large pan and cook the onion until soft. Add the chicken and, when browned, stir in the curry powder and cumin seeds for 2 minutes. Add the extra flour and stir for 30 seconds. Remove from the heat and gradually stir in the stock. Return to the heat and stir until the sauce boils and thickens. Reduce the heat and simmer for 2–3 minutes, until reduced and very thick. Stir in the chutney and coriander leaves. Season and cool.
4 Preheat the oven to moderate 180°C (350°F/ Gas 4). Divide the filling among the pies and brush the edges with water. Join the tops by pressing around the edges with the tip of a sharp knife. Slash each top to allow steam to escape. Brush with milk and bake for 30 minutes. Cool slightly before removing from tins. Serve warm.

LAMB KORMA PIES

Preparation time: 30 minutes + chilling
Total cooking time: 1 hour 20 minutes
Makes 24

3 cups (375 g/12 oz) plain flour, sifted
2 tablespoons caraway seeds
180 g (6 oz) butter, chopped
1 tablespoon olive oil
1 small onion, finely chopped
1 clove garlic, crushed
2 tablespoons bottled mild curry paste
250 g (8 oz) lamb fillets, trimmed, finely diced
1 small potato, finely diced
¼ cup (40 g/1¼ oz) frozen baby peas
¼ cup (60 g/2 oz) natural yoghurt
1 egg, lightly beaten
2 tablespoons chopped fresh coriander

1 Combine the flour and caraway seeds in a large bowl. Rub in the butter using just your fingertips, until the mixture resembles fine breadcrumbs. Make a well, add 4 tablespoons water and mix with a flat-bladed knife, using a cutting action, until the mixture comes together in beads. Lift onto a floured surface and gather into a ball. Flatten slightly into a disc, wrap in plastic wrap and chill for 20 minutes.
2 Heat the oil in a heavy-based pan, add the onion and garlic and stir over medium heat for 3–4 minutes, or until the onion is soft. Add the curry paste and stir for 1 minute. Increase the heat to high and add the lamb, potato and peas, stirring for 5 minutes, or until the lamb is well browned all over. Add the yoghurt, bring to the boil, then reduce the heat and simmer, covered, for 30 minutes, or until the lamb is tender. Uncover and simmer for 10 minutes, or until the sauce thickens. Remove from the heat and allow to cool.
3 Preheat the oven to 180°C (350°F/Gas 5). Lightly grease two 12-hole mini muffin tins. Roll two-thirds of the dough between baking paper to 2 mm (⅛ inch) thick. Cut 24 rounds with a 7 cm (2¾ inch) cutter and ease into the tins. Spoon the lamb into the cases. Roll out the remaining pastry into a rectangle. Cut 24 strips 1 x 20 cm (½ x 8 inches) and twist onto the top of each pie. Brush with the egg and bake for 25–30 minutes, or until golden brown. Cool slightly before removing from the tins. Serve warm, sprinkled with fresh coriander.

PEAS
This popular vegetable is used throughout the world. The juicy seeds, encased in a pod, are removed, except in varieties such as snow peas (mangetout) and sugar snap peas, which both have tender, edible pods. Frozen peas, including sweet-flavoured baby peas, are commonly used for convenience. Fresh peas take longer to cook than frozen.

OPPOSITE PAGE: Curried chicken pies (left); Lamb korma pies

INDIAN TEMPURA

Preparation time: 20 minutes + standing
Total cooking time: 25 minutes
Serves 8

★★

Batter

1⅓ cups (145 g/5 oz) besan flour
75 g (2½ oz) rice flour
1 teaspoon ground turmeric
1 teaspoon chilli powder
¼ teaspoon kalonji (nigella) seeds

2 potatoes
300 g (10 oz) pumpkin
300 g (10 oz) eggplant (aubergine)
2 small onions
15 baby English spinach leaves
oil, for deep-frying
besan flour, for dusting
sweet chilli sauce, for serving

ABOVE: Indian tempura

1 Sift the besan flour, rice flour, turmeric, chilli powder and ½ teaspoon salt into a large bowl and make a well in the centre. Gradually add 1 cup (250 ml/8 fl oz) water, whisking to make a smooth, thick batter. Stir in the kalonji seeds, cover and leave for 10 minutes.

2 Cut the potatoes and pumpkin into batons about 8 cm (3 inches) long. Cut the eggplant into thin slices and each slice into quarters. Cut the onions into quarters and separate the sections into individual pieces, discarding the centre. Wash and pat dry the baby spinach leaves.

3 Check the consistency the batter. It should be like cream so, if it is too thick, add a little extra water. Fill a heavy-based pan one third full of oil and heat to 180°C (350°F). Test the oil by cooking ¼ teaspoon of batter. If it keeps its shape and sizzles while rising to the top, the oil is ready. Make sure the oil stays at the same temperature and does not get too hot. The tempura should cook through as well as brown.

4 Dip batches of the vegetables in the besan flour, shake well, then dip in the batter and fry until golden brown. The cooking time will vary for each type of vegetable. Drain each batch on crumpled paper towel, sprinkle with salt and keep warm in a slow 150°C (300°F/Gas 2) oven. Serve immediately with sweet chilli sauce.

NOTE: Kalonji (nigella) seeds are available where Indian and Lebanese ingredients are sold.

PURIS WITH CORIANDER RELISH

Preparation time: 40 minutes
Total cooking time: 10–15 minutes
Makes 32

★★

¾ cup (90 g/3 oz) plain flour

¾ cup (110 g/3½ oz) wholemeal plain flour

1 teaspoon salt

1 tablespoon cracked black pepper

3 tablespoons oil or ghee

1 teaspoon kalonji (nigella) seeds

oil, for deep-frying

Coriander relish

60 g (2 oz) fresh coriander leaves

20 g (¾ oz) fresh mint leaves

½ small onion

1 green chilli

2 tablespoons lemon juice

1 Sift the flours and salt and pepper into a large bowl. Add the oil or ghee and rub it into the flour with your fingertips until it resembles fine breadcrumbs. Stir in the kalonji seeds. Make a well, add 3–4 tablespoons hot water and mix with a flat-bladed knife. It should be rough but hold together. Form into a ball.

2 Divide the dough into 4 and then each portion into 8 pieces, making 32 altogether. On a lightly floured surface, roll one piece at a time into a 6 cm (2½ inch) round. Keep the rest covered with a damp tea towel or plastic wrap. Don't worry about the cracked edges.

3 Heat 2.5 cm (1 inch) of oil in a wok or large heavy-based frying pan to 180°C (350°F). The oil is ready when a cube of bread dropped into the oil turns golden brown in 15 seconds. Fry 3 or 4 puris at a time, turning them halfway through. They will only take a few seconds to turn golden on each side. Remove from the oil and drain on crumpled paper towel while you fry the remainder.

4 For the coriander relish, process all the relish ingredients together in a food processor until smooth. Serve with the puris.

ABOVE: Puris with coriander relish

LEMON GRASS PRAWN SATAYS

Preparation time: 20 minutes + chilling
Total cooking time: 15 minutes
Makes 24

1 tablespoon oil

1 clove garlic, crushed

1 tablespoon grated fresh ginger

1 tablespoon finely chopped lemon grass, white part only

1 onion, finely chopped

1 tablespoon tandoori curry paste

4 kaffir lime leaves, finely shredded

1 tablespoon coconut cream

2 teaspoons grated lime rind

600 g (1¼ lb) raw prawns, peeled and deveined

12 stems lemon grass, cut into 15 cm (6 inch) lengths, halved lengthways

1 Heat the oil in a frying pan, add the garlic, ginger, lemon grass and onion and stir over medium heat for 3 minutes, or until golden.
2 Add the tandoori paste and kaffir lime leaves to the pan and cook for 5 minutes, or until the tandoori paste is fragrant. Allow to cool slightly. Transfer to a food processor, add the coconut cream, lime rind and prawns and mix until finely minced. Divide into 24 portions and, with wet hands, shape one portion around each piece of lemon grass stem, leaving about 3 cm (1¼ inches) uncovered at each end. The mixture is quite soft, so take care when handling it. Using wet hands makes the mixture easier to manage. Refrigerate for 1 hour.
3 Grill the satays under a medium heat for 5 minutes, or until cooked through.
IN ADVANCE: The prawn mixture can be frozen up to a month ahead. Thaw in the refrigerator and mould onto the lemon grass. The satays can be prepared a day ahead.

LEMON GRASS

This fresh herb is popular for its distinct lemon fragrance and flavour. The white base of the long stem is used in curries and the leaves make a refreshing cup of tea. To prepare lemon grass for cooking, cut off all the green top and a few of the tough outer leaves, rinse the white bulb and slice or chop according to the recipe. Store in the crisper section in the refrigerator.

RIGHT: Lemon grass prawn satays

MINI SPICY BURGERS

Preparation time: 30 minutes
Total cooking time: 15 minutes
Makes 24

6–8 rounds of naan bread

600 g (1¼ lb) lean beef mince

1 green chilli, chopped

1 tablespoon curry powder

3 cloves garlic, crushed

2 teaspoons finely chopped fresh ginger

1 tablespoon peanut oil

3 tablespoons thick natural yoghurt

3 tablespoons mango chutney

24 fresh mint leaves

1 Heat the oven to warm 160°C (315°F/ Gas 2–3). Using a 6 cm (2½ inch) round cutter, mark the naan bread into 48 rounds, then cut with scissors. Loosely wrap in foil and warm in the oven while you make the patties.

2 In a bowl, combine the beef mince, chopped chilli, curry powder, garlic and ginger. Season with salt and black pepper. With wet hands, form the meat into 24 patties, about 6 cm (2½ inches) in diameter.

3 Heat the oil in a large frying pan and cook the burgers in batches, for 2–3 minutes each side, or until done to your liking. Drain on crumpled paper towels.

4 Place 24 of the warm rounds of naan on a serving platter, top each with a beef patty, then some yoghurt, mango chutney and a mint leaf. Top with the remaining rounds of naan and serve immediately.

NOTE: Prepared naan bread can be bought at most supermarkets where you find pita bread and lavash bread. These can be substituted if naan is unavailable.

IN ADVANCE: The burger mixture can be made a day ahead and formed into patties, then stored, covered, in the refrigerator. Alternatively, the patties can be frozen in a single layer on a baking tray and, when frozen, transferred to a plastic bag, sealed and returned to the freezer. Thaw in a single layer in the refrigerator before cooking.

NAAN BREAD
This traditional Indian bread is slightly puffed, flattish and teardrop-shaped. Traditionally, the leavened dough is shaped, then slapped on the sides of a tandoor oven where it cooks quickly. However, it can be baked in a normal oven, then grilled lightly until brown. It is usually served warm or hot.

ABOVE: Mini spicy burgers

EASTERN APPETIZERS

When the chefs of Sung Dynasty China created a vast array of succulent bite-sized morsels to titillate the pampered palates of their Imperial rulers, little did they know that they were inventing the tradition of yum cha. These tiny snacks have survived the centuries and are now served with tea and much loved throughout China and in Chinatowns the world over. And the other countries of Asia are not standing back shyly, letting China take all the culinary glory... Japanese sushi, Thai fish cakes and Indonesian gado gado all have their place at the table of Eastern favourites.

bread dropped into the oil turns brown in 15 seconds. Add the bread and cook, prawn-side-down, for 2–3 minutes. Turn over and cook the other side for 1 minute, or until crisp. Drain on crumpled paper towels. Serve immediately.

WARM DUCK AND CORIANDER TARTS

Preparation time: 35 minutes + chilling
Total cooking time: 20 minutes
Makes 24

1¹/₂ cups (185 g/6 oz) plain flour
125 g (4 oz) chilled butter, chopped
3 tablespoons sesame seeds
2 tablespoons chopped fresh coriander, plus
    extra sprigs to garnish

Filling
1 large Chinese roasted duck
2 tablespoons orange marmalade
1 tablespoon kecap manis
2 teaspoons sesame oil
1 tablespoon grated fresh ginger
5 finely sliced green spring onions

1 Lightly grease two 12-hole round-based patty tins. Sift the flour and ¹/₂ teaspoon salt into a large bowl and add the butter. Rub in with your fingertips until the mixture resembles fine breadcrumbs. Stir in the sesame seeds. Make a well and add up to 2 tablespoons iced water and mix with a flat-bladed knife until the dough just comes together. Turn out onto a lightly floured surface and gather into a ball.
2 Preheat the oven to hot 210°C (415°F/ Gas 6–7). Roll the pastry out thinly on a lightly floured work surface until 3 mm (¹/₈ inch) thick. Prick lightly all over. Cut 24 rounds with a 6 cm (2¹/₂ inch) fluted cutter. Re-roll the pastry if necessary. Line the tins with pastry. Bake for 10 minutes, or until the pastry is golden brown, remove from the tins and allow to cool.
3 For the filling, remove the duck meat from the bones and shred the meat. Put the marmalade in a pan and stir over low heat until smooth. Add the remaining ingredients, including the shredded duck, and mix well. Stir until warmed through.
4 Arrange the pastry shells on a warm serving platter and add the warm filling. Garnish with

PRAWN AND CORIANDER TOASTS

Preparation time: 25 minutes
Total cooking time: 15 minutes
Makes 32

500 g (1 lb) peeled raw prawns
8 spring onions, chopped
1 stem lemon grass, white part only, chopped
1 clove garlic, crushed
1 egg white
1 tablespoon oil
1 tablespoon chopped fresh coriander
1 tablespoon fish sauce
2 teaspoons chilli sauce
1 teaspoon lemon juice
8 slices of stale bread, crusts removed
oil, for shallow-frying

1 Finely chop the prawns, spring onion, lemon grass, garlic, egg white, oil, coriander, sauces and lemon juice together in a food processor.
2 Spread the mixture over the bread, right to the edge, and cut each slice into 4 triangles.
3 Heat 2 cm (³/₄ inch) of oil in a pan to 180°C (350°F). The oil is hot enough when a cube of

ABOVE: Prawn and coriander toasts

the fresh coriander and serve immediately.
NOTE: The skin from the duck can also be used in the filling. However, all visible fat should be removed. Kecap manis is an Indonesian sweet soy sauce, available in most supermarkets.

COMBINATION DIM SIMS

Preparation time: 1 hour + chilling + standing
Total cooking time: 30 minutes
Makes about 30

★

6 dried Chinese mushrooms
200 g (6¹/2 oz) lean pork mince
30 g (1 oz) pork fat, finely chopped
100 g (3¹/2 oz) peeled raw prawns, finely chopped
2 spring onions, finely chopped
1 tablespoon sliced bamboo shoots, finely chopped
1 celery stick, finely chopped
3 teaspoons cornflour
2 teaspoons soy sauce
1 teaspoon caster sugar
30 won ton or egg noodle wrappers
chilli or soy sauce, for serving

1 Put the mushrooms in a small heatproof bowl, cover with boiling water and leave for 10 minutes. Drain, discard the stems, and finely chop.
2 Mix the mushrooms, pork mince, pork fat, prawns, spring onion, bamboo shoots and celery in a bowl. Combine the cornflour, soy, sugar and salt and pepper into a smooth paste in another bowl. Stir into the pork mixture, cover and refrigerate for 1 hour.
3 Work with 1 wrapper at a time, keeping the rest covered with a tea towel. Place 1 tablespoon of filling in the centre of each, then moisten the edges with water and gather the edges into the centre, pressing together to seal. Set aside on a lightly floured surface.
4 Line the base of a bamboo steamer with a circle of baking paper. Arrange the dim sims on the paper, spacing them well (they will need to be cooked in batches). Cover the steamer and cook over a pan of simmering water for 8 minutes, or until the filling is cooked. Serve with chilli or soy sauce.

COMBINATION DIM SIMS

Soak the dried mushrooms in hot water for 10 minutes, to rehydrate them.

Gather the wrapper up to the centre to enclose the filling, then press together to seal.

Arrange a circle of baking paper in the base of a bamboo steamer.

LEFT: Combination dim sims

VIETNAMESE FRESH SPRING ROLLS

Preparation time: 50 minutes + soaking
Total cooking time: 25 minutes
Makes about 20

20 large cooked prawns
100 g (3 1/2 oz) dried mung bean vermicelli
   (cellophane noodles)
20–25 rice paper wrappers, about 16 cm
   (6 1/2 inches) round
40 fresh mint leaves
10 garlic chives, cut in halves

Dipping sauce
2 tablespoons satay sauce
3 tablespoons hoisin sauce
1 red chilli, finely chopped
1 tablespoon chopped roasted unsalted peanuts
1 tablespoon lemon juice

BELOW: Vietnamese fresh spring rolls

1 Peel the prawns and gently pull out the dark vein from the backs, starting at the head end. Cut all the prawns in half.
2 Soak the vermicelli for 5 minutes in a bowl with enough hot water to cover. Drain well and use scissors to roughly chop the noodles into shorter lengths.
3 Working with one rice paper wrapper at a time, dip into a bowl of warm water, leave for about 30 seconds, or until the wrapper becomes soft and pliable, then remove. Be careful as the wrappers can tear easily when softened.
4 Place 1 softened wrapper on a work surface and spoon about 1 tablespoon of the noodles along the bottom third of the wrapper, leaving enough space at the sides to fold the wrapper over. Top with 2 mint leaves and 2 prawn halves. Fold in the sides towards each other and firmly roll up the wrapper, adding the piece of garlic chive as you roll so it points out of one side. Repeat with the remaining wrappers and ingredients and place the spring rolls, seam-side-down, on a serving plate.
5 For the dipping sauce, mix the ingredients in a small bowl. Serve with the spring rolls.

PORK AND LEMON GRASS WON TONS

Preparation time: 40 minutes + chilling
Total cooking time: 20 minutes
Makes 56

 ★ ☆

400 g (13 oz) pork mince
1 teaspoon finely chopped fresh ginger
1 stem lemon grass, white part only, finely
   sliced
230 g (7¹/₂ oz) can water chestnuts, drained and
   finely chopped
2 tablespoons finely chopped fresh garlic chives
¹/₂ teaspoon chilli paste
2 tablespoons plum sauce
1 teaspoon chilli oil
1 teaspoon sesame oil
1 tablespoon cornflour
56 x 8 cm (3 inch) won ton wrappers
   (about 2 packets)
oil, for deep-frying

Dipping sauce
¹/₂ cup (125 ml/4 fl oz) light soy sauce
¹/₄ cup (60 ml/2 fl oz) balsamic vinegar
1 teaspoon finely grated fresh ginger
1 teaspoon chilli oil

1 Put the mince, ginger, lemon grass, water chestnuts, garlic chives, chilli paste, plum sauce, chilli and sesame oils and cornflour in a bowl. Mix with your hands. Cover; chill for 1 hour.
2 For the dipping sauce, combine the ingredients in a jug.
3 Work with 1 won ton wrapper at a time, keeping the rest covered. Spoon 2 teaspoons of the filling onto the centre of each wrapper and lightly brush the edges of the wrapper with water. Gather up the ends, bring the edges together in the centre and press firmly to seal. Repeat with the remaining wrappers and filling.
4 Fill a deep heavy-based pan one third full of oil. Heat the oil to 180°C (350°F). The oil is ready when a cube of bread dropped into the oil turns golden brown in 15 seconds. Deep-fry batches of won tons for 3–4 minutes, until lightly browned. Remove with a slotted spoon, drain on crumpled paper towels and serve hot with the sauce.

ABOVE: Pork and lemon grass won tons

COCONUT RICE IN BANANA LEAVES

Preparation time: 40 minutes
Total cooking time: 1 hour 30 minutes
Makes about 12

2–3 young banana leaves, or foil
2 cups (400 g/13 oz) glutinous rice
3/4 cup (185 ml/6 fl oz) coconut milk

Chicken filling

2 tablespoons oil
2–3 cloves garlic, crushed
6 curry leaves
1 teaspoon dried shrimp paste
2 teaspoons ground coriander
2 teaspoons ground cumin
1/2 teaspoon turmeric
250 g (8 oz) chicken mince
3 tablespoons coconut milk, extra
1 teaspoon lemon juice

ABOVE: Coconut rice in banana leaves

1 With a sharp knife, cut away the central ribs of the banana leaves. The leaves will split into large pieces—cut into pieces about 15 cm (6 inches) square. Blanch in boiling water briefly to soften them, then spread out on a tea towel and cover.
2 Wash the rice, drain and put in a large heavy-based pan with 1 3/4 cups (440 ml/14 fl oz) water. Bring slowly to the boil, reduce the heat to very low, cover tightly and cook for 15 minutes.
3 Put the coconut milk and 1/2 cup (125 ml/ 4 fl oz) water in a small pan and heat without boiling. Stir through the rice with a fork. Transfer to a bowl and set aside to cool.
4 For the chicken filling, heat the oil in a large heavy-based frying pan, add the garlic and curry leaves and stir for 1 minute over medium heat. Add the shrimp paste, coriander, cumin and turmeric and cook for another minute. Add the chicken mince and cook and break up with a fork for 3–4 minutes, or until the chicken changes colour. Add the extra coconut milk and continue to cook over low heat for 5 minutes, or until absorbed. Remove the curry leaves. Add the lemon juice and salt and pepper, to taste. Cool.
5 Place 1 heaped tablespoon of rice in the centre of each piece of banana leaf and flatten to a

4 cm (1½ inch) square. Top with a heaped teaspoon of filling. Roll the leaf into a parcel and place, seam-side-down, in a steamer lined with leftover banana leaf scraps. Steam, in batches, for 15 minutes. Serve at room temperature with chopsticks or small forks.

NOTE: Banana leaves are used throughout Asia to wrap foods for steaming or baking. They keep the food moist and impart a mild flavour. They can be bought at Asian food stores if you don't have access to fresh leaves from a plant.

IN ADVANCE: Can be made in advance and refrigerated for up to 2 days.

CHICKEN WITH NORI

Preparation time: 25 minutes + marinating
Total cooking time: 20 minutes
Makes about 30 pieces

★★

400 g (13 oz) chicken breast tenderloins
¼ cup (60 ml/2 fl oz) Japanese soy sauce
¼ cup (60 ml/2 fl oz) mirin
4 cm (1½ inches) fresh ginger, very
   finely grated
1 sheet nori, finely chopped or crumbled into
   very small pieces
⅓ cup (40 g/1¼ oz) cornflour
1 cup (250 ml/8 fl oz) oil, for frying

1 Carefully trim and discard any sinew from the chicken, then cut the chicken into bite-sized pieces and put them in a bowl.
2 Combine the soy sauce, mirin and ginger in a small jug, pour over the chicken and toss until evenly coated. Marinate in the refrigerator for 15 minutes, then drain off any excess marinade.
3 Mix the nori with the cornflour and, using your fingertips, lightly coat the chicken.
4 Heat the oil in a heavy-based pan to 180°C (350°F). The oil is ready when a cube of bread dropped into the oil turns golden brown in 15 seconds. Fry 6–7 pieces of chicken at a time until golden, turning regularly. Drain on crumpled paper towels. Garnish with extra strips of nori, if desired.

NOTE: Nori is the most common form of dried seaweed used in Asian cookery. It is available in speciality stores. Use scissors or a very sharp knife to cut it.

CRISPY VERMICELLI CAKES WITH SESAME VEGETABLES

Preparation time: 20 minutes
Total cooking time: 15 minutes
Makes about 12

★

400 g (13 oz) rice vermicelli
oil, for shallow-frying
2 teaspoons sesame oil
2 carrots, cut into matchsticks
1 red pepper (capsicum), cut into matchsticks
2 zucchini (courgettes), cut into julienne strips
4 spring onions, cut into julienne strips
½–1 tablespoon oyster sauce

1 Soak the vermicelli for 3 minutes in a bowl with enough boiling water to cover, then drain thoroughly until very dry.
2 Heat the oil in a large heavy-based frying pan over medium heat. Shape tablespoons of the noodles into flat discs and shallow-fry in batches for 3 minutes, or until crisp and golden. Drain on crumpled paper towels.
3 Heat the sesame oil in a wok and stir-fry the vegetables for 3 minutes until softened slightly. Stir in the oyster sauce and cook for 2 minutes. Serve the cakes topped with the vegetables.

ABOVE: Chicken with nori

117

SATAYS & KEBABS

If you are using wooden skewers, soak them in water for 30 minutes beforehand so

that they don't burn before the food is cooked. The ends can be wrapped in foil.

LIME PRAWNS

Using 12 canned sugar canes, cut into 5 mm (¼ inch) thick strips 10 cm (4 inches) long. Peel and devein 48 raw king prawns. Thread 2 prawns onto each sugar cane skewer. You may need to make small cuts in the prawns to make it easier. Brush lightly with some lime juice and cook on a lightly oiled preheated chargrill pan for 2–3 minutes each side, or until cooked through. Makes 24.

BEEF WITH BLACK BEAN SAUCE

Cut 1 kg (2 lb) rump steak into 2 cm (¾ inch) cubes and make small slits in the meat with a sharp knife. Trim bay leaf stems of leaves and thread the meat onto the stems. Brush lightly with ⅓ cup (80 ml/2¾ fl oz) black bean sauce. Cook on a preheated oiled chargrill pan for 2–3 minutes on each side, brushing with any remaining black bean sauce during cooking. Makes 28.

GARLIC LAMB

Cut 600 g (1¼ lb) trimmed lamb steaks into 2 cm (¾ inch) cubes and 6 cloves of garlic into thick slices. Thread 2 pieces of lamb and 2 slices of garlic alternately onto 35 small metal skewers. Mix together 1 chopped red chilli, 2 crushed cloves garlic and 3 tablespoons oil. Heat a chargrill pan and lightly brush with oil. Cook the skewers for 2–5 minutes, brushing occasionally with the garlic and chilli marinade. Makes 35.

CHILLI VEGETABLES

Halve 12 shiitake mushrooms, 12 baby corn cobs and 12 snow peas (mangetout). Thread alternately onto 24 small wooden skewers. Combine 2 tablespoons oil with 1 crushed clove garlic and 1 tablespoon sweet chilli sauce in a bowl and mix well. Brush over the skewers and cook the skewers in a preheated chargrill pan for 1–2 minutes, brushing with the sauce during cooking. Makes 24.

SALMON AND TUNA

Cut 600 g (1¼ lb) salmon fillet and 500 g (1 lb) fresh tuna into 2 cm (¾ inch) cubes and season with salt and pepper. Thread alternately onto small wooden skewers, using 3 pieces on each. Heat a chargrill or frying pan and brush lightly with oil. Cook the skewers for 3–4 minutes, turning frequently and squeezing with a little lime or lemon juice as they cook. Makes 18–20.

CHICKEN AND LEMON GRASS

Cut 1 kg (2 lb) chicken thigh fillets into 2 cm (¾ inch) cubes. Trim the leaves off 6 lemon grass stems. Cut the thicker ends of the stems into 10 cm (4 inch) lengths, then into quarters lengthways. Cut 12 spring onion bulbs into quarters. Make a small slit in the centre of each chicken cube and through the onion pieces, to make threading easier. Thread pieces of chicken and onion onto the lemon grass stems alternately, using 2 pieces of each for each stem. Mix together 3 tablespoons soy sauce, 3 tablespoons mirin and 2 tablespoons sugar. Heat a chargrill or frying pan and cook the skewers for 3–5 minutes. Brush with half the soy mixture as they cook, turning frequently. Add 1 finely sliced stem lemon grass (white part only) and 1 seeded and finely chopped red chilli to the remaining soy mixture and serve with the skewers, for dipping. Makes 24.

MUSHROOMS AND PROSCIUTTO

Wipe 48 Swiss brown mushrooms (sometimes called chestnut mushrooms) with a damp cloth, then cut them in half. Melt 80 g (2¾ oz) butter in a frying pan and add the mushrooms and a pinch of salt. Cook, stirring, over medium heat for 1 minute. Add ½ cup (125 ml/4 fl oz) port and cook, stirring, until it evaporates completely. Remove from the heat and set aside. Cut 18 slices of prosciutto into 4 pieces each. Thread 4 pieces of mushroom and 3 rolled pieces of prosciutto alternately onto wooden skewers and serve. Makes 24.

FROM LEFT: Lime prawns; Centre plate: Beef with black bean sauce; Chilli vegetables; Garlic lamb; Right-hand plate: Chicken and lemon grass; Mushrooms and prosciutto; Salmon and tuna

SCALLOPS

Sold in their half shells, scallops are generally still attached to their shells with a muscle. To remove from the shell, slip a small sharp knife between the shell and the scallop and gently cut away. Trim off the dark vein and white muscle before cooking. Scallops should be cooked for a short time only, otherwise they will become tough. They will turn white when cooked.

ABOVE: Dim sum scallops

DIM SUM SCALLOPS

Preparation time: 10 minutes
Total cooking time: 10 minutes
Makes 24

24 scallops in the half shell

Marinade
2 tablespoons teriyaki sauce
1 tablespoon soy sauce
1 tablespoon dry sherry
2 spring onions, finely chopped
2 teaspoons lemon or lime juice
2 teaspoons oyster sauce
1 teaspoon sesame oil
1 clove garlic, crushed
1/2 teaspoon grated fresh ginger

1 Preheat the oven to moderate 180°C (350°F/ Gas 4). Place the scallops, in the shells, on a baking tray.
2 Combine the marinade ingredients together in a bowl and drizzle some of the mixture over each scallop. Put the scallops on a baking tray and bake for 5–10 minutes, or until the scallops are tender and white.
NOTE: If you prefer, the scallops can be cooked under a preheated hot grill for 5 minutes instead.
IN ADVANCE: The marinade can be made a day ahead, covered and refrigerated.

SATAY SAUCE

Heat 1 tablespoon oil in a pan. Add 1 finely chopped large onion and 1 finely chopped garlic clove and stir for 8 minutes over low heat. Add 2 finely chopped red chillies and 1 teaspoon shrimp paste and cook for 1 minute. Remove from the heat. Add 250 g (8 oz) peanut butter, return to the heat and stir in 1 cup (250 ml/8 fl oz) each of coconut milk and water. Bring to the boil over low heat, stirring so that it does not stick. Add 2 teaspoons kecap manis or thick soy sauce and 1 tablespoon tomato sauce; simmer for 1 minute. Cool. Serve with skewers of chicken, meat or vegetables.

STUFFED PRAWNS IN CRISPY WON TON

Preparation time: 40 minutes
Total cooking time: 10 minutes
Makes 24

30 won ton wrappers
24 large raw prawns
400 g (13 oz) raw prawn meat
8 spring onions, very finely chopped
100 g (1 3/4 oz) pork fat, finely chopped
2 egg whites
1 cup (125 g/4 oz) cornflour
2 eggs, lightly beaten
oil, for deep-frying

1 Using a very sharp knife, finely shred the won ton wrappers. Place on a plate and cover with a damp tea towel until required. Peel the prawns, leaving the tails intact. Discard the heads. Using the tip of a small sharp knife, pull out the dark vein. Cut a shallow pocket along the inside of each prawn.
2 Combine the prawn meat, spring onion and pork fat on a chopping board. Using a large sharp knife, chop the mixture until very smooth. (Alternatively, you can use a food processor.) Place the mixture in a bowl and add the egg white, 3 teaspoons of the cornflour and a little salt and pepper and mix together well with your fingertips.
3 Using a knife, spread about 1 tablespoon of the prawn mixture along each prawn, pressing as much mixture as possible into the pocket. With wet hands, press any remaining mixture around the prawn. Coat the prawns in the remaining cornflour, lightly dip in egg, then loosely sprinkle with won ton shreds, pressing on very firmly.
4 Heat 4 cm (1½ inches) oil in a wok or pan to 180°C (350°F). The oil is hot enough when a cube of bread dropped into the oil turns golden brown in 15 seconds. Add the prawns in batches and cook for 4 minutes or until golden brown. Drain on crumpled paper towels and serve immediately.
NOTE: Pork fat is available in the refrigerator section of Asian supermarkets.
IN ADVANCE: The prawns can be cleaned and filled with stuffing up to a day in advance. Store in the refrigerator. Coat the prawns with shredded won ton just before frying.

STUFFED PRAWNS IN CRISPY WON TON

Finely shred the won ton wrappers with a sharp knife.

Cut a shallow incision along the underside of each prawn to make room for the stuffing.

LEFT: Stuffed prawns in crispy won ton

CRISPY CHICKEN AND FISH WRAPS WITH SWEET AND SOUR SAUCE

Preparation time: 30 minutes
Total cooking time: 4 minutes per batch
Makes 30

Sweet and sour sauce
1/2 cup (125 g/4 oz) sugar
1/2 cup (125 ml/4 fl oz) white vinegar
1 tablespoon tomato sauce
1 tablespoon cornflour

30 won ton wrappers
oil, for deep-frying

Filling
100 g (3 1/2 oz) chicken, finely chopped
100 g (3 1/2 oz) fish fillets, finely chopped
1/2 stalk celery, finely chopped
1 small spring onion, finely chopped
2 teaspoons light soy sauce

1 To make the sauce, combine the sugar, vinegar and tomato sauce with 3/4 cup (185 ml/ 6 fl oz) water in a small saucepan. Blend the cornflour with 1 tablespoon of water in a small bowl. Add to the saucepan and stir over low heat until the mixture boils and thickens and the sugar has dissolved.
2 Combine the filling ingredients with 1/4 teaspoon salt. Place 1 teaspoon of mixture onto each won ton wrapper. Brush the edges lightly with water. Fold to form a triangle. Dab water onto the left front corner of the triangle. Fold the two bottom corners across, one on top of the other, and press together lightly with your finger.
3 Fill a deep heavy-based pan one third full of oil. Heat the oil to 180°C (350°F). The oil is hot enough when a cube of bread dropped into the oil turns golden brown in 15 seconds. Deep-fry in batches until crisp and golden brown. Shake off the excess oil and drain on crumpled paper towel. Serve with the sauce.

PORK DUMPLINGS

Preparation time: 30 minutes
Total cooking time: 45 minutes
Makes 50

250 g (4 oz) pork mince
125 g (4 oz) raw prawn meat, finely chopped
60 g (2 oz) bamboo shoots, chopped
3 spring onions, finely chopped
3 mushrooms, finely chopped
1 stick celery, finely chopped
1/2 pepper (capsicum), finely chopped
1 tablespoon dry sherry
1 tablespoon soy sauce
1 teaspoon sesame oil
1/2 teaspoon chopped chilli
50 won ton wrappers
soy sauce, for dipping

1 Put the mince, prawn, bamboo shoots, spring onion, mushrooms, celery, pepper, dry sherry, soy sauce, sesame oil and chilli in a bowl and mix well. Place a heaped teaspoon of the filling in the centre of each won ton wrapper. Brush the edges with a little water, then gather the wrapper around the filling to form a pouch, slightly open at the top.
2 Steam in a bamboo or metal steamer over a pan of simmering water for 15 minutes, or until cooked through. Serve with soy sauce.

CHICKEN DUMPLINGS

Preparation time: 30 minutes
Total cooking time: 45 minutes
Makes 50

375 g (12 oz) chicken mince
90 g (3 oz) ham, finely chopped
4 spring onions, finely chopped
1 stick celery, finely chopped
3 tablespoons bamboo shoots, chopped
1 tablespoon soy sauce
1 clove garlic, crushed
1 teaspoon grated fresh ginger

1 Combine all the ingredients in a bowl, then use to fill 50 won ton wrappers as above.

CRISPY CHICKEN AND FISH WRAPS WITH SWEET AND SOUR SAUCE

Lightly brush the edges of the won ton with water, then fold it over the filling to form a triangle.

Fold the two bottom corners across, one on top of the other, and press together lightly.

OPPOSITE PAGE: Crispy chicken and fish wraps with sweet and sour sauce (top); Dumplings

EGGS

Eggs, apart from being enjoyed boiled, poached, fried and scrambled, are an essential ingredient used to thicken or aerate many dishes such as soufflés, omelettes, frittata and mayonnaise. They are also used to glaze or bind and in many other ways. To successfully hard-boil eggs for dishes such as gado gado, first bring them to room temperature, then put them in a saucepan, cover with cold water and bring to the boil over high heat. Simmer over low heat for 7–8 minutes. Stirring the eggs in the first few minutes helps centre the yolk. When cooked, stand the eggs under cold running water to stop them cooking any further. If boiled eggs have dark rings around the yolk, they have been cooked too long. Keep fresh eggs refrigerated until you need them, then bring them to room temperature before using them.

ABOVE: Gado gado

GADO GADO

Preparation time: 30 minutes
Total cooking time: 35 minutes
Serves 6–8

6 new potatoes
2 carrots, cut into batons
250 g (8 oz) snake beans, cut into 10 cm
   (4 inch) lengths
2 tablespoons peanut oil
250 g (8 oz) firm tofu, cubed
100 g (3¹/₂ oz) baby English spinach leaves
2 Lebanese cucumbers, cut into thick strips
1 large red pepper (capsicum), cut into
   thick strips
100 g (3¹/₂ oz) bean sprouts
5 hard-boiled eggs

Peanut sauce

1 tablespoon peanut oil
1 onion, finely chopped
²/₃ cup (160 g/5¹/₂ oz) peanut butter
¹/₄ cup (60 ml/2 fl oz) kecap manis
2 tablespoons ground coriander
2 teaspoons chilli sauce
³/₄ cup (185 ml/6 fl oz) coconut cream
1 teaspoon grated palm sugar
1 tablespoon lemon juice

1 Cook the potatoes in boiling water until tender. Drain, cool slightly, then cut into quarters. Cook the carrots and beans separately until just tender. Drain, plunge into iced water, then drain thoroughly.
2 Heat the oil in a non-stick frying pan and cook the tofu all over in batches until crisp. Drain on crumpled paper towels.
3 To make the peanut sauce, heat the oil in a pan over low heat and cook the onion for 5 minutes, or until golden. Add the peanut butter, kecap manis, coriander, chilli sauce and coconut cream. Bring to the boil, reduce the heat and simmer for 5 minutes. Stir in the sugar and juice, stirring until dissolved.
4 Arrange all the vegetables and tofu on a plate. Cut the eggs in half and place in the centre around the bowl of sauce.

FISH TEMPURA

Preparation time: 10 minutes
Total cooking time: 20 minutes
Makes 24

500 g (1 lb) boneless fish
1 sheet nori
1 tablespoon tempura flour

Tempura batter
1 cup (250 ml/8 oz) iced water
2 cups (250 g/8 oz) tempura flour
oil, for deep-frying

1 Cut the fish into bite-sized pieces and set aside. Using scissors, cut the nori into tiny squares and combine on a plate with the tablespoon of tempura flour.
2 For the batter, quickly mix the iced water with the tempura flour. It will be slightly lumpy. If it is too thick, add more water. Fill a heavy-based pan one third full of oil and heat to 180°C (350°F). The oil is ready when ¼ teaspoon of batter dropped into the oil keeps its shape, sizzles and rises to the top. Make sure the oil stays at the same temperature and does not get too hot. The fish should cook through.
3 Dip the fish in batches into the nori and flour, then in the batter. Fry until golden, then drain on crumpled paper towels. Season with salt and keep warm in a single layer on a baking tray in a very slow 120°C (240°F/Gas 1) oven. The fish can be served with shoyu (Japanese soy sauce), for dipping.
NOTE: Tempura flour is available at Asian supermarkets. If unavailable, substitute with 1½ cups (185 g/6 oz) plain flour and ½ cup (90 g/3 oz) rice flour. This recipe can also be made using chicken or vegetable pieces.

TEMPURA
Tempura was introduced to Japan by Portuguese and Spanish traders in the sixteenth century. However, chefs in Japan improved the batter, resulting in the special crispness with which it is associated today. The very light thin batter is made with iced water to ensure that it puffs up as soon as it hits the oil. Special tempura flour also ensures a light batter.

BELOW: Fish tempura

GINGER

If ginger is fresh when you buy it, the flesh should be juicy, not shrivelled or dried out. To prepare it for cooking, just peel with a vegetable peeler or sharp knife and cut. You can rub the skin off some very fresh ginger with your fingers. For grating, don't fuss about the irregular-shaped knob, just peel as much as you need from any part, grate on a ginger grater and return the rest to the crisper in the refrigerator. Ceramic ginger graters have little sharp teeth that grate the ginger off as you rub it up and down. Bamboo graters look like small versions of old-fashioned washboards, made with angled strips of bamboo for rubbing the ginger against.

ABOVE: Yakitori

YAKITORI
(SKEWERED CHICKEN)

Preparation time: 20 minutes + soaking
Total cooking time: 10 minutes
Makes about 25 skewers

1 kg (2 lb) chicken thigh fillets
1/2 cup (125 ml/4 fl oz) sake
3/4 cup (185 ml/6 fl oz) Japanese soy sauce
1/2 cup (125 ml/4 fl oz) mirin
2 tablespoons sugar
1 cup (65 g/2 1/4 oz) spring onions, cut diagonally
   into 2 cm (3/4 inch) pieces

1 Soak 25 wooden skewers for about 30 minutes in water, then drain and set aside.
2 Cut the chicken fillets into bite-sized pieces. Combine the sake, soy sauce, mirin and sugar in a small pan, bring to the boil, then remove the pan and set aside.
3 Thread 3 chicken pieces onto wooden skewers, alternating with pieces of spring onion. Place the skewers on a foil-lined tray and cook under a

preheated grill or barbecue, turning and brushing frequently with the sauce for about 7–8 minutes, or until the chicken is cooked through. Serve.
NOTE: The yakitori can be served with a bottled Asian dipping sauce.

THAI NOODLE BALLS WITH ASIAN DIPPING SAUCE

Preparation time: 20 minutes + soaking
Total cooking time: 20 minutes
Makes 40

Asian dipping sauce
1/4 cup (60 ml/2 fl oz) sweet chilli
   sauce
1/4 cup (60 ml/2 fl oz) lime juice
2 tablespoons fish sauce
1 teaspoon soft brown sugar
2 teaspoons kecap manis
4 cm (1 1/2 inch) piece fresh ginger,
   cut into julienne strips

500 g (1 lb) Hokkien noodles

75 g (2½ oz) snake beans, finely chopped

3 spring onions, finely chopped

2 cloves garlic, crushed

50 g (1¾ oz) fresh coriander leaves, chopped

¼ cup (60 ml/2 fl oz) sweet chilli sauce

2 tablespoons fish sauce

2 tablespoons fresh lime juice

250 g (8 oz) pork mince

3 eggs, lightly beaten

1 cup (125 g/4 oz) plain flour

oil, for deep-frying

1 Mix the dipping sauce ingredients in a bowl.
2 Break up the noodles and cut with scissors into short lengths. Soak in a bowl of boiling water for 2 minutes, then drain well. Combine with the beans, spring onion, garlic, coriander, sauces, lime juice, mince, eggs and flour and mix well.
3 Fill a deep heavy-based pan one third full of oil and heat the oil to 180°C (350°F). The oil is ready when a cube of bread dropped into the oil turns golden brown in 15 seconds. Roll heaped tablespoons of mixture into balls and deep-fry in batches for 2 minutes, or until deep golden. Drain on crumpled paper towels. Serve with sauce.
IN ADVANCE: The dipping sauce can be made several days ahead and the noodle mixture the day before required. Fry close to serving time.

PRAWN PARCELS

Preparation time: 30 minutes
Total cooking time: 20 minutes
Makes 24

★★

1 tablespoon oil

2 cloves garlic, crushed

1 tablespoon grated fresh ginger

2 spring onions, chopped

500 g (1 lb) raw prawns, peeled and chopped

½ teaspoon fish sauce

½ teaspoon sugar

1 tablespoon lemon juice

2 tablespoons chopped fresh coriander

6 large spring roll wrappers, cut into quarters

oil, for deep-frying

fresh chives, for serving

sweet chilli sauce, for serving

1 Heat the oil in a frying pan, add the garlic and ginger and cook over low heat for 2 minutes. Add the spring onion and cook for 2 minutes. Increase the heat to high, add the prawns and stir-fry for 2 minutes, or until the colour just changes. Be careful not to overcook the prawns or they will become tough once deep-fried.
2 Add the fish sauce, sugar, lemon juice and coriander to the pan. Toss with the prawns for 1 minute. Remove from the heat; cool slightly.
3 Divide the cooled mixture into 24 portions. Place one portion in the centre of each piece of spring roll wrapper. Brush the edges with water and fold to form a parcel.
4 Fill a deep heavy-based pan one third full of oil. Heat the oil to 180°C (350°F). The oil is hot enough when a cube of bread dropped into the oil turns golden brown in 15 seconds. Deep-fry the parcels one at a time, holding them with tongs for the first few seconds to keep them intact. Cook until golden brown. Drain on crumpled paper towels. Tie with lengths of chives. Serve with sweet chilli sauce.
NOTE: If the spring roll wrappers are very thin, you may need to use two together.

ABOVE: Prawn parcels

RICE
Apart from various colours, tastes and textures, different types of rice are preferred for certain recipes because of their behaviour when cooked. Short-grain rice, with small oval grains, is high in starch and is used in recipes such as sushi where you want a rice that sticks together. It is also easier to eat using chopsticks, so is popular in some Asian countries. Other recipes are better with rices whose grains stay separate when cooked.

SCALLOP POCKETS

Preparation time: 40 minutes
Total cooking time: 15 minutes
Makes 25

25 large scallops
1 tablespoon oil
5 cm (2 inch) piece fresh ginger, grated
4 spring onions, finely chopped
1 tablespoon Shaosing (Chinese) wine or
   dry sherry
2 teaspoons sesame oil
1 teaspoon cornflour
25 won ton or egg noodle wrappers
oil, for shallow frying
15 g (½ oz) garlic chives, blanched, for serving

1 Carefully slice or pull off any vein, membrane or hard white muscle from the scallops, leaving any roe attached.
2 Heat the oil in a pan, add the ginger and spring onion and cook over medium heat for 2 minutes, stirring occasionally. Increase the heat and, when the pan is very hot, add the scallops and stir-fry, tossing quickly, for 30 seconds. Remove the pan from the heat.
3 Blend the wine, sesame oil, cornflour and a little salt and pepper in a small bowl until it forms a smooth paste. Pour over the scallops, return to the heat and toss over high heat for 30 seconds or until the liquid has thickened. Cool completely.
4 Working with one wrapper at a time and keeping the rest covered, brush the edge of each lightly with water. Place a scallop in the centre, bring up the sides and pinch together to form a pouch with a frill at the top. Put on a paper-covered baking tray and repeat with the remaining wrappers and filling.
5 Heat 2 cm (¾ inch) oil in a pan to 180°C (350°F). The oil is hot enough when a cube of bread sizzles and turns golden brown in 15 seconds. Cook the scallop pouches, in batches if necessary, for 5 minutes, or until golden brown. Drain on paper towels. Tie a blanched garlic chive around each and serve immediately.
IN ADVANCE: The scallop pockets can be filled a day ahead, covered and refrigerated. Don't deep-fry until just before serving.

PORCUPINE BALLS

Preparation time: 40 minutes + soaking
Total cooking time: 30 minutes each batch
Makes 24

1 cup (220 g/7 oz) short-grain rice
5 dried Chinese mushrooms
250 g (8 oz) beef mince
250 g (8 oz) pork mince
60 g (2 oz) finely chopped water chestnuts
4 spring onions, finely chopped
1–2 cloves garlic, crushed
1 teaspoon grated fresh ginger
1 tablespoon soy sauce
1 egg, lightly beaten

Dipping sauce
3 tablespoons light soy sauce
2 tablespoons soft brown sugar
2 tablespoons grated fresh ginger

1 Soak the rice in cold water in a large bowl for at least 2 hours, then drain and spread to dry on paper towels.
2 Place the mushrooms in a heatproof bowl and cover with boiling water. Leave for 20 minutes, squeeze dry, discard the stems and chop the mushrooms finely. Combine in a large bowl with both minces, water chestnuts, spring onion, garlic, ginger, soy sauce, egg and ½ teaspoon salt. Mix with your hands.
3 Divide the mixture into 24 portions and with wet hands, shape into small balls. Roll each in the rice until well coated. Line a bamboo steamer base with baking paper and put the balls in the steamer, leaving room for the rice to swell (cook in batches, depending on the size of the steamer). Place the steamer over a wok half-filled with boiling water. Steam for 30 minutes, or until the rice and meatballs are cooked through, adding more water to the wok when necessary. Serve immediately with dipping sauce.
4 For the dipping sauce, mix the ingredients with 3 tablespoons water. Serve in a small bowl.
IN ADVANCE: The mince mixture can be made a day ahead or frozen for 2 months. Roll in rice close to cooking time.

OPPOSITE PAGE:
Scallop pockets (left);
Porcupine balls

SUSHI

These rolls of nori (dried seaweed) with rice and savoury fillings are ideal for serving as finger food. Sushi looks difficult and impressive but is not hard once you have mastered the basic technique.

TO MAKE SUSHI RICE

The rice in sushi is not just plain rice. It has been cooked, then specially dressed for use. To make good sushi, you must first prepare good sushi rice. Use white short-grain rice—in Japan they use Japonica rice. Wash 2½ cups (550 g/1 lb 2 oz) short-grain rice under cold running water until the water runs clear, then leave in the strainer to drain for an hour. Put the rice in a pan with 3 cups (750 ml/24 fl oz) water and bring to the boil. Cook for

5–10 minutes, or until tunnels form on the surface of the rice, then reduce the heat to low, cover and cook the rice for 12–15 minutes, or until tender. Remove from the heat, remove the lid from the pan, cover the rice with a clean tea towel and leave for 15 minutes. To make the dressing, mix 5 tablespoons rice vinegar, 1 tablespoon mirin, 3 tablespoons sugar and 2 teaspoons salt and stir until the sugar has dissolved. Spread the rice over the base of a hangiri (a flat shallow

wooden bowl) or a non-metallic dish or bowl, pour the dressing over the top and use a rice paddle or spatula to mix the dressing through the rice, separating the grains. Fan the rice until it cools to room temperature. Cover with a clean tea towel until ready to use. One quantity is enough to make each of the following sushi recipes. To prevent rice sticking to your hands when assembling sushi, dip your fingers in a bowl of warm water with a few drops of rice vinegar added.

MAKI ZUSHI

Maki zushi is probably the most well-known sushi roll—the one that you will usually find in a Japanese lunchbox. It is ideal for serving as finger food and can be filled with a variety of ingredients such as strips of sashimi tuna or salmon (available from good fishmongers), cucumber, pickled daikon, dried mushrooms (soaked in hot water for 20 minutes, so they swell up), kampyo (dried gourd), pickled ginger, omelette or sesame seeds. Place one sheet of nori on a bamboo mat with the shiny side facing down. (You will need 8 sheets of nori for this recipe. Nori is the most common form of seaweed used in Japanese and Korean cooking. It comes in paper-thin sheets, plain or roasted. If you toast it lightly over an open flame before use it will have a good nutty flavour.) Spread cooled sushi rice about 1 cm thick over the nori, leaving a 1 cm (1/2 inch) border on each side. Make

a shallow groove down the centre of the rice towards one short end. Spread a small amount of wasabi (an extremely hot paste, also known as Japanese horseradish) along the groove in the rice. Place a selection of strips of your filling ingredients on top of the wasabi.
Lift up the edge of the bamboo mat and roll the sushi, starting from the edge nearest to you. When you've finished rolling, press the mat to make either a round or square roll. Push in any rice that may be escaping from the ends. Wet a sharp knife, trim the ends and cut the roll in half and then each half into three. Repeat with the remaining seven sheets of nori, sushi rice and fillings. Makes 48.

NOTE: Bamboo mats are not expensive and are available at Asian grocery stores. There isn't really a substitute, if you want to make successful sushi.

INSIDE OUT ROLLS

These are made with the same technique and ingredients as the maki zushi, but with the rice on the outside. Use 8 sheets of nori and one quantity of sushi rice. Place a sheet of nori on the bamboo mat and spread 1 cm (1/2 inch) rice over the top of it, leaving a 1 cm (1/2 inch) border. Cover with a sheet of plastic wrap, slightly larger than the nori. In one quick motion, turn the whole thing over, then place it back on the mat, so the plastic wrap is under the rice and the nori on top. Spread a little wasabi along the short end of the rice, about 4 cm (1 1/2 inches) from the edge. Lay strips of cucumber, avocado and crab on top of the wasabi, then roll up from this end, using the plastic as a guide. Rewrap in plastic, then roll up in the mat to make a neat roll. Remove the plastic and roll in sesame seeds. Cut in half, trim the ends, and cut each half into three. Serve with shoyu.

SUSHI

NIGIRI ZUSHI

Trim 250 g (8 oz) sashimi tuna or salmon into a neat rectangle, removing any blood or connective tissue. Using a sharp knife, cut paper-thin slices of fish from the trimmed fillet, cleaning your knife in a bowl of water and lemon juice after cutting each slice. Form a tablespoon of your sushi rice into an oval about the same length and width as your rectangles of fish. Place a piece of fish on the open palm of your left hand, then spread a small dab of wasabi over the centre of the fish. Place the rice on the fish and gently cup your palm to make a curve. Using the middle and index fingers of your right hand, press the rice onto the fish, firmly pushing with a slight upward motion to make a neat shape. Turn over and repeat the shaping process, finishing with the fish on top of the rice. Nigiri zushi can be served with a strip of seaweed tied around the centre. Makes 16–20.

INARI ZUSHI

Combine 1 cup (250 ml/8 fl oz) dashi stock, 220 g (7 oz) sugar, 1/3 cup (90 ml/ 3 fl oz) shoyu and 1/4 cup (60 ml/2 fl oz) sake in a pan and stir over low heat until the sugar has dissolved. Bring to the boil, reduce the heat and add 16 half inari pouches (these are also known as tofu pouches and are thin slices of tofu that have been fried). Simmer for 5 minutes, allow to cool and then drain. Open the braised pouches and fill with sushi rice. Serve, cut-side-down, as they are, or tied with a blanched chive. Makes 16.

HAND ROLLS

These are small cone-shaped rolls of nori filled with rice and selected fillings. Your choice of fillings could include strips of pickled daikon, strips of cucumber,

pickled ginger, strips of omelette, peeled strips of prawns, strips of tuna/salmon, strips of eel, strips of inari, crab meat and strips of avocado. You will need 8 sheets of nori for each quantity of sushi rice. Cut each sheet of nori into quarters. Place a small amount of rice diagonally across the centre of the square of nori. Place a small amount of wasabi on your finger and spread along the length of the rice (remember that wasabi is VERY HOT so don't overdo it). Top with a couple of the suggested fillings, which will poke out of the top of the finished roll. Then roll the nori up into a cone shape to enclose the filling. Serve with shoyu as a dipping sauce. Makes 32.

SUSHI FOR A CROWD

This is a very simple sushi which is ideal for serving large quantities of guests. Lightly oil a 23 cm (9 inch) square baking tin and line with plastic wrap. Line the base of the tin with sheets of nori, trimming the sheets to fit neatly. Spread half of your sushi rice over the nori, taking it right to the edge. Spread a very thin scraping of wasabi over the rice. Top with thinly slice sashimi salmon or smoked salmon (you will need 250 g/ 8 oz altogether) and then another layer of nori. Top these with 3 tablespoons pickled ginger and 2 thinly sliced cucumbers (slice the cucumbers lengthways). Top with the remaining rice and another layer of nori. Cover with plastic wrap. Top with a slightly smaller

tin (so it sits directly onto the sushi) and weigh down with tins, to flatten the sushi. Refrigerate for at least 1 hour, or overnight. Turn out onto a chopping board and peel away the plastic wrap. Cut the sushi into squares. Makes 36.

NOTE: Shoyu is Japanese soy sauce. It is much lighter and sweeter than Chinese soy. As it is naturally brewed, it should be refrigerated after opening. It is available, with all the other Japanese ingredients and utensils, at speciality food stores and Asian supermarkets.

FROM LEFT: Nigiri zushi (tuna); Nigiri zushi (salmon); Inari zushi; Hand rolls; Sushi squares (for a crowd)

SPICY PRAWN FRITTERS

Preparation time: 25 minutes
Total cooking time: 15 minutes
Makes 20–25

300 g (10 oz) raw prawns, peeled and deveined
1 egg
1 tablespoon fish sauce
1 cup (125 g/4 fl oz) plain flour
50 g (1¾ oz) dried rice vermicelli
¼ teaspoon shrimp paste
3 spring onions, sliced
1 small red chilli, finely chopped
oil, for deep-frying
sweet chilli sauce, for serving

1 Process half the prawns in a food processor until smooth. Chop the remaining prawns and mix in a bowl with the processed prawns.
2 In a small jug, beat the egg and fish sauce with ¾ cup (185 ml/6 fl oz) water. Sift the flour into a bowl and make a well. Gradually add the egg mixture, whisking to make a lump-free batter.
3 Soak the vermicelli in boiling water in a bowl for 5 minutes. Drain and cut into short lengths with scissors. Mix with the prawns, shrimp paste, spring onion and chilli and stir into the batter.

4 Fill a deep heavy-based pan one third full of oil. Heat the oil to 180°C (350°F). The oil is hot enough when a cube of bread dropped into the oil turns golden brown in 15 seconds. Drop tablespoons of mixture into the oil and deep-fry in batches for 3 minutes, or until crisp and golden. Remove with a slotted spoon. Drain on crumpled paper towels. Repeat with the remaining mixture. Serve with sweet chilli sauce.

TONKATSU (CRUMBED PORK)

Preparation time: 35 minutes + chilling
Total cooking time: 12 minutes
Makes 40–50 slices

500 g (1 lb) pork schnitzels, trimmed of sinew
½ cup (60 g/2 oz) plain flour
5 egg yolks
2 cups (120 g/4 oz) Japanese dried breadcrumbs
1 sheet nori
oil, for shallow-frying
1 cup (250 ml/8 fl oz) Tonkatsu sauce

1 Sprinkle the pork with a good pinch each of salt and pepper and lightly coat with flour.
2 Beat the egg yolks with 2 tablespoons water,

CHILLIES

Chillies come in many shapes, sizes and colours. Generally, the smaller the hotter, the tiny red bird's eye chilli being the hottest of all. The small red chillies, about 5 cm (2 inches) long are also very hot, the medium red chillies 10–15 cm (4–6 inches) long are less overpowering, while the large red and green chillies 15–20 cm (6–8 inches) long are not very hot. As tolerance to the heat of chillies varies, they should be used according to taste. If you don't like too much, reduce the quantity in the recipe and, if you are cooking for a crowd, use your discretion. Deseeding chillies reduces the heat intensity. To avoid skin irritation, handle chillies with rubber gloves or thoroughly wash your hands when finished, and don't rub your eyes or touch your face.

RIGHT: Spicy prawn fritters

Use a melon baller to scoop the flesh from the zucchini, leaving a shell of flesh to hold in the filling.

Use a couple of teaspoons to spoon the mixture into the zucchini shells.

Steam the stuffed zucchini until the filling is cooked and the zucchini tender.

dip each schnitzel in the egg, then in the breadcrumbs, pressing on to ensure an even coating. Refrigerate the pork in a single layer on a plate, uncovered, for at least 2 hours.

3 Using a sharp knife, shred the nori very finely and then break into strips about 4 cm (1½ inches) long. Set aside until serving time.

4 Heat 2 cm (¾ inch) oil in a deep heavy-based pan to 180°C (350°F). The oil is ready when a cube of bread dropped into the oil turns golden brown in 15 seconds. Cook 2–3 schnitzels at a time until golden brown on both sides, then drain on crumpled paper towels. Repeat the process with the remaining schnitzels. Slice the schnitzels into 1 cm (½ inch) strips and reassemble into the original shape. Sprinkle with nori strips. Serve with the Tonkatsu sauce.

STUFFED ZUCCHINI
(COURGETTE)

Preparation time: 30 minutes
Total cooking time: 10 minutes
Makes about 24

4 large zucchini (courgette)
125 g (4 oz) pork mince
60 g (2 oz) peeled raw prawns, finely chopped
2 cloves garlic, crushed

2 tablespoons finely chopped fresh coriander
½ teaspoon sugar
2 kaffir lime leaves, finely chopped, or
  1 teaspoon grated lime rind
2 Asian shallots, finely chopped
3 tablespoons coconut cream
2 teaspoons fish sauce
1 tablespoon roasted unsalted peanuts,
  finely chopped

1 Cut the zucchini into 4 cm (1½ inch) thick slices. Scoop out the centre with a melon baller, leaving 5 mm (¼ inch) of flesh around the inside of the skin as well as on the bottom of each slice.

2 In a small bowl, combine the pork mince, chopped prawn meat, garlic, coriander, sugar, kaffir lime leaves, Asian shallots, 2 tablespoons of the coconut cream and the fish sauce. Spoon into the zucchini shells, then cover and refrigerate until close to serving time.

3 Place in a bamboo or metal steamer over a pan of boiling water, cover and steam for 10 minutes or until the filling is cooked and zucchini tender. Serve dotted with a little coconut cream and sprinkled with chopped peanuts.

ABOVE: Stuffed zucchini

PRAWNS IN RICE PAPER

Preparation time: 35 minutes
Total cooking time: 5–10 minutes
Makes 20

20 rice paper wrappers
350 g (11 oz) raw prawn meat
4 cm (1 1/2 inch) piece fresh ginger, grated
2 cloves garlic, crushed
3 spring onions, finely chopped
1 tablespoon rice flour
1 egg white, beaten
2 teaspoons sesame oil
2 tablespoons cornflour
oil, for deep frying
2 tablespoons sesame seeds, toasted
plum sauce, for serving, optional

1 Place 4 rice paper wrappers on a work surface. Brush generously with water, then leave for 2 minutes, or until soft and pliable. Gently transfer to a plate (they may be stacked on top of each other at this stage). Repeat the brushing with the remaining wrappers, then cover with plastic wrap.
2 Finely chop the prawn meat and combine with the ginger, garlic, spring onion, rice flour, egg white, sesame oil and some salt and pepper. Mix very well with your fingertips. Blend the cornflour with 2 tablespoons water in a small bowl. Working with one wrapper at a time, spread one tablespoon of prawn mixture across the wrapper, just below the centre. Fold up the bottom section to encase the filling. Roll the wrapper over once, lightly pushing down to flatten out the filling. Fold in the sides and brush the edges with cornflour mixture, then wrap to form a parcel. Put on double thickness paper towels and repeat with the remaining wrappers and filling.
3 Fill a deep heavy-based pan one third full of oil and heat to 180°C (350°F). The oil is ready when a cube of bread dropped into the oil turns golden brown in 15 seconds. Add several parcels and cook for 4–5 minutes, or until golden brown. Remove with a slotted spoon or tongs, drain on crumpled paper towels and repeat with the remainder. Sprinkle with sesame seeds. Serve with plum sauce, if desired.
NOTE: Rice paper wrappers are available in some speciality shops and Asian supermarkets.
IN ADVANCE: Filling can be prepared a day ahead. Wrap in rice paper several hours ahead.

PLUM SAUCE
This is a sweet-sour, jam-like condiment used in Chinese cooking and sometimes served as a dip. Plum sauce is made from dark red plums, garlic, ginger, sugar, vinegar and spices.

PORK SAN CHOY BAU

Preparation time: 25 minutes + soaking
Total cooking time: 5 minutes
Makes 25

1 tablespoon oil
400 g (13 oz) pork mince
230 g (7 1/2 oz) can water chestnuts, drained and chopped finely
125 g (4 oz) canned bamboo shoots, drained and chopped finely
6 spring onions, finely chopped
2 tablespoons dry sherry
1 tablespoon soy sauce
2 teaspoons sesame oil
2 teaspoons oyster sauce
tiny lettuce leaves (cos, iceberg or witlof)
chopped fresh mint, for serving

Sauce
2 tablespoons plum sauce
1 tablepoon hoisin sauce
1 teaspoon soy sauce

1 Heat the oil in a pan or wok, add the pork and cook, stirring, over high heat until brown all over. Break up any lumps of mince with the back of a fork. Add the water chestnuts, bamboo shoots and spring onion, toss well and cook for 1 minute.
2 Combine the sherry, soy sauce, sesame oil and oyster sauce, add to the wok, toss well and cook for 2 minutes. Remove from the heat.
3 To make the dipping sauce, stir all the ingredients in a bowl with 2 tablespoons water.
4 To serve, put about 1 tablespoon of warm pork mixture on each lettuce leaf. Sprinkle with the chopped mint. Serve with the sauce, for drizzling over the top.
IN ADVANCE: The pork mince can be prepared early in the day and refrigerated. Reheat to serve. The dipping sauce can be mixed the day before required and refrigerated.

OPPOSITE PAGE: Prawns in rice paper (top); Pork san choy bau

CHILLI PRAWN SKEWERS

Preparation time: 25 minutes
Total cooking time: 10 minutes
Makes 30

30 large raw prawns
60 g (2 oz) butter
1 clove garlic, crushed
2 teaspoons soft brown sugar
2 tablespoons lemon or lime juice
2 tablespoons fresh coriander sprigs, finely
   chopped
2 tablespoons fresh basil leaves, finely chopped
1 tablespoon sweet chilli sauce

1 Remove the heads from the prawns, then peel, leaving the tails intact. With a sharp knife, slit each prawn down the back and devein.
2 Heat the butter in a large frying pan or wok. Add the garlic, sugar, juice, coriander, basil and sweet chilli sauce. Mix thoroughly, add the prawns in batches, then cook over medium heat for 5 minutes, or until the prawns turn pink and are cooked through.
3 Thread the prawns onto bamboo skewers or strong toothpicks. Serve warm.

*BELOW: Chilli
prawn skewers*

IN ADVANCE: Prepare the prawns several hours ahead. Cook just before serving. They are also delicious grilled. Thread onto skewers and grill for 2–3 minutes. Brush with butter mixture during cooking. Scallops or oysters can be used instead of prawns, or alternate pieces of fish with prawns. You can use other fresh herbs such as dill and parsley.

THAI CHICKEN CAKES

Preparation time: 15 minutes
Total cooking time: 20 minutes
Makes 36

4 eggs, lightly beaten
2 tablespoons finely chopped fresh coriander
1 tablespoon fish sauce
2 tablespoons oil
500 g (1 lb) chicken mince
3 stalks lemon grass, white part only,
   finely chopped
2 cloves garlic, crushed
4 spring onions, chopped
1/4 cup (60 ml/2 fl oz) fresh lime juice
30 g (1 oz) coriander leaves and stems,
   chopped, extra
2 tablespoons sweet chilli sauce
1 tablespoon fish sauce
1 egg, extra, lightly beaten
1/2 cup (125 ml/4 fl oz) coconut milk
6 red chillies, seeded and finely sliced,
   to garnish

1 Preheat the oven to moderately hot 200°C (400°F/Gas 6). Lightly grease three 12-hole shallow patty tins.
2 In a bowl combine the eggs, coriander and fish sauce. Heat the oil in a large 25–28 cm (10–11 inch) frying pan and pour in the egg mixture. Cook over medium heat for about 2 minutes each side, or until golden. Roll up and shred finely. Set aside.
3 Mix the chicken mince, lemon grass, garlic, spring onion, lime juice, extra coriander, sauces, extra egg and coconut milk in a food processor until fine but not smooth. Spoon into the patty tins and top with a little shredded omelette. Bake for 15 minutes, or until cooked through. Rotate the trays once to ensure the chicken cakes all cook through. Serve hot, garnished with chilli.

LIMES
This citrus fruit is smaller than a lemon and has a fresh tart taste. In many Asian countries, the juice from limes is more commonly used than lemon juice. It is used in much the same way as lemons, for its unique flavour and as a tenderizer, and can be used as a substitute for lemons in most recipes. The juice is favoured as a beverage, often sweetened and added to soda. The rind is also grated into some dishes, as with lemons.

THAI FISH CAKES

Preparation time: 25 minutes
Total cooking time: 5–10 minutes
Makes about 24

500 g (1 lb) firm white fish fillets
4 kaffir lime leaves, finely shredded
1 tablespoon chopped fresh Asian basil
2 tablespoons red curry paste
100 g (3½ oz) green beans, very finely sliced
2 spring onions, finely chopped
oil, for shallow-frying

Cucumber dipping sauce
1 Lebanese cucumber, finely chopped
3 tablespoons sweet chilli sauce
2 tablespoons rice vinegar
1 tablespoon chopped unsalted roasted peanuts
1 tablespoon chopped fresh coriander

1 Briefly chop the fish in a food processor until smooth. Add the lime leaves, basil and curry paste and process for 10 seconds. Transfer to a large bowl, add the beans and spring onion and mix well. Wet your hands and form level tablespoons of the mixture into small, flattish patties.
2 Mix all the sauce ingredients in a bowl.
3 Heat the oil in a heavy-based frying pan over medium heat. Cook the fish cakes, in batches, until golden brown on both sides. Drain on paper towels and serve with the dipping sauce.

ABOVE: Thai fish cakes

PEKING DUCK WITH MANDARIN PANCAKES

Preparation time: 1 hour + drying
Total cooking time: 1 hour
Makes 20

★ ★ ★

1.7 kg (3½ lb) duck
1 tablespoon honey
1 small Lebanese cucumber
12 spring onions
2 tablespoons hoisin sauce

Mandarin pancakes

2½ cups (310 g/10 oz) plain flour
2 teaspoons caster sugar
1 tablespoon sesame oil

1 Wash the duck and remove the neck and any large pieces of fat from inside the carcass. Hold the duck over the sink (wear thick rubber gloves to protect your hands) and very carefully and slowly pour 3 litres of boiling water over it, rotating the duck so the water scalds all the skin. You may need another lot of boiling water.

2 Put the duck on a cake rack placed over a baking dish. Mix the honey and ½ cup (125 ml/4 fl oz) hot water and brush two coats of this glaze over the duck, ensuring it is entirely covered. Dry the duck, preferably hanging it up in a cool, airy place. (Alternatively, use an electric fan on a cool setting, positioned a metre or so away.) The skin is sufficiently dry when it is papery to touch. This may take 2–4 hours.

3 Remove the seeds from the cucumber and slice the flesh into matchsticks. Take an 8 cm (3 inch) section from each spring onion and make fine parallel cuts from the centre towards the end. Place in iced water—the spring onions will open into 'brushes'.

4 Preheat the oven to hot 210°C (415°F/ Gas 6–7). Bake the duck on the rack over a baking dish for 30 minutes. Turn the duck over carefully, without tearing the skin, then bake for another 30 minutes. Remove and leave for a minute or two. Place on a warm dish.

5 To make the mandarin pancakes, combine the flour and sugar in a bowl and pour in 1 cup (250 ml/8 fl oz) boiling water. Stir a few times to just combine and leave until lukewarm. Knead the mixture on a lightly floured surface to make a smooth dough, cover and set aside for 30 minutes.

6 Roll two level tablespoons of dough at a time into balls, then roll out to 8 cm (3 inch) rounds. Lightly brush one round with sesame oil and place another on top. Re-roll to make a thin pancake about 15 cm (6 inches) in diameter. Repeat with the remaining dough and oil to make about 10 'double' pancakes.

7 Heat a frying pan and cook the pancakes one at a time. When small bubbles appear on the surface, turn over and cook the second side, pressing the surface with a clean tea towel. The pancakes should puff up when done. Transfer to a plate. When cool enough to handle, peel each pair into two, stack on a plate and cover at once to prevent them drying out.

8 To serve, remove the crisp skin from the underside of the duck and cut into thin strips. Thinly slice the breast and leg meat and place on a warm serving plate. Arrange the cucumber sticks and spring onion brushes on a serving plate. Pour the hoisin sauce into a small dish. Place the pancakes and finely sliced duck on separate plates. Each person takes a pancake, spreads a little sauce on it, using the spring onion brush, and adds a couple of pieces of cucumber, a spring onion brush and finally a piece of duck and crisp duck skin. The pancake is then folded over into an envelope shape to hold the filling. Follow the same procedure with the remaining pancakes and duck.

NOTE: Traditionally, these pancakes are paper-thin. Once you have mastered the technique of making them, use 1 level tablespoon of the dough for each and proceed as before.
Barbecued ducks are available at Asian barbecue shops and ready-made pancakes are also available where you buy the duck.

IN ADVANCE: The pancakes can be made a few hours ahead and kept covered in a cool place. Reheat briefly just before serving—either steam in a colander lined with a clean tea towel or wrap securely in foil and heat in a moderate 180°C (350°F/Gas 4) oven for 2 minutes.

PEKING DUCK
In traditional Chinese restaurants, Peking Duck is made by a master chef with years of experience. To obtain the required crispness, the duck skin is gently loosened from the flesh by massaging back and forth, making sure there are no holes in the skin. A small tube is used to blow air between the skin and carcass, which is then sealed. When the boiling water is poured over the duck, the skin plumps up and then becomes crisp when cooked. Some restaurants require 24 hours notice for serving Peking Duck.

OPPOSITE PAGE: Peking duck with mandarin pancakes

SUSHI CREPES

Pour enough egg mixture into a pan to lightly cover the base.

Cook the short-grain rice until small tunnels begin to appear on the surface.

Roll the crepe up firmly around the filling, using a sushi mat or greaseproof paper to help you.

SUSHI CREPES

Preparation time: 1 hour
Total cooking time: 30 minutes
Makes about 40

★★

4 eggs

Sushi

1 cup (220 g/7 oz) short-grain rice

2 tablespoons rice vinegar

1 tablespoon sugar

1 tablespoon mirin or dry sherry

a little wasabi paste

125 g (4 oz) sashimi tuna, cut into thin strips

1 small cucumber, peeled and cut into matchsticks

1/2 avocado, peeled and cut into matchsticks

3 tablespoons pickled ginger, cut into thin strips

soy sauce, for dipping

1 To make the egg crepes, gently whisk the eggs with 2 tablespoons cold water and a pinch of salt in a bowl until combined. Heat and lightly oil a small crepe pan, and pour enough of the egg mixture into the pan to lightly cover the base. Cook over low heat for 1 minute, being careful not to allow the crepe to brown. Turn the crepe over and cook for 1 minute. Transfer to a plate and cook the remaining mixture.

2 To make the sushi, put the rice in a pan with 2 cups (500 ml/16 fl oz) water, bring to the boil, then reduce the heat and simmer for 5 minutes, or until small tunnels begin to appear in the rice. If using gas, cover and turn the heat to very low, and continue cooking for 7 minutes, or until all the liquid is absorbed. If using an electric stovetop, remove the pan from the heat, cover and leave the rice to steam for 10–12 minutes (this prevents the rice from catching on the bottom of the pan and burning).

3 Combine the rice vinegar, sugar, mirin and 1 teaspoon salt in a jug and gently stir through the rice until well coated. Spread the rice evenly over a baking tray and cool at room temperature.

4 Place one egg crepe on a sushi mat or a piece of baking paper. Spread 4 tablespoons of the sushi rice over a third of the crepe, using a spatula or the back of a spoon.

5 Spread a tiny amount of wasabi along the

ABOVE: Sushi crepes

centre of the rice, taking care when doing this as the wasabi is extremely hot. Place some tuna, cucumber, avocado and ginger over the wasabi.
6 Using the sushi mat or paper to help you, fold the crepe over to enclose the filling and roll up firmly in the mat or paper. Trim the ends with a sharp knife and cut the crepe roll into 2 cm (³/₄ inch) rounds with a sharp knife. Serve with soy sauce for dipping.

NOTE: Sashimi tuna is the freshest, highest quality tuna and is available from good seafood outlets. If you find the rice sticking to your hands, keep them moist by dipping in a small bowl of warm water with a squeeze of lemon added to it.

IN ADVANCE: Crepes can be made ahead and stored in an airtight container in the refrigerator. Do not slice until serving or they may dry out.

GRILLED MUSHROOMS WITH SESAME SEEDS

Preparation time: 15 minutes
Total cooking time: 10 minutes
Makes 30–35

1 tablespoon sesame seeds
400 g (13 oz) medium, flat mushrooms or
    shiitake mushrooms
2 tablespoons teriyaki sauce
2 tablespoons mirin or sweet sherry
1 tablespoon sugar
1 tablespoon finely chopped chives
1 teaspoon sesame oil
10 chives, cut into short lengths

1 Preheat the oven to moderate 180°C (350°/Gas 4). Sprinkle the sesame seeds on a baking tray and bake for 10 minutes, or until golden. Remove from the tray.
2 Wipe the mushrooms with a damp cloth and discard the stalks. Put the mushrooms in a shallow dish. Combine the teriyaki sauce, mirin, sugar, chives and sesame oil, pour over the mushrooms and leave for 5 minutes.
3 Put the mushrooms on a greased baking tray, brush with half the marinade and grill under a preheated hot grill for 5 minutes. Turn the mushrooms over, brush with the remaining marinade and grill for another 5 minutes or until browned. Garnish the mushrooms with the roasted sesame seeds and chopped chives.

SPICY WON TON STRIPS

Cut fresh won ton wrappers into 1 cm (¹/₂ inch) strips with scissors. Fill a deep heavy-based pan one third full of oil and heat to 180°C (350°F), or until a cube of bread dropped into the oil turns golden brown in 15 seconds. Deep-fry the won ton strips quickly in batches until golden brown, remove with a slotted spoon and drain on crumpled paper towels. While hot, sprinkle with a mixture of Chinese five-spice powder and salt. When cold, store in an airtight container. The quantity you make will depend on the number of people you are entertaining. Serve with drinks.

ABOVE: Grilled mushrooms with sesame seeds

FAR EASTERN PANTRY

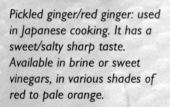

Pickled ginger/red ginger: used in Japanese cooking. It has a sweet/salty sharp taste. Available in brine or sweet vinegars, in various shades of red to pale orange.

Tamarind: an essential flavour in many Asian dishes. It is available as a rich brown liquid or compressed blocks of pulp that must be soaked, kneaded and seeds removed before use.

Shrimp paste (blachan): made from shrimps that have been dried, salted and pounded to form a paste. It is sold in a block or in jars. Store in an airtight container.

Wasabi paste: also known as Japanese horseradish. An extremely hot paste made from the knobbly green root of the wasabi, native to Japan. Also comes in powdered form.

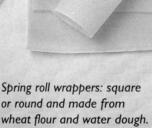

Rice paper: edible paper-thin dry rounds made from rice flour, water and salt. Only available in dry form. Must be moistened before use to make them pliable.

Spring roll wrappers: square or round and made from wheat flour and water dough. Also called egg roll wrappers.

Gow gee wrappers: rounds of dough made from wheat flour and water.

Won ton wrappers: thin squares of wheat flour and egg dough.

Asian basil: three varieties of aromatic basil are used in Asian cooking, all with their own distinct flavour, but fresh sweet basil is a good all-purpose one.

Cha plu: sometimes referred to as betel leaves. Sold in bunches at Asian shops. Traditionally used in Thai cuisine as a wrapping for snacks.

Water spinach: grown extensively throughout Asia. Not related to the spinach family, though English spinach can be used in its place. Requires only minimal cooking.

Vietnamese mint: also called laksa leaf and Cambodian mint, this trailing herb has a flavour more akin to coriander than its namesake.

Asian/golden shallots: small mild members of the onion family. Coppery brown and about the size of a large walnut. Prepare as onions.

Galangal: pinkish in colour with a distinctive peppery flavour. Available fresh (peel and slice as you would fresh ginger) or sliced, dried (must be soaked in hot water before use).

Daikon: a large elongated Asian carrot-shaped radish with quite a sweet flavour. Similar in taste and texture to ordinary radish. Also available pickled in jars.

Kampyo: thinly shaved dried strips of gourd, soaked until pliable and used as a filling in sushi or to tie wrapped food.

Bean curd skins: the skin that forms on heated soya bean milk and is then dried. Brush with water to soften. Comes in large sheets to cut to size. Use to wrap food before deep-frying, steaming or braising.

Star anise: dried star-shaped seed pod of a tree native to China. Adds aniseed taste to simmered meat and poultry. Available whole or ground.

Shiitake mushrooms: have a rich smoky flavour and are available fresh and dried. The dried variety must be soaked in boiling water for at least 20 minutes to soften before use.

Tempura flour: Available in packets in Asian grocery stores. Made up with iced water. Plain flour can be substituted but the batter won't be quite as light.

ABOVE: Spring rolls

SPRING ROLLS

Preparation time: 45 minutes + soaking
Total cooking time: 20 minutes
Makes 20

★ ★

4 dried Chinese mushrooms
1 tablespoon oil
2 cloves garlic, crushed
1 tablespoon grated fresh ginger
150 g (5 oz) fried bean curd, cut into strips
1 large carrot, cut into very fine matchsticks
70 g (2¼ oz) water chestnuts, chopped
6 spring onions, chopped
150 g (5 oz) Chinese cabbage, shredded
1 tablespoon soy sauce
1 tablespoon cornflour
10 large spring roll wrappers
oil, for deep-frying

1 Soak the dried mushrooms in boiling water for 20 minutes. Drain and squeeze to remove any excess liquid. Slice the mushroom caps and discard the hard stems.

2 Heat the tablespoon of oil in a large wok, swirling gently to coat the base and side. Stir-fry the garlic, ginger, bean curd, carrot and water chestnuts for 30 seconds, over high heat. Add the spring onion and cabbage and cook for 1 minute, or until the cabbage is just softened. Add the soy sauce and some salt, white pepper and sugar, to taste; cool. Add the sliced mushroom caps.

3 Mix the cornflour with 2 tablespoons of water to form a paste. Keep the spring roll wrappers covered with a clean damp tea towel while you work. Place two wrappers on a board, one on top of the other. (The rolls are made with two layers of wrappers.) Cut the large square into four squares. Brush the edges of each square with a little cornflour paste. Place about 1 tablespoon of the filling in the centre of one square. With a corner facing you, roll up the wrapper firmly, folding in the sides as you roll. Repeat with the remaining wrappers and filling.

4 Fill a deep heavy-based pan one third full of oil and heat the oil to 180°C (350°F). The oil is ready when a cube of bread dropped into the oil turns golden brown in 15 seconds. Deep-fry the spring rolls, about four at a time, for 3 minutes, or until golden. Drain on crumpled paper towels.

BABY SQUASH WITH RICE STUFFING

Preparation time: 20 minutes
Total cooking time: 10 minutes
Makes 24

24 baby yellow squash
1 tablespoon oil
2 teaspoons Thai red curry paste
1 spring onion, finely chopped
1 small red pepper (capsicum), finely chopped
1 cup (185 g/6 oz) cooked jasmine rice
1 tablespoon finely chopped fresh coriander
2 kaffir lime leaves, finely shredded
24 fresh coriander leaves, to garnish

1 Blanch or steam the squash for 5 minutes, or until just tender.
2 Cut a thin slice off the base of each squash to allow it to stand upright, then slice a thin piece off the top to make a lid. Set aside.
3 Using a melon baller, scoop out the flesh from the squash, leaving a thin shell. Discard the flesh.
4 Heat the oil in a wok, then add the curry paste, spring onion and red pepper and stir-fry for 2–3 minutes. Add the rice and stir-fry for another 2–3 minutes. Add the chopped coriander and kaffir lime leaves and toss to combine.
5 Remove from the heat and spoon 1 teaspoon of rice into each of the yellow squash. Garnish each with a coriander leaf and gently arrange the lids on top. Arrange on a platter and serve.
NOTE: For 1 cup (185 g/6 oz) jasmine rice, you will need to cook 1/3 cup (65 g/2 1/4 oz) of rice in boiling water for about 10 minutes.
IN ADVANCE: The filling and squash can be prepared a day ahead. Cover and store separately in the refrigerator. Assemble several hours before you are serving.

BELOW: Baby squash with rice stuffing

GARLIC

Although some people love the pungent flavour of garlic, while others hate it, it is indispensable as a flavouring for many recipes. It has been used for thousands of years and is renowned for its medicinal properties. It was used as an antiseptic before antibiotics. A member of the onion family, the bulb consists of a cluster of cloves surrounded by a thin skin. The cloves, with their skin on, are easily separated as required. The cloves are easier to peel if you lay them on a board and squash them slightly with the flat side of a broad knife. Crush or chop the clove with a knife or a garlic crusher. To add a subtle flavour to salads, cut a clove and rub round the inside of the salad bowl, or add a whole peeled clove to the salad dressing, then remove before serving.

OPPOSITE PAGE: Crusted tuna crisps (left); Pork gyoza dumplings

CRUSTED TUNA CRISPS

Preparation time: 45 minutes + chilling
Total cooking time: 15 minutes
Makes 24

Wasabi cream
1/4 cup (60 ml/2 fl oz) cream
2 tablespoons sour cream
1 tablespoon wasabi powder
1/2 tablespoon lemon juice
1 tablespoon rice wine vinegar
1/2 teaspoon sugar

12 round gow gee wrappers
oil, for deep-frying
500 g (1 lb) tuna steaks, 2.5 cm (1 inch) thick
1/2 cup (80 g/2³/4 oz) sesame seeds

Salad
125 g (4 oz) watercress
1 Lebanese cucumber
3 radishes
1 teaspoon grated fresh ginger
3 teaspoons rice wine vinegar
1 tablespoon sesame oil
1 tablespoon peanut or corn oil

1 For the wasabi cream, whisk the cream until it thickens, then gently stir in the sour cream, wasabi powder, lemon juice, rice wine vinegar and sugar. Season with salt and pepper. Refrigerate for at least 30 minutes.
2 Cut each gow gee wrapper in half. Fill a deep heavy-based saucepan one third full of oil and heat the oil to 180°C (350°F). The oil is ready when a cube of bread dropped into the oil turns golden brown in 15 seconds. Fry batches of gow gee wrappers until slightly brown and crisp, about 30 seconds per side. Drain on crumpled paper towels.
3 Cut the tuna steaks into 4 cm (1¹/2 inch) wide strips (about 2 or 3 pieces). Lightly brush with 2 teaspoons of oil, season with salt and pepper and toss in the sesame seeds. Refrigerate.
4 Divide the watercress into small sprigs. Use a vegetable peeler to slice the cucumber into thin strips. Rotate the cucumber and stop when you get to the seeds. Use the peeler to slice the radishes into thin pieces. Combine the cucumber, radish and watercress and set aside. Combine the ginger, rice wine vinegar, sesame and peanut oils

in a small non-metallic bowl. Season; set aside.
5 Heat 1 tablespoon oil in a heavy-based pan over medium heat. Sear the tuna on all sides for 1 minute per side. The sesame seeds should be golden brown and the centre of the tuna pink. Slice the tuna crossways into 24 pieces.
6 When ready to serve, stir the ginger dressing, then toss through the watercress, cucumber and radish. Place a small pile of salad on the wrappers, followed by a piece of tuna and some wasabi cream. Serve at room temperature.

PORK GYOZA DUMPLINGS

Preparation time: 40 minutes
Total cooking time: 10 minutes per batch
Makes 40

Filling
400 g (13 oz) minced pork
15 garlic chives, chopped
2 cloves garlic, crushed
1 teaspoon sesame oil

40 gyoza or round gow gee wrappers
1/2 cup (125 ml/4 fl oz) soy sauce
1 tablespoon sesame seeds
oil, for frying

1 To make the filling, place all the ingredients in a bowl, mix well and season, to taste.
2 Place a teaspoon of filling in the centre of each wrapper, dampen the edges with water, fold over and pleat to seal. Place on a lightly oiled tray and repeat with the remaining wrappers and filling. Before steaming, lightly brush the dumplings with a little oil.
3 Half fill a wok or pan with water, cover and bring to the boil. Place batches of dumplings, not touching each other, in a bamboo steamer lined with lightly oiled baking paper. Steam for 10 minutes.
4 Combine the soy sauce and sesame seeds in a small serving dish.
5 Heat the oil in a large frying pan. Cook the gyoza dumplings in batches for about 2 minutes on one side, or until golden brown. Do not turn over. Remove from the pan and serve hot with soy sauce for dipping.
NOTE: These are quick and easy if you use a dumpling press, available at kitchen shops. You can buy the wrappers at Asian supermarkets.

FRIED SPICY TEMPEH

Preparation time: 30 minutes + standing
Total cooking time: 40 minutes
Serves 4-6

★ ★

4 small red chillies, seeded
2 stalks lemon grass, white part only
2 fresh kaffir lime leaves
1/2 cup (125 ml/4 fl oz) oil
10 Asian red or golden shallots, finely sliced
2 large cloves garlic, finely chopped
500 g (1 lb) tempeh, sliced into matchsticks
4 cm (1 1/2 inch) piece fresh galangal, peeled and thinly sliced
3 teaspoons tamarind purée
1 teaspoon salt
60 g (2 oz) palm sugar, grated

ABOVE: Fried spicy tempeh

1 Slit the chillies lengthways and remove the seeds and membrane. Finely slice the chillies diagonally. Bruise the lemon grass and lime leaves with the back of a large knife.

2 Heat 2 tablespoons of the oil in a wok or pan and fry the shallots and garlic in batches over medium-low heat for 2–3 minutes, or until crisp. Drain on crumpled paper towels. Heat the remaining oil and fry the tempeh in batches for 3–4 minutes, or until very crisp (you may need to add a little more oil). Drain on crumpled paper towels. Discard all the oil except 2 teaspoons.

3 Heat the reserved oil in the wok and add the chilli, lemon grass, galangal and lime leaves. Cook over medium heat for 2 minutes, or until fragrant. Add the tamarind purée, salt, palm sugar and 1 tablespoon water. Cook for 2–3 minutes, or until the sauce is thick and has caramelized.

4 Add the crispy shallots, garlic and tempeh and stir-fry for 1–2 minutes, or until all the liquid has evaporated. Turn off the heat, spread the mixture in the wok and leave to cool. Remove and discard the lemon grass, galangal and lime leaves. Store in an airtight container for up to 5 days.

NOTE: Soft brown sugar can be used instead of palm sugar. Tempeh is an easily digestible source of protein made from soya beans. It is available at Asian speciality stores and some supermarkets.

THAI BEEF SALAD IN CUCUMBER CUPS

Preparation time: 25 minutes + marinating
Total cooking time: 5–10 minutes
Makes 30

Marinade
¹/₃ cup (80 ml/2³/₄ fl oz) kecap manis
¹/₃ cup (80 ml/2³/₄ fl oz) lime juice
1 red chilli, finely sliced
1 tablespoon sesame oil

250 g (8 oz) piece beef eye fillet
7 Lebanese cucumbers

Salad
¹/₂ stem lemon grass, white part only, finely
   chopped
¹/₄ cup (60 ml/2 fl oz) lime juice
1–2 fresh red chillies, finely sliced
20 g (³/₄ oz) fresh mint leaves, finely chopped

20 g (³/₄ oz) fresh coriander leaves, finely
   chopped
1 tablespoon fish sauce

1 Mix together the marinade ingredients. Put the beef eye fillet in a non-metallic bowl, pour in the marinade and refrigerate for 2 hours, or overnight. Allow the meat to come back to room temperature before cooking.

2 Heat a barbecue or chargrill pan and cook the beef. For medium, cook for 7 minutes. Cook less for rare and longer for well-done. Allow to cool, then finely slice into thin strips and mix with the rest of the salad ingredients.

3 Cut off the ends of the cucumber and slice about 3 cm (1¹/₄ inches) thick. Using a melon baller, scoop out the flesh from each slice to make a 'cup' about 1 cm (¹/₂ inch) thick. Fill each cup with the Thai beef salad.

IN ADVANCE: Prepare the salad and scooped out cucumber slices separately, refrigerate, then fill at the last minute.

THAI BEEF SALAD IN CUCUMBER CUPS

Trim the Lebanese cucumbers at both ends, then cut the cucumbers into short pieces.

Use a melon baller to scoop out the flesh, leaving a border of flesh on the base and sides to make a cup for the filling.

LEFT: Thai beef salad in cucumber cups

SPINACH AND WATER CHESTNUT DUMPLINGS

Preparation time: I hour 30 minutes + cooling
Total cooking time: 50 minutes
Makes 30

★★

Filling
I tablespoon peanut oil
I teaspoon sesame oil
I clove garlic, crushed
2.5 cm (I inch) piece fresh ginger, grated
2 tablespoons chopped fresh garlic chives
30 g (I oz) water spinach, chopped into
   I cm (1/2 inch) lengths
120 g (4 oz) can water chestnuts, drained,
   finely chopped
I tablespoon soy sauce

Pastry
2 cups (350 g/11 oz) rice flour
2/3 cup (85 g/3 oz) tapioca starch
2 tablespoons arrowroot flour
I tablespoon glutinous rice flour

Dipping sauce
1/2 teaspoon sesame oil
1/2 teaspoon peanut oil
I tablespoon soy sauce
I tablespoon lime juice
I small red chilli, seeded and finely chopped

tapioca flour, for dusting

I For the filling, heat the oils over medium-low heat in a wok. Add the garlic and ginger and cook, stirring, for 1 minute, or until fragrant but not brown. Add the chives, water spinach, water chestnuts and soy sauce and cook for 2 minutes. Remove from the pan and cool for about 5 minutes. Drain away any liquid.
2 Combine the pastry ingredients in a large pan with 2 1/2 cups (600 ml/20 fl oz) water, stirring to remove any lumps. Stir over low heat for 10 minutes, or until thick. Cook stirring, for another 5 minutes, or until the liquid is opaque. Turn onto a work surface dusted liberally with tapioca flour and cool for 10 minutes. (You will need to use the tapioca flour to continually dust the surface and your hands while kneading.) With floured hands, knead the dough for

ABOVE: Spinach and water chestnut dumplings

10 minutes. Divide into two, covering one half with plastic wrap.

3 Roll out the dough to 2 mm (1/8 inch) thick. Cut out 9 cm (3 1/2 inch) rounds with a cutter. Place a heaped teaspoon of filling in the centre of each circle, dampen the edge, fold over and pleat to seal. This is very easy with a dumpling press. Place on a lightly floured board or tray and repeat with the remaining dough and filling. Do not re-roll any pastry scraps. Before steaming, lightly brush the dumplings with oil.

4 Half fill a wok or pan with water, cover and bring to the boil. Place the dumplings, leaving a gap between each, in a bamboo steamer lined with lightly oiled baking paper. Cover and steam for 10 minutes, or until the pastry is opaque. Repeat until all the dumplings are done, then serve with the dipping sauce on the side.

5 For the sauce, whisk all the ingredients together in a small bowl.

NOTE: Water spinach, also known as kangkung, is available at Asian greengrocers. Rice flour, tapioca starch, arrowroot flour and glutinous rice flour are available from large Asian food stores and some supermarkets.

THAI CHICKEN ROLLS

Preparation time: 25 minutes
Total cooking time: 10 minutes
Makes 30

★★

600 g (1 1/4 lb) chicken mince
4 stalks lemon grass, finely chopped
4 red chillies, seeded and finely chopped
6 Asian red shallots, finely chopped
2 tablespoons finely chopped fresh
    Vietnamese mint
3 tablespoons finely chopped fresh coriander
2 tablespoons fish sauce
2 tablespoons fresh lime juice
100 g (3 1/2 oz) packet bean curd skin
oil, for deep frying
4 kaffir lime leaves, finely shredded,
    to garnish

 Mix the chicken mince, lemon grass, chopped chilli, shallots, mint, coriander, fish sauce and lime juice (this can be done with sharp knives or in a food processor). Cut thirty 10 x 16 cm (4 x 6 1/2 inch) rectangles from the bean curd skin. Brush the bean curd skin lightly with water to soften it for rolling. Roll 1 tablespoon of chicken mixture into a log and place on each bean curd rectangle. Roll up from the short end, folding in the ends as you roll.

2 Fill a deep heavy-based pan one third full of oil and heat to 180°C (350°F). The oil is ready when a cube of bread dropped into the oil turns golden brown in 15 seconds. Deep-fry the chicken rolls for 1 minute, or until golden brown and cooked through. If the bean curd skin is browning before the chicken is cooked, turn the heat down. Drain well on crumpled paper towels. Serve garnished with finely shredded kaffir lime leaves. Serve immediately to retain crispness.

ABOVE: Thai chicken rolls

BEEF CHA PLU PARCELS

Preparation time: 25 minutes
Total cooking time: 10 minutes
Makes about 45

★ ★

1 medium leek, trimmed
250 g (8 oz) lean beef mince
1 Lebanese cucumber, finely chopped
1/2 red onion, finely chopped
5–6 fresh Vietnamese mint leaves, finely
    chopped
2 tablespoons lime juice
2 tablespoons fish sauce
2 tablespoons desiccated coconut, toasted
500 g (1 lb) cha plu (betel leaves)
1 cup (250 ml/8 fl oz) sweet chilli sauce,
    for dipping

1 Cut the leek in half lengthways, wash thoroughly and discard the outer layers and any hard core. Put the leek in a bowl, pour boiling water over it and soak for 5 minutes, or until softened. Drain well and set aside.
2 Heat 1 tablespoon of oil in a frying pan and cook the beef mince, breaking up any lumps with the back of a fork, for 5–8 minutes, until cooked through and browned. Remove from the heat and cool slightly.
3 Combine the mince with the cucumber, onion, mint, lime juice, fish sauce and coconut. Toss well and set aside.
4 Cut the base off the leek and cut the leek lengthways into thin strips about 5 mm (1/4 inch) wide. Trim the required amount of betel leaves (larger ones are better for making into parcels), wash and dry well.
5 Place 1 teaspoon of mixture in the centre of each leaf and fold in the sides to form a parcel, or draw up the sides to form a pouch. Carefully tie with pieces of leek. Repeat with all the leaves. Arrange on a platter with sweet chilli sauce to dip and serve immediately.
NOTE: Betel leaves and Vietnamese mint can be found in Asian fruit and vegetable stores as well as in some greengrocers. If unavailable, use blanched Chinese cabbage leaves instead of the betel leaves and normal mint to replace the Vietnamese mint.

BLACK SATIN CHICKEN

Preparation time: 15 minutes + soaking
Total cooking time: 1 hour
Makes about 25 pieces

★

3 dried Chinese mushrooms
1/2 cup (125 ml/4 fl oz) dark soy sauce
1/4 cup (45 g/1 1/2 oz) soft brown sugar
2 tablespoons Shaosing (Chinese) wine
1 tablespoon soy sauce
1 teaspoon sesame oil
1/4 teaspoon Chinese five-spice powder
1.4 kg (2 lb 13 oz) chicken drumettes
4 cm (1 1/2 inch) piece fresh ginger, grated

1 Put the mushrooms in a small heatproof bowl, cover with boiling water and leave to soak for 20 minutes, or until softened. Drain, reserving the liquid. Combine the liquid with the dark soy sauce, sugar, wine, soy sauce, sesame oil and five-spice powder in a small pan and bring to the boil, stirring continuously.
2 Rub the chicken with ginger and 1 teaspoon salt and put in a large pan. Cover with the soy marinade and mushrooms, turning to coat evenly. Cover and cook over low heat, turning regularly, for 20 minutes or until the juices run clear when pierced with a skewer. Remove the chicken and allow to cool briefly. Boil the sauce over high heat until thick and syrupy. Discard the mushrooms.
3 Arrange the chicken on a platter, brush lightly with the syrupy sauce and serve the remaining sauce for dipping.
NOTE: Dark soy sauce is thicker in consistency than regular soy and is available from Asian food speciality stores. Drumettes are the meaty part of the wing with the two smaller joints cut off.

BEEF CHA PLU PARCELS

Spoon 1 teaspoon of mixture into the centre of the underside of each leaf.

Draw up the sides of each leaf to form a pouch, or fold to form a parcel, then tie with strips of leek.

OPPOSITE PAGE: Beef cha plu parcels (top); Black satin chicken

and pour the lemon juice over. Cover and refrigerate for 15 minutes. Drain and pat dry.
2 Combine the cornflour, salt, pepper and sugar in a bowl. Dip the squid into the egg white and dust with the flour mixture, shaking off any excess. Fill a deep heavy-based pan one third full of oil and heat to 180°C (350°F), or until a cube of bread dropped into the oil turns golden brown in 15 seconds. Deep-fry the squid, in batches, for 1–2 minutes, or until the squid turns white and curls. Drain on crumpled paper towels. Serve immediately.

STEAMED CHINESE MUSHROOMS WITH PRAWNS

Preparation time: 40 minutes + soaking
Total cooking time: 40 minutes
Makes about 20

60 g (2 oz) dried shiitake mushrooms
2 tablespoons soy sauce
3 tablespoons sesame oil
1 tablespoon grated palm sugar
1 kg (2 lb) large raw prawns, peeled and deveined
6 spring onions, finely chopped
1/2 large celery stick, finely chopped
2 tablespoons finely chopped fresh coriander
2.5 cm (1 inch) piece fresh ginger, grated
1/2 teaspoon fish sauce
1 red chilli, finely chopped
1/4 teaspoon sesame oil

1 Soak the mushrooms in boiling water for 20 minutes, then drain, reserving the liquid. Remove and discard the stems. To 1 cup (250 ml/4 fl oz) of the reserved liquid, add the soy sauce and 1 tablespoon of the sesame oil.
2 Heat the remaining sesame oil in a wok or frying pan and cook the mushrooms, on the pale side only, until lightly browned. Sprinkle with the palm sugar and cook for another minute. Add the reserved seasoned liquid and cook, covered, for about 15 minutes over low heat. Drain, reserving any remaining liquid, and cool.
3 Roughly chop the prawn meat in a food processor, then transfer to a bowl and mix with the spring onion, celery, coriander, ginger, fish sauce, chilli and sesame oil.
4 To assemble, put 1 dessertspoon of paste on each mushroom and smooth into a dome shape. Place in a steamer. Bring the reserved liquid to

SALT AND PEPPER SQUID

Preparation time: 30 minutes + marinating
Total cooking time: 10 minutes
Serves 10

1 kg (2 lb) squid tubes, halved lengthways
1 cup (250 ml/8 fl oz) lemon juice
2 cups (250 g/8 oz) cornflour
1 1/2 tablespoons salt
1 tablespoon ground white pepper
2 teaspoons caster sugar
4 egg whites, lightly beaten
oil, for deep-frying
lemon wedges, for serving
fresh coriander leaves, to garnish

1 Open out the squid tubes, wash and pat dry. Lay on a chopping board with the inside facing upwards. Score a fine diamond pattern on the squid, being careful not to cut all the way through. Cut into pieces about 5 x 3 cm (2 x 1 1/4 inches). Place in a flat non-metallic dish

ABOVE: Salt and pepper squid

the boil in a pan and steam the mushrooms over the liquid, adding water if necessary, for about 15 minutes, or until the filling is cooked through.

MIXED TEMPURA

Preparation time: 20 minutes
Total cooking time: 10 minutes
Makes about 30

12 raw king prawns
1 sheet nori, cut into 12 thin strips
2 cups (250 g/8 oz) tempura flour or
   plain flour
2 cups (500 ml/16 fl oz) iced water
2 egg yolks, lightly beaten
oil, for deep-frying
flour, for coating
60 g (2 oz) broccoli florets
100 g (3½ oz) button mushrooms
1 red pepper (capsicum), cut into thin strips
soy sauce, for serving

1 Peel and devein the prawns, leaving the tails intact. Cut a slit in the underside of each prawn (this will prevent them curling) and wrap a piece of nori around the base of the tail.
2 Sift the flour into a bowl, make a well in the centre and add the iced water and egg yolk. Stir with chopsticks until just combined. The batter should be slightly lumpy.
3 Fill a deep heavy-based pan one third full of oil and heat to 180°C (350°F), or until a cube of bread dropped into the oil turns golden in 15 seconds.
4 Dip the prawns in flour to coat, shake off any excess, then dip in the batter. Cook the prawns in batches until crisp and light golden. Drain on crumpled paper towels. Repeat with the vegetables. Serve the tempura immediately with soy sauce for dipping.
NOTE: Tempura should have a very light batter and needs to be served as soon as it is cooked. Be sure that the water is ice cold as this helps to lighten the batter. If you are unsure, add a few ice cubes. If you use plain flour, add a little extra water to help thin the batter.

BELOW: Mixed tempura

STEAMED PORK BUNS

Flatten the dough portions slightly, making them slightly thinner around the edges.

Pull the dough up around the pork filling to enclose, pinching firmly to seal.

Place each bun on a piece of greaseproof paper and place in a steamer.

ABOVE: Steamed pork buns

STEAMED PORK BUNS

Preparation time: 40 minutes
Total cooking time: 15 minutes
Makes about 24

★★

3 cups (450 g/14 oz) char sui pork bun flour
1 cup (250 ml/8 fl oz) milk
1/2 cup (125 g/4 oz) caster sugar
1 tablespoon oil

Filling

2 teaspoons oil
1 clove garlic, crushed
2 spring onions, finely chopped
3 teaspoons cornflour
2 teaspoons hoisin sauce
1 1/2 teaspoons soy sauce
1/2 teaspoon caster sugar
150 g (5 oz) Chinese barbecued pork,
   finely chopped

1 Set aside two tablespoons of flour. In a small pan, combine the milk and sugar and stir over low heat until dissolved. Sift the remaining flour into a large bowl and make a well in the centre. Gradually add the milk, stirring until it just comes together. Lightly dust a work surface with some of the reserved flour. Turn out the dough and knead for 10 minutes, or until smooth and elastic. Gradually incorporate the tablespoon of oil by kneading it into the dough a little at a time, kneading for about 10 minutes. Cover with plastic wrap and refrigerate for 30 minutes.

2 For the filling, heat the oil in a pan, add the garlic and spring onion and stir over medium heat until just soft. Blend the cornflour with 1/3 cup (80 ml/2 3/4 fl oz) water, the sauces and sugar and add to the pan. Stir over medium heat until the mixture boils and thickens, remove from the heat and stir in the pork. Allow to cool.

3 Divide the dough into 24 portions and flatten slightly, making the edges slightly thinner than the centre. Place teaspoons of filling in the centre of each and pull up the edges around the filling to enclose, pinching firmly to seal. Place each bun on a small square of greaseproof paper and place 3 cm (1 1/4 inches) apart on a bamboo or metal steamer. Place over a large pan of simmering water and steam in batches for 15 minutes, or until the buns have risen and are cooked through.

NOTE: Char sui pork bun flour is available at Asian food stores. It gives a finer, lighter texture.

STIR-FRIED NOODLES WITH CORN AND PEANUTS

Preparation time: 25 minutes
Total cooking time: 10 minutes
Makes 35

★ ★ ★

1/2 cup (90 g/3 oz) roasted peanuts
1/4 cup (60 ml/2 fl oz) coconut milk
2 tablespoons lime juice
1/2 teaspoon ground turmeric
1/4 cup (60 ml/2 fl oz) oil
3 eggs, lightly beaten
125 g (4 oz) dried rice vermicelli
3 cloves garlic, crushed
1 tablespoon finely chopped fresh ginger
2 teaspoons shrimp paste (blachan)
6 spring onions, thinly sliced
400 g (13 oz) can baby corn, drained,
    quartered lengthways
150 g (5 oz) bean shoots
500 g (1 lb) Chinese cabbage, hard stems
    removed, thinly sliced
1/2 small red pepper (capsicum), thinly sliced
10 g (1/4 oz) fresh coriander leaves
11/2 tablespoons fish sauce
2–3 large banana leaves, for serving
1/2 cup (90 g/3 oz) roasted peanuts, extra,
    chopped, to garnish
lime wedges, for serving

1 Mix the peanuts, coconut milk, lime juice and turmeric in a food processor until combined, but so the peanuts are only roughly chopped.
2 Heat 1 tablespoon of the oil in a large wok. Add the eggs and tilt the uncooked egg to the outside edge of the wok. Cook until firm, then remove from the wok and roll up firmly. Cut into thin slices.
3 Place the vermicelli in a bowl, cover with boiling water and soak for 5 minutes. Drain and cut into short lengths with scissors.
4 Heat the remaining oil in the wok. Add the garlic, ginger and shrimp paste and stir-fry for 30 seconds, or until aromatic. Add the vegetables and stir-fry until tender. Add the vermicelli and stir-fry until heated through. Stir in the peanut mixture and stir-fry until well combined and heated through. Turn off the heat and gently stir in the omelette and coriander leaves and fish sauce.

5 Cut the banana leaves into 11 cm (41/2 inch) squares and blanch them in hot water for 10–15 seconds. Hold one corner of a square down on a flat surface with your finger, then fold one side of the banana leaf across, overlapping it into a cone shape. Secure down the side through to the base with a toothpick. Repeat to make 35 cones.
6 Spoon the filling into the cones, sprinkle with the extra peanuts and serve with lime wedges.
NOTE: Banana leaves are available in the fruit and vegetable section of most supermarkets or in Asian or Pacific Island stores.

ABOVE: Stir-fried noodles with corn and peanuts

TAPAS & MEZE

Tapas and meze are those delicious little appetizers served throughout the balmy Mediterranean. Tapas are at the heart of the gregarious Spanish social life. The word comes from *tapa*, 'to cover', and at first this is exactly what tapas were—slices of bread or ham placed on top of glasses of sherry in a bar to keep off the flies. Thankfully tapas have evolved somewhat since then and are often now the main reason to visit a Spanish tavern. Meze is directly translated from the Greek for 'tasty morsels' and celebrates the flavours of Greece, Turkey and the Middle East. Originally served before the main meal, a meze platter is now recognised as a magnificent feast in its own right.

PRAWN FRITTERS

Preparation time: 20 minutes
Total cooking time: 10 minutes
Makes about 30

★ ★

²/₃ cup (85 g/3 oz) plain flour
¹/₃ cup (40 g/1¹/₄ oz) self-raising flour
2 spring onions, chopped
2 tablespoons chopped fresh flat-leaf parsley
pinch of cayenne pepper
³/₄ cup (185 ml/6 fl oz) soda water
125 g (4 oz) small cooked prawns, peeled and chopped
olive oil, for deep-frying

1 Sift the flours into a large bowl. Add the spring onion, parsley, cayenne pepper and some salt and mix well. Make a well in the centre and gradually add the soda water, whisking to form a smooth lump-free batter. Add enough soda water to form a batter that will drop from a spoon. Add the prawns and stir until combined.

2 Fill a deep heavy-based pan one third full of oil and heat to 180°C (350°F), or until a cube of bread dropped into the oil browns in 15 seconds. Drop half tablespoons of the batter into the hot oil in batches and cook for 1–2 minutes, turning, until puffed and evenly browned all over. Remove with a slotted spoon and drain on crumpled paper towels. Serve hot.

OLIVE TWISTS

Finely chop 1 tablespoon of capers and 4 anchovy fillets and mix with 2 tablespoons olive paste, some chopped fresh parsley and a drizzle of oil, to form a smooth paste. Spread 2 sheets of ready-rolled puff pastry with the paste and cut into 1.5 cm (⁵/₈ inch) strips. Twist each strip about 4 times and bake on baking paper covered trays in a moderately hot 200°C (400°F/Gas 6) oven for about 5–10 minutes, or until golden brown. Makes about 50.

ABOVE: Prawn fritters

HAM AND MUSHROOM CROQUETTES

Preparation time: 35 minutes + cooling + chilling
Total cooking time: 20 minutes
Makes 36

90 g (3 oz) butter
1 small onion, finely chopped
110 g (3½ oz) cap mushrooms, finely chopped
¾ cup (90 g/3 oz) plain flour
1 cup (250 ml/8 fl oz) milk
¾ cup (185 ml/6 fl oz) chicken stock
110 g (3½ oz) ham, finely chopped
½ cup (60 g/2 oz) plain flour, extra
2 eggs, lightly beaten
½ cup (50 g/1¾ oz) dry breadcrumbs
olive oil, for deep-frying

1 Melt the butter in a pan over low heat and cook the onion for 5 minutes, or until translucent. Add the mushrooms and cook, stirring occasionally, over low heat for 5 minutes. Add the flour and stir over medium–low heat for 1 minute, or until the mixture is dry and crumbly and begins to change colour.

2 Remove the pan from the heat and gradually stir in the milk and stock. Return to the heat, stirring constantly until the mixture boils and becomes very thick. Stir in the ham and some black pepper, then transfer to a bowl to cool for about 2 hours.

3 When completely cool, roll tablespoons of the mixture into croquette shapes. Place the extra flour, beaten eggs and breadcrumbs in three shallow bowls. Toss the croquettes in the flour, then in the eggs, allowing the excess to drip away, then toss in the breadcrumbs. Place on a baking tray covered with paper and refrigerate for about 30 minutes.

4 Fill a deep heavy-based pan one third full of oil and heat to 180°C (350°F), or until a cube of bread dropped into the oil browns in 15 seconds. Deep-fry the croquettes, in batches, for about 3 minutes each batch, until they are browned all over and heated through. Drain each batch on crumpled paper towels. Serve the croquettes warm or hot.

BELOW: Ham and mushroom croquettes

BOREK OF ASPARAGUS

Cut the puff pastry sheets into rectangles and put one trimmed asparagus spear on each.

Fold in the short ends, then roll the pastry up like a parcel so the asparagus is sealed in.

OPPOSITE PAGE: Scallop ceviche (top); Borek of asparagus

SCALLOP CEVICHE

Preparation time: 20 minutes + marinating
Total cooking time: Nil
Makes 15

15 scallops on the half shell
1 teaspoon finely grated lime rind
2 cloves garlic, chopped
2 red chillies, seeded and chopped
1/4 cup (60 ml/2 fl oz) lime juice
1 tablespoon chopped fresh parsley
1 tablespoon olive oil

1 Take the scallops off their half shells. If the scallops need to be cut off the shells, use a small, sharp paring knife to carefully slice the attached part away from the shell, being careful to leave as little scallop meat on the shell as possible. Remove the dark vein and white muscle from the scallops, and wash the shells.
2 In a bowl, mix together the lime rind, garlic, chilli, lime juice, parsley and olive oil and season with salt and freshly ground black pepper. Place the scallops in the dressing and stir to coat evenly. Cover with plastic wrap and marinate in the refrigerator for 2 hours to 'cook' the scallop meat.
3 To serve, slide each of the scallops back onto a half shell and spoon the dressing over the top. Serve cold.

BOREK OF ASPARAGUS

Preparation time: 20 minutes
Total cooking time: 25 minutes
Makes 16

16 fresh asparagus spears
1/2 teaspoon salt
1/2 teaspoon black pepper
2 tablespoons finely grated lemon rind
2 sheets ready-rolled puff pastry
1 egg yolk
1 tablespoon sesame seeds

1 Preheat the oven to moderately hot 200°C (400°F/Gas 6).
2 Add the asparagus to a large pan of lightly salted boiling water and simmer for about 3 minutes, then drain and refresh under cold running water. Trim to 10 cm (4 inch) lengths.
3 Combine the salt, black pepper and lemon rind in a shallow dish and roll each asparagus spear in this mixture.
4 Cut the puff pastry sheets into 12 x 6 cm (5 x 2½ inch) rectangles and place one asparagus spear on each piece of pastry. In a bowl, combine the egg yolk with 2 teaspoons water and brush some on the sides and ends of the pastry. Roll the pastry up like a parcel, enclosing the sides so that the asparagus is completely sealed in. Press the joins of the pastry with a fork.
5 Place the parcels on lightly greased baking trays. Brush with the remaining egg and sprinkle with sesame seeds. Bake for 15–20 minutes, or until golden. These parcels are delicious served warm or cold, with tzatziki (see page 167).

BOREK OF MUSHROOM

Preparation time: 40 minutes + cooling
Total cooking time: 40 minutes
Makes 24

4 rashers bacon
250 g (8 oz) mushrooms
1 tablespoon olive oil
1 onion, chopped
1/4 teaspoon paprika
6 sheets ready-rolled puff pastry

1 Chop the bacon and mushrooms into 5 mm (1/4 inch) cubes. Heat the olive oil in a frying pan over medium heat, and cook the onion and paprika for 3 minutes, without browning. Add the bacon and cook for 3 minutes. Add the mushroom and cook for another 5 minutes, or until all the ingredients are tender. Season with salt and cracked black pepper, then spoon into a bowl. Set aside and allow to cool completely.
2 Using a 10 cm (4 inch) pastry cutter, cut 4 rounds out of each sheet of pastry. Refrigerate to make handling them easier. Preheat the oven to moderately hot 200°C (400°F/Gas 6).
3 Spoon 1 tablespoon of the mushroom and bacon into the centre of each round of pastry. Draw up the pastry to form four sides. To seal, pinch the sides together with wet fingertips. Repeat with the remaining pastry and filling.
4 Bake on baking trays covered with baking paper for 20–30 minutes, or until the pastry is golden and brown. Serve hot or warm.

SPANISH-STYLE BEEF KEBABS

Preparation time: 15 minutes + marinating
Total cooking time: 5 minutes
Makes 18–20

★ ★

1 kg (2 lb) rump steak
3 cloves garlic, chopped
1 tablespoon chopped fresh flat-leaf parsley
1/3 cup (80 ml/2³/4 fl oz) lemon juice
1/2 teaspoon black pepper
18–20 small wooden skewers

Paprika dressing

2 teaspoons paprika
large pinch of cayenne pepper
1/2 teaspoon salt
2 tablespoons red wine vinegar
1/3 cup (80 ml/2³/4 fl oz) olive oil

1 Trim the excess fat from the rump steak and cut into 2 cm (³/4 inch) pieces. Combine the steak, garlic, parsley, lemon juice and pepper in a bowl, cover with plastic wrap and marinate for 2 hours in the refrigerator. Meanwhile, soak the skewers in water for about 1 hour to ensure they don't burn during cooking.

2 To make the paprika dressing, whisk the paprika, cayenne pepper, salt, vinegar and oil together until well blended.

3 Preheat a lightly oiled barbecue hotplate or grill. Thread the pieces of marinated meat onto the skewers, then cook the kebabs, turning occasionally for about 4–5 minutes, or until cooked through. Drizzle with the paprika dressing and serve hot with wedges of lemon.

HALOUMI

This is a firm, stretched-curd cheese that is matured in brine (salt water). It has a salty, sharp taste, similar to feta. Haloumi can be served as part of a cheese platter, together with fresh fruit. It can also be pan-fried in olive oil, or brushed with oil before grilling. It has a smooth and creamy texture when melted.

ABOVE: Spanish-style beef kebabs

BARBECUED HALOUMI

Lightly brush 10 slices of French bread on both sides with olive oil and barbecue until brown. Cut 250 g (8 oz) haloumi cheese into 5 mm (1/4 inch) slices. Combine a little oil and crushed garlic and brush over the cheese. Barbecue on a hotplate for 1 minute, or until soft and golden underneath. Use an egg slide to remove the cheese and place some on each piece of toast. Drizzle with a little olive oil and sprinkle with chopped mint and cracked black pepper. Makes 10.

BABA GANOUJ
(EGGPLANT/AUBERGINE DIP)

Preparation time: 15 minutes + standing
Total cooking time: 35 minutes
Makes about 1 cup (250 ml/8 fl oz)

★ ★

2 medium eggplants (aubergines)
3–4 cloves garlic, crushed
2 tablespoons lemon juice
2 tablespoons tahini
1 tablespoon olive oil
sprinkle of paprika, to garnish

1 Halve the eggplants (aubergines) lengthways, sprinkle with salt and leave to stand for 15–20 minutes. Rinse and pat dry with paper towels. Preheat the oven to moderate 180°C (350°F/Gas 4).
2 Place the eggplants on a baking tray and bake for 35 minutes, or until soft. Peel away the skin and discard. Place the flesh in a food processor with the garlic, lemon juice, tahini and olive oil and season, to taste, with salt and pepper. Process for 20–30 seconds. Sprinkle with paprika and serve with pieces of Lebanese bread.

NOTE: The reason eggplants are sprinkled with salt and left to stand before using is that they can have a bitter taste. The salt draws out the bitter liquid from the eggplant. Slender eggplants do not need to be treated in this way before you use them. Tahini is a paste made from crushed sesame seeds and is available at the supermarket.

TZATZIKI
(MINTED CUCUMBER DIP)

Finely grate 1 Lebanese cucumber and squeeze out the excess moisture. Mix together in a bowl with 2 crushed cloves of garlic, 250 g (8 oz) natural yoghurt, 1 teaspoon white vinegar and a teaspoon each of chopped dill and mint. Add salt and black pepper, to taste. Serve with pitta or Turkish bread or crudités.

BELOW: Baba ganouj

BAKED POLENTA
WITH SPICY RELISH

Whisk the polenta into the boiling milk, pouring the polenta in a thin stream, until it thickens.

When the mixture is thick, stir continuously with a wooden spoon for 20 minutes, or until it leaves the side of the pan.

BAKED POLENTA WITH SPICY RELISH

Preparation time: 20 minutes + chilling
Total cooking time: 1 hour
Makes 48

600 ml (20 fl oz) milk
2/3 cup (100 g/3 1/2 oz) polenta
25 g (3/4 oz) butter, diced
1 tablespoon olive oil
1 tablespoon polenta, extra

Spicy relish

1 tablespoon oil
2 red onions, roughly chopped
500 g (1 lb) Roma (egg) tomatoes, roughly chopped
1 large red chilli, finely chopped
1/4 teaspoon Mexican chilli powder, or to taste
1 tablespoon soft brown sugar
1 tablespoon red wine vinegar

1 Lightly grease a 30 x 20 cm (12 x 8 inch) cake tin. Bring the milk to the boil in a pan. Reduce the heat to medium and whisk in the polenta, pouring it in a stream, until it thickens, then stir continuously with a wooden spoon for 20 minutes, or until it leaves the side of the pan. Remove from the heat and stir in the butter. Season, to taste.
2 Spread the polenta into the tin and smooth the top. Refrigerate for 2 hours, or until set.
3 To make the spicy tomato relish, heat the oil in a pan, add the onion and cook, stirring, over high heat, for 3 minutes. Add the tomato, chilli, chilli powder, sugar and vinegar. Simmer, stirring occasionally, for 20 minutes, or until thickened. Season with salt.
4 Preheat the oven to moderately hot 200°C (400°F/Gas 6). Turn the polenta out onto a board, cut into 5 cm (2 inch) squares, then into triangles. Place on a baking tray covered with paper, brush with olive oil and sprinkle with the extra polenta. Bake for 10 minutes, or until the polenta is golden and has a crust. Serve hot or warm with the warm relish.
NOTE: You can also use instant polenta which only takes about 3 minutes to cook.

TOMATO AND ANCHOVY TOASTS

Preparation time: 10 minutes
Total cooking time: 5 minutes
Makes 16

16 x 1 cm (1/2 inch) thick slices Italian bread
3 cloves garlic, halved
8 ripe vine-ripened tomatoes
1/3 cup (80 ml/2 3/4 fl oz) extra virgin olive oil
2 x 45 g (1 1/2 oz) cans anchovy fillets, drained and sliced lengthways

1 Toast the bread on both sides until golden. While warm, rub both sides of the toast with the cut garlic.
2 Cut the tomatoes in half and rub each side of the toast with them, so that the juice and seeds soak well into the toast but do not saturate it. Chop the remaining tomato and pile it on the toast.
3 Drizzle each toast with the oil and top with anchovy fillets. Sprinkle with salt and ground black pepper and serve.

FETA SPREAD

Preparation time: 10 minutes
Total cooking time: Nil
Makes about 1 cup (250 ml/8 fl oz)

175 g (6 oz) crumbled feta
100 g (3 1/2 oz) ricotta
3 tablespoons olive oil
15 g (1/2 oz) fresh mint, chopped
crusty bread, for serving.

1 Combine the feta, ricotta and olive oil in a bowl and mash with a fork until well combined. The mixture should still contain a few small lumps of cheese.
2 Add the mint and some cracked black pepper, to taste. Store in an airtight container in the refrigerator for up to 5 days. Toast the crusty bread and serve with the spread.
NOTE: These could be topped with slices of roasted tomato or pepper (capsicum).

OPPOSITE PAGE: Baked polenta with spicy relish (top); Tomato and anchovy toasts

GRILLED SARDINES WITH CUCUMBER

Preparation time: 20 minutes + marinating
Total cooking time: 10 minutes
Makes 30

★ ★

30 butterflied sardines, without heads
   (see Note)
2 tablespoons olive oil
2 tablespoons vegetable oil
2 tablespoons lemon juice
2 cloves garlic, sliced
1 tablespoon fresh oregano leaves
1 Lebanese cucumber
1/4 teaspoon sugar

1 Place half the sardines in a single layer in a non-metallic dish. Combine the olive and vegetable oils, lemon juice, garlic and oregano leaves and pour half over the sardines. Top with the remaining sardines and pour over the rest of the oil mixture. Cover with plastic wrap and marinate for 30 minutes in the refrigerator.
2 Meanwhile, using a wide vegetable peeler, peel strips lengthways off the cucumber, making four even sides and avoiding peeling off any cucumber with seeds. You should end up with about 15 slices of cucumber. Cut in half to make 30 strips the same length as the sardines.
3 Lay the cucumber strips flat around the sides and base of a colander and sprinkle with sugar and a little salt. Place over a bowl. Leave for 15 minutes to drain off any juices.
4 Preheat the grill. Wash the cucumber well and pat dry with paper towels. Place one strip of cucumber on the flesh side of each sardine and roll up like a pinwheel. Secure with toothpicks.
5 Place half the sardines under the grill and cook for 5 minutes, or until cooked through. Repeat with the remaining sardines. Serve warm, with tzatziki (see page 167) if desired.
NOTE: Butterflied sardines are sardines that have been gutted, deboned and opened out flat.
IN ADVANCE: The sardines can be rolled in the cucumber a day ahead. Keep covered in the refrigerator.

ABOVE: Grilled sardines with cucumber

CHICKEN ROLLS

Preparation time: 1 hour 15 minutes
Total cooking time: 1 hour 5 minutes
Makes about 40

60 g (2 oz) butter
1 large onion, chopped
2 cloves garlic, crushed
2 tablespoons plain flour
1/2 cup (125 ml/4 fl oz) chicken stock
1/2 cup (125 ml/4 fl oz) milk
1 large barbecued chicken, skin removed and
   flesh shredded
1/4 cup (25 g/3/4 oz) grated Parmesan
2 teaspoons fresh thyme leaves
1/4 cup (25 g/3/4 oz) dry breadcrumbs
2 eggs, lightly beaten
13 sheets filo pastry, cut into thirds crossways
140 g (4 1/2 oz) butter, extra, melted

1 Melt the butter in a pan and add the onion.
Cook over low heat for 12 minutes, or until soft,
stirring occasionally. Increase the heat to
medium–high and add the garlic. Cook, stirring,
for 1 minute, then add the flour and cook for
1 minute. Remove from the heat and gradually
stir in the stock and milk. Return to the heat and
stir constantly until the sauce boils and thickens.
Boil for 1 minute, then remove from the heat
and add the chicken, Parmesan, thyme,
breadcrumbs, salt and pepper. Cool, then stir in
the eggs.
2 Preheat the oven to hot 220°C (425°F/Gas 7).
Lightly grease three baking trays.
3 Put one piece of filo pastry on the bench with
the short end closest to you (cover the remaining
pieces with a damp tea towel). Brush with the
extra melted butter and place a level tablespoon
of chicken mixture on the base end closest to
you. Fold in the sides, brush along the length
with butter and roll up tightly to form a roll
8 cm (3 inches) long. Put onto the baking tray
and brush the top with some of the butter.
Repeat with the remaining filo, butter and
chicken mixture.
4 Bake for 15 minutes in the top half of the
oven until well browned. Serve hot.

BELOW: Chicken rolls

STUFFED MUSSELS

Scrub the mussels with a stiff brush and pull off the hairy beard. Discard any open or broken mussels.

Spoon the mussel mixture into the shells, top with white sauce and smooth with a flat-bladed knife.

STUFFED MUSSELS

Preparation time: 40 minutes + cooling
Total cooking time: 16 minutes
Makes 18

✲ ✲

18 black mussels
2 teaspoons olive oil
2 spring onions, finely chopped
1 clove garlic, crushed
1 tablespoon tomato paste (tomato purée)
2 teaspoons lemon juice
3 tablespoons chopped fresh flat-leaf parsley
1/3 cup (35 g/1 1/4 oz) dry breadcrumbs
2 eggs, beaten
olive oil, for deep-frying

White sauce

40 g (1 1/4 oz) butter
1/4 cup (30 g/1 oz) plain flour
1/3 cup (80 ml/2 3/4 fl oz) milk

1 Scrub the mussels and remove their beards. Discard any open ones that do not close when given a sharp tap. Bring 1 cup (250 ml/8 fl oz) water to the boil in a medium saucepan, add the mussels, cover and cook for 5 minutes, shaking occasionally. Strain the liquid into a jug until you have 1/3 cup (80 ml/2 3/4 fl oz). Discard any unopened mussels. Remove the mussels from their shells and discard half the shells. Finely chop the mussels.

2 Heat the oil in a pan, add the spring onion and cook for 1 minute. Add the garlic and cook for 1 minute. Stir in the mussels, tomato paste, lemon juice and 2 tablespoons of parsley. Season with salt and pepper and set aside to cool.

3 To make the white sauce, melt the butter in a pan over low heat, add the flour and cook for 1 minute, or until pale and foaming. Remove from the heat and gradually stir in the reserved mussel liquid, the milk and some pepper. Return to the heat and stir constantly until the sauce boils and thickens and leaves the side of the pan. Transfer to a bowl to cool.

4 Spoon the mussel mixture into the shells. Top with the sauce and smooth so it is heaped.

5 Combine the crumbs and remaining parsley. Dip the mussels in the egg, then the crumbs, pressing on to cover the top.

6 Fill a deep heavy-based pan one third full of oil and heat to 180°C (350°F), or until a cube of bread dropped into the oil browns in 15 seconds. Cook the mussels in batches for 2 minutes, or until brown. Remove with a slotted spoon and drain on crumpled paper towels. Serve hot.

ABOVE: Stuffed mussels

STUFFED MUSHROOMS

Preparation time: 25 minutes + cooling
Total cooking time: 25 minutes
Makes about 30

850 g (1 lb 12 oz) cap mushrooms

40 g (1¼ oz) butter

1 small onion, finely chopped

100 g (3½ oz) pork mince

60 g (2 oz) chorizo sausage, finely chopped

1 tablespoon tomato paste (tomato purée)

2 tablespoons dry breadcrumbs

1 tablespoon chopped fresh flat-leaf parsley

1 Remove the stalks from the mushrooms, then finely chop the stalks. Set aside.
2 Melt the butter in a frying pan over low heat, add the onion and cook, stirring occasionally, for 5 minutes, or until soft. Increase the heat to high, add the pork mince, and cook for 1 minute, stirring constantly and breaking up any lumps. Add the mushroom stalks and chorizo and continue cooking for 1 minute, or until the mixture is dry and browned. Add the tomato paste and ½ cup (125 ml/4 fl oz) water. Bring to the boil, then reduce the heat to low and simmer

for 5 minutes, or until thick. Stir in the breadcrumbs, then transfer to a bowl and cool.
3 Preheat the oven to hot 210°C (415°F/ Gas 6–7). Lightly grease a baking tray. Spoon about 1½ teaspoons of the cooled meat into the mushroom caps, smoothing the top with a flat-bladed knife so that the filling is slightly domed. Place on the tray and bake in the top half of the oven for 10 minutes. Sprinkle with the parsley and serve hot.

RED PEPPER (CAPSICUM) AND WALNUT DIP

Quarter and seed 2 red peppers (capsicums). Grill skin-side-up until the skin is black and blistered. Cool in a plastic bag, then peel. Heat 1 tablespoon olive oil in a pan, add 1 chopped onion and 1 crushed clove garlic and cook until soft. Stir in ½ teaspoon dried chilli flakes. Process ½ cup (60 g/2 oz) walnuts until fine and add the peeled peppers, onion mixture, 3 tablespoons olive oil, 2 teaspoons red wine vinegar and ¼ teaspoon salt. Process until fine and almost smooth. Can be made up to 5 days ahead and chilled in an airtight container. Makes 1 cup (250 ml/8 fl oz).

ABOVE: Stuffed mushrooms

CAULIFLOWER FRITTERS

Preparation time: 15 minutes + standing
Total cooking time: 15 minutes
Makes about 40 pieces

600 g (1 1/4 lb) cauliflower
1/2 cup (55 g/2 oz) besan flour
2 teaspoons ground cumin
1 teaspoon ground coriander
1 teaspoon ground turmeric
pinch of cayenne pepper
1 egg, lightly beaten
1 egg yolk
oil, for deep-frying

1 Cut the cauliflower into bite-sized florets. Sift the flour and spices into a bowl, then stir in 1/2 teaspoon salt and make a well in the centre.
2 Combine 1/4 cup (60 ml/2 fl oz) water with the egg and egg yolk and gradually pour into the well, whisking to make a smooth lump-free batter. Cover and leave for 30 minutes.
3 Fill a deep heavy-based pan one third full of oil and heat to 180°C (350°F), or until a cube of bread dropped into the oil browns in 15 seconds. Holding the florets by the stem, dip into the batter, draining the excess back into the bowl. Deep-fry in batches for 3–4 minutes, or until puffed and brown. Drain, season and serve hot.

CHEESY ZUCCHINI FLOWERS

Preparation time: 1 hour 20 minutes + standing
Total cooking time: 10 minutes
Makes 24

1 1/2 cups (185 g/6 oz) plain flour
7 g (1/4 oz) dry yeast or 15 g (1/2 oz) compressed fresh yeast
24 zucchini with flowers
50 g (1 3/4 oz) kefalotyri cheese or Parmesan
8 anchovy fillets in oil, drained
oil, for deep-frying

1 Sift the flour and 1 1/4 teaspoons salt into a bowl and make a well. Whisk the yeast and 1 1/4 cups (315 ml/10 fl oz) warm water in a bowl until dissolved and pour into the well. Gradually stir with the whisk to form a thick batter. Cover with plastic wrap and leave in a warm place for 1 hour, or until frothy. Do not stir.
2 Gently open the zucchini flowers and remove the centre stamens. Wash and drain. Cut the cheese into 1 cm (1/2 inch) cubes. Cut the anchovies into 1.5 cm (5/8 inch) pieces.
3 Put a cube of cheese and a piece of anchovy into the centre of each flower. Fold the petals around them. Fill a deep pan one third full of oil and heat to 180°C (350°F), or until a cube of bread dropped into the oil browns in 15 seconds. Dip the flowers into the batter, turning to coat and drain off the excess. Deep-fry in batches for 1–2 minutes, or until puffed and lightly brown. Drain on crumpled paper towel. Serve hot.

SPANISH TORTILLA

Preparation time: 20 minutes
Total cooking time: 30 minutes
Makes 16 wedges

1/2 cup (125 ml/4 fl oz) olive oil
2 large potatoes (600 g/1 1/4 lb), peeled and cut into 5 mm (1/4 inch) slices
2 large onions, sliced
3 eggs
1/2 teaspoon salt
1/2 teaspoon pepper

1 Heat the oil in a 20 cm (8 inch) diameter, 5 cm (2 inch) deep non-stick frying pan. Place alternate layers of potato and onion in the pan, cover and cook for 8 minutes over low heat. Using tongs, turn the layers in sections (it doesn't matter if they break up). Cover and cook for 8 minutes, without allowing the potato to colour.
2 Place a strainer over a bowl and drain the potato mixture, reserving 1 tablespoon of the oil. (The rest can be used for cooking another time, it will have a delicately sweet onion flavour.)
3 Place the eggs, salt and pepper in a bowl and whisk to combine. Add the potato mixture, pressing down with the back of a spoon to completely cover with the egg.
4 Heat the reserved oil in the same frying pan over high heat. Pour in the egg mixture, pressing down to even it out. Reduce the heat to low, cover with a lid or foil and cook for 12 minutes, or until set. Gently shake the pan to ensure the tortilla is not sticking. Leave for 5 minutes, then invert onto a plate. Cut into wedges. Serve hot.

ANCHOVY FILLETS
The anchovy is a small saltwater fish which has been popular in Italy for centuries. Supplies from the waters of southern Europe have almost been depleted so now they often come from Africa and South America. There is also an Australian anchovy. Anchovies have a slightly oily flesh and a strong taste. If you find them too salty, they can be soaked in milk or water for about 20 minutes before use. They are commonly sold in jars and cans, preserved in and marinated in oil, or preserved in salt.

OPPOSITE PAGE:
Cauliflower fritters (top);
Cheesy zucchini flowers

STUFFED PEPPERS

Spoon filling onto the end of each pepper strip, then roll up and push a toothpick through.

Coat the peppers in flour, then dip in egg, drain off the excess and roll in the breadcrumbs to coat.

STUFFED PEPPERS (CAPSICUMS)

Preparation time: 40 minutes + cooling
Total cooking time: 25 minutes
Makes 20

★★

5 large red peppers (capsicums)
60 g (2 oz) butter
I small pickling onion, finely chopped
I clove garlic, crushed
1/4 cup (30 g/I oz) plain flour
I cup (250 ml/8 fl oz) milk
3 x 100 g (3 1/2 oz) cans tuna in oil, drained
I tablespoon chopped fresh flat-leaf parsley
2/3 cup (85 g/3 oz) plain flour, extra
2 eggs, lightly beaten
1/2 teaspoon paprika
2/3 cup (65 g/2 1/4 oz) dry breadcrumbs
olive oil, for deep-frying

1 Preheat the grill. Cut the peppers into quarters. Cook, skin-side-up, under a hot grill until the skin is black and blistered. Place in a plastic bag and leave to cool, then peel away the skin.

2 Heat the butter in a pan over medium heat. Add the onion and cook, stirring occasionally, for 2 minutes, or until soft. Add the garlic and cook for 1 minute. Add the flour and cook, stirring, for 1 minute, or until bubbly and just beginning to change colour. Remove from the heat and gradually stir in the milk. Return to the heat and stir constantly until the mixture boils and thickens and leaves the side of the pan. Stir in the tuna, parsley and some salt. Transfer to a bowl to cool.

3 Spoon 1 tablespoon of the filling onto the base end of each pepper strip, roll up and secure the end with a toothpick. Place the extra flour in a shallow dish, the eggs in a shallow bowl and combine the paprika and breadcrumbs in another shallow dish.

4 Coat the peppers in the flour, then the eggs, allowing the excess to drip away, then toss in the crumbs.

5 Fill a deep, heavy-based pan a third full of oil and heat to 180°C (350°F). The oil is ready when a cube of bread dropped in the oil browns in 15 seconds. Cook in batches for 2 minutes, or until golden. Remove with a slotted spoon, drain on crumpled paper towels and remove the toothpicks. Serve warm or hot.

ABOVE: Stuffed peppers

TAHINI AND CHILLI PALMIERS

Preparation time: 25 minutes + chilling
Total cooking time: 20 minutes
Makes 32

¹/₂ cup (135 g/4¹/₂ oz) tahini
I fresh red chilli, seeded and finely chopped
¹/₂ teaspoon paprika
2 sheets ready-rolled puff pastry, thawed

I Preheat the oven to moderately hot 200°C (400°F/Gas 6).
2 Put the tahini, chilli and paprika in a bowl, season with some salt and stir to combine. Spread half the paste evenly over each pastry sheet, making sure the paste goes all the way to the edges.
3 Take one pastry sheet and fold from opposite sides until the folds meet in the middle. Then fold one side over the other to resemble a closed book. Repeat with the remaining pastry sheet and tahini mixture. Refrigerate the pastry at this stage for at least 30 minutes, to firm it up and make it easier to work with.
4 Cut the pastry into 1 cm (¹/₂ inch) slices. Cover two baking trays with baking paper and place the palmiers on them, making sure that the palmiers are not too close to one another as they will spread during cooking.
5 Bake the palmiers for 10–12 minutes on one side, then flip them over and bake for another 5–6 minutes, or until golden and cooked through. They are delicious served at room temperature or cold.
NOTE: To freeze the palmiers, place the sliced, uncooked palmiers on a tray and freeze until firm, then seal in plastic bags. Allow to thaw on trays and cook as above. Cooked palmiers can be stored in an airtight container for up to 1 week. If the palmiers soften, recrisp in a moderate oven for 3–5 minutes, then cool on a wire rack. Tahini is a paste made from crushed sesame seeds and is available from most supermarkets and health food stores.

TAHINI
This thick smooth paste, made from crushed sesame seeds, originated in the Middle East. Tahini is often used as an ingredient in hummus and other dips and sauces. It is also used in the making of confectionery such as halva, as well as in biscuits and cakes.

LEFT: Tahini and chilli palmiers

OLIVES
All these recipes will keep in the fridge for 3 months if stored in properly sterilized jars. Wash jars and lids thoroughly in boiling water, rinse in boiling water and dry in a slow 150°C (300°F/Gas 2) oven for 30 minutes.

OLIVES WITH HERBS DE PROVENCE
Rinse and drain 500 g (1 lb) Niçoise or Ligurian olives. Put 1 crushed clove garlic, 2 teaspoons chopped fresh basil, 1 teaspoon each chopped fresh thyme, rosemary, marjoram, oregano and mint, 1 teaspoon fennel seeds, 2 tablespoons lemon juice and ½ cup (125 ml/4 fl oz) olive oil in a bowl and mix together. Layer the olives and marinade in a wide-necked, 3-cup (750 ml/24 fl oz) sterilized jar, adding extra olive oil to cover the olives. Seal and marinate in the refrigerator for at least 1 week before using. Serve at room temperature.

HONEY CITRUS OLIVES
Mix together the rind of 1 lemon, lime and orange, 2 tablespoons lime juice, 4 tablespoons lemon juice, 1 tablespoon orange juice, 1 tablespoon honey, 2 teaspoons wholegrain mustard, ½ cup (125 ml/4 fl oz) extra virgin olive oil, 2 thinly sliced cloves garlic, ¼ teaspoon dried oregano or 1 tablespoon chopped fresh oregano leaves and 6 thin slices of lemon and lime. Add 1½ cups (265 g/ 8½ oz) drained unpitted black olives, 1½ cups (265 g/8½ oz) drained unpitted green olives and 2 tablespoons chopped fresh parsley. Place in a wide-necked, 3-cup (750 ml/24 fl oz) sterilized jar, then seal and marinate in the refrigerator for at least 1 week before using. Serve at room temperature.

LEMON OLIVES WITH VERMOUTH

Combine 3 tablespoons dry vermouth, 1 tablespoon lemon juice, 2 teaspoons shredded lemon rind and 2 tablespoons extra virgin olive oil. Rinse 1 cup (170 g/5½ oz) of Spanish green or stuffed olives and pat dry. Add to the marinade and toss well. Cover and refrigerate overnight. Serve at room temperature.

DILL, GARLIC AND ORANGE OLIVES

Combine 500 g (1 lb) Kalamata olives with 3 tablespoons coarsely chopped fresh dill, 1 bruised clove garlic, 4 thin slices of orange cut into eighths and 2 torn bay leaves. Spoon into a 1-litre sterilized jar and pour in about 1¾ cups (440 ml/14 fl oz) olive oil or enough to cover the olives completely. Seal and marinate in the refrigerator for at least 2 days. Serve at room temperature.

CHILLI AND LEMON OLIVES

Combine 500 g (1 lb) cured black olives (olives with wrinkled skin) with 2 teaspoons finely grated lemon rind, 2 teaspoons chopped fresh oregano and 3 teaspoons dried chilli flakes. Transfer to a 3-cup (750 ml/24 fl oz) sterilized jar; cover with olive oil. Seal; chill for at least 2 days. Serve at room temperature.

SUN-DRIED TOMATO OLIVES

Rinse 500 g (1 lb) Spanish black olives; pat dry. Score or crack the olives. Layer in a 3-cup (750 ml/24 fl oz) sterilized jar, with 100 g (3½ oz) drained and chopped sun-dried tomatoes (reserve the oil), 2 crushed cloves garlic, 2 bay leaves, 3 teaspoons fresh thyme leaves and 2 teaspoons red wine vinegar. Pour over the reserved oil and 1 cup (250 ml/ 8 fl oz) extra virgin olive oil, or enough to cover. Seal and refrigerate overnight. Serve at room temperature.

MIXED OLIVE PICKLES

Combine 200 g (6½ oz) jumbo green olives, 4 gherkins, thickly sliced diagonally, 1 tablespoon capers, 2 brown pickling onions, quartered, 2 teaspoons mustard seeds and 1 tablespoon fresh dill sprigs in a bowl. Spoon into a 2-cup (500 ml/16 fl oz) sterilized jar and pour in ½ cup (125 ml/4 fl oz) tarragon vinegar. Top with about ½ cup (125 ml/4 fl oz) olive oil, or enough to cover completely. Seal and refrigerate for at least 2 days. Shake the jar occasionally. Serve at room temperature.

CLOCKWISE, FROM TOP LEFT: Olives with herbs de provence; Honey citrus olives; Lemon olives with vermouth; Dill, garlic and orange olives; Chilli and lemon olives; Sun-dried tomato olives; Mixed olive pickles

PINE NUTS

The trees on which pine nuts grow do not yield a heavy crop until the trees are at least 70 years old. This is part of the reason they are expensive. The pine trees they come from are native to southern Europe, Mexico and some parts of the United States. Pine nuts are high in protein, iron, phosphorous and thiamin.

VEGETARIAN DOLMADES

Preparation time: 1 hour + cooling
Total cooking time: 1 hour 15 minutes
Makes about 50

★★★

1/2 cup (125 ml/4 fl oz) olive oil
6 spring onions, chopped
3/4 cup (150 g/5 oz) long-grain rice
1/4 cup (15 g/1/2 oz) chopped fresh mint
2 tablespoons chopped fresh dill
2/3 cup (170 ml/5 1/2 fl oz) lemon juice
1/4 cup (35 g/1 1/4 oz) currants
1/4 cup (40 g/1 1/4 oz) pine nuts
240 g (7 1/2 oz) packaged vine leaves (about 50)
2 tablespoons olive oil, extra

1 Heat the oil in a medium pan. Add the spring onion and cook over medium heat for 1 minute. Stir in the rice, mint, dill, half the lemon juice, and season, to taste. Add 1 cup (250 ml/8 fl oz) water and bring to the boil, then reduce the heat, cover and simmer for 20 minutes. Remove the lid, fork through the currants and pine nuts,

cover with a paper towel, then the lid and leave to cool.
2 Rinse the vine leaves and gently separate. Drain, then dry on paper towels. Trim any thick stems with scissors. Line the base of a 20 cm (8 inch) pan with any torn or misshapen leaves. Choose the larger leaves for filling and use the smaller leaves to patch up any gaps.
3 Place a leaf shiny-side-down. Spoon a tablespoon of filling into the centre, bring in the sides and roll up tightly from the stem end. Place seam-side-down, with the stem end closest to you, in the base of the pan, arranging them close together in a single layer.
4 Pour in the rest of the lemon juice, the extra oil and about 3/4 cup (185 ml/6 fl oz) water to just cover the dolmades. Cover with an inverted plate and place a tin on the plate to firmly compress the dolmades and keep them in place while they are cooking. Cover with the lid.
5 Bring to the boil, then reduce the heat and simmer for 45 minutes. Cool in the pan. Serve at room temperature.
NOTE: Store, covered with the cooking liquid, in the refrigerator for up to 2 weeks.

ABOVE: Vegetarian dolmades

FELAFEL

Preparation time: 2 hours 15 minutes
  + overnight soaking
Total cooking time: 15 minutes
Makes about 16

250 g (8 oz) dried chickpeas
4 spring onions, chopped
2 cloves garlic, crushed
1/2 cup (15 g/1/2 oz) chopped fresh flat-leaf parsley
1/4 cup (15 g/1/2 oz) chopped fresh mint
1/2 cup (25 g/3/4 oz) chopped fresh coriander
1/4 teaspoon cayenne pepper
2 teaspoons ground cumin
2 teaspoons ground coriander
1/2 teaspoon baking powder
oil, for deep-frying

1 Put the chickpeas in a large bowl, cover with plenty of cold water and soak overnight. Drain.
2 Combine the chickpeas, spring onion, garlic, parsley, mint, coriander, cayenne, cumin, ground coriander, baking powder and 1 teaspoon salt. Process batches in a processor for 30–40 seconds, or until finely chopped and the mixture holds together. Refrigerate, uncovered, for 2 hours.
3 Press 2 tablespoons of mixture together in the palm of your hand and form into a patty. Fill a deep heavy-based pan one third full of oil and heat to 180°C (350°F), or until a cube of bread dropped into the oil browns in 15 seconds. Deep-fry the felafel in batches for 3–4 minutes, or until well browned. Drain on crumpled paper towels and serve hot with hummus.

LABNEH

Preparation time: 20 minutes + 4 days chilling
Total cooking time: Nil
Makes 12

2 cups (500 g/1 lb) thick Greek-style natural
   yoghurt
2 teaspoons sea salt
1 tablespoon dried oregano
2 teaspoons dried thyme leaves
11/3 cups (350 ml/11 fl oz) olive oil
1 bay leaf

1 Fold a 60 x 30 cm (24 x 12 inch) piece of muslin in half to make a 30 cm (12 inch) square.
2 Combine the yoghurt, salt and 1 teaspoon black pepper in a bowl. Line a bowl with the muslin and spoon the mixture into the centre. Bring the corners together and, using a piece of kitchen string, tie as closely as possible to the yoghurt, leaving a loop at the end. Thread the loop through the handle of a wooden spoon and hang over a bowl to drain in the fridge for 3 days.
3 Combine the oregano and thyme in a shallow bowl. Pour half the oil into a 2-cup (500 ml/ 16 fl oz) jar and add the bay leaf.
4 Roll level tablespoons of the yoghurt into balls. Toss in the combined herbs and place into the jar of oil. Pour in the remaining oil to cover the balls completely, seal and refrigerate for at least 1 day. Serve at room temperature, with chunky bread.

*ABOVE: Felafel (top);
Labneh*

FRIED CHICKPEAS

Preparation time: 30 minutes +overnight soaking
Total cooking time: 15 minutes
Makes about 2¹/₂ cups (600 g/20 oz)

 ✫✫

300 g (10 oz) dried chickpeas
oil, for deep-frying
¹/₂ teaspoon mild or hot paprika, to taste
¹/₄ teaspoon cayenne pepper

1 Put the chickpeas in a large bowl, cover with plenty of cold water and soak overnight. Drain well and pat dry with paper towels.
2 Fill a deep heavy-based pan one third full of oil and heat to 180°C (350°F), or until a cube of bread dropped into the oil browns in 15 seconds. Deep-fry half the chickpeas for 3 minutes. Remove with a slotted spoon. Drain on crumpled paper towel and repeat with the rest of the chickpeas. Partially cover the pan as some beans may pop. Don't leave the oil unattended.
3 Reheat the oil and fry the chickpeas again in batches for 3 minutes each batch, or until browned. Drain. Season the paprika with salt and cayenne pepper, and sprinkle over the hot chickpeas. Cool.

HUMMUS

Preparation time: 30 minutes + overnight soaking
Total cooking time: 1 hour
Makes about 2 cups (500 g/16 oz)

 ✫✫

125 g (4 oz) dried chickpeas
1 tablespoon olive oil
1 small finely chopped onion
1¹/₂ teaspoons ground cumin
pinch of cayenne pepper
2 tablespoons lemon juice
¹/₂ cup (125 ml/4 fl oz) olive oil, extra
3 cloves garlic, crushed

1 Put the chickpeas in a large bowl, cover with plenty of cold water and soak overnight. Rinse well and transfer to a pan of boiling water. Cook, covered, over medium heat for 1 hour, or until tender. Drain and return to the pan. Add the tablespoon of olive oil, onion, cumin and cayenne pepper to the pan and cook over high heat for 1 minute. Transfer to a food processor, add the lemon juice, extra olive oil and garlic, season with salt and process until smooth. Add water if you prefer a thinner consistency.

HUMMUS
Hummus means chickpeas in Arabic. You will see it spelt in many ways including homos, houmus, houmous and humus. The well-known recipe from Syria, *Hummus-bi-tahina,* has the addition of tahini. To make this classic dish, add 2 tablespoons of tahini to the recipe on this page. Add to the cooked chickpeas just before processing. Tahini, a paste made from crushed sesame seeds, is available at most supermarkets.

ABOVE: Fried chickpeas

MEAT PATTIES WITH HALOUMI FILLING

Preparation time: 25 minutes + chilling
Total cooking time: 10 minutes
Makes 24

★ ★

8 slices (125 g/4 oz) white bread, crusts
    removed
700 g (23 oz) lamb or beef mince
1 tablespoon chopped fresh flat-leaf parsley
3 tablespoons chopped fresh mint leaves
1 onion, grated
2 eggs, lightly beaten
140 g (4¹/₂ oz) haloumi cheese (see Note)
¹/₃ cup (40 g/1¹/₄ oz) plain flour
olive oil, for shallow-frying

1 Put the bread in a bowl, cover with water and then squeeze out as much water as possible. Place the bread in a bowl with the mince, parsley, mint, onion, egg, pepper and ¹/₂ teaspoon salt. Knead the mixture by hand for 2–3 minutes, breaking up the mince and any large pieces of bread with your fingers. The mixture should be smooth and leave the side of the bowl. Cover and refrigerate for 30 minutes.
2 Cut the haloumi into 24 rectangles, 3 x 1 x 1 cm (1¹/₄ x ¹/₂ x ¹/₂ inch). Place the flour in a shallow dish. Divide the mince mixture into level tablespoon portions. Roll a portion into a long shape and flatten in the palm of your hand. Place the cheese in the centre and top with another portion of mince. Pinch the edges together and roll into a torpedo 6 cm (2¹/₂ inches) long. Repeat with the remaining mince.
3 Heat 2 cm (³/₄ inch) oil in a deep heavy-based frying pan to 180°C (350°F), or until a cube of bread dropped into the oil browns in 15 seconds. Toss the patties in flour, shake off the excess and fry in batches for 3–5 minutes, or until brown and cooked through. Drain on crumpled paper towels. Serve hot.
NOTE: Haloumi is a creamy white sheep's milk cheese kept in brine. It can be bought from delicatessens and supermarkets.

BELOW: Meat patties with haloumi filling

ABOVE: *Fried whitebait*

FRIED WHITEBAIT

Preparation time: 10 minutes + chilling
Total cooking time: 10 minutes
Serves 6–8

500 g (1 lb) whitebait

2 teaspoons sea salt

1/3 cup (40 g/1 1/4 oz) plain flour

1/4 cup (30 g/1 oz) cornflour

2 teaspoons finely chopped fresh
    flat-leaf parsley

olive oil, for deep-frying

1 lemon, cut into wedges, for serving

1 Combine the whitebait and sea salt in a bowl and mix well. Cover and refrigerate.
2 Combine the sifted flours and chopped parsley in a bowl and season well with cracked pepper. Fill a deep heavy-based pan one third full of oil and heat to 180°C (350°F), or until a cube of bread browns in 15 seconds. Toss a third of the whitebait in the flour mixture, shake off the excess and deep-fry for 1½ minutes, or until pale and crisp. Remove with a slotted spoon and drain well on crumpled paper towels. Repeat with the remaining whitebait, cooking in two batches.
3 Reheat the oil and fry the whitebait a second time in three batches for 1 minute each, or until lightly browned. Drain on crumpled paper towels and serve hot with lemon wedges.

TARAMASALATA

Remove the crusts from 4 slices of white bread. Put the bread in a bowl, cover with water, drain and squeeze out as much water as possible. Place in a bowl. Finely grate a small onion into the bowl and add 100 g (3½ oz) tarama (cod roe), 2 tablespoons freshly squeezed lemon juice, 3 tablespoons olive oil and a pinch of black pepper. Mix with a fork until well combined. Alternatively, process the ingredients until smooth. Taramasalata can be made up to 3 days ahead and stored in an airtight container in the refrigerator. Makes about 1 cup (250 ml/8 fl oz).

BACALAO CROQUETTES WITH SKORDALIA

Preparation time: 50 minutes + 8 hours soaking
Total cooking time: 55 minutes
Makes 24

400 g (13 oz) dried salt cod or bacalao
  (see Note)
300 g (10 oz) floury potatoes, unpeeled
1 small brown pickling onion, grated
2 tablespoons chopped fresh flat-leaf parsley
1 egg, lightly beaten
oil, for deep-frying

Skordalia

250 g (8 oz) floury potatoes, unpeeled
2 cloves garlic, crushed
1 tablespoon white wine vinegar
2 tablespoons olive oil

1 Remove the excess salt from the cod by placing in a large bowl, covering with cold water and leaving to soak for 8–12 hours, changing the water three times. Drain on crumpled paper towels.
2 To make the skordalia, boil or steam the 250 g potatoes until tender, peel and mash. Cool and add the garlic, vinegar and oil. Season with salt and cracked black pepper, mix well and set aside.
3 Put the cod in a pan, cover with water, bring to the boil, then reduce the heat and simmer for 15 minutes. Drain well and dry on paper towels. When cool enough to handle, remove the skin and bones from the cod and flake with your fingers into a bowl. Meanwhile, boil or steam the potatoes until tender, peel and mash well.
4 Add the mashed potato to the cod with the onion, parsley, egg and ½ teaspoon cracked pepper. Mix well with a wooden spoon to form a thick mixture. Taste before seasoning with salt.
5 Fill a deep heavy-based pan one third full of oil and heat to 180°C (350°F), or until a cube of bread dropped into the oil browns in 15 seconds. Drop level tablespoons of the mixture into the oil and cook in batches for 2–3 minutes, or until well browned. Drain on crumpled paper towel. Serve hot with skordalia.
NOTE: Dried bacalao or salted cod is available at delicatessens or fish markets. The skordalia can be made up to 4 days ahead and kept covered in the refrigerator until needed.

POTATOES
The texture, whether waxy or floury when cooked, is the main concern when selecting the type of potato for a recipe. Waxy potatoes, such as Desiree and Bintji, have a high moisture content and are low in starch. Most have a creamy, dense flesh and are suitable for salads and gratins as they hold together. They are not suitable for chips. Floury potatoes, such as the Russet and King Edward, have a lower moisture content and are higher in starch, with coarser flesh. This makes them good for mashing, baking and chip-making. There are more varieties of potato being sold, some of them good all-rounders.

LEFT: Bacalao croquettes with skordalia

1 Lightly oil a 3 cm (1¼ inch) deep baking tin with a base measuring 26 x 17 cm (10½ x 6½ inches).

2 Sift the flour and ½ teaspoon salt into a bowl. Rub the butter into the flour until it resembles fine breadcrumbs. Pour in the oil and rub it in by lifting the flour mixture onto one hand and lightly rubbing the other hand over the top. The mixture should clump together. Make a well in the centre and, while mixing by hand, add enough water to form a firm supple dough. Knead gently to bring the dough together—it may not be completely smooth. Cover with plastic wrap and chill for 1 hour.

3 Trim away the bottom quarter from the spinach stalks. Wash and shred the remaining leaves and stalks. Pile the spinach onto a clean tea towel, twist as tightly as possible and squeeze out as much moisture as possible. Put into a bowl with the leek, nutmeg, dill, feta, breadcrumbs and ½ teaspoon cracked black pepper.

4 Preheat the oven to hot 220°C (425°F/Gas 7). Roll out just over half the dough on a lightly floured surface until large enough to line the base and sides of the tin. Lift the dough into the tin, pressing evenly over the base and sides.

5 Add the eggs and oil to the spinach mixture. Mix with your hand, but do not overmix or the mixture will become too wet. Spoon into the pastry-lined tin.

6 Roll out the remaining pastry on a lightly floured surface until large enough to cover the tin. Lift onto the tin and press the two pastry edges firmly together to seal. Trim the excess pastry with a sharp knife from the outer edge of the tin, then brush the top with a little extra olive oil. Using a sharp knife, mark into three strips lengthways and then diagonally into diamonds. Make two or three small slits through the top layer of pastry to allow the steam to escape during cooking.

7 Bake the pie on the centre shelf for 45–50 minutes, or until well browned. Cover with foil if the pastry is overbrowning. The pie is cooked if it slides when you gently shake the tin. Turn out onto a wire rack to cool for 10 minutes, then transfer to a cutting board or back into the tin to cut into diamonds. Serve warm or cold.

SPINACH PIE DIAMONDS

Preparation time: 50 minutes + chilling
Total cooking time: 50 minutes
Makes about 15

★★

2 cups (250 g/4 oz) plain flour
30 g butter, chopped
¼ cup (60 ml/2 fl oz) olive oil
½ cup (125 ml/4 fl oz) warm water

Filling

420 g (14 oz) English spinach
1 leek, white part only, halved lengthways and thinly sliced
¼ teaspoon ground nutmeg
2 teaspoons chopped fresh dill
200 g (6½ oz) feta, crumbled
1 tablespoon dry breadcrumbs
3 eggs, lightly beaten
2 tablespoons olive oil

ABOVE: Spinach pie diamonds

KIBBEH

Preparation time: 45 minutes + cooling + chilling
Total cooking time: 25 minutes
Makes 15

★★★

1⅓ cups (235 g/7½ oz) fine burghul wheat
150 g (5 oz) lean lamb, chopped
1 onion, grated
2 tablespoons plain flour
1 teaspoon ground allspice

Filling

2 teaspoons olive oil
1 small onion, finely chopped
100 g (3½ oz) lean lamb mince
½ teaspoon ground allspice
½ teaspoon ground cinnamon
⅓ cup (80 ml/2¾ fl oz) beef stock
2 tablespoons pine nuts
2 tablespoons chopped fresh mint

1 Put the burghul wheat in a large bowl, cover with boiling water and leave for 5 minutes. Drain in a colander, pressing well to remove the water. Spread on paper towels to absorb the remaining moisture.

2 Process the wheat, lamb, onion, flour, and allspice until a fine paste forms. Season well, then refrigerate for 1 hour.

3 For the filling, heat the oil in a frying pan, add the onion and cook over low heat for 3 minutes, or until soft. Add the mince, allspice and cinnamon, and stir over high heat, for 3 minutes. Add the stock and cook, partially covered, over low heat for 6 minutes, or until the mince is soft. Roughly chop the pine nuts and stir in with the mint. Season well with salt and cracked pepper, then transfer to a bowl and allow to cool.

4 Shape 2 tablespoons of the wheat mixture into a sausage shape 6 cm (2½ inches) long. Dip your hands in cold water, and with your finger, make a long hole through the centre and gently work your finger around to make a shell. Fill with 2 teaspoons of the filling and seal, moulding it into a torpedo shape. Smooth over any cracks with your fingers. Place on a foil-lined tray and refrigerate, uncovered, for 1 hour.

5 Fill a deep heavy-based pan one third full of oil and heat the oil to 180° (350°F), or until a cube of bread dropped into the oil browns in 15 seconds. Deep-fry the kibbeh in batches for 2–3 minutes, or until well browned. Drain on crumpled paper towels. Serve hot.

ONIONS
A member of the lily family, onions are one of the staples in the pantry. The colour, shape and intensity of flavour varies greatly. Raw onions have a strong flavour which is mellowed when cooked. Many savoury recipes, including soups, sauces, tarts, casseroles and curries, call for an onion or two to enhance their flavour. They are also used raw in salads and are fried, baked or boiled as a vegetable in their own right. Although, there are many varieties, most people choose by the colour, the brown being the most commonly used, followed by white, yellow and red.

LEFT: Kibbeh

1 Mix the yeast, sugar, 2 tablespoons of the plain flour and ¼ cup (60 ml/2 fl oz) warm water in a bowl. Cover with plastic wrap and leave in a warm place for 10 minutes, or until frothy.

2 Sift the remaining flours and cinnamon into a large bowl, return the husks to the bowl and stir through the sesame seeds and ½ teaspoon salt. Pour in the oil and rub it in by lifting the flour mixture onto one hand and lightly rubbing the other hand over the top. Make a well in the centre and add the yeast mixture and about ¼ cup (60 ml/2 fl oz) warm water, or enough to mix to a soft but not sticky dough. Knead on a floured surface for about 2 minutes, or until smooth and elastic. Place in a lightly oiled bowl, turning the dough to coat in the oil. Cover loosely with plastic wrap and leave in a warm place for 45–60 minutes, or until doubled in bulk.

3 Preheat the oven to moderately hot 200°C (400°F/Gas 6). Lightly grease a baking tray. Punch down the dough to expel the air, divide it into three portions and roll each on a lightly floured surface into a long sausage shape about 30 cm (12 inches) long. Place the first roll on the baking tray. Cut through almost to the base of the roll at 2 cm (¾ inch) intervals with a serrated knife (about 15 portions). Repeat with the remaining rolls.

4 Cover with a tea towel and leave in a warm place for 30 minutes, or until well risen. Bake for 30 minutes, or until browned underneath and the rolls sound hollow when tapped. Reduce the oven temperature to very slow 120°C (250°F/Gas ½). Cool the rolls on the tray for 5 minutes. Transfer each roll to a cutting board and cut through the markings. Place cut-side-up on two baking trays. Bake for 30 minutes, or until the tops feel dry. Turn each biscuit and bake for another 30 minutes, or until completely dry and crisp. Cool. Store in an airtight container for up to 3 weeks.

5 Dunk each biscuit quickly into cold water and place on a tray. Top with the combined tomato and feta. Drizzle with the combined oil and vinegar and sprinkle with oregano. Season.

NOTE: To make another delicious topping, combine 1 sliced roasted pepper (capsicum), 10 pitted and quartered Kalamata olives and 2 tablespoons chopped flat-leaf parsley. Season. Combine 3 tablespoons of extra virgin olive oil and 1 tablespoon of red wine vinegar and drizzle over the top.

OLIVE OIL BISCUITS

Preparation time: 30 minutes + standing
Total cooking time: 1 hour 30 minutes
Makes about 45

★★★

7 g (¼ oz) dried yeast or 15 g (½ oz) fresh
1 teaspoon sugar
1½ cups (185 g/6 oz) plain flour
1½ cups (225 g/7 oz) plain wholemeal flour
1 teaspoon ground cinnamon
1½ tablespoons sesame seeds, toasted
½ cup (125 ml/4 fl oz) olive oil

Topping
4 ripe tomatoes, diced
160 g (5½ oz) feta, crumbled
⅓ cup (80 ml/2¾ fl oz) extra virgin olive oil
2 tablespoons red wine vinegar
1 teaspoon dried oregano

ABOVE: Olive oil biscuits

CALAMARI ROMANA

Preparation time: 10 minutes + chilling
Total cooking time: 10 minutes
Makes about 30

350 g (11 oz) cleaned small squid hoods
1/2 teaspoon salt
1/3 cup (40 g/11/4 oz) plain flour
1/4 teaspoon black pepper
oil, for deep-frying
lemon wedges, for serving

1 Cut the squid into 1 cm (1/2 inch) wide rings. Combine the squid rings with the salt, cover and refrigerate for about 30 minutes, then dry on crumpled paper towels.
2 Combine the flour and pepper in a bowl. Fill a deep, heavy-based pan a third full of oil and heat to 180°C (350°F). The oil is ready when a cube of bread dropped in the oil browns in 15 seconds. Flour a few squid rings and cook, turning with a long-handled spoon, for 3 minutes, or until lightly browned and crisp. Flour the remaining batches just before frying. Drain on crumpled paper towels and serve hot with the lemon wedges.

ZUCCHINI PATTIES

Preparation time: 20 minutes
Total cooking time: 15 minutes
Makes about 25

2 medium zucchini, grated
1 small onion, grated
1/4 cup (30 g/1 oz) self-raising flour
1/3 cup (35 g/11/4 oz) grated kefalotyri cheese
    or Parmesan
1 tablespoon chopped fresh mint
2 teaspoons chopped fresh parsley
pinch of ground nutmeg
1/4 cup (25 g/3/4 oz) dry breadcrumbs
1 egg
olive oil, for shallow-frying

1 Put the zucchini and onion into the centre of a clean tea towel, twist as tightly as possible and squeeze dry. Combine the zucchini, onion, flour, cheese, mint, parsley, nutmeg, breadcrumbs and egg in a large bowl. Season well with salt and cracked black pepper, and mix with your hands to a stiff mixture that clumps together.
2 Heat the shallow-frying oil in a large pan over medium heat. Drop level tablespoons of the mixture into the pan and shallow-fry for 2–3 minutes, or until well browned all over, turning once. Drain well on paper towels and serve hot. The patties can be served plain sprinkled with salt or are delicious served with tzatziki (see page 167).
NOTE: Kefalotyri is a pale hard sheep's milk cheese originating in Greece. In this recipe, Parmesan or pecorino cheeses can be substituted.
IN ADVANCE: This recipe is best prepared close to cooking. Cooked patties can be reheated on a baking tray covered with baking paper. Heat in a moderate 180°C (350°F/Gas 4) oven for 3–5 minutes, or until warmed through.

ABOVE: Calamari Romana

FETA

Feta is a semi-hard cheese with a crumbly texture. It is not matured but preserved in a liquid made up of its whey and brine. It originated in Greece where it was made from the milk from goats or ewes and is an essential ingredient in the Greek salad, as well as being used in pies, tarts and in fillings for stuffed vegetables.

MEATBALLS

Preparation time: 25 minutes + chilling
Total cooking time: 20 minutes
Makes about 28

★ ★

4 slices white bread, crusts removed
150 g (5 oz) pork mince
150 g (5 oz) veal mince
1 tablespoon chopped fresh flat-leaf parsley
1 tablespoon chopped fresh mint
1 onion, grated
1/2 teaspoon ground cumin
1 egg
1/4 cup (25 g/3/4 oz) grated kefalotyri cheese or Parmesan
1/2 cup (60 g/2 oz) plain flour
olive oil, for shallow-frying

1 Cover the bread with water in a bowl, then squeeze out as much water as possible. Place in a large bowl with the mince, parsley, mint, onion, cumin, egg and cheese. Season. Knead the mixture by hand for 2–3 minutes until smooth. Cover and refrigerate for 30 minutes.
2 Put the flour in a shallow dish. With wet hands, roll level tablespoons of the meatball mixture into balls. Heat the oil over medium heat. Toss the meatballs in the flour. Shallow-fry in batches for 3–5 minutes, or until the meatballs are browned and cooked through. Drain on crumpled paper towels. Serve hot.

CHEESE PASTRIES

Preparation time: 40 minutes
Total cooking time: 20 minutes
Makes 16

★

160 g (5 1/2 oz) feta, grated
60 g (2 oz) ricotta
2 tablespoons chopped fresh mint
1 egg, lightly beaten
2 spring onions, finely chopped
2 tablespoons dry breadcrumbs
4 sheets ready-rolled puff pastry
1 egg, extra, lightly beaten
1 tablespoon sesame seeds

1 Preheat the oven to hot 220°C (425°F/ Gas 7). Lightly grease two baking trays.
2 Put the feta, ricotta, mint, egg, spring onion, breadcrumbs and 1/2 teaspoon cracked black

ABOVE: Meatballs

Use poultry shears to cut down the side of the backbones of the quails.

Place the quails on the work surface and gently press down to flatten them.

Cut the quails in half through the breasts, then cut that half in half again.

pepper in a bowl and mix with a fork to combine and break up the ricotta.

3 Using a pastry cutter or saucer, cut 10 cm (4 inch) rounds from the pastry sheets. Spoon level tablespoons of the cheese mixture into the centre of each round and lightly brush the edges with water. Fold over to enclose the filling, expelling any air, and firmly seal with the prongs of a fork to form a crescent shape. Brush with the extra egg and sprinkle with sesame seeds.

4 Put the crescents on the baking trays and bake for 15–20 minutes, or until well browned and puffed. Serve hot.

BARBECUED QUAIL

Preparation time: 40 minutes + chilling
Total cooking time: 10 minutes
Makes 24

★★★

6 quails
1 cup (250 ml/8 fl oz) dry red wine
2 sticks celery, including tops, chopped
1 carrot, chopped
1 small onion, chopped
1 bay leaf, torn into small pieces
1 teaspoon allspice
1 teaspoon dried thyme leaves
2 cloves garlic, crushed
2 tablespoons olive oil
2 tablespoons lemon juice
lemon wedges, for serving

1 To prepare the quails, use poultry shears to cut down either side of the backbone, then discard the backbone. Remove the innards and neck, wash the insides and pat dry with paper towels. Place breast-side-up on the bench, open out flat and gently press to flatten. Using poultry shears, cut in half through the breast then cut each half in half again into the thigh and drumstick piece and breast and wing piece.

2 In a non-metallic bowl, combine the wine, celery, carrot, onion, bay leaf and allspice. Add the quail and stir to coat. Cover and refrigerate for 3 hours, or preferably overnight, stirring occasionally. Drain and sprinkle with thyme, salt and pepper.

3 Whisk the garlic, oil and lemon juice in a small bowl.

4 Heat a lightly oiled barbecue plate until hot or heat a grill to its highest setting. Reduce the heat to medium and cook the quail breast pieces for 4–5 minutes on each side and the drumstick pieces for 3 minutes each side, or until tender and cooked through. Brush frequently with the lemon mixture. Serve hot with lemon wedges.

ABOVE: Barbecued quail

OREGANO

This herb grows along the ground on long stems. It has a small, strong-flavoured leaf which is very popular in Greek and Italian cookery. It blends well with tomatoes, eggplant and other vegetables, beef, lamb, fish, and is, of course, used in many sauces and on pizzas. Oregano is easy to grow in your own garden. Dried oregano has a full flavour if fresh is not available.

PAN-FRIED CHEESE SLICES

Preparation time: 10 minutes
Total cooking time: 5 minutes
Makes about 12

250 g (8 oz) kefalograviera (see Note)
2 tablespoons plain flour
1/4 cup (60 ml/2 fl oz) olive oil
1/2 teaspoon dried oregano
1/2 lemon, cut into wedges, for serving

1 Cut the cheese into 1 cm (1/2 inch) slices. The pieces can be as large as you wish, as they can be cut smaller for serving.
2 Put the flour in a shallow dish and season well with cracked pepper. Toss the cheese in the flour. Heat the oil over high heat in a frying pan until hot. Add the cheese to the pan and cook for 1 minute, or until browned and crusty underneath. Carefully turn the cheese to brown the other side. Lift onto a serving plate and sprinkle with oregano. Serve hot with lemon wedges and fresh bread.
NOTE: Kefalograviera and kefalotyri are pale hard sheep's milk cheeses originating in Greece.

ABOVE: Pan-fried cheese slices

TOMATO AND EGGPLANT (AUBERGINE) BOREK

Preparation time: 50 minutes + chilling
Total cooking time: 1 hour
Makes 30

75 g (2½ oz) butter, melted
1/3 cup (80 ml/2¾ fl oz) olive oil
1½ cups (185 g/6 oz) plain flour

Filling
250 g (8 oz) tomatoes
2 teaspoons olive oil
1 small onion, chopped
1/2 teaspoon ground cumin
300 g (10 oz) eggplant (aubergine), cut into 2 cm (3/4 inch) cubes
2 teaspoons tomato paste (tomato purée)
1 tablespoon chopped fresh coriander
1 egg, lightly beaten

1 Put the butter, oil and 1/3 cup (80 ml/2¾ fl oz) water into a bowl. Season well with salt. Gradually add the flour in batches, mixing with a wooden spoon to form an oily, lumpy dough that leaves the side of the bowl. Knead gently to bring the dough together, cover with plastic wrap and refrigerate for 1 hour.

2 Core the tomatoes and cut a small cross at the base. Plunge into a pan of boiling water and leave for 1 minute. Drain, plunge into cold water, then remove the peel. Halve the tomatoes, squeeze over a bowl to remove the seeds, and finely chop the flesh.

3 Heat the oil in a frying pan, add the onion and cook, stirring, over low heat for 2–3 minutes, or until soft. Add the cumin, cook for 1 minute, then add the eggplant and cook, stirring, for 8–10 minutes, or until the eggplant begins to soften. Stir in the tomato and tomato paste. Cook over medium heat for 15 minutes, or until the mixture becomes dry. Stir occasionally. Season and stir in the coriander. Cool.

4 Preheat the oven to moderate 180°C (350°F/ Gas 4). Lightly grease two baking trays.

5 Roll out half the pastry on a lightly floured surface to 2 mm (1/8 inch) thick. Using an 8 cm (3 inch) cutter, cut rounds from the pastry. Spoon 2 level teaspoons of the mixture into the centre of each round, lightly brush the edges with water and fold over the filling, expelling any air. Press firmly and crimp the edge with a fork to seal. Place on the trays and brush with the beaten egg. Bake in the top half of the oven for 25 minutes, or until golden brown and crisp.

HAM AND OLIVE EMPANADILLAS

Preparation time: 45 minutes + cooling
Total cooking time: 25 minutes
Makes about 15

2 hard-boiled eggs, roughly chopped
40 g (1 1/4 oz) stuffed green olives, chopped
95 g (3 oz) ham, finely chopped
30 g (1 oz) Cheddar, grated
3 sheets ready-rolled puff pastry
1 egg yolk, lightly beaten

1 Preheat the oven to hot 220°C (425°F/Gas 7). Lightly grease two baking trays. Combine the eggs with the olives, ham and Cheddar in a bowl.

2 Cut the puff pastry sheets into 10 cm (4 inch) rounds (about five rounds from each sheet.) Spoon a tablespoon of the mixture into the centre of each round, fold over the pastry to enclose the filling and crimp the edges to seal.

3 Place the pastries on the trays 2 cm (3/4 inch) apart. Brush with egg yolk and bake for 15 minutes, or until brown and puffed. Swap the trays around after 10 minutes. Cover loosely with foil if browning too much. Serve hot.

EGGPLANT (AUBERGINE)
Eggplants are common in the Mediterranean region and are used in many recipes. The skin varies from dark purple (almost black) to paler and even to white. Inside, the flesh is creamy-white, sometimes tending to pale green. Eggplants come in many shapes, from long and thin, to fat and round, and some the size of grapes. When you buy them, they should be quite firm. The larger eggplants can taste slightly bitter so, to draw out the bitter juices before cooking, cut or slice as required for the recipe, sprinkle generously with salt, then leave for about half an hour before rinsing, drying and cooking. The slender eggplants do not require salting.

LEFT: Ham and olive empanadillas

193

TEX-MEX

The border between Mexico and Texas may separate two very different countries but where food is concerned the line blurs. Tex-Mex cooking is as bright and colourful as sunny Texas and Mexico where it originated. While an antipasto platter or a tray of canapés might signify a certain type of calm and sophisticated gathering, an array of fiery Tex-Mex food seems to call out 'party'. It begs loud conversation, colourful characters and jugs of cold Margaritas—although you might want to persuade your guests to leave their sombreros at home. So, if you want your party to go with a sizzle, bring out the jalapenos. Olé.

SAVOURY POTATO EMPANADAS

Preparation time: 1 hour
Total cooking time: 40 minutes
Makes 32

⭐⭐

3 tablespoons olive oil

1 small onion, finely diced

2 spring onions, thinly sliced

1 clove garlic, crushed

100 g (3½ oz) beef mince

1 teaspoon ground cumin

1 teaspoon dried oregano

125 g (4 oz) potatoes, cubed

4 sheets ready-rolled puff pastry

50 g (1¾ oz) black olives, pitted and quartered

1 hard-boiled egg, finely chopped

1 egg, separated

pinch of paprika

pinch of sugar

1 In a heavy-based frying pan, heat 1 tablespoon of the oil, add the onion and spring onion and stir for 5 minutes. Stir in the garlic and cook for 3 minutes. Remove from the pan and set aside.

2 Heat another tablespoon of oil in the pan, add the beef mince and stir over medium heat until browned, breaking up any lumps with a fork. Add the onion mixture and stir well.

3 Add the cumin, oregano, and ½ teaspoon each of salt and pepper, and stir for another 2 minutes. Transfer to a bowl and cool. Wipe out the pan.

4 Heat another tablespoon of oil in the pan, add the potato and stir over high heat for 1 minute. Reduce the heat to low and stir for 5 minutes, or until tender. Cool slightly and then gently mix into the beef mixture.

5 Preheat the oven to moderately hot 200°C (400°F/Gas 6). Cut rounds from the pastry with an 8 cm (3 inch) cutter. Grease two baking trays.

6 Spoon heaped teaspoons of the beef mixture onto one side of each pastry round (leaving a border wide enough for the pastry to be folded over). Place a few olive quarters and some chopped egg on top of the beef mixture. Brush the border with egg white. Carefully fold the pastry over to make a half moon shape, pressing firmly to seal. Press the edges with a floured fork, to decorate, and then gently transfer to the baking trays. Stir the egg yolk, paprika and sugar together and brush over the empanadas. Bake for 15 minutes, or until golden brown and puffed.

IN ADVANCE: The puffs can be made 2 days ahead or frozen for 2 months.

EMPANADAS

These pies vary in the way they are made. Sometimes they are sold in wedges cut from large flat pies, but they are also often made as small turnovers. The fillings range from savoury to sweet, or a mixture of both. Empanadas are shallow-fried or baked.

ABOVE: Savoury potato empanadas

SPICY TORTILLA TRIANGLES

Preparation time: 20 minutes
Total cooking time: 5 minutes
Makes 24

2 x 23 cm (9 inch) round flour tortillas
¼ cup (60 ml/2 fl oz) oil

Topping

1 onion, finely chopped
2 cloves garlic, crushed
2 small red chillies, finely chopped
425 g (14 oz) can pinto beans, drained,
    mashed roughly
1 cup (250 ml/8 fl oz) thick and chunky
    bottled salsa
2 tablespoons chopped fresh coriander leaves
90 g (3 oz) Cheddar, grated

1 Cut the tortillas into quarters and cut each quarter into three triangles.
2 Heat 2 tablespoons of the oil in a frying pan. Add a few triangles to the pan, cook for 30 seconds on each side, or until crisp and golden brown. Remove from the pan and drain on paper towels. Repeat with the remaining triangles, adding extra oil as necessary.
3 For the topping, heat 1 tablespoon of oil in a medium pan, add the onion, garlic and chilli and stir over medium heat for 3 minutes, or until the onion is tender. Stir in the pinto beans, salsa and fresh coriander. Remove from the heat and leave to cool.
4 Spread the topping on the triangles, leaving a border around the edges, and sprinkle with Cheddar. Grill for 1 minute, or until the cheese has melted.
NOTES: Tortilla triangles can be cooked in the oven instead of fried and grilled. Place the triangles on a baking tray in a preheated moderate 180°C (350°F/Gas 4) oven for 5 minutes or until crisp. Add the topping and cook for another 3–5 minutes, or until the cheese has melted.

Red kidney beans can be used instead of pinto beans.
IN ADVANCE: Tortilla triangles can be made a day ahead; store in an airtight container. The topping can be made a day ahead and stored in the refrigerator. Assemble the triangles up to 1 hour ahead. Grill just before serving.

TORTILLAS

Mexican flour tortillas are small flat pancakes traditionally made from a dough using masa harina (cornmeal). They are cooked on both sides and are the basis of popular dishes such as tacos, burritos, enchiladas and tostadas. For all of these, the flour tortillas are either rolled or folded around a filling, or fried until crisp, then topped or filled with the traditional mixtures of cooked meats, vegetables and spices.

ABOVE: Spicy tortilla triangles

2 To make the batter, sift the flour into a large bowl, stir in the cornmeal and make a well in the centre. Gradually add the combined egg, oil and 1½ cups (375 ml/12 fl oz) water, whisking to make a smooth, lump-free batter.

3 Fill a deep heavy-based pan one third full of oil and heat to 180°C (350°F). The oil is ready when a cube of bread dropped into the oil turns golden brown in 15 seconds. Dip the frankfurts into the batter a few at a time; drain off the excess batter. Using tongs, gently lower the frankfurts into the oil. Cook over medium–high heat for 1–2 minutes, or until golden and crisp and heated through. Carefully remove from the oil. Drain on crumpled paper towels and keep warm. Repeat with the remaining frankfurts. Serve with tomato sauce.

NOTE: You can add a teaspoon of chopped fresh chilli or a pinch of chilli powder to the batter.

BAKED HONEY AND GARLIC RIBS

Preparation time: 20 minutes + marinating
Total cooking time: 55 minutes
Makes about 30

1.5 kg (3 lb) American-style pork spare ribs
½ cup (175 g/6 oz) honey
6 cloves garlic, crushed
5 cm (2 inch) piece fresh ginger, finely grated
¼ teaspoon Tabasco
3 tablespoons chilli sauce
2 teaspoons grated orange rind

1 Cut the ribs into small pieces, with about 1 bone per piece. Place in a large dish. Combine the remaining ingredients and pour over the ribs. Stir until well coated. Refrigerate for several hours, or overnight.

2 Preheat the oven to moderately hot 200°C (400°F/Gas 6). Drain the ribs and place the marinade in a small pan. Place the ribs in one or two large shallow ovenproof dishes in a single layer.

3 Bring the marinade to the boil and simmer gently for 3–4 minutes, or until it has thickened and reduced slightly.

4 Brush the ribs with the marinade and bake for 50 minutes, basting with the marinade three or four times. Cook until the ribs are well browned and tender. Serve the ribs hot with any remaining marinade.

MINI CORN DOGS

Preparation time: 10 minutes
Total cooking time: 8–10 minutes
Makes 16

★★★

8 large frankfurts
8 wooden skewers
cornflour, for dusting
oil, for deep-frying
tomato sauce, for dipping

Batter

1¾ cups (220 g/7 oz) self-raising flour
¼ cup (35 g/1¼ oz) cornmeal
1 egg, lightly beaten
1 tablespoon oil

1 Cut the frankfurts in half crossways. Cut 8 wooden skewers in half and insert one half through each frankfurt, leaving some of the skewer sticking out for a handle. Dust the frankfurts with a little cornflour.

ABOVE: Mini corn dogs

STARS AND STRIPES BARBECUED RIBS

Preparation time: 30 minutes + overnight marinating
Total cooking time: 15 minutes
Makes about 30

1/2 teaspoon dry mustard, or prepared English mustard
1/2 teaspoon ground sweet paprika
1/4 teaspoon ground oregano
1/4 teaspoon ground cumin
1 1/2 tablespoons peanut oil
1 teaspoon Tabasco sauce
1 clove garlic, crushed
1/2 cup (125 ml/4 fl oz) tomato sauce
2 tablespoons tomato paste (tomato purée)
2 tablespoons soft brown sugar
1 tablespoon Worcestershire sauce
2 teaspoons brown vinegar
1.5 kg (3 lb) American-style pork spare ribs

1 For the sauce, combine the mustard, paprika, oregano, cumin and oil in a pan. Add the remaining ingredients, except the ribs. Cook, stirring, over medium heat for 3 minutes, or until combined. Allow to cool.

2 Coat the ribs with sauce and marinate overnight. Cook on a hot barbecue grill, turning frequently, until firm and well done. Cut into individual ribs before serving.

NOTE: Get very lean pork spare ribs as fatty ones tend to flare up and burn. You can use beef spare ribs if you prefer but first simmer until tender, then drain.

FRIED CHICKEN

Mix 1 kg (2 lb) chicken drumettes in a bowl with 2 cups (500 ml/16 fl oz) buttermilk. Cover and refrigerate for 2 hours, turning occasionally. Half fill a large, deep heavy-based pan with oil and heat to 180°C (350°F). The oil is ready when a cube of bread dropped into the oil turns golden brown in 15 seconds. Place 1 1/2 cups (185 g/6 oz) plain flour in a shallow dish and season. Drain the chicken and shake off any excess buttermilk, then coat in the flour. Deep fry in batches for 6–8 minutes, making sure the oil is not too hot or the chicken won't cook through. Drain on paper towels. Makes about 20.

TOMATOES
Tomatoes are sold fresh, in cans, or processed and sold as sauces and pastes with various consistencies, sometimes with flavourings added. Tomato paste, known in the U.K. as tomato purée, is strained concentrated tomatoes which have been cooked for several hours until they form a very thick, dark paste. Salt is added, and sometimes sugar. The intense flavour is used sparingly to flavour stews, stocks, sauces and soups. Some are slightly more concentrated than others so experiment to find which you prefer. Tomato sauce is a much thinner consistency than the paste and is often blended with sugar, salt, spices and other flavourings.

LEFT: Stars and stripes barbecued ribs

HOT CORN CAKES WITH AVOCADO AND PRAWNS

Preparation time: 25 minutes
Total cooking time: 15–20 minutes
Makes 32

³/4 cup (110 g/3¹/2 oz) frozen corn kernels, thawed, roughly chopped
1¹/2 canned chipotle peppers, roughly chopped, and 2 teaspoons of the sauce
¹/2 cup (60 g/2 oz) plain flour
¹/3 cup (50 g/1³/4 oz) polenta (cornmeal)
¹/2 teaspoon baking powder
¹/4 teaspoon bicarbonate of soda
1 teaspoon salt
¹/2 teaspoon sugar
1 cup (250 ml/8 fl oz) buttermilk
20 g (³/4 oz) butter, melted
1 egg
32 cooked medium prawns, peeled, deveined
32 fresh coriander leaves, to garnish

Avocado sauce

1 ripe avocado, roughly chopped
2 tablespoons lime juice
1 canned chipotle pepper, in sauce
¹/2 cup (15 g/¹/2 oz) fresh coriander leaves
1 clove garlic, chopped
¹/2 teaspoon salt
1 teaspoon ground cumin
2 tablespoons sour cream

1 Roughly chop the corn and chipotle peppers, using short bursts of a food processor.
2 Combine the dry ingredients in a large bowl and make a well. Whisk the buttermilk, butter and egg together in a jug, gradually add to the dry ingredients and whisk until thoroughly incorporated. Stir in the chopped corn and chipotle pepper. (The batter should have the consistency of pancake batter.) Add a tablespoon of water to thin the batter if necessary. Set aside.
3 Purée all the sauce ingredients in a food processor until very smooth. Season.
4 Heat a lightly greased frying pan over medium heat. Spoon tablespoons of the corn cake batter into the pan, forming 5 cm (2 inch) cakes, cooking in batches. Cook until golden brown, about 1 minute per side. Remove from the pan and repeat with the remaining batter. Keep the cakes warm until ready to serve. Alternatively, you can make the corn cakes up to 2 days ahead of time, wrap well in plastic wrap and refrigerate. Place a single layer on a baking sheet and reheat in a warm 170°C (325°F/Gas 3) oven for 5 minutes, or until warmed through. (Corn cakes can also be served at room temperature.)
4 To assemble, dollop a heaped teaspoon of avocado sauce on the warmed corn cakes. Place one cooked prawn on top of the avocado sauce. Garnish with coriander leaves.

MINI TORTILLAS WITH CHORIZO SALSA

Preparation time: 25 minutes
Total cooking time: 12–15 minutes
Makes about 30

4 x 20 cm (8 inch) round flour tortillas
2 tablespoons olive oil
250 g (8 oz) chorizo sausages
¹/3 cup (90 g/3 oz) Greek-style natural yoghurt
20 g (³/4 oz) finely chopped fresh coriander
1 ripe avocado
1 large tomato, seeded
¹/4 red onion
2 teaspoons balsamic vinegar
1 tablespoon virgin olive oil
30 small fresh coriander leaves, to garnish

1 Preheat the oven to moderate 180°C (350°F/ Gas 4). Cut 7–8 circles from each tortilla with a 5.5 cm (2¹/4 inch) cutter, or cut into triangles. Heat 1 tablespoon of the oil in a large non-stick frying pan, add one third of the mini tortillas and cook in a single layer, turning once, until crisp and golden. Drain on crumpled paper towels. Repeat with the remaining oil and tortillas.
2 Chop the sausages into small cubes and bake on a baking tray for 10 minutes, or until cooked through. Cool; drain on crumpled paper towel.
3 Meanwhile, combine the yoghurt and chopped coriander in a small bowl; set aside.
4 Chop the avocado, tomato and onion into small cubes and combine in a bowl. Add the sausage, vinegar, oil and salt and pepper, to taste, and gently stir to combine.
5 To assemble, spoon the sausage onto tortillas and top with yoghurt and coriander leaves.

OPPOSITE PAGE: Hot corn cakes with avocado and prawns (left); Mini tortillas with chorizo salsa

CHARRED PRAWNS WITH PEPPER (CAPSICUM) MAYONNAISE

Preparation time: 20 minutes + marinating
Total cooking time: 40 minutes
Makes 24

★★

1 kg (2 lb) large raw prawns

4 cloves garlic, crushed

3 tablespoons lime juice

1 teaspoon ground cumin

3 tablespoons chopped fresh coriander

lime wedges, for serving

Pepper (capsicum) mayonnaise

1 small red pepper (capsicum)

6 cloves garlic, unpeeled

1 tablespoon olive oil

1/3 cup (90 g/3 oz) whole-egg mayonnaise

1 tablespoon lime juice

ABOVE: Charred prawns with pepper mayonnaise

1 Peel and devein the prawns, leaving the tails intact. Combine the garlic, lime juice, cumin and coriander in a bowl, place the prawns in the marinade and mix well. Cover and refrigerate for at least 2 hours.

2 To make the pepper mayonnaise, preheat the oven to moderately hot 190°C (375°F/Gas 5). Cut the red pepper into quarters and remove the seeds and membrane. Place on a baking tray with the garlic and drizzle with the olive oil. Cook for 20–30 minutes, or until the skin blisters on the pepper and the garlic is soft but not burnt. Place in a plastic bag until cool, then peel the red pepper and garlic.

3 Combine the red pepper and garlic in a food processor with the mayonnaise until smooth. Transfer to a bowl and stir in the lime juice. Add salt, to taste.

4 Preheat a lightly oiled chargrill or heavy-based pan until it just starts to smoke. Drain the prawns, discarding the marinade and cook in batches for 2 minutes on each side, or until cooked. Serve the prawns with the mayonnaise and a wedge of lime.

EMPANADAS

Preparation time: 45 minutes + cooling
Total cooking time: 1 hour
Makes 48

★★

oil, for frying
1 small onion, finely chopped
1 small green pepper (capsicum), finely chopped
1 clove garlic, crushed
350 g (11 oz) beef mince
200 g (6¹/₂ oz) pork mince
³/₄ cup (185 ml/6 fl oz) tomato passata, or
   chopped canned tomatoes
110 g (3³/₄ oz) pitted green olives, chopped
8 frozen sheets shortcrust pastry, thawed

1 Heat a little oil in a frying pan and cook the onion over low heat for 3 minutes, or until soft. Add the green pepper, cook for 3 minutes, then add the garlic and cook for another minute. Add the minces and cook, breaking up any lumps with a fork, until browned.

2 Stir in the tomato passata and green olives and bring to the boil. Reduce the heat and simmer for 10 minutes, stirring occasionally, or until most of the liquid has evaporated. Remove from the heat, season to taste, and allow to cool completely.

3 Cut six 8 cm (3 inch) rounds from each sheet of pastry. Place 2 heaped teaspoons of the filling onto each round and fold over to enclose. Press the edges down with a fork to seal.

4 Heat 2 cm (³/₄ inch) of oil in a deep frying pan to 180°C (350°F). The oil is ready when a cube of bread dropped into the oil turns golden brown in 15 seconds. Cook the empanadas in batches until crisp and golden, then drain well on crumpled paper towels. Alternatively, bake in a moderately hot 200°C (400°F/Gas 6) oven for 20–25 minutes, or until puffed and golden.

IN ADVANCE: These can be made up to 2 days ahead, or frozen, uncooked.

ONIONS

Brown onions, which keep well, have a strong flavour and are best cooked, while white onions are usually milder and sweeter and hence can be used in salads as well as cooked. Red and yellow onions, which don't keep as long as other onions, are used in salads for their colour and sweetness. Chopped or sliced onions should be cooked slowly over medium-low heat to soften and sweeten them.

LEFT: Empanadas

CEVICHE

Preparation time: 20 minutes + overnight chilling
Total cooking time: Nil
Makes about 48 cubes

600 g (1 1/4 lb) very fresh, skinless, firm
   white-fleshed fish such as snapper fillets
1/3 cup (80 ml/2 3/4 fl oz) lime juice
1/2 red onion, very finely diced
1 teaspoon finely chopped red chilli
1 teaspoon finely chopped green chilli
1 tomato, seeded and chopped into very
   small dice
2 tablespoons finely chopped fresh parsley

1 Remove any bones from the fish with
tweezers. Cut the fish into bite-sized pieces and
place in a shallow glass bowl. Pour the lime juice
over the fish, cover with plastic wrap and
refrigerate overnight.
2 Toss the diced onion, chilli, tomato and
chopped parsley through the fish.
3 Arrange on a serving plate and serve
immediately, providing cocktail sticks for guests
to help themselves.

TEX-MEX CHEESE CRISPS

Preparation time: 20 minutes + chilling
Total cooking time: 12 minutes
Makes 80

1 3/4 cups (215 g/7 oz) plain flour
1 teaspoon chilli powder
1 teaspoon garlic salt
1/2 teaspoon ground paprika
200 g (6 1/2 oz) butter, chopped
1 egg, lightly beaten
200 g (6 1/2 oz) Cheddar, grated

1 Preheat the oven to hot 210°C (415°F/
Gas 6–7). Lightly brush two baking trays with
melted butter.
2 Sift the flour, chilli powder, garlic salt and
paprika into a large bowl. Rub the butter into
the flour with your fingertips until the mixture
resembles fine breadcrumbs. Add the egg and
cheese and stir until the mixture comes together.
Turn onto a lightly floured surface and gather
together into a ball. Cover the dough with
plastic wrap and refrigerate for 20 minutes.
3 Roll the dough on a lightly floured surface to
3 mm (1/8 inch) thickness. Cut into shapes with
a 6 cm (2 1/2 inch) star-shaped biscuit cutter. Place
on the trays, allowing room for spreading. Bake
for 12 minutes, or until crisp and golden brown.
Leave on the trays for 2 minutes before
transferring to a wire rack to cool.

TORTILLA FLUTES

Preparation time: 25 minutes
Total cooking time: 15 minutes
Makes 24

1/4 cup (60 ml/2 fl oz) olive oil
2 small onions, finely chopped
2 garlic cloves, crushed
1/2 teaspoon chilli powder
2 teaspoons ground cumin
1 kg (2 lb) cooked chicken, finely chopped
2 tablespoons finely chopped fresh
   coriander
24 soft flour or corn tortillas
oil, for shallow-frying
red or green chilli sauce, for serving
1 avocado, sliced, for serving

1 Heat the olive oil in a frying pan and fry the
onion and garlic over medium heat for
2–3 minutes, or until the onion is just tender
but not soft. Add the chilli powder and cumin
and stir for 1 minute.
2 Add the chicken and mix well. Cook over
medium heat until just heated through. Stir in
the coriander and remove from the heat.
3 Soften the tortillas, one at a time, by heating
in a dry heavy-based frying pan over high heat
for about 30 seconds each side.
4 Lay a tortilla flat on a work surface and place
a large spoonful of chicken mixture along the
centre. Carefully roll up to form a flute.
5 Pour oil in a deep frying pan to 5 cm
(2 inches) deep and heat the oil to 180°C
(350°F). The oil is ready when a cube of bread
dropped into the oil turns golden brown in
15 seconds. Holding the flute together with
tongs (or fasten with toothpicks), cook one at
a time until slightly crisp. Drain on crumpled
paper towels. Serve with chilli sauce and
avocado slices.

CEVICHE
Ceviche was originally a
Peruvian dish, consisting of
small pieces of raw fish
marinated or 'cooked' in
a mixture that includes
lime or lemon juice—this
tenderises and flavours the
fish. Normally, the dish is
served cold with toast, or
in lettuce cups with
cooked sweet potato and
corn cobs.

OPPOSITE PAGE,
CLOCKWISE FROM TOP:
Ceviche; Tortilla flutes;
Tex-Mex cheese crisps

GUACAMOLE

This is a Mexican dip or spread made by mixing mashed ripe avocado with lime or lemon juice as well as chopped onion, tomato and chilli. Sometimes other ingredients are added. Traditionally, the dip is served with tortillas or nachos but you can have it with your favourite chips or dipping biscuits.

MEXICAN LAYERED DIP

Preparation time: 1 hour + chilling
Total cooking time: Nil
Serves 12

★★

Guacamole

3 ripe avocados

1 small tomato

1–2 red chillies, finely chopped

1 small red onion, finely chopped

1 tablespoon chopped fresh coriander

1 tablespoon lime or lemon juice

2 tablespoons sour cream

1–2 drops habanero or Tabasco sauce

450 g (14 oz) can refried beans

35 g (1¼ oz) packet of taco seasoning mix

300 g (10 oz) sour cream

200 g (6½ oz) ready-made salsa sauce

60 g (2 oz) Cheddar, grated

2 tablespoons chopped pitted black olives

200 g (6½ oz) corn chips

chopped fresh coriander leaves, to garnish

1 For the guacamole, roughly chop the avocado flesh, then mash lightly with a fork. Cut the tomato in half horizontally. Using a teaspoon, scoop out the seeds and discard. Finely dice the flesh and add to the avocado. Stir in the chilli, onion, coriander, lime juice, sour cream and sauce. Season with salt and cracked black pepper. Cover and refrigerate until required.

2 Using a fork, mix the refried beans and taco seasoning together in a small bowl.

3 To assemble, spread the beans in the centre of a large platter (we used a 30 x 35 cm/12 x 14 inch dish), leaving a border for the corn chips. Spoon the sour cream on top, leaving a small border of bean mixture showing. Repeat with the guacamole and salsa sauce so that you can see each layer. Sprinkle the top with cheese and olives.

4 Arrange some of the corn chips around the edge just before serving and garnish with the coriander. Serve with the remaining corn chips.

NOTE: Tabasco and habanero sauces are both made from fiery hot chillies, so taste before adding too much.

IN ADVANCE: This dip can be made 2 hours ahead, and refrigerated, covered. Surround with corn chips close to serving time.

ABOVE: Mexican layered dip

CORN FRITTERS

Preparation time: 15 minutes
Total cooking time: 20–25 minutes
Makes 20

1¼ cups (155 g/4½ oz) plain flour
1½ teaspoons baking powder
½ teaspoon ground coriander
¼ teaspoon ground cumin
130 g (4½ oz) can corn kernels, well drained
130 g (4½ oz) can creamed corn
½ cup (80 ml/2¾ fl oz) milk
2 eggs, lightly beaten
2 tablespoons chopped fresh chives
½ cup (125 ml/4 fl oz) olive oil

Dipping sauce

1 tablespoon brown vinegar
3 teaspoons soft brown sugar
1 teaspoon chilli sauce
1 tablespoon chopped fresh chives
salt, to taste

1 Sift the flour, baking powder, ground coriander and cumin into a bowl and make a well in the centre. Add the corn kernels, creamed corn, milk, eggs and chives all at once. Stir until the ingredients are combined and the mixture is free of flour lumps. Season, to taste, with salt and pepper.

2 Heat the oil in a large frying pan to 180°C (350°F). The oil is ready when a cube of bread dropped into the oil turns golden brown in 15 seconds. Drop heaped tablespoons of mixture into the pan about 2 cm (¾ inch) apart and flatten slightly with the back of a spoon. Cook in batches over medium–high heat for 2 minutes, or until the underside is golden. Turn over and cook the other side. Remove from the pan and drain on crumpled paper towels. Repeat the process with the remaining mixture. Serve the fritters with the dipping sauce.

3 For the dipping sauce, heat the vinegar, sugar and chilli sauce in a small pan for 1–2 minutes, until the liquid is heated through and the sugar is dissolved. Stir in the chives and season with salt, to taste.

IN ADVANCE: The fritters can be made several hours ahead. Reheat on baking trays covered with baking paper in a moderate 180°C (350°F/ Gas 4) oven for 5 minutes.

LEFT: Corn fritters

CORNMEAL CHILLIES

Preparation time: 40 minutes + chilling
Total cooking time: 2–3 minutes each batch
Makes 24

2 x 330 g (11 oz) jars mild whole chillies
125 g (4 oz) Cheddar, grated
200 g (6¹/₂ oz) cream cheese, softened
²/₃ cup (85 g/3 oz) plain flour
4 eggs, lightly beaten
1¹/₄ cups (185 g/6 oz) cornmeal
1¹/₄ cups (125 g/4 oz) dry breadcrumbs
oil, for deep-frying
sour cream, for serving

1 Select 24 large, uniform chillies. Drain well and dry with paper towels. With a sharp knife, cut a slit down the length of one side of each chilli. Remove the seeds and membrane.

2 Combine the Cheddar and cream cheese and spoon some into each chilli. Put the flour on a large plate and the beaten egg in a small bowl. Combine the cornmeal and breadcrumbs on a flat dish. Roll each chilli in the flour, shake off the excess, dip in the egg and roll in the crumb mixture to coat thoroughly. Refrigerate for 1 hour. Re-dip in egg and re-roll in breadcrumbs. Refrigerate for another hour.

3 Fill a deep heavy-based pan one third full of oil and heat the oil to 180°C (350°F). The oil is ready when a cube of bread dropped into the oil turns golden brown in 15 seconds. Deep-fry the chillies in small batches until golden brown. Drain on crumpled paper towels. Serve with sour cream.

IN ADVANCE: These can be prepared up to 3 hours ahead.

ABOVE: Cornmeal chillies

PRAWN AND CORN CAKES WITH LIME MAYONNAISE

Preparation time: 40 minutes + chilling
Total cooking time: 10 minutes
Makes 30

★★★

500 g (1 lb) cooked prawns
1 tablespoon light olive oil
2 jalapeno chillies, seeded and finely chopped
1 teaspoon ground coriander
4 spring onions, finely chopped
20 g (³/4 oz) fresh coriander leaves, chopped
130 g (4¹/2 oz) can corn kernels, drained
130 g (4¹/2 oz) can creamed corn
1 egg, lightly beaten
¹/3 cup (90 g/3 oz) sour cream
2¹/2 cups (200 g/6¹/2 oz) fresh breadcrumbs
oil, for shallow-frying

Lime mayonnaise
2 egg yolks
1 clove garlic, crushed
¹/3 cup (80 ml/2³/4 fl oz) vegetable oil
¹/3 cup (80 ml/2³/4 fl oz) olive oil
2 tablespoons lime juice
1 small green chilli, finely chopped

1 Peel, devein and finely chop the prawns. Heat the oil in a pan over medium heat. Add the chilli, ground coriander and spring onion and fry for 2–3 minutes, until soft and fragrant. Remove the pan from the heat and add the fresh coriander, prawns, corn kernels and creamed corn. Mix, then transfer to a bowl.
2 Add the egg, sour cream and 1 cup (80 g/ 2³/4 oz) of breadcrumbs, mix and season, to taste. Cover and refrigerate for 2 hours.
3 Shape level tablespoons of mixture into patties. Coat all over with the remaining breadcrumbs and refrigerate for another 30 minutes.
4 Heat 2 cm (³/4 inch) oil in a large frying pan and cook the patties in batches for 3–4 minutes each side, or until golden brown. Drain on crumpled paper towels.
5 For the lime mayonnaise, combine the egg yolks and garlic in a bowl. Slowly add the vegetable oil, one drop at a time, whisking continuously to form a smooth mixture. When all the vegetable oil has been added, slowly add the olive oil in a thin stream, whisking continuously. Add the lime juice and chilli and mix well. Season well with salt and pepper and refrigerate, covered, until needed. Serve with the chilli prawn and corn cakes.
NOTE: The corn cake mixture is very soft and needs gentle handling. To make the cakes firmer, freeze for 30 minutes. To save time, buy whole egg mayonnaise and stir in some grated lime rind, chopped chilli and garlic.

PRAWNS
Whole unpeeled cooked prawns can be frozen in a large block. Put them in a plastic container, such as an ice cream tub, fill with icy cold water and freeze. When ready to use, thaw the prawns in a large bowl in the fridge.

LEFT: Prawn and corn cakes with lime mayonnaise

QUESADILLAS
Use flour tortillas from the bread section of your supermarket to make these Mexican snacks. And stun your guests with your authentic pronunciation... 'kay-sah-dee-yah'.

GUACAMOLE ROLLS

Mix a 450 g (14 oz) can of refried beans with 90 g (3 oz) grated Cheddar. Cut 7 flour tortillas into rounds, using an 8 cm (3 inch) cutter. Wrap in foil and cook in a moderate 180°F (350°F/Gas 4) oven for 2–3 minutes, until warmed through. To make the guacamole, mash 2 avocados and mix with 1 small chopped red onion, 1 tablespoon mayonnaise, 1 chopped red chilli, 1 tablespoon lime juice and 1 tablespoon chopped fresh coriander. Spread a little bean mixture over the base of each tortilla and roll up like a horn. Place, seam-side-down, on a baking tray and bake for another 5 minutes, or until crisp. Spoon a teaspoon of guacamole into the open end and serve. Makes 42.

CHEESE QUESADILLAS

Roast 2 jalapeno chillies by holding with tongs over a flame until blackened and blistered. You can also roast chillies under a hot grill. Put in a plastic bag and when cool, you will find the skin peels away easily. Finely chop the chilli flesh and mix with 250 g (8 oz) grated Cheddar and 75 g (2½ oz) grated mozzarella cheese. Spread evenly over 3 flour tortillas, then top with another 3 tortillas. Cut out rounds with a 6 cm (2½ inch) cutter, then fry in a little oil for 1–2 minutes, or until golden brown on each side. Serve with home-made salsa. Makes about 25–30.

TACO CHICKEN QUESADILLAS

In a large frying pan, heat 1 tablespoon oil, add 1 finely chopped red onion and 1 finely diced red pepper (capsicum). Cook until the onion has softened. Add 2 crushed cloves garlic, ¼ teaspoon paprika, 1 teaspoon ground cumin and 1 teaspoon ground coriander and cook for 2 minutes. Add 400 g (13 oz) chicken mince and cook for 5–8 minutes, until brown, breaking up any lumps. Add a 400 g (13 oz) can chopped tomatoes and simmer for 20 minutes, or until thick. Cut 7 flour tortillas into rounds with an 8 cm (3 inch) cutter. Place a teaspoon of the mixture on one half of each round. Sprinkle with 220 g (7 oz) grated Cheddar. Bake in a moderate 180°C (350°F/Gas 4) oven for 1 minute, or until the cheese has melted. Fold over and hold for a few seconds to stick. Garnish with sliced spring onion. Makes 42.

CORN, TOMATO AND BEAN QUESADILLAS

Combine 1 finely chopped red onion, 2 chopped tomatoes, a 310 g (10 oz) can drained and rinsed corn kernels and 1 diced red pepper (capsicum). Drain and rinse a 425 g (14 oz) can pinto beans and mash with a fork. Place 3 flour tortillas on a work surface, spread the pinto beans evenly over the tortillas, top with the corn and tomato mixture and sprinkle with 90 g (3 oz) grated Cheddar. Top with 3 more flour tortillas. Heat 2 teaspoons oil in a 25 cm (10 inch) frying pan and cook the stacks for 3–4 minutes each side, until golden brown. Remove from the pan and cut into 12 triangles. Makes 36.

CHILLI BEEF QUESADILLAS

Heat 1 tablespoon oil in a frying pan and cook 1 chopped onion and 2 crushed cloves garlic for 2–3 minutes. Add 400 g (13 oz) beef mince and cook for 5–7 minutes until brown, breaking up any lumps. Stir in a 325 g (11 oz) bottle of Mexican black bean salsa. Bring to the boil, reduce the heat and simmer for 3–4 minutes, or until the mixture reduces and thickens. Season. Place 3 flour tortillas on a work surface and sprinkle with 125 g (4 oz) grated Cheddar. Spoon the mince evenly over the cheese, then top with another 3 tortillas. Heat 2 teaspoons oil in a 25 cm (10 inch) frying pan and cook the stacks for 3–4 minutes each side, or until golden brown. Remove from the pan, trim off the sides and cut into 5 cm (2 inch) squares. Makes about 36.

FROM LEFT: Guacamole rolls; Cheese quesadillas; Taco chicken quesadillas; Corn, tomato and bean quesadillas; Chilli beef quesadillas

CORNBREAD WITH BEANS

Preparation time: 1 hour
Total cooking time: 30 minutes
Makes 24

⭐ ⭐

1 large green chilli
1 large red chilli
1 cup (150 g/5 oz) cornmeal (polenta)
1 cup (125 g/4 oz) self-raising flour
1/2 cup (60 g/2 oz) grated Cheddar
1 egg, lightly beaten
3/4 cup (185 ml/6 fl oz) milk
310 g (10 oz) can creamed corn
Tabasco sauce, for serving
fresh coriander leaves, to garnish

Topping

1 cup (230 g/7 1/2 oz) refried beans
2 tablespoons sour cream
1/2 teaspoon ground cumin
1/2 teaspoon ground coriander
1/2 teaspoon paprika

REFRIED BEANS
Although you would never guess from the name, these are dried beans (pinto, red kidney or black beans) that have been boiled until tender, then fried until very soft. Refried beans actually translates as 'well-fried'.

ABOVE: Cornbread with beans

1 Preheat the oven to moderately hot 200°C (400°F/Gas 6). Grease a 20 x 30 cm (8 x 12 inch) shallow baking tin. Roast the chillies by holding them with tongs (one at a time) over a gas flame, until well blackened. Alternatively, cut the chillies in half, remove the seeds and membrane, flatten out and grill skin-side-up until black and blistered. Place in a plastic bag until cool, then peel, cut in half and chop finely.
2 Combine the cornmeal, flour, Cheddar, chilli flesh and 1 teaspoon salt in a bowl. Make a well in the centre and add the egg, milk and creamed corn. Stir until just combined, being careful not to overbeat.
3 Pour into the tin and bake for 20 minutes, or until lightly browned and firm to touch. Turn onto a wire rack to cool.
4 For the topping, mix all the ingredients in a small bowl until well combined.
5 Using a serrated knife, trim the edges of the cornbread. Cut into 3 cm (1 1/4 inch) squares. Place on a platter and top each square with a teaspoon of topping. Sprinkle each with a drop of Tabasco and garnish with a coriander leaf.
IN ADVANCE: The topping can be made the day before and stored, covered, in the refrigerator.

MEXICAN MEATBALLS

Preparation time: 30 minutes
Total cooking time: 35 minutes
Makes about 28

2 slices white bread, crusts removed
3 tablespoons milk
250 g (8 oz) veal or beef mince
250 g (8 oz) pork mince
1 small onion, grated
1 egg, lightly beaten
1 teaspoon cumin seeds
2 tablespoons chopped fresh coriander
1 litre beef stock
2 tablespoons tomato paste (tomato purée)
sprigs of fresh coriander, to garnish

Tomato chilli sauce
3–4 red serrano chillies (or to taste)
1 small onion, finely chopped
2 cloves garlic, crushed
400 g (13 oz) can chopped tomatoes
2 teaspoons sugar

1 Roughly tear the bread into a bowl and soak in the milk for about 2 minutes. Squeeze, then break the bread into small pieces. Combine with the minces, onion, egg, cumin and fresh coriander. Season. The mixture will be sloppy. Mix well with your hands, then roll into about 28 small balls.

2 Mix the stock and tomato paste in a large saucepan and bring to the boil. Add the meatballs and return to the boil, then reduce the heat and simmer over low heat for 20 minutes, or until cooked through. Remove the meatballs with a slotted spoon, place in a warm serving bowl and provide cocktail sticks for serving. Garnish with coriander to serve. Strain and reserve the cooking liquid for another use, or freeze.

3 For the sauce, cut the chillies in half, discard the seeds, then finely chop. Heat a little oil in a pan and cook the onion over low heat for about 3 minutes, until soft and golden. Stir in the garlic and chilli for 1 minute. Stir in the tomato and sugar and simmer for 15 minutes. Cool slightly, then purée in a food processor. Season with salt and pepper and serve with the meatballs.

NOTE: Moisten your fingers with water when rolling the meatballs, to help prevent them sticking to you.

LEFT: Mexican meatballs

CHICKEN TAMALES

Preparation time: 45 minutes
Total cooking time: 1 hour 15 minutes
Makes 12

Dough

100 g (3½ oz) butter, softened
1 clove garlic, crushed
1 teaspoon ground cumin
1½ cups (210 g/7 oz) masa harina
⅓ cup (80 ml/2¾ fl oz) cream
⅓ cup (80 ml/2¾ fl oz) chicken stock

Filling

1 corn cob
2 tablespoons oil
150 g (5 oz) chicken breast fillets
2 cloves garlic, crushed
1 red chilli, seeded and chopped
1 red onion, chopped
1 red pepper (capsicum), chopped
2 tomatoes, peeled and chopped

1 To make the dough, beat the butter with electric beaters until creamy. Then add the garlic, cumin and 1 teaspoon salt and mix well. Add the masa harina and combined cream and stock alternately, beating until combined.
2 To make the filling, add the corn to a pan of boiling water and cook for 5–8 minutes, or until tender. Cool, then cut off the kernels with a sharp knife. Heat the oil in a frying pan and cook the chicken until golden. Remove, cool and shred finely. Add the garlic, chilli and onion to the pan and cook until soft. Add the red pepper and corn and stir for 3 minutes. Add the chicken, tomato and 1 teaspoon salt and simmer for 15 minutes, or until the liquid has reduced.
3 Bring a large pan of water to the boil and place a large bamboo steamer over it, making sure it doesn't touch the water.
4 Cut 12 pieces of baking paper 20 x 15 cm (8 x 6 inches). Spread a thick layer of dough over each piece, leaving a border at each end. Place some filling in the centre, roll up and secure both ends with string. Cook in the steamer for 35 minutes, or until firm.
IN ADVANCE: The filling can be made a day ahead. Assemble on the day of serving.

TAMALE BEEF AND BEAN PIES

Preparation time: 1 hour
Total cooking time: 50 minutes
Makes 30

1 tablespoon oil
1 small onion, finely chopped
250 g (8 oz) beef mince
1 clove garlic, crushed
¼ teaspoon chilli powder
200 g (6½ oz) canned crushed tomatoes
1½ cups (375 ml/12 fl oz) beef stock
300 g (10 oz) can red kidney beans, drained
2½ cups (360 g/11½ oz) masa harina
1 teaspoon baking powder
125 g (4 oz) butter, cut into cubes and chilled
125 g (4 oz) Cheddar, grated
sour cream, for serving

1 Heat the oil in a frying pan. Add the onion and cook over low heat for 3–4 minutes, or until soft. Increase the heat, add the mince and cook until browned all over. Add the garlic, chilli, tomato and ½ cup (125 ml/4 fl oz) stock. Bring to the boil, then reduce the heat and simmer for 35 minutes, or until the liquid has evaporated to a thick sauce. Stir in the beans and cool.
2 Lightly grease 30 holes in deep mini muffin tins. Sift the masa harina, baking powder and ½ teaspoon salt into a bowl. Rub the butter into the flour with your fingertips until it resembles fine breadcrumbs. Make a well in the centre and, with a flat-bladed knife, mix in the remaining stock, then use your hands to bring the mixture together into a ball. Divide into thirds and roll two thirds between 2 sheets of baking paper and cut out rounds with a 7 cm (2¾ inch) cutter. Line the muffin tins. Trim the edges and reserve any leftover pastry.
3 Preheat the oven to moderately hot 200°C (400°F/Gas 6). Spoon the filling into the pastry cases and sprinkle with the Cheddar. Roll out the remaining pastry and reserved pastry as above. Cut into 4 cm (1½ inch) rounds to cover the tops of the pies. Brush the edges with water and place over the filling. Trim the edges and press the pastry together to seal. Bake for 20–25 minutes, or until the pastry is crisp and lightly browned. Serve with sour cream.

CHICKEN TAMALES

Combine the dough ingredients, then beat the mixture until smooth.

Spread a thick layer of dough over each piece of baking paper.

Put some filling in the centre and roll the tamales up firmly.

Tie both ends of the paper securely with short pieces of string.

OPPOSITE PAGE: Chicken tamales (top); Tamale beef and bean pies

TOSTADAS WITH EGG AND CHORIZO

Preparation time: 15 minutes
Total cooking time: 10 minutes
Makes 28

4 flour tortillas

25 g (³/4 oz) butter, melted

1 teaspoon olive oil

1 chorizo sausage, peeled and finely chopped

25 g (³/4 oz) butter

5 eggs, lightly beaten

3 tablespoons milk

1 tablespoon chopped fresh coriander,
   to garnish

1 To make the tostadas, preheat the oven to moderately hot 200°C (400°F/Gas 6). Cut the tortillas into 28 rounds with a 6 cm (2½ inch) cutter. Line two baking trays with baking paper and brush the tortilla rounds with melted butter. Bake on the trays for 5–6 minutes, or until golden and crisp. Take care not to burn. Transfer to a serving platter.

2 Meanwhile, heat the oil in a small saucepan and cook the chorizo until crispy. Drain on crumpled paper towels. Wipe out the saucepan with paper towel and gently melt the butter. Add the combined eggs and milk and cook gently over low heat, stirring constantly until soft and creamy.

3 Remove from the heat and spoon the mixture into a warm bowl. (This is to stop the eggs from cooking further.) Fold the chorizo through and season, to taste, with salt and black pepper. Pile 2–3 teaspoons of the egg and chorizo mixture onto each tostada, scatter with fresh coriander and serve immediately.

IN ADVANCE: You can cook the tostadas ahead of time. Just before serving, warm them in the oven, wrapped in foil, for a few minutes. You will have to cook the egg and chorizo at the last minute.

ABOVE: Tostadas with egg and chorizo

CHICKEN DRUMSTICKS WITH RANCH DRESSING

Preparation time: 25 minutes + marinating
Total cooking time: 10 minutes
Makes 32

32 small chicken drumsticks
1 tablespoon cracked black pepper
1 tablespoon garlic salt
1 tablespoon onion powder
olive oil, for deep-frying
1 cup (250 ml/8 fl oz) tomato sauce
1/3 cup (80 ml/2 3/4 fl oz) Worcestershire sauce
40 g (1 1/4 oz) butter, melted
1 tablespoon sugar
Tabasco sauce, to taste

Ranch dressing
1 cup (250 g/8 oz) whole egg mayonnaise
1 cup (250 g/8 oz) sour cream
1/3 cup (80 ml/2 3/4 fl oz) lemon juice
1/3 cup (20 g/3/4 oz) chopped fresh chives

1 Remove the skin from the chicken and use a cleaver or large knife to cut off the knuckle. Wash the chicken thoroughly and pat dry with paper towels. Combine the pepper, garlic salt and onion powder and rub some into each piece of chicken.

2 Fill a deep heavy-based pan one third full of oil and heat the oil to 180°C (350°F). The oil is ready when a cube of bread dropped into the oil turns golden brown in 15 seconds. Cook the chicken in batches for 2 minutes each batch, remove with tongs or a slotted spoon and drain on paper towels.

3 Transfer the chicken to a large non-metal bowl or shallow dish. Combine the sauces, butter, sugar and Tabasco, pour over the chicken and stir to coat. Refrigerate, covered, for several hours or overnight. Prepare and heat the barbecue 1 hour before cooking.

4 Place the chicken on a hot lightly oiled barbecue grill or flatplate and cook for 20–25 minutes, or until cooked through. Turn and brush with the marinade during cooking. Serve with the ranch dressing.

5 For the ranch dressing, mix together the mayonnaise, sour cream, juice, chives, and salt and pepper, to taste.

TABASCO
This is a very hot spicy red sauce made using red chillies grown specially in Louisiana in America. The chillies are ground with vinegar and salt, then matured for 3 years in oak barrels. The result is the peppery sauce which is used as a condiment in Tex-Mex and other cuisines, as well as for spicing some cocktails.

LEFT: Chicken drumsticks with ranch dressing

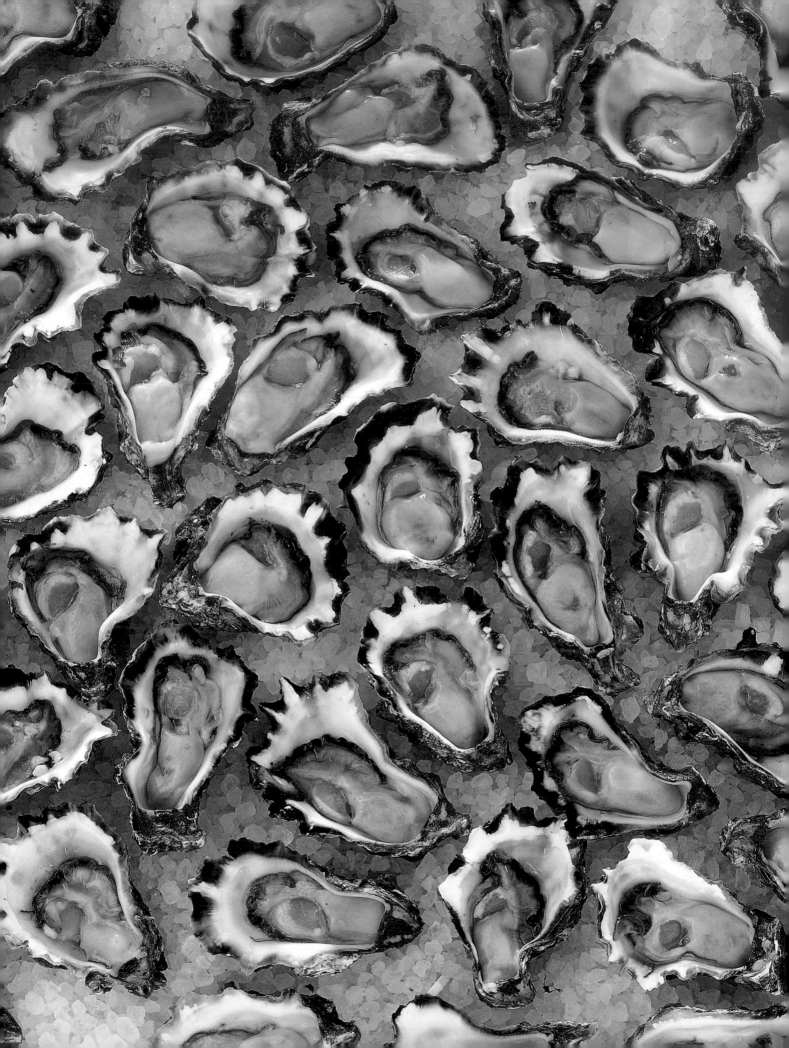

PARTY TIME

So, you've written the invitations and now there's no denying it... it's not a 'gathering', not just a 'few friends coming over', it's a fully-fledged party. And with the word 'party' comes the anticipation, the excitement and the thrill. Keep calm and don't overdo it: a selection of five or six of the following ideas (double or treble the recipes as necessary) will keep you cooler than a frenzy of twenty different dishes. Ring the changes by serving miniature versions of food your guests expect to be 'big'—tiny meat pies and mini pan-fried sandwiches. Alternatively, push the boat out and serve nothing but the best Champagne and a sophisticated range of seafood to be eaten straight from the shell.

HERBS

As dried herbs have a stronger flavour than fresh, they are used more sparingly. If a recipe calls for fresh herbs that are unavailable, in many cases you can use dried if you adjust the quantity. For every tablespoon of chopped fresh herbs, substitute 1 teaspoon of dried. Store dried herbs in an airtight container in a cool dark place. When in plentiful supply, fresh herbs can be chopped, then frozen in ice cube trays with a little water. You can use the frozen cubes in sauces.

MINI MEAT PIES

Preparation time: 20 minutes
Total cooking time: 25 minutes
Makes 24

6 sheets ready-rolled shortcrust pastry
2 small tomatoes, sliced
1/2 teaspoon dried oregano leaves

Filling

1 tablespoon oil
1 onion, chopped
2 cloves garlic, crushed
500 g (1 lb) beef mince
2 tablespoons plain flour
1 1/2 cups (375 ml/12 fl oz) beef stock
1/3 cup (80 ml/2 3/4 fl oz) tomato sauce
2 teaspoons Worcestershire sauce
1/2 teaspoon dried mixed herbs

1 Preheat the oven to moderately hot 200°C (400°F/Gas 6). Cut the pastry into 48 circles (if making traditional pies, only 24 if making uncovered pies) using a 7 cm (2 3/4 inch) round cutter. Press 24 circles into two lightly greased 12-hole patty tins.
2 To make the filling, heat the oil in a heavy-based pan, add the onion and garlic and cook over medium heat for 2 minutes, or until the onion is soft. Add the mince and stir over high heat for 3 minutes, or until well browned and all the liquid has evaporated. Use a fork to break up any lumps of mince.
3 Add the flour, stir until combined, then cook over medium heat for 1 minute. Add the stock, sauces and herbs and stir over the heat until boiling. Reduce the heat to low and simmer for 5 minutes, or until the mixture has reduced and thickened; stir occasionally. Allow to cool.
4 Divide the filling among the pastry circles. Top each with two half slices of tomato and sprinkle with oregano. Bake for 25 minutes, or until the pastry is golden brown and crisp. For traditional pies, place the remaining pastry rounds over the tomato and oregano topping and seal the edges with beaten egg before baking. Serve hot.

ABOVE: Mini meat pies

CHICKEN AND CORN BITES

Preparation time: 15 minutes
Total cooking time: 15 minutes
Makes 50

1 1/2 cups (185 g/6 oz) self-raising flour
2 teaspoons chicken stock powder
1/2 teaspoon chicken seasoning salt
60 g (2 oz) butter, chopped
50 g (1 3/4 oz) corn chips, finely crushed
2 eggs, lightly beaten
chicken seasoning salt, extra

1 Preheat the oven to moderate 180°C (350°F/
Gas 4). Line a baking tray with baking paper.
2 Sift the flour, stock powder and seasoning salt
into a large bowl and add the butter. Rub into
the flour with your fingertips until the mixture
resembles fine breadcrumbs. Stir in the corn
chips. Make a well in the centre, add the eggs
and mix with a flat-bladed knife, using a cutting
action until the mixture comes together in beads.
3 Gently gather the dough together, lift out
onto a lightly floured surface and press together
into a ball. Roll out to 4 mm (1/4 inch) thickness.
Cut the dough into shapes with a plain or fluted
biscuit cutter.
4 Place on the tray and sprinkle with chicken
salt. Bake for 15 minutes, or until lightly
browned. Cool on the tray.
IN ADVANCE: Store in an airtight container for
up to 2 days or freeze.

POLENTA SQUARES WITH SMOKED TURKEY AND CRANBERRY SAUCE

Preparation time: 25 minutes + chilling
Total cooking time: 20 minutes
Makes 35

1 litre chicken stock
1 1/2 cups (250 g/8 oz) instant polenta
150 g (5 oz) sliced smoked turkey breast,
   finely shredded
3/4 cup (185 g/6 oz) whole egg mayonnaise
2 tablespoons cranberry sauce
1 clove garlic, crushed
1/2 teaspoon finely grated lime rind

2 teaspoons lime juice
1 teaspoon finely chopped fresh thyme
oil, for deep-frying
thyme leaves, extra, to garnish

1 Lightly grease a 20 x 30 cm (8 x 12 inch)
shallow baking tin. Place the chicken stock in a
large pan and bring to the boil. Reduce the heat
and gradually add the polenta, stirring constantly.
Cook for 2 minutes, over medium heat, until the
polenta becomes thick. Spread into the tin and
refrigerate for 30 minutes, or until firm.
2 Combine the turkey, mayonnaise, cranberry
sauce, garlic, lime rind, juice and thyme in a
bowl, then add salt and pepper, to taste.
3 Cut the polenta into 35 squares. Fill a deep
heavy-based pan one third full of oil and heat the
oil to 180°C (350°F). The oil is ready when a
cube of bread dropped in the oil turns golden
brown in 15 seconds. Deep-fry the polenta in
several batches until lightly browned and crisp.
Drain on crumpled paper towels. Top the
polenta squares with the turkey mixture and
garnish with thyme leaves. Serve warm.
IN ADVANCE: Topping and polenta can be made
a day ahead. Cook the polenta close to serving.

*ABOVE: Chicken
and corn bites*

SPICY SAUSAGE ROLL-UPS

Preparation time: 20 minutes
Total cooking time: 20 minutes
Makes about 25

2 sheets frozen shortcrust pastry
2 tablespoons French mustard
5 sticks cabanossi
1 egg yolk, beaten

1 Preheat the oven to hot 200°C (400°F/Gas 6). Cut each pastry sheet in half. Cut triangles with bases of 6 cm (2½ inches). Place a small dob of mustard at the base of each pastry piece. Cut the cabanossi into 7 cm (2¾ inch) lengths and place across the mustard on the pastry triangles.
2 Dampen the tips of the triangles with a little water. Working from the base, roll each pastry triangle around the pieces of cabanossi. Press lightly to secure the tip to the rest of the pastry.
3 Place the roll-ups on a lightly greased baking tray and brush with a mixture of egg yolk and 2 teaspoons cold water. Bake for 15–20 minutes, or until the roll-ups are golden brown.
IN ADVANCE: These can be made up to 2 days ahead, refrigerated, then gently reheated in the oven when required.

GLAZED CHICKEN WINGS

Preparation time: 30 minutes + marinating
Total cooking time: 45 minutes
Makes about 40

2 kg (4 lb) chicken wings
½ cup (125 ml/4 fl oz) barbecue sauce
½ cup (160 g/5½ oz) apricot jam
2 tablespoons white vinegar
2 tablespoons soy sauce
2 tablespoons tomato sauce
1 tablespoon sesame oil
2 cloves garlic, crushed

1 Trim excess fat from the wings. Stir the barbecue sauce, jam, vinegar, soy sauce, tomato sauce, oil and garlic in a small pan over low heat until just combined. Cool slightly, pour over the chicken wings and mix well. Cover and marinate in the refrigerator for at least 2 hours.
2 Preheat the oven to moderate 180°C (350°F/ Gas 4). Drain the excess marinade from the wings and reserve. Bake the wings in a lightly greased baking dish for 45 minutes. To prevent sticking, you can add a little water. Turn halfway through the cooking time, brushing occasionally with the reserved marinade.

RIGHT: Spicy sausage roll-ups (left); Glazed chicken wings; Zucchini boats

ZUCCHINI (COURGETTE) BOATS

Preparation time: 20 minutes
Total cooking time: 10 minutes
Makes 30

5 large zucchini (courgettes)
1 large tomato, finely chopped
2 spring onions, finely chopped
1 tablespoon chopped fresh parsley
2 slices salami, finely chopped
1/2 cup (60 g/2 oz) grated Cheddar

1 Cut each zucchini into three equal pieces, about 4 cm (1½ inches) long. Cut each piece in half lengthways.
2 Using a teaspoon, scoop a small hollow from each piece. Add the zucchini to a pan of simmering water for about 3 minutes, or until tender; drain. Refresh under cold water, then pat dry with paper towels.
3 Combine the tomato, onion, parsley, salami and Cheddar in a small bowl. Spoon the filling into the zucchini boats. Cook under a preheated grill until the Cheddar has melted and the boats are warmed through. Serve immediately.

CHILLI PRAWNS WITH SHREDDED COCONUT

Preparation time: 40 minutes + marinating
Total cooking time: 8–10 minutes
Makes about 18

1 cup (250 ml/8 fl oz) tomato sauce
3 cloves garlic, crushed
1 teaspoon ground chilli
1/4 cup (60 ml/2 fl oz) lemon juice
2 teaspoons finely grated lemon rind
2 tablespoons soy sauce
2 tablespoons honey
1 tablespoon oil
2 kg (4 lb) raw king prawns, peeled and deveined
1 cup (60 g/2 oz) shredded coconut

1 In a large bowl, mix the tomato sauce, garlic, chilli, lemon juice, rind, soy sauce and honey. Add the prawns and marinate in the refrigerator for at least 2 hours. Drain. Reserve the marinade.
2 Heat the oil in a large frying pan. Add the prawns and coconut and cook until the prawns turn pink. Stir in the marinade and cook for 2 minutes, or until heated through. Stir in the coconut. Serve on a platter.

COCONUT
Used extensively in Asian and Indian cuisines, as well as many others, coconut is available in many forms including milk, cream, oil, shredded, flaked and desiccated, or powdered. High in saturated fat, it is not good if you are watching your weight.

ABOVE: Chilli prawns with shredded coconut

SWEET POTATO ROSTI

Preparation time: 30 minutes
Total cooking time: 45 minutes
Makes 30

3 sweet potatoes, unpeeled
2 teaspoons cornflour
40 g (1 1/4 oz) butter
150 g (5 oz) mozzarella cheese, cut
   into 30 cubes

1 Boil or microwave the sweet potatoes until almost cooked, but still firm. Set aside to cool, then peel and coarsely grate into a bowl. Add the cornflour and 1/2 teaspoon salt and toss lightly to combine.
2 Melt a little of the butter in a frying pan. Place teaspoons of the potato in the pan and put a cube of cheese in the centre of each mound. Top with another teaspoon of potato and gently flatten to form rough circles. Increase the heat to medium and cook for about 3 minutes each side, or until golden. Repeat with remaining potato mixture and mozzarella cubes.
IN ADVANCE: The sweet potatoes can be cooked and grated up to 2 hours ahead and set aside, covered, until serving time. Assemble and cook the rosti close to serving time.

CORN AND RED PEPPER (CAPSICUM) TARTS

Preparation time: 20 minutes
Total cooking time: 25 minutes
Makes about 36

3 sheets frozen puff pastry, thawed
310 g (10 oz) canned corn kernels, drained
150 g (5 oz) Red Leicester cheese, grated
1 small red pepper (capsicum), finely chopped
2 eggs, lightly beaten
1/4 cup (60 ml/2 fl oz) buttermilk
2/3 cup (170 ml/5 1/2 fl oz) thick (double) cream
1 teaspoon Dijon mustard
dash of Tabasco sauce

1 Preheat the oven to moderately hot 200°C (400°F/Gas 6). Lightly grease three 12-hole round-based patty tins. Using a 6 cm (2 1/2 inch) round pastry cutter, cut circles from the pastry sheets. Press the circles into the prepared tins and prick the bases all over with a fork.
2 Combine the corn, cheese and red pepper in a bowl and season with salt and freshly ground pepper. Whisk the eggs, buttermilk, cream, mustard and Tabasco sauce in a jug. Spoon some of the vegetable mixture into the pastry cases, then pour the egg mixture over the top until the cases are almost full. Bake for 20–25 minutes, or until well risen and set. The tarts can be served hot or cold. Garnish with herbs of your choice if you wish.
IN ADVANCE: The tarts can be made up to a day ahead and refrigerated, covered, in an airtight container, or frozen for up to 2 months.

EGGS WITH SALMON AND CAPERS

Preparation time: 20 minutes
Total cooking time: 10 minutes
Makes 24

12 eggs
1 tablespoon drained capers, finely chopped
1 tablespoon finely chopped fresh dill
1/2 cup (125 g/4 oz) whole egg mayonnaise
200 g (6 1/2 oz) sliced smoked salmon
extra dill, to garnish

1 Put the eggs in a saucepan, cover with cold water and slowly bring to the boil. Gently stir the eggs while boiling to centre the yolk. Cook for 7 minutes, rinse under cold water and peel. Cut the eggs in half lengthways.
2 Remove the yolk from the egg halves, press the yolks through a sieve or grate finely into a bowl, then combine with the capers, dill and mayonnaise. Mix with a fork until well combined. Season, to taste.
3 Using a 1 cm (1/2 inch) star nozzle, pipe a small rosette of the egg mixture into each of the egg halves.
4 Shred the salmon slices and pile on top of the egg halves. Garnish with dill sprigs and black pepper, to taste. Serve.

OPPOSITE PAGE: Sweet potato rosti (top); Corn and red pepper tarts

SANDWICHES Sandwiches don't have

to be ungainly chunks of bread filled with salmon paste or cheese spread. Welcome

to the sophisticated party sandwich. It could just be the star of your show.

HAM AND CORN RELISH RIBBONS

Mix 1 cup (250 g/8 oz) sour cream with ½ cup (140 g/4½ oz) corn relish and spread on 8 slices of white bread. Top each with a slice of dark seed bread. Top that with sliced ham, then sandwich with a buttered slice of white bread. Remove the crusts and slice each sandwich into three. Makes 24 ribbon sandwiches.

VEGETABLE TRIANGLES

Cut 500 g (1 lb) butternut pumpkin into chunks, put in a baking dish, drizzle with oil and bake in a moderately hot 200°C (400°F/Gas 6) oven for 1 hour, or until tender. Cool, then mash. Spread 4 slices of soy and linseed bread with 1 tablespoon of tomato salsa. Top each with sliced marinated eggplant, coriander leaves and sliced spring onion. Spread 4 more slices of bread with the mashed pumpkin and place on top. Remove the crusts and cut into triangles. Makes 16.

226

CHICKEN AND GUACAMOLE SQUARES

Mash 2 avocados with 1 tablespoon mayonnaise, 1 teaspoon chopped chilli, 1 tablespoon lemon juice, 1 small chopped tomato and 1/2 finely chopped red onion. Spread over 8 slices of wholemeal bread and top with 250 g (8 oz) sliced smoked chicken breast. Add trimmed snow pea (mangetout) sprouts. Sandwich with more bread, remove the crusts and cut into squares. Makes 32.

TURKEY AND BRIE TRIANGLES

Trim the crusts from 8 slices bread. Spread 4 with cranberry sauce. Using 120 g (4 oz) turkey breast, 120 g (4 oz) sliced brie and 4 butter lettuce leaves, make into sandwiches. Cut into triangles. Makes 16.

ROAST BEEF, PATE AND ROCKET FINGERS

Trim the crusts from 16 slices of bread. Spread 160 g (5 1/2 oz) cracked pepper paté over half the bread. Make sandwiches using 250 g (8 oz) sliced rare roast beef, 160 g (5 1/2 oz) semi-dried tomatoes and rocket leaves. Cut each into three fingers to serve. Makes 24.

LEMON SANDWICHES WITH PRAWNS

Wash and dry 1 1/2 thin-skinned lemons and slice finely. Make lemon sandwiches with 10 slices of multi-grain bread. Cut each sandwich into 8 triangles. Remove the crusts and serve with 500 g (1 lb) peeled and deveined cooked king prawns, leaving the tails intact. Makes 40.

CHICKEN, ROCKET AND WALNUT SANDWICHES

Fry 250 g (8 oz) chicken breast fillets and 500 g (1 lb) chicken thigh fillets until cooked. Cool, then chop finely. Mix with 1 cup (250 g/8 oz) mayonnaise, some finely chopped celery and chopped walnuts. Season. Make into sandwiches with 20 slices bread, adding trimmed rocket to each. Remove the crusts and cut the sandwiches into fingers. Makes 30.

CLOKWISE, FROM BOTTOM LEFT: Chicken and guacamole squares; Vegetable triangles; Ham and corn relish ribbons; Turkey and brie triangles; Roast beef, pâté and rocket fingers; Chicken, rocket and walnut sandwiches; Lemon sandwiches with prawns

MARINATED ROASTED VEGETABLE DIP

Preparation time: 55 minutes + marinating
Total cooking time: 50 minutes
Serves 8

★ ★

1 small eggplant (aubergine), sliced

2 zucchini (courgettes), sliced

3 red peppers (capsicums)

¹/₂ cup (125 ml/4 fl oz) extra virgin olive oil

2 cloves garlic, sliced

2 Roma tomatoes

200 g (6¹/₂ oz) canned artichoke hearts, drained

7 g (¹/₄ oz) fresh oregano leaves

250 g (8 oz) ricotta cheese

45 g (1¹/₂ oz) black olives, pitted and sliced

1 Place the eggplant and zucchini in a colander over a bowl, sprinkle generously with salt and leave for 15–20 minutes. Meanwhile, cut the red peppers into large flat pieces, removing the seeds and membrane. Cook, skin-side-up, under a hot grill until the skin is black and blistered. Cool in a plastic bag, then peel. Reserve about a quarter of the peppers to use as a garnish and place the rest in a large non-metallic bowl.

2 Place half the olive oil in a bowl, add 1 garlic clove and a pinch of salt and mix. Rinse the eggplant and zucchini and pat dry with paper towels. Place the eggplant on a non-stick or foil-lined tray and brush with the garlic oil. Cook under a very hot grill for 4–6 minutes each side, or until golden brown, brushing both sides with oil during grilling. The eggplant will burn easily, so keep a close watch. Allow to cool while grilling the zucchini in the same way. Add both to the red pepper in the bowl.

3 Slice the tomatoes lengthways, place on a non-stick or foil-lined baking tray and brush with the garlic oil. Reduce the temperature slightly and grill for 10–15 minutes, or until soft. Add to the bowl with the other vegetables.

4 Cut the artichokes into quarters and add to the bowl. Mix in any remaining garlic oil along with the remaining olive oil. Stir in the oregano and remaining garlic. Cover with a tight-fitting lid or plastic wrap and refrigerate for at least 2 hours.

5 Drain the vegetables and place in a food processor. Add the ricotta and process for 20 seconds, or until smooth. Reserve a tablespoon of olives to garnish. Add the rest to the processor. Mix in a couple of short bursts,

ABOVE: Marinated roasted vegetable dip

228

then transfer to a non-metallic bowl and cover with plastic wrap. Chill for at least 2 hours.
6 Slice the reserved roasted red pepper into fine strips and arrange over the top of the dip with the reserved olives.

HERBED SCALLOP KEBABS

Preparation time: 1 hour + soaking
Total cooking time: 10 minutes
Makes 24

24 scallops
6 large spring onions, green part only
2 zucchini (courgettes)
2 carrots
20 g (³⁄₄ oz) butter, melted
2 teaspoons lemon juice
1 tablespoon white wine
2 teaspoons mixed dried herbs
¹⁄₄ teaspoon onion powder

1 Soak 24 wooden skewers in cold water for 30 minutes. Wash the scallops, slice or pull off any vein, membrane or hard white muscle, then pat dry with paper towels. Cut the spring onions in half lengthways, then into 8 cm (3 inch) lengths. Line a baking tray with foil.
2 Using a vegetable peeler, slice the zucchini and carrots lengthways into thin ribbons. Plunge the vegetable strips into a bowl of boiling water, leave for 1 minute, then drain. Plunge into a bowl of iced water and leave until cold. Drain and pat dry with paper towels.
3 Roll each scallop in a strip of onion, carrot and zucchini and secure with a wooden skewer.
4 Combine the butter, juice and wine in a small bowl. Brush over the scallops. Sprinkle with the combined herbs and onion powder. Place under a hot grill for 5–10 minutes, or chargrill or barbecue until the scallops are tender and cooked through.
IN ADVANCE: Scallops can be prepared several hours ahead. Refrigerate, covered, until needed.

SCALLOPS
World-wide, there are more than 400 species of this popular bivalve mollusc. Both the roe and the muscle that opens and closes the shell are edible. The attractive fan-shaped fluted shells, which vary in colour, make ideal serving dishes.

LEFT: Herbed scallop kebabs

CRAB-STUFFED MUSHROOMS

Preparation time: 25 minutes
Total cooking time: 6 minutes
Makes 24

24 small cap mushrooms
30 g (1 oz) butter, softened
4 spring onions, chopped
200 g (6 1/2 oz) can crab meat, drained
2 tablespoons lemon juice
1/2 teaspoon chilli powder
1 cup (250 g/8 oz) sour cream
25 g (3/4 oz) Parmesan, grated
125 g (4 oz) Cheddar, grated
pinch of paprika

1 Preheat the oven to moderate 180°C (350°F/Gas 4). Remove the mushroom stalks and chop finely; set aside. Place the mushroom caps on a baking tray.
2 Combine the butter, spring onion, crab, lemon juice, chilli powder and freshly ground pepper, to taste, in a bowl.
3 Mix in the mushroom stalks, sour cream and Parmesan. Spoon even amounts into the mushroom caps and sprinkle with the combined Cheddar and paprika.
4 Bake for 5–6 minutes, or until the Cheddar has melted and the mushrooms heated through. Serve warm.

CAVIAR EGGS

Preparation time: 20 minutes
Total cooking time: 7 minutes
Makes 40

20 eggs
1 tablespoon curry powder
1 1/2 cups (375 g/12 oz) whole egg mayonnaise
45 g (1 1/2 oz) jar red caviar
45 g (1 1/2 oz) jar black caviar

1 Put the eggs in a saucepan, cover with cold water and slowly bring to the boil. Gently stir the eggs while boiling to centre the yolk. Cook for 7 minutes, rinse under cold water and peel.
2 Cut the eggs in halves lengthways, remove the yolks and push the yolks through a fine sieve

into a bowl. Blend in the curry powder and mayonnaise, stirring until the mixture is smooth.
3 Put the filling in a piping bag fitted with a 1 cm (1/2 inch) star nozzle. Pipe the mixture into the egg cavities. Garnish with red and black caviar just before serving.
IN ADVANCE: The eggs can be prepared hours ahead, covered and refrigerated. Decorate with caviar close to serving.

SESAME CHICKEN STICKS

Preparation time: 25 minutes + overnight marinating
Total cooking time: 25 minutes
Makes about 32

4 chicken breast fillets, cut into strips
1/4 cup (60 ml/2 fl oz) teriyaki sauce
1 tablespoon chilli sauce
1 tablespoon natural yoghurt
2 teaspoons curry powder
2 cups (100 g/3 1/2 oz) crushed cornflakes
1/4 cup (40 g/1 1/4 oz) sesame seeds
35 g (1 1/4 oz) Parmesan, grated

Sweet and sour sauce
1 tablespoon cornflour
1/2 cup (125 ml/4 fl oz) white vinegar
1/2 cup (125 g/4 oz) caster sugar
1/4 cup (60 ml/2 fl oz) tomato sauce
1 teaspoon chicken stock powder

1 Combine the chicken strips in a bowl with the teriyaki sauce, chilli sauce, yoghurt and curry powder. Mix well, cover and refrigerate overnight.
2 Preheat the oven to moderately hot 190°C (375°F/Gas 5). Combine the cornflakes, sesame seeds and Parmesan in a shallow dish. Drain the excess marinade from the chicken. Coat each chicken strip in the crumb mixture.
3 Place the strips in a single layer on a greased baking tray. Bake for 20–25 minutes, or until crisp and golden. Serve hot with the sauce.
4 To prepare the sauce, blend the cornflour with the vinegar and combine with the remaining ingredients and 1 cup (250 ml/8 fl oz) water in a small saucepan. Stir over medium heat until the mixture boils and thickens.
IN ADVANCE: Crumbed chicken strips can be frozen in a single layer for 2 months.

CAVIAR
True caviar, which is very expensive, is the roe or eggs from the sturgeon family of fish. The size of the roe varies according to the type of fish, and the colour ranges from light grey to black. Red caviar comes either from salmon, the roe of which is naturally red, or from lumpfish. Lumpfish roe is tiny and pink and is dyed black or red and sold as Danish or German caviar.

OPPOSITE PAGE, FROM LEFT: Crab-stuffed mushrooms; Caviar eggs; Sesame chicken sticks

1 Preheat the oven to moderate 180°C (350°F/Gas 4). Spread the almonds and pecans on a large baking tray and bake for 5–10 minutes, or until they are crisp and lightly coloured. Remove and allow to cool.

2 Combine the sugar, salt and spices in a small bowl and mix well.

3 Heat a large non-stick frying pan and add the almonds and pecans. Sprinkle the spice mixture over the nuts and stir over medium heat for 5 minutes, or until the nuts turn golden. The sugar will melt and coat the nuts. Gently shake the frying pan often to ensure even cooking. If the nuts stick together, separate them with a wooden spoon. When the nuts are cooked, remove from the heat and spread them on a lightly oiled baking tray to cool.

NOTE: If you use a small frying pan, cook the nuts in batches. Cashews, macadamias or peanuts can be used or, if you prefer, just one variety.

IN ADVANCE: Transfer the cooled nuts to tightly sealed jars or containers. They will keep for a couple of weeks.

GOATS CHEESE TARTS WITH PEPPER (CAPSICUM) AND CARAMELIZED ONION

Preparation time: 20 minutes + chilling
Total cooking time: 55 minutes
Makes about 48

2 cups (250 g/8 oz) plain flour

125 g (4 oz) butter, chopped

1 red pepper (capsicum)

150 g (5 oz) firm goats cheese, grated

1 cup (250 g/8 oz) sour cream or
    crème fraîche

2 eggs

1 clove garlic, crushed

2 teaspoons finely chopped fresh lemon thyme

30 g (1 oz) butter

1 large red onion, halved and finely sliced

2 teaspoons soft brown sugar

1 teaspoon balsamic vinegar

1 Preheat the oven to moderately hot 190°C (350°F/Gas 4). Lightly grease two 12-hole round-based patty tins.

2 Sift the flour with a pinch of salt into a large bowl. Add the butter and rub into the flour with

SWEET AND SALTY PARTY NUTS

Preparation time: 20 minutes
Total cooking time: 15 minutes
Serves 6-8

250 g (8 oz) blanched almonds

250 g (8 oz) pecans

1/4 cup (60 g/2 oz) sugar

1 teaspoon salt

1 teaspoon ground cinnamon

pinch of ground cloves

1/2 teaspoon curry powder

1/4 teaspoon ground cumin

1/2 teaspoon ground black pepper

ABOVE: Sweet and salty party nuts

your fingertips until the mixture resembles fine breadcrumbs. Make a well in the centre and stir in up to 4 tablespoons water to form a firm dough. Gently gather together and lift onto a lightly floured surface. Press into a ball, then flatten into a disc. Wrap in plastic wrap and refrigerate for 30 minutes.

3 Roll out half the dough on a lightly floured surface to 2 mm (⅛ inch) thick and cut out 24 rounds with a 5 cm (2 inch) cutter. Place into the patty tins and refrigerate for 10 minutes.

4 Cut the pepper into quarters and remove the seeds and membrane. Cook, skin-side-up, under a hot grill until the skin is black and blistered. Place in a plastic bag until cool, then peel. Cut the flesh into thin strips.

5 Mix together the goats cheese, sour cream, eggs, garlic, thyme and salt and pepper and set aside.

6 Melt the butter in a frying pan and cook the onion for 5 minutes, or until golden brown. Add the sugar and vinegar and cook for another 5 minutes, or until caramelized.

7 Divide half the goats cheese mixture evenly onto the pastry rounds and top with half the pepper strips and half the caramelized onion. Bake for 20 minutes, or until golden brown. Repeat with the remaining pastry and filling. Serve immediately.

DEVILS ON HORSEBACK

Preparation time: 10 minutes + soaking
Total cooking time: 6 minutes
Makes 24

8 bacon rashers
12 pitted prunes
12 oysters, on the shell or bottled
2 tablespoons Worcestershire sauce
Tabasco sauce, to taste

1 Soak 24 wooden skewers in water for 30 minutes. Trim the rind from the bacon and cut each rasher into three pieces. Wrap a portion of bacon around each prune and secure with a skewer.

2 Remove the oysters from their shells, or drain from the bottling liquid. Sprinkle lightly with Worcestershire sauce and ground black pepper, to taste. Wrap each oyster in bacon, securing with a skewer as before.

3 Cook under a preheated grill or lightly oil the outer edge of a preheated barbecue flatplate. Cook the savouries, turning occasionally, until the bacon is crisp. Serve warm, sprinkled with a dash of Tabasco sauce.

DEVILS ON HORSEBACK
There are two versions of this party piece. One has oysters wrapped in bacon before being cooked, while the other has prunes instead of oysters. The prunes are sometimes cooked in wine, then stuffed with mango chutney or an almond. The addition of hot Tabasco sauce turns *Angels on Horseback* into little devils.

ABOVE: Devils on horseback

POTATO AND ROSEMARY PIZZETTAS

Preparation time: 25 minutes + standing
Total cooking time: 12–15 minutes
Makes 48

1 teaspoon dried yeast
1/2 teaspoon sugar
2 1/2 cups (310 g/10 oz) plain flour
1/3 cup (80 ml/2 3/4 fl oz) olive oil
400 g (13 oz) pontiac potatoes, unpeeled
2 tablespoons olive oil, extra
1 tablespoon fresh rosemary leaves

1 Place the yeast, sugar and 1/3 cup (80 ml/ 2 3/4 fl oz) water in a small bowl, cover and leave in a warm place until foamy.
2 Sift the flour and 1/4 teaspoon salt into a large bowl. Make a well in the centre and stir in the yeast mixture, the oil and 1/3 cup (80 ml/ 2 3/4 fl oz) water; mix to a soft dough. Turn out onto a lightly floured surface and knead for 5 minutes, or until the dough is smooth and elastic. Place the dough in an oiled bowl, cover and leave in a warm place for about 1 hour, or until the dough has doubled in size.
3 Preheat the oven to hot 220°C (425°F/Gas 7). Punch down the dough to expel the air. Turn out and knead for 1 minute, or until smooth. Divide into 48 portions and roll each portion to a 5 cm (2 inch) round. Place on lightly greased baking trays.
4 Cut the potatoes into slices. Cover each dough round with a slice of potato, leaving a 1 cm (1/2 inch) border. Brush the pizzettas with the extra olive oil and sprinkle with rosemary leaves and salt. Bake on the highest shelf in the oven for 12–15 minutes, or until the pastry is crisp and lightly browned. Serve immediately.
IN ADVANCE: Best made close to serving. The dough can be prepared ahead on the day of serving and refrigerated, covered, up to the point of second kneading. Alternatively, at this stage, the dough can be frozen. When hard, remove from the trays and seal in plastic bags. Place on lightly greased baking trays to thaw. The pizzas can be baked several hours ahead and reheated in a moderate 180°C (350°F/Gas 4) oven for 5 minutes, or until warmed through.

POTATO BASKETS WITH CHEESE

Preparation time: 15 minutes
Total cooking time: 55 minutes
Makes about 40

20 small new potatoes
250 g (8 oz) ricotta cheese
35 g (1 1/4 oz) Cheddar, grated
25 g (3/4 oz) Parmesan, shredded
oil, for spraying or brushing
15 g (1/2 oz) fresh chives, finely chopped, to garnish

1 Preheat the oven to moderately hot 200°C (400°F/Gas 6). Boil or steam the potatoes for 10 minutes, or until just tender when tested with a skewer (do not overcook or the potatoes will fall apart when you are preparing them). Drain well and cool completely.
2 Meanwhile, in a small bowl combine the ricotta, Cheddar and Parmesan. Season, to taste, and set aside.
3 Cut the cooled potatoes in half and use a melon baller to scoop out the flesh, leaving a 5 mm (1/4 inch) border. Discard the flesh.
4 Lightly spray the potato halves with oil and bake on baking trays for 30–45 minutes, or until crisp and golden. Heat the grill to high.
5 Fill each potato shell with a teaspoon of the cheese mixture and grill for 5–8 minutes, or until the tops are lightly golden and the cheese has melted. Arrange on a serving dish and garnish each with chopped chives. Serve immediately.
IN ADVANCE: The potatoes can be cooked and filled in advance, then grilled just before serving.

CUCUMBER BITES

Cut 1 cm (1/2 inch) rounds of telegraph cucumber. You can leave as is or cut into shapes with a decorative cutter. Top with dollops of taramasalata (see page 184) or creamy salmon dip (see page 236). Sprinkle with chopped fresh dill and decorate with small pieces of sliced lemon. Cooked, peeled and deveined prawns can be put on top, or small pieces of smoked salmon. Refrigerate until ready to serve.

ROSEMARY
This fragrant herb is native to the Mediterranean region. The silvery-grey spiky leaves complement many foods including lamb, fish, tomatoes and vegetables. Because of its strong flavour the herb should be used sparingly. The leaves are also available dried or ground.

OPPOSITE PAGE: Potato and rosemary pizzettas (top); Potato baskets with cheese

DIPS
These are a favourite at any gathering. Serve them up with crudités, crackers or crusty bread and watch your guests hovering around the bowl trying not to look too greedy.

CREAMY SALMON
Combine 200 g (6½ oz) cream cheese with 100 g (3½ oz) chopped smoked salmon and 5 tablespoons cream in a food processor and mix until smooth. Season with pepper and sprinkle with a few chopped chives. Keep refrigerated until ready to use.
Makes about 1½ cups.

HOT APPLE CHUTNEY
Beat ¼ cup (60 g/2 oz) sour cream, ½ cup (125 g/4 oz) natural yoghurt, ¼ cup (70 g/2¼ oz) ready-made hot apple chutney and 1 teaspoon maple syrup together until smooth. Season, to taste, with salt and pepper and refrigerate until ready to serve.
Makes about 1½ cups.

BLUE CHEESE AND CREAM
Mix 250 g (8 oz) blue cheese in a food processor with ½ cup (125 ml/4 fl oz) cream until smooth. Transfer to a bowl, stir in another ½ cup (125 ml/4 fl oz) cream and 2 teaspoons apple cider vinegar and mix well. Season with salt and pepper, cover and refrigerate until ready to use. Makes about 1½ cups.

SWEET AND SOUR

Beat 1 cup (250 g/4 oz) natural yoghurt and 1/3 cup (80 ml/2¾ fl oz) bottled sweet and sour sauce together until smooth. Add 1 tablespoon finely chopped fresh chives and season, to taste, with salt and pepper. Cover and keep refrigerated until ready to use. Makes about 1½ cups.

CUCUMBER AND PEAR

Beat 2 tablespoons whole egg mayonnaise, 2 tablespoons natural yoghurt, 1 tablespoon sour cream and 1 teaspoon Dijon mustard together until well combined and smooth. Finely dice half a pear and 1/4 of a small cucumber and stir into the mixture with 1 teaspoon of lemon juice. Season, to taste, with salt and freshly ground black pepper. Cover and keep refrigerated until ready to use. Makes about 1 cup.

REFRIED BEANS

Combine a 460 g (14 oz) can refried beans and 1/4 cup (60 g/2 oz) sour cream in a food processor and mix until smooth, adding salt and pepper, to taste. Cover and keep at room temperature until ready to use. Makes about 1½ cups.

AVOCADO AND HERB

Place 1 avocado, 1 tablespoon each of sour cream, lemon juice and light olive oil, 1 small seeded tomato and 3/4 cup (25 g/3/4 oz) coriander leaves in a food processor and mix until smooth. Season with salt and pepper. Transfer to a glass bowl, lay plastic wrap directly onto the surface of the dip (to prevent a skin forming) and keep refrigerated until ready to use. Try to make this dip close to serving time, so it doesn't discolour. Makes about 2 cups.

CORN AND BACON

Cut the corn kernels from 2 cobs of corn and cook in boiling water, covered, for about 10 minutes, then drain. Meanwhile cook 250 g (8 oz) lean finely chopped bacon in a non-stick pan until very crispy and drain on paper towels. Put the corn in a food processor with 1 crushed clove garlic and mix until quite smooth. Add 250 g (8 oz) spreadable cream cheese and process until well combined. Spoon into a serving dish, cool to room temperature and sprinkle the bacon and some chopped chives over the top. Makes about 2 cups.

CLOKWISE, FROM TOP LEFT: Creamy salmon; Blue cheese and cream; Cucumber and pear; Avocado and herb; Corn and bacon; Refried beans; Sweet and sour; Hot apple chutney

mustard in a small bowl. Peel the eggs, and toss lightly in the flour.

3 Divide the chicken mixture into 24 even portions. Using damp hands, wrap each portion around an egg. Brush each wrapped egg with the beaten egg, and then roll in breadcrumbs, shaking off any excess.

4 Fill a deep heavy-based pan one third full of oil and heat the oil to 180°C (350°F). The oil is ready when a cube of bread dropped in the oil turns golden brown in 15 seconds. Deep-fry the coated eggs until golden brown, then drain on crumpled paper towels. Serve hot, either whole or cut in half.

IN ADVANCE: The eggs can be assembled up to 4 hours ahead and refrigerated, covered, until required. Deep-fry just before serving and garnish with fresh herb sprigs.

RATATOUILLE TRIANGLES

Preparation time: 45 minutes + chilling
Total cooking time: 40 minutes
Makes 18

3 tablespoons oil
1 spring onion, finely chopped
1–2 cloves garlic, crushed
1 eggplant (aubergine), diced
1 red pepper (capsicum), diced
2 zucchini (courgettes), diced
6 button mushrooms, diced
1 tomato, peeled, seeded and chopped
1 tablespoon chopped capers
2 tablespoons chopped fresh parsley
50 g (1³/4 oz) Parmesan, grated
2 sheets ready-rolled puff pastry

1 Heat the oil in a heavy-based frying pan, add the spring onion and garlic and stir for 2 minutes. Add the eggplant, red pepper, zucchini and mushrooms and cook, stirring, for 10 minutes, or until softened.

2 Remove from the heat and add the tomato, capers and parsley. Cool and add the Parmesan. Cut each sheet of pastry into 3 equal strips and each strip into 3 triangles. Roll up a thin border on each side of the triangle and twist the corners to seal. Place on a greased baking tray and prick all over with a fork. Cover and chill for 10–15 minutes.

3 Preheat the oven to moderately hot 190°C (375°F/Gas 5) and bake the triangles for

SCOTCH QUAIL EGGS

Preparation time: 30 minutes
Total cooking time: 20 minutes
Makes 24 whole eggs or 48 halves

24 quail eggs
600 g (1¹/4 lb) chicken mince
2 teaspoons grated fresh ginger
2 tablespoons chopped fresh chives
2 teaspoons Dijon mustard
¹/2 cup (60 g/2 oz) plain flour
2 eggs, lightly beaten
1 cup (100 g/3¹/2 oz) dry breadcrumbs
oil, for deep-frying

1 Place the eggs in a pan and cover with water. Place over medium heat, stirring the eggs gently until the water boils (this centres the yolks). Cook for 5 minutes once boiling. Drain, place in a bowl of cold water and set aside to cool.

2 Mix the chicken mince, ginger, chives and

ABOVE: Scotch quail eggs

15 minutes, or until crisp. Place a tablespoon of filling into each pastry triangle and reheat for 5–10 minutes.

IN ADVANCE: These ratatouille triangles can be made up to 2 days ahead. Store the pastry triangles and ratatouille separately, covered, in the refrigerator. When required, fill the triangles and reheat briefly on greased baking trays in a moderate 180°C (350°F/Gas 4) oven.

POTATO NOODLE NIBBLES

Preparation time: 30 minutes + cooling
Total cooking time: 40 minutes
Serves 6

⭐ ⭐

450 g (14 oz) floury potatoes, peeled
  and chopped
40 g (1¼ oz) butter, softened
2 tablespoons grated Parmesan or
  Pecorino cheese
100 g (3½ oz) besan (chickpea flour)
2 teaspoons ground cumin
2 teaspoons garam masala
1 teaspoon ground coriander
1 teaspoon chilli powder
1 teaspoon cayenne pepper
1½ teaspoons ground turmeric
oil, for deep-frying

1 Boil or steam the potato until tender. Drain and cool for 15–20 minutes, then mash with the butter and cheese. Add the besan, cumin, garam masala, coriander, chilli powder, cayenne, turmeric and ¾ teaspoon of salt and mix with a wooden spoon until a soft, light dough forms. Turn out and knead lightly 10–12 times, until quite smooth.
2 Fill a deep heavy-based pan one third full of oil and heat to 180°C (350°F). Test the temperature by dropping a small ball of dough into the oil. The oil is ready if the dough rises immediately to the surface.
3 Using a piping bag with a 1 cm (½ inch) star nozzle, pipe short lengths of dough into the oil, cutting the dough off with a knife. Cook in manageable batches. They will rise to the surface and turn golden quickly. Remove with a slotted spoon and drain on crumpled paper towels. Serve the nibbles within 2 hours of cooking.

SMOKED SALMON AND ROCKET ROLLS

Preparation time: 20 minutes
Total cooking time: Nil
Makes 36

⭐

200 g (6½ oz) ricotta cheese
¼ cup (60 g/2 oz) crème fraîche or
  sour cream
2 teaspoons wasabi paste
1 tablespoon lime juice
12 slices brown bread, crusts removed
300 g (10 oz) smoked salmon
100 g (3½ oz) baby rocket, trimmed
rocket leaves, extra, to garnish

1 Mix together the ricotta, crème fraîche, wasabi and lime juice.
2 Roll the bread out with a rolling pin to flatten.
3 Spread the ricotta over the bread, then top with the smoked salmon and rocket leaves, leaving a border. Roll up lengthways, wrap tightly in plastic wrap to hold the shape, then refrigerate for 30 minutes.
4 Unwrap, trim the ends and cut into 2 cm (¾ inch) slices. Garnish with rocket leaves.

POTATO NOODLE
NIBBLES

Spoon the mixture into a piping bag with a star nozzle and pipe short lengths of dough into the oil, in small batches. Cut the dough off with a knife.

ABOVE: Potato noodle nibbles

239

DILL

This is a tall annual herb with delicate, long, thin leaves which have an intense aroma and distinctive taste. The leaves are chopped and served with fish, potatoes and other vegetables, or added to butters and sauces. The flavour also complements some soups and salads. The seeds are also used in cookery and are reminiscent of aniseed.

OPPOSITE PAGE: Baby potatoes (centre); Beef rolls

BABY POTATOES

Preparation time: 10 minutes
Total cooking time: 40 minutes
Makes 30

30 baby new potatoes (see Note)
1 cup (250 g/8 oz) sour cream
2 tablespoons caviar

1 Preheat the oven to moderately hot 200°C (400°F/Gas 6). Prick the potatoes with a fork and place on a baking tray. Bake for 40 minutes, or until tender. Cool to room temperature.
2 Cut a large cross in the top of each potato, squeeze open, and top with a small dollop of sour cream and a little caviar.
IN ADVANCE: Cook the potatoes up to 4 hours ahead. Prepare up to 30 minutes before serving.
NOTE: Choose very small potatoes of the same size, so they take the same time to cook and are easy to eat. Use red or black caviar, or a combination. Caviar comes in different varieties and you may like to try various ones.

BEEF ROLLS

Preparation time: 30 minutes
Total cooking time: 30 minutes
Makes about 20

500 g (1 lb) beef fillet, 8 cm (3 inch) in diameter
3 tablespoons olive oil
1 1/2 tablespoons horseradish cream
1 1/2 tablespoons wholegrain mustard
1 zucchini (courgette), cut into fine strips
1 small carrot, cut into fine strips
1 small red pepper (capsicum), cut into fine strips
60 g (2 oz) snow peas (mangetout), cut into fine strips

1 Preheat the oven to moderately hot 200°C (400°F/Gas 6). Trim the beef of excess fat and sinew and brush with a little of the oil. Heat a heavy-based frying pan over high heat and brown each side of the beef fillet quickly, to seal in the juices. Transfer to a baking dish and bake for 20 minutes. Remove and set aside to cool.
2 Slice the cooled beef very thinly. Combine the horseradish cream and the mustard, then spread a little over each slice of beef.
3 Heat the remaining oil in a pan and cook the zucchini, carrot, pepper and snow peas quickly over high heat, and then allow to cool. Place a small bunch of the cooked vegetable strips on the end of each beef slice and roll up. Arrange on a platter and serve.
IN ADVANCE: The beef can be cooked and the vegetables prepared up to 2 hours in advance. Don't cook the vegetables or fill the rolls any earlier than 30 minutes before serving.

CORN MINI MUFFINS WITH PRAWNS AND DILL MAYONNAISE

Preparation time: 15 minutes
Total cooking time: 40 minutes
Makes about 50

2 cups (250 g/8 oz) plain flour, sifted
3/4 cup (110 g/3 1/2 oz) cornmeal
1 tablespoon baking powder
1/4 cup (60 g/2 oz) sugar
2 eggs, lightly beaten
125 g (4 oz) butter, melted
1 cup (250 ml/8 fl oz) milk
3 tablespoons finely chopped fresh dill
1 tablespoon lemon juice
1 teaspoon horseradish cream
1 1/2 cups (375 g /12 oz) whole egg mayonnaise
300 g (10 oz) small cooked prawns

1 Preheat the oven to moderately hot 200°C (400°F/Gas 6) and oil or spray two 12-hole mini muffin pans. Sift the flour into a large bowl and mix with the cornmeal, baking powder, sugar and 1/2 teaspoon salt. Add the eggs, butter and milk. Stir until just combined. Spoon small amounts into the muffin tins, filling the holes three-quarters full. Cook for 15–20 minutes, or until lightly browned. Turn onto a cake rack to cool. Repeat until you have used all the mixture.
2 Mix the dill, lemon juice and horseradish cream into the mayonnaise and add plenty of salt and black pepper.
3 When the muffins are cool, cut a circle from the top, as you would with a butterfly cake, and spoon a little dill mayonnaise into the cavity. Top with a prawn and some freshly ground black pepper.

PARSLEY

Parsley is probably the most commonly used herb in the kitchen. Two different types are cultivated. This one, the curly-leafed variety, is commonly grown in the garden and is milder than the flat-leafed parsley. Parsley is used to flavour many sauces, vegetables, soups and casseroles and makes an attractive garnish. Parsley is a good source of some vitamins and minerals.

HERBED CHEESE CRACKERS

Preparation time: 40 minutes
Total cooking time: 8 minutes each tray
Makes 20

Biscuit pastry

1 cup (125 g/4 oz) plain flour
1/2 teaspoon baking powder
60 g (2 oz) butter
1 egg, lightly beaten
60 g (2 oz) Cheddar, grated
1 teaspoon chopped fresh chives
1 teaspoon chopped fresh parsley

Cheese filling

80 g (2 3/4 oz) cream cheese, softened
20 g (3/4 oz) butter
1 tablespoon chopped fresh chives
1 tablespoon chopped fresh parsley
1/4 teaspoon lemon pepper
90 g (3 oz) Cheddar, grated

1 Preheat the oven to moderately hot 190°C (375°F/Gas 5). Line two baking trays with baking paper.
2 To make the biscuit pastry, sift the flour and baking powder into a large bowl and add the chopped butter. Rub in with your fingertips, until the mixture resembles fine breadcrumbs.
3 Make a well in the centre and add the egg, cheese, herbs and 1 tablespoon iced water. Mix with a flat-bladed knife, using a cutting action until the mixture comes together in beads. Gently gather together and lift out onto a lightly floured surface. Press together into a ball.
4 Roll the pastry between sheets of baking paper to 3 mm (1/8 inch) thickness. Remove the top sheet of paper and cut the pastry into rounds, using a 5 cm (2 inch) cutter. Place the rounds onto the trays. Re-roll the remaining pastry and repeat cutting. Bake for about 8 minutes, or until lightly browned. Transfer to a wire rack to cool.
5 To make the filling, beat the cream cheese and butter in a small bowl with electric beaters until light and creamy. Add the herbs, pepper and cheese and beat until smooth. Spread half a teaspoon of filling on half of the biscuits and sandwich together with the remaining biscuits.
NOTE: You can use freshly chopped lemon thyme instead of parsley.
IN ADVANCE: The biscuits can be made 2 days ahead and stored in an airtight container, or frozen. The filling can be made a day ahead and stored, covered, in the refrigerator.

ABOVE: Herbed cheese crackers

EGG AND CAVIAR
MOULDED DIP

Spread half the softened cream cheese over the egg layer with a spatula.

When set, gently ease the side of the tin away from the dip.

EGG AND CAVIAR MOULDED DIP

Preparation time: 1 hour + chilling
Total cooking time: 7 minutes
Serves 8–12

✷ ✷

7 eggs

3 tablespoons finely chopped fresh parsley

3 tablespoons whole egg mayonnaise

80 g (2³/4 oz) chives, finely chopped

500 g (1 lb) cream cheese, softened to room temperature

90 g (3 oz) black caviar

300 g (10 oz) sour cream

extra chives, snipped, and black caviar, for serving

 Fill a pan with cold water and gently add the eggs. Bring to the boil, then reduce the heat and simmer for 7 minutes. Drain and plunge the eggs in cold water to stop the cooking process. Cool thoroughly and drain.

2 Line a deep loose-based fluted flan tin (about 18 cm/7 inches in diameter) with plastic wrap, leaving a wide overhang to help you remove the moulded dip from the tin.

3 Peel and mash the eggs, add the parsley and mayonnaise, and season with salt and pepper.

4 Divide the egg mixture in half. Spoon one half into the lined tin. Firmly press down and smooth the surface with a spatula or the back of a spoon, pressing well into the side of the tin. Sprinkle with half the chives, pressing them down into the dip. Using a clean, warm spatula, spread with half the cream cheese to form another layer. Spoon half the caviar over the cream cheese and press down gently.

5 Repeat the layering with the remaining egg mixture, chives, cream cheese and caviar. Cover the moulded dip with plastic wrap, pressing down firmly so the layers stick together, and refrigerate for 2 hours.

6 Remove the top cover of plastic wrap and place a plate over the mould. Flip over onto the plate while holding the tin and gently ease the tin off. Carefully remove the plastic wrap, trying not to damage the fluted edges.

7 Spoon dollops of sour cream over the top of the mould and spread a little. Decorate with the extra snipped chives and a few spoonfuls of caviar. Serve with water crackers.

ABOVE: Egg and caviar moulded dip

243

PATES
Not strictly finger food—you will need a knife to spread them lusciously over crunchy toast—however, no occasion would be quite complete without a stylish pâté.

GRAND MARNIER PATE
Melt 90 g (3 oz) butter in a pan and cook 1 chopped onion and 1 crushed clove of garlic until the onion is tender. Add 250 g (4 oz) trimmed duck or chicken livers and cook for 5–10 minutes. Spoon into a food processor or blender with 2 tablespoons orange juice, 1 tablespoon Grand Marnier (or port or liqueur of your choice), 1 tablespoon sour cream and freshly ground pepper, to taste.

Process until smooth. To prepare the topping, arrange 2 orange slices (cut into quarters if you wish), and fresh chives or parsley in the base of a 2-cup (500 ml/ 16 fl oz) capacity serving dish. Sprinkle 1½ teaspoons gelatine over ½ cup (125 ml/4 fl oz) hot chicken stock and whisk vigorously with a fork to dissolve. Pour over the oranges to a depth of 1 cm (½ inch). Refrigerate until set. Spoon the pâté over the gelatine layer, tap gently

and smooth the top. Refrigerate until set. Unmould onto a serving plate. Serve with crackers or Melba toast. (Pâté can also be made without the gelatine topping, and served on cracker biscuits.) Serves 12–15.

SMOKED TROUT PATE
Mix 250 g (8 oz) skinned and boned smoked trout, 125 g (4 oz) softened butter and 125 g (4 oz) softened cream

cheese in a food processor for 20 seconds, or until smooth. Add 1 tablespoon lemon juice, 1 teaspoon horseradish cream, 15 g (½ oz) each of finely chopped fresh parsley and fresh chives and process for 10 seconds. Add salt and freshly ground black pepper, to taste, and more lemon juice, if liked. Transfer to a small serving dish. Serve with hot toasted brown bread. Serves 8–10.

LEMON PRAWN PATE

Melt 100 g (3½ oz) butter in a frying pan. When it sizzles, add 3 crushed cloves garlic and 750 g (1½ lb) peeled and deveined raw prawns and stir for 3–4 minutes, or until the prawns are pink and cooked through. Cool. Transfer to a food processor, add 1 teaspoon grated lemon rind, 3 tablespoons lemon juice and ¼ teaspoon grated nutmeg and process for 20 seconds, or until roughly

puréed. Season and add 2 tablespoons each of mayonnaise and finely chopped fresh chives, then process for 20 seconds, or until combined. Spoon into a dish and chill for at least 1 hour, or until firm. Serves 6–8.

MUSHROOM PATE

Melt 40 g (1¼ oz) butter and 1 tablespoon oil in a large frying pan. Add 400 g (13 oz) chopped field mushrooms and 2 crushed cloves garlic. Cook until the mushrooms have softened and the mushroom liquid has evaporated. Stir in 3 chopped spring onions. Allow to cool, then process with 1 tablespoon lemon juice, 100 g (3½ oz) ricotta cheese, 100 g (3½ oz) soft cream cheese and 2 tablespoons chopped fresh coriander leaves. Process until smooth. Season, to taste, then spoon into a serving dish, cover and chill for 2 hours. Serves 8–10.

SOFT CHEESE PATE

Roughly chop 150 g (5 oz) toasted pine nuts in a food processor, add 500 g (1 lb) crumbled feta cheese, ¾ cup (185 ml/6 fl oz) cream and 2 teaspoons coarsely ground pepper and mix until smooth. Add 30 g (1 oz) each of chopped fresh mint, dill and parsley and process until just combined. Line a 3-cup (750 ml/24 fl oz) capacity bowl with plastic wrap. Transfer the mixture to the bowl and press in firmly. Refrigerate, covered, for at least 1 hour, or until firm. Turn out onto a plate and smooth the surface with a knife. Serve with toast triangles. Serves 12–15.

PATES, CLOCKWISE, FROM LEFT: Grand Marnier; Smoked trout; Lemon prawn; Soft cheese; Mushroom

1 Combine the flour and seasoning in a plastic bag and toss with the chicken strips to coat; remove and shake off excess.

2 Beat the eggs lightly in a shallow bowl, and put the breadcrumbs in a plastic bag.

3 Working with a few chicken strips at a time, dip into the beaten egg, then toss in the breadcrumbs. Transfer to a baking tray covered with baking paper and refrigerate for about 30 minutes.

4 Heat 3 cm (1 1/4 inches) oil in a large frying pan to 180°C (350°F/Gas 4), or until a cube of bread dropped into the oil turns golden brown in 15 seconds. Fry the strips in batches for 3–5 minutes, or until golden brown. Drain on crumpled paper towels. Serve with the sauce.

5 For the sauce, combine the juice, vinegar, soy sauce, sugar and tomato sauce in a small pan. Stir over low heat until the sugar has dissolved. Blend the cornflour with 1 tablespoon water, add to the pan and stir constantly, until the mixture boils and thickens. Reduce the heat and simmer for 2 minutes.

BASIC SAUSAGE ROLLS

Preparation time: 30 minutes
Total cooking time: 15 minutes
Makes 36

3 sheets ready-rolled puff pastry

2 eggs, lightly beaten

750 g (1 1/2 lb) sausage mince

1 onion, finely chopped

1 clove garlic, crushed

1 cup (80 g/2 3/4 oz) fresh breadcrumbs

3 tablespoons chopped fresh parsley

3 tablespoons chopped fresh thyme

1/2 teaspoon each ground sage, nutmeg, black pepper and cloves

1 Preheat the oven to 200°C (400°F/Gas 6). Cut the pastry sheets in half and lightly brush the edges with some of the beaten egg.

2 Mix half the remaining egg with the remaining ingredients in a large bowl, then divide into six even portions. Pipe or spoon the filling down the centre of each piece of pastry, then brush the edges with some of the egg. Fold the pastry over the filling, overlapping the edges and placing the join underneath. Brush the rolls with more egg, then cut each into 6 short pieces.

CHICKEN STRIPS WITH SWEET AND SOUR SAUCE

Preparation time: 30 minutes + chilling
Total cooking time: 30 minutes
Makes 35–40

1/2 cup (60 g/2 oz) plain flour

1 tablespoon chicken seasoning salt

4 chicken breast fillets, cut into 2 cm (3/4 inch) wide strips

2 eggs

1 1/2 cups (150 g/5 oz) dry breadcrumbs

oil, for shallow-frying

Sweet and sour sauce

1 cup (250 ml/8 fl oz) pineapple juice

3 tablespoons white wine vinegar

2 teaspoons soy sauce

2 tablespoons soft brown sugar

2 tablespoons tomato sauce

1 tablespoon cornflour

ABOVE: Chicken strips with sweet and sour sauce

3 Cut two small slashes on top of each roll and place on lightly greased baking trays and bake for 15 minutes, then reduce the oven temperature to moderate 180°C (350°F/Gas 4) and bake for another 15 minutes, or until puffed and golden.

For a different flavour, select a filling from the recipes below and follow the method outlined for the basic sausage roll.

CURRIED PORK AND VEAL

Soak 3 dried Chinese mushrooms in hot water for 30 minutes, squeeze dry and chop finely. Cook 4 finely chopped spring onions, 1 crushed clove garlic, 1 finely chopped small red chilli and 2–3 teaspoons curry powder in 1 tablespoon oil. Transfer to a bowl and mix with 750 g (1½ lb) pork and veal mince, 1 cup (90 g/3 oz) fresh breadcrumbs, the dried mushrooms, 1 lightly beaten egg, 3 tablespoons chopped coriander and 1 tablespoon each soy and oyster sauce.

SPICY LAMB

Mix 750 g (1½ lb) lamb mince, 1 cup (90 g/ 3 oz) fresh breadcrumbs, 1 small grated onion, 1 tablespoon soy sauce, 2 teaspoons each of grated fresh ginger and soft brown sugar, 1 teaspoon ground coriander, ½ teaspoon each of ground cumin and sambal oelek. Lightly sprinkle the pastry rolls with poppy seeds after glazing and before baking.

SAUCY BEEF

Cook 1 finely chopped onion and 1–2 crushed cloves garlic in 20 g (⅔ oz) butter until the onion is softened. Mix 750 g (1½ lb) lean beef mince, the sautéed onion and garlic, 3 tablespoons finely chopped fresh parsley, 3 tablespoons plain flour, 3 tablespoons tomato sauce, 1 tablespoon each of Worcestershire and soy sauces and 2 teaspoons ground allspice until well combined.

CHUTNEY CHICKEN

Mix 750 g (1½ lb) chicken mince, 4 finely chopped spring onions, 1 cup (80 g/2¾ oz) fresh breadcrumbs, 1 finely grated carrot, 2 tablespoons fruit chutney and 1 tablespoon each of sweet chilli sauce and grated ginger. Sprinkle the pastry with sesame seeds after glazing, before baking.

BELOW: Basic sausage rolls (left); Sausage rolls with chutney chicken filling

SALMON SATAY WITH GINGER LIME MAYONNAISE

Preparation time: 30 minutes + chilling
Total cooking time: 4 minutes
Makes 24 skewers

500 g (1 lb) Atlantic salmon (or ocean trout) fillet
24 small wooden skewers
light olive oil

Ginger lime mayonnaise
1 cup (250 g/8 oz) whole egg mayonnaise
1/4 cup (60 g/2 oz) natural yoghurt
1 teaspoon finely grated fresh ginger
1 teaspoon finely grated lime rind
2 teaspoons lime juice

1 Remove the skin from the salmon. Use kitchen tweezers to remove any bones from the fish, then wrap the fish in plastic wrap and freeze for 1 hour. Soak small wooden satay sticks in cold water for 30 minutes (this will prevent them burning during cooking).
2 Cut the salmon fillets into 5 cm (2 inch) strips. Thread the strips loosely onto the satay sticks and place them on an oiled tray. Brush all over with oil and season, to taste, with salt and freshly ground pepper. Grill in two batches for 2 minutes, taking care not to overcook. Serve with the ginger lime mayonnaise.
3 To make ginger lime mayonnaise, place the mayonnaise in a small bowl and stir until smooth. Add the yoghurt, ginger and lime rind and juice. Add salt and pepper, to taste, and stir until blended thoroughly. Chill for at least 1 hour.
IN ADVANCE: The skewers can be assembled up to 1 hour in advance and refrigerated. Cook just prior to serving. Make the mayonnaise up to 2 days ahead and store, covered, in the refrigerator. The prepared skewers can be frozen in a single layer for up to 2 months.

MINI LENTIL BURGERS WITH TOMATO RELISH

Preparation time: 40 minutes
Total cooking time: 55 minutes
Makes 32

1 cup (185 g/6 oz) brown lentils
1 bay leaf
1 onion, roughly chopped
1 clove garlic, crushed
1 small leek, finely sliced
1 small carrot, finely grated
1 cup (80 g/2 3/4 oz) fresh breadcrumbs
2 egg yolks
2 tablespoons chopped fresh coriander
2 tablespoons oil
8 slices bread, cut into 4 cm (1 1/2 inch) squares
ready-made tomato relish, for serving

1 Place the lentils and bay leaf in a pan, cover with plenty of water, bring to the boil and simmer for 20–30 minutes, or until tender; drain well and discard the bay leaf.
2 Combine half the cooked lentils with the onion and garlic in a food processor until the mixture forms a smooth paste. Transfer to a bowl and mix with the remaining lentils, leek, carrot, breadcrumbs, egg yolks and coriander; season with salt and freshly ground black pepper. Form level tablespoons of the mixture into mini burgers.
3 Heat some of the oil in a non-stick frying pan and fry the mini burgers in batches until browned on both sides, adding more oil as necessary. Drain on paper towels and serve warm, on the bread squares (or toast), with a dollop of tomato relish on top. Garnish with fresh herbs.

OYSTERS WITH SALMON ROE

Spread rock salt all over a large plate to cover. Arrange 1 dozen freshly shucked oysters on the plate. Spoon 1 teaspoon of crème fraîche onto each oyster and top with 1/2 teaspoon salmon roe (you will need about 60 g/2 oz salmon roe). Season with black pepper. Garnish with fresh dill. Serve with lime wedges. (See cover illustration.)

BROWN LENTILS
Lentils come in various colours including brown, green and red. Some lentils are much bigger than others. Lentils have been used for thousands of years and are a good source of protein, fibre, potassium, magnesium and zinc, as well as some of the B vitamins. To prepare, lentils need to be picked over to remove any small stones, then, depending on the type, either soaked to soften before cooking, or simply cooked until soft. They are used in many recipes, including soups, casseroles, dhal and salads.

OPPOSITE PAGE: Salmon satay with ginger lime mayonnaise (top); Mini lentil burgers with tomato relish

CORNED BEEF, PARSNIP AND MINT PATTIES

Preparation time: 20 minutes
Total cooking time: 25 minutes
Makes 24

★★

2 parsnips, chopped

1 cup (100 g/3½ oz) dry breadcrumbs

200 g (6½ oz) piece cooked corned beef, finely chopped

1 egg yolk

¼ small onion, finely chopped

20 g (¾ oz) fresh mint leaves, finely chopped

1 tablespoon lemon juice

3 teaspoons wholegrain mustard

2 tablespoons plain flour

1 egg

1 tablespoon milk

¼ cup (60 ml/2 fl oz) olive oil

½ cup (140 g/4½ oz) spicy tomato chutney

24 small fresh mint leaves, to garnish

ABOVE: Corned beef, parsnip and mint patties

1 Cook the parsnip in a large pan of boiling water for 10 minutes, or until tender. Drain and mash until smooth. Set aside to cool.

2 Mix the parsnip with ⅓ cup 35 g (1¼ oz) of the breadcrumbs, the corned beef, egg yolk, onion, mint, lemon juice, mustard and salt and freshly ground black pepper.

3 Shape into 24 patties, pressing firmly together. Dust with flour and shake off any excess. Dip into the combined egg and milk, then coat in the remaining breadcrumbs.

4 Heat the oil in a large frying pan over medium-low heat and cook the patties in batches for 2–3 minutes each side, or until golden brown and heated through. Drain on crumpled paper towels. Spoon 1 teaspoon of tomato chutney onto each patty and top with a mint leaf. Serve immediately.

IN ADVANCE: The patties can be prepared a day ahead. Keep covered in the refrigerator until ready to cook.

MARINATED LAMB CUTLETS WITH SALSA VERDE

Preparation time: 30 minutes + marinating
Total cooking time: 20–25 minutes
Makes 24

2 lemons
4 tablespoons virgin olive oil
1 tablespoon Dijon mustard
3 racks of 8 small lamb cutlets (about 1.1 kg),
   trimmed of fat
40 g (1¼ oz) flat-leaf parsley
3 drained anchovy fillets, finely chopped
1 clove garlic, crushed
1 tablespoon olive oil
1½ tablespoons baby capers, rinsed
   and drained

1 Finely grate the rind of the lemons and squeeze the juice from the fruit. Combine 1 teaspoon of the rind and 2 tablespoons of the juice with half the virgin olive oil and the mustard in a large bowl. Add the lamb racks and turn to coat thoroughly. Cover and refrigerate for at least 3 hours, or overnight.

2 To make the salsa verde, mix the parsley, anchovies, garlic, 1 tablespoon of the remaining lemon juice and 1 teaspoon of the rind in a food processor until finely chopped. With the motor running, add the remaining virgin olive oil and process until smooth and thickened. Transfer to a bowl, cover and refrigerate for at least 2½ hours.

3 Preheat the oven to moderately hot 200°C (400°F/Gas 6). Drain the lamb and discard the marinade. Heat the olive oil in a large baking dish over medium-high heat, add the lamb racks and cook, turning occasionally, for 5 minutes, or until the lamb is browned all over. Transfer the dish to the oven and bake for 15–20 minutes, or until the lamb is tender. Set aside for at least 10 minutes before slicing between the bones. Arrange in a single layer on a plate, top with salsa verde and sprinkle with capers.

NOTE: When you buy the racks of lamb, ask the butcher to cut through the bones at the base to make slicing into cutlets easier.

IN ADVANCE: Lamb can be prepared a day ahead, refrigerated, then brought to room temperature just before slicing and serving. Salsa verde can be made a day ahead and refrigerated until use.

OLIVE OIL
Olive oil is made by pressing olives from olive trees, native to the Mediterranean region. There are two methods of pressing olives. If cold-pressed, they are simply crushed, producing unrefined oil, whereas if pressed with the help of heat and treated in other ways, including the addition of preservatives, refined oil is the result. Olive oil is sold in different grades, which have different uses. Extra virgin olive oil, considered one of the best, is made from specially selected olives that are cold-pressed. It is used mainly for salad dressings or flavouring. Virgin olive oil is made with more mature olives and used in cooking and dressings. The cheaper all-purpose olive oil is made by the hot pressing method, sometimes with olives left after making extra virgin olive oil.

LEFT: Marinated lamb cutlets with salsa verde

FROM THE SHELL Some

foods need little dressing up—they seem to have been born to party. Shellfish are a

wonderful example—drizzle with sauce and serve in the shells nature gave them.

OYSTERS WITH PROSCIUTTO AND BALSAMIC VINEGAR

Place 24 fresh oysters on a baking tray and sprinkle with 2–3 tablespoons of balsamic vinegar. Chop 6 slices of prosciutto and sprinkle over the oysters. Sprinkle with cracked black pepper and place under a hot grill for 1 minute, or until the prosciutto is starting to crisp. Makes 24.

OYSTERS WITH TARRAGON

Remove 24 fresh oysters from their shells. Wash the shells and set aside. Combine the oysters with 1 tablespoon chopped fresh tarragon, 1 small finely chopped spring onion, 2 teaspoons white wine vinegar, 1 tablespoon lemon juice and 2 tablespoons extra virgin olive oil, cover and refrigerate for 30 minutes. Place the oyster shells on a serving plate

and spoon an oyster back into each shell. Drizzle with any remaining viniagrette. Makes 24.

SCALLOPS WITH LIME HOLLANDAISE SAUCE

Using a sharp knife, carefully cut 24 scallops from their shells, as cleanly as possible, and remove the veins. Wash the shells in warm water and warm

through on a baking tray in a moderate 180°C (350°F/Gas 4) oven for 5 minutes. Chargrill or fry the scallops for 2–4 minutes, then return to their shells. For the sauce, mix 1 egg yolk and 1 tablespoon lime juice in a food processor for 30 seconds. With the motor running, add 45 g (1½ oz) melted butter in a thin stream. (Beat in a bowl if you prefer.) Transfer to a bowl, add 1 tablespoon snipped chives and season with salt and pepper. Spoon 1 teaspoon over each scallop and serve. Makes 24.

CITRUS SAUCY SCALLOPS

Using a sharp knife, carefully cut 24 scallops from their shells, as cleanly as possible, and remove the veins. Wash the shells in warm water and warm through on a baking tray in a moderate 180°C (350°F/Gas 4) oven for 5 minutes.

Chargrill or fry the scallops for 2–4 minutes and return to their shells. For the sauce, combine 3 tablespoons lime juice, 1 tablespoon lemon juice, 1 finely chopped red chilli, 1 tablespoon fish sauce, 2 teaspoons sugar, 3 teaspoons chopped fresh coriander and 2 teaspoons chopped fresh mint. Spoon 1 teaspoon over each scallop and serve. Makes 24.

MUSSELS WITH BLOODY MARY SAUCE

Scrub 24 black mussels and remove the beards (discard any mussels which are open and don't close when tapped). Place in a large heavy-based pan with the juice of a lemon and 1 tablespoon water. Cover and steam over medium-low heat for 2–3 minutes, removing them as they open. (Discard any which haven't opened in that time.) Remove and discard the

top shell. Run a small knife along the shell under the mussel to detach it from the shell. Place the mussels in their shells on a baking tray which has been spread with a layer of salt (to keep them level and stop the filling falling out). For the sauce, combine 2 tablespoons vodka, 2 tablespoons tomato juice, 1 tablespoon lemon juice, 2 teaspoons Worcestershire sauce, a dash of Tabasco and ¼ teaspoon celery salt. Spoon 1 teaspoon into each shell and grill for a few seconds, or until the sauce is warm. Serve with a sprinkle of freshly ground black pepper. Makes 24.

FROM LEFT: Oysters with prosciutto and balsamic vinegar; Oysters with tarragon; Scallops with lime hollandaise sauce; Citrus saucy scallops; Mussels with bloody mary sauce

253

MINI EGGS FLORENTINE

Preparation time: 15 minutes + chilling
Total cooking time: 30 minutes
Makes 24

Hollandaise sauce
3 egg yolks
2 tablespoons lime or lemon juice
125 g (4 oz) butter, melted

6–8 slices bread
oil spray
24 quail eggs
250 g (8 oz) English spinach, trimmed

1 Preheat the oven to moderate 180°C (350°F/Gas 4). To make the hollandaise sauce, blend the yolks and juice in a food processor for 5 seconds, then gradually add the melted butter. Transfer to a bowl and refrigerate for about 30 minutes, until thickened.

2 Cut 24 rounds of bread with a 4 cm (1½ inch) cutter. Place on a baking tray, spray with oil and bake for 10 minutes. Turn over and bake for another 5 minutes, until dry and crisp.

3 Put about 2.5 cm (1 inch) water in a large non-stick frying pan and bring to simmering point. Reduce the heat so the water is not moving. Carefully crack the eggs into the water. Spoon a little water onto the top of the eggs as they cook, and when set, remove from the pan and drain on paper towels.

4 Steam or microwave the spinach for 2 minutes, or until wilted, then drain well. To assemble, put some spinach on the bread rounds, then top with egg and drizzle with hollandaise. Serve immediately.

NOTE: Quail eggs are available from speciality food stores or can be ordered from poultry shops. You can use bottled hollandaise. Any leftover hollandaise will keep in the refrigerator, covered, for up to five days.

HOLLANDAISE SAUCE
Although the origins of rich creamy hollandaise sauce are unknown, it translates from French into *Dutch sauce*. It was actually known by that name as long ago as the 16th century and until as recently as the early 20th century. Hollandaise sauce is used to embellish fish, eggs and vegetables, especially asparagus.

RIGHT: Mini eggs florentine

PAN-FRIED CHEESE SANDWICHES

Preparation time: 20 minutes
Total cooking time: 20 minutes
Makes about 40

20 thick slices white bread
2–3 tablespoons Dijon mustard
12 slices Cheddar
oil, for shallow-frying
plain flour, for dusting
3 eggs, lightly beaten
watercress, to garnish

1 Remove the crusts from the bread. Spread the bread with mustard, place a slice of cheese on top, then finish with another bread slice.
2 Heat a little oil in a frying pan. Dust the sandwiches lightly with flour and dip quickly into the beaten egg.
3 Cook the sandwiches on both sides until golden; drain on paper towels. Cut into quarters and garnish with watercress. Serve hot.
IN ADVANCE: Assemble the sandwiches up to 4 hours in advance, but don't dust with flour and dip in the egg until just before frying.

ALMOND-CRUSTED CHEESE BITES

Preparation time: 30 minutes + chilling
Total cooking time: 20 minutes
Makes 24

★ ★

500 g (1 lb) Cheddar, grated
250 g (8 oz) cold mashed pumpkin
1/3 cup (40 g/1 1/4 oz) plain flour
1 clove garlic, crushed
2 tablespoons chopped fresh chives or parsley
2 egg whites
250 g (8 oz) flaked almonds, roughly crushed
oil, for deep-frying

1 Combine the cheese, pumpkin, flour, garlic and chives in a large bowl. Beat the egg whites in a bowl until stiff, then stir into the pumpkin.
2 Mould small spoonfuls with your hands to form balls. Roll in the almonds, place on baking trays and refrigerate for 1 hour.
3 Fill a deep heavy-based pan one third full of oil and heat the oil to 180°C (350°F), or until a cube of bread dropped into the oil turns golden brown in 15 seconds. Deep-fry the balls in batches until golden brown; drain on crumpled paper towels.

PUMPKIN
This winter squash is sweet-tasting and very versatile. It can be baked, steamed, mashed or puréed, used in risotto and also made into a delicious soup. A whole pumpkin keeps in a cool, dark place for about six weeks. Once cut, however, it will tend to deteriorate quickly. Remove the seeds, wrap in plastic and refrigerate. Pumpkin is available in a variety of types and shapes, some of which are huge, others tiny, some round and fat, and others, such as the butternut, elongated. Make sure pumpkins are firm and heavy for their size when you buy them.

ABOVE: Pan-fried cheese sandwiches

255

OLIVE BASIL CHEESE SPREAD

Preparation time: 15 minutes
Total cooking time: Nil
Makes 2 cups

250 g (8 oz) cream cheese, softened
200 g (6¹/₂ oz) feta cheese
20 g (³/₄ oz) basil leaves
3 tablespoons olive oil
15 Kalamata olives, pitted and roughly chopped

1 Combine the cream cheese, feta cheese, basil, 1 tablespoon of the oil and ¹/₄ teaspoon cracked black pepper in a bowl and mix until smooth.
2 Fold in the olives and spoon into a serving bowl. Smooth the top with the back of the spoon. Pour the remaining oil over the top. Garnish with a little more cracked pepper and serve with warm bruschetta.

SMOKED SALMON PATE WITH CHIVE PIKELETS

Preparation time: 30 minutes + standing
Total cooking time: 40 minutes
Makes about 30

125 g (4 oz) smoked salmon
2 teaspoons softened butter
1 small onion, chopped
1¹/₂ teaspoons horseradish cream
30 g (1 oz) soft butter, extra
3 teaspoons chopped tarragon
1 lime, cut into tiny wedges
red or black caviar, to garnish

Chive pikelets
¹/₂ cup (60 g/2 oz) self-raising flour
1 tablespoon coarsely chopped chives
1 egg yolk, lightly beaten
¹/₂ cup (125 ml/4 fl oz) milk

1 Roughly chop the salmon. Heat the butter in a small pan, add the onion and cook until soft. Put the smoked salmon, onion, horseradish cream and extra butter in a food processor. Season with salt and freshly ground black pepper and mix until smooth. Add the tarragon and process until the pâté is just combined.

2 For the pikelets, sift the flour and a pinch of salt into a bowl. Stir in the chives and make a well in the centre. Gradually whisk in the yolk and enough milk to form a smooth lump-free batter, the consistency of thick cream. Set aside for 15 minutes, then lightly grease a non-stick frying pan and drop teaspoons of the batter into the pan. When bubbles appear on the surface of the pikelets, turn them over and brown the other side. Transfer to a wire rack to cool. Repeat with the remaining batter.
3 Pipe or spread the pâté onto the pikelets, garnish with a slice of lime and some caviar.
IN ADVANCE: The pikelets may be assembled up to 3 hours ahead, covered and refrigerated.

OLIVE AND ALMOND PALMIERS

Preparation time: 30 minutes
Total cooking time: 20 minutes
Makes about 24

75 g (2¹/₂ oz) black olives, pitted and chopped
95 g (3¹/₄ oz) ground almonds
25 g (³/₄ oz) Parmesan, grated
2 tablespoons chopped fresh basil
3 tablespoons olive oil
2 teaspoons wholegrain mustard
2 sheets frozen puff pastry, thawed
¹/₄ cup (60 ml/2 fl oz) milk

1 Preheat the oven to moderately hot 200°C (400°F/Gas 6). Line two baking trays with non-stick baking paper. In a food processor, process the olives, almonds, Parmesan, basil, oil, mustard, ¹/₄ teaspoon salt and ¹/₂ teaspoon cracked black pepper until they form a paste.
2 Spread out one sheet of pastry and cover evenly with half the olive-almond paste. Fold two opposite ends into the centre to meet.
3 Fold the same way again. Brush the pastry with milk. Repeat the process with the remaining pastry and filling. Cut into 1.5 cm (⁵/₈ inch) thick slices. Shape the slices into a V-shape, with the two sides curving out slightly. Bake on baking trays, leaving room for spreading, for 15–20 minutes, or until puffed and golden. Serve warm or at room temperature.
IN ADVANCE: Palmiers can be cooked up to 6 hours ahead and stored in an airtight container. Serve at room temperature, or warm.
NOTE: You can use ready-made olive paste.

PALMIERS
Traditional palmiers are small sweet puff pastry biscuits shaped a little like butterflies. Literally the word means 'palm tree' and it is believed their inventor thought the shape was reminiscent of the topknot of leaves on a palm. We have broken with tradition and given a savoury version.

OPPOSITE PAGE: Olive basil cheese spread (top); Smoked salmon pâté with chive pikelets

SWEET POTATO CREPES WITH DUCK FILLING

Bake the duck breasts on a wire rack in a baking dish until tender.

Measure the batter into a pan and quickly spread with the back of a spoon.

Fold the crepes in half to enclose the filling, then fold over into quarters.

ABOVE: Sweet potato crepes with duck filling

SWEET POTATO CREPES WITH DUCK FILLING

Preparation time: 25–30 minutes + chilling
Total cooking time: 55 minutes
Makes 24

★ ★ ☆

1 cup (125 g/4 oz) plain flour

1/2 teaspoon bicarbonate of soda

3 eggs, lightly beaten

1 1/2 cups (375 ml/12 fl oz) milk

1 tablespoon light olive oil

2 teaspoons ground cumin

3 duck breast fillets (about 450 g/14 oz)

1/4 cup (60 ml/2 fl oz) olive oil

2 tablespoons orange juice

1 tablespoon lime juice

1 teaspoon pomegranate molasses

1/4 teaspoon finely grated orange rind

1/2 teaspoon sugar

pinch of ground cumin

60 g (2 oz) orange sweet potato, finely grated

2 tablespoons chopped fresh coriander

fresh coriander leaves, extra

1 Preheat the oven to moderately hot 200°C (400°F/Gas 6). Sift the flour and soda into a large bowl and make a well in the centre. Gradually add the combined eggs, milk, light olive oil and cumin, whisking to make a smooth, lump-free batter. Cover and refrigerate for 30 minutes.

2 Season the duck all over with salt and pepper. Heat a non-stick frying pan, brown the duck over medium-high heat, then bake, skin-side up, on a wire rack in a baking dish for 20 minutes, or until tender. Rest the duck in a warm place for at least 5 minutes. .

3 Combine the olive oil, juices, molasses, orange rind, sugar and cumin in a screw-top jar and shake until well combined.

4 Discard the duck skin, then finely slice the duck across the grain or shred into thin pieces. Wrap in foil and keep warm in the oven.

5 Press the sweet potato between sheets of paper towel to extract as much moisture as possible. Stir into the batter with the coriander leaves. Spoon 1 tablespoon of batter into a non-stick or greased crepe pan. Quickly spread with the back of a spoon so the crepe measures about 12 cm (5 inches) across. Cook for 1 minute, or until lightly browned underneath. Turn and brown on the other side. Repeat to make 24 crepes. The crepes can be stacked, wrapped loosely in foil and kept warm in the oven.

6 To assemble, lay the crepes flat, and pile even amounts of duck in one quarter of each. Drizzle with pomegranate dressing and top with the extra coriander leaves. Fold the crepes in half to enclose the filling, then into quarters. Serve.
NOTE: Pomegranate molasses is available from gourmet speciality stores.
IN ADVANCE: The crepes and duck can both be prepared a day ahead, covered separately in the refrigerator, then reheated in foil. The dressing can be made a day ahead, refrigerated and brought to room temperature before serving.

CHIPOLATA SAUSAGES WITH HORSERADISH CREAM

Preparation time: 15 minutes
Total cooking time: 25 minutes
Makes 12

2 tablespoons virgin olive oil
2 red onions, cut into thin wedges
2 tablespoons dark brown sugar
3 teaspoons balsamic vinegar
100 g (3 1/2 oz) spreadable cream cheese

1 tablespoon horseradish cream
12 chipolata sausages
12 par-baked mini bread rolls
100 g (3 1/2 oz) rocket leaves, stalks removed

1 Preheat the oven to hot 220°C (425°F/Gas 7). Heat 1 1/2 tablespoons olive oil in a small pan. Add the onion and 1 1/2 tablespoons water, cover, and cook over medium heat for about 10 minutes, stirring occasionally, until the onion is soft and starting to brown. Stir in the sugar and vinegar and cook, uncovered, for 3 minutes, or until thick. Season and keep warm.
2 Meanwhile, in a small bowl, mix the cream cheese and horseradish cream until smooth.
3 Heat the remaining oil in a large frying pan and cook the sausages in batches over medium-low heat for 6–8 minutes, or until brown and cooked. Remove; drain on crumpled paper towels.
4 Meanwhile, heat the bread rolls according to the manufacturer's instructions. When hot, slice vertically, three-quarters of the way through, and spread with the horseradish mixture. Fill the rolls with rocket and a sausage, then onion. Serve.
NOTE: If you can't get chipolatas, you can use thin sausages and twist them through the centre.

BALSAMIC VINEGAR
Good-quality balsamic vinegar is quite expensive because of the length of time involved in processing the Trebbiano grapes from which it is made. Genuine balsamic vinegar, which is aged for 30–50 years, is made by about 40 families in Italy, so only a small quantity is produced. You can usually tell the quality by the price. However, some of the cheaper vinegars, although not aged for as long, are still quite good. Avoid especially cheap ones as they are poor imitations. Balsamic vinegar is used in many salad dressings, marinades and sauces, and is also brushed directly onto food before grilling.

ABOVE: Chipolata sausages with horseradish cream

259

CHICKPEAS

The chickpea is the seed of a leguminous plant, native to Asia. Chickpeas are an excellent source of protein as well as dietary fibre, iron, B vitamins and potassium and so are an excellent staple in a vegetarian diet. As dried chickpeas need overnight soaking before being cooked, sometimes it is easier to use canned chickpeas, which are readily available.

CHICKEN FELAFEL WITH TABBOULI CONES

Preparation time: 30 minutes + standing
Total cooking time: 20 minutes
Makes 24

☆ ☆ ☆

¹/₄ cup (45 g/1¹/₂ oz) cracked wheat (burghul)
4 pieces Lavash bread 30 x 23 cm (12 x 9 inch)
2 spring onions, thinly sliced
1 large tomato, seeded, finely chopped
1 small Lebanese cucumber, finely chopped
15 g (¹/₂ oz) fresh flat-leaf parsley, chopped
1 tablespoon lemon juice
1 tablespoon virgin olive oil
1 tablespoon olive oil
1 onion, finely chopped
1 clove garlic, crushed
2 teaspoons ground coriander
1 teaspoon cumin seeds
¹/₂ teaspoon ground cinnamon
250 g (8 oz) chicken mince
300 g (10 oz) can chickpeas, rinsed, drained
    and mashed

10 g (¹/₄ oz) fresh flat-leaf parsley, extra, chopped
10 g (¹/₄ oz) fresh mint leaves, chopped
2 tablespoons plain flour
vegetable oil, for shallow-frying
¹/₄ cup (60 g/2 oz) Greek-style natural yoghurt

1 Soak the cracked wheat in hot water for 20 minutes. Slice the bread into thirds widthways, then cut in half. Keep the bread covered with a damp cloth to prevent it drying out. Cut some baking paper the same size as the bread. Roll the paper up around the bottom half of the bread to form a cone and secure. Twist at the bottom. You will need 24 bread cones.
2 Drain the wheat in a fine mesh sieve, pressing out as much water as possible. Transfer to a bowl and mix with the onion, tomato, cucumber, parsley, lemon juice and virgin olive oil. Season.
3 Heat the olive oil in a pan, add the onion and garlic and cook, stirring over medium–low heat, for 5 minutes, or until the onion is soft. Add the spices and cook for another minute, or until the spices are aromatic.
4 Place the onion mixture, chicken mince, chickpeas, parsley and mint in a bowl, season with salt and pepper and mix until combined.

ABOVE: Chicken felafel with tabbouli cones

Shape into 24 patties, pressing firmly together. Toss in the flour and shake off the excess.

5 Fill a deep, heavy-based pan one third full of oil and heat to 180°C (350°F), or until a cube of bread dropped into the oil turns golden brown in 15 seconds. Cook the felafels in batches for 3–4 minutes each side, or until golden and heated through. Drain on crumpled paper towels.

6 To assemble, place a felafel in each bread cone, top with tabbouli, then ¹/₂ teaspoon yoghurt.

IN ADVANCE: The salad is best made on the day of serving. The felafel can be prepared up to a day ahead and cooked just before serving.

FRIED CALAMARI WITH TARTARE SAUCE

Preparation time: 30 minutes
Total cooking time: 10 minutes
Serves 8

1 kg (2 lb) small, cleaned calamari tubes
4 tablespoons cornflour
4 eggs, lightly beaten
2 cloves garlic, crushed
1 tablespoon grated lemon rind
2 cups (200 g/6¹/₂ oz) dry breadcrumbs
oil, for deep-frying

Tartare sauce
1 cup (250 g/8 oz) mayonnaise
2 tablespoons chopped chives
2 small pickled onions, finely chopped
1 tablespoon seeded mustard

1 Thinly slice the calamari, toss in cornflour and shake off the excess. Dip into the combined egg, garlic and lemon rind. Coat with breadcrumbs and shake off the excess.

2 Fill a deep heavy-based pan one third full of oil and heat the oil to 180°C (350°F). The oil is ready when a cube of bread dropped into the oil turns golden brown in 15 seconds. Gently lower small batches of calamari into the oil and cook for 1 minute, or until just heated through and lightly browned. Remove with a slotted spoon. Drain on crumpled paper towels and keep warm while cooking the remainder.

3 To make tartare sauce, combine the mayonnaise, chives, pickled onions and mustard. Mix well and serve with the calamari.

ABOVE: Fried calamari with tartare sauce

PARSNIP AND CHICKEN PATTIES WITH CRISPY LEEK

Preparation time: 15 minutes
Total cooking time: 25 minutes
Makes 24

1 large parsnip, chopped
500 g (1 lb) English spinach leaves
250 g (8 oz) chicken mince
4 spring onions, thinly sliced
1 egg yolk
1/2 cup (50 g/1 3/4 oz) dry breadcrumbs
1 tablespoon lemon juice
2 teaspoons chopped fresh thyme
2 tablespoons polenta
1 leek
1/4 cup (60 ml/2 fl oz) light olive oil
1/2 cup (125 g/4 oz) light sour cream
50 g (1 3/4 oz) creamy blue cheese

1 Cook the parsnip in a large pan of boiling water for 10 minutes, or until tender. Drain and mash until smooth. Set aside to cool.
2 Trim the spinach, rinse and add to a pan of boiling water. Boil for 1 minute, drain and rinse under cold water; drain thoroughly. Squeeze the spinach with your hands to remove as much liquid as possible; chop finely.
3 In a bowl, mix the parsnip, spinach, chicken, spring onion, egg yolk, breadcrumbs, lemon juice, thyme and salt and pepper. Shape into 24 patties, pressing firmly together. Dust with polenta and shake off any excess.
4 Remove the tough green portion of the leek and trim the base. Cut the leek widthways into 6 cm (2 1/2 inch) lengths, then cut lengthways into thin strips. Heat the oil in a large frying pan over medium-high heat and cook the leek until golden brown; drain on crumpled paper towels. Add the patties to the pan and cook, in batches, for 3–4 minutes each side, or until golden and heated through. Drain on crumpled paper towels.
5 Meanwhile, combine the sour cream and blue cheese in a small bowl and season with salt and pepper. To assemble, spoon 1 teaspoon of blue cheese mixture on top of each patty and top with crispy leek. Serve immediately.
IN ADVANCE: The patties can be made a day ahead and covered in the refrigerator until ready to cook, or frozen for up to 2 months. Crispy leek is best made close to serving.

HONEY VEAL TAGINE ON PAPPADUMS

Preparation time: 20 minutes
Total cooking time: 1 hour 10 minutes
Makes 24

2 tablespoons olive oil
650 g (1 lb 5 oz) whole piece leg veal, cut into small cubes
1 onion, chopped
2 cloves garlic, crushed
1 cinnamon stick
2 teaspoons ground cumin
1 teaspoon coriander seeds, crushed
1/4 teaspoon ground cardamom
1 1/4 cups (315 ml/10 fl oz) chicken stock
24 small pappadums
3 pitted dates, thinly sliced
4 pitted prunes, finely chopped
3 teaspoons honey
1/2 cup (125 g/4 oz) Greek-style natural yoghurt
fresh coriander leaves, to garnish

1 Heat 1 tablespoon of the olive oil and brown the veal in batches over high heat. Transfer the veal and any juices to a bowl.
2 Heat the remaining oil in the same pan, add the onion and garlic and stir over medium heat for 5 minutes, or until the onion is slightly softened. Add the spices and cook for another minute, or until the spices are aromatic. Return the veal to the pan, pour in the stock and bring to the boil. Reduce the heat and simmer, covered, over low heat for 30 minutes.
3 Uncover and simmer for 30 minutes, or until the mixture is thickened and the veal is tender. Meanwhile, cook the pappadums according to the manufacturer's instructions.
4 Stir the dates, prunes and honey into the veal mixture. To assemble, spoon the veal tagine in the centre of the pappadums, top each with 1 teaspoon of yoghurt and sprinkle with coriander leaves. Serve immediately.
IN ADVANCE: Veal tagine can be prepared a day ahead, refrigerated and reheated just before serving. Pappadums can be cooked a day ahead and stored in an airtight container.

LEEKS
This vegetable has a long history, dating back at least as far as Ancient Egypt when leeks were part of the rations given to the builders of the pyramids. The leek is the national emblem of Wales and, in a battle in the seventh century, the Welsh wore leeks in their caps as identification so they wouldn't kill the wrong fighters. On St David's Day, Welsh men wear pieces of leek in their buttonholes in memory of this victory. Leeks can be steamed, braised, used in soups, pies and stir-fries, or added to dressed salads.

OPPOSITE PAGE: Parsnip and chicken patties with crispy leek (left); Honey veal tagine on pappadums

VEGETABLE FRITTATA WITH HUMMUS AND BLACK OLIVES

Preparation time: 30 minutes
Total cooking time: 35 minutes
Makes 30

⭐⭐

Hummus
425 g (14 oz) can chickpeas, drained
2 cloves garlic, crushed
1/3 cup (80 ml/2¾ fl oz) lemon juice
2 tablespoons natural yoghurt

2 large red peppers (capsicums)
600 g (1¼ lb) orange sweet potato
500 g (1 lb) eggplant (aubergine)
3 tablespoons olive oil
2 leeks, finely sliced
2 cloves garlic, crushed
250 g (8 oz) zucchini (courgettes), thinly sliced
8 eggs, lightly beaten
2 tablespoons finely chopped fresh basil
125 g (4 oz) Parmesan, grated
60 g (2 oz) black olives, pitted and halved, to garnish

1 In a food processor, purée the chickpeas, garlic, lemon juice, yoghurt and black pepper.
2 Quarter the peppers, remove the seeds and membrane and cook, skin-side-up, under a hot grill until the skin is black and blistered. Cool in a plastic bag, then peel.
3 Cut the sweet potato into 1 cm (½ inch) thick slices and cook until just tender; drain.
4 Cut the eggplant into 1 cm (½ inch) slices. Heat 1 tablespoon oil in a 23 cm (9 inch) round, high-sided frying pan and stir the leek and garlic over medium heat for 1 minute, or until soft. Add the zucchini and cook for another 2 minutes. Remove from the pan and set aside.
5 Heat the remaining oil in the same frying pan and cook the eggplant slices, in batches, for 1 minute each side, or until golden. Line the base of the pan with half the eggplant and spread the leek over the top. Cover with the roasted peppers, remaining eggplant and sweet potato.
6 Combine the eggs, basil, Parmesan and some black pepper in a jug, pour over the vegetables and cook over low heat for 15 minutes, or until almost cooked. Place the frying pan under a preheated grill for 2–3 minutes, until the frittata is golden and cooked. Cool for 10 minutes before inverting onto a cutting board. Trim the edges and cut into 30 squares. Top with hummus and olives. Serve cold or at room temperature.

FRITTATA
This is an Italian version of an omelette but differs in the way it is cooked. The filling ingredients are mixed with the egg instead of being folded inside, and the egg is cooked slowly until set, not served soft and creamy. Frittata is cooked on both sides, not folded over. It can be flipped, but most people cook the underside, then put the pan under a grill to cook the top.

RIGHT: Vegetable frittata with hummus and black olives

BAGUETTE WITH EGG, DILL PESTO AND PROSCIUTTO

Preparation time: 20 minutes
Total cooking time: 25 minutes
Makes 30

★★

8 thin slices prosciutto

45 g (1 1/2 oz) fresh dill sprigs

75 g (2 1/2 oz) pine nuts, toasted

60 g (2 oz) Parmesan, finely grated

2 cloves garlic, crushed

1/3 cup (80 ml/2 3/4 fl oz) virgin olive oil

1 French bread stick, sliced diagonally

2 teaspoons butter

7 eggs, lightly beaten

1/3 cup (80 ml/2 3/4 fl oz) milk

1 tablespoon light sour cream

1 Preheat the oven to moderately hot 200°C (400°F/Gas 6). Spread the prosciutto on a baking tray lined with baking paper. Bake for 5 minutes, or until sizzling and lightly crisp. Set aside.
2 Finely chop the dill, pine nuts, Parmesan and garlic together in a food processor. With the motor running, add the oil in a thin stream and process until smooth. Season.
3 Arrange the bread on baking trays and grill until golden on both sides. Spread with dill pesto.
4 Heat the butter in a large non-stick frying pan over low heat. Add the combined eggs and milk. As the egg begins to set, use a wooden spoon to scrape along the base with long strokes to bring the cooked egg to the surface in large lumps. Repeat several times over 10 minutes, or until the mixture is cooked but still creamy-looking. Remove from the heat and stir in the sour cream. Season with salt and pepper.
5 Divide the egg among the toasts and top with torn prosciutto. Serve immediately.
IN ADVANCE: Pesto can be made 3 days ahead and refrigerated. Use at room temperature.

SOUR CREAM
Sour cream, used in many recipes, was originally made by leaving cream at room temperature to sour. Today, commercial sour cream is made by adding a lactic acid culture to cream, thus providing the characteristic slightly acidic tang. Keep sour cream refrigerated and discard if any mould forms.

ABOVE: Baguette with egg, dill pesto and prosciutto

SOMETHING SWEET

Where on earth did the phrase 'sweet nothings' arise from? What a dreadful contradiction in terms. For most of us, sweet food is definitely not 'nothing'; it is one of life's greatest pleasures. The sensation of chocolate melting on the lips, cream oozing from a tiny pastry, or the tang of fresh berries catching on the tastebuds, is not something to be taken lightly. So round off your evening with a platter of sweet treats and watch your guests' eyes light up. Or, for those with a really sweet tooth, do away with the savoury food altogether and have a 'sweets only' party.

TEARDROP CHOCOLATE CHERRY MOUSSE CUPS

Just before the chocolate sets, bring the short edges together to form a teardrop shape. Hold together with your fingers.

Use a small sharp knife to trim around the outer edge of each teardrop, then leave until set completely.

TEARDROP CHOCOLATE CHERRY MOUSSE CUPS

Preparation time: 1 hour
Total cooking time: Nil
Makes about 24

★ ★ ★

glossy contact paper
200 g (6¹/₂ oz) dark chocolate melts or buttons
³/₄ cup (150 g/5 oz) stoneless black cherries, well drained

Chocolate mousse
60 g (2 oz) dark cooking chocolate, melted
1 tablespoon cream
1 egg yolk
¹/₂ teaspoon gelatine
¹/₃ cup (80 ml/2³/₄ fl oz) cream, extra
1 egg white

1 Cut glossy contact into 24 rectangles 4 x 11 cm (1¹/₂ x 4¹/₂ inches). Line a tray with baking paper.
2 Place the chocolate melts in a small heatproof bowl. Bring a small pan of water to the boil and remove from the heat. Sit the bowl over the pan, making sure the bowl does not touch the water. Stir occasionally until the chocolate has melted and the mixture is smooth. Using a palette or flat-bladed knife, spread a little of the chocolate over one of the contact rectangles. Just before the chocolate starts to set, bring the short edges together to form a teardrop shape. (Leave the contact attached.) Hold together with your fingers until the shape holds by itself and will stand up. Repeat with some of the remaining chocolate and rectangles. (The chocolate will need to be re-melted several times. To do this, place the bowl over steaming water again.)
3 Spoon about 1¹/₂ teaspoons of the remaining chocolate on the tray and spread into an oval about 5 cm (2 inches) long. Sit a teardrop in the centre of it and press down gently. Repeat with the remaining teardrops. Allow to almost set.
4 Using a sharp small knife or scalpel, cut around the outer edge of each teardrop. Allow the cups to set completely before lifting away from the baking paper. Carefully break away the excess chocolate from the bases to form a neat edge on the base. Carefully peel away the contact. Set the cups aside. Cut the cherries into quarters and drain on crumpled paper towels.
5 For the mousse, mix the chocolate, cream and yolk in a bowl until smooth. Sprinkle the gelatine in an even layer over 2 teaspoons water in a small heatproof bowl and leave until spongy. Bring a small pan of water to the boil, remove from the

ABOVE: Teardrop chocolate cherry mousse cups

heat and place the bowl over the pan. The water should come halfway up the side of the bowl. Stir the gelatine until clear and dissolved. Stir into the chocolate mixture.

6 Working quickly, so the gelatine does not set, beat the extra cream with electric beaters until soft peaks form; fold into the chocolate. Using electric beaters, beat the egg white in a clean dry bowl until soft peaks form. Fold into the chocolate.

7 Place a few pieces of cherry inside each teardrop cup. Spoon the chocolate mousse over the cherries. (Fill to slightly over the brim as the mousse will drop during setting.) Chill until set.

CHOCOLATE CUPS WITH CARAMEL

Preparation time: 40 minutes
Total cooking time: 5–10 minutes
Makes 24

✧ ✧ ✧

150 g (5 oz) dark chocolate melts
24 small foil confectionery cups
80 g (2³/4 oz) Mars® bar, chopped
¹/4 cup (60 ml/2 fl oz) cream
50 g (1³/4 oz) white chocolate melts

1 Place the dark chocolate in a small heatproof bowl. Bring a small pan of water to the boil and remove from the heat. Sit the bowl over the pan, making sure the bowl does not touch the water. Stir occasionally until the chocolate has melted and the mixture is smooth.

2 Using a small new paintbrush, brush a thin layer of chocolate inside the foil cases. Stand the cases upside-down on a wire rack to set. (Return the remaining chocolate to the pan of steaming water for later use.)

3 Combine the Mars® bar and cream in a small pan and stir over low heat until the chocolate has melted and the mixture is smooth. Transfer to a bowl and leave until just starting to set, then spoon into each cup leaving about 3 mm (about ¹/4 inch) of space at the top.

4 Spoon the reserved melted chocolate into the caramel cases and allow the chocolate to set. Melt the white chocolate in the same way as the dark chocolate. Place in a small paper piping bag and drizzle patterns over the cups. Carefully peel away the foil when the chocolate has set.

NOTE: Ensure the chocolate is set before piping the white chocolate on the top.

IN ADVANCE: Caramel cups can be made up to 3 days ahead.

ABOVE: Chocolate cups with caramel

269

thickness of 3 mm (¼ inch). Cut out rounds with a 5 cm (2 inch) fluted cutter. Lift gently with a flat-bladed knife and line each muffin hole with pastry. Spread the pine nuts onto a flat baking tray and bake for 2–3 minutes, or until just golden. Remove from the tray and cool; divide the nuts among the pastry cases.

4 Combine the melted butter, syrup and sugar in a jug and whisk with a fork, then pour over the pine nuts. Bake for 15 minutes, or until golden. Cool in the trays for 5 minutes before lifting out onto a wire rack to cool completely. Dust with icing sugar before serving, if desired.

NOTE: You can use chopped walnuts or pecans instead of the pine nuts.

IN ADVANCE: The tarts can be made up to 8 hours ahead. Store in an airtight container.

GULAB JAMUN

Preparation time: 20 minutes
Total cooking time: 25 minutes
Makes 35

1 cup (100 g/3½ oz) milk powder
50 g (1¾ oz) blanched almonds, ground
150 g (5 oz) plain flour
1 teaspoon baking powder
½ teaspoon ground cardamom
30 g (1 oz) butter, chopped
¼ cup (60 g/2 oz) natural yoghurt
oil, for deep-frying
1 cup (250 g/4 oz) sugar
a few drops of rose water

1 Sift the dry ingredients into a large bowl and add the butter. Rub the butter into the flour with your fingertips until the mixture resembles fine breadcrumbs. Make a well, then add the yoghurt and 2–3 tablespoons of water. Mix with a flat-bladed knife to form a soft dough (alternatively, use a food processor). Shape the dough into small balls about the size of quail eggs, cover with a damp cloth and set aside.

2 Fill a heavy-based pan one third full of oil and heat to 180°C (350°F). The oil is ready when a cube of bread dropped into the oil turns golden brown in 15 seconds. Deep-fry the jamuns in several batches until deep brown. Do not cook them too quickly or the middle won't cook through. They should puff up a little. Drain in a sieve set over a bowl.

PINE NUT TARTS

Preparation time: 25 minutes
Total cooking time: 15 minutes
Makes 24

½ cup (60 g/2 oz) plain flour
60 g (2 oz) butter, chopped
40 g (1¼ oz) pine nuts
20 g (¾ oz) butter, melted
½ cup (175 g/6 oz) golden syrup
2 tablespoons soft brown sugar

1 Preheat the oven to moderate 180°C (350°F/ Gas 4). Grease two 12-hole mini muffin tins.

2 Sift the flour into a bowl and add the chopped butter. Rub into the flour with your fingertips until the mixture comes together. Turn onto a lightly floured surface and gather together.

3 Roll out on a lightly floured surface to a

3 Place the sugar and 1½ cups (375 ml/12 fl oz) water in a heavy-based pan and stir until the sugar has dissolved. Bring to the boil, reduce the heat and simmer for 5 minutes. Stir in the rose water. Place the warm jamuns in a deep bowl and pour the syrup over. Leave to soak and cool until still slightly warm. Drain and serve piled in a small bowl.

BAKLAVA FINGERS

Preparation time: 30 minutes
Total cooking time: 20 minutes
Makes 24

Filling
90 g (3 oz) walnuts, finely chopped
1 tablespoon soft brown sugar
1 teaspoon ground cinnamon
20 g (¾ oz) butter, melted

8 sheets filo pastry
50 g (1¾ oz) butter, melted

Syrup
1 cup (250 g/8 oz) sugar
2 tablespoons honey
2 teaspoons orange flower water, optional

1 Preheat the oven to hot 210°C (415°F/ Gas 6–7). Brush a baking tray with oil or melted butter.
2 To make the filling, place the walnuts, sugar, cinnamon and butter in a small bowl and stir until combined.
3 Remove one sheet of filo and cover the rest to prevent drying out. Place the sheet of filo pastry on a work bench, brush with melted butter and fold in half. Cut the sheet into three strips and place a heaped teaspoon of filling close to the front edge of the pastry. Roll up, tucking in the edges. Place on the prepared tray and brush with melted butter.
4 Repeat with the remaining pastry sheets. Bake for 15 minutes, or until golden brown.
5 To make the syrup, combine the sugar, honey and ½ cup (125 ml/4 fl oz) water in a small pan. Stir over low heat, without boiling, until the sugar has completely dissolved. Bring to the boil, reduce the heat and simmer for 5 minutes. Remove from the heat and add the orange flower water.

6 Transfer to a wire rack over a tray and spoon the syrup over the pastries while both the pastries and syrup are still warm.
IN ADVANCE: Store in an airtight container for up to 2 days.

CHOCOLATE STRAWBERRIES

Brush 250 g (8 oz) strawberries with a dry pastry brush to remove any dirt. Melt 150 g (5 oz) dark chocolate in a small heatproof bowl over a pan of steaming water and dip the bottom half of each strawberry in the chocolate. Place on a baking paper-covered baking tray and leave to set. When set, melt 100 g (3½ oz) white chocolate in a small bowl, dip the tips of the strawberries in the chocolate and allow to set.

ABOVE: Baklava fingers

RICH CHOCOLATE TRUFFLES

Preparation time: 40 minutes + chilling
Total cooking time: 5 minutes
Makes about 30

3/4 cup (185 ml/6 fl oz) thick (double) cream
400 g (13 oz) dark chocolate, grated
70 g (2 1/4 oz) butter, chopped
2 tablespoons Cointreau
dark cocoa powder, for rolling

1 Place the cream in a small pan and bring to the boil. Remove from the heat and stir in the chocolate until it is completely melted. Add the butter and stir until melted. Stir in the Cointreau. Transfer to a large bowl, cover and refrigerate for several hours or overnight, or until firm enough to roll.
2 Quickly roll tablespoons of the mixture into balls, and refrigerate until firm. Roll the balls in the cocoa, shake off any excess and return to the refrigerator. Serve at room temperature.
IN ADVANCE: Truffle mixture can be made and rolled up to 2 weeks ahead. You will need to roll the balls in cocoa again close to serving time.

RUM-AND-RAISIN TRUFFLES

Preparation time: 30 minutes + soaking
  and chilling
Total cooking time: 5 minutes
Makes about 40

60 g (2 oz) raisins, finely chopped
1/4 cup (60 ml/2 fl oz) dark rum
200 g (6 1/2 oz) chocolate-coated wheatmeal
  biscuits, crushed
1/3 cup (60 g/2 oz) soft brown sugar
1 teaspoon ground cinnamon
50 g (1 3/4 oz) pecans, finely chopped
1/4 cup (60 ml/2 fl oz) cream
250 g (8 oz) dark chocolate, chopped
1/4 cup (90 g/3 oz) golden syrup
125 g (4 oz) pecans, finely ground

1 Marinate the raisins in the rum in a small bowl for 1 hour. Put the biscuits, sugar, cinnamon and pecans in a large bowl and mix until combined.

2 Stir the cream, chocolate and golden syrup in a pan over low heat until melted. Pour onto the biscuit mixture, add the raisins and rum mixture and stir until well combined. Refrigerate until just firm enough to roll into balls.
3 Roll tablespoons of the mixture into balls, then roll the balls in the ground pecans. Refrigerate until firm.
IN ADVANCE: Truffles can be made up to 2 weeks ahead.

WHITE CAKE TRUFFLES

Preparation time: 25 minutes
Total cooking time: Nil
Makes about 25

2 cups (250 g/8 oz) Madeira cake crumbs
2 tablespoons chopped glacé orange peel or
  glacé apricots
1 tablespoon apricot jam
2 tablespoons cream
100 g (3 1/2 oz) white chocolate, melted

Chocolate coating
150 g (5 oz) white chocolate, chopped
20 g (3/4 oz) white vegetable shortening
  (Copha), chopped

1 Line a baking tray with foil. Combine the cake crumbs in a bowl with the chopped peel or apricots, jam, cream and melted chocolate. Mix until smooth, then roll into balls using 2 teaspoons of mixture for each.
2 To make the chocolate coating, combine the chocolate and shortening in a heatproof bowl. Bring a pan of water to the boil, remove from the heat and sit the bowl over the pan, making sure the bowl does not touch the water. Stir occasionally until the chocolate and shortening have melted. Dip the balls in chocolate, wipe the excess off on the edge of the bowl and leave them to set on the tray. Decorate with gold leaf, if desired.
NOTE: For decorating, you can buy 24 carat edible gold leaf from speciality art shops or cake decorating suppliers.
IN ADVANCE: These truffles can be made up to 2 weeks ahead.

WHITE CHOCOLATE
White chocolate is not strictly a chocolate as it contains no cocoa liquor. It is a blend of cocoa butter, sugar, vanilla flavouring, milk solids and a stabilizer. It is softer than real chocolate and is not as easy to handle. Because of its different chemistry, it cannot be easily substituted for other chocolates in recipes.

OPPOSITE PAGE: Rich chocolate truffles (top); Rum-and-raisin truffles

CASTER SUGAR
Often used on baking day in cakes, meringues and biscuits, caster sugar is simply finely ground white sugar. It is used because it dissolves more easily and is also good to use when making custards or sauces. In America, it is called superfine sugar.

ABOVE: Amaretti

AMARETTI

Preparation time: 15 minutes + standing
Total cooking time: 20 minutes
Makes 40

1 tablespoon plain flour

1 tablespoon cornflour

1 teaspoon ground cinnamon

2/3 cup (160 g/5 1/2 oz) caster sugar

1 teaspoon grated lemon rind

1 cup (185 g/6 oz) ground almonds

2 egg whites

1/4 cup (30 g/1 oz) icing sugar

1 Line two baking trays with baking paper. Sift the plain flour, cornflour, cinnamon and half the caster sugar into a large bowl; add the lemon rind and ground almonds.
2 Place the egg whites in a small, dry bowl. With electric beaters, beat the egg whites until soft peaks form. Add the remaining caster sugar gradually, beating constantly until the mixture is thick and glossy, stiff peaks form and all the sugar has dissolved. Using a metal spoon, fold the egg white into the dry ingredients. Stir until the ingredients are just combined and the mixture forms a soft dough.
3 With oiled or wetted hands, roll 2 level teaspoons of mixture at a time into a ball. Arrange on the prepared tray, allowing room for spreading. Set the tray aside, uncovered, for 1 hour before baking.
4 Heat the oven to moderate 180°C (350°F/ Gas 4). Sift the icing sugar liberally over the biscuits. Bake for 15–20 minutes, or until crisp and lightly browned. Transfer to a wire rack to cool.
IN ADVANCE: The biscuits can be stored in an airtight container for up to 2 days.
NOTE: You can use orange rind instead of lemon rind. These biscuits have a chewy texture and are perfect served with coffee.

STUFFED FIGS

Preparation time: 20 minutes
Total cooking time: 5 minutes
Makes 30

100 g (3½ oz) blanched almonds
30 soft dried figs
⅔ cup (125 g/4 oz) mixed peel
200 g (6½ oz) marzipan, chopped

1 Preheat the oven to moderate 180°C (350°F/ Gas 4). Place the almonds on a baking tray and bake for 5 minutes, or until lightly golden. Leave to cool.
2 Remove the hard stem ends from the figs. Cut a cross in the top of each fig halfway through to the base and open out like petals.
3 Chop the mixed peel and almonds in a food processor until fine. Add the marzipan and process in short bursts until fine and crumbly.
4 With your hands, press 2 teaspoons of marzipan filling together to make a ball. Place a ball inside each fig and press back into shape around it. Serve at room temperature.
IN ADVANCE: Store the stuffed figs in a single layer in a covered container in the refrigerator for up to 2 days. Return to room temperature before serving.
NOTE: As a variation, you can dip the bases of the figs into melted chocolate.

PANFORTE

Preparation time: 15 minutes
Total cooking time: 40 minutes
Makes about 32 pieces

115 g (4 oz) blanched almonds, toasted
70 g (2¼ oz) hazelnuts, toasted
60 g (2 oz) walnuts
90 g (3 oz) raisins
180 g (6 oz) glacé apricots, cut into 8 pieces
45 g (1½ oz) mixed peel
⅔ cup (85 g/3 oz) plain flour
2 tablespoons cocoa powder
1 teaspoon ground cinnamon
50 g (1¾ oz) dark chocolate, chopped
⅓ cup (90 g/3 oz) caster sugar
⅓ cup (115 g/4 oz) honey

1 Preheat the oven to warm 160°C (315°F/ Gas 2–3). Lightly grease a shallow 20 cm (8 inch) round cake tin and cover the base with non-stick baking paper. Combine the almonds, hazelnuts, walnuts, raisins, apricots and peel in a large bowl. Add the sifted flour and cocoa and cinnamon to the fruit mixture and stir to combine.
2 Combine the chocolate, sugar and honey in a small pan and stir over low heat until melted. Make a well in the centre of the dry ingredients and add the melted mixture. Mix until all the ingredients are just combined. You will need to use your hand after the initial mixing with a spoon, as the mixture will be very stiff.
3 Press the mixture evenly into the prepared tin. Wet your hand slightly to prevent the mixture sticking. Smooth the top with the back of a spoon. Bake for about 35 minutes, or until the panforte is just firm to touch in the centre. Allow to cool completely in the tin.
4 When cold, remove from the tin, dust generously with icing sugar and cut into thin wedges for serving.

ABOVE: Stuffed figs

MINI PARIS-BREST

Preparation time: 30 minutes
Total cooking time: 35 minutes
Makes 15

1/2 cup (60 g/2 oz) plain flour
60 g (2 oz) butter, chopped
2 eggs, lightly beaten

Custard filling

1 1/4 cups (315 ml/10 fl oz) milk
3 egg yolks
2 tablespoons caster sugar
1 tablespoon plain flour
1 tablespoon custard powder
few drops almond essence, to taste

Toffee

1 cup (250 g/8 oz) caster sugar
2/3 cup (60 g/2 oz) flaked almonds,
  lightly toasted

1 To make choux pastry, sift the flour onto a sheet of baking paper. Put the butter in a pan with 1/2 cup (125 ml/4 fl oz) water, stir over low heat until melted, then bring to the boil. Remove from the heat, add the flour in one go and quickly beat it into the water with a wooden spoon. Return to the heat and continue beating until the mixture forms a ball and leaves the side of the pan. Transfer to a large clean bowl and cool slightly. Beat with electric beaters to release any more heat. Gradually add the beaten egg, about 3 teaspoons at a time. Beat well after each addition until all the egg has been added and the mixture is smooth and glossy.

2 Preheat the oven to moderately hot 190°C (375°F/Gas 5). Line 3 baking trays with baking paper. Place the choux pastry into a piping bag with a 5 mm (1/4 inch) star nozzle. Pipe 3 cm (1 1/4 inch) circles of choux onto the paper. Bake for 10 minutes then reduce the heat to moderate 180°C (350°F/Gas 4). Bake for 15–20 minutes more, or until well browned and puffed. Pierce the sides to allow the steam to escape and cool on a wire rack.

3 For the filling, heat 1 cup (250 ml/8 fl oz) milk to simmering point in a pan. In a bowl, whisk together the remaining milk, egg yolks, sugar, flour and custard powder and slowly pour on the hot milk, whisking vigorously until well combined. Pour back into the clean pan and stir over medium heat until the mixture boils and thickens. Stir in the essence. Transfer to a bowl, cover and cool.

3 To make the toffee, combine the sugar and 1/2 cup (125 ml/4 fl oz) water in a small pan, stirring constantly over low heat until the sugar has dissolved. Bring to the boil and boil rapidly without stirring for about 10 minutes, or until just golden. Place the pan immediately over another pan of hot water to stop the toffee setting.

4 Immediately dip the choux tops into the toffee, decorate with a few toasted flaked almonds and place on a wire rack to set. Split the choux rings in half, pipe or spoon the filling in and top with the toffee lids.

PETITS PITHIVIERS

Preparation time: 40 minutes + chilling
Total cooking time: 15 minutes
Makes 26

Almond filling

45 g (1 1/2 oz) butter
1/3 cup (40 g/1 1/4 oz) icing sugar
1 egg yolk
70 g (2 1/4 oz) ground almonds
1 teaspoon finely grated orange rind
few drops almond essence

3 sheets puff pastry
1 egg, lightly beaten

1 To make the filling, beat the butter and icing sugar with electric beaters until light and creamy. Add the egg yolk and beat well. Stir in the ground almonds, rind and essence.

2 Preheat the oven to hot 210°C (415°F/Gas 6–7) and lightly grease 2 baking trays. Lay the puff pastry on a work surface and cut into 5 cm (2 inch) circles with a cutter. Divide the almond filling among half the circles, using about 1 1/2 teaspoons filling for each. Leave a 5 mm (1/4 inch) border. Brush the border with egg.

3 Place the remaining pastry circles over the filling and press the edges firmly to seal. Transfer to the baking trays and chill for 30 minutes. With a blunt-edged knife, press up the edges gently at intervals. Carefully score the tops of the pastries into wedges, then brush with beaten egg. Bake on the greased trays for 10 minutes, or until lightly golden.

PARIS-BREST
This classic French pastry is meant to resemble the wheel of a bicycle and the name is taken from a bicycle race that was run in the late 19th century between the two cities Paris and Brest.

OPPOSITE PAGE: Mini Paris-Brest (top); Petits pithiviers

TINY TREATS
There is only one thing better than a huge cheesecake, and that's a plateful of miniature cheesecakes... so you can sneak back and eat as many as you want without anyone noticing.

CHOCOLATE LIQUEUR CHEESECAKES

Grease four deep 12-hole patty tins and place a thin strip of baking paper in the bases, extending up the sides. Finely crush 250 g (8 oz) sweet biscuits, stir in 125 g (4 oz) melted butter, then firmly press 1 heaped teaspoon into each base. Refrigerate. Dissolve 3 teaspoons gelatine in 1/4 cup (60 ml/2 fl oz) boiling water. Beat 250 g (8 oz) soft cream cheese with 1/3 cup (90 g/3 oz) caster sugar, then add 150 g (5 oz) melted chocolate, 2 teaspoons grated orange rind and 3 tablespoons Tia Maria and beat until smooth. Stir in the gelatine, spoon onto the bases and refrigerate for 2 hours, or until firm. Whip 300 ml (10 fl oz) cream, spoon over the cheesecakes and garnish with chocolate curls. Makes 48.

BAKED CHEESECAKES

Preheat the oven to warm 160°C (315°F/ Gas 2–3). Grease three deep 12-hole patty tins and place a thin strip of baking paper in the bases, extending up the sides. Finely crush 250 g (8 oz) sweet biscuits, stir in 125 g (4 oz) melted butter, then firmly press 1 heaped teaspoon into each base. Refrigerate. Beat 250 g (8 oz) soft cream cheese, 1/2 cup (125 g/4 oz) sour cream and 1/2 cup (125 g/4 oz) caster sugar, until smooth. Mix in 2 egg yolks, 1 tablespoon lemon juice and 2 teaspoons plain flour. Beat 2 egg whites until stiff peaks form, then fold through the cream cheese mixture. Spoon 1 tablespoon filling into each base and bake for 15–20 minutes, until set. Cool. Makes 36.

CUSTARD AND FRUIT TARTS

Preheat the oven to moderate 180°C (350°F/Gas 4). Grease three shallow 12-hole patty tins. Using a 7 cm (2³/4 inch) round cutter, cut rounds from 4 sheets of ready-rolled sweet shortcrust pastry. Place in the tins and prick the bases several times with a fork. Bake for 12–15 minutes, or until golden brown. Remove and cool. Cut a vanilla pod in half and place in a saucepan with 1¹/4 cups (315 ml/10 fl oz) milk. Slowly bring to the boil, remove from the heat and cool slightly. In a large heatproof bowl whisk 2 egg yolks and 2 tablespoons sugar until thick and pale. Add 3 tablespoons plain flour, then gradually whisk in the vanilla milk. Return to a clean pan and heat slowly, stirring constantly for 5–10 minutes, or until it boils and thickens. Allow to cool, then spoon evenly into each pastry case and top with some sliced fruit. Glaze with warmed sieved apricot jam. Makes 36.

MINI LIME MERINGUE PIES

Preheat the oven to moderate 180°C (350°F/Gas 4). Grease three shallow 12-hole patty tins. Cut rounds with a 7 cm (2³/4 inch) cutter from 4 sheets of ready-rolled sweet shortcrust pastry. Place in the tins and prick the bases well with a fork. Bake for 12–15 minutes, or until golden brown, then cool. Put ¹/2 cup (125 g/4 oz) caster sugar, ¹/4 cup (30 g/1 oz) cornflour, 2 teaspoons lime rind, ¹/3 cup (80 ml/2³/4 fl oz) lime juice and ³/4 cup (185 ml/6 fl oz) water in a large pan. Stir over medium heat until the mixture boils and thickens. Remove from the heat and add 30 g (1 oz) butter, then mix. Gradually mix in 2 egg yolks. Spoon heaped teaspoons into each pastry case. Beat 3 egg whites into stiff peaks, gradually add ¹/2 cup (125 g/4 oz) sugar and beat until the sugar dissolves and is glossy. Spoon 1 tablespoon over each tart. Bake for 4–5 minutes, or until lightly golden. Makes 36.

PEACH AND ALMOND STRUDELS

Preheat the oven to moderate 180°C (350°F/Gas 4). Grease two deep patty tins. Mix a 425 g (14 oz) can pie peaches, 60 g (2 oz) slivered almonds, 60 g (2 oz) sultanas and 1 tablespoon soft brown sugar. Brush a sheet of filo pastry with melted butter, then top with another sheet. Cut into 4 and cut each piece into 4 again. Repeat with another 4 sheets of filo. Place 4 squares in each base and bake for 10 minutes. Place 1 tablespoon of filling in each pastry case, sprinkle with cinnamon and bake for 5–10 minutes, until the pastry is golden. Makes 24.

FROM LEFT: Chocolate liqueur cheesecakes; Baked cheesecakes; Custard and fruit tarts; Mini lime meringue pies; Peach and almond strudels

SACHER CAKE

The original Sacher Torte was a two-layered dense chocolate cake separated by apricot jam and covered with smooth chocolate. Created by Franz Sacher, chief pastrycook to the Austrian statesman Metternich during the Congress of Vienna (1814–15), the cake was later the subject of a protracted argument between some of Sacher's descendants and Vienna's famous Demel pâtisserie as to whether in its true form it had two layers or was just a cake spread with jam and iced.

BELOW: Sacher squares

SACHER SQUARES

Preparation time: 1 hour
Total cooking time: 40 minutes
Makes 24

★★★

Base

1 cup (125 g/4 oz) plain flour
60 g (2 oz) butter, chopped
1/4 cup (60 g/2 oz) sugar
2 egg yolks, lightly beaten

Cake

1 cup (125 g/4 oz) plain flour
1/3 cup (40 g/11/4 oz) cocoa powder
1 cup (250 g/4 oz) caster sugar
100 g (31/2 oz) butter
2 tablespoons apricot jam
4 eggs, separated
1 cup (315 g/10 oz) apricot jam, extra

Topping

250 g (4 oz) dark chocolate
3/4 cup (185 ml/6 fl oz) cream

1 Preheat the oven to moderate 180°C (350°F/Gas 4). To make the base, sift the flour into a large bowl and add the butter. Rub in until the mixture resembles fine breadcrumbs. Stir in the sugar and make a well in the centre. Add the egg yolks and 1½ teaspoons iced water and mix with a flat-bladed knife, using a cutting action, to a firm dough, adding more water if necessary. Gently gather the dough together and lift onto a lightly floured surface. Roll out the pastry to an 18 x 28 cm (7 x 11 inch) rectangle. Bake on a tray covered with baking paper for 10 minutes, or until just golden. Cool completely.

2 To make the cake, keep the oven at moderate 180°C (350°F/Gas 4). Lightly grease a shallow 18 x 28 cm (7 x 11 inch) tin and line the base and side with baking paper, extending over two sides. Sift the flour and cocoa into a large bowl. Make a well in the centre. Combine the sugar, butter and jam in a small pan and stir over low heat until the butter has melted and the sugar has dissolved. Remove from the heat. Add the butter mixture to the dry ingredients and stir until just combined. Mix in the egg yolks.

3 Place the egg whites in a small clean dry bowl and beat with electric beaters until soft peaks form. Using a metal spoon, fold the egg whites into the cake mixture. Pour into the prepared tin

and bake for 30 minutes or until a skewer comes out clean when inserted into the centre of cake. Leave in the tin for 15 minutes before turning out onto a wire rack to cool.

4 Warm the extra jam in a microwave or in a small pan, then push through a fine sieve. Brush the pastry base with 3 tablespoons of the jam. Place the cake on the base. Trim the sides evenly, cutting the hard edges from the cake and base. Using a serrated knife, cut into 24 squares.

5 Brush the top and sides of each square with apricot jam. Place the squares on a large wire rack, over a piece of baking paper, leaving at least 4 cm (1½ inches) between each.

6 To make the topping, break the chocolate into small pieces and place in a small bowl. Place the cream in a small pan and bring to the boil. Remove from the heat, pour over the chocolate and leave for 5 minutes, then stir until the mixture is smooth. Cool slightly. Working with one at a time, spoon the topping over each square and use a flat-bladed knife to cover completely. Scrape the excess topping from the paper, with any left over, and spoon into a small paper piping bag. Seal the open end, snip off the tip and pipe an 'S' onto each square.

IN ADVANCE: Store for up to 5 days in an airtight container.

WALNUT CHOCOLATES

Preparation time: 30 minutes + chilling
Total cooking time: 2–3 minutes
Makes 30 ~15
★

100 g (3½ oz) walnut pieces
½ cup (60 g/2 oz) icing sugar
2 teaspoons egg white
200 g (6½ oz) dark chocolate
30 walnut halves

1 Chop the walnut pieces in a food processor. Sift the icing sugar and process with the walnuts and egg white until a moist paste forms. Cover and refrigerate for 20 minutes.

2 Roll teaspoons of walnut paste into balls and flatten slightly. Place the chocolate in a heatproof bowl. Bring a pan of water to the boil and remove from the heat. Sit the bowl over the pan, making sure the base of the bowl does not sit in the water. Stir occasionally until the chocolate has melted.

3 Dip the walnut rounds in the chocolate and transfer to a piece of greaseproof paper or foil. Press the walnut halves gently into the top of each round and leave to set.

IN ADVANCE: Can be made 4 days ahead.

WALNUTS
Various types of walnut have been used in cookery for thousands of years. The most commonly available is believed to have originated in Persia and been transported to Europe. Other types are native to Asia, America and Europe. Many other countries now grow walnuts. Store the peeled walnuts in the refrigerator or freezer.

ABOVE: Walnut chocolates

oil and heat the oil to 180°C (350°F). The oil is ready when a cube of bread dropped into the oil turns golden brown in 15 seconds. Fry 3 or 4 khvorst at a time, until golden brown on both sides. Drain on crumpled paper towel. Sift icing sugar over the pastry after it is fried but before it gets cold.

IN ADVANCE: These will keep for up to 2 weeks in a dry airtight container.

BABY FLORENTINES

Preparation time: 20 minutes
Total cooking time: about 50 minutes
Makes about 50

★★

90 g (3 oz) butter
1/2 cup (125 g/4 oz) caster sugar
1 tablespoon honey
45 g (1 1/2 oz) slivered almonds, chopped
55 g (2 oz) dried apricots, finely chopped
2 tablespoons chopped glacé cherries
45 g (1 1/2 oz) mixed peel
1/2 cup (60 g/2 oz) plain flour
150 g (5 oz) dark chocolate

1 Preheat the oven to 180°C (350°F/Gas 4). Cover two baking trays with non-stick baking paper. Melt the butter, sugar and honey in a saucepan. Remove from the heat and stir in the almonds, apricots, glacé cherries, mixed peel and the flour. Mix well to combine (the mixture may feel oily).
2 Roll teaspoonfuls into balls and place on the prepared trays, allowing plenty of room for spreading. Press lightly with your fingertips into 3 cm (1 1/4 inch) rounds.
3 Bake for 8–10 minutes, or until golden brown. Cool on the trays until slightly firm, then using a spatula, carefully remove and cool completely on wire racks. Repeat with the remaining mixture.
4 Bring a pan of water to the boil and remove from the heat. Put the chocolate in a heatproof bowl and sit the bowl over the pan, making sure the base of the bowl does not sit in the water. Stir occasionally until the chocolate has melted. Spread a thin layer of chocolate quickly over the backs of the florentines. A little of the chocolate will come through the florentine. Leave to set chocolate-side-up. When set, store in an airtight container in a cool place or keep refrigerated for up to 2 weeks .

SWEET TWISTS

Preparation time: 40 minutes
Total cooking time: 10 minutes
Makes 45

★★

1 egg
1 1/2 tablespoons sugar
1/2 cup (125 ml/4 fl oz) milk
2 cups (250 g/8 oz) plain flour
oil, for deep-frying
1 3/4 cups (215 g/7 oz) icing sugar

1 Beat the egg with the sugar in a bowl, then stir in the milk. Sift the flour with 1/2 teaspoon salt and mix in to form a stiff dough, adding more milk if necessary. Roll out on a lightly floured work surface. Cut into strips about 10 cm (4 inches) long and 3 cm (1 1/4 inches) wide. Make a slit along the length, like a buttonhole. Tuck one end through the slit and pull through to make a twist.
2 Fill a deep heavy-based pan one third full of

ABOVE: Sweet twists

PETITS FOURS

Preparation time: 45 minutes
Total cooking time: 20 minutes
Makes 32

2 eggs
¹/₄ cup (60 g/2 oz) caster sugar
²/₃ cup (85 g/3 oz) plain flour
30 g (1 oz) butter, melted

Topping

1 cup (315 g/10 oz) apricot jam, warmed
   and strained
2 teaspoons liqueur
200 g (6¹/₂ oz) marzipan
400 g (13 oz) ready-made soft icing, chopped

1 Preheat the oven to moderate 180°C (350°F/ Gas 4). Brush two 26 x 8 x 4.5 cm (10¹/₂ x 3 x 1³/₄ inch) bar tins with melted butter or oil. Line the bases and sides with baking paper.
2 Using electric beaters, beat the eggs and sugar in a bowl for 5 minutes, until very thick and pale. Fold in the sifted flour and melted butter quickly and lightly, using a metal spoon. Divide between the tins and bake for 15 minutes, until lightly golden and springy to the touch. Leave in the tins for 3 minutes before turning out onto a wire rack to cool.
3 Using a 3 cm (1¹/₄ inch) round cutter, cut shapes from the cakes. Brush the top and sides of each with the combined jam and liqueur. Roll the marzipan out to a thickness of 2 mm (¹/₈ inch) and cut out rounds and strips to cover the top and sides of the cakes.
4 Place the icing and 2 tablespoons water in a heatproof bowl and stand the bowl over a pan of simmering water. Stir until the icing has melted and the mixture is smooth; cool slightly.
5 Place the marzipan-covered cakes on a wire rack over a tray. Spoon the icing over each cake and use a flat-bladed knife to spread evenly over the base and sides. Reheat the icing over the pan if it begins to thicken. Leave the cakes to set. Carefully lift from the rack and place each in a paper petit four case. Decorate with small coloured fondant flowers if desired.
NOTE: Fondant flowers for decorating are found in some supermarkets and in speciality shops.
IN ADVANCE: Petits fours will keep for up to 2 days in an airtight container in a cool, dark place. Store in a single layer.

MINI TOFFEE APPLES

Peel 2 large apples and use a melon baller to cut out balls, or cut the apples into cubes. Push a cocktail stick into each ball or cube. Sprinkle 200 g (6¹/₂ oz) sugar in an even layer over the base of a pan and melt over low heat, slowly tipping the pan from side to side to make sure the sugar melts evenly. Keep the sugar moving so it does not start to colour on one side before the other side has melted. When the caramel starts to colour, keep swirling until you have an even colour, then remove the pan from the heat and stop the cooking by plunging the base into cold water. Reheat the caramel gently until runny. Dip each piece of apple in the caramel, coating completely. Leave to dry, standing upright on a piece of baking paper. Reheat the caramel when necessary.

PETITS FOURS
A petit four is a small dainty biscuit, cake or sweet, often decorated or iced. It is usually served at the end of a meal. The French term *petit four* literally means 'small oven' and probably refers to the fact that the little cakes or biscuits were baked at a low temperature.

ABOVE: Petits fours

EGG TARTS

Place the inner dough on the centre of the outer dough and fold over the edges to enclose.

When cooled slightly, slip a knife down the side of each tart and transfer the tarts to a wire rack.

EGG TARTS

Preparation time: 10 minutes + standing
Total cooking time: 20 minutes
Makes 18

★★★

Outer dough

1¹/₃ cups (165 g/5¹/₂ oz) plain flour
2 tablespoons icing sugar
2 tablespoons oil

Inner dough

1 cup (125 g/4 oz) plain flour
100 g (3¹/₂ oz) lard, chopped

Custard

¹/₄ cup (60 g/2 oz) caster sugar
2 eggs, lightly beaten

1 Preheat the oven to hot 210°C (415°F/Gas 6–7). Lightly grease 18 holes in shallow 12-hole patty tins.
2 For the outer dough, sift the flour and sugar into a bowl. Make a well and pour in the oil and ¹/₃ cup (80 ml/2³/₄ fl oz) water. Stir quickly, then knead to form a soft dough. (If the dough is very dry, you may need a little extra water.) Cover and set aside for 15 minutes.
3 For the inner dough, sift the flour into a bowl. Add the lard and rub in with your fingertips until the mixture resembles coarse breadcrumbs, then press together to form a very short-textured pastry. Cover and set aside for 15 minutes.
4 On a lightly floured surface, roll the outer dough into a rectangle 20 x 10 cm (8 x 4 inch). Roll the inner dough on a lightly floured surface into a rectangle one-third the size of the other. Place the inner dough on the centre of the outer dough. Fold over the edges to thoroughly enclose, then pinch the ends together to seal.
5 Roll the dough out on a lightly floured surface into a long rectangle, about half as thick as it was previously. Take the left-hand edge and bring it towards the centre. Repeat with the right-hand edge. Wrap the dough in plastic wrap and leave in a cool place for 30 minutes.
6 For the custard, place the sugar and ¹/₃ cup (80 ml/2³/₄ fl oz) water in a pan and bring to the boil. Reduce the heat and simmer, uncovered, until the sugar has dissolved. Cool for 5 minutes, then whisk into the eggs until just combined. Strain into a jug.
7 Turn the pastry so that the fold is on the left-hand side. Working on a lightly floured surface, roll the pastry out to a rectangle about 3 mm

RIGHT: Egg tarts

(¹/8 inch) thickness. Cut out rounds with a 7 cm (2³/4 inch) fluted cutter and put in the tins.

8 Fill each pastry case two thirds full of egg custard, then cook for 15–18 minutes. Do not overcook; the filling should be just set. Leave for 3 minutes, then slip a flat-bladed knife down the sides to lift out onto a rack. Serve warm or cold.

NOTE: If you prefer, use 3 sheets of ready-rolled shortcrust pastry.

IN ADVANCE: Can be cooked 2 days ahead and stored in an airtight container.

THAI STICKY RICE

Preparation time: 15 minutes + overnight soaking
Total cooking time: 1 hour
Makes 25–30

★★

2¹/2 cups (500 g/1 lb) glutinous rice
2¹/2 cups (600 ml/20 fl oz) coconut milk
¹/2 cup (125 g/4 oz) caster sugar

Topping

1 cup (90 g/3 oz) desiccated coconut
¹/4 cup (60 ml/2 fl oz) coconut milk, heated
90 g (3 oz) palm sugar, grated

1 Put the rice in a large glass bowl and cover with water. Soak for 8 hours or overnight; drain. Line a 30 x 20 cm (12 x 8 inch) shallow tin with baking paper, overlapping the two long sides. Line a large bamboo steamer with baking paper.

2 Spread the steamer base with rice, cover and place over a wok. Half-fill the wok with boiling water. Steam for 45–50 minutes, or until the grains are softened. Top up the wok with water when necessary.

3 Put the rice, coconut milk and sugar in a large heavy-based pan. Stir over low heat for 10 minutes, or until all the coconut milk is absorbed. Spoon into the tin and flatten the surface. Set aside to cool and firm.

4 For the topping, put the coconut in a small bowl and mix in the coconut milk. Put the palm sugar and 3 tablespoons water in a small pan and stir over low heat for 3 minutes, or until the sugar has dissolved and the syrup has thickened slightly. Stir in the coconut and continue to stir until the mixture holds together. Cover and set aside to cool. Spread the topping over the rice base. Cut into diamonds for serving. Serve at room temperature.

NOTE: These are best eaten on the same day. Chilling firms the mixture and it loses its flavour. Glutinous rice and palm sugar are available from Asian speciality stores. Palm sugar can be crushed with a rolling pin.

GLUTINOUS RICE
As no rice contains any gluten, this name is a bit of a misnomer. Sometimes it is called *sticky rice*. The stickiness comes from a particular type of starch highly prevalent in sticky rice. This type of rice is most commonly used for making sweets, but in parts of Laos, Cambodia and Vietnam it is the main crop and the preferred rice for all dishes. Most sticky rices are short-grained.

ABOVE: Thai sticky rice

SORBET BALLS

Scoop out balls of sorbet, put on a tray and push a cocktail stick into each ball.

Thoroughly coat each frozen sorbet ball with melted chocolate.

SORBET BALLS

Preparation time: 15 minutes + overnight freezing
Total cooking time: 35 minutes
Makes 24

★★★

400 g (13 oz) sorbet
250 g (8 oz) dark chocolate melts or buttons

1 Soften the sorbet slightly (if you do this step as soon as you get home it will probably be the right consistency and will save having to refreeze it) and spread it out in a shallow container to a depth of about 2.5 cm (1 inch). Put in the freezer until solid.
2 Cover a baking tray with baking paper and place in the freezer. Using a melon baller, scoop out tiny balls of sorbet and place them on the prepared tray. Put a cocktail stick in each sorbet ball. Cover the tray tightly with plastic wrap, ensuring it is completely covered (see Note), then refreeze overnight so the balls are solid.
3 Place the chocolate in a heatproof bowl. Bring a pan of water to the boil, then remove the pan from the heat. Sit the bowl over the pan, making sure the base of the bowl does not touch the water. Stir occasionally until the chocolate has melted. Remove the bowl and set aside to cool a little.
4 The next part is quite tricky so you need to be careful. Ladle some of the chocolate into a separate bowl so that if anything goes wrong you won't ruin the whole batch. Work with just a few balls at a time so they do not melt. Dip each sorbet ball in the chocolate, making sure it is thoroughly coated and place it back on the tray. Return to the freezer. Reheat the chocolate if necessary. It must be liquid enough not to coat too thickly. Add more melted chocolate to the bowl when necessary, but if it seizes, start with a new bowl and a new batch. Freeze until you are ready to serve.
NOTE: In a frost-free freezer, the sorbet will dry out if not properly covered.

Serve these on a bed of dry ice or pile them into a bowl set inside an ice bowl. To make an ice bowl, fill a bowl half full of water and float some flower petals and herb leaves in it, place another bowl inside and weight it down so it sits down in the water but does not sink to the bottom. The water should form a bowl-shaped layer between the two bowls. Freeze overnight. Separate the bowls by rubbing a cloth dipped in hot water over them and twisting them apart.

MINI PAVLOVAS

Preparation time: 50 minutes
Total cooking time: 50 minutes
Makes 35–40

3 egg whites
1 cup (125 g/4 oz) icing sugar
150 g (5 oz) dark chocolate, melted
1 cup (250 ml/8 fl oz) thick (double) cream
1 tablespoon icing sugar, extra
1 teaspoon finely grated orange rind
assorted fresh fruit for garnish, such as
    strawberries, cut into thin wedges, sliced
    pawpaw and kiwi fruit, and passionfruit pulp

1 Preheat the oven to slow 150°C (300°F/ Gas 2). Place the egg whites in a large bowl and beat until stiff peaks form. Set the bowl over a large pan of simmering water and add the icing sugar to the egg whites while continuing to beat. Add it carefully or it will fly all over the place. At this stage it is best to use electric beaters as you must now beat the meringue until thick and very solid.
2 Using a cutter as a guide, draw 4 cm (1½ inch) circles onto two sheets of baking paper, then invert these sheets onto baking trays (so the pencil won't come off on the base of the pavlovas). Spread a little of the meringue mixture over each round—this will be the base of the pavlova. Spoon the remaining meringue into a piping bag fitted with an 5 mm (¼ inch) plain piping nozzle.
3 Pipe three small circles on top of each other on the outer edge of each base, leaving a small hole in the centre. Bake for 30 minutes, or until firm to touch. Leave to cool in the oven with the door slightly ajar.
4 When cold, dip the bases of the meringues into the melted chocolate to come about 2 mm (⅛ inch) up the sides of the meringues, then place on trays covered with baking paper and allow to set.
5 Combine the cream, extra icing sugar and rind, stirring until just thick. If necessary, beat slightly. Spoon into a piping bag fitted with a small plain nozzle and pipe into the meringues. Top with fruit and passionfruit pulp.
IN ADVANCE: Chocolate-dipped meringues without the filling can be made up to a week ahead and stored in an airtight container. Fill them close to serving time, otherwise they will soften.

OPPOSITE PAGE: Sorbet balls (top); Mini pavlovas

CHOCOLATE PRALINE TRIANGLES

When the praline mix is cold and set, break it up roughly, put it in a plastic bag, then crush with a rolling pin.

Spread the chocolate praline over the prepared loaf tin and smooth the surface. Tap gently on the bench to level.

Press a whole toasted almond onto each triangle. Lift each triangle with two forks and dip into the melted chocolate to coat.

ABOVE: Chocolate praline triangles

CHOCOLATE PRALINE TRIANGLES

Preparation time: 40 minutes + chilling
Total cooking time: 3 minutes
Makes 36

60 g (2 oz) slivered almonds
1/2 cup (125 g/4 oz) caster sugar
150 g (5 oz) dark chocolate, chopped
40 g (1 1/4 oz) butter
1/4 cup (60 ml/2 fl oz) cream
80 g (2 3/4 oz) blanched almonds, toasted
200 g (6 1/2 oz) dark compound chocolate,
   melted
50 g (1 3/4 oz) white compound chocolate,
   optional

1 Line a baking tray with foil and brush lightly with oil. Line a 20 x 10 cm (8 x 4 inch) loaf tin with foil.
2 Combine the almonds and sugar in a small pan and place over low heat. Watch carefully, without stirring, for 3–5 minutes, until the sugar is melted and golden. (Swirl the pan slightly to dissolve the sugar.) Pour onto the tray and leave until set and completely cold. Break into chunks, place in a plastic bag and crush with a rolling pin, or chop in a food processor until crumbly.
3 Put the chopped chocolate in a heatproof bowl. Combine the butter and cream in a small pan and stir over low heat until the butter melts. Bring to the boil, then remove from the heat. Pour the hot cream mixture over the chocolate. Leave for 2 minutes, then stir until the chocolate is smooth. Cool slightly, then stir in the crushed praline.
4 Spread the mixture into the loaf tin and smooth the surface. Tap gently on the bench to level. Cover with plastic wrap, then refrigerate for 1 hour, or until set. Lift from the tin, peel away the foil and cut into 36 small triangles.
5 Line a tray with foil. Press a whole toasted almond onto each triangle. Using two forks, dip the triangles one at a time into the chocolate to coat. Lift out, drain off the excess chocolate and place on the tray to set. Pipe with white chocolate to decorate, if desired.
NOTE: Refrigerate in warm weather.

EGGS
Many recipes call for just egg yolks but you don't have to waste the white as it is easily transformed into tempting little sweet meringues. To make them successfully, make sure you bring the egg whites to room temperature, that the bowl and utensils are clean, and be careful when separating the eggs that no yolk slips into the white.

CHOCOLATE MERINGUE KISSES

Preparation time: 20 minutes
Total cooking time: 40 minutes
Makes 25

2 egg whites, at room temperature
¹/₂ cup (125 g/4 oz) caster sugar
¹/₄ teaspoon ground cinnamon

Filling
125 g (4 oz) dark chocolate melts or buttons
¹/₃ cup (90 g/3 oz) sour cream

1 Preheat the oven to slow 150°C (300°F/ Gas 2). Line two oven trays with baking paper.
2 Using electric beaters, beat the egg whites in a small clean dry bowl until soft peaks form. Gradually add the sugar, beating well after each addition until stiffened and glossy peaks form. Add the cinnamon and beat until just combined.
3 Transfer the mixture to a piping bag fitted

with a 1 cm (¹/₂ inch) fluted nozzle. Pipe small stars of 1.5 cm (⁵/₈ inch) diameter onto the trays, 3 cm (1¹/₄ inches) apart. Bake for 30 minutes, or until pale and crisp. Turn off the oven and leave the meringues to cool in the oven with the door ajar.
4 To make the filling, place the chocolate and sour cream in a small heatproof bowl. Bring a pan of water to the boil, remove from the heat and sit the bowl over the pan, making sure the bottom of the bowl does not sit in the water. Stir occasionally until the chocolate has melted. Remove from the heat and cool slightly. Sandwich the meringues together with the chocolate filling.
NOTE: You can use white chocolate instead of dark and other ground spices such as ground cloves, allspice or nutmeg. Meringues should be cooked slowly. The ideal texture is crunchy on the outside and soft inside.
IN ADVANCE: Unfilled meringues can be made several days ahead. Store in an airtight container, between sheets of greaseproof paper.

ABOVE: Chocolate meringue kisses

1 teaspoon of chocolate in each. Use a small new paintbrush to coat the inside with chocolate, making sure it is thick and there are no gaps. Turn the cups upside down on a wire rack and leave until firm. Set the remaining chocolate aside.

3 Combine the cream, white chocolate and Tia Maria in a heatproof bowl. Stir over a pan of simmering water until smooth. Cool slightly, then spoon into the chocolate cups. Press half a coffee bean into each cup. Allow to set.

4 Remelt the reserved chocolate. Spoon it over the filling and tap to level, then leave to set.

CHOCOLATE CLUSTERS

Preparation time: 35 minutes
Total cooking time: Nil
Makes about 40

125 g (4 oz) dark chocolate melts
125 g (4 oz) white chocolate melts
²/₃ cup (125 g/4 oz) dried mixed fruit
125 g (4 oz) glacé ginger, chopped
30 g (1 oz) each dark chocolate and white
    chocolate melts or buttons, extra, melted

1 Put the dark chocolate in a heatproof bowl. Bring a pan of water to the boil, remove from the heat. Sit the bowl over the pan, making sure the base of the bowl is not touching the water. Stir occasionally until the chocolate has melted. Cool slightly. Repeat with the white chocolate.
2 Stir the mixed fruit into the dark chocolate. Combine the ginger with the white chocolate.
3 Drop spoonfuls of the mixtures onto foil-lined trays, and leave to set at room temperature. Drizzle with the extra melted chocolate.

CHOCOLATE-COFFEE CUPS

Preparation time: 40 minutes
Total cooking time: 10 minutes
Makes 20

200 g (6¹/₂ oz) dark chocolate melts
20 foil cups
1 tablespoon cream
50 g (1³/₄ oz) white chocolate, chopped
1 tablespoon Tia Maria
10 coffee beans, halved

1 Put the dark chocolate in a heatproof bowl. Bring a pan of water to the boil, remove from the heat and sit the bowl over the pan, making sure the base of the bowl does not sit in the water. Stir occasionally until the chocolate has melted. Cool slightly.
2 Working with one foil cup at a time, put

ABOVE: Chocolate clusters (top); Chocolate-coffee cups

FRUIT BITES WITH WARM CHOCOLATE SAUCE

Thread two or three chopped pieces of fresh fruit onto small skewers and serve with warm chocolate sauce. In a small pan, combine 250 g (8 oz) good quality dark chocolate, 3/4 cup (185 ml/6 fl oz) cream, 50 g (1³/₄ oz) butter, 1 tablespoon golden syrup and 2 tablespoons coffee-flavoured liqueur. Stir over low heat until melted and serve in a bowl beside the fruit.

CHOCOLATE TARTS

Preparation time: 40 minutes + chilling
Total cooking time: 30 minutes
Makes about 45

1¼ cups (155 g/5 oz) plain flour
75 g (2½ oz) butter, chopped
¼ cup (60 g/2 oz) caster sugar
2 egg yolks
250 g (4 oz) dark chocolate, finely chopped
1 cup (250 ml/4 fl oz) cream
1 tablespoon orange-flavoured liqueur
1 orange
½ cup (125 g/4 oz) caster sugar, extra

1 Lightly grease two 12-hole tartlet tins. Sift the flour into a large bowl and add the butter. Rub in with your fingertips until the mixture resembles fine breadcrumbs. Stir in the sugar. Make a well and add the egg yolks and up to 2 tablespoons water. Mix with a flat-bladed knife using a cutting action, until the mixture comes together in beads. Gather together and lift out onto a lightly floured work surface. Press into a ball and flatten slightly into a disc. Wrap in plastic and refrigerate for 20 minutes.

2 Preheat the oven to moderate 180°C (350°F/Gas 4). Roll the dough between two sheets of baking paper and cut rounds with a 5 cm (2 inch) cutter. Press into the tins.

3 Bake for about 10 minutes, or until lightly browned. Remove from the tins and cool. Repeat to use all the pastry. Allow to cool.

4 Put the chocolate in a heatproof bowl. Bring the cream to the boil in a small pan and pour over the chocolate. Leave for 1 minute, then stir until the chocolate has melted. Stir in the liqueur. Allow to set, stirring occasionally until thick.

5 Meanwhile, thinly peel the orange, avoiding the bitter white pith, and cut into short thin strips. Combine the extra sugar, rind and ½ cup (125 ml/4 fl oz) water in a small pan, stir over heat until the sugar has dissolved, then simmer for about 5–10 minutes, or until thick and syrupy. Remove the rind with tongs and drain on baking paper; allow to cool.

6 Spoon the chocolate mixture into a piping bag fitted with a 1 cm (½ inch) plain piping nozzle. Pipe three small blobs of ganache into the pastry case, pulling up as you pipe so the ganache forms a point. Dust with cocoa, decorate with the orange rind and refrigerate until ready to serve.

ORANGES

Oranges are in plentiful supply all year round with different varieties available in opposite seasons. Summer and spring are *Valencia* time, whereas autumn through to spring are the times for the seedless *Navel* orange. Blood oranges, with red flesh, and the *Seville*, a bitter orange used for marmalade, are available in winter. Navel oranges have thick, easy to peel skin, whereas the Valencia skin is smooth and thin. Valencias are ideal for making juice, with a high yield. Store oranges in the refrigerator or in a dry, cool area.

LEFT: Chocolate tarts

BRANDY SNAPS
WITH COFFEE
LIQUEUR CREAM

Drop level teaspoons of mixture onto the covered tray and spread into rounds using the broad side of a knife.

While the biscuits are still hot, wrap them around the handle of a wooden spoon.

Spoon the cream mix into a piping bag and fill the cooled biscuits.

BRANDY SNAPS WITH
COFFEE LIQUEUR CREAM

Preparation time: 12 minutes + chilling
Total cooking time: 20 minutes
Makes 25

★★☆

60 g (2 oz) butter
2 tablespoons golden syrup
1/3 cup (60 g/2 oz) soft brown sugar
1/4 cup (30 g/1 oz) plain flour
1 1/2 teaspoons ground ginger
80 g (2 3/4 oz) dark chocolate, melted

Coffee liqueur cream
2/3 cup (170 ml/5 1/2 fl oz) cream
1 tablespoon icing sugar, sifted
1 teaspoon instant coffee powder
1 tablespoon coffee liqueur

1 Preheat the oven to moderate 180°C (350°F/ Gas 4). Line two baking trays with baking paper. Combine the butter, syrup and sugar in a small pan. Stir over low heat until the butter has melted and the sugar has dissolved; remove from the heat. Add the sifted flour and ginger and, using a wooden spoon, stir until well combined; do not overbeat.

2 Drop 1 level teaspoon of mixture at a time onto the trays, about 12 cm (5 inches) apart. (Prepare only three or four biscuits at a time.) Use a palette knife to spread the mixture into 8 cm (3 inch) rounds. Bake for 6 minutes, or until lightly browned. Leave on the trays for 30 seconds, then lift off the tray and wrap around the handle of a wooden spoon while still hot. If the biscuits harden on the trays, return to the oven to soften again, then roll. Set aside to cool. Repeat with the remaining mixture.

3 To make the coffee liqueur cream, combine all the ingredients in a small bowl and stir until just combined. Cover with plastic wrap and refrigerate for 1 hour. Using electric beaters, beat until the mixture is thick and forms stiff peaks. Fill the biscuits. (You can spoon the cream into a small paper icing bag, seal the open end and snip off the tip, then pipe into the snaps.) Pipe or drizzle with melted chocolate before serving.
IN ADVANCE: Store in an airtight container for up to 2 days, or freeze snaps for up to 1 month without filling.

ABOVE: Brandy snaps with coffee liqueur cream

CHINESE FORTUNE COOKIES

Preparation time: 15 minutes
Total cooking time: 5 minutes each tray
Makes about 30

★★

3 egg whites
1/2 cup (60 g/2 oz) icing sugar, sifted
45 g (1 1/2 oz) butter, melted
1/2 cup (60 g/2 oz) plain flour

1 Preheat the oven to moderate 180°C (350°F/Gas 4). Line a baking tray with baking paper. Draw three 8 cm (3 inch) circles on the paper. Turn the paper over.
2 Place the egg whites in a bowl and whisk until just frothy. Add the icing sugar and butter and stir until smooth. Add the flour and mix until smooth. Set aside for 15 minutes. Using a flat-bladed knife, spread 1 1/2 level teaspoons of mixture over each circle. Bake for 5 minutes, or until slightly brown around the edges.

3 Working quickly, remove from the trays by sliding a flat-bladed knife under each round. Place a folded written fortune message inside each cookie.
4 Fold in half, then in half again over a blunt-edged object. Allow to cool on a wire rack. Cook the remaining mixture the same way.
NOTE: Make only two or three fortune cookies at a time, otherwise they will harden too quickly and break when folding. If this happens, return the tray to the oven and warm through.
IN ADVANCE: The fortune cookies can be cooked up to 2 days ahead and stored in an airtight container.

CHINESE
FORTUNE COOKIE
This is a small biscuit or cake containing a slip of paper with a horoscope, joke or proverb printed on it. Chinese Americans invented the idea early in the 20th century.

ABOVE: Chinese fortune cookies

INDEX

Page numbers in *italics* refer to photographs. Page numbers in **bold** type refer to margin notes.

Cover illustration (from top): Asparagus Boats (p.72); Beef en Croute with Béarnaise (p.79); Cucumber Bites (p.235); Caviar Eggs (p.230); Smoked Salmon Pikelets (p.47); Marinated Trout and Cucumber Tarts (p.80)

ACKNOWLEDGEMENTS

HOME ECONOMISTS: Miles Beaufort, Anna Beaumont, Anna Boyd, Wendy Brodhurst, Kerrie Carr, Rebecca Clancy, Bronwyn Clark, Michelle Earl, Maria Gargas, Wendy Goggin, Kathy Knudsen, Michelle Lawton, Melanie McDermott, Beth Mitchell, Kerrie Mullins, Justine Poole, Tracey Port, Kerrie Ray, Jo Richardson, Maria Sampsonis, Christine Sheppard, Dimitra Stais, Alison Turner, Jody Vassallo

RECIPE DEVELOPMENT: Roslyn Anderson, Anna Beaumont, Wendy Berecry, Janelle Bloom, Wendy Brodhurst, Janene Brooks, Rosey Bryan, Rebecca Clancy, Amanda Cooper, Anne Creber, Michelle Earl, Jenny Grainger, Lulu Grimes, Eva Katz, Coral Kingston, Kathy Knudsen, Barbara Lowery, Rachel Mackey, Voula Mantzouridis, Rosemary Mellish, Kerrie Mullins, Sally Parker, Jacki Passmore, Rosemary Penman, Tracey Port, Jennene Plummer, Justine Poole, Kerrie Ray, Jo Richardson, Tracy Rutherford, Stephanie Souvilis, Dimitra Stais, Beverly Sutherland Smith, Alison Turner, Jody Vassallo

PHOTOGRAPHY: Jon Bader, Paul Clarke, Joe Filshie, Andrew Furlong, Chris Jones, Andre Martin, Luis Martin, Andy Payne, Hans Sclupp, Peter Scott

STYLISTS: Marie-Helene Clauzon, Georgina Dolling, Kay Francis, Mary Harris, Donna Hay, Vicki Liley, Rosemary Mellish, Lucy Mortensen, Sylvia Seiff, Suzi Smith

The publisher wishes to thank the following for their assistance in the photography for this book:

The Bay Tree Kitchen Shop, NSW;
Made in Japan, NSW;
MEC-Kambrook Pty Ltd, NSW;
Orson & Blake Collectables, NSW;
Royal Doulton Australia Pty Ltd, NSW;
Ruby Star Traders Pty Ltd, NSW;
Sunbeam Corporation Ltd, NSW;
Villery & Boch Australia Pty Ltd, NSW;
Waterford Wedgwood Australia Ltd, NSW.